ESSAYS FOR RICHARD ELLMANN:
OMNIUM GATHERUM

ESSAYS FOR RICHARD ELLMANN

Omnium Gatherum

Editors

Susan Dick
Declan Kiberd
Dougald McMillan
Joseph Ronsley

McGill-Queen's University Press
Kingston and Montreal

Published in Canada by
McGill-Queen's University Press

ISBN 0-7735-0707-8

Legal deposit 1st quarter 1989
Bibliothèque nationale de Quebec

Printed in Great Britain

Published in Great Britain in 1989 by
Colin Smythe Limited,
Gerrards Cross,
Buckinghamshire SL9 8XA
ISBN 0-86140-288-X

Canadian Cataloguing in Publication Data
Main entry under title:
Essays for Richard Ellmann: Omnium Gatherum
Includes bibliographical references.
ISBN 0-7735-0707-8
   1. English literature – History and criticism
   2. Ellmann, Richard, 1918–1987
   I. Ellmann, Richard 1918-1987
   II. Dick, Susan, 1940–
PN85.046 1988   820'.9   C88.090410-0

Contents

Photographs

Preface

This book was conceived, and work begun on it, in February, 1987, three months before Richard Ellmann's death on 13 May. In fact, the book's conception was two-fold: Susan Dick and Dougald McMillan had the idea at about the same time Declan Kiberd and I did. We are all Ellmann's former students. Inevitably, we discovered each other almost immediately, and, each group modifying its concept slightly, we combined our efforts. The collaboration has been a happy one. Our final weekend editorial meeting in Montreal during November, 1987, was marked by intellectual stimulation, harmony in point of view, and a strong sense of cordial camaraderie enhanced by Dick Ellmann's spirit which was pervasive throughout the weekend. We were all motivated from the beginning by deep feelings of admiration, gratitude, and affection, and had hoped Dick would be able to see the book, which was intended originally as a tribute on the occasion of his seventieth birthday, to occur on 15 March 1988. The depth of our grief at news of his death was considerable. Sylvan and Gigi Schendler, Dick's very close friends, had told him about the book shortly before he died; they say he was very pleased to hear about it.

Our intention was to include pieces by people who had worked with Dick one way or another—as colleagues, collaborators on books and other projects, his former students, and in some cases simply as good friends. We have pretty well held to this. It is not surprising that some of the contributors are among the most distinguished people in their fields. Nor is it surprising that the editors found no difficulty in getting them to contribute; the affection we felt, and grief at Dick's death, was widely shared. The book is comprised mainly of essays on twentieth-century literature, where Dick's primary interest lay. It is quite large, and also quite diverse, which we feel is appropriate in light of the range and dimension of our teacher's contribution to literary study. In addition to the essays on twentieth-century literature, we have included a few poems and essays that are biographical and personal, about the man himself, essays which, because their subject is what it is, turn out to be important contributions to literary history.

Jane Lidderdale OBE, a close friend of Dick's, was unable to provide material for this volume, but wished very much to be associated with it. She writes of her disappointment, and recalls that 'one of his traits that won my attention and regard was his artistry in opening a lecture: a challenging and often witty first sentence, accompanied by a little turn of the head, a signal to his listeners that he was glad to be addressing them'.

The editors are most grateful to people and institutions that have helped generously and enthusiastically to produce this collection and tribute. Dick's daughters, Maud and Lucy Ellmann, have gone to considerable trouble to provide us with important information and with photographs of their father. Sylvan and Virginia Schendler have taken an interest in the project from the start; they have given us support and provided us with contacts. Gigi's portraits of Dick can be found on the dust jacket and in the photo section. Jamie W. O'Connor, Graduate Secretary for the Department of English at Northwestern University, provided us with a list of people who had completed PhDs under Dick's supervision there. The Reference Department of McGill University's McLennon Library, and especially librarians Lonnie Wetherby and Elaine Yarosky, have contributed an enormous amount of time and effort assembling the bibliography, and, along with Mary Mason, Carol Marley, and Jewel Lowenstein, providing other information. Richard Ellmann's radio talk 'Joyce as Letter Writer' was kindly provided by Seán Ó Mórdha and transcribed from the tape by Robert M. Head. Joanne Ronsley contributed welcome editorial assistance, Rosita Fanto helped with contacts, and Mark Rosenberg helped with correspondence between Montreal and Kingston.

The pages from Samuel Beckett's notebooks in Dougald McMillan's essay are reproduced by permission, from the originals in the Samuel Beckett Collection in the University of Reading Library.

The letters of Mrs. W.B. Yeats in Professor Saddlemyer's article are published by kind permission of Anne Yeats and Michael B. Yeats.

We are grateful to the McGill Faculty of Graduate Studies and Research and the Queen's School of Graduate Studies and Research for grants that helped the editorial process, and to the Faculty of Arts and Science at Queen's University, The Faculty of Graduate Studies and Research at McGill University, and, through a gift to McGill, to the Max Bell Foundation for grants to subsidize publication. Finally, we wish to thank Mr William Turner, Chairman of the Consolidated-Bathurst Corporation of Montreal, for that Company's generous support of the publication of this book. Consolidated-Bathurst sponsors a distinguished lecture series, entitled 'The Literary Imagination', at McGill University, devoted to literature, theatre, and the film. Richard Ellmann spoke in this series on 7 October 1985, on 'Adventures and Misadventures of a Joyce Biographer'. Such corporate support for literature and the arts is the mark of an enlightened, humane, and civilized culture, and is appropriate to the memory of the man honoured by this collection.

Joseph Ronsley
Montreal
December 1987

Richard Ellmann: The Critic as Artist

It is the destiny of original minds to seem less and less remarkable in direct proportion to their success in changing conventional ideas. A moment is reached when nobody can remember what life was like before they came upon the scene. People start to quote their words without always recollecting the source, and at this point the original mind seems no longer to evoke a person but a whole climate of opinion.

Such a mind was Richard Ellmann's. It is not true that he invented the 'Modern Tradition'—it just sometimes seems as if he had. By now the poetry of Yeats, the plays and criticism of Wilde, the prose of Joyce seem inseparable from his explanations of them. At a period when the new critics asserted the absolute self-sufficiency of the literary text, he was steadfast in his insistence on the ultimate connections between an artist's life and work. In his studies of Yeats, Wilde and Joyce, he shrewdly fused the celebratory techniques of Victorian biography with the close analytic methods of the New Criticism, essentially advancing an inclusive approach to literature, quite innovative when he began, and comprising a synthesis in a dialectical process. Hence the double meaning of 'The Identity of Yeats'—identity in the sense of personal hallmark of the author, but also of internal consistency of the work. In this he showed the way for others. His celebration of the author James Joyce and his character Leopold Bloom as womanly man seemed eccentric when he offered it in 1959, but within a decade had been endorsed by the counter-culture. They had learned to be Ellmann's contemporaries as well as Joyce's.

Few students today can have a clear conception of the critical innovation wrought by Richard Ellmann and his friends. Ellsworth Mason's essay in this volume helps to clarify this picture. When Ellmann began his university work, Robert Browning was still regarded by his academic mentor as an instance of the modern poet. It took courage, as well as an extraordinary perspicacity, for a young graduate student to stake his career on the poetry of W.B. Yeats. The sheer complexity of Yeats's art, the wayward sophistication of his sensibility, and the apparent eccentricity of many of his ideas were formidable obstacles to full appreciation of his achievement. But Richard Ellmann and a small number of gifted contemporaries accepted the challenge of modernism to occupy themselves with 'the fascination of what's difficult'. They launched themselves into a systematic explanation of the texts of high modernism with an audacity which must, at times, have unnerved not just their teachers but also themselves. Almost like monks of some unproven new religion, they undertook exegesis of seemingly impenetrable works with no certainty that the wider world would concur that these texts were sacred. (In later years as a teacher with avid students, Ellmann would half-jokingly refer to his habit of taking up examination papers from each student individually as a 'laying on of hands'.) Before the masterworks of Yeats and Joyce they vibrated with an intensity and vulnerability which constituted a wholly new tone in the discourse of literary criticism.

Ellmann's immense skill as a biographer sometimes obscured the range and originality of his thought. But it is now recognized that the chapters of almost pure criticism in the Joyce biography (on the backgrounds to 'The Dead' and *Ulysses*, for example) stand as definitive essay-length treatments of their subjects, and that he had managed to say more in a hundred pages of *Eminent Domain* than other capable critics might articulate at far greater length. In its particulars Ellmann's criticism not only explained the difficult works of modernism, it defined and established them. His lucid readings of Yeats's poems and his reasoned presentation of the ancillary texts behind them provided the basis for the recognition of Yeats as a major genius rather than a brilliant Irish eccentric. His discussions of *Ulysses* laid to rest the prevalent interpretation that Leopold Bloom was only a debased satirical contrast with Odysseus and not a true hero. He articulated the 'mythic method' so central to modernism in a sentence worthy of Eliot or Joyce. 'We walk in darkness on familiar roads', he wrote. Even in the pattern of ordinary lives in progress, the outlines of the true heroism of the past is discernible. And throughout his criticism—as for example in identifying the significance of the final 'yes' of *Ulysses* and later establishing that the 'word known to all men' is 'love' rather than 'death' as others argued—he has helped to define as a major tenet of high modernism its affirmation of life in the face of a full presentation of human imperfection.

He was later to make a more direct and comprehensive effort to define the essential elements of modernism. In conjunction with Charles Feidelson he assembled and edited an important collection of the texts which provide the intellectual backdrop to twentieth-century literature. *The Modern Tradition* is a massive volume whose contents are of a scope and quality commensurate with the ambition of its title. The selections almost unerringly epitomize their authors' thoughts, the introductions cover their subjects with wit, elegance and economy, and the masterly linkage between sections in notes provide a deceptively subtle and unobtrusive continuity.

Ellmann's reverence before his chosen texts was one of his most impressive features during his years as a teacher at Northwestern University. To his students he was prismatic. In the classroom, his delicate, inquiring intellect manifested itself in the form of genuine questions rather than coercive statements. In the face of a knotty textual crux, Ellmann asserted his conviction that the lines of a great writer will always yield a satisfactory explanation. 'Let us take the poet's part', he would urge his students, asking them as far as possible to see the artist as he saw himself. The scholarly scruple which characterizes every page of his own writing is expressed by the memorable phrases with which he described the common traits of Stephen Dedalus and Leopold Bloom: passivity in act, energy in thought, tenacity in conviction.

He believed in the potential of his own students, whom he treated in the same spirit that governed his approach to texts. He treated both with tact, respect, and an exacting scrutiny. He inspired by his always evident commitment and involvement, by thoughtful shared enquiry, and by the casually stated pressure of his own almost naively high expectations. He asked of students not much less than he demanded of himself ('take a look at Heidegger' or 'you should read Ibsen in Norwegian') and, by believing the best of them, evoked from them qualities they never knew they had. Behind the imposing expectations was also the understanding and protective mentor. His stealthy acts of kindness on behalf of many were often discovered only in retrospect and by accident.

His personal grace and the genuineness of his humanity inspired not just confidence but love. His strong sense of family must have reassured those who favoured him with access to private papers and personal confidences that, in his rigorous researches into the lives of authors, he would not give unnecessary offense to relations or friends. In fact he remained on excellent terms with the families and friends of his subjects even after his. books were published.

Despite his almost legendary reputation as a thorough and persistent biographical researcher, moreover, his repect for the personal lives of his subjects matched his respect for their artistic achievements. In 1975 he published the Fontency Street letters of Joyce. These pornographic letters were written to Nora Barnacle during a crisis in their relationship, and their inclusion in a special one-volume paperback edition of the letters evoked anger among Joyce's admirers not only in Dublin but in Paris. Most of that anger was subsequently dispelled by the explanation that another scholar had been on the verge of putting the letters into print anyway. He pre-empted this act by publishing them with a detailed preface establishing the wider context of marital fidelity and reawakened love which these very letters helped to restore. In protecting Joyce's reputation in this way, he was simply keeping faith with the closing claim in the biography that Joyce had two over-riding concerns, his family and his work—and that, as the first gave his work its human sympathy, so the second raised a somewhat disorderly life to dignity and high dedication. Nevertheless, the inevitable controversy and the harsh criticisms rankled, not least because they fed the suspicion still widespread in Britain, that Joyce was a 'smutmonger'.

In consequence of the clarity and readability of his style and his genuine illumination of the texts, his audience extended well beyond the academy. His successful collaborations with radio and television producers were a further testimony to his ability to reach a wide public. He had the gift not of simplification, but of explanation. For television, he collaborated on texts which captured the full complexity of his subjects (Wilde, Joyce, Beckett) in a prose which was never put to shame by their company. His words were always simple, his thought invariably sophisticated, and the more complex his syntax became, the more straightforward the diction.

From Joyce, he had learned that literature is recorded speech, and counselled that 'Nobody has read *Ulysses* until he has read it aloud'. (He revelled in his own retelling of the account of Joyce reading aloud from 'Cyclops' and asked at the end 'How's that for low?') In Yeats he chronicled the search for the passionate syntax and rhythm of everyday speech, summoned from the adage that a poet should try to think like a wise man, but to express himself like the common people. And he recognised a similar impulse in the witticisms of Wilde which were characterized as 'a kind of aristocratic folklore'. Ellmann's own writings betrayed a similar tendency toward the spoken word, just as his public lectures seemed to have a polished and writerly quality about them.

This fascination with oral tradition so alive in Ireland may explain to some extent his intimate and lifelong obsession with Irish authors. Unlike some of the scholars who invaded Dublin in the 1940s, Richard Ellmann came not in search of 'Irishness' but of the greatest modern artists who just happened to be Irish. By the time he arrived in Dublin in 1942 the realist reaction against the 'harp-and-shamrock' phase of the Irish Literary Revival was well and truly under way. Part of his appeal for writers like Sean O'Faolain and Frank O'Connor, by whom he was quickly befriended, was his refusal to have any truck with 'shamrockery' or 'paddywhackery', with what was known in Dublin as 'Irishness'. 'Irishness', said one writer, with painful memories of too many stage-Irish authors still ringing in his head, 'is a form of anti-art, a way of posing as an artist without being one'.

While thoughts of national identity were never paramount for him, by explicating major Irish artists Ellmann helped Irish people to know themselves. Ireland, rightly famous for great writers, had produced no critic commensurate with their capacity for complexity, and so this gifted foreign scholar became the interpreter of Irish genius for himself and, later, for the world. Not all Irish persons proved immediately or unqualifiedly grateful, however. There were the predictable wisecracks about Americans with file-index boxes. And Ellmann believed that his pious Bloomsday pilgrimage, which he made at the outset of his work on the Joyce biography, was the butt of Patrick Kavanagh's poetic ridicule in 'Who Killed James Joyce?':

> Who killed James Joyce?
> I said the scholar.
> I killed James Joyce
> For my graduation.
>
> What weapon was used
> To slay might Ulysses?
> The weapon that was used
> Was a Harvard thesis.
>
> . . .
>
> And did you get high marks?
> The PhD?
> I got the B Litt
> And my Master's degree.
>
> Did you get money
> For your Joycean Knowledge?
> I got a scholarship
> To Trinity College.

In fact Ellmann got much more than the Trinity B Litt, for he was, in due time, accorded an honorary Doctorate (one of eight in all, received during his career) by the National University of Ireland in 1976.

He was by then, and despite his English domicile, something of a legendary figure in Dublin literary and academic circles. After a particularly grave injustice at an Irish University one young scholar asked: 'Why are professors such cantankerous bowsies?' 'Because', he answered, smiling gently, 'the stakes they play for are so low'.

His persistence and intuitive knack for being in the right place to benefit from fortuitous discoveries that would have eluded others gave rise to many anecdotes about the making of his biographies. His favourite was of an early attempt to establish the life-models for the main characters in *Ulysses*. After weeks of bootless searching, one hot summer, he had almost despaired of finding the prototype for Blazes Boylan. He needed a man who had worn a straw hat and been a boxer. Nothing doing anywhere. Even the old-timers of Dublin were baffled. So, chagrined, he booked a plane out of the city one Friday, but just before leaving paid a call to a shopkeeper on the Liffey quay. Box after dusty box of photographs were produced, but nothing useful turned up. The man sympathized civilly, as Ellmann consulted his watch for the last time and conceded defeat. Then, as he was going out the door, he noticed a photograph on the wall, of a dapper young man in a straw boater, his arms in a somewhat pugilistic pose. 'Who is that?' he asked with faint curiosity. 'That's myself', smiled the shopkeeper before waving the critic into the taxi.

When he was appointed to the Goldsmith's Chair of Modern Literature at Oxford in 1970—the first American to gain the distinction of a Chair in Literature at Oxford—he approached his new position with an unavowed sense of mission. He had replaced his friend Lord David Cecil, an expert on Jane Austen and the novel of nineteenth-century England. As the new man, Ellmann began to modernize the curriculum. Even in the 1970s there were few native British Joyceans and there were many modern literature courses in British universities in which the writings of Joyce did not feature. 'You know, Joyce still isn't fully accepted here', he complained to an Oxford class in 1974. And he spoke out in general for the modernist periphery of Irish and American writers, and the French Symbolists that had been held at arms' length by a conservative faculty.

Ellmann was born, as a critic, into an age of New Criticism and he died in an age of critical theory. Though he had friends and even close relations in both camps—as is clear from the rich diversity of essays in this volume—he never fully belonged to either. He always strove for ethical standards, but he was too sophisticated and good-natured to state in categorical terms what those standards might be. And he never proclaimed a hard and fast critical method, preferring to allow each of his chosen texts to dictate its own special terms, but he was always willing if asked to do so, to examine the assumptions on which his practices were based.

Throughout his life he remained engaged in constant dialogue with himself and with the world. He celebrated the spoken qualities of Irish writing; he held opposing viewpoints actively in mind; he advised readers to 'cross over' into the mind of their artists; he believed that the quarrel with the self was unending, like the mediations between the male and female components of a full personality; and he saw each of his essays as a response to some previous statement or question. His gift for hearing other voices engendered a liberal, humanistic perspective which pervaded his life and work. The debate about Yeats's alleged fascism left him completely unmoved, because to him an artist who saw that there were two sides to every story could never be deemed guilty of the hopeful simplicities of totalitarian thought.

This same perspective which so marked his thinking was also expressed in his actions. He was unstinting in his support for victims of spiritual intolerance, whether it took the form of literary censorship in the United States or legal repression of homosexual persons in Ireland. Long before it became *de rigueur* to espouse feminist ideals, he admired the 'androgynous angel' Leopold Bloom, the Yeatsian resort to the female voice in Crazy Jane, the Wildean antithesis between the manly woman and the womanly man. Such commitments must have seemed unavoidable to a man married to the author of *Thinking About Women*. So from the outset he offered encouragement to the women in his classes and in his profession, and he took great pleasure in the steady rise of an increasing number of gifted woman scholars.

The art Richard Ellmann most admired was that whose principles are central but unexpressed, and unexpressed because they are manifest in symbolic action. So, too, with his criticism, which he frequently raised to the level of art. He established, for two generations, the contexts of modern writing, and his own works have become a fundamental part of the context of modern criticism. In an age when brilliant practitioners succumbed increasingly to the temptation of producing interpretations which, in their rigour and ingenuity, seemed to outstrip the texts which they claimed to illuminate, Ellmann's dialogues with authors, students and readers represent a critical legacy as remarkable for its sympathy and humility as for its achievement.

Susan Dick
Declan Kiberd
Dougald McMillan
Joseph Ronsley
December 1987

Acknowledgements

The publishers are most grateful to the Society of Authors on behalf of the James Joyce Estate for their permission to quote from *Finnegans Wake*, and *Selected Letters of James Joyce*. Acknowledgement is also made to Jonathan Cape Ltd. for quotations from *Stephen Hero*, and *The Essential James Joyce* (ed. Harry Levin, containing *Portrait of the Artist as a Young Man*, and *Collected Poems*); to Faber & Faber Ltd. for quotations from James Joyce's letters and critical writings; and the Bodley Head for extracts from *Ulysses*. For the United States of America acknowledgement is made to Viking Press for extracts from *Finnegans Wake, the Portable James Joyce* (ed. Harry Levin, containing *A Portrait of the Artist as a Young Man* and *Collected Poems*), and *Selected Letters of James Joyce*; New Directions for *Stephen Hero*; and Random House for quotations from *Ulysses*.

The publishers are grateful to Messrs. A. P. Watt Ltd. on behalf of Michael B. Yeats and Macmillan London Limited, and for the Macmillan Publishing Company and Anne Yeats, for their permission to quote from the writings of W. B. Yeats in their respective territories.

'Heroic Work, Heroic Being': Avoid the Valedictory

Sylvan Schendler

> learn the
> right words . . .
> avoiding elevated
> generics like *misery*,
> *wretchedness*.
> William Meredith

Richard Ellmann completed *Samuel Beckett: Nayman of Noland*, in time for Beckett's eightieth birthday, on April 13, 1986. He may have been conscious of moderate difficulty in enunciation when reading the essay at the Library of Congress. During the winter at Oxford his voice had been unaccountably hoarse for too long. Before that, he had fallen twice when jogging. In June, when he travelled to McGill for an honorary degree, his speech was slurred. He was having difficulty with his posture.

Uncertain of the reason for his deterioration, he and Mary could still be amused when they remembered Captain Carpenter dismembered by life:

> To any adversary it is fame
> If he risk to be wounded by my tongue
> Or burnt in two beneath my red heart's flame
> Such are the perils he is cast among.

> But if he can he has a pretty choice
> From an anatomy with little to lose
> Whether he cut my tongue and take my voice
> Or whether it be my round red heart he choose.

He believed in what he observed when he thought of Beckett—the balancing force of wit in facing the grimness of existence. The spokesman for 'the decrepit and maimed and inarticulate, men and women at the end of their tether' chose a garbage can for his pulpit, and set flashes of irreverent detail against the darkness of the human condition.

'Praise Art . . . Praise Life'

The conclusion to *The Man and the Masks*, and the essay on Yeats almost forty years later: from praise of life and praise of art to the late vision. Images of

1

desolation, of abandonment, of death, succeed one another in the essay where he marks the beatific vision, but sense it overbalanced, in moments, by pain and nullification, 'not completion, not the abounding horn', but 'blankness, futility, emptiness'. The poet, facing death, knows pain, and the void. 'All men live in suffering', says the wild old wicked man who finds solace for a time in women, not in God. But his work stands, and the critic's admiration is not nullified, whatever the poet's despair:

> 'Let the fools rage, I swerved in naught,
> Something to perfection brought';
> But louder sang that ghost, 'What then?'

At The Door

Mary at the front entry with her walker. He had gone out. He had not said where. Wind and rain. Headline: Gales of Death Pound Britain. Then he is at the door, tall, twisted, thin, head drooping, he does not speak, busies himself peeling away the neck brace. Now the voice, the difficult line of words, phrases, the enunciation of muscles and nerves destroyed, the brain working behind its miraculous barrier to the disease. He repeats, the old effort to form speech, and tries again. Then punches out a sentence emerging on a tape.

He has been reading Dickens, *Old Curiosity Shop, Dombey and Son*.

What do you look for?
Head back, smiling: Varieties of imagination.
Are you troubled by sentimentality?
No, I like, it. He recalls Wilde: I cannot read of the death of Little Nell without laughing.

Beyond Yeats, Beyond Beckett

He was still physically strong when he wrote of Beckett, 'It is somehow salutary to know the horrors in store for us'. Beckett seconds Samuel Johnson's conviction that 'the predominant element in life is misery', and comes to approve the later Wilde who found that 'the secret of life is suffering'. The health in Richard Ellmann, the immense capacity for assimilating the accidents of existence to some large encompassing vision of life and of art, was not lost. A wild virus, a dark twist of the biologic order, made him drool, bent him over, destroyed the sounds of words. But not language. Nor even his delight in number.

What joke is apposite to such a condition? He recalls the story of the infirm gent, unable to bend over, who dropped a fifty cent coin in the lobby of the Fontainebleau. He refused to acknowledge his loss. 'Why should I pay a bell-hop a dollar to pick it up?' He taps out the punch line.

Mary fought back after a stroke. He felt himself falling apart and pressed for diagnosis. When it was revealed, there was nothing to fight it with. He tried acupuncture and Chinese drugs. The director of this therapy in England disagreed with the doctor in Tientsin who prescribed different formulas, and another use of the needles.

Avoid the Valedictory

What did he make of John Carey's review of *Four Dubliners*? Mary: he objected to it. He felt it was valedictory.

'Words', Beckett has said, 'are a form of complacency'. These four short studies show, however, that Ellmann's are not. His gift for uniting critical insight with biography is as freshening, as undogmatical and as humane as ever. (*Times*, 3/29/87).

He looks at his hands, then speaks in phrases and rhythms that enforce intelligibility: 'Time hath, my lord, a wallet on his back, bearing alms for oblivion'.

The Work Place

The first floor library, study. On the sofa, the floor, the table, the chairs, the shelves, hurricane of papers. Now fixed. Stacks of words. All arguing the uncomplacent mind. He produces the certificates. Come to this, has it? Numbers. Well, we can deal with number, and suppose connection, beneath number.

There are no things here, no objects to catch the eye. 'Poverty and possessions are the same thing, possessions being only meaningless arrests in time, and time itself an illusion.' For Beckett. The biographer marks the years, essays the man, knows Dublin. So distinguishes himself. This is an austere place, where the meaningless arrests of time have no place.

Ellmann's Road to Xanadu

Ellsworth Mason

In days of yore, when the Ivy League was still made of solid ivy, and before the Second World War shattered forever what was a very stable world, there lived in the nooks of Yale's English department three remarkable graduate students—William K. Wimsatt, Norman Holmes Pearson, and Richard Ellmann. Wimsatt kept very much to himself, bent hard on swiftly upgrading his prep school teaching status, and just missing by a hair compiling a bibliography of Colley Cibber as his dissertation. He had yet to emerge with curved beak and great wings flapping. Norman Pearson was by no means unlettered. He had already edited the Modern Library edition of Hawthorne's complete novels, and, with William Rose Benét, the *Oxford Anthology of American Literature*, a pioneering work and a best seller. But he was still undoctored, a parlous state for a scholar in 1939 requiring prompt treatment. He was warm and interested in people, even graduate students, but since he did not live in the Hall of Graduate Studies he was seen only occasionally.

These two were old men, past thirty (Pearson jokingly referred to himself as 'the oldest *living* graduate student'), and to the young and chipper, who for years had been watching Franklin D. Roosevelt turn over the economy monthly with a compost fork, they seemed part of another generation. In contrast Ellmann was one of us, bright, young, draft-bait, and as interesting as Pearson. With his graciousness and charm he was always visible, always companionable, and full of delights from off the beaten track. Ellmann knew, as most of us did not, that another major movement in English literature had occurred between the end of the first world war and the beginning of the second. Though his interests ranged broadly, he would slip into any conversation information about contemporary poetry. He was close to the undergraduates who launched *Furioso* magazine, including James Angleton (later of CIA fame, to our huge surprise), John Pauker, and Reed Whittemore. Ellmann was friend and magnet to anyone who would listen to a good word about 20th century literature. In William DeVane's Victorian Literature seminar his papers always invoked comparisons with contemporary writing.

And what contemporary writing! The literary production of 1939 to 1942 dropped on our doorstep (to skim off only the very top of the offerings) such items as:

Joyce—*Finnegans Wake* (1939).
Eliot—*The Family Reunion* (1939), *Burnt Norton* and *The Dry Salvages* (1941), *Little Gidding* (1942).

4

Yeats—*Last Poems and Two Plays* (1939), *If I Were Four-and-Twenty* (1940).
Auden—*The Double Man* and *New Year Letter* (1941), *Another Time* (1940).
Faulkner—*The Wild Palms* (1939), *The Hamlet* (1940), *Go Down, Moses* (1942).
Frost—*Collected Poems* (1939), *A Witness Tree* (1942).
Graves—*No More Ghosts* and *Sergeant Lamb of the Ninth* (1940), *Proceed, Sergeant Lamb* (1941).
Hemingway—*For Whom the Bell Tolls* (1940).
D.H. Lawrence—*Poems* (1939).
Marianne Moore—*What Are the Years?* (1941).
Pound—*Cantos LII-LXXI* (1940).
Shaw—*In Good King Charles's Golden Days* (1939).
Sitwell—*Poems New and Old* (1940), *Street Songs* (1942).
Stevens—*Notes Toward a Supreme Fiction* and *Parts of a World* (1942).
Thomas—*The Map of Love* (1939), *Portrait of the Artist as a Young Dog* (1940).
William C. Williams—*In the Money* (1940), *The Broken Span* (1941).
Woolf—*Between the Acts* (1941), *The Death of the Moth* (1942).

In looking back it is hard to realize that none of our mentors encouraged the reading of contemporary writing. Twentieth century literature was just beginning to emerge in the universities. At Harvard Harry Levin's course on Joyce, Proust and Mann had begun in 1939. At Yale, a half-year course in the contemporary British novel was first offered in 1937, taught by Arnold Whitridge, a grandson of Matthew Arnold. The first seminar in 20th century literature ever offered in the Yale graduate school was given by Cleanth Brooks in September 1947. I was in it. Ellmann's dissertation on Yeats in 1947 was the first ever accepted on a 20th century subject, and mine on Joyce in 1948 was the second. Ellmann had no formal instruction in 20th century literature during his study for three degrees at Yale, but he was working on it by himself. In 1939 he formed a small group, into which he had instilled the proper enthusiasm, which met in the large lounge area of Wimsatt's suite in Silliman College which he made accessible to us once a week. I can remember all of us poking in a crude way at the first three lines of 'Ash Wednesday' for an hour at a time, week after week, in the Spring of 1941 with no great success. They constitute a total of eight words, and at this distance it is hard to realize how remote they were from our reading experience. The second world war was to change all of that.

Much of the new literature was not appreciated at the time because no one could read difficult poetry well. The modernist movement was not clearly recognized, and certainly none of it was appraised at its true stature. Joyce, like Dante, was considered a great genius, but despite all the copies of *Ulysses* slipped into the United States illegally in the 1920s and its liberation in the 1934 Random House edition, nobody really read it (like Dante today). Nobody knew how to read it. About *Finnegans Wake* nobody could say anything sensible and only a few reviewers tried.[1] Moore, Sitwell, Stevens and Williams were almost unnoticed.[2] Woolf was looked at askew. Pound was considered a crackpot, Faulkner, a lightweight writer of overdramatic prose on sensational subjects. Graves and Lawrence, who wrote in fairly conventional styles, could not be considered seriously by anyone taken with the new writing of Auden and his circle. Indeed, the Auden circle was front and centre for those brave souls willing to wade into poetry they could not read. This was partly because they reflected the social concerns of England, which was much more depressed by the Depression than the United States and therefore much more radical, and partly because Auden et al. were adept at arrogant public relations.

Writers who were easily read were noticed, often for the wrong reasons. Shaw because he was fun and wrote lively prefaces, Frost because he was considered bucolic, hoe in one hand and pen in the other. Hemingway because he was a late Romantic and wrote about wars. *For Whom the Bell Tolls* made a big splash because it was about the Spanish Civil War, the central cause of the liberals of the 1930s, and because the quotation from Donne used as its epigraph and title reeked of brotherly love (as it does not in Donne's context). Sales certainly weren't hurt by a story that circulated widely shortly after the novel's publication. It seems that in great exuberance Hemingway came into the Stork Club in New York one night, waved his advance check for the book under the cashier's nose, and asked if she could cash it. It was for $100,000 in 1940 money. 'No we can't, Mr Hemingway', she said, 'but if you come back about ten o'clock we will.' Recognition of the novel as Hemingway's greatest was scant. Thomas, a full-blown Romantic, was viewed with interest tempered by his obscure writing.

Besides the Auden group, who excited us all, the two who could not be ignored were Eliot and Yeats. Eliot was all wrong for the times, a conservative in politics, profoundly religious in an arid secular climate, and concerned with ultimate things rather than government actions to patch up the surface of the world. Yet the deep rumble of his genius emerged from his poetry even when you couldn't understand it. I remember asking Ellmann, who had led me to Eliot, when I was going to start liking him, since I had been reading him for a month. He observed that so long as something kept me coming back to the poetry, I was moving in the direction of liking it.

Yeats was a queer one. Irish. All queer ones. He didn't really sound Irish, but he tried to. He had good Romantic credentials, though they had changed shortly after Queen Victoria died, and although much of his poetry was hard to read, not all of it was. Besides, by 1939 he was properly dead, an essential condition to be considered literature at the time. He had written many books and they were all around. In 1940 one of my jobs in the Yale University Library was setting out for public use duplicate booksellers' catalogues from the acquisitions department. Ellmann was already heavily into Yeats, and when I noticed him looking at the catalogues I volunteered to call his attention to all Yeats items in the catalogues I handled. From an ample allowance he was able to buy most of what I found, and had bought more than two-thirds of Yeats in first editions at prices from $3.50 to $8.00 before he left Yale for war service in 1942.

An event in the Spring of 1942 made us realize that when the army talked about able-bodied men they meant *us*. Charles Feidelson was among the first of the graduate students to be drafted. He was Ellmann's roommate, and probably had the most deeply intelligent mind of us all. The very flower of the intellectual crop that burgeoned at the end of the Great Depression, he had been top student in his Yale class and had won a Henry Fellowship to Oxford. He was keenly sensitive in his perceptions, and could think of nothing but the broadest, deepest philosophical implications, in all their subtleties, of any subject he approached, a fact about which he complained because it slowed him down. Now he was a GI in the army. We deplored this cosmic injustice, but we also looked at our draft cards again.

We'd signed up for the draft the year before in the opulent lounge of the Hall of Graduate Studies, with its twenty-foot high oak-beamed ceiling, its cushioned seats at great bay windows looking out onto grassy courts, and its splendid grand piano standing guard at the lounge entrance. There in the bright morning sunshine, we were dutifully registered for the draft by nice, well-groomed Yale departmental secretaries at the long dark-oak tables from which tea-and-cakes were dispensed each weekday afternoon. Who could think that this had anything to do with war? Our generation had been thoroughly infected by the powerful propaganda of the peace movement[3] that had grown out of disillusionment about Europe following the ruthless treaty imposed by the Allies on Germany after the first world war. The lying propaganda issued by the Allies during the war, much of it written by England's leading literary figures, had been thoroughly exposed, and we were convinced that Europe's great powers were a bunch of thugs who should be allowed to bash each other's brains out without our getting involved in it at all. This feeling tended to slow down the perception in this country of the extreme brutality of the Nazi regime, and despite the superb heroism of the British people in fending off all alone the Nazi airforce in 1940, we still suspected that somehow that tiny country must have some imperial motives hovering around in the background. Little did we suspect that the United States would be subjected to the same view forty years later.

Ellmann participated in these general attitudes, and although immediately after Pearl Harbour a number of graduate students rushed off to volunteer as officers, many of us were not at all sure that we wanted to get involved in the armed services, rather than preserving our sacred bodies and choice (and modest) minds for rebuilding the world after the war. Consequently, in June 1942, after being duly tagged with the highest degrees for which we could qualify, many of us sought government jobs in Washington, DC that could mollify our conscience and our draft status. Among the Yale biggies already in government service was Wilmarth Lewis, and to him at one time or other trotted the English graduate students, clutching in their MA'ed fists a recommendation from Fredrick Pottle, then Director of Graduate Studies in English (and a longstanding friend of Lewis), who had the remarkable ability of writing an honest two-sentence recommendation that made his candidate seem glowing. Lewis was the head of a section of the Coordinator of Information (a new government agency that became the Office of Strategic Services, and later the CIA) that was amassing into an ordered file information from all

sources including the FBI and Army and Navy intelligence, and writing
reports from it. Ellmann became a unit head in this section in March, 1942.
The switch from the intellectual world to the world of practical power was a
heady one for many academicians, as noted in Auden's poem written after the
war, 'Under Which Lyre':

> Professors back from secret missions
> Resume their proper eruditions,
> Though some regret it;
> They liked their dictaphones a lot,
> They met some big wheels, and do not
> Let you forget it.

The practical world, however, had its own difficulties, and Ellmann never
felt comfortable in it, complaining about the rigid channels of bureaucracy,
petty jealousies among employees, and the politics that infuse everything in
our nation's capital. He was trying to get an assignment involving writing, and
reported having composed and delivered 'a mildly satiric poem to my office
staff' which improved its morale, adding 'I have hitched my muse to an index
system'.[4] Ellmann tried to find me a job in his section but was blocked by a
budget freeze on staff. However, when I went to be interviewed by Wilmarth
Lewis I had made the rounds of other agencies and on June 29, 1942 I joined
the Board of Economic Warfare in Washington. For the next two months I saw
Ellmann frequently at lunch or dinner, often with other Yale friends, and
conversation would divide about equally between 20th century literature and
the antics of Washington.

In August Ellmann accepted an instructorship at Harvard that he felt he
couldn't refuse, and by the end of that academic year 'the draft boards
Damocletian sword' was hanging heavily over his head. At the same time, he
was reading Hone's biography of Yeats which he pronounced 'competent and
safe'.[5] September 1943 brought a shocker in the form of a postal card from
Camp Peary, Virginia, on its picture side the half-fun, half-corny emblem of
the US Navy Seabees and on the writing side Ellmann's complaint that he was
'stuck in this sailor's desert'. Of all the incongruities of the war none was
greater than Richard Ellmann in the US Navy Construction Battalions (CBs=
Seabees), whose principal function was to build and maintain airstrips and
related military facilities in the Pacific. My depression over this gross miscar-
riage was soon diverted by my own affairs. Three weeks later I was inducted
into the Navy and joined Ellmann as a Seabee at Camp Peary!

Ellmann hated with passion his service as a Navy enlisted man, although it
led in time to one of the two greatest strokes of luck in his life. Though most of
us had been inducted at the lowest rank in the Navy, he had been made
Yeoman Third Class, equal to the lowest grade of army sergeant, but he always
felt demeaned by his non-officer status throughout the war. I first realized this
one evening as we were walking in his barracks area and a fellow yeoman
approached us with Ensign Bubenick, from Oregon he said, and Ellmann did
something extraordinary to avoid saluting that officer. He pulled off his sailor's

hat! While an enlisted man does not have to salute an officer when he is not wearing a hat (to avoid popping salutes continually indoors), the fact of not wearing a hat outdoors constitutes being out of uniform, a condition punishable under the regulations of the Navy, but this Ellmann risked to avoid the salute. 'This Pool is hell', he remarked about the Stevedore Pool to which he was initially assigned,[6] and when he was transferred in June 1944 to the Headquarters of the 6th Naval District in Charleston, SC, he pronounced it 'a couple of steps closer to dementia praecox or psychoneurosis than Peary'.[7]

However, the same letter contained the first deep stirrings of intellectual life I had seen in him for a year, a poem entitled 'In Dispraise of Parents', with an epigraph from Hart Crane, 'The mind is brushed by sparrow wings', and some fine lines like:

> In the clutch, in the blow,
> Power lies, but truly lies
> In the tickle, the scratch,
> Using the Christian name,
> Jollying to weakness.

For the next year our correspondence maintained a highly intellectual flavour. Ellmann sent a stream of his poems, one emerging from Yeats's use of the word 'clambers', one heavily under the influence of Auden, and one with an epigraph from Valery's Le Cimetière Marin. Three of these poems were published in the Kenyon Review in 1945, following which Dodd, Mead offered to publish a book of his poems. Since he did not have enough for a book he turned them down.[8] We had an extended discussion of Koestler's Arrival and Departure which revealed to me for the first time the full range of his remarkable mind, the precision and subtlety and comprehensiveness of his understanding. By early 1945 he was in touch with Henri Michaux and had begun to translate his works.[9]

By April 1945 I was well into my tinkering with Joyce. I had sent to me in Eniwetok in the Marshall Islands my copy of the Portrait, and the newly published Stephen Hero, and had bought from a mate a copy of the Modern Library Ulysses that he'd found on the beach at Santa Barbara. Desultorily, I began to read it by chapters randomly and suddenly realized that the material of every chapter is intimately connected to every other chapter, and that as familiarity with its details develops the difficulty of reading Ulysses disappears. My discoveries were shared with Ellmann, about the interconnections between the Portrait and Ulysses, about Stephen's aesthetic theory, about Levin's book and an article that James T. Farrell published in the New York Times. To all this Ellmann replied rather casually, little realizing his future as a Joycean.

The most important chance in his life emerged after the war had ended. Ellmann had obtained a transfer out of the CBs and was assigned to Washington for about six months. Then at the beginning of 1945 he was transferred to the Headquarters staff of the Commander of the US Naval Forces, France, in Paris, and while complaining about 'this lousy typing and filing' he observed that 'this is a pretty exciting place to be'.[10] Shortly thereafter he ran into

Norman Pearson on the streets of Paris, and Pearson, who was head of a section of the (now) Office of Strategic Services in London, arranged to have Ellmann assigned by the Navy to work for him in London. The rest of the story is told in full in the Preface to the 1979 edition of *Yeats, The Man and the Masks*. In September 1945 Ellmann was granted unrestricted access by Mrs W.B. Yeats, who was much taken with him, to about 50,000 manuscript sheets of Yeats's writings, letters and diaries, much of it never published. He was the first scholar to confront what was substantially the entire body of manuscripts of a major 20th century writer.

After transfer back to Washington, where he continued to work for the OSS on assignment from the Navy, Ellmann returned to Ireland immediately after his discharge in May 1946, replete with a Rockefeller Foundation fellowship which sustained him through thirteen months of research for his dissertation. Ellmann got to know every significant figure in Irish letters in the country and was admitted to membership in the United Arts Club, where he lived while in Dublin.

Beginning in 1947, after passage of the Fulbright Act in 1946, dissertationeers descended on Ireland like a plague of locusts,[11] but in May 1946 Ellmann was far ahead of them in time and in the vital connections he quickly established with the Irish. A few Irish and English scholars were sniffing around Yeats, but none of them had his ability or his broad range of reading in 20th century literature.

Ellmann was writing his dissertation, that is to say he was fulfilling an academic requirement to prove that he had sufficient knowledge of research methods to become a valid scholar. The product was expected to be refinable into a neophyte publication, to be put behind as one climbed higher. Ellmann never thought in these limited terms. He had fallen into a gold mine and was fully confident that he would emerge from it with most of the important nuggets already shaped into imperishable form. Six months after his return to Ireland he wrote, 'It is hard to know how revolutionary my ideas are, but I do feel that I shall produce the definitive book on Yeats for many years to come'.[12]

The magnitude of his intentions were made clear in a letter of November 11, 1946, warning me not to write my dissertation on Joyce, who was 'fine as a hobby but not dissertation material'. It was impossible to work on him outside of Dublin, Paris and Zürich. I would have to get hold of letters and talk to people who knew him, would have to do a very careful study of Catholic doctrine and literature, and there were other problems, too. 'You can't work on a man so recently dead without being a constant prey of his friends' misconceptions. Exegesis with Joyce is in an earlier stage even than in Yeats, and your problems would therefore be greater than mine, which are, God knows, great enough.' Was I prepared to do the biographical work necessary for any new study of Joyce? 'Every creative artist has a life so bound up with his work that the questions of value are constantly impinging upon facts of his life.' While this reflects his preoccupations in his work on Yeats, it also shows that six years before he began his biography of Joyce, Ellmann already had rough-hewn at the edge of his mind the central problems he would attack in writing that book.

Ellmann didn't write a dissertation; he wrote a book which he submitted as a dissertation before he published it. It was a pioneering book in 20th century studies. In demonstrating how Yeats evolved a new way of writing poetry and seeing his development as inseparable from that of modern poetry Ellmann set forth a seminal view of forces that shaped the modernist movement. His was the first literary study to show the gigantic dislocations in thought and personal confidence that followed the impact of 20th century science and materialism on 19th century ideas. Yeats, who was born the year that our Civil War ended and died the year the second world war began, straddled both worlds. He intensely desired to belong to the world of the mind and imagination and to reject the outside world. Yet he was so much a 20th century product that he would subject the validity of occult ideas and symbols to empirical tests by observations in daily life. In *A Vision*, despite all of its occult trappings, Yeats tried to wrap all of history up in a numerical, almost mathematical, quasi-geometrical mantle. Ellmann's book was the first ambitious attempt to see a 20th century poet in the 20th century, and in the process he began to define our understanding of modernism.

Six years later he continued this definition in *The Identity of Yeats*, a far more philosophical book which refined his approach to an understanding of modernism. In these two books we see a modern tradition that reaches into romanticism and interacts with it in a variety of ways. We see a poet who elevated the individual above society, and passion, will and unconscious feeling above consciousness and intellection. We see the struggle of a man who rails at the culture around him but does not reject society, clinging fast to custom and established ritual. Throughout, we see in Yeats the myth-making tendency that pervades modernism in a number of different guises, the myths sometimes wearing masks of their own.

Eleven years later in 1965, in collaboration with Charles Feidelson, Ellmann published *The Modern Tradition*, an anthology of discursive statements across the entire spectrum of thought, which is probably the most important book in exposing the kinds of ideas that underlie 20th century art, and beyond that the world of practical action and human culture. The book presents the groundwork for a general theory of modernism, suggesting in its topical headings central criteria for such a theory, and demonstrating how wide is the range of ideas that must be taken into consideration in developing such a theory. Yeats is represented by six contributions in this collection. It came at a pivotal year in our culture, 1965, and reading it in light of subsequent developments makes clear that modernist art was prophetic of what was to come in its ideas and attitudes.

Eight years later, in collaboration with Robert O'Clair, Ellmann published *The Norton Anthology of Modern Poetry*, which in its span, its selection and its editorial apparatus (we're still in the exegesis stage) is one of the most remarkable anthologies of all time. In its comments and footnotes, it continues the definition of modernism and the reaction against it. Many voices have spoken about modernism during the past thirty years, but none of them has been more cogent, or persistent than Ellmann's.

Ellmann's enormous scholarly productivity was subsidized to some extent by foundations, but mostly by the universities where he taught. He returned from Ireland in 1948 as Briggs-Copeland Assistant Professor of English Composition at Harvard, one of the few named posts for young instructors, and after he gave a paper on a panel with Auden and Eric Bentley at the Modern Language Association annual meeting in December 1948, job offers began to come in. After two years at Harvard he was offered a full professorship at the University of Iowa to succeed Austin Warren, but since he had been granted a sabbatical and a Guggenheim fellowship he turned it down. A year later, as he was being interviewed by Northwestern University, he slipped the fact of this offer into the negotiations and 'it perceptibly raised the tone of conversation' and raised the rank they offered him to full professor. During his seventeen years at Northwestern he was continually pursued by other offers,[13] many of them as department head (which he would not have enjoyed), and although he thought that Northwestern just fell short of being a first rate university, he remained there because it steadfastly topped every other salary he was offered and allowed him princely teaching loads. Toward the end of his tenure there he was teaching one course the first semester and two courses the second semester with every third year off with full pay. When American friends asked him why he prolonged his stay at Oxford University, where he originally intended to stay a few years, he replied that he had gotten used to the Oxford academic teaching load, which was 'forty-eight hours a year'. ·

The results of all this academic generosity emerged in twenty-one distinguished books, three of which (including the Wilde) will remain monuments in their fields. Although his academic lectures varied in quality with the pressure of his writing, those prepared for public presentation were always remarkable—real mind-stretchers from beginning to end, artfully constructed in their exposition, with details finely chiselled from the range of his subject and melded into a mosaic of shining brilliance. He is the only one in history who has been invited to give the Gertrude Clarke Whitall Poetry Lecture at the Library of Congress four different times. I believe that he is the only author who received a *New York Times Book Review* front page article for both the first and the second edition of a book (the Joyce biography). Ellmann was a rare man, the finest teacher and scholar of my generation, and those of us who knew him will not see his like again.

With Dick in Dublin, 1946

John V. Kelleher

It bothers me that I don't remember how we met or who introduced us, though I presume it was some Yale friend of his, then a graduate student at Harvard, who knew that we both intended to go to Ireland as soon as we could. Anyway, we did meet in the spring of 1946 and arranged to travel together.

We left New York in late May, I think, and it was on shipboard that I really got to know Dick and to appreciate his charm and tact. The old Cunarder on which we sailed was unconverted from its wartime role as troop transport so the passengers slept in big rooms—separate quarters for men and women—and each had a five-tiered bunk to himself and could occupy whichever level he chose. There were only a few stewards (just the right number) and one could stand at the rail and watch the grey tossing waves without being lassoed for activities. Such organized entertainment as there was was incited and directed by a lively, bossy British Navy wife who was returning from five or six years in New Zealand. One day she came up to me as I was looking hopefully for whales and said, 'Really, I don't know what you teach your American college students. We've been playing Twenty Questions and no one could guess Bonar Law!' 'Well', I said, 'suppose they were British students and the answer was Benjamin Harrison.' 'Well, who was *he*?' 'A President of the United States.' 'Well, surely you don't mean to compare a President of the United States to a Prime Minister of the British Empire?' And she stalked angrily away. (Unfortunately I could not recommend that she look at Robert Blake's *The Unknown Prime Minister: The Life and Times of Andrew Bonar Law, 1858-1923* because it hadn't been written yet, but it may be doubted that even that would have had much effect.) A little later, though, I saw her indignantly laying the case before Dick. He soothed her. He listened smilingly and a little pensively, then began to chuckle softly—not at her, not at me, not at the questions, but at the situation. The things people get themselves involved in. Presently she began to laugh too. By the next afternoon she had forgiven me almost fully, though for what I could never quite figure out. That was the first time I saw Dick's tact in operation. It was wholly personal, quite instinctive, and as far as I could observe it always worked.

On the last morning of the voyage, as the ship was moving at reduced speed along the Cork coast, he and I stood at the rail and watched as a mile-high curtain of brown fog lifted slowly to reveal great hills curving smoothly down to the sea. It was a moment of emotion for me—seeing for the first time what my grandparents and great-grandparents had seen for the last time seventy-five or a hundred years before, so I didn't notice till Dick nudged me and pointed

him out that a steward was coming down the deck selling chances on a ship's
pool as to the minute when the pilot would be picked up. As we watched him
come, Dick lectured me quietly on the foolishness of throwing money away on
something with the odds so stacked against the bettor. Maybe because I knew
the odds as well as he did, or maybe because I was feeling lucky, I at once paid
my dollar when approached and chose my minute from among those still left.
Dick was disgusted. All that sound advice gone to waste.

A couple of hours later when the ship came to anchor off Cobh we were
edified to see that the approaching tender was the *John Joyce*, surely a good
omen for a couple of students of Irish literature, even if it was unlikely that the
craft was named for John Stanislaus, father of James. Then there was another
omen. The steward came running up, calling my name, and handed me fifty
dollars. Dick was torn between dismay and hilarity. He never forgot it,
counting it afterwards as one of the two occasions on which I had clearly bested
him.

I would accept that there were only two, for I had learned very early on in our
association that in most ways he was distinctly the more competent. He had
been to Dublin, on leave from his Navy assignment in London, the year
before; and in that short visit he had made, as I was soon to discover, a
surprising number of acquaintances. Again, since I was a stammerer, with a
stammerer's shyness, his ready address and his ability to talk easily on the
telephone were of great service to me, as was his practical gift for solving the
problems that daily confront tourists. Nearly every day I had fresh cause to
bless the luck that had brought us together.

I might say, too, that we were not at all in competition. He was there to work
on his biography of Yeats. I had come to learn as much about Ireland as I could
and possibly to meet some of the writers—in particular Sean O'Faolain, Frank
O'Connor and Austin Clarke—in whose work I was then most interested.
Three years earlier I had had an exchange of letters with O'Faolain and I now
thought I might write him, asking for an interview. How to go about trying to
meet O'Connor and Clarke I had no clear notion. As it turned out, I needn't
have worried.

After a night in Cork we came to Dublin by train. At my insistence we took a
jaunting car from Kingsbridge Station to the Shelbourne Hotel where we were
to spend our first week. For me it was an amazing ride. I had the map of Dublin
in my head and I had studied guidebooks, photograph albums, city histories,
and of course *Ulysses*, but as we trotted along the south side quays, then up to
Dame Street and through College Green, everything I looked at was the wrong
size or a strange colour or somehow misplaced. As we swung into Grafton
Street and approached the hotel, I suddenly realized that I had forgotten
whether twelve or twenty related to pounds or pence or how much any coin was
worth in American money. When I paid the jarvey he smiled broadly and
wished us the happiest of times. Dick said, 'You'd better let me handle the
money for the next day or two'.

Twenty minutes later, as I stared out the window of our room at the pond in
Stephen's Green, Dick made a telephone call. Not long afterwards a maid

rapped on the door to announce a Mr Montgomery. A slim man, with a derby and umbrella, came in, sat on the bed, talked rapidly for ten minutes, and left us with an invitation to dinner at his home on the following evening. Though I didn't realize it, from that moment Ireland began opening up for me. Niall Montgomery was soon, and would long remain, a much to be cherished friend.

The next day Dick, having made more use of the telephone, brought me to the Palace Bar in Fleet Street, then a great haunt of Dublin literateurs, and introduced me to Frank O'Connor and his wife, Evelyn, while less-known writers stared over their shoulders at us. I proposed a drink, but O'Connor said, 'No, let's get the hell out of here first!' which we did; and on the way up to Davy Byrne's in Duke Street I began learning that Irish writers were not all a band of brothers.

Things happened very rapidly that first week. The day after we met O'Connor we had lunch at the Bailey with Sean O'Faolain for whom my longstanding admiration was instantly confirmed and indeed doubled. Niall meanwhile was arranging that I should call on Austin Clarke. All this without my having had to lift a finger on my own behalf.

Presently Dick brought me to meet Mrs Yeats. She was not at all what I would have expected of a great poet's wife, being a large woman with a hearty laugh and much kindness and humour. With Dick I saw her on three or four occasions, at her home, at the Cuala Press, and once at the Unicorn, a new smart little restaurant, where she insisted on treating us to lunch. Though I have clear recollections of her, I would not presume to place them beside that warm and wonderfully accurate appreciation that Dick added as preface to the last edition of *Yeats, the Man and the Masks*, a noble essay, equally honourable to both.

Before the week was out Dick had found lodgings for us at the United Arts Club in Upper Fitzwilliam Street. We had separate rooms on the top floor, good-sized rooms, adequately furnished, and soon found ourselves happily settled in. There were a few other lodgers, some regulars came to dinner nearly every night, and other members drifted in from time to time. We got to know them all, a most pleasant lot of people.

None, I might say, were arty. In fact some had no perceptible connection with art in any form and apparently were accounted none the worse for that—which was understandable, for the Dublin arty crowd of that period, known at once by the uniform (for men, beards, corduroys, and heavy sandals; for women, heavy sandals and peasant skirts), were a painful lot. Niall had a story about an old pub-owner, a friend of his father's, whose two sons and two daughters all went arty on him and advertised their scorn of the old Philistine on whom they battened. Finally he called them into conference. 'I just wanted to tell yez one thing', he said. 'Yer mother and I was never married, and yez is nothing but a get of bastards.' The story delighted Dick, not least for its revelation of so useful a collective: nide of pheasants, pride of lions, get of bastards. There was one sturdy beard we used to pass nearly every morning in Baggot Street. He glared at us, apparently sensing that there was something wrong about our smiles.

I had one complaint about the club. Every morning the maids brought breakfast to our rooms, lugging the heavy trays up three flights from the kitchen. Not only did I detest breakfast in bed, there was the ideological aspect. Being waited on like that placed us against our will and certainly against our wishes in a most undemocratic position. Yet I found that Dick, though he too would have preferred to eat at the table, accepted the arrangement philosophically. We had, he reminded me, been asked how we would like breakfast, and we had both said we would come down for it at whatever time was most convenient for the staff. Whereupon they, having politely ascertained our wishes, had proceeded to do what they would have done anyway. 'You see', he explained, 'they find it easier to bring up the trays than to set up the dining-room for breakfast and then change it again for dinner.' He was right of course, but how did he find that out? Though doubtless the maids talked to him more readily than they would to me, it wasn't until about a month later that I saw that he, without a drop of Irish blood in his veins, had at once grasped a principle I had to learn the hard way. One could call it the certainly-sir-whatever-you'd-like principle. When I was cycling around Ireland and putting up at country hotels I tried again and again to get off to an early start. Could I, I would ask, have my shaving water by, say, seven and breakfast shortly afterwards? 'Your shaving water at seven? Certainly, sir.' Next morning the bedroom door would open slightly at half past nine and an arm reach in and place a brass jug of hot water on the floor. Then, after a hearty breakfast, I would get on the road about eleven, just as the last of the local shopkeepers was taking down his shutters and smiling at the dawn of a new day.

Jack Yeats the painter, the poet's younger brother, dined at the club at least once a week, a tall slender old man who used to arrive wearing a sailor's pea-jacket. He was treated with marked respect, though I learned that some found it rather tedious when he got onto a favourite subject like children's games or the art of sailing paper boats. He spoke in a low even voice with the same basic accent one can hear on W.B.'s surviving records, but with none of the roll and drama. He lived and had his studio in Fitzwilliam Square, and once Niall brought me to one of his Thursday afternoons. A half dozen other guests were there, talking over tea with the painter and his wife. His easel, with a paper rose at the top, was at the other end of the long room, and after a while I walked over to look at the painting it held—'The Tired Boxer', an exhausted fighter slumped on his stool with his arms spread limply on the ropes. Then I went behind the easel. Another man was there, a lean, pleasant man with whom I got into a conversation about the American army. Presently he said he had to leave and he introduced himself, Samuel Beckett.

One bright afternoon soon after, Dick and I walked out to Roebuck to call on Madame Maud Gonne MacBride who was then in her early eighties. On the way Dick shared various warnings about what not to say, what subjects not to raise, that had been given him by Mrs Yeats and others. These, added to my awareness that my sympathies in Irish politics were almost diametrically opposed to those of Madame MacBride, insured that I scarcely opened my mouth during the entire visit. But as I recall Dick hadn't much to say either. Opportunity seldom offered.

Madame MacBride had published her autobiography, *A Servant of the Queen*, in 1938, so not unnaturally any question about past events called forth a reasonably close recitation of the relevant pages of the book, and since one topic led on to another there were few intervals for the insertion of further questions. She was very alert; she clearly enjoyed a fresh audience, and, sitting in a low easychair before the tiled fireplace with her hands clasped around one knee, she talked on in as lovely a voice as I have ever heard, truly a flute-like voice. She spoke of Willie Yeats and herself, pre-revolutionary politics and herself, the Easter Rising and herself, herself and the bitter aftermath of the Civil War. As for her long quarrel with Yeats over his support for the Irish Free State which she as a Republican utterly rejected, that was now past and, though he had been so miserably in the wrong, she spoke of him with entire friendliness. As for the poems he had written about her, she seemed not to resent those that likened her to 'an old bellows full of angry wind' or to put special value on the many earlier lyrics that had sung her half-divine beauty. It was if she had always taken men's notice for granted and was half indifferent to it.

I thought her then the vainest woman I had ever encountered. In particular I was put off by her describing one of my heroes, James Connolly, the Labour leader executed in 1916, as 'that little man', in what seemed exactly the words and tone used by women in America when boasting of having discovered some fink who would do cut-rate painting or plumbing. But I was wrong about that. She, who was six feet tall, simply meant that Connolly was quite short, and when I re-read *A Servant of the Queen* I found that she called him 'the bravest man I ever knew'. Courage, surely, was something she was well able to judge of.

As we walked back I wondered if Dick thought he had got anything useful out of the interview, but he hadn't much to say except to agree that Yeats's luck had held when Maud had turned him down for the last time and he had married Georgie Hyde-Lees. It wasn't till much later that I realized that in these interviews he could perceive clearly many things, small significant traits of personality for instance, that I, with my all-too-ready judgments, might miss completely.

We went into Trinity College to call briefly on H.O. White, the Professor of English, a friendly man who was most helpful to Dick and who had remarked to us that day that 'Yeats is still everywhere in this town'. Signs on it, he was right. In Kildare Street we stopped to watch a platoon of greenclad infantry slogging along glumly behind a small band that was playing 'Down by the Salley Gardens', a lovely air but the least foot-stirring of marches. Not as hopeless, though, as the 'Three Marching Songs' Yeats had written for the Blue Shirts, the words set to the tune of 'O'Donnell Abu' according to the notion of a tone-deaf man who had never done any marching himself.

Now the time had come for me to get out of Dublin and explore Ireland. I bought a three-speed bike, leather panniers, a rain-cape, and various straps for fastening gear to the carrier, and having got much advice, all good but not all followable, I set off across the Wicklow mountains one warm, muggy day in July. Though I had tried to prepare with practice runs, by the third evening, when I got to Waterford, I was distinctly saddlesore. From there on, as I painfully made my way, cycling standing up or pushing the bike for long distances, the thought grew that when I got to Cork I should have to enter the hospital and have my behind amputated. However, after three days in Cork, walking everywhere in the little city to discover the settings of short stories and novels by Corkery, O'Faolain, and O'Connor, I suddenly realized that my seat had indurated. From there on cycling was no trouble and my daily runs got longer and longer. There were only two botherments: the weather—1946 was a very wet year and sometimes I was rained in for a day or two—and the lack of reading matter. O'Faolain had stressed the need to stock up on Penguins in Cork, warning that I would find few, if any, books between there and Limerick. He might have added that when one is stuck in a big dark bedroom with a single 15-watt bulb hanging from the middle of the ceiling one might as well crawl into the damp bed and forget about reading anyway.

These small matters apart, I enjoyed myself tremendously. It was a great time for such a tour. The roads were good, the people wonderfully kind and friendly, there were few automobiles and those driven slowly to conserve scarce petrol, and once I had discovered that the way to get meat and potatoes was to find where the commercial travellers ate, I was able to avoid unbroken runs of bacon and eggs, tea, toast, and jam for breakfast, lunch, and high tea. Before that I had had thirteen such meals in a row.

In Limerick I called on O'Connor's friend, Standish Stewart, to pick up the mail I had had forwarded to his house. He kept me for a week, introduced me to his great circle of friends, and at last sent me on with advice, introductions, and most precise instructions for finding all sorts of antiquities—dolmens, crosses, forts, sheelanagigs, everything. As with Niall, there was another great opening-up before me and another lifelong friend.

From Galway I took the train back to Dublin and found to my pleasure that I had acquired considerable kudos as an American who was really seeing Ireland and seeing it the right way. Dick I now saw less of for he had finished talking with those he needed to interview in Dublin and was working steadily at Mrs Yeats's house on the Yeats papers. We dined together nearly every night but no longer travelled together around the city. In any case, after a week or so, I went back to Galway to resume the trek.

It had been raining steadily in Galway when I had left it, and rain was descending with grim determination when I returned. However, after waiting a day or two I took to the roads again. Sometimes cycling, sometimes travelling by bus with the bike on the roof, I at last came to Sligo. There the rain really came down. After three days in the hotel, listening to arguments between a combative American priest and a retired British major, I went to the station and bought a ticket for Dublin. On the train I got talking with a young farmer, a man about my own age, who had spent all spring and half the summer trying to keep his ditches open while the rain relentlessly flattened his crops in the fields. He was going up to Dublin to see some movies. At Mullingar, as we stared out at the grey rain-soaked square beyond the station, a wide square in which the only sign of life was a grey rain-soaked dog, the farmer sighed and said, 'Ah, well, as the Turks say, "Fatima, it is fate"'.

Dick, I found, had decided to go with me when I should set out on the next leg of the trip. It may have been that story which delighted him. It may have been that he was stirred to emulation of my feats. Certainly it was partly because he felt he should talk with some of Yeats's Sligo relatives and he might as well do so now. A more compelling reason, though, was that Horse Show week was impending and our rooms at the club were wanted for regular members who would be coming up from the country. Anyway, he hired a bike and did a bit of practising, and, since the rain had let up, we took the train west.

I know that he thoroughly enjoyed the next several days, which were full of warm golden sunshine. We cycled the four miles to Knocknarea and climbed that thousand-foot hill to the great cairn under which, Yeats had declared, 'passionate Maeve lies stony still'. Actually its name in Irish is *Measgán Meidhbhe*, 'Maeve's mess, or butterpat', but neither of us knew that then, and we stood on top of the cairn looking reverently out over the entire landscape of Yeats's early writings. The next day we went to Drumcliffe, saw the old stone cross under which Yeats would be reburied when his body was brought back from France, and climbed Ben Bulben. I remember the hares darting out of the grass and fanning out before us as we mounted the slope. That evening I went with him as he called on the Middletons to whom Mrs Yeats had given him letters of introduction.

Though none of them seemed particularly interested in cousin Willie—one *was* interested in the fact that we often saw Jack at the Arts Club, but though he evidently liked Jack he had nothing to say about him—on that occasion I really came to understand and appreciate what Dick was doing. His way was to come armed with more, and generally more detailed and reliable, knowledge than he could expect the person interviewed to have, yet never to bring this forward, never to contradict, scarcely ever to interrupt. He let them talk; he showed himself grateful for what they told him; now and then with a quiet question he would elicit some particular point of information, and in leaving would express his thanks again. He left them smiling and thinking, what a nice young man!

Though I then wondered that he thought the trouble worth it, for in view of what he already knew the ore he could extract from these interviews would scarcely assay at one-percent, when, a year later, I was reading his book in typescript I saw how much this constant concern for small facts, minor interrelations, contributed to the consistency and authority of the portrait.

I am afraid (indeed I know all too well) that as we cycled north from Sligo Dick's enjoyment of the trip dwindled rapidly. We were then beyond Yeats country—in picturesque landscape, to be sure, but I don't think Dick was much of a man for landscape—and from the way he got off the bike at every opportunity, electing to push it up even rather small hills, I recognized that he was finding little to lift his spirits. We spent the night in Ballyshannon, the hometown of William Allingham. Even this association with a poet who had greatly interested the young Yeats and from whose verse he had lifted a number of rhythms failed to stir Dick. He wasn't much of a man for minor poets either. And the following evening, after a very slow day's ride to Donegal town, he announced flatly that wherever I went the next day he would follow by bus.

We agreed that we would meet at Dungloe. I would start early, cycle ahead, and get us a room at Sweeney's hotel. His bus should get there in the late afternoon. I marvel now to think that I made that long run in such quick time, for I got to Dungloe before two. The girl at the desk brought me through long passages to the room, and I, having been led through many such passages, memorized the pictures on the walls so that I could find the room again. I went out then, found the cobbler, got my boots tapped, and came back to the hotel. When I opened the room door a priest glared at me. I reported this at the desk. The girl stuck her knuckles between her teeth and giggled. 'Oh, I forgot to tell you. Father MacK—always has that room, so I moved you to another.' She brought me to the other and I memorized a new series of pictures. After that I went out to the street to wait for the bus. It came more or less on time, and Dick, looking very disgruntled, descended painfully from it and waited for his bike to be handed down from the roof.

He made little conversation as I conducted him to our new room. I opened the door, and a woman in her underwear let out a shriek. This time the girl at the desk was less apologetic. 'Tis how Mrs So-and-so always has that room when she comes, so I moved you again.' Clearly, as with the British Navy wife, the fault was somehow mine. Anyone in his right mind ought to have known about Mrs So-and-so.

My contretemps somewhat cheered Dick, and we had a pleasant supper and a slow walk around the little town, but I knew that he dreaded the next day and I knew why. He had my warm sympathy.

Actually he did very well, partly because we made a long day of it, pushing the bikes and talking as we went up the straight, slowly rising road past Glenveagh Castle, but again that night at Letterkenny he told me he would take the bus to Londonderry and meet me there.

We spent two days in Londonderry. The second evening we went to a show at the Guildhall, a group of one-acters put on by a travelling company of the Abbey Theatre making their first appearance in the North since before the war. There was good attendance, a most friendly audience, and I particularly noticed that an Inspector of the Royal Ulster Constabulary in full uniform was roaring with laughter at the boasting of Dolphie Griggs, the comic Orangeman, in O'Casey's *The Shadow of a Gunman*. As we went out of the Guildhall past the statue of Victoria in the lace dress (of all lace dresses the most perfectly carved in marble)—hall and statue now, alas, no more—a hand was laid on my arm and a voice said, 'What happened you? We waited nearly two hours for you at the bottom of the pass'. Two young Derrymen I had met in Kerry and had travelled with for a couple of days. From Dingle we had started over the Conor Pass together, but on the far side I got a flat tire, couldn't succeed in repairing it myself, and was at last saved by a quarryman who stopped to help. He took a big piece of patching out of his pocket, cut off a chunk, and, as it seemed to me, spat on it and stuck it on the tube. The patch held for the rest of the trip, but I never caught up with the Derry lads.

The coincidence of this meeting amazed Dick and set him talking about how different everything is in a small country than in such places as London or the United States. Yet, years afterwards, when I mentioned the incident to him, I was even more amazed to find that he remembered nothing about Londonderry or Letterkenny and had even forgotten Mrs So-and-so in the room at Dungloe. Even at the time, though, I should have realized from his pensive expression when we parted at the station in Londonderry that his mind was on the biography and all that remained to be done in Dublin and London and, even more immediately, that he was looking ahead to travelling on a cushioned seat, with no need ever again to bestride a bicycle.

By the time I had finished cycling through the North and down to Dublin it was nearing the time for both of us to leave. Dick was to go to London; I, back to my wife and two small daughters after an absence of more than three months. There was, though, one joint-project I thought we might manage in the days remaining. Except for Night-town, the brothel quarter, which had been pretty well demolished, and O'Connell Street where so many of the buildings had been burned out in 1916 and 1922, much of Dublin looked just about the same as it had in Joyce's youth. Even in O'Connell Street the General Post Office had been restored and the statues and Nelson's Pillar were unchanged. People dressed differently, to be sure, and that would be a problem, but on the other hand the trams were still running, there was plenty of horsedrawn traffic, and if one was careful it should be fairly easy to avoid photographing automobiles. How would it be, then, if we got a movie-camera and two men dressed in black, one of medium build and wearing a derby, the other, tall and slim, with a wide black hat. The derbied man, as Leopold Bloom, could walk a few yards ahead of the camera as we filmed his journeys through the city. The fellow with the hat would stroll as Stephen Dedalus.

Dick demurred. Doubtless he was still much too busy with the Yeats documents, but the reasons he gave were that neither of us knew anything about film-making and, besides, that I was such a rotten photographer. (In that opinion he was not alone. Stan Stewart had a generic name for a bad picture, such as one taken out of focus in a rainstorm. It was 'a Kelleher'.) So the proposal died a-borning, but I still think the idea was good. No matter how fuzzy the film of that now vanished Dublin might have turned out, it would nowadays be an accepted classic on the college circuit.

I decided to carry out what I could of the scheme with still photography. My own camera had disappeared somewhere in Mayo, so I borrowed Dick's and in the course of two sunny days and a lot of hiking I shot Joycean scenes by the dozen—7 Eccles Street, the Volta Cinema, the house outside of which Stephen and Cranly listened to the scullery maid singing 'Sweet Rosie O'Grady', to name only a few buildings that are now vanished. I took three rolls but I didn't get them developed till I was home. Then I discovered that if I was the world's worst photographer, Dick was the owner of the world's worst camera, for it had a hole in the bellows, and every snap came out with a great white spot in the middle and with only a fringe of blurry detail to identify the scene.

In the years immediately after, we were both Assistant Professors at Harvard—Dick, alas, only on a five-year Briggs-Copeland appointment. Naturally we saw much of each other, and a day came when I called at their flat to behold and praise his and Mary's firstborn, Stephen. Even before I was admitted I could hear the baby within, howling without pause and with a vigour that should allay any fears for his health. Dick opened the door. His brow was knotted with anxiety and he murmured something about perhaps calling in a child psychologist. Mary was the picture of distraction and worry. As the experienced father now of three, all good howlers on occasion, I picked Stevie up, laid him over my shoulder, and firmly patted his diaper. An enormous burp erupted. He gave one last yip and dropped into sound, sweet sleep.

Mary of course absorbed the whole lesson instantly. As for Dick, I watched his face reassembling itself stage by stage as he took in, considered, comprehended, and assimilated all the levels of meaning and guidance in this demonstration. Then he began to laugh, chuckling softly in his wonted way.

Richard Ellmann's Michaux:
A Publisher's Recollections

James Laughlin

One of the ornaments of the New Directions list in the early Fifties was Richard Ellmann's translations of *The Selected Writings of Henri Michaux* (1951).[1] At that time, although Michaux had been writing for over twenty years and had an established reputation in France, his work was scarcely known in the United States except through a few translations in small magazines. In 1949, New Directions had published Sylvia Beach's translation of Michaux's *A Barbarian in Asia*, the ironic and highly diverting account of his travels in the Far East as a young man, but that did not reach much of the poetry public. It was Dick's book which made Michaux in this country, by its sensitive translations and perhaps even more by the long introduction which so brilliantly analysed Michaux's writing[2] in terms of his life, personality and literary background. That essay still stands as the definitive treatment of Michaux in English; the acuteness of its perceptions foreshadowed what Dick would later be able to do with a subject as difficult as Joyce.

Perhaps I might say something about my own interest in French poetry because translations from the French became such an important part of our program at New Directions. In 1929 my parents shipped my brother and me off to a Swiss boarding school to spare us 'the unpleasantness' of the Depression in Pittsburgh. I arrived with very little French but since that was all that was permissibly spoken I had to bear down and learn some. Le Rosey, near Geneva, was quite a culture shock. There were students from twenty-two countries, including Pahlevi, as we called him, the heir to the throne of Iran. Not a lovable fellow. All he cared about was ice hockey, and we were jealous of his royal privileges; Saturday nights his bodyguards would drive him off to Geneva for amusement.

At Rosey, poetry was taught by Monsieur Jacquet, who was also the hockey coach. He would give us a passage to study and then we would have dictation. Jacquet would read the poem very slowly and we would try to copy it correctly in our blue *cahiers*, in ink. When our copies were returned to us corrected we had to recopy. Well, it was a way of learning some words, though seldom very useful ones. Finally, we were assigned certain passages to memorize and read in class, with many comments on our accents. Jacquet's taste was not bad for a hockey coach. I can still vaguely remember a few lines from two of his favourites. One very sad poem was by Sully Prudhomme. It ended:

> Des yeux sans nombre ont vu L'aurore;
> Maintenant ils dorment au fond des tombeaux.[3]

Another passage I recall was more exciting. It comes from Victor Hugo's poem about the biblical Cain:

> Lorsqu' avec ses enfants vêtus de peaux de bêtes
> Cain s'est enfui de devant Jehovah . . .

God's eye followed poor Cain wherever he went, but we never read to the end to find out what happened. Monsieur Jacquet was of stern demeanour but he did have to laugh when the class wit, the young Prince Metternich, in his recitation substituted 'peaux de phoques' for 'peaux de bêtes'. 'Peaux de phoques' were the long strips of sealskin which we strapped to the bottom of our skis to make them climb as we trudged up the mountain for our afternoon skiing, the ski lift having not yet been invented.

Of course my taste for poetry improved rapidly when I went to Choate where there were great English masters such as Carey Briggs and Dudley Fitts. My particular slant came when, after Freshman year at Harvard, I had the good luck in 1934 to be enrolled in Ezra Pound's 'Ezuversity' at Rapallo. Pound taught by his canon of the innovators, those who brought something new to poetry. The canon is set out in his *How to Read* (1931). Here, for French poetry, are certain troubadours, Villon[4] and then a long jump to Théophile Gautier, Corbière, Laforgue (these three an enthusiasm shared with Eliot) and Rimbaud.[5]

Pound told his students that they must have at least three languages to be good poets, to make use of more than one tradition. Certainly this exhortation influenced me when in 1936 at Pound's suggestion I started New Directions. Getting good French books translated became one of the major objectives. Skimming through the bibliography, I see that in fifty years New Directions has done thirty-five French authors, often with several books: fourteen poets (usually bilingual) and twenty-one prose writers. (For this worthy labour I received in due course my little red ribbon, with kisses on both cheeks from the French Consul. The ribbon actually has some utility—for getting good service in snooty Paris restaurants—and the grandchildren are impressed when I tell them that the military-looking medal is from an order founded by Napoleon . . . but less so when I explain that any stationmaster in France who doesn't derail a train during his career gets one too.) Whether Dick got one for his *Michaux* I don't know; he certainly deserved it for the book which gave American readers a great French poet.

I met Michaux through Sylvia Beach in 1947. Shakespeare and Company, at 12 rue de L'Odéon, was a shrine for any young literary person coming to Paris. I visited it at once and was received with a welcome that made me imagine I might be another Hemingway. What a charming, intelligent, perceptive, energetic and helpful lady she was. And how happy I was to find that she had a shelf of the better New Directions books in stock. Sylvia and her close friend Adrienne Monnier had been friends with the Michaux for some years. They took my wife and me to call on them, which I could hardly have arranged myself because Michaux received few visitors. He mixed very little with literary people and didn't frequent the cafés. He and his beautiful wife had a life of their own in a modest but comfortable apartment in the rue Séguier on the Left Bank near the Seine. Their self-absorption was much like that of Estlin and Marion Cummings in Patchin Place in Greenwich Village. There was even a physical and some temperamental resemblance between Michaux and Cummings. Both were rather slight, a bit bald, and mobile in their body language. They were lively, amusing talkers, both witty, though Cummings could be rather sarcastic while Michaux's tone was essentially ironic. And both were ardent painters. Cummings was never recognized as an important artist but Michaux was. He had frequent shows, even several in New York, and his work sold. I couldn't attempt to describe it. Like Klee, he was concerned with mental imagery, which was at once anguished and humorous; this was true also of characters in his writing. His technique was quite his own, sparing of colour, usually a soft wash over charcoal or ink for the figures. His figures are mysterious. The paintings are hermetic statements. He did many tiny ink drawings (his handwriting was small and almost indecipherable) often in a page of boxes, rigidly simplified little figures, inventions of his imagination. These figures are almost ideoglyphic. Michaux was fascinated by Chinese calligraphy. One of his last books, and one which greatly impressed Pound, was *Ideograms in China* (1975), in which Michaux analysed in terse, poetic paragraphs 'the way traced by writing'.

I had only that one visit with Michaux. He could not have been more hospitable but I sensed and respected his need for quiet, for work and meditation. As Ellmann points out, Michaux, in his own particular way, was a mystic. He knew the literature of mysticism and acknowledged Ruysbroek, Pascal and Lao Tse among his masters. Michaux, I think, was seeking a kind of 'nothingness' that would also liberate and reinforce his creativity. As Ellmann puts it, 'nothingness and the millenium had this in common: in both one is finally at one with the universe, by unconsciousness if . . . "he is drained of the abscess of being somebody", and by hyperconsciousness if he is a visionary'.

I heard from Michaux only when he had points to make about *Barbarian in Asia* or the *Selected Writings*. Then, in 1948, came word from Sylvia of a devastating event, the death of Madame Michaux. Her peignoir had become entangled in a heater and she suffered burns which proved fatal. I doubt that the despair of this loss had too much to do with an important phase of Michaux's later work, his experiments with mescalin and other hallucinatory drugs as a stimulus to composition and his detailed reporting on them. His first mescalin book, *Miserable Miracle* did not appear until 1956.[6]

What I may say about Michaux is of small importance. But Dick's introduction is a masterpiece of analysis and critical interpretation. For those readers who are unlikely to look up the *Selected Writings*, though New Directions keeps it in print in paperback, let me quote a few passages, chosen more or less at random.

Reading Michaux makes one uncomfortable. The world of his poems bears some relation to that of everyday, but it is hard to determine what. If we try to reassure ourselves by calling it fantasy, we have to ignore the scalpel which is playing about our insides. On the other hand, the term satire at first seems equally inappropriate, for the *point d'appui* is hidden, and no obvious appeal to law, convention, or common sense provides a focus for an attack on human ways. And to call Michaux's world obsessive or neurotic, as we may also be tempted momentarily to do, is to disregard the pervasive wit, a wit which is too keen, and implies too much control, to confirm a psychiatric explanation.

What makes his writing so difficult to categorize is not his concern with the self's wobblings and grapplings, which Proust had made familiar enough; rather it is his habit of casting pyschological insights into physical instead of mental terms, or into a system of images which at first appear arbitrary. The frame of reference is subtly displaced.
. . .

Michaux resembles allegorical writers in that he finds the internal world more important than the external one; he differs from them, however, in being unable or unwilling to keep the two separate. They merge disconcertingly.
. . .

Working independently of a writer like Kafka, he has arrived at a view of life which at many points is comparable. The same veneer of logicality overlies *The Space Within* as *The Castle* or *The Trial*. While both authors exert literary control over their material, that material is nothing if not the uncontrolable. Unknown or scarcely known forces dominate helplessly resisting or unresisting characters; yet the bleak landscape is relieved by the steady light of a sardonic humor, which restores a kind of equilibrium, a kind of normalcy, imparts detachment, and in the end suggests that man is more than a creature thrown into a mine without tools, flashlight, or map.

Michaux diverges from Kafka by implying no general guilt; he posits no god or devil to explain what is going on in the world. Instead he clearly and clinically presents the algebra of suffering; in spare, almost antiseptic, terms, he works out the equation: man being man, here is what happens.
. . .

Michaux writes in free verse, prose poems and prose, and the distinction between them seems to him of no consequence. He accentuates their informality by occasionally odd syntax, by frequent shifts between conversational and literary tenses, by idioms invented *ad hoc* and used as if known to everybody, by a colloquial overuse of the neuter gender, by an unusual concentration of verbs at the expense of other parts of speech, by exclamations, slang terms, and sentence fragments. But his iconoclasm is not so great as to prevent his occasionally introducing a formal note with remarkable results.
. . .

Michaux declares that we are multiple, carried this way or that by influences of different intensity from various sources . . . 'There is no one self. Self is only a position of equilibrium'. . . . When this fluid, elastic self attempts to come to grips with the world of objects, it is necessarily incapable of dominating them; they slip away. The attitude in the poems is one of non-acceptance of the world, of constant struggle against disintegration by the world.
. . .

The posture [of the poems] is nearly always one of attack. In some of them the attack is directed, as Michaux says, against all that is 'congealed and established'. . . . In others the attack is directed against words themselves. It is not waged in behalf of chaos, but of something beyond man, which the present setup of things does not make room for.
. . .

None of these characters is round or full. Plume might be an American as easily as a Frenchman; the details which could single him out have been resolutely cut away. For Michaux deals in flat planes, never in the third dimension. His people and situations alike come out of nothingness; they have no background and exist in a narrow space.
. . .

His words are as severely constricted in their meaning as his pictures in their detail . . . For all his stylistic freedom, he rigidly disavows those metaphorical connotations and allusions that most contemporary poets insist upon. With Michaux the poetry is not in the metaphor of words, but of situations. The statement itself is prosaic, but the tensions created are ultimately equivalent to those created by poems.

Dick was a publisher's dream to work with. He knew exactly what kind of book he wanted and how it should be layed out. He was a good proofreader and understood printing problems. Above all he was patient about delays which went far beyond the *retard normal*. It took over three years to get the book produced. It was a painful comedy of errors. At that time New Directions was suffering through one of its periods of extreme penury. The quotations we had from printers in New York for setting the French side of the bilingual text were frighteningly high. So I decided to print in France. Through a friend in Paris I met the benevolent Monsieur Henri Marchand, who had a small printshop out near the Lion de Belfort where he employed only the deaf and dumb, at low wages, since he was training them to be printers. His apprentices did well enough with the French pages but they had to compose the English letter by letter. Thus there were four sets of proofs for Dick to correct before all was right. Beyond that, because they knew no English, the young printers could not match up the English that was facing the French. (This is a constant problem with bilingual books since one language will inevitably run longer or shorter than the other). Dick had to sort that out. Worst of all, when the type was paged up it was discovered that, through an inaccurate cast off, too large a type had been chosen. The book would not fit into the 320 pages which had been agreed upon. Some poems had to be cut. Many authors would have raised the roof, but Dick understood our situation and went along with it. Fortunately he was in Paris when this crisis developed. He took Michaux out to Monsieur Marchand's and together they did the amputation. Although Routledge in London took a few hundred of our first printing, the book didn't sell out until 1967. The following year we brought out a paperback edition for which Dick made some corrections and supplied a new foreword. This we keep in print.

In the following years Dick and I corresponded about this and that. I had asked him in 1951 if he would like to write a book for our Makers of Modern Literature Series, short bio-critical volumes aimed especially at college students. This series got off to a great start with Harry Levin's *James Joyce* and ran to some dozen titles, including Trilling's *E.M. Forster* and Nabokov's somewhat curious *Gogol*. Dick at first suggested Hemingway but I felt that was premature; I was sure Hem still had some great books in him. Dick then suggested George Moore, whom he saw as 'an important link between French and English literature'. I was receptive, but Dick became involved in the Joyce letters project.

It is one of my little vanities that Dick gave me a footnote in his monumental biography of Joyce. I had told him about my visit to Joyce in Paris. In 1938 I had published Stuart Gilbert's translation of Edouard Dujardin's *Les Lauriers sont coupés (We'll to the Woods No More)*, a novella written in the 1880's, which is often cited as the first stream-of-consciousness novel. Typically, Joyce said little about the influence of *Les Lauriers* but he did tell the story of how he came on the book. Joyce loved singing. He learned that a remarkable tenor was to sing in the cathedral at Tours. He took with him a young friend, a Siamese prince who had adopted the name 'Ulysse' in his honour. He bought *Les Lauriers* at a kiosk on a station platform. Dick pursued this lead and identified the Siamese as authentic. This relieved my worry that I had been the victim of a Joycean leg-pull.

Dick had always been interested in the work of Pound. In 1968 he asked if I could help him explore the possibility of his doing a biography. By that time Ezra had gone into deep depression—there was the famous 'silence', he would speak only a few words a day—and he was not answering letters. My correspondence about his publishing affairs was with his wife, Dorothy Shakespear. Dorothy's reply asked quite bluntly the question I had feared: was Ellmann a Jew? If so he would be unacceptable to Ezra. It took me several letters to convince her that this was immaterial because Dick's *Joyce* had proved him to be the best scholar-biographer in the field. The next problem was whether Dick could have access to Pound's papers stored in one of the towers of his daughter's Brunnenburg castle near Merano. Mary de Rachewiltz was cooperative because she didn't really care for Noel Stock's biography and she had read the Joyce. The final question was whether Ezra would or could give any interviews. Even when he was well Pound had had little time for scholars unless they would talk about economics. There was no point in making the trip to Italy if Pound wouldn't converse. Things looked dim. But then, out of the blue, I heard from Lewis Freedman, the producer of cultural films, that he had raised money from a foundation to do a documentary on Pound, and that Ezra and Olga Rudge, Mary's mother, would soon be flying to New York. If he would talk in the film perhaps he would talk to Dick. Too good to be true, I thought. It was. Ezra wasn't strong enough to make the trip.

After Dick took up his chair at Oxford I saw little of him, except when now and then he came to New York, where he always stayed with our friends Gigi and Sylvan Schendler. And now he is gone. I miss him very much.

Richard Ellmann and Film Collaboration

Seán Ó Mórdha

As I think of Richard Ellmann at the end of this year of sadness for the Ellmann family, his monumental study of Oscar Wilde has scored a most wonderful critical and commercial success. Readers and critics alike have seen his new biography as the book of the year, perhaps, of the decade. Posthumously, Richard Ellmann has hit the jackpot sending Oscar forth triumphantly from the debris of the Victorian nineties to his rightful place as the first of the moderns.

My great film adventure with Dick Ellmann began in 1981 as I was preparing a documentary profile of James Joyce for the centenary celebrations. I was met with great courtesy at New College, Oxford, and later brought to 38 St Giles—that warm house of great talk, much humour, many books. So began a collaboration with Richard Ellmann on three major film portraits—James Joyce, Samuel Beckett, and Oscar Wilde. We also managed a Bloomsday celebration of Nora Barnacle and a delightful literary conversation on location in Dublin with Seamus Heaney.

Working with Dick Ellmann was fun. His great intelligence was energetically and enthusiastically released in the quest for the best possible results in the restricted time allocated by production schedules. As he covered well-trodden ground Dick was ever patient and encouraging. Having viewed a fine-cut of the Joyce documentary on the editing bench for two and a half hours, he made no comment, but simply asked if he could see the film from the top again. As I got to know him better I realised that this was Dick's way of giving himself time to reflect on what he had viewed. Over dinner that night and, when least expected, he gave his reaction to the film. He was always on the lookout for a new lead. The seemingly unimportant was important. He once laughingly said to me—'don't you think the way a genius knots his tie is important?'

We had many a leisurely meal and drink—'how I envy your wonderful Irish bladders' was his response as I ordered a second pint. We also occasionally tried our hands at the horses. He loved to get tips on Irish horses running in major English races. The fact that our winning streak never lasted very long did not bother him. If the horse put up a good show he was pleased to cheer him on. When we triumphed as we did so memorably with Dawn Run in the Cheltenham Gold Cup it was a cause for great jubilation and much replaying on his newly acquired video recorder. When Vincent O'Brien carried off yet

29

another top classic prize Dick was proud of his new reputation in Oxford—'I developed a considerable reputation in New College because of Caerleon—one of the porters was in the betting shop and saw me collect my winnings!'

Film was a completely new experience for Dick and he took to it with boyish enthusiasm. He understood its power, was fascinated by its techniques, and was not hindered by its limitations. He saw it as the modern way to communicate with a mass audience. One effect of the films is that Ireland has given a sort of national recognition to its great exiled writers. People are reading their works more than ever before. Irish insularity has been a little diminished by a sense of what modern literature is.

We had begun work on W.B. Yeats, the fourth Dubliner—'I'll write soon about self, alter ego and the tertium quid—that strange unknown who does Yeats's decision-making'. In October 1986 Dick told me he had Motor Neurone disease. Facing the inevitable with energy and tenacity, there was a heroic persistence in the way he managed to finish his *Oscar Wilde* in the months that were left.

This last great book, elegant and eloquent, has all the distinctive qualities we seek in Richard Ellmann's writings—a range of scholarship that dazzles, meticulous research that wins respect, and a wonderful way with words that is both uplifting and delightful. Richard Ellmann was a literary man with a passion for the modern movement. His many books, written with humour and compassion, will remain among the most penetrating and influential on the literature of our century.

The Oscar Wilde Playing Cards

Rosita Fanto

Juggling between fiction and reality, Richard Ellmann could transform even predictable schmalz into sophisticated entertainment. 'Clever', he said, delighted with the drawings. We went to his study in Wolfson College where we started on the Odyssey of the Oscar Wilde Playing Cards. We both were intoxicated by the novelty of this project—the pictorial form of a normally serious subject—and were urging each other on into a world of humorous fantasy.

Then Dick became a voice on the long distance telephone between Oxford and Monte Carlo where I had locked myself up to concentrate on the intricate scheme he had devised. To the profitable joy of the telephone company we spent hours late into the night deciding which of the drawings to use. We each had a set with a number for each drawing, and our visual imaginations did the rest.

At first Dick was cautious and shy in his comments. As he was getting more and more involved he surprised me not only by his artistic knowledge, but also by his instinct for fun. During that period he was sending joyful notes, at times mocking my working marathon, as on 27 January 1986: 'Are you working furiously, as I suspect? You must, with [Anthony] Burgess, be the hardest working people in Monte Carlo. The House of Grimaldi would be outraged if they knew of this treasonable industriousness.' Or, providing sympathy and amusement, on 27 February 1986:

I feel a bit conscience-stricken at leaving you so much to do, while I sit inertly in Oxford. Maybe there will be something later on with which I can help. Anyway, I hope it goes well. I sent you the program for Salome, and you will see a picture of a Herod with a headdress, which seemed to me impressive. Did I tell you that the conductor doesn't like Salome, so I got his parking place—en face de Covent Garden!

Or encouragement when it was badly needed, on the letterhead of the British Academy, on 25 March 1986: 'This stationery should give our midnight gambols respectability . . . I agree with you about . . . but as Blake says, "The fool who persists in his folly becomes wise".'

I knew that time was running out, but I did persist. The publishing date of the Oscar Wilde Playing Cards was 16 Ocober 1986. The event was celebrated at the Cadogan in London, where Lillie Langtry had lived and where Wilde was arrested. It was Dick's last public appearance. His illness was already greatly diminishing his strength. This was the last book he saw printed and signed, the last party he enjoyed as if everything was going to be eternal. The only consolation is that until the end, on 13 May 1987, encouragement and laughter were constantly there, despair only an underlying leitmotif.

Poems

Andonis Decavalles

SOLACE

How to fill the void of your corner in its sorrow?
What to tell our eyes as they search for your invulnerable
your endless smile that used to ripple like a rivulet
under the forest of your eyelashes? What to tell our
perplexed fingers that had known the motions of your own?

Cross-legged, with unbroken calm, your Greek britches
folded up, you had the sun a gold thread in your shuttle
to darn the tattered hours strolling on the pier. Knot after knot,
thought after thought, and memory after memory, you mended
all the wounds and losses of your net dragged from the deepest
spiny crags of the impenetrable.

                            You must be sitting now
at a shaded corner of the sky where, to fill our void,
the shuttle of your smile weaves a silken ladder to be lowered
for us to climb. Your unwounded net must lie deep down into
the sky's briny fathoms, capturing the voice of the voiceless,
the deathless throb. As for your hours, they must all have grown
into a single one of morning dressed forever in its Sunday clothes.

HINTERLAND

In lack of other stars, take those of memory
to help you with their glimmer in the dark impasses.
I would have said the sun, had he not been too honest
and enemical to recollection. After all, a sound you are,
and I can see you only through the hearing beyond sound.

You'll traverse the dark in sundry miles, your purling
body clear as a pebble, a first uttering to release the heave
in ocean's swell. But mind you, don't be touched when you
leave the shore behind. You will have to wash away
the dream's anguish, to dredge the wrecks of roofs,
to help the souls come down their crosses; let
the highways reach their outlets, mend the broken bridges
and unbury rivers from their putrid graves.

Don't forget, you are the remote sea. Set out
and come, and I shall let sleep usurp my body.
Only my ears will be wide awake and alert by their
secret casement to receive communion, your whisper.

33

YOU CAN SAFELY DRIVE

You can safely drive through a darkness
stigmatized by scraps and particles of light,
chtonic flares fallen in the puddles;
but I am frightened, shattered, lost
in their diffusions, for I know
light and dark apart and cannot guess
what contrivances hide in their nettings.

Are there eyeglasses, I should inquire,
to disentangle fears on roads where
light and dark have lost their identity?

LAST RITES

From what encounter that bitter
curve of the lips?
Was it from here or from across?
Was it from the silence that
spared us of a life's detriment
or was it from the howl unheard
for what emerged in the beyond?
Was it the spasm of farewell
for the deserting soul?

A curve of earth was written
on his lips, a sorrow bowing
downwards. And if the skill
of obsequies tried to reverse
the curvature into the hollow
of a smiling calm, what was indeed
the final face that he delivered?

Poem

Brendan Kennelly

THE SCHOLAR'S RETREAT

I live at the end
Of a crooked road,
My chosen part of the valley.

My field (a euphemism
For a patch of rock,
Heather, scutch grass

And honest-to-God muck)
Borders the road.
My house is on a height above.

The floor of my room is made of stone.
The roof is open,
All the beams exposed

On the hill of the adulterers
Opposite
The glen of the beer.

Away at the back
Bog opens to the mountains.
There's a river below,

A forest
And two brooks.
One vanishes into the forest,

The other makes exquisite
Twists and turns
For my delight.

The deer whistle and bark
When they mate in winter.
I am no stranger here.

My best friend is music.
I track the dead
Through the crooked roads in my head.

What I seek
Survives the cards I shuffle till dawn,
The talk of sheep,

Shy words of distant neighbours,
Drinkers' hectic prattle
In the Queen's and Jack's and Joker's hours.

It flows under
And through such things.
I swear there is more wonder

In it now
Than when I started out.
On a frosty April night

It is a hungry fox
Snouting through still fields,
Sidestepping the brittle sticks

Of winter. It might be
From another world
It moves so silently.

It passes my house
Bonewhite in the moonlight.
The rhythm of its paws

Is more regular than my heart
Measuring the dark.
It strikes and kills in the damp grass

And vanishes,
The body of the lamb
Thrilling its jaws.

'Oranges—Apples—Sugarsticks . . .' Joycean Associations: An Interview with Richard Ellmann[1]

Christie McDonald

Christie McDonald: In your book, *James Joyce*,[2] you refer to one of the most widely known devices used in *Ulysses*, the internal monologue. Could you describe how this device allows Joyce to construct character by 'odds and ends, by minutiae', and constitute thereby a notion of personality new to the novel as a form? If this method results in an 'islanded' character, one whose mind is neither tied to authorial dictates nor grounded in his context, does it not effectively prevent the reader from reaching a view of character, and the truth of that character, as a totality?

Richard Ellmann: The internal monologue transfers the burden of prose narrative from the author to his character. In Edouard Dujardin's *Les Lauriers sont coupés*,[3] which Joyce read at the outset of his literary career, the leading character might be said to think the whole book; no other voice intervenes . . . The weather, the Paris streets, the arranged and the chance encounters are registered in his consciousness and filtered through that to the reader. Joyce could see that the method made for awkwardness. Because Dujardin rigorously excluded everything except the subjective world of his hero, the external situation had to be laboriously established when the hero's thoughts were obsessively on his mistress.

Joyce brilliantly decided to modify the monologue. Only Molly Bloom's at the end of *Ulysses* is done without any outside intervention. It is after midnight, she is in bed, her eyes closed, and the world outside is absent. The other monologues, of Bloom and Stephen, are dotted with stage directions. These are often ironical, as when one of them says of Bloom, 'His slow feet walked him riverward, reading'. (Dujardin's hero would have had to say, 'I must as I read walk to the river'.) Bloom's feet take on a ludicrous autonomy, and the ambiguous subject of the participle 'reading' offers a mind-body interfusion which suited Joyce's view of consciousness. Such comments cross the subjective monologue widdershins.

Joyce also thickened the internal monologue with a much wider range of associations than Dujardin had provided. He allowed Bloom's character to

37

divulge itself by odds and ends, by minutiae, resuscitating the accumulation of debris from his day. These details appear random, but are not so. A multitude of small bells is set ringing, and they tintinnabulate in various sequences throughout the book. Prejudices, convictions, superstitions, observations of passing phenomena, sensations of hunger and lust, memories of embarrassment and joy, anxieties about infidelity, twists of the tongue, resistance to authorities, worries about death, acts of forgetting, sneezing, breaking wind, defecating, urinating, masturbating, taste in food or dress, liking for small animals, love, all clang together in the mind's campanile. Yet as one reads one becomes aware of large harmonies. Hunger for food and for sexuality intertwine, for example, and the images associated with the one transfer easily to the other. Bloom recalls the seedcake which Molly Bloom passed from her mouth to his during their courtship, and remembers her 'gumjelly lips'. By the end of the book, details that had appeared disparate coalesce into a multifarious unity.

In the new edition of *Ulysses*, the editor found words in a daydream of Bloom's which had been left out by accident. The earlier edition reads: 'heave under embon senorita young eyes Mulvey plump years dreams return.' The new edition amplifies this: 'heave under embon senorita young eyes Mulvey plump bubs me breadvan winkle red slippers she rusty sleep wander years of dreams return.' This confusion of sensations has its precise origins in several earlier passages in the book. Bloom, who is half asleep, confuses what he participated in and what he read, what he dreamt and what he was told. He remembers a game of charades that he played with Molly before they married, and attributes to her now as before, 'the same young eyes'. 'Rip Van Winkle we played. Rip: tear in Henry Doyle's overcoat. Van: breadvan delivering. Winkle: cockle and periwinkles. Then I did Rip Van Winkle coming back [. . .] Twenty years asleep in Sleepy Hollow. All changed. Forgotten. The young are old. His gun rusty from the dew.' This memory is related to the book, *Fair Tyrants*, by James Lovebrich that Bloom had perused earlier the same day. Two sentences had excited him: 'Hands felt for the opulent . . .' and 'The beautiful woman threw off her sabletrimmed wrap, displaying her queenly shoulders and heaving embonpoint . . .' He had had a dream the night before: 'Dreamt last night . . . Something confused. She had red slippers on. Turkish!' Finally, he remembers two other things that Molly had said to him. First: 'I always thought I'd marry a lord or a gentleman with a private yacht. Buenas noches, senorita . . .' He answered this by asking her: 'Why me?' She had replied: 'Because you were always so foreign from the others.' Then, the other was an amorous experience that Molly had mentioned: 'Molly, Lieutenant Mulvey that kissed her under the Moorish wall beside the gardens. Fifteen she told me. But her breasts were developed.' The rhythm of the associative passage calms down slowly, suggesting the growing somnolence of Bloom and the reconciliation of these divergent threads.

In the Circe episode some of these details come back in a surrealistic manner. Bloom 'contracts his face so as to resemble many historical personages', including Rip Van Winkle, and, later on, Bello says to him: 'No, Leopold

Bloom, all is changed by woman's will since you slept horizontal in Sleepy Hollow your night of twenty years. Return and see.' A stage direction follows in parenthesis: '(Old Sleepy Hollow calls over the world.) "Rip Van Winkle! Rip Van Winkle!"' The theme of the past which returns, and the details of Mulvey and the 'plump bubs', are all taken up again at the end of Molly Bloom's monologue in which, having recalled how Mulvey had embraced her near the Moorish wall at Gibraltar, she comes back to the memory of a moment when she finds herself in the arms of Bloom: 'and first I put my arms around him yes and drew him down to me so he could feel my breasts all perfume yes and his heart was going like mad and yes I said yes I will Yes.' So that the details which seem to join together by chance strategically produce a coalescing union in the mind of the two Blooms.[4]

Joyce was not satisfied with intensifying and extending the internal monologue. He made use of other devices as well, traditional and untraditional. So he usually refers to Bloom as 'Mr Bloom', the Mister being almost a Homeric epithet. The excessive formality gives Bloom burgher status and also, by its mocking repetition, undercuts that status. Bloom's counterpart, Stephen Dedalus, is not called Mr Dedalus by the author, but 'Stephen' or 'Stephen Dedalus', for a different emphasis on his youth, his as yet unsettled position in society.

Many episodes in *Ulysses* use the internal monologue little or not at all. The Cyclops episode is recounted by two narrators, one with a poison pen, the other with a sirupy one; the Nausicaa episode is told, at least in the first half, by someone in a tone of rapturous idealization; The Wandering Rocks offers an account of Dublin that pretends to be objective but is actually ironical; the Circe episode gives Bloom's oddities a vaudeville extrapolation. Like many early readers, T.S. Eliot exaggerated the degree to which the internal monologue was used. 'Bloom tells us nothing', he said. 'Indeed, this new method of giving the psychology proves to my mind that it doesn't work. It doesn't tell as much as some casual glance from outside often tells.' Joyce anticipated this difficulty, and so he allows Bloom to be seen not only in his own terms, but through other people's casual or studied scrutiny, sometimes mocking, sometimes celebratory or acceptant.

Joyce thought of the internal monologue as a stylization, rather than a total exposition, of consciousness. He said to Stuart Gilbert, 'From my point of view, it hardly matters whether the technique is "veracious" or not; it has served me as a bridge over which to march my eighteen episodes, and once I have got my troops across, the opposing forces can, for all I care, blow the bridge sky high'.

The internal monologue imitates some of the mind's workings; that it does not imitate all is demonstrated by the chapters in which it is not used.

Christie McDonald: I wonder if you could bring together several thoughts, concerning parallelism in Joyce's work to Freudian dream analysis and the use of association. I think especially of the moment when you quote him on the analogy between writing a novel and composing music, in which the same elements recur: 'A man might eat kidneys in one chapter, suffer from a kidney disease in another, and one of his friends could be kicked in the kidney in another' (*Joyce*, p. 436). What role does the memory play, either in the narrator or the reader, that permits or blocks, as the case may be, recognition and understanding through repetition?

Richard Ellmann: From the beginning Joyce attached importance to dreams, as he demonstrated by some dream poems and some dream epiphanies among his earliest writings. In Trieste he evidently heard about psychoanalysis from his friend and English pupil, Ettore Schmitz, whose nephew Edoardo Weiss introduced it into Italy in 1910. Joyce's library in Trieste included three pamphlets, by Freud, Jung, and Ernest Jones, dated between 1909 and 1911. Subsequently, he made experiments in word associations, using his wife as his subject. On November 12, 1913, one of the notes for *Exiles* clearly refers to words which she has concatenated:

'Blister—amber—silver—oranges—apples—sugarstick—hair—spongecake—ivy—roses—ribbon.'
He then offers a gloss:

The blister reminds her of the burning of her hand as a girl. She sees her own amber hair and her mother's silver hair. This silver is the crown of age but also the stigma of care and grief which she and her lover had laid upon it . . . Oranges, apples, sugarstick—these take the place of the shunned thoughts and are herself as she was, being her girlish joys. Hair . . . the softly growing symbol of her girlhood. Spongecake: a weak flash again of joys which now begin to seem more those of a child than those of a girl. Ivy and roses: she gathered ivy often when out in the evening with girls. Roses grew then a sudden scarlet note in the memory which may be a dim suggestion of the roses of the body . . . Ribbon for her hair . . .

In 1916 he records three of her dreams and offers an interpretation of two of them. He apparently thought that the unconscious mind was composed of condensed fragments of the conscious mind. There were no accidental associations—he so far agreed with Freud—and an artist could find their secret links and exploit them in his writings. He evidently conceived of some analogy between the dream, which recalls in displaced and undigested form bits of the remembered past, and the reverie induced in the reader whereby disassociated bits of the text could cluster and reverberate.

Christie McDonald: I am curious about the role that the epiphanies, defined as the 'sudden revelation of the whatness of a thing' or the moment in which the 'soul of the commonest object . . . seems to us radiant', played in the development of the artist: both in his own sketches, or 'isolated spasms of insight', and through their insertion in *Stephen Hero*. Where is the artist to look for these apparently uneventful moments? And when they read, as you say, like 'messages in an unfamiliar tongue', how are they to become intelligible within the narrative structure? Do they lead to the creation of new aesthetics as system?

Richard Ellmann: Joyce took the religious term 'epiphany' and secularized it. He agreed with Aristotle that everything has its form, its whatness, and thought that the artist's task was to reveal it. 'Signatures of all things I am here to read', says Stephen Dedalus. What was novel about this aesthetic was that it gave warrant to the presentation of a common event 'in the vulgarity of speech or of gesture', so long as that event disclosed its shape and inner meaning. Epiphanies were not however confined to naturalistic moments; they also included 'memorable phases of the mind itself', which might occur in dreams or reveries, and were closer to symbolism than naturalism.

At first Joyce planned to collect his epiphanies into a book. There were various reasons why he decided in the end against this. One was that, deprived of context, the vulgar incidents might sound cheaply satirical, and the mind's memorable phases sentimental. Another was that he found the disconnection of the epiphanies hard to justify, even in the light of a central consciousness. He did not give up his idea entirely. *Giacomo Joyce*, which he never published, could be thought of as a series of epiphanies. His other books have many semi-isolated moments which were originally epiphanic. At the end of *A Portrait of the Artist as a Young Man*, for example, the two paragraphs beginning, 'Faintly under the heavy night' and 'The spell of arms and voices', were originally epiphanies, of the more symbolistic variety. They escape (though barely) the charge of fine writing because of the naturalistic context in which they are imbedded. Their meaning is somewhat cryptic, and useful to Joyce at this point because his hero's departure is metaphysical as well as physical. The mysterious relations of the soul and the body are implicit, and if they cannot be defined, they can at least be particularized.

A Portrait of James Joyce's Biographer

William K. Robertson

Interview published in the Miami Herald *on 21 March 1982*

In the novel *A Portrait of the Artist as a Young Man*, the hero, Stephen Dedalus, is about to leave Dublin—and his youth—behind to set out on a special mission. His purpose is nothing less than to form the collective conscience of his race.

Stephen, of course, is the alter ego of his creator, James Joyce. In 1982, the centenary of Joyce's birth, it is still open to discussion how well he accomplished Stephen's ambitious, arrogant quest, but there is no doubt that the author has been as influential on the course of modern literature as any writer of our age. A prominent Joycean expert remarked earlier in this year that literature without Joyce would be akin to physics without Einstein.

The comparison could hardly be more precise. As Einstein changed the way we regard the external world of nature, Joyce reshaped our perception of the internal workings of human nature. In his three major works—*A Portrait of the Artist as a Young Man* (1916), *Ulysses* (1922) and *Finnegans Wake* (1939)—he revolutionized the novel, abandoning the traditions of plot, style and character and offering instead a narrative approach that refuses to compromise with the reader. It's your job to understand him, and damned if he'll make it easy for you. Not in *Ulysses*, which in a rush of more or less conventional language attempts to describe the lives of several Dubliners, who stand for all of us as they think and feel their way through a single, long day. Certainly not in *Finnegans Wake*, which redefines language itself, portraying night dreams that encompass all of history and all of man.

If James Joyce hadn't been a writer, a lot of people would be out of work, for Joyce belongs not so much to ordinary readers these days as to a priesthood of professors who feel called to explain him. Occasionally the best of them manage to do it, guiding us to the riches of a Joycean word-heap we might otherwise have thought gibberish.

One of the most persuasive of these scholars is Richard Ellmann, whose *James Joyce* is the standard biography of the writer. The study won the National Book Award in 1960 and a revised version, based on another 20 years of research, will be published this fall.

An American who has devoted his professional life to the extraordinary flowering of writers in the late 19th and early 20th centuries known as the Irish literary renaissance, Ellmann has taught at Harvard, Yale and Northwestern and now holds a chair at New College, Oxford. He was in South Florida last week to lecture at Florida Atlantic University's Conference on the Fantastic in the Arts and took time out to discuss biography and the life and art of the writer who captured his imagination years ago and has held it ever since.

What follows is an edited transcript of the conversation:

Q Let's talk about the subject of biography for a moment. We know that fiction has several formal systems of criticism. To my knowledge anyway, there are no systematic ways of looking at biography in a critical sense. Do you think there should be a criticism of biography?

A You mean whether there should be a methodology?

Q Right.

A I've never been able to work out one. I've only done full-length studies of Yeats and Joyce—and Wilde I've more or less done. But my impression is that each of them requires a quite different method and emphasis and that half of the job of the biographer is to devise a new method for each subject. But I don't feel altogether satisfied with it. I mean a good deal of what the biographer does, at least if there's material available, is to make connections, which you haven't understood before, between the life and the work. Everybody supposes that life and work are in some sense related, but in some sense they aren't related. I suppose that is the point: that they're not the same. At the same time, I suppose that the way in which you respond to experience must somehow connect to the way in which you write your books. Also the experiences themselves must somehow suit your personality in some way. They must somehow, at least in retrospect, seem to be adjusted to you. Joyce himself had a very peculiar attitude towards his own life. When he was young he had a lot of experience that forced itself in upon him. He didn't have to do very much. But I think later on he began to feel that he had to cue himself, and the way to do this was to have certain kinds of experiences he might not otherwise have had. I think he did feel to some extent that his philandering would be a prompt-book for his work.

Q As a biographer yourself, what do you look for in a biography? Not necessarily about a literary figure.

A I think one would like to feel that the writer did have a very special relationship with the subject and that he could either know or almost know what the subject was thinking at any given time. But I don't like it when the biographer claims omniscience. I think it's better for him to allow a certain distance between himself and the subject. I mean he offers his views, but I always feel he has some duty to present material so that a reader can judge it independently. I always put in a fair number of letters of Joyce. I felt that even if my own construction of his situation at a given time might be valid, it was just as well to see how he was writing himself about it. Not that one necessarily would agree with everything he said either, but at any rate one could have some sort of check upon the biographer's interpretation. At the same time, I think when biographers don't interpret, they're not much use. I think with literary biographies in particular you must somehow offer a view of the man which will in some sense illuminate his works: You will see how this particular kind of guy would write these particular works.

Q So that would be what basically distinguishes literary biography from most other types?

A It's different when people are historical characters because there the personal life, the relationship to your surroundings, seems to be somewhat different. You have to build up a much bigger construct of the environment and all. But I think there's something very peculiar about literary work, that it is a private matter, and while you're no doubt affected by everything that's going on—Joyce was terribly interested in politics, religion and everything else—you're at the same time alone with a piece of paper in the way that a historical character isn't.

Q　Which biographers have been influential in your own work?

A　It seems rather conventional to say it, but when I wrote my first book about Yeats, I was inclined to pooh-pooh the material circumstances in which Yeats lived, as he did himself. I felt the really important thing was what went on in his mind. I didn't entirely do that. I did talk about Irish politics and I did talk about his friendships and his love affairs and so on, but I guess I did think of his literature as a kind of working out of problems with only slight reference to external circumstances. But when I was working on Joyce I realized I really must try and deal, as he did, with external things, too, because he attaches so much importance to external things. And I thought: If I could only get hold of these things, and perhaps find out what people said to him or what he had said to people, if I could only get his remarks about what he was doing in his work but also get any kind of quotation. I suppose at this point I had Boswell in mind as much as anybody. Not that I could emulate him because he, after all, besides being a marvellous writer, was also able to construct situations. You can't do that with a dead man. But I did go about Europe, seeking out Joyce's friends, struggling to catch little bits of conversation.

Q　How did you get interested in the Irish renaissance in the first place?

A　Well, I think it was quite accidental with me to get onto Irish literature. I didn't really think of it as particularly distinct from English literature. I had an instructor in college [Yale] who gave us some anonymous poems, one of which was by Yeats, and it made a tremendous impression upon me. So I got interested in Yeats and read a good deal of him and when I was trying to think of what to write a doctoral dissertation on, why there was this Irish friend of mine who said, 'You're working on Yeats, aren't you?' and I said, 'Yes', and that was when I discovered it. But then I finally found out what it was to the Irish or at least a little bit of what it was to the Irish and it gradually became apparent that unless I enlisted something of Irish history and life I wouldn't fully grasp what Yeats was up to. And then from Yeats I went onto Joyce because Mrs Yeats showed me an unpublished preface that her husband had written in which he talked about this young man who had knocked at his door and told him that he was all out of date and he'd got to do something new and, of course, it was Joyce. There had been many stories about their first meeting. Most of the stories said that Joyce had ended up saying, 'How old are you?' and Yeats told him and he said, 'I thought so; you're too old for me to help you'.

And essentially that was more or less borne out by this account which Yeats wrote evidently very soon after their meeting. I wrote something about them and then when I was out in Evanston, Ill, [after moving from Harvard to Northwestern] and a lawyer called me and said, 'Come and see my Joyce collection', and it occurred to me that one might be able to do another biography. The only one at that time was by Gorman, Herbert Gorman. That was written while Joyce was alive and under great restrictions. He didn't know about half of Joyce's life and there were big gaps which he filled in by telling what was going on in the rest of the world. And so I thought, well, I can do better than this, even if I just use this secondary material that has accumulated. But then I went over to Dublin and met Joyce's sisters, who I was told would not speak to anybody about their brother—were very much ashamed of him—but actually they were not ashamed of him; they were very pleased to talk to me, and then his brother, Stanislaus, in Trieste, was a great help, though he was writing his own book. I saw him in '53 and '54 and then he died in '55. And after his death I did edit his unfinished memoir of James and I helped his widow sort out all the Joyce papers—an enormous trunkful of stuff, most of which is now at Cornell—and this really made the book possible.

Q Getting around to your revised biography: It was in 1959 that it first came out. What new facts have come to light since then and have you had to revise any of your major notions about Joyce?

A No. The fabric of the book, I think, is pretty much intact. But I put in about 100 pages of insertions of one kind or another. I've also made some modifications, I will admit that, but I don't think in major matters. I once thought that his love affair with the woman in Zurich was, as she always told her niece, a platonic affair. It became clear that while nothing very much happened it was not platonic.

Anyway, his philandering is represented somewhat more specifically and largely in this version. Another thing that I have is some other interesting statements to his brother about what he was doing in his books and how he was trying to change *A Portrait* particularly. He felt very dissatisfied with *A Portrait*. He re-wrote it several times over. Even after he had done that he still felt unhappy about it.

Q What was the basis of his unhappiness?

A The basis was that he thought anyone reading it would realize that he was still writing in the groove of what he had read. He was evidently determined not to do this [laughter], and by the time he finished rewriting *A Portrait*, why it isn't in the groove, I think. He's starting a new groove. Yeah, I think you get much more sense of his stops and starts from this new information and the fact that it didn't come so easy, you know. But by the time he got to *Ulysses* he set himself such difficult problems that he really had to do all kinds of things that had never been done before in order to solve the problems. I don't think he ever thought of himself as an experimenter. I think he felt that this was the only way in which you could solve these problems and I think he would have felt they were consolidations rather than experiments.

I also have a certain amount more material on his daughter and her troubles, and I have more stuff on his relations with his wife, which were always a bit tumultuous because of his tendency to get drunk.

Q I have a notion that modernism, which is so heavily indebted to Joyce, has trickled down even into the popular fiction we read today. I'm thinking, for instance, of someone like John Irving. Would you think that idea has some validity?

A I'm sure it has. I'm always amused when Anthony Burgess, whom I suppose you could consider a popular novelist, says that Joyce has had no influence whatsoever. He says it over and over. And every time he publishes another novel, why there is Joyce. I don't mean he doesn't have his own flair, but he's certainly very much affected by Joyce. You know, Bloom has a bowel movement, Burgess's character has a bowel movement, that sort of thing. It's so obvious to anyone else, but Burgess always denies it very vigorously. But I think the main thing is exactly what you say, that it has trickled down. To everybody, whether they've read Joyce or not. Not all of them have read him, but they still have to decide whether they're going to write a traditional novel or not, and this is a decision they didn't use to have to make. Some of them still opt for tradition, especially in England, but over here I think they're less likely to be so traditional; they seem to recognize that modern consciousness does require different techniques. Irving, I'm sure, has been affected by Joyce and by Joyce's successors because there are lots of people who have also innovated.

Q There has been a lot of discussion lately about the bankruptcy of modernist consciousness. Do you dispute that? Do you think that modernism has run its course?

A Well, I wouldn't think that was true. I suppose it's true that it has been very difficult for subsequent writers to go further than Joyce did. I always like the way in which his book ends. Gide says somewhere that many writers sort of show a slow decline from the mountain of their principal work but with Joyce you get his final work as really the most looming of the crags of all his stuff. The [largest part] of his genius seems to be incorporated in *Finnegans Wake*, which is a kind of radical attack upon language itself. Most writers have been content to use language without modifying it. Some of them have hard words like Nabokov or Beckett. Some of them have easy words. But whichever they use, it's the conventional dictionary. Whereas Joyce seems to have felt that if you really wanted to represent the nightworld of humanity, you would have to represent what is going on during the night, which, when you come to think of it, is a very remarkable kind of work. The words that I'm speaking are obviously a blend of many different languages. How did they all come together? I don't think the linguists have ever really explained this process, but Joyce obviously felt that it was clear that it had taken place. I think the notion in *Finnegans Wake* was to have it all take place in a single night instead of over hundreds of years. All of a sudden, you know, the tongue slips, and nobody knows why, and Latin turns to French. How did it all happen? Extraordinary process. Joyce, I think, was the first to look into this and get hold of it. I do think it's a great innovative work. I think that my favourite of his books is *Ulysses* but I think that *Finnegans Wake* has such challenges for literature.

Q   How long did it take you to master *Finnegans Wake*?
A   Well, I wouldn't say I have mastered it.
Q   Or to even be comfortable with it?
A   I'm uncomfortable with it, but I think that when you read it, as many people do—I did—with a group—everybody reading aloud trying to figure out what things mean (it's useful to have people around who know languages), why things do become clearer. The main outlines of the book are probably understood. It's only a great deal of detail that is still blurred. But I think one can get pleasure out of that detail. Joyce once said until he'd read *The Waste Land* he'd really not regarded Eliot as a great poet and a woman said to him, 'I don't understand it'. He said, 'You don't have to understand it.' I once had a chance to tell this story to Eliot who agreed completely [laughter]. I think it's true that you get a lot out of *Finnegans Wake* without really understanding it. It's funny, and it's lyrical, and it has all sorts of wonderful games going on, linguistic games, and one does feel that he's probably in some sense getting into areas of the mind that other writers have left alone.

Q   Do you think that there are any literary inheritors of Joyce—I mean direct inheritors—writing today?
A   I think the exploration of consciousness, both the nighttime in *Finnegans Wake* and the daytime in *Ulysses* is something that Joyce carried further than anyone else. He once described his work as 'extravagant excursions into forbidden territory'. And I suppose what he meant by that was that he had not only done what other writers have done, which is to say what his character is thinking, in the most obvious way—everybody's done that, somebody says that the interior monologue began with the Book of Job—but I don't think they realize that what he does is more than that. I mean he not only describes the consecutive thoughts but he describes all the pauses, all the hesitations, all the lapses of memory, all the fleeting sexual desires, feelings of hunger, the way in which you respond to the weather, the fact that you get depressed when there are clouds and when the sun comes out you feel a little better. I mean all the twists and turns of consciousness and pre-consciousness seem to be implied in this and it seems to me there is a great deal of this in literature. I suppose the most obvious of his heirs is Faulkner, who once said to me that he considered himself to be the heir of Joyce in *The Sound and the Fury*. I think one can

see that that book derives partly from the first pages in *A Portrait of the Artist*, where Joyce describes the beginning consciousness of the child, the smells and the sounds, and the way in which words begin to reverberate and become succeeded by other words and so on. All that seems to be implied in the Benjy section of *The Sound and the Fury*. I asked Faulkner if he had read *Ulysses*. He said, no, he hadn't but people had told him about it [laughter].

Q   Did you believe him?

A   I think he couldn't have resisted looking at it a little. He was very reverent toward Joyce. He told me he was in a café in Paris and there was Joyce at another table, but he didn't have the courage to approach him at all. He obviously thought he was marvellous. I think that would be an example of the effect, and then you'd have to say whom did Faulkner influence? Of course Faulkner has influenced a whole lot of writers, in foreign countries, too. Then the whole French *nouveau roman* seems to be affected. And, of course, Beckett is really very much affected by Joyce, even though I think he has his own flair, as to some extent Burgess does, too. No, I think it's a world-wide influence.

Q   Of course Joyce is not just a cottage industry in academia, but a major industry. Is there a lot of politics involved in Joycean scholarship?

A   It's a very hotly contested field and the animosities engendered are considerable. I suppose it's much more full of [pause] . . . it's a much more competitive field than almost any other modern writer. There are modern writers about whom the scholars all seem to be more or less agreed, or at least respectful of each other, whereas Joyce arouses much more frantic passion. But I think that also there is some rather special bond between Joyce's readers, and one loves to go to all the places Joyce writes about. I think we do this with all writers. But I think we do it even more with Joyce. There's something rather indrawn about Joyce that makes one long for an intimacy that he doesn't easily extend.

In a *Portrait of the Artist*, after visiting the rector's office, he [Stephen Dedalus] leaves and goes down the long corridor, you may remember. At the end of the corridor he bumps his elbow against the door. Well, I was recently talking with people in Clongowes Wood [the school Dedalus attended, as did Joyce] and they said that generations of boys have bumped their elbow against the door. You begin to feel how accurate Joyce often is. He's insistent upon getting things right. I think he said to somebody—I believe it's quoted in my book—that if Dublin were destroyed, it could be reconstructed from his books. But in fact many writers, like George Eliot, describe things in a way that's much more reconstructable than Joyce. What he does is describe the places where the elbows bump or lean. He glances at things. You don't see the whole building. You see a corner of the building. You get a smell or a touch.

Q   Now that you've finished the revisions on the Joyce biography, do you have any plans to tackle another major figure?

A   Well, I am doing a book on Wilde. I have written a draft of it, and I think that will be my . . . [pauses] well, that's the only long work I have in mind to do. I think after that I might well do some short things. I have a feeling it might be nice to write short essays in which I indicate how long books could be written.

Q   Are you going to return to America from Oxford?

A   I've been coming to Emory in Atlanta every spring for five or six weeks. That's for the last four years. I probably will continue to do that. I don't have very many years to go at Oxford. Retirement there is at 67 and I'm 64. So at that point perhaps we'll come back.

Q   Do you enjoy English life?

A   Well at first I found it very peculiar. Oxford seems from a distance to be so gentlemanly. But of course it has fangs. One can have very unpleasant experiences there. But I've gradually come to roll with Oxford. After the first two years I decided I'd stay for five. After five years I decided I'd stay for seven or eight. Here it's 12 years now and, as I say, I only have three years more, at most, to go. And I wouldn't be surprised if I stayed for those. There are some very pleasant aspects to life there. I miss some of the intimacy, as it seems to me, of American life. I think one has it in England only if you've met people in childhood, forming life-long friendships. If you go at the age of 50 or so, you never feel quite so much a part of a situation.

Q   As the custodian of the reputation of the man who changed the way we perceive literature, what do you forsee as the future of the written word? That's a nice cosmic, and closing, question.

A   I think people will never give up the making of fantasies or the writing of them down. I just can't believe that's ever going to stop. I think the imagination will require that as long as man exists. So I would think literature is with us to stay. I expect that there will be all kinds of twists and turns in it that, in a way, Joyce has opened the door to a Pandora's box of all kinds of possibilities. But I should think it is going to last. I recognize the effect of television has been perhaps to reduce the amount of reading, but I believe that television cannot be a substitute for what literature does. You get a much more complete world in the world of fiction than television can offer with its limited screen and limited compass. So I should think that the imagination will require that the novel go on. As for poetry, which of course is an even more concentrated form, this will never be superceded by any of the more obvious technological developments in our time. If you really want to get the concentrated experience of the race, you'll have to get it from poetry rather than from any of the other things.

The Concept of Modernism

Christopher Butler

Henry James tells us in his Preface to *The Awkward Age* (1899) that

> We are shut up wholly to cross-relations all within the action itself, no part of which is related to anything but some other part—save of course by the relation of the total to life.

This is a suitable warning to anyone wishing to write about twentieth century 'Modernism'. It suggests at least the appalling complexity of a subject which should bring together the concerns of artists working in all the main cities of Europe. But James ends with an assurance more typical of the nineteenth century than of the twentieth: and it arises from that realistic mode which Modernism was to challenge. For he thinks that the 'total' may be satisfactorily related to something 'out there' which is 'life'. He is modernist and relativist enough to see the difficulty of this—but not its theoretical impossibility. For by now any attempt to write about Modernism will provide us with no more than another narrative, to rival its predecessors, and not with a 'realist' history. Of course it will be structured by many generally accepted facts, but it will essentially be an interpretation of them. For there are many Modernisms, as there are many Modern movements, and their beginnings and their possible endings are a good subject for endless disputes.

The 'Modern' becomes familiar to cultural historians as a self-conscious slogan or battle cry used at the turn of the century by many who felt the repression of earlier traditions. The study of Modernism could thus be the study of generational identity and conflict. It could also be the history of a self-conscious avant garde, in a period in which the social world and its moral standards are in a state of perpetual change. For much of the basic philosophical and technological reorientation of the period after 1900 was so profound, that as Kern shows, even the basic categories of time and space were reinterpreted in a way that affected the very feel and texture of everyday life, let alone of that experimental art which we associate with 'Modernism'.[1]

Nor does the Modern, in all the senses we still need to investigate, have an agreed chronological end. We are uncertain whether it has yet fully metamorphosed into the post-Modern or not. We may need an entirely new word to describe the epoch of contemporary art, or we may still be in a late or decadent phase of the age of Modernism after all. For the Modern is still for us the focus of a set of values; and many critics believe that present day avantgardism, with its apparently aimless and disordered search for new styles, may be merely epigonal to Modernism.[2]

The 'Modern' is thus most unlikely to turn out to be our name for anything very stable. That is why so many of the generalisations we find about it in the scholarly literature fail to stand up to examination, useful though they may be in illuminating parts of the field. I am thinking of those pseudo definitions of Modernism as the 'dramatisation of self doubt', or as the attempt to make opposites cohere, or as a collective search for an underlying myth, or as inherently indeterminate and 'slippery', or as a neo-romantic attempt to escape from the constraints of society. They are all open to severe objections, of which the simplest but most devastating is the counter example. Peter Gay thus attacks the neo-romantic view, which

sees a great transvaluation of values beginning, roughly, with the Impressionists and ending, roughly, with the Surrealists, as the impassioned protest of civilised artists and thinkers against the mechanisation, the ugliness, the rootlessness, the sheer vulgarity of technological civilisation. Modernism, in this view, is the hatred of the modern world, the rebellion of culture against culture. Its name is the Waste Land; its dominant emotions are alienation, ambivalence and anxiety; its principal victims the illusions of liberalism; and its chief adversaries those supreme representatives of the genteel age, the bourgeois.[3]

There is no way this description is going to apply to the Futurists, to Apollinaire, to Cendrars, to Stravinsky, to Picasso, Léger, Delaunay, Mondrian, . . . and so on and so on. For by no means all Modernists could be described as anti-technology, alienated, anxious, or even antibourgeois, and very few were all four at once.

The concept of Modernism then, in so far as we have a single word to cover such disparate phenomena, is likely to turn out to be one with all sorts of sufficient conditions for its application, but no necessary ones. And all of the sufficient conditions, which may well satisfy particular interpretative strategies, will turn out to be 'fuzzy at the edges' when confronted by an alternative strategy. Thus Lunn in his *Marxism and Modernism* quite reasonably offers definitions of Modernism that will allow him to reveal themes central to a later debate concerning its nature between Lukács, Brecht, Benjamin, and Adorno.[4]

Such restrictive critical presuppositions, which always carry more or less disguised political commitments, are obviously enough not going to allow us to satisfy any desire we may have to understand an historical period in detail. They see Modernist art too obviously through adventitiously interpretative schemas, however strong, and justifiable, their pragmatic aims within academic politics may be. Of course we are *all* subject to conscious or unconscious intellectual and hence political bias; but one way of attempting to minimise its effect may be to adopt a rather different strategy, of attempting to see Modernism first through its works of art, and to attempt to work outward from them to the types of intellectual context we have indicated rather than vice versa.[5]

This means that some type of canon formation will, paradoxically enough, be an essential first step in the study of any period of art. But how is the canon to be formed? This leads to questions of theory which have recently been very much disputed, for any canon looks like a preferred 'tradition', but I am going to sidestep them for the time being by appealing to the consensual judgement of my readers so far as the main candidates are concerned. That is, it seems to me to be a suitable first step to fix upon some generally accepted instances of Modernist art, and then to make sure that any generalisations we are tempted to make at least do not fail to be significantly tested by them. We will also have to recognise of course that any list of 'canonic' works will draw into consideration others which are associated with them by reason of influence and family resemblance. These groups of works will tend to fall within what we call (recognising the trickiness of their devotion to change) 'movements', such as Fauvism, Expressionism, Cubism, Neoclassicism, Neue Sachlichkeit, and Surrealism.

Any analysis of early Modernism up to 1914, then, should be adequate to *at least* the examples which follow, and those which can be demonstrated to resemble them: in painting; to Matisse's evolution from the 'Lady in a Hat' to the 'Portrait of Madame Matisse' (1913) and 'Piano Lesson' (1916); to Picasso's 'Demoiselles d'Avignon' and cubist portraits; to Kandinsky's 'Improvisations' and 'Compositions'; to Boccioni's 'Stati d'Animo'; to Delaunay's 'Fenêtre' series, and so on. In music to works like Schoenberg's *Erwartung* and *Pierrot Lunaire*; Stravinsky's *Petrushka, Le Sacre du Printemps* and *Les Noces*; Berg's *Three Orchestral Pieces*; Webern's *Five Orchestral Pieces op 10*; Satie's *Parade*, and so on. And in literature to the Imagists; to Apollinaire's *Alcools*; to prewar German expressionist drama and poetry by Benn and Stramm; to Eliot's *Prufrock*; Cendrar's *Prose du TransSibérien*; Joyce's *Portrait*, and so on. So far, the most that I can hope for is some kind of intuitive consent from the knowledgeable.

One of the features to emerge strongly after the construction of even so sketchy a canonical list, is the lack of any obvious common denominator of subject matter; and yet there must have been some criteria for exclusion. The most important of these concerns the definition of the historical period with which we are concerned, and most particularly the proposal of a particular starting point. For the canon I suggest refuses to include those ancestors who contributed to the definition of the *modernité* of the nineteenth century. Thus Baudelaire, Rimbaud and Mallarmé can only be admitted to consideration when they have a demonstrable influence on a canonic work: as for example did Rimbaud's 'Ophelia' upon Heym's 'Black Visions I' and Benn's 'Schöne Jugend'. And later Rimbaud has a more general influence upon Surrealist poetry, Baudelaire upon *The Waste Land*, and so on.

For the chronology of the canon I propose shows that I am thinking of the generation which succeeded that of Debussy, Yeats, Proust, James and Valéry. The point of choosing this generation, whose major works begin to appear in the twentieth century, rather than their predecessors as 'modernists', would then depend on the success of the demonstration that they significantly come *after*: after Romanticism, after English Victorianism (or equally repressive attitudes in other countries, as the careers of Ibsen, Wedekind and Gide would show), after 'bourgeois' Realism or Naturalism, and, most importantly and immediately, after Symbolism. The Modernism I am concerned with might then partly be defined as what cannot be wholly identified with any of these. It thus runs counter to earlier accounts of Modernism, which explain it as essentially a continuation of Romanticism or of Symbolism.[6]

The concept of Modernism I am urging then has a contrastive rather than a continuative use: and it will involve our concentration upon the dialectic between Modernism in the arts and preceding traditions, with which artists are often most deeply involved, just at the point at which they attempt to exceed them. It is this sense of contrast with what has gone before which seems to me to have an essential theoretic status for the description of an artistic period.

I can perhaps make this clearer by following a hint of Northrop Frye's in suggesting that in the following sequence, each work has a direct relationship to earlier Symbolist thinking; but it is 'Symbolist' compared to its successors, and 'Modernist' as compared to its predecessors: *Paludes*, *The Golden Bowl*, *Salomé*, *Neue Gedichte*, *Elektra*, *Erwartung*, *Tod in Venedig*, *Pierrot Lunaire*, *Alcools*, *Prufrock*, *A Portrait of the Artist*.[7]

Thus even though one may argue that Debussy, Cézanne and Mallarmé are 'à la racine de toute Modernité', as Boulez remarks, it is, as he further indicates, the manner of their later metamorphosis that will offer us further clues to the definition of Modernism:

Le symbolisme est dissipé par Apollinaire, puis par la révolution surréaliste; le cubisme met à nu Cézanne; le basson du *Sacre* se substitue á la flûe du *Faune* tandis que Pelléas émigre de Paris à Vienne.[8]

It is precisely this willed dissipation or disruption, the stripping down and primitivisation of the 'poetic', and most particularly the way in which artistic evolution attains a European, migratory flavour, that is symptomatic of the emergence of Modernism as a distinct epoch in cultural history.

I do not deny then, that much of the very early work of the major Modernists is *fin de siècle* and Symbolist in sensibility. Indeed one of the most remarkable characteristics of the generation I discuss is the way in which it masters and reproduces the previous tradition in elaborated forms, in works like Matisse's 'Luxe Calme et Volupté' and 'Bonheur de Vivre', Picasso's 'La Vie' and 'Saltimbanques', Kandinksy's 'Motley Life', Schoenberg's *Verklärte Nacht* and *Gurrelieder* and *Pelléas and Mélisande*, Stravinsky's *King of the Stars* and *Firebird* and *Petrushka*, Joyce's *Stephen Hero*, Eliot's Laforguean verse, and in much of the early poetry of Pound and Apollinaire.

The Symbolist strain is thus an important provocation within the larger Modernist tradition. *Pierrot Lunaire* (1912), for example, uses *fin de siècle* texts, but accompanies them with a distinctively Modernist atonal technique; and Bartok's *Bluebeard's Castle* (written 1911, performed 1918) adapts a version of Maeterlinck's Symbolist drama *Ariane et Barbe-bleu*, and thus combines an inward and Symbolist psychological action with a much more aggressive, expressionist development of Hungarian elements in its music. However, what seems to me most important in the Symbolist contribution to Modernism, is its surprising re-emergence in its strongest form at a very late stage, in the High Modernist period of the 1920s, with works like Rilke's *Duino Elegies* (1923), and Stevens' *Harmonium* (1923). It is also of course sustained throughout the period by W.B. Yeats, whose Modernism is problematic, and has a late efflorescence in Eliot's *Four Quartets*. But this relationship to Symbolism is only a part of the Modernist enterprise.

For the artists we cited above went on to produce works which made a decisive break with previous tradition. Hence Matisse's 'Open Window at Collioure', Picasso's 'Demoiselles', Kandinsky's 'Composition IV', Schoenberg's *Erwartung*, Stravinsky's *Rite*, Pound's Imagism, Eliot's *Prufrock*, Apollinaire's *Zones*. Futurist poetry and painting after their *passéiste* divisionism of 1909-10, and the opening of *A Portrait of the Artist as a Young Man*. Any investigation of Modernism would thus have to distinguish carefully between the selective mastery of tradition, and a later, growingly self-conscious sense of being 'new' or original, which led to a peculiarly aggressive avantgardism, most particularly in the Manifestos, if not in all the works, of the Futurists; and they were indeed the most explicitly opposed of all early Modernists to the Symbolist aesthetic.

*   *   *

We have so far only gestured at the nature of Modernism, in suggesting that there are significant 'breaks' to be analysed within an historical sequence of works, and something 'new' or 'surprising' (Apollinaire's term) which characterises them. Our next problem is to find the general terms to describe these changes. To do so, I think, we have to look at the background, and then the foreground—that is, at the history of ideas, and then at artistic technique. I shall argue that it is the relationship between the two that is essential to our understanding of those breaks with previous tradition that help to define the Modern period. Any such approach through the history of ideas may seem to meet an immediate setback, for there is an obvious conclusion to be drawn from our candidates for the Modernist 'canon'. There is no *single* aesthetic, or philosophy, or *weltanschauung* running behind them. For the avowedly bourgeois hedonism of Matisse, the primitivism of Picasso in his African period and of Stravinsky in the *Rite*, the sexual anatagonisms of Kokoschka and Schoenberg, the antifeminism and advocacy of war of the Futurists, the challenge to the transformation of man in early German expressionist poetry and drama, the apolitical minimalism of the Imagists, and the occultism of Kandinsky (simply to concentrate on the climactic period of early Modernism from circa 1909-1914) can hardly be seen as emanating from a single philosophical source, or as sharing a common philosophical attitude.

This lack of a single specifiable philosophical impulse behind Modernism may arise for an interesting reason. For it has frequently been argued that twentieth-century Modernism contests the totalising religious and political frameworks of the nineteenth century in favour of a growing scepticism, pragmatism or pluralism (and was much encouraged to do so by Nietzsche and Ibsen). Thus Malcolm Bradbury believes that with Modernism

Art . . . tends to lose many of its powers to assert a coherent wisdom, sustain a coherent myth or assert the veracity of its own perception. The artist, like the thinker, tends therefore to dramatise his own self-scepticism. His work tends to become self-critical, ironic or game-like in disposition.

Modernist intellectuals thus tend to see themselves as critical, as somehow divorced from and marginal to the society in which they live. This judgement applies quite obviously to the professional critics of society within the period, whether they belonged to the left or the right, such as Shaw, Wells, Spengler, Kraus, Benda, and Maurras. But an equally critical and more subtle growth of sceptical distance is found in the literature of the period. One might instance the evolution of Marcel's consciousness in A la Recherche du temps perdu from a naïve acceptance of social norms to a detached, subjectivist criticism of them, or the aristocratic political scepticism of Conrad's later work; or Gide's and Heinrich Mann's advocacy of very different kinds of dissentient morality. Even the work of so unlikely a figure as Schoenberg arises, as he acknowledged in his Harmonienlehre of 1911, from the critical intellectual matrix provided by Nietzsche, Weininger, Kraus and others.

There is a deep connection between this turn of the century scepticism and the stylistic autonomy of much Modernist art. Its diverse stylistic commitments are, furthermore, often essentially subjective, and indeed intuitive. Thus Kandinsky for example judges that

When religion, science and morality are shaken, the two last by the strong hand of Nietzsche, man turns his gaze from externals in on himself.[10]

The results of this subjective self reliance are also to be seen in the placing of line and volume in cubism, without reference to representation; in the correlation of atonal procedures in music with subjective impulses which are often neurotic (as in Erwartung and later in Wozzeck); and in the post Strindbergian antagonism of the sexes, to be found in works like Kokoschka's Mörder Hoffnung der Frauen, which is expressed indeed in a speech which is hardly intelligible.

These aspects of Modernism often draw upon the growing influence of subjectivism in philosophy, in Nietzsche's plea for a transvaluation of all values in a world without God, in the work of Bergson (Essai sur les données immédiates de la conscience 1889) and in a growing insistence on divisions within personality, of which the psychology of Freud, (Traumdeutung 1899, 1900) is perhaps the most influential symptom. A more refined subjectivism is also to be found in the work of Mach on sensation, which influenced Musil. It is this withdrawal into subjective concerns that provides the most characteristic underpinning for the evolving Symbolism and intuitionism of Kandinsky, for the (Bergsonian) thoughts of Eliot's early personae, for Leopold Bloom's neo-Freudian self-revelation in Nighttown, for the irrational gestures of Lewis's hero Tarr, and very obviously indeed for Dada, Surrealism, and the occultism of 'The Bride Stripped Bare', It also underwrites Pound's doctrine of the Image, as 'that which presents an intellectual and emotional complex in an instant of time'. For Pound is careful to call such influences in support, by continuing: 'I use the word "complex" rather in the technical sense employed by the new psychologists, such as Hart.'[11]

I wish to suggest that this subjectivism arises partly from a sceptical withdrawal from social consensus and the morality it implied. Of course the situation this sort of analysis presupposes has its roots well back in the nineteenth century. In England alone, we find Arnold remarking as early as 1863 in his essay on Heine that

Modern times find themselves with an immense system of institutions, established facts, accredited dogmas, customs, rules, which have come to them from times not modern. In this system their life has to be carried forward, yet they have a sense that this system is not of their own creation, that it by no means corresponds exactly with the wants of their actual life, that for them, it is customary not rational. The awakening of this sense is the awakening of the modern spirit.[12]

One result of this is Arnold's notorious wish to give 'culture' the overall responsibilities of religion. This is a confused and confusing demand, felt in various forms all over Europe, which has some of its most peculiar consequences in the displaced religiosity of many early Modern works; in the occultism of Yeats and Kandinsky, the displaced rituals of Stravinsky (in the *Rite* and in *Les Noces*), and in many crucified artist redeemers from Schoenberg's *Die Gluckliche Hand* to the poet hero of Toller's *Die Wandlung*.

Other Modernist thinkers and artists were less concerned to save Christianity from itself, and were in different ways sceptical questioners of the morality and social arrangements of the previous generation. (Here the influence of things like those heralded by Georg Brandes in his *Men of the Modern Breakthrough* [1880]—Ibsen, Bjornson, Jacobson, Drachman, Flaubert, Renan and J.S. Mill—is crucial.) Such considerations obviously inspire the youthful protagonists of many early Modern works, in the plays of Wedekind, Musil's *Young Torless*, Gide's *Immoralist*, and Mann's *Toni Kröger*, who says

Literature is not a calling, it is a curse, believe me! . . . It begins by your feeling yourself set apart, in a curious sort of opposition to the nice, regular people; there is a gulf of ironic sensibility, of knowledge, scepticism, disagreement, between you and the others; it grows deeper and deeper, you realise that you are alone; and from then on any rapprochement is simply hopeless! What a fate![13]

The young Dedalus of *Stephen Hero*, (1904-1906) has also inherited the Arnoldian awareness, 'that though he was nominally in amity with the order of society into which he had been born, he would not be able to continue so'. He tells his friend Cranly that the modern spirit is a 'vivisective' seeing of things as they really are:

The ancient spirit accepted phenomena with a bad grace. The ancient method investigated law with the lantern of justice, morality with the lantern of revelation, art with the lantern of tradition. But all these lanterns have magical properties: they transform and disfigure. The modern method examines its territory by the light of day.

This, we remember, is the Ibsenite Stephen, who has been told, by a priest admittedly, that his paper devoted to Ibsen on 'Art and Life', 'represents the sum of modern unrest and modern freethinking'.[14]

The critical scepticism of the young is obviously part of the Modern in its most extended sense, in the history of ideas: hence Babbit recalls Goethe, Renan, Sainte Beuve, and Arnold, when he defines the Modern as the 'positive and critical spirit, the spirit that refuses to take things on authority'.[15] When the generation of Jung Wien rose up against the previous generation, in what Schorske describes as 'a kind of collective Oedipal revolt', they re-enacted a drama from the past, even to evoking the older generation of Nietzsche and others in their aid.[16]

I must seem by now to be slipping into contradiction, in suggesting that there are indeed overarching subjectivist and sceptical epistemological explanations of the early impulse to Modernism. However, I think that any such explanation by reference to scepticism should be very carefully qualified, not least because it defends the 'new' by reference to one of our most cherished and yet deceptive myths of origin, the myth that we are all descended from a period of certainties superior to our own.[17]

For what scepticism does in this sort of case is favour change so that Stephen can go beyond Ibsen, the children of Wedekind and Musil can prepare the way for Freud's notions concerning childhood sexuality and so on. And the artist who breaks with the past has to be very positive indeed about the things that are being found out. One has only to think of the convinced *fin de siécle* 'spiritualisms' of Yeats, Kandinsky or Scriabin, the Christianity (by 1926) of Eliot, the competing definitions of the 'new man' in expressionist drama, the 'economics' of Pound, the historical visions of Yeats and Joyce, the neo-Freudianism of such different figures as Lawrence and Breton, and the propaganda of the Futurists and Apollinaire, to realise that strong intellectual commitments remained possible. These need to be set alongside the ironic scepticism of writers like Proust, Thomas Mann, Kafka and Joyce, or the retrospective search for a perpetually receding philosophical (and even mystical) solution of Musil. And even these 'ironic' and sceptical writers move towards totalising, even mystical explanations, in Marcel's revelations concerning memory, Hans Castorp's vision in the snow, Musils's erotic mysticism, the theological allegory of *The Castle*, or Joyce's final dream world in which all languages connect.

Nor should we forget the influence on the early Modernists of exciting new fields of knowledge, such as relativity theory, Freudianism, the critique of language initiated by Mauthner and Wittgenstein, the world revealed by photography, or the new appreciation of primitive art, all of which are taken by various Modernists as support for artistic change. It cannot then be said that the Modernists believed *less* than their fathers. On the contrary, they often thought that they *knew* a great deal more, even if in a much more relativist historical perspective, as we can see if we look, for example, at the history of the study of primitive cultures and myth, through Frazer, Malinowski, Freud and Jung, and its effects on the work of Yeats, Eliot, Pound and others.

I argue then that although Modernist scepticism may have deprived artists of that generally acceptable social consensus (which perhaps only really 'exists' for conservative artists anyway) it didn't in the least deprive them of intellectual commitments. Musil puts this rather well when he looks back on the pre-1914 period:

Out of the oilsmooth spirit of the last two decades of the nineteenth century, suddenly throughout Europe there arose a new kindling fervour. Nobody knew exactly what was on the way; nobody was able to say, whether it was to be a new art, a new man, a new morality, or perhaps a reshuffling of society. So everybody made of it what he liked. But people were standing up on all sides to fight against the old way of life.[18]

* * *

The great variety of the commitments we have indicated does however show the loss of those modes of discourse which can express a shared culture, or at least that ideal of it, which Realism and Naturalism (and Impressionism and Symbolism) presupposed, however tentatively. This sense of loss extends to the postmodern period as the 'crisis of legitimation' of which Lyotard and others speak. For the intellectual concerns of the Modernist period break apart into highly specialised and often esoteric cultural formations.[19]

Without this implicit confidence in a common language, the way is laid open for those stylistic contortions which express the subjectivist individual vision to which I have referred. For there is an important sense in which all our canonic works deviate radically from a previous common language, and often enough also from common sense. Thus music abandons the natural 'Pythagorean' language of tonality, Cubism abandons the methods of Renaissance perspective, and the alogical poetry of Apollinaire, Cendrars, Benn, van Hoddis, Stramm and others, and the stream of consciousness writing of Joyce, Woolf and the surrealists abandons that language of rational control which had been so heroically exercised in the introspections of nineteenth-century heroes and heroines like Dorothea Brooke and Isobel Archer. Indeed this last opposition, to the very language of reason, leads inexorably through the early Modernist period to the rise of Dada and Surrealism.

All of these manifestations of Modernist experiment deny the public consensual languages which continue in the conservative art which underlies and runs alongside Modernism, and thus claim the freedom to invent new styles of expression (eighteen of them indeed, in *Ulysses*, as Joyce proudly claimed). It is this huge diversity of artistic styles within Modernism which allows me to bring to the fore the not-so-hidden common denominator of my canonical works, which is their experimentalism of technique. This of course is hardly a surprising or original conclusion, but given the considerations I have advanced above, it is not nearly as simple as it looks. Modernism very rarely aims at the provision of a uniquely 'aesthetic experience' (here Roger Fry lost his way).

For we need to show in each case what the change in technique was for; how, to echo Schoenberg, 'style' is related to significant changes in 'idea'. We have in technique a good focus for historical relationships of influence and evolution: thus cubism partly evolves from Cézanne, atonalism from Wagnerian chromaticism and Mahlerian polyphony, Imagism from Symbolism, and stream of consciousness from *erlebte rede*. But what intervenes within such technical change is the new idea, the shift in the conceptual scheme that makes a Kuhnian revolution, and sustains the artist's sense of the significance of formal discovery.

The symptom of these shifts is often enough a change in the function of the work of art, which brings the artist into a new and often initially adversarial relationship to an audience. Thus cubism usurps the social arrangements surrounding the representational portrait; Imagism discards the discursive (and moral) interpretability of previous verse; the stream of consciousness is symptomatic of the growth of post-Freudian assumptions about the significance of the buried mental life; some Futurist painting imitates the new photographic methods for recording the movement of an object, and justifies that by an ideology of dynamism; Léger's tubular designs embody new ideas of social order, and Brechtian alienation effects seek to evoke a critical attitude to political problems in its audience.

These relationships between technique and idea, innovation and avant gardist revolution, are not always obvious, and were particularly difficult to appreciate at the time. For the innovatory work of art calls into question the viewer's, hearer's or reader's very identity. This is because a newly abstract painting, or twelve-tone music, or a Dada gesture subverting the institution of art itself, will bewilder its audience because it is unsupported by those modes of discourse that were previously common to the consumer and the work, and bound them together. One final example will have to suffice to suggest the sorts of consideration that may be involved here.

If we look at a Symbolist picture like Moreau's 'Salomé' we find that it is laden with an interpretative meaning which is accessible to its audience from literature.[20] Hence Huysmanns' description in his *A Rebours* (1884):

she was no longer just the dancing girl who extorts a cry of lust and lechery from an old man by the lascivious movement of her loins; who saps the morale and breaks the will of a king with the heaving of her breasts, the twitching of her belly, the quivering of her thighs. She had become, as it were, the symbolic incarnation of undying Lust, the Goddess of Immortal Hysteria, the accursed Beauty exalted above all other beauties by the catalepsy that hardens her flesh and steels her muscles, the monstrous Beast, indifferent, irresponsible, poisoning, like the Helen of ancient myth, everything that approaches her, everything that sees her, everything that she touches.[21]

Braque's 'Grand Nu' (1908), on the other hand, (a painting which may show part of his reaction to Picasso's 'Demoiselles d'Avignon') is not laden with this kind of cultural meaning at all. Her meaning is more technical and painterly than literary and erotic, as Braque himself points out, in a passage which links together our themes of technique, of subjectivity in expression, and the refusal of realism. It is deeply indebted to the formal considerations which painters inherited from Cézanne:

I couldn't portray a woman in her natural loveliness . . . I haven't the skill. No one has. I must, therefore, create a new sort of thing, the beauty that appears to me in terms of volume, of line, of weight, and through that beauty interpret my subjective impression. Nature is a mere pretext for decorative composition, plus sentiment. It suggests emotion, and translates that emotion into art. I want to express the Absolute, and not merely the factitious woman.[22]

In the transition between these two works, the function of the naked within painting is subverted, as the conventions of the erotic are abandoned to realism and the photograph. Braque's remarks are also important for the way in which they ask the viewer to appreciate his technical means. (This becomes of crucial importance to Cubism.) Indeed I wish to suggest, finally, that the growth of technical talk of this kind within the interpretation of works of art, becomes dominant with early Modernism. That is to say, the avantgardist attempt to bind an *élite* of critical interpreters to innovatory works of art grows significantly in the Modern period, to the point where the typically Modernist aesthetic, variously understood, is dominant in intellectual circles. Cubist paintings, atonal music, novels and poems like *Ulysses* and *The Trial, The Waste Land* and the *Cantos*, are produced for an audience which is capable, not alone of grappling with new ideas, but of decoding the relationships within the work between its stylistic medium and its message. The Modernist epoch thus inaugurates a process of comprehension which, in growing alliance with the Academy, leads inexorably to the theory dominated, abstract and conceptualist art of the postmoderns. In this later art the critical response itself may even come to dominate the merely exemplifying aesthetic object, so that our perception of art is mediated through theory, which helps to give it an institutional or avantgardist credibility.[23]

Modernist art, because of its technical concerns, begins this process of constructing that technically or theoretically oriented critical community that now sustains the institutions of the art world. The early development of this situation, in which the commitments of 'technique' disrupt the idea of a socially agreed reflective content, is to be found in the early Modernism whose features I have attempted to explore, very provisionally, in this essay.

A Modernist Noesis

Bruce Johnson

In Virginia Woolf's *To The Lighthouse*, Andrew describes his father's work to
Lily Briscoe as ' "Subject and object and the nature of reality . . . Think of a
kitchen table then," he told her, "when you're not there" '.[1] Mr Ramsay, we
later learn, has promised 'to talk "some nonsense" to the young men of Cardiff
about Locke, Hume, Berkeley, and the causes of the French Revolution'.(p. 70) Lily Briscoe, however, in a tangibly different spirit subsequently
wonders while 'sitting on the floor with her arms round Mrs Ramsay's knees'
whether there might be a 'device for becoming, like waters poured into one jar,
inextricably the same, one with the object one adored?'(pp. 78, 79) And Mrs
Ramsay in a related mood 'could not help attaching oneself to one thing
especially of the things one saw'. Often she sits and looks 'until she became the
thing she looked at—that light, for example'.(p. 97) Readers seldom realize
that in the section called 'Time Passes' we are pointedly invited to think of a
kitchen table—or more precisely of a whole vacation house—'when you're not
there', as though Woolf were subjecting her various renderings of consciousness to the very test that Andrew imagines his father has found congenial: a
kind of measurement against reality-in-itself.

One of my colleagues, a distinguished Renaissance scholar, has often
remarked that he resents the 'splendid solipsistic isolation' of consciousness as
it had been represented in the great modernist narrative experiments—in
Joyce, Woolf, and Conrad to name only salient examples. But in Woolf, at
least, there is both confused pleasure and despair at the possibility of ever
really sharing the private consciousness of another, and she no less than Joyce
and Conrad writes against the background of a massively influential late-
Victorian and Edwardian crisis, one that is perhaps most conveniently epito-
mized in T.S. Eliot's doctoral dissertation on F.H. Bradley. Finished and sent
from England in April 1916, the general argument of the thesis concerns the
so-called subject-object split and affirms Bradley's sense that what he calls
'immediate experience' is prior to any separation of the event into 'subject' and
'object'.[2] Bradley and Eliot agree that—to quote Eliot—'We have no right,
except in the most provisional way, to speak of *my* experience, since the I is a
construction out of experience, an abstraction from it; and the *thats*, the
browns and hards and flats, are equally ideal constructions, as ideal as atoms'.[3]
As Sanford Schwartz demonstrates, Eliot goes on to suggest that Edwardian
psychology persistently objectified the subjective and that much of Romantic
and Victorian poetry persistently subjectified the objective, until excesses in

both directions left the artist in 1916 looking for antidotes. Swinburne is of course often mentioned as one of the culprits for—as Schwartz says—his 'habit of expressing emotion with words detached from objective reference'.[4] Schwartz argues convincingly that many of Eliot's most cherished critical principles, especially the idea of a 'dissociation of sensibility' and of the 'objective correlative' derive from Eliot's preoccupation with this unwelcome Cartesian inheritance. In fact, Schwartz suggests that the term 'objective correlative' may come from Husserl's *Logische Untersuchungen* (1900) rather than—as has been supposed—from Meinong; both were, after all, eager students of Franz Brentano.

Whether the term has been borrowed from Husserl is less important than the larger perception that both Eliot and Husserl are struggling against the rigidity of the subject-object frame. In October 1914 Eliot says in a letter to the Chairman of the Harvard philosophy department: 'I have been plugging away at Husserl, and find it terribly hard, but very interesting, and I like very much what I think I understand of it.'[5]

Despite the enormously tortured German sentences that Eliot must have been reading, he was probably already into *Ideen, Ideas* (1913) and well beyond *Logische Untersuchungen* (or at least beyond its preliminary spirit), and had read enough to see that the German philosopher too had recognized the onus of the Cartesian 'Cogito, ergo sum': its attempt to isolate reflexive consciousness as the first truly modern and undoubtable criterion for being—'ergo sum'. As William Barrett says, 'It is a strange affirmation of consciousness, this of Decartes, that begins by abolishing our everyday world'. 'The exhaltation of self-consciousness, which Hegel admires, splits the mind off from a realm of objects, which it proceeds now to understand in quantitative terms very different from those of everyday life.'[6] Barrett sees this moment as the origin of technology, the will to power over these now estranged objects, and Eliot must have seen in Husserl an ally who in developing the idea of consciousness's 'intentionality' and later of the *Lebenswelt* was reaching for the same rapprochement that Eliot saw in the concept of the objective correlative and that Hulme, Ezra Pound and even some of the Imagists sought in a theory of concrete diction. Husserl, despite the potentially estranging effect of the *epoché*, the bracketing or suspension of questions of 'existence', saw that the essential structure of consciousness was always to intend beyond itself, even beyond its most intimate introspection, and that in doing so it denied the Cartesian 'two worlds' in favour of one immediately lived and everyday world.

So many names—Edwardian artists, philosophers, and psychologists such as Bergson, Bradley, William James, Nietzsche, Meinong, Brentano—are associated with this belated reaction against the Cartesian 'two worlds' that it is really quite astonishing to find so little mention of it as a background for the great narrative experiments of Modernism. It has only recently come into its own in the discussion of post-impressionist painting, particularly with regard to the layered planes of Cézanne which nervously blend human and nonhuman, sitter and table top, in demonstration that there were not two worlds but one. Yet even Stephen's aesthetic in *A Portrait of the Artist as a Young Man* is hard to place in the context of modernism without some sense of the 'two worlds' anxiety, a concern that by 1916 had crossed the boundaries of so many disciplines that it deserves to be called a 'cultural' crisis, particularly if Barrett is right about its connection with technology. Joyce's sense of the need for a 'dramatic' equivalent for what might otherwise be only the *language* of feeling and meaning is very close to Eliot's 'objective correlative' and to Husserl's and Heidegger's sense of consciousness habitually projecting beyond itself to its own talismanic objects and to the experience of human becoming in the daily world of immediate experience.

Many of the important philosophers and artists in this 'two worlds' crisis echo the early anthropologists (evolutionary, most of them: Darwin himself, Edward Tylor, Frazer, Jesse Weston,) in pointing out that apparently no other culture in the world had created an equivalent split. Most were, in fact, peculiarly animistic in dissolving any such gap between consciousness and the lived world. But, upon close examination, so are the great experiments in rendering consciousness that we recognize as the modern novel.

Although one might choose Joyce's *Ulysses* as readily as Conrad's Marlow to explore this crisis, Woolf will in a brief exposition serve me better. In the 'Time Passes' section of *To The Lighthouse* she tries, as I suggested above, to imagine a table, a house, 'when you're not there' (Mrs Ramsay having died in brackets one night), when Mr Ramsay, his children and his guests have all departed and are prevented from returning not only by more death and war but by some cosmic entropy. Woolf's coy characterization of that entropy as 'certain airs' serves only to intensify the steady threat.

Mr Ramsay seems to represent at least in part the spirit of the 'two worlds'—whatever the opposite of a Bergsonian or Bradleyan recovery of 'pure duration' or 'immediate experience' might have meant to Woolf. He specializes in the empirical, associationist philosophers and their assertion that mental abstraction at its best corresponds to the reality of sensation impressed on an otherwise blank tablet, and at its worst wanders away from that original correspondence into 'notions'. His approach to philosophy ('He reached Q. Very few people in the whole of England ever reach Q') suggests a kind of Laputian, dehumanized quest for the nature of reality-in-itself apart from human perception ('Think of a kitchen table . . . when you're not there'), an acceptance nonetheless of the 'two worlds' ('subject and object', says Andrew) and, in short, a contradiction to Woolf's and—in general—modernism's instrumentalist theory of knowledge, wherein the criterion of value can range from Nietzsche's 'power' to William James' 'usefulness' or 'cash value' or Woolf's and Forster's sheer human connection. In such instrumentalist theories mental abstractions have no 'correspondence' to reality (and are at least Kantian in that partial sense) but are judged better or worse as they allow the philosopher's or artist's central value to flourish. If Mr Ramsay's signposts of philosophic progress are the abstract letters of the alphabet, Woolf's are connected human beings, Nietzsche's, degrees of radical self-possession and so on. The crucial point is not that Mr Ramsay can be identified with a specific philosophic school or position but that the reader sense Woolf's own instrumentalist attitude toward knowledge and its uses in the human community.

One of Mrs Ramsay's talents, like some of E.M. Forster's characters in *Howards End*, is to become a place, an object, a searching lighthouse beam, a dinner party—consciousness so indistinguishable from the material world it inhabits that one is hard pressed to say which inhabits the other. As Woolf eases into this section of the novel, the traditional philosophic terms are very much on her mind: 'There was scarcely anything left of body or mind by which one could say, "This is he" or "This is she".' The paradox of the whole section (and it is a paradox critical of Mr Ramsay's quality of mind) is that as the author withdraws all characters from the scene, some sort of consciousness nevertheless remains in the material world before us. The 'point of view' in this scene may well be unique in modern fiction, if not in all narrative, because it does not seem to belong to the 'author' in any tidy sense of that concept, not even in a structuralist sense. Many readers will testify to its haunting indeterminacy: some have even agreed with Gayatri Spivak that there is a hint of madness in the technique of the section.[7] At the very least we may say that no easy omniscience has been intended. With only the once-inhabited material world left to draw near to (as she had to the consciousnesses present when they were available), she continues nonetheless to draw near! 'Certain airs' question 'gently' not only the red and yellow roses on the wallpaper but 'the torn letters in the wastepaper basket, the flowers, the books, all of which were now open to them and asking, Were they allies? Were they enemies? How long would they endure?' The 'airs' seem to become small creatures nosing through the house and frustrated in their eventual conquest by the presence of sleeping people. After the family has gone, the quiet conquest of the house by time and Nature proceeds relentlessly despite occasional cleaning forays by Mrs McNab. Prue dies and Andrew dies, both in brackets (*pace* Husserl), and human categories and distinctions die: 'Giant artichokes towered among roses, a fringed carnation flowered among the cabbages.' Not even this densely inhabited bit of the material world can ultimately withstand Woolf's mindless time and tide. Even the stroke of the lighthouse has begun to lose its identification with Mrs Ramsay, though that inhabited bit of the material world remains sentient longer than any other. Saved from entropy at the last possible moment by the return of cleaners, repairmen, and finally of family and guests, the house has nonetheless collapsed easy distinctions between 'subject' and 'object' and impressed most readers with the clear sense that both concepts are indeed abstractions from an 'immediate experience' far more seminal than either. For the high-modern novel at least, the criterion of human 'being' is no more limited to 'cogito, ergo sum', to the nuclear certainty of reflexive consciousness, than it is in Husserl or Heidegger. If Woolf's 'wedge-shaped core of darkness' is consciousness in its remotest privacy, the quality of human 'being' lives no more intensely there than it does in James's boar skull, in the great brown pot of Boeuf en Daube, or in the wedge-shaped lighthouse beam that seems a symmetrical counterpart in the material world for that 'wedge-shaped core of darkness within'. The individual 'wedges' of consciousness die within

brackets; the wedge-like stroke from the lighthouse lives on to inhabit other
consciousness. If, as Mrs Ramsay supposes, two of the many books she has
failed to read, 'Croom on the Mind and Bates on the Savage Customs of
Polynesia', are neither of them books that one could send to the lighthouse, we
might nonetheless suppose that many a 'savage' could teach Croom a thing or
two about the nature of 'mind' and just who was savaging what by isolating
'mind'. Many a 'savage' could understand at once how whole being arises from
a lived place, how Alexandria produces its lovers, the Marabar its wary
Godboles, Howards End its generations of yeoman inheritors. Woolf stands
plainly with those modernists (not the least of them D.H. Lawrence) who want
to put Humpty Dumpty together again.

It is well known that in the transition from the late-Victorian and Edwardian
novel to the modern, Thomas Hardy and his follower D.H. Lawrence both
insist on an expansion of human character beyond its Victorian social definition ('I associate, therefore I am?') to its allotropic participation in cosmic
forces and structures, an allotropy that in both writers once again binds
'subject' to the 'objective' world of places and things, somewhat in the manner
of the ancient pastoral. The *noesis*, to use Husserl's term, the structure of the
conscious 'intention' that drives much of the symbolic meaning of both
Hardy's and Lawrence's world, is thus all but defined by a determination to
dissolve the Cartesian two worlds in favour—as Jeffrey M. Perl might say—of a
typically modernist 'nostos', a return to a lost home where there were never
two worlds, but one.[8] One might even venture a guess that one of the most
basic noetic structures of high modernism, if it is not Perl's pervasive sense of
nostos, of a return to a kind of lost classicism, is not Cartesian 'doubting', as we
have so often been told, but an heroic zeal for the *ur-alt*. The modernist seeks
not only *nostos*, a return home to an original classic wholeness of mind and
body, as Perl suggests and as the cyclical motifs of so much modernist art
would confirm, but a return to primordial 'origins' of all sorts. For the
modernist, Christianity is not old, and even the spirituality of Christian faith
must be discovered to rest upon Fisher Kings and fertility cults that are not
merely old but *ur-alt*. As Hugh Kenner suggests, with modernism comes the
study of word origins and language origins, the archeological method of
philology. With Hardy and then Lawrence we move into the countryside in
order to probe progressively deeper, beneath Roman ruins to 'Celtic' structures and on down—as Hardy once described an excavation of his beloved
Maumbury Ring—to flints of which one could hardly say whether they were
manmade or natural.[9] With Joseph Conrad we must go upriver toward the
'beginnings of time' and to the most seminal well-springs of human consciousness. And so on and on in a manner that many studies of modernism will
already have revealed, whether of Yeats and Pound or of analytic cubism.

Because of this fundamental noetic structure (and no doubt there are a few
other structures equally intrinsic to High Modernism) one of the feelings most
common to modernist art is the artist's nagging doubt whether he or she has
ever been fundamental *enough*, an anxiety displayed everywhere in Woolf's
presentation of consciousness but particularly in the strange 'Time Passes'

section, or even more clearly—to cite painting again for a moment—in Picasso's 'Les Demoiselles d'Avignon', where the viewer is invited to move from almost conventionally abstracted Western faces to increasingly 'barbaric', African abstraction. Chins and noses become scimitars, as though Picasso were conducting us back in time through ever more atavistic revelations. In both the Woolf section and the Picasso painting (both classics of High-Modernist spirit) the *process* of recovering the most fundamental elements becomes the subject, and the process is fraught with anxiety not only about what we shall find when we get there (whether id or reconstructed Indo-European language) but about whether we have somehow been conned into stopping too soon.

Of course also fundamental to this modernist noetic structure is a partial sense of *déjà-vu* that is sometimes mistaken for a *nostos*. Early modernists—not the least of them Joseph Conrad and Freud himself—had asserted that, far from outgrowing primordial origins, we carry them constantly and actively within, and this realization, whether in *Heart of Darkness* or in the case of the Wolf Man had, after all, been one of Modernism's greatest contributions to epistemology. Even Structuralism (especially in its early manifestation, Russian Formalism) grew out of typically fundamentalist language theory to bypass specific content in order to find the non-specific 'deep structure', a deep structure that presumably lies so far down in the ur-mind as to realize itself again and again in *all* forms of cultural activity, basket-making no less than myth-making, cooking no less than love-making. Even the individual personality and ego is dissolved in the presence of a 'first cause' so fundamental that it can have no specific content and 'uses' individual personality rather than being used by it.

We know we are in the presence of this particular *noesis* when what is allegedly most modern, even avant-garde, seems simultaneously most ancient. If there is one word more than any other that undergoes a crescendo in modernist texts, it is the adjective and noun 'primordial'. Beginning as early as Impressionism in 1874, Monet and other key figures speak of a return to a 'primordial' way of seeing free of superimposed conceptions generated by the mind rather than the eye alone (perspective and line, drawing, despised perhaps above all others). The eye itself, unencumbered by intellectual baggage, will lead the way to a new kind of seeing that is at once—*must* have been, says Monet—also the original way of seeing, before what is not-eye intervened.[10] Critics and philosophers of the time as diverse as Emile Littré (an outspoken Positivist), Hippolyte Taine, and Jules Laforgue all argued that 'subject' and 'object' were secondary constructions that must yield to the primordial act of consciousness, to the 'impression' that contains and precedes both. Their arguments show real affinities with both Husserl and T.S. Eliot, despite the staggering differences in background and personality, and suggest that we are indeed dealing with a cultural crisis that develops as early as the late 1860s and for at least thirty years after pivots on the work of Impressionist and Post-Impressionist painters. At about the same time, Thomas Hardy offers Egdon Heath as at once the only suitable landscape for the ultra-modernist

Clym (disillusioned and irretrievably infected with cosmic *angst*) and yet also the most ancient and enduring 'survival' imaginable, its geology and botany so exquisitely modulated that it has remained untouched by geological forces that might have produced cataclysm in another topography. The 'irrepressible New' and the eternally enduring 'survival'—the word used in its rather precise anthropological sense—are not only kin but, in many of Hardy's images, seem to embrace one another or, more fundamentally, to be phenomenologically identical.[11]

Even in the most recent issue of *Art News* we are not surprised to read that viewers of the sculpture of a very avant-garde New York artist 'might have assumed that they had stumbled on an exhibition of totemic or ritual artifacts from some obscure ancient civilization . . .' (May '87, p.83) Students of architecture had after all correctly begun fifty years ago to see 'Aztec' and Mayan forms in Frank Lloyd Wright's most advanced California style, and the influence of African and tribal art, of so-called 'primitive' art, on early modernist work had been institutionalized (and some said wildly chauvinized) by the 1985 MOMA exhibition and the massive two-volume catalogue-text that went with it. Evidence for this essential characteristic of one modernist *noesis* crowds in from all sides. Even when we look at the visually and technically enormous difference between, for example, Russian Formalist (constructivist) paintings and Impressionist canvases—recognizing that both would have laid fervent claim to being aggressively modernist—their equal share in a 'return to primordial origins' is apparent: the Russians in a politicized, abstractly structuralist mode that they share with Propp and Shklovsky in folkloric and literary matters, the impressionists in their drive toward pure seeing, however naive such 'purity' may seem to us today. The sense of the primordial is of course different for each, as are the ends to which the recovery will be turned, but the *noesis* is apparently the same. The Russian Formalism is the manifestation in painting and sculpture of structuralist abstraction quite as much as Impressionism represents a faith that the eye comes before intellection and abstraction—certainly (an ardent impressionist would say) before the despised 'line' of even the most inspired formalist geometry.

It may be that the most important element of this particular modernist *noesis* is a spirit of 'recognition', just the sort of recognition widely attributed to both the Joycean 'epiphany' and the phenomenologist's *aletheia*: a sudden awareness of an incarnate, embodied but previously hidden truth; an awareness putatively beyond the need for rhetoric, for authorial persuasiveness, and almost beyond the need for either explanation or even words. But this 'recognition', even when it is incarnate in Eliot's 'objective correlative', is nonetheless so often full of submerged rhetorical intentions that one might want to speculate about its being, in fact, a defensive claim of recognition: the artist fully working in this particular modernist *noesis* wants the reader (or viewer) to feel not that the artist has established some fresh truth by the power and efficacy of his art, but that the reader, having always in some sense been already in possession of origins (the mistaken idea that ontogeny recapitulates phylogeny was current) needs almost in the Platonic sense only to 'remember'. If that recognition, that alleged recognition in the mode of remembering, will genuinely stand alone (as Hemingway too thought it could), why do so many readers nonetheless feel the presence of so much covert rhetoric?

My description of this modernist *noesis* so far would help to explain why so much modern art leading us up to the recognition/remembering seems like an excavation or stripping off of somehow 'secondary' imposed qualities (one also no doubt thinks here of Robbe-Grillet or even of Beckett). Hardy says that when the excavation of Maumbury Ring had gone below the Roman and 'Celtic' artifacts and down to flints on which the human touch could hardly be discerned, the 'blood of us onlookers ran cold'.[12] When Conrad conducts us closer and closer to the atavistic 'heart of darkness' he protects himself with an impression of an impression: Impressionism, in a sense, as both revelation and defensive distancing. One of the results of the modernist's alleged 'recognition' is that it annihilates one sense—and that the most disturbing sense—of the word and concept 'new'. If the new is actually our re-recognition of the primordial, indeed of origins, then there is really nothing hitherto unknown in it. One has this sense strongly in Freud's texts. The modernist has tamed the new or protected himself against its most untoward implications and threats by recognizing in it not merely a resurgent 'classicism' (as Pound would have it and as Jeffrey Perl argues so persuasively in his case for a modernist *nostos*) but the *ur-alt*, the virgin springs before even a classicism could form. Mercea Eliade suggests that mythology is inevitably 'origin stories', because to know the origin of something is to believe oneself able to control it: a kind of metaphysical blackmail.

Thus one of the most important structural aspects of this modernist *noesis* is the connection between recognition/remembering and the protective value (against the truly unknown inherent in absolute newness) of knowing origins. A radical but interesting speculation might then be that the repressed and concealed structural element of such a *noesis* is its desire to annihilate—not merely to control and defend against—the newness itself. Lest this speculation seem unpardonably deconstructionist, let me wonder further whether Derrida's attack on Husserl's claims for self-evident *aletheia* (a denial that extends finally to all Western metaphysics and that truly lies at the origins of deconstructionism) is not an exercise in oneupmanship well within the modernist project of a return to origins. There will be a revelation, a showing-forth, says Husserl, not from some god but from the bracketed thing itself. And when we have this, he implies, we shall be in the inner sanctum, at the self-evident source of meaning. The source of meaning, says Derrida to the contrary, is Peirce's discovery that the only explication of a sign is another sign. To use another of Husserl's terms (the companion term for *noesis*), the two men are really talking about the same *noema*, object of intention, and through the same *noesis*: the *true* remembering of origins, whatever the truth of it may be.

The most moving tribute to this return/recognition/remembering that I know of comes in Hemingway's *The Sun Also Rises*, when Bill and Jake and Harris reluctantly leave their fishing and manage to walk up to the village of

Roncesvalles, the Roncevaux of Roland's death in a defeat by Saracen forces and, of course, the symbolic fountainhead of Charlemagne's tradition of chivalric heroism in the manner of the *Chanson de Roland*. The allusiveness of the reference is large but falls here on ears that are tuned to a different though no less heroic song. After Bill and Harris have agreed that it is a 'remarkable place' and Harris has noted that he has 'been intending coming up each day', Bill offers a source of value more congenial to this group: 'It isn't the same as fishing, though, is it?' Bill's earlier conversation with Jake while fishing has been full of the names of men who, like Cohn, live by second-hand preconceptions, their lives imitating someone else's convention or art: William Jennings Bryan, Mencken, even one A.E.W. Mason, a romantic hack whose story Jake reads, about a woman who waits twenty-four years for her dead fiancé to melt out of a glacier before she will marry her new true love; he of course waits with her patiently at the bottom of the glacier.

The juxtaposition of A.E.W. Mason and Charlemagne's and Roland's Roncevaux is astonishingly obscure until one realizes that for Hemingway and Jake both are decadent traditions and literary conventions, the heroic chivalric no less than the pulp romantic. The passage takes no notice of the towering differences beween the sentimental Victorian cliché and the spiritually rich chivalric tradition. Both fail for Hemingway because now they can only be received already packaged; one cannot now experience origins through them, if once that were possible even through sentimentalism (perhaps in its latitudinarian origins in someone like Henry Fielding). For Hemingway one must find a way to take experience first-hand. Whether the pre-conception (and hence filter) be a distinguished tradition of chivalric valour, Cohn's worship of W.H. Hudson's *Green Mansions*, or an official wartime corruption of language ('honour', 'valour', 'patriotism', all the 'big words' that Hemingway has purged), so great is Hemingway's contempt that all are lumped together—or almost so, Roland alone meriting quiet respect. No convention, not Charlemagne's struggle against an alien Moorish consciousness (his echo, if you will, of Herodotus' point about the significance of the Persian Wars) can compete with the primordial sensations of the clean, precise action-ethic of fishing and the brotherhood of those who can go back to the uncontaminated well springs, the cold mountain streams that come before even ideas, words, traditions.

Both men immediately recognize what Bill means and, of course, refuse even to consider talking about it. No persuasion is necessary; the recognition is all. The whole counterpoint of the scene is between those who can touch the origins (and recognize at once when they are there), and those who take experience through learned categories and formulae, even if they once were Roland's formulae. The hero is not only the one who can 'return' and 'recognize' but one who can additionally defeat the snares of a false or partial return. For Hemingway the capacity to observe, for example, that icy wine, cold from a mountain stream, makes the 'eyes ache' is a safer mooring amidst modern chaos than even Roncevaux—an arrogant claim to be sure, and one that can hardly be substantiated with the destruction of straw men such as

Cohn (who pick one up in the approved Princeton manner before they knock one down again) but nevertheless a claim in the familiar modernist *noesis*.

What makes Woolf's 'Time Passes' different within the same noetic structure is that we must follow her to the edge of signification, nearly to the breakdown of human categories (carnations flower among cabbages). In the vacation house lies the possibility of the deepest return of all, to a point beyond any 'recognition' or remembering, a point which begins the madness of non-human order. 'Time Passes' is a radical vision of an 'instrumental' theory of knowledge, as Sanford Schwartz calls it, and indeed as it is ordinarily called.[13] Our conceptualizations cannot correspond to reality-in-itself but are no less powerful metaphors and models for using it, as many modernists from Hulme and William James to Nietzsche and John Dewey had said. If there is any recognition in this scene it is of an absolutely 'other'. Like Kant, Woolf implies that we can never know the thing itself, but unlike Kant, for Woolf the mind is not structured according to the essences of Newton and Euclid. The Nature which is about to overwhelm the house is not a wonderfully precise Newtonian machine. It is much more like Nietzsche's welter of sensation before we will the power to conceptualize and use it. Mr Ramsay does not recognize the 'will to power' in what purports to be his disinterested philosophic enquiry. Yet the 'break of brass' is applied as unrelentingly to his theory of knowledge as it is to Andrew. 'Time Passes' cries out for a recognition of motives, of the will to one kind of power or another, within an allegedly abstract conceptualization. Even the distinction between 'subject' and 'object' must be made to reveal its underlying motives, the *motive* for the abstraction, as William James too would have agreed with Nietzsche. It is as though 'Time Passes' had been addressed to those who imagine some human abstractions truly reflect reality-in-itself and may lead them past 'Q' to 'R' or even to 'Z', the alphabet of the philosophy being also the alphabet of reality-in-itself. But the passage leads us on the contrary to a point of origin very suggestive of the 'boum' in Forster's Marabar caves, which in Woolf has become—speaking generically—carnations flowering among the cabbages. Recognition has become its opposite—an apprehension of the wholly 'other', the definitively alien.

The particular modernist *noesis* we have been examining seems to require this final 'turn', where origins are seen as the end or the beginning of human differentiation (all words and human categories can become merely 'boum') and the illusion that our conceptualization reflects reality-in-itself is finally shattered.

This realization (for me best accomplished in 'Time Passes', in the Marabar caves, and in Kurtz's career in *Heart of Darkness*) leads to a new sense of 'home', even of *nostos* if you will, now contemplated under the new fellowship possible to strangers in an alien land, in an alien cosmos. We are shown what may be a new basis for human community—not any daunting gap between subject and object in the old Cartesian sense, but the heroic possibilities in recognizing the human motives behind even that kind of abstraction. Mr Ramsay's philosophy-as-charge-of-the-light-brigade had yielded to Woolf's modernist version of eighteenth-century 'right reason'. This modernist return/ recognition in short deconstructs itself, at least in the sense that the return to end all returns no longer finds anything to recognize in reality-in-itself (unlike Mr Ramsay's Locke, Hume, and Berkeley). Having cultivated the noetic mode of 'recognition' with a peculiar loyalty, the modernist, like Crusoe digging and deepening his protective cave, comes frighteningly out the other side.

In seeking something aboriginally prior to the abstractions of 'subject' and 'object', a whole half-century had turned against Descartes with an enthusiasm that we ignore at our peril in the study of modern philosophy and art. Even more important to our sense of modernism, however, is the passion for a reapprehension of origins that led to this revision of Descartes and also— beyond much doubt—to Husserl's proposal of 'pure subjectivity' as the only possible basis for a 'presuppositionless' philosophy, a basis so archaic and seminal as to be unchallengeable. True to the noetic structure we have been examining, Husserl often said that Descartes' key fault had been that he had not gone far enough (had been seduced into stopping the 'return' too soon) and thus had not recognized that the truly primordial act of consciousness lay even prior to the imagined coherence of the 'I' and to any abstraction from immediate experience. A student of the whole period from at least 1874 through high modernism in the 1920s might have great difficulty deciding who among the critics, philosophers, and artists believed most fervently that he or she had been truly 'presuppositionless'—that is, without presuppositions: Husserl or Hemingway, Monet or in some important respects T.S. Eliot, Laforgue or Woolf as she leads us to the very edge of human order and then draws back to show us where we have been, to show us our 'recognition' turned inside-out or into some sort of Möbius strip where the concept of inside and outside is shown to be an abstraction from more fundamental and immediate experience.

Northrop Frye and the Bible

Frank Kermode

Northrop Frye does not practise literary criticism as most of us know it. For him, literature is a manifestation of the human plot against the inhuman—a secondary universe we make to give ourselves the possibility of accommodating ourselves to a world we never made. Like Blake, the poet he so cherishes, he constantly believes that our life in the world we never made can be made tolerable, can be transformed, by the human imagination. Like Wallace Stevens, another very congenial poet, he thinks that without our imagination version of the world—what Stevens calls a *mundo* rather than the world as objectively conceived—we must live in poverty, if indeed we can live at all. 'Natives of poverty, children of malheur, / The gaiety of language is our seigneur.' But unlike Stevens, he not only meditates systems, he makes them—systems for studying the systems of the *mundo*. These secondary systems are all his own, for, again like Blake, he must have his own system lest he be enslaved by another man's.

This is a way of saying that he studies the possibility of human freedom, a freedom conferred by myth and operative in the *mundo* of myth. He studies mythology as 'part of the imaginative insulation that separates us from our environment'. His work is therefore far from the spirit of Roland Barthes's, for example; Barthes's modern mythologies are ways of cheating, inducements to the acceptance of corrupt cultural products as natural. For Frye the natural is another thing; we have discourses for dealing with it that are not mythological. But among these discourses poetry survives, an apparent atavism, our stubborn way of retaining some remnant of mythological thinking—in its broadest connotations, the means by which we preserve that insulation, and the means by which we might conceivably construct a tolerably human world. With all his habitual irony, his sometimes sad little jokes, Frye is a kind of Utopian thinker. He has a Viconian view of history, but the first phase of language survives into the others. The wheel will turn, and the large plot is the restoration of metaphor and of paradise.

The *Anatomy of Criticism* gave us the essentials of his method. It is, in a word, taxonomical but not static. Criticism is a physics, literature is the nature it studies. This means that in one phase of the operation the world of literature is conceived as static, as having, like the inhuman world, 'spatial' dimensions. But there is also a dimension of time, as when myth is progressively displaced, or when one mode of discourse melts into another. There are fluid borderlines, like that between tragedy and irony; inversions, as when the curve of comedy is transformed into the curve of tragedy, or when metaphor yields to metonymy, or metonymy to the demotic or descriptive. The entire system is accordingly in constant and complicated motion. It looks almost Ptolemaic. It does not give us the world as we might see it without the benefit of insulation; it is perhaps some kind of parody of that world, and at any rate a world in itself.

In *The Secular Scripture*, published in 1976, Frye offered 'a summary geography lesson in what I call the mythological or imaginative universe'. In so doing he speaks of two scriptures, one secular and one divine. These are in conflict, but each is an aspect of *the* mythological universe. The secular scripture owes some aspects of its structure to the older divine scripture, 'the great code' as Blake called it. Frye is aware that discrepancies of texture and structure call for discussion, but it is clear in any case that the full expression of his system, the final accounting for the 'mythological or imaginative universe', called imperatively for a study of the Bible.

It is an ancient myth that the world is like a book—possibly *legato con amor in un volume*—and the notion that the Bible is a world is almost equally ancient and enormously developed. The rabbinical tradition provides a physics of Torah, treating its world as an inexhaustible mass of correspondences, of interpretanda, of challenges to the human imagination, which can prove itself by the detection of relationships previously undetected. Such zealous applications recur in more secular studies, as in certain speculations on word and world in the period immediately before the triumph of Newtonian physics. To apprehend the world as systematic is the aim of those who study the Book of Nature; students of the other Book will also seek its systems. In so doing, Frye claims his place in a long and honoured tradition.

His version of the Bible is a *mundo*, though it isn't rabbinical and it isn't obviously 'poetic', for he expresses it in a demotic mode. This world is fictive. Just as he exiled questions of value from the *Anatomy*, he exiles from his biblical criticism questions of belief. The correspondence of this *mundo* is with the human, not the divine mind, though perhaps the human at its full extent is all we can know of the divine. Like his admired Stevens in this also, he suggests that the final belief must be in a fiction, a fiction that clothes a reality it would not be tolerable, even if it were possible, to perceive in its nakedness.

What I shall now say about *The Great Code* will be very inadequate, not merely because of the inadequacy of the expositor, but because we have as yet only the first of the two volumes promised. We are asked to regard the first as prolegomena, and the second volume will obviously address issues that may seem to be neglected in the first. However, the first is all one has to talk about and to dissent from; and I shall do so freely, pausing to affirm that whatever doubts I have about parts of this book I have none about Frye's stature. He is the best writer among modern anglophone critics, never writing an idle sentence, never bullying but always arguing finely, always assured of the truth of his own thought, and assured, too, that what he has achieved by long and independent study is what we unconsciously know and can bring to consciousness without his needing to do more than explain it. Then we too can extract from the 'flawed speech and stubborn sounds' of language that imaginative truth by which the world is to be understood and transformed. The ambition is entirely noble, and a measure of dissent from Frye's performance cannot diminish its nobility.

There is a sense in which all Frye's books are, to use a word of his own, 'centripetal'. Their structures have a completeness and internal correspondence that make them wholes—whole myths, whole metaphors. This can be a disadvantage to his followers. They must either remain within his system (and so be 'enslaved') or write parodies of it, or build their hovels with his stones, or abjure him altogether in favour of the many new kinds of critical discourse, uneasy blends of the demotic and the mandarin, that now fascinate the coteries. But however they may deal with the difficulty, it is true to say that *The Great Code* is a centripetal work.

Frye spends little time on the claim that the Bible is a single book and not merely a collection of books. It is, of course, a claim indispensable to his position: the Bible is a world, therefore one. The dispatch with which he makes this necessary point is admirable. He doesn't refer to the current dispute among professional biblical critics on this very issue. In their tradition (for which Frye says he hasn't much time, though he hints that it will get a fuller showing in volume 2) it has been the general custom over a couple of centuries to reduce the Bible to its constituent *biblia*, and then, if possible, reduce those parts to hypothetical lost earlier versions, always with the object of getting behind the books themselves to the events described in them. This historico-critical method remains the dominant strain in biblical criticism, though it is at present under strong challenge from the so-called 'canonical' critics. The argument in progress is extremely interesting, and important in its implications for literary history generally. The canonical critics do not deny the value of historical scholarship but argue that however the canons were founded they were validated by the devotion and study of many generations (not by some imagined single fiat) and that to ignore this long and venerable process of validation, to ignore that in a perfectly intelligible way the Bible is one book, is perverse.

This is a problem in hermeneutics, for one party dedicates itself to the recovery of an original meaning, while to the other it is the essence of scripture that its truth and meaning emerge when it is applied to circumstances different from those of its origin. This defence of 'application' strikes the advocates of the original sense as dishonest, not 'application' so much as 'wrongful appropriation'. The argument is acrimonious and complicated—but Frye ignores it. Of the 'original meaning' view he merely says that even if it is true it isn't important; 'what matters is that "the Bible" has traditionally been read as a unity, and has influenced Western imagination as a unity. It exists if only because it has been compelled to exist.' And in any case, whoever reads the Bible through will see that it has the kind of unity that interests Frye—a beginning, when time begins, an end when time ends, and in between much middle matter which can be seen as self-replicating structural patterns of narrative and imagery that make of the scattered *biblia* in which they occur a coherent whole.

I have no quarrel with this prior assumption, which is in some respects quite like that of the anthropologist Sir Edmund Leach in his biblical studies, though it has to be said that his patterns are very different. For both of them the Bible is a universe of myth, though for Frye it is not merely made up of self-replicating motifs; there is progression to an end, as well as a cyclical movement. Here, as everywhere, he is dealing with a 'mythological universe, a body of assumptions and beliefs developed by man from his existential concerns. Most of this is held unconsciously; which means that our imaginations may recognize elements of it when presented in art or literature, including the Bible, without consciously understanding what it is that we recognize'. For example, to put it very simply, the Bible helps us to understand our sense that there is something wrong about our having to die, and our sense that we can imagine a better world as having existed before and capable of existing again. Or rather, we can recognise these feelings when we meet them in the Bible; it is the task of the critic to bring them to light, to understand what obstructs the passage of our understanding into consciousness, so that we may perceive, in our poverty, the means by which we are able to imagine human happiness.

To imagine the fully human world is the business of poets, who are the surviving instruments of metaphor, which is the language of myth. When language has declined (or, if you prefer, moved on) into its later phases, the dialectic and then the demotic, then it becomes the critic's task to translate the metaphors of imagination into these later dialects. Much of *The Great Code* is devoted to an explanation of a metaphorical discourse largely displaced by prose, and the consequent separation of the observing subject from an objective world with which he formerly identified himself. Among other things, the Bible provides much metaphorical discourse of this kind. Moreover the Bible, and its readers, have had much to do with the shaping and development of all subsequent discourses, and that is another reason why it was necessary for the author of the *Anatomy* to give it independent examination.

'If we "freeze" the Bible into a simultaneous unit, it becomes a single, gigantic, complex metaphor . . .' Frye perceives his affinities with a mythographic tradition stretching from antiquity to Ruskin, and argues that however aberrant its manifestations may seem, this tradition had the merit of recognising mythical thinking as 'universal or poetic thinking'. And that is his main interest. He will not concern himself with the pretence of descriptive history: 'if anything is historically true in the Bible, it is not there because it is historically true but for different reasons.' It is myth, and the truth of myth is inside the structure, not outside. Authority rests in words, not events. And despite its formal differences from poetry, the Bible derives its authority from its language and not from what it talks about.

We are still near the beginning of Frye's exposition, but this is the moment to enter a couple of caveats. Here are two points that have, I think, more than local importance. The first is this: although he has a lot to say about *figura*, though under another name, he is apparently not very interested in Auerbach, whose name does not appear in the index, though there is a passing mention of it in the book. I have in mind Auerbach's perception, in its time original and influential, that the Gospels contain *figurae* of great range and depth—as Frye of course knows very well—and that these *figurae* are expressed in discourse of a demotic and descriptive character. This combination of mystery with demotic language, with *sermo humilis*, Auerbach regarded as an innovation of great importance in the subsequent history of literature. It may well be that those famous pages now require refinement, but Auerbach was certainly right to affirm the novelty of the Gospel discourse, obscured for most readers of the Bible by their ignorance of the *koine*, and perhaps also by a failure to understand the types for what they really were. The language of translations, whether Latin or vernacular, cannot reproduce the demotic of the original, with its barbarisms and simplicities; and the ingrained habit of accepting the fulfilments recorded in the Gospels as being simply that—evidence of the veracity of Old Testament prophecies, demonstrations that all took place 'according to the Scriptures'—prevented the perception that much of the writing, especially in the Passion narratives, was a careful development of those ancient 'testimonies', a matter of imaginative writing rather than the record of fact. I don't doubt that Frye could, if he chose, make much of this early fusion of the mythical and the demotic; indeed he may do so in his second volume. But at present there appears to be a lacuna in the system.

My second objection is more specific; and concerns a single text, John 1:14: 'And the Word became flesh . . .' It is important to Frye's conception of the metaphoric phase that it should be the *word* that has the power, as opposed to the metonymic phase where the word lacks direct access to the object and becomes instead the agent of dialectical discourse. He uses the text of John as an example of the word in its metaphoric phase, where to say that 'the Word became flesh' is no less intelligible than to say 'the boy became a man' or 'the ice became water'. However, says Frye, in the descriptive (i.e. the third) phase of discourse John's statement becomes unintelligible, making no more sense than 'the apple became an orange'. Here Frye completely ignores the context of the statement. John has taken the trouble to ensure that we associate the *logos* with the verb 'was': *en arché én ho logos*; reserving for created things, including flesh, the verb 'became'—*egeneto*, which happens to be the verb used in the Greek Genesis in the account of the creation. Verse 14 is the first in which *logos* and *egeneto* converge. The effect is not commonplace, not ice turning into water, but shocking; the words are a violent paradox. The Word which *was* in the beginning, which *was* with God, which *was* God, suddenly, almost incomprehensibly, enters the realm of becoming, the world of time, death and darkness. The catachresis is so drastic that, like the event it enacts, it could never be repeated.

The point might not be worth dwelling upon if this were a mere passing failure of perception. But it surely indicates the way in which system can crush individual texts, or, more generally, force linguistic and typological characteristics into conformity. It was a complaint made of the *Anatomy* that to systematize a great profusion of observations the author, and after him the reader, had to stand back so far that the fine detail was lost, the painting apparently without brushwork.

However, it is of little use to complain that Frye, the Blakean system-maker, reduces things to fit systems or fantasticates systems to fit things. It is not a surprise to his readers that he arranges his Bible book on a mirror principle (the principle on which the Bible itself is arranged) calling his chapters Language I, Myth I, Metaphor I, Typology I, Typology II, Metaphor II, Myth II, Language II. It is equally in character that he should discover in the Bible seven phases of revelation: Creation, Exodus, Law, Wisdom, Prophecy, Gospel and Apocalypse: seven phases, on the pattern of the apocalyptic seals and trumpets. It is further to be expected that this sequence is not *simply* a sequence; each phase is the type of the phase that follows it, and the antitype of the phase that precedes it. And although typological thinking implies a certain linearity, this sequence may be thought of as possibly cyclical, since Creation can be perceived as the antitype of Apocalypse. However, linearity is the stronger force, since interpretations are said to be the antitypes of the texts to which they are addressed, and presumably are themselves the types of what people later say about them.

Typology is at the heart of the system, the principle of its structure. When Frye takes up a familiar idea or term he often transforms it for his own ends. His use of 'typology' bears only a slight resemblance to other usages, which is why he can make what is on the face of it the extraordinary observation that typology is a neglected subject. It is not at all neglected, except in the definition he has invented for it. Never wholly absent from Christian thought, it has in the last century or so undergone a revival in a modernised form. There have been many versions of it; some have thought that only typological inferences that had direct New Testament validation—mostly in the Pauline epistles and the Epistle to the Hebrews—were justified, the rest being what Chillingworth in *The Scarlet Letter* called 'typical illusions'. But the tradition in general has been more liberal, and nowadays typology is regarded as part of the instrumentation of New Testament narrative. Much work is devoted to the subject, by people who have a right to suppose that each knows what the others are talking about, but Frye's typology isn't part of that conversation, which is why he can call the subject 'neglected'. His affinities are less with modern biblical scholars than with certain visionaries who carried the typological habit to extremes condemned by the medieval church. Frye knows this, and makes allusion to Joachim of Fiore, a writer on whom one would like to hear him expatiate more fully. Joachim, as elaborated or fantasticated by his thirteenth-century followers, regarded the New Testament as the antitype of the Old, the Testament of a *status* of Love fulfilling a *status* of Law, and expected a *tertius status* of the Spirit to follow as the antitype of the New Testament, which (as his followers believed) would have its own Gospel, the Everlasting Gospel mentioned in Revelation. Such ideas, varied by ignorance and ingenuity, have enjoyed long life, and acquired new importance in the nineteenth century, when they were disseminated by Michelet, Renan and George Sand; George Eliot and Matthew Arnold found them attractive, and both Yeats and D.H.

Lawrence worked them into their own systems. Some of Frye's patterns and diagrams have a Joachimite air, and he may in the end be associated with this speculative tradition, as Blake has been before him.

A book that is a system of mirrors is going to be, like the Bible, an inward-looking book, and rather unlike most other books. 'Mirror on mirror mirrored is all the show', as Yeats remarked. 'How do we know the Gospel is true? Because it confirms the prophecies of the Old Testament. But how do we know the prophecies of the Old Testament are true? Because they are confirmed by the Gospel story . . . The two Testaments form a double mirror, each reflecting the other but neither the world outside.' So there is obviously no other book quite like the Bible, not even *The Great Code* itself, for it treats its own past as an image of its future, and vice versa; theoretically anything in the Old Testament can turn out to be a type, as Zechariah's thirty pieces of silver are fulfilled by the price paid to Judas, or Jonah's sojourn in the fish by the entombment and resurrection of Christ (a typological interpretation which has the highest authority of all).

Yet if we cannot expect other books to work in quite that way, we may find in some fairly unexpected places a tendency toward typological elaboration. Frye finds such a tendency in the works of Plato and in the history of Marxism, since the nineteenth-century prophecies of Marx and Engels are fulfilled in Lenin's organisation of the Bolshevik revolution. This thesis remains undeveloped, but it gives one an idea of the way the Bible affects Frye—it provides, in one volume, a model of the ways in which the human imagination works to provide us with our necessary shelters against meaningless history and meaningless reality. In the later phases of discourse, type and antitype were unfortunately supplanted by more modern notions of causality; but just as metaphor survives (as poetry) into a demotic age, so typology continues to work as it were underground, even in an epoch of post-typological theology. And of course even a post-typological theology is an antitype of biblical types. It may be even revolutionary in character, like the Reformation or like Marxism; for 'revolution is the antitype of history as a whole', much like the *tertius status* of Joachim.

Since all its patterns, progressions, descents and fulfilments occur nowhere except in its language, it follows that the language of the Bible is a matter of concern to Frye, who discusses it with his usual gentle dogmatism. He is aware of the formidable complexity of the topic, rightly observing that Christianity is a religion of translation. Its founding texts are in Hebrew, Aramaic and Greek; it has been generally read in Latin or in the vernaculars. Since we are all conscious of the inadequacy of translations, especially of poetry, how can we be sure we know the Bible aright, and can discern its designs? Frye holds that all we can truly translate is its *langage*, not its *langue*, the former referring to the signified that is common to all the signifiers. Simply by being human we have a common stock of such signifiers, and so are able to translate a 'common sense'. However, *langage* itself varies from epoch to epoch—at first metaphoric, then dialectic (here enters continuous prose) and then demotic or descriptive. The Bible uses all these modes—poetry and aphorism from the first, hieratic prose from the second, something, though very little, from the third. The modes can coexist, and here, at any rate, they do.

An example of what happens to a hieroglyphic or metaphoric word in its displaced condition is the Greek *pneuma*, which, like the Hebrew *ruach*, means 'air' or 'wind' or 'breath' as well as 'spirit'. The Authorised Version has the Jesus of John say, 'The wind bloweth where it listeth . . . so is everyone that is born of the spirit', but in the Greek the word for 'wind' is the same as the word for 'spirit': *pneuma*. The metaphorical compactness of the original is lost when the translation separates the two senses. In modern English car tyres are pneumatic, and the French call them 'pneus', but we can still use 'pneumatic' to mean 'relating to spirit or spiritual existence' (*O.E.D.*), and 'pneumatology' is not the study of tyres. Some affinity between the senses persists, but the separation is not altogether loss, and may even enrich the vernacular; Swift's *A Tale of a Tub* turns partly on the etymological identity of 'wind' and 'spirit'. This is worth mentioning because Frye's book is in a way controlled by nostalgia for the compact metaphor—as when he maintains that because the Bible is *logos* and Christ is *logos* also, they are one and the same, metaphorically, unlike tyres and ghosts. He thinks this identity enables us to recover an ancient feeling for 'the radically metaphoric' and makes us conscious of 'the presence of a numinous personality in the world'. Indeed this is what he wishes to do for us, though compelled to use the discourse of a later phase, which has more in common with the *Timaeus* than with Genesis, though one would have to add a dash of the demotic. He wants to tell us how it was when everything was hieroglyphic, but to tell us in continuous prose; thus may the literary critic restore to us some sense of the lost satisfactions of *numen*.

Frye's nostalgia for compaction seems to exist in a dialectical relationship with his urge to expand, to qualify by systematic elaboration. Thus, having set out the three main orders of discourse, he explains that the Bible cannot be wholly accounted for in their terms, and at once invents a fourth order, which he calls *kerygma*. This word is familiar in more orthodox modern biblical criticism, where it has a technical sense: deriving from the original Greek sense of a herald's proclamation, it is now used to mean roughly that part of the gospel which makes a direct appeal to the spirit of the individual, the message which is independent of the mythological wrappings. Frye acknowledges this sense, but uses the expression quite differently, to mean that of which myth is the linguistic vehicle. Certainly we should never understand *kerygma* in this sense, or as a fourth mode of discourse, without reading Frye. His is indeed a centripetal work, even one might say, a geocentric work, with *kerygma* a very characteristic epicycle. The epicycle is a symptom of the contrary movements, one seeking compaction, the other—forced, as it were, unwillingly into service—is expansion. The more urgent the vision of oneness, the more necessary the epicycles.

And here I am perhaps getting closer to the true nature of my doubts about an author I so much admire. I am uneasy when persuasively invited to accept arguments which, devised to meet the challenge of his own scepticism, increasingly summon up my own. Here is another example. Frye has always, for his own good reasons, been exercised about the resemblances and differences between myths and folktales, roughly because the latter cannot be thought to meet the quasi-divine demands he makes on myth (though folktales might be said to be an interesting example of *langage*). In *The Secular Scripture* he calls folktale the basis of romance, which *is* the secular scripture. As A.C. Hamilton has pointed out in one of the best articles on Frye,[2] this seems to be a departure from the formulations of the *Anatomy*, which distinguished 'canonical' from 'apocryphal' myth, the first being capable of greater 'metaphorical identification'. We had better avoid the question whether the myth is a myth by virtue of being in a canon, or whether the canon is canonical because it contains only myths. The immediate issue in Frye's Bible book is the book of Judges, in which there are episodes analogous to uncanonical folktales. He settles it in this way: there is 'no consistent structural difference' between myths and folktales, but there is a difference of use, since myths have to do with revelation and folktales with entertainment.

Thus the story of Samson is a myth because it belongs to 'the central body of sacrosanct biblical legend' and presumably because it has been read, traditionally, as bearing upon revelation (Samson is an Old Testament 'saint', a type of Christ, etc). If it were not in the Bible it would be simply a folktale. Here we have an interesting idea, which is to define the cultural and religious status of a story entirely in terms of the particular form of attention we pay to it. In a developed form this idea might have resounding implications for the whole body of Frye's theory, for it suggests that myths are myths only in so far as we choose to confer on them a particular form of attention. Moreover, there is a further implication that the story of Samson is a myth for some and not for others—the presumably large number of people who do not concern themselves with canonicity and may be merely entertained by the idea that Samson is a Christ-figure. But Frye himself goes on to speak as if the status of Samson as myth were quite independent of the kind of attention paid it. Its mythiness is inherent in it. And he will not allow us to say even that there is a myth *behind* the Samson story, describing this as a false or 'metonymic' assumption. He dismisses the idea that because 'Samson' resembles Semetic words for 'sun', and because Samson burns crops and spends time in a prison-house, we can say we are dealing with a variation on a solar myth. After all, he observes, we can say of Napoleon that he reached the zenith of his fame and had his fortunes eclipsed, without needing to call him a solar myth. But such expressions are the worn change of conversation or journalism. In the Samson story something more seems to be going on: 'Delilah' is probably connected with an early Semitic word meaning 'night', and it is she who makes Samson impotent and blind. This renders the Napoleon comparison less persuasive, and the idea that Samson is a folktale founded on a myth (even if later granted mythical status by inclusion in the canon) more difficult to dispose of.

The impulse behind such rather peremptory clearing operations is evidently to leave the system free of clutter, of anything that might obscure its lines, however complicated the lines may be. And the effect is to encourage suspicion that the system is to some extent arbitrary and self-centred however much we may continue to admire the intellectual energy devoted to its elaboration and to its simplification.

When all is arranged, and the machine begins to work, we see that we are in the presence of an apocalypse. If the Exodus is the dominant type, the Apocalypse is the dominant antitype, the climax, philosophically and psychologically as well as typologically. It sums up the whole type-series, is the end towards which everything tends; and it is a figure for Frye's own ideal world, representing 'the way the world looks after the ego has disappeared'. This formula rather strongly recalls Freud's dictum, 'Where Id was, Ego shall be', though the inversion isn't perfect, since what takes the place of Ego in the Frye millennium can't be thought of as Id, at any rate in the Freudian sense. Still, we may perhaps call it an antitype of Freud's remark, or even a parody, unless we take Freud's remark to be a parody, *avant la lettre*, of Frye's. Of course the biblical modes are susceptible to demonic parody, Apocalypse most of all; it may even contain its own demonic self-parody, as perhaps Lawrence was hinting when he said that the Woman Clothed with the Sun and the Whore of Babylon were two versions of the same original, the second a parody of the first.

What of the total structure of this single but multiple book? Between beginning and end there are repeated structural patterns, echoing the grand design, which is U-shaped, like that of Comedy: 'apostasy . . . followed by descent into disaster and bondage . . . followed by repentance, then by a rise through deliverance to a point more or less on the level from which the descent began.' This, the shape of the whole Bible, is echoed in its episodes, in the stories of Israel's historical vicissitudes, which, as we have seen, can be reduced to seven movements, the archetype of them all being Exodus. Since this up and down motion can be thought of as coming to a stop in the up position, the Bible is a comedy, but it is possible to concentrate on the down position, so that the movement can be tragic too, and accommodate such genuinely tragic heroes as Saul. 'All the high points and all the low points are metaphorically related to one another', so that however one reads the book it repeats the pattern of ups and downs until the last up, which is the kingdom of God, with which we reach the level of the original Eden. Even the short stories that come in between, such as those of Job and Samson, follow in smaller compass the same design.

Anybody who has not actually read Frye might be forgiven for supposing that I am making his book sound too complicated and too schematic, but those who have read it will complain with more justice of my oversimplifications. Since the Bible is a myth that covers the whole of time and all human vicissitude, it isn't surprising that a diagrammatic account of it will be pretty complex. It is the myth which encapsulates all our imaginative dealings with the world, our social constructions of reality. It is both homogeneous and endlessly receptive to our reading, which, says Frye, is why a great preacher can, by meditating a single text, meditate the whole. Frye of course isn't doing that, but merely trying to explain why it is possible, that it is so because the

Bible is a full human world. 'Happy creature! For it is he who has invented the gods.' Frye writes partly in pity for man's darkening thought, in a time when the gods have been disinvented, but partly out of a robust conviction that the gods invented by men are good gods for men, and that the metaphors by which they were made can still be potent, not least as a *démenti* of the rumour that God is dead.

To this powerful and original book I have made some objections, which in summary can be reduced to two. First, a system, if it is to be truly inclusive, will distort detail; and, as Aby Warburg liked to say, the good God dwells in detail. Secondly, the contrary movement of Frye's speculation—on the one hand the desire to recover numinous metaphorical compaction, to roll the universe up into one ball, and on the other the unrestricted proliferation of auxiliary systematic patterns, three of this and seven of that—is often quite beautiful and entertaining, but never compels belief. His myth, that is, may be called apocryphal rather than canonical. We may come to think of it as we think of the systems of Joachim or Blake or Yeats. It may be the fate of *The Great Code* (and which critic would refuse such a destiny?) to make the transition—of which Gibbon's *Decline and Fall* is Frye's chosen example— from secondary to primary writing: it may survive not as what it announces itself to be but as 'a classic of English literature, or at any rate of English cultural history'. Or, to quote Frye one last time, 'as a Cimabue painting of the Crucifixion comes to be, in the course of time, more important as a picture than as an icon of the death of Christ'.

Poe's Angels

Charles A. Huttar

By the end of the eighteenth century, with help from Voltaire and others,[1] the angels had left the universe. That enabled them to survive to the twentieth century in poetry,[2] but only by becoming very different beings from what they had been in the epic imaginations of Dante, Milton, and Blake. In the intervening period, which in some ways, at least, may rightly be called 'transitional', the figure of central significance is Edgar Allan Poe. The Enlightenment's depopulating of the spiritual world had quickly brought on Romantic reaction: in Wordsworth, for example, who lamented the loss of a sensibility capable of recognizing spiritual presences, of looking at the sea and catching sight of Proteus;[3] or in Shelley, who proclaimed that 'the awful presence of some unseen Power/Floats thought unseen among us'.[4] Thus begins a magnificent statement of one of the great Shelleyan themes, a lament for the human condition, imprisoned in a world of matter and unable to enjoy any sustained union with the world of truer reality. The Platonic Idea of Beauty which Shelley hymned was taken up by Poe and directly associated with angels, but the mood is no longer one of lament. For Poe, the fact that the angels can no longer be believed in is, by implication at least, positive: it is what gives them value as a poetic symbol.

On the surface Poe's angels are fairly traditional, though with some teasing heterodox twists. The popular misconception—found nowhere in serious theology—that the souls of departed humans, on taking up their abode in heaven, turn into angels is echoed several times in Poe ('Lenore', 'The Conversation of Eiros and Charmion', 'The Colloquy of Monos and Una', 'The Power of Words').[5] With that exception, however, Poe's emphasis is on the radical difference between man and angels. The line 'seraphim whose foot-falls tinkled on the tufted floor' ('The Raven')—a sensory effect scarcely imaginable in the real physical world—is a brilliant, if trivial, instance. All of Poe's angelic dialogues are set in some remote part of the heavens, either after the earth has been destroyed ('The Conversation of Eiros and Charmion', 'The Colloquy of Monos and Una', 'The Power of Words') or on a star which once was but is no more ('Al Aaraaf': Tycho Brahe's nova of 1572). Poe blames Science for having 'driven the Hamadryad from the wood/To seek a shelter in some happier star' ('Sonnet: To Science', the opening poem in the *Al Aaraaf* volume, 1.91); this angel-like creature is no longer accessible, as she was, however fleetingly, to Wordsworth and Shelley. Platonic Beauty has been removed to the star Al Aaraaf which no longer exists: which means that attainment of it is out of space, out of time ('Dream-Land'). In short, the angelic function of messenger, essential to orthodoxy, has disappeared. Between Poe's angels and humans there is, instead, an impassable gulf—or one that can be bridged in only one direction, and that by death. Thus we see that the theological misconception mentioned above, though it seems to blur the distinction between the human and angelic orders of being—a distinction which mattered a great deal so long as the Great Chain of Being was a living cultural motif—is not an exception after all to the general observation that Poe's angels are radically separate from his humans.

Yet Poe's angel, a symbol of the hopelessly unattainable, at the same time represents the poet's deepest longings. As a man Poe would abandon the earth and live where his angels are 'among Platonic forms'.[6] As a poet he fantasizes changing places with Israfel, sweetest singer of all the angels—even though that must involve a suffering perhaps tantamount to death, for Israfel's lute, like Roderick Usher's, is his own heartstrings. Nor does the poet's ambition end there. Israfel, a sort of Orpheus figure among the angels, even has power over creation:

> And the giddy stars (so legends tell)
> Ceasing their hymns, attend the spell
> Of his voice, all mute.
>
> (1.175)

But in the prose sketch 'The Power of Words' Poe goes still further. There one angel shows the other a whole world he has created, *ex nihilo* apparently, speaking it into being 'with a few passionate sentences' (3.1215). Further, he accomplished this some three centuries since, while still human, before becoming an angel. The implied claim for the creative power of the poetic intellect may, when reduced to sober propositions, be little more than Coleridge's doctrine of Imagination,[7] yet the language in which the claim is couched certainly justifies Allen Tate's description of it as 'grandiose angelic [or, to use his own later qualification, "superangelic"] presumption on the part of man' (p. 250, 251).

Moreover, the presumption is intensified by Poe's implicit renunciation of divine holiness in favour of the maculate values of (fallen) human life. The angel Agathos is unabashedly satisfied with 'his' star, created as it is out of the extremes of human emotion. 'The greenest and yet most terrible', this star contains flowers which are 'the dearest of . . . dreams' and volcanoes which are 'the passions of the most turbulent and unhallowed of hearts' (3.1215). In this closing phrase, without any hint of how to reconcile 'unhallowed' with the angel's name, Agathos, 'Good', Poe throws down the ethical gauntlet. This attitude finds its poetic parallel in 'Annabel Lee', where the 'seraphs of Heaven' kill the child lover out of envy because she and the speaker enjoy a love and a happiness which are beyond their reach (1.479). Morally flawed, they are also weak: they cannot succeed in separating the two lovers' souls.

The symbolism of Poe's angels, then, is full of tensions. They represent an ideal world impossibly remote and unattainable, yet one that is intensely desired; they represent a spiritual consummation whose price is the rejection of the physical world; they represent the transformation of the Shelleyan longing for union into an incipient solipsism;[8] they represent the creative artist in a role which challenges Deity, not only as the sole Almighty but also as the author of moral value; they represent, that is, the highest aspiration yet also a dejection almost to the point of nihilism. Poe's appetite for images of decay and horror suggests, in fact, and his antagonism to transcendental philosophy[9] corroborates, a deep psychological kinship with the despairing Victorian, James Thomson.[10] Far from making any effort to reduce these tensions, Poe makes them the very soul of his poetry. It is no wonder Poe's angels reveal to us with intensity the disintegration of personality which Tate (p. 241) finds to be a central motif of his writings and, indeed, of his life.

The influence of Poe crossed the Atlantic and was strongest among the French Symbolists. Mallarmé's initial attraction to angelic images was independent of that influence, reflecting instead a Christian orientation in his earliest verse, but there is no doubt that the example of Poe, whom Mallarmé honoured as a guide, helped steer it in a new direction.[11] From Mallarmé the line may be traced to—these poets, at least—Valéry, Rilke, and Stevens, in whose poetry angels are recurrent and prominent, but not objects of belief.

Isabel Archer:
The New Woman as American

Declan Kiberd

Henry James was the nicest old lady I ever knew
William Faulkner.

In the expansionist economy of the nineteenth century, the American male devoted himself to mastering the machine and pursuing vast profits, while his wife became a pampered consumer of gadgets, fashions and money. The protracted intricacies of traditional courtship were not for the new generation of capitalists, who won their ladies in hasty moments snatched from their busy lives in factory or marketplace.[1] In consequence, a disastrous chasm opened between the sexes who were now doomed to lead virtually separate lives. American men were so busy earning money that they scarcely found time to experience the pleasure of spending it with wives, whose conspicuous consumption became further testimony to the manliness of their partners.

In Henry James's novel *The Portrait of a Lady*, Mrs Touchett seldom sees the husband whose wealth she spends in travelling the world. She nakedly admits that her idea of marriage is to make use of a man. She may boast that she has never sacrificed her husband to another, but that, as her associate Madame Merle knows, is because 'you never did anything for another'. Egotism is the only code of these cynical American matrons who, if they were not so selfish, might pass for middle-aged feminists:

'Poor American ladies!' cried Mrs Touchett with a laugh.
'They're the slaves of slaves.'
'They're the companions of freemen', Henrietta retorted.
'They're the companions of their servants—the Irish chambermaid and the Negro waiter. They share their work.'
'Do you call the domestics in an American household "slaves"?' Miss Stackpole inquired. 'If that's the way you desire to treat them, no wonder you don't like America.'
'If you've not good servants you're miserable', Mrs Touchett said.

The plight of the displaced American leisure class in Europe is illuminatingly compared by Madame Merle with the ambiguous predicament of the new American woman. 'We're mere parasites crawling over the surface; we haven't our feet in the soil. At least one can know it and not have illusions. A woman perhaps can get on; a woman, it seems to me, has no natural place anywhere;

wherever she finds herself she has to remain on the surface and, more or less, to crawl.'

Such a statement of material self-interest is based on values as aggressively masculine as those of the *laissez-faire* economy which makes such amorality necessary. There lies the paradox of sexual relations, for the manly American evokes in his wife or lover not an answering femininity but a tough-minded business acumen. He seeks a lover but, in the very nature of his brief and brutal wooing, he discovers another competitor. His wealth may deny his woman the chance of material self-sufficiency, but she achieves an absolute self-reliance in the world of feeling and in the life of the mind. Henceforth, her emotions have little to do with her 'absentee husband', but are invested instead in the education and formation of young minds.[2] In *Huckleberry Finn* the civilisation of the riverbank amounted to nothing more than a conspiracy of Christian widows, aunts and spinsters, but the same conditions prevail in the upper-class world inhabited by the characters of Henry James. It has often been asserted that James was opposed to the growing feminisation of American life. The canonical text, in this regard, is the outburst of Basil Ransom to the suffragette whom he woos and wins at the end of *The Bostonians*:

My interest is in my own sex; yours evidently can look after itself. That's what I want to save . . . From the most damnable feminisation! I am so far from thinking, as you set forth the other night, that there is not enough woman in our general life, that it has been pressed home to me that there is a great deal too much. The whole generation is womanised; the masculine tone is passing out of the world; it's a feminine, a nervous, hysterical, chattering, canting age, an age of hollow phrases and false delicacy and exaggerated solicitudes and coddled sensibilities, which, if they don't soon look out, will usher in the reign of mediocrity, of the feeblest and flattest and most pretentious that has ever been. The masculine character, the ability to dare and endure, to know and yet not fear reality . . . that is what I want to preserve, or rather, as I may say, to recover; and I must tell you that I don't in the least care what becomes of you ladies while I make the attempt.

It must be emphasized, however, that this crude and windy eloquence is not the modulated voice of Henry James, who opens his affectionately conde-scending portrait of this spirited Southerner with the warning that 'he was very provincial'. James is by no means against feminisation, but rather against the doctrine that the world of work should be exclusively male and the world of society rigorously female. *The Portrait of a Lady* chronicles the cost to sexual relations of such a division which turns men and women into terrifying strangers to one another.

At much the same time as Alfred Adler was propounding his theory of 'masculine protest', James began to describe the workings of the phenomenon. He knew that the feminisation, which Ransom ritually deplored, was simply the attempt by a woman, denied the dignity of work, to apply her time and talent in the alternative spheres of education and society. She exploited her newly acquired leisure hours in order to study and ponder the wrongs of her condition. By this very act, according to William Bysshe Stein, she invaded the male preserve of 'thought'; and he sees it as but a further step to the rejection of her biological destiny as wife and mother.[3] There is evidence to support this rather extreme reading of *The Portrait of a Lady*. Mrs Touchett's relations with her son, Ralph, are almost as perfunctory as those with her husband. Though she will experience belated pain at Ralph's early death, it is qualified by the advice which she passes on to Isabel Archer: 'Go and thank God you've no child.' The more her husband showered her with wealth, the more did she reject her assigned female role and assert her right to exploit that wealth in the world of travel and property. As she grew older, she rejected the fripperies of femininity and the male element in her personality found its inevitable expression. In similar fashion, after years of aggressive money-getting in the banking system, the long-suppressed female within her husband emerged, to the delight of his admiring son Ralph: 'His father, as he had often said to himself, was the more motherly; his mother, on the other hand, was paternal, and even, according to the slang of the day, gubernatorial.' So it is left to the father to adopt the role of absentee mother and to urge on his son the vital importance of marriage and procreation. If everybody became over-scrupulous about whom they married, says the old man on his death-bed, 'the human race would die out'. It is an avowal strikingly at odds with his own wife's repudiation of motherhood. Too late does old Mr Touchett realise that a macho-culture may sow the seeds of its own destruction by its attempt at a total differentiation of the sexes.

A mysterious aura of remoteness enhances the attraction of each sex to the other, but the cultivation of an excessive sense of difference may become a barrier to true communication. The early married life of the Touchetts fell victim to such a malaise and from the beginning of the novel the reader has a premonition that Isabel will repeat the mistake. Her manifest inexperience and romantic longings leave her easy prey to a code which sees love not in terms of liking somebody near and known, but as a blinding flash of passion for someone remote. Her reasons for refusing the personable Lord Warburton are curiously phrased: 'she was so conscious of liking him that she ventured to assure herself it was the very softness, and the fine intelligence, of sympathy. She liked him too much to marry him, that was the truth.' Her view of love is infinitely theatrical and dramatic, for she confides to the bemused Englishman that she cannot escape her fate. What this actually means is that she does not believe in the possibility of communication between male and female. Her fate, as it turns out, is a vacuous and vicious dilettante named Gilbert Osmond. James has often been criticized for his failure to supply an adequate account of Isabel's motivation in entering upon the marriage, but far from being an artistic flaw, this is part of his novel's innermost theme. The marriage is the *acte gratuit* of a young woman who blindly decides that this is her destiny. It was as unmotivated for Isabel as it is for the reader. Indeed, James anticipated the criticisms of his future detractors by explaining just how little she knew of her man. 'This would have been a rather dry account of Mr Osmond's career if Isabel had fully believed it; but her imagination supplied the human element which she was sure had not been wanting.' Just how a heroine of spellbinding intelligence could marry a brute like Osmond in the belief that she was hitching herself to a remote star is made clear by James's account of her notion of the proper partner for a marriage. She is an extreme example of the American as idealist and 'often reminded herself that there were essential reasons why one's ideal could never become concrete. It was a thing to believe in, not to see—a matter of faith, not of experience'. These are illusions possible only in a society where men and women speak a different language and see one another as inhabitants of different worlds. It is no accident that when Mr Touchett gazes with fondness on Isabel, his feeling is complicated by the awareness that 'she reminded him of his wife when his wife was in her teens'. She is about to repeat the old woman's mistake.

In *The Portrait of a Lady* James keeps his focus on Isabel Archer and the surrounding American expatriates to such an extent that the European characters, except for Lord Warburton, are sketched in the most shadowy manner. Not only are the reprehensible characters American, like Osmond and Madame Merle, but so are the innocent like Mr Touchett, Henrietta Stackpole and Caspar Goodwood himself—a fact often noted.[4] The difference is that the latter group work, whereas the others are simply the idle not-so-rich. Isabel's first response to the inanity of expatriate life is thoroughly American in its puritan insistence on the virtues of hard work: 'You all live here this way, but what does it lead to? It doesn't seem to lead to anything and I should think you'd get very tired of it.' Mrs Touchett thought the question worthy of the feminist Henrietta Stackpole, but the reader has already noted that Henrietta is the only woman in the book who works for a living. More than halfway through the narrative, Isabel still subscribes to this work ethic, when she asks Ralph Touchett about Gilbert Osmond:

'He lives in Florence', Ralph said.
'What is he besides?'
'Nothing at all. Oh yes, he's an American, but one forgets that, he's so little of one.'

So, even the Oxford-educated Ralph still cleaves to some values of his mother country, for his own indolence is enforced by chronic ill-health. However, by prevailing on his father to settle a substantial legacy on the unsuspecting Isabel, he ensures the eventual loss of her critical perspective on this way of life. By the end of the novel, she too will be living a life of boredom and bad temper on the basis of unearned income, the epitome of the nineteenth-century American wife with more money than comfort.

But not at the start, where Henrietta stars for Isabel in the role of New Woman as American, the very embodiment of the self-sufficiency to which her young friend aspires. 'Henrietta for Isabel was chiefly a proof that a woman might suffice to herself and be happy.' In keeping with this feminism, Isabel's first thought on the subject of marriage is a conviction of the vulgarity of thinking too much of it—a fatal flaw which will bring dire results:

From lapsing into eagerness on this point she earnestly prayed she might be delivered. She held that a woman ought to be able to live to herself, in the absence of exceptional flimsiness, and that it was perfectly possible to be happy without the society of a more or less coarse-minded person of another sex. Something pure and proud there was in her—something cold and dry . . . Deep in her soul . . . lay the belief that if a certain light should dawn she could give herself completely; but this image, on the whole, was too formidable to be attractive.

There is an uncanny slide in the second sentence from a robust self-sufficiency to an altogether more dainty aversion to 'a coarse-minded person of another sex'. It suggests that Isabel's feminism may simply be the attempt to rationalize a fastidious repudiation if not of sex itself, then at least of hairy and thrusting males. Isabel proudly tells Ralph that Henrietta doesn't care a straw what men think of her, so it doesn't matter whether he loves or hates her. She might have been speaking of her own early dismissal of Caspar Goodwood, which is couched in the same terms: 'I don't need the aid of a clever man to teach me how to live. I can find it out for myself.' Goodwood's reply is full of the wisdom of true love: 'Find out how to live alone? I wish that, when you have, you'd teach me.' Such honest intensity is lost on the radical who sees marriage as a trap rather than a liberation. Her view seems close to that of Verena Tarrant in *The Bostonians*, whose gloomy image of matrimony 'consisted of a tired woman holding a baby over a furnace register that emited lukewarm air'. Goodwood claims that it is to make Isabel independent that he wishes to marry her, since an unmarried woman is hampered at every step. Isabel sees this as the beautiful sophism that it surely is, for she knows that the successful industrialist wants a wife who will wear his wealth in tribute to his manly powers of accumulation. With the ardour of a born radical, Isabel turns even the disabilities of her current position into grounds for an abstract demonstration of her independence:

I'm not in my first youth—I can do what I choose—I've neither father nor mother; I'm poor and of a serious disposition, I'm not pretty. I therefore am not bound to be timid and conventional; indeed I can't afford such luxuries. Besides I try to judge things for myself; to judge wrong, I think, is more honourable than not to judge at all.

Those disadvantages which might impel a lesser woman into a safe and early marriage are seized gratefully by Isabel as further reasons for maintaining her freedom. These are sentiments which ought to win the support of Henrietta Stackpole, but do not. Henrietta may be a feminist, but she is that only because she is first and foremost an American. She sees that, in spurning the industrialist who loves her, Isabel has repudiated the American who is still a part of herself. Little by little, she is being assimilated into the dessicated circle of Osmond and Madame Merle, unlike Henrietta who shuttles back and forth to and from America, engaged in the honest toil of a newspaperwoman.

Yet, the dismissal of Goodwood is founded on a paradox. Isabel justifies her rejection by an appeal to the ultimate American value of self-reliance. Like her fellow-countrymen who have read and believed their constitutional guarantee, Isabel comes to Europe 'to be as happy as possible', almost as if she conceived of pursuit as the ultimate happiness. The virtues of America are those of committed feminists, and so are the vices. Philip Rahv sees Isabel as an essential American in that she preaches self-reliance as a duty *and* seeks happiness by right.[5] But, as Basil Ransom says in *The Bostonians* in defence of the conservative south, 'There was one happiness they always had—that of having learned not to think about it too much, and to make the best of their circumstances'. Like Goodwood, Ransom also attempts to break down the resistence of a desirable young woman, whose mind has been filled with radical theories by a feminist mentor. Verena Tarrant desired to prove that Olive Chancellor was right in her conviction 'that a woman *could* live on persistently, clinging to a great, vivifying, redemptory idea, without the help of a man'. There is a major difference between the two plots, however. Ransom finally puts Olive Chancellor to rout and wins his girl in the face of the feminist's anguish, whereas Goodwood fails to win Isabel even with the enthusiastic support of Henrietta Stackpole.

As a character, Henrietta Stackpole is a great deal more complex than she has often seemed to a generation of readers, who saw her buttonlike eyes as James's warning that she was not to be taken very seriously. But her views are by no means as fixed or as predictable as the other characters make them seem. Coming from a feminist, her aid to Goodwood's suit is as unpredictable as her eventual marriage to Mr Bantling is surprising. It is *she*, rather than the other characters, who manages to learn from experience. The woman who began with 'clear-cut views on most subjects' ends by openly conceding what Isabel will never admit—that some of those views were wrong. She marries a man whom her sophisticated friends deem 'a very simple organism'. But the very words in which she explains her marriage to Isabel show just how free of illusions and false sentiment her relationship with Bantling is. He may not be 'intellectual', but he 'appreciates intellect'. Moreover, without even trying to, he has educated his partner into a proper awareness of the limited claims of the mind, an awareness which Henrietta admits to be lacking in the United States. The radical newspaperwoman confounds her protegé by conceding that Americans are infatuated with mere brainpower, a weakness to which Isabel succumbed from the start.

The marriage which Henrietta contracts is based on mutual understanding over a long period of friendship. Not for her the lightning flash of sudden destiny. In the end, Henrietta boasts that she has seen right through her man and still can like him, just as he finds her faults almost as rewarding as her virtues. She laughingly recognises the strange reversal of traditional sexual roles in their relationship, a reversal which Bantling finds as amusing and as fulfilling as she. Henrietta's account of the affair to Isabel, at a fairly early stage in the novel, shows her to be a great deal more sophisticated an organism than spectators like Ralph might think. She exudes enthusiastic intelligence in describing the androgynous nature of her relation with Bantling:

Mr Bantling, who was of rather a slow and discursive habit, relished a prompt, keen, positive woman, who charmed him by the influence of a shining, challenging eye . . . Henrietta, on the other hand, enjoyed the society of a gentleman who appeared somehow, in his way, made by expensive, roundabout, almost 'quaint' processes, for her use, and whose leisured state, though generally indefensible, was a decided boon to a breathless mate.

One cannot imagine Isabel offering a similarly probing self-analysis at the start of her infatuation with Osmond. She can only love a stranger.

It is this which prevents her from admitting to herself that she loves Ralph Touchett and that he is, moreover, her ideal mate. She likes him far too much to admit that she loves him. Yet he loves her and it is only on his deathbed that he learns that the feeling might have been reciprocated. That love is never consummated, for Isabel is far more conventional than she would like to think. She cannot believe it to be her destiny to marry a passive and unhealthy male, whom she might lead through life. Only a Henrietta would have the courage to take the lead from the start, and Isabel is no Henrietta. Yet she and Ralph, taken as a couple, might have achieved an alignment very similar to that of Henrietta and Mr Bantling, for they also are characters who invert many of the customary sexual roles.

This is a fact true of many of the heroes and heroines in the novels of Henry James, who are as repelled as their creator by the extremities of 'male' and 'female'. The aversion has been brilliantly described by Philip Sicker in terms of James's desire 'to create a man who was, at once, masculine enough to stimulate a woman's sympathetic love and feminine enough to return it with equal depth and intensity. What was needed was a sensitive but still unformed male mind. The act of loving could provide identity through relation only if the consciousness of both lovers was fluid, only if the lovers had not yet learned to see themselves fixed in arbitrary social and sexual roles'.[6] Henrietta and Bantling have the necessary fluidity. So has Ralph Touchett and it is his tragedy that he does not speak his love until it is too late. While Isabel is like the traditional male hero in her mobility, spontaneity and apparent freedom of choice, Ralph is like the old-fashioned heroine in his enforced passivity, formality and apparent restriction of opportunity. An early critic of the book remarked on the underlying similarity between their seemingly differing predicaments:

The very limitations upon her freedom, the dependency of her position, give to the adventures of a brave woman an attaching pathos, and even a spiritual richness, which a man's can seldom have . . . Ralph Touchett shares this advantage in disadvantage. And I am willing to grant him a very large measure of the attractiveness of the generous fettered woman.[7]

The early scene in which they both take out a boat defines the nature of their possible relationship, as the lady rows and Ralph enjoys her skill, to the outrage of the more manly Warburton. There are moments in her first week at Gardencourt when Isabel, like Ralph's own father, tries to goad the young man into a more aggressive attitude:

'It's not absolutely necessary to suffer; we were not made for that.'
'You were not, certainly.'
'I'm not speaking of myself.' And she wandered off a little.

No sooner has she spoken than she regrets her implicit challenge to his manliness, as the mark of a possible callousness in herself: 'Only if you don't suffer they call you hard.' Being alone with Isabel in the thickening London dusk is for him a moment of unrepeatable charm, for 'it made her seem to depend on him and to be in his power'. When she leaves him a short while later, he feels desolated.

Precisely because Ralph has such a highly developed female side to his personality, he alone of men can feel an interest in Isabel as a person rather than a woman. That which distinguishes her from the everyday woman is what fascinates him: 'But what was she going to do with herself? This question was irregular, for with most women one had no occasion to ask it.' If feminism is the struggle to be human rather than female, then Ralph is arguably the most committed feminist in the book. In that sense, he has much in common with his creator, who, according to Carolyn Heilbrun, looked at women rather as women look at them. 'Women look at women as persons', says Heilbrun in *Towards a Recognition of Androgyny*, 'men look at them as women'.[8] It was this same gift which James celebrated in *his* biography of Hawthorne, whose Zenobia he praised as 'the nearest approach that Hawthorne has made to the complete creation of a *person*'.

In *The Bostonians* James was at pains to show how few feminists, not to mention men, have achieved this degree of discrimination. Perhaps the most engaging lady in that entire book is Dr Prance who, subject to the tirades of suffragettes, is 'bored with being reminded, even for the sake of her rights, that she was a woman—a detail that she was in the habit of forgetting, having as many rights as she had time for. It was certain that whatever might become of the movement at large, Doctor Prance's own little revolution was a success'. Late in *The Bostonians*, Dr Prance acidly observes that her radical friends think women the equals of men, but are a great deal more pleased when a man joins their ranks than when a woman does. This is borne out in the case of Olive Chancellor who, fearing that she will lose Verena, abandons her feminist principles and criticises the impecunious Ransom for his audacity in proposing to a woman. Indeed, Olive goes so far as to engage in some traditional muckraking at the expense of those men who support the feminists. 'They are not really men', she assures the bemused Verena, 'and I wouldn't be sure even of them.' So the womanly man receives his come-uppance from a woman who secretly wishes that she were male. Olive is a feminist who envies men their virility, rather than one who seeks to recreate in herself a truly androgynous blend of opposites. As James observes with an ill-concealed wink, 'it was a curious incident in her zeal for the regeneration of her sex that manly things were, perhaps on the whole, what she understood best'.

Not so her creator who saw all people, especially artists, as androgynous. Heilbrun notes how James recreated many features of his own childhood and youth in the career of Isabel Archer, his grandmother's house, his Dutch school, his peach trees, and so on. Indeed, James's biographer argues that Isabel's predicament is similar to that of the author when he wrote the book; and the question, 'What will she do?', is the same issue which James faced concerning his literary gift after his arrival in Europe.[9] Some feminist critics have found the question coldly observational, arguing that James has a clinical psychologist's interest in the way his women think and feel rather than a sympathetic awareness of the fundamental injustice of their situation.[10] This takes no account of the way in which the author felt himself implicated in Isabel's situation, nor of his repeated analyses of what it actually means to be born a woman, analyses which stung that arch-traditionalist William Faulkner to make his famous jibe.

Ralph Touchett had the grace to treat Isabel as a person. When she throws in her lot with Gilbert Osmond, he laments her capitulation in decidedly feminist terms. What did Isabel now represent? he asked himself and the answer was 'Gilbert Osmond'. His woeful complaint that she was meant for something better than to keep guard over the sensibilities of a sterile dilletante is more a criticism of her than of Osmond—and it is followed at once by a downright declaration of love. It is clear by now (although she tries to deny it to herself) that Isabel has fallen in love with Ralph and that what appeals to her is his passive nature, which is the perfect complement to her own masterful temperament. Isabel has been called sexless and cold by feminist critics, who claim that, for James, fineness and passion cannot coexist in a woman. Patricia Stubbs has even argued that sexlessness is a handicap which James inflicts only on women like Isabel and that his novels show not so much an indifference to sex as a refusal to recognise woman's sexual nature.[11] Against this, one might cite the case of Isabel, a heroine who positively vibrates with passion, collapsing into tears after each encounter with Goodwood. Her passions are not of the surface, but only those who experience deep emotions feel the need to control them so strictly. If Isabel is finally sexless, then so is Ralph Touchett and, for that matter, Gilbert Osmond. In fact, she is not so much sexless as sexually reticent. Far from refusing to recognise woman's sexual nature, James has shown it to be a blend of conflicting desires and fears. Isabel is not frightened of sex, as male critics so monotonously maintain,[12] but she *is* unnerved by the hypermasculine personality of Caspar Goodwood and by the self-confident manliness of Lord Warburton. She rejects the virile suitor because it is her nature to seek out and love the womanly man.

Isabel's ladylike distaste for 'coarse-minded' males makes the idea of sexual surrender too formidable to be attractive. The woman who ponders these thoughts has already found Caspar Goodwood too masculine to interest her: 'it was part of the influence he had upon her that he seemed to deprive her of the sense of freedom. There was a disagreeably strong push, a kind of hardness of presence, in his way of rising before her.' She can see him only as a stubborn fact who for all his patent sincerity, would seek to possess her as a chattel. He is a Gerald Crich of his era, rejoicing in machines, organisation and mastery of other humans in a communal enterprize. He embodies the ultimate threat posed by American capitalism to an emancipated womanhood and to Isabel he seems cast in the same hard steel which runs his factories: 'She wished him no ounce less of his manhood, but she sometimes thought he would be rather nicer if he looked, for instance, a little differently. His jaw was too square and set and his figure too straight and stiff: these things suggested a want of easy consonance with the deeper rhythms of life.' By their next meeting in London,

Goodwood has learned enough about Isabel to see that she is more likely to be drawn to the passively suffering male and so he changes his suitor's pitch. James is positively satiric in his depiction of the ploy and of its immediate effect on Isabel:

This immediately had a value—classic, romantic, redeeming, what did she know?—for her, 'the strong man in pain' was one of the categories of the human appeal, little charm as it might exercise in the given case.

Yet, even during this exchange, Isabel cannot avoid the sense of 'having to defend herself against a certain air he had of knowing better what was good for her than she knew herself'. So she sends him packing once again. She knows that what he offers is the same kind of bogus freedom that Mr Touchett brought to his wife. Indeed, Isabel's fear of opening the floodgates of emotion in the presence of Goodwood is phrased in language remarkably similar to that used of Mrs Touchett's inability to mourn her dead son: 'On the other hand, perhaps she was afraid; if she should begin to show remorse at all, it might take her too far . . . '

Because Isabel can never befriend or know Caspar Goodwood, each of his proposals has the nightmarish quality of an assault on her spiritual and bodily integrity. When Ralph asks the depressed Isabel if she would leave Rome with himself and Goodwood, she replies that she cannot—not because she fears her husband, or Goodwood, but because she is 'afraid of myself', that is, afraid of her own weakness in their presence. At the very end, when Goodwood embraces her for the first time, his urgent expression of tenderness seems to her an act of violence. She knows now that Goodwood loves her, though there is no evidence that she could love him. He asks why she must return to her hollow marriage in Rome:

'To get away from you!' she answered. But this expressed only a little of what she felt. The rest was that she had never been loved before. She had believed it, but this was different; that was the hot wind of the desert, at the approach of which the others dropped dead, like mere sweet airs of the garden. It wrapped her about; it lifted her off her feet, while the very taste of it, as of something potent, acrid, and strange, forced open her set teeth.

There is far more revulsion than fascination in the final lines, for what Isabel is experiencing is the aggressive act of possession which she always dreaded in Goodwood. When finally she submits to his awful kiss, 'it was extraordinarily as if, while she took it, she felt each thing in his hard manhood that had least pleased her, each aggressive fact of his face, his figure, his presence, justified of its intense identity and made one with this act of possession. So had she heard of those wrecked and under water following a train of images before they sank. But when darkness returned she was free'. So she flees this scene of her violation, for she knows that Goodwood offers nothing that she hasn't had before, the spurious emancipation of unearned wealth. He is simply pleading for the right to repeat the mistake made by Ralph. Moreover, his American notion of the sovereignty of a self, untouched by 'the bottomless idiocy of the world', is an argument that Isabel knows from experience to be utterly invalid. She who thought she was forging her own destiny now finds that it has been shaped by virtually everyone except herself. Goodwood's conviction that they can do absolutely as they please, owing nothing to anybody, strikes her as the innocence of a simple man who has yet to learn that the world is small and can be traversed by Mrs Touchett in a matter of months.

If Goodwood is spurned for his machismo, then Warburton also loses for much the same causes. His first proposal shocks Isabel for the good reason that she hardly knows him. Her coldness of response was no coy effect, insists James, but 'came from a certain fear'. Warburton, with the 'manly figure' of an 'explorer', is too traditional a suitor for Isabel's tastes. Moreover, he is deeply patronising and silly, when he suspects that Isabel might be rejecting him because his house has a moat. His charm is undeniable, but it unnerves Isabel, who accuses herself of coldness for failing to be properly captivated; but the final effect of Warburton's manly overtures is indistinguishable from Goodwood's, for they leave Isabel 'really frightened at herself'. She fears frigidity in herself and it is only through her refusals (which seem to surprise herself as much as everyone else) that she begins to learn of the truly androgynous nature of her own sexuality. Her lover, when he comes, will have to be more tentative and refined. All this is not fully clear, however, when she refuses Warburton. She is simply baffled that she could have rejected Goodwood for not being 'delightful', when Warburton decidedly was. 'It was certainly strange', she muses. So she is forced to advance some public justification, while her subconscious sorts the real reasons out.

The rejection of an English lord by a penniless American can have only one purpose—to display Isabel's independence of social convention at a time when no English aristocrat felt complete without an American spouse. The idea of marriage to Warburton failed 'to support any enlightened prejudice in favour of the free exploration of life that she had hitherto entertained'. Yet there is something rather stagey about the way in which she monitors her own refusals, marvelling at the fact that it cost her so little to spurn so magnificent a chance. James has already warned us that his heroine was liable to the sin of self-esteem and that 'she treated herself to occasions of homage'. But reasons have to be given and Isabel explains that marriage to Warburton would exempt her 'from the usual chances and dangers, from what most people know and suffer'. This desire for suffering is as irrational as her contradictory assumption of the right to happiness. Warburton assures her that he offers no exemption from the tragedies of life and that he seeks her as a man who runs all the risks of being human, but she can never quite forget that she is rejecting a lord. No sooner has she sent him away than she begins to give 'poor Lord Warburton' the benefit of an ephithet. She describes him as 'a collection of attributes and powers' and permits herself to question the sincerity of a radical lord who, in Ralph's words, can neither abolish himself as a nuisance or maintain himself as an institution. She deems his liberalism to be skin-deep, a parade of refined sentiment, but lacking true substance. Ironically, this *will* be true of Osmond, the man she does marry. To old Mr Touchett, Isabel implies that Warburton's liberalism is a matter of pure theory, but the paradox is—as Warburton points out—that it is Isabel who is hopelessly theoretical. 'I never saw a person judge things on such theoretic grounds', he exclaims, and he is proven right when she marries Osmond, who suffers from all those aristocratic fetishes which she falsely imputed to Warburton. Osmond lives high on a hill, above the squalor of the poor, a connoisseur of the fastidious.

The settlement of a fortune on Isabel by the Touchetts seems, at first, to be the outcome of an innocent wish by a dying son to a dying father. Ralph wants Isabel to be rich and he calls people rich when they are able to meet the requirements of their imaginations. Like a self-effacing but proud wife, Ralph asks no more than the spectacle of what his lucky partner will make of this new-found wealth. His gesture is similar in quality to the quixotic whims of Isabel, a compound of idealism and self-indulgence. It leaves him open to the same accusation with which most critics convict Madame Merle, that of interfering with the natural course of a life. Isabel's marriage to Osmond is a performance as theatrical as Ralph's ostentatious reticence about confessing his love. In both cases, they are enacting the puritan drama of renunciation and self-sacrifice. In waiving part of his inheritance, Ralph has given Isabel a model for conspicuous self-sacrifice; to a certain extent, he has also anticipated Osmond in his desire to use Isabel for his own imaginative ends. But it isn't just obnoxious characters like Osmond and Merle, or amiable meddlers like Ralph and his father, who interfere with lives and violate the sanctity of the human heart. It is also, most crucially, Isabel Archer herself who uses Osmond as much as he uses her, just as she 'used' Warburton and will always 'use' Goodwood, as occasions for a stagey demonstration of glorious self-denial. How else do we explain her masochistic return to Rome? What is wrong with Isabel is what ails most of the expatriates in the book, the fact—noted by Dorothy Van Ghent—that they base their actions on aesthetic rather than moral considerations.[13] To the newly arrived Isabel on the threshold of Europe, suffering is an artistic performance rather than a moral fact. She tells old Mr Touchett that in a revolution she would like to be a loyalist, because 'they've a chance to behave so exquisitely', i.e. losing their heads. When Ralph asks if she wants to drain the cup of experience (as she had implied in the reasons for refusing Warburton), she replies 'No! It's a poisoned drink. I only want to see for myself'. Pondering this, Ralph comes up with the shrewd formulation: 'You want to see but not to feel.' This is what links her fatally to Osmond, this desire to be a connoisseur rather than an exponent of her own emotions, to monitor her own performance with the same delicacy of judgement with which Osmond sizes up his antiques.

The critical attack on Osmond centres on the way in which he treats his wife as the latest addition to his collection, 'as smooth to his general need of her as handled ivory to the palm'. But few readers have noticed that this is precisely how she treats him. He is simply the latest recruit to that growing collection of males who provide her with opportunities to display her fastidiousness and self-sacrifice. James is unambiguous on the point: 'She had married him because he was better than anyone else. The finest manly organism she had ever known had become her property, and the recognition of her having but to put out her hands and take it had been originally a sort of act of devotion.' Indeed, her trip to the antiquities of the East seemed but a rehearsal for the time when she would take her place in Osmond's collection. On her return, she felt as if she were 'worth more' for it, 'like some curious piece in an antiquary's collection'. In such a fashion, the 'emancipated' woman is forced to contemplate herself through male eyes as a precious object to be possessed rather than as a living person to be known. A crudely sexist culture has built its replica in Isabel's own mind and, even after years of bitterness, she is still astonished at the happiness she feels in procuring a pleasure for her husband. No wonder that Osmond judges her aesthetically, likening her intelligence and imagination to silver objects which he could tap with his knuckle to make them ring. Yet Osmond is no more than the extreme carrier of a virus which afflicts all the Europeanised Americans. Even Ralph's first response to Isabel is to celebrate the moral in terms of the aesthetic: 'a character like that is finer than a Greek bas-relief.' (James qualifies this negative implication two hundred pages later by remarking that such connoisseurship was in Ralph a humorous anomaly, whereas for Osmond it was the key to his whole being.) Rosier likens Pansy to a Dresden china shepherdess, although he later proves his love by his readiness to sacrifice his artistic gems on the off-chance of winning his lover. It is his ambiguous fate to have to express a true feeling in this stylized and rather insincere way, a fate which finally overtakes Mrs Touchett, when she can find neither words nor gestures adequate to the loss of her son. All of these portraits amount to an indictment by James of a leisured class which cultivates art for art's sake, and which views life with the detachment of the connoisseur rather than the reverence of authentic feeling.[14] The world of these dessicated expatriates has little room for a healthy sexuality. Ralph abstains; Rosier yearns and waits; Isabel makes refusal her most memorable performance and then marries a man who insists that she knock on his door before entering. 'We don't live decently together', she protests, as they quarter in separate rooms, but her fate was implicit in the sexual arrest of Mrs Touchett's marriage to her husband. One way or another, most of the Americans avoid sex with the same manic conviction that they shirk an honest day's work.

But not Isabel, whose protest against their idleness is now compounded by her protest against marital asexuality. It is not true to say, as one critic has, that marriage to Osmond provides 'a home for her uncertain womanhood' or that it is a result of 'a defection from the biological function of woman in nature'.[15] Isabel is neither frigid nor asexual, but clearly desires a full physical relation with a man and is deeply frustrated by Osmond's failure to satisfy her. She who felt unnerved by the hypermasculine suitor had hoped for fulfilment with a more sensitive man, but, in the event, Osmond's sensitivity is indistinguishable from selfishness. Isabel had dreamed of uniting her power of cash and character to his refined sensibility: 'she would launch his boat for him, she would be his providence.' All of this Osmond perfectly understood. By nature, he was as aggressive and competitive as any male, finding it proper that his chosen lady should have spurned belted earls and hard-nosed industrialists.

But his proposal is a masterly impersonation of that very powerlessness which Isabel seeks:

I've too little to offer you. What I have—it's enough for me; but it's not enough for you. I've neither fortune, nor fame, nor extrinsic advantages of any kind. So I offer nothing.

In this rhetorical tour-de-force, Osmond makes the same virtue of disadvantage which Isabel had employed to such crushing effect when she spurned Goodwood. He understands how sumptuous is destitution to an imagination like Isabel's and, in the manner of Henry James himself, he presents himself as 'the individual who abjures power by clothing it in meekness and deceptive docility'.[16] There is only one other person in the book who understands the fatal charms of self-effacement and Ralph is quick to spot Osmond's ploy. He knows that 'having invented a fine theory about Gilbert Osmond, she loved him not for what he really possessed, but for his very poverties dressed out as honours.' But that very passivity which affords Ralph such a bleak insight into the relationship leaves him powerless to act in defence of the woman he loves.

Moreover, Ralph lacked the intelligence to foresee Isabel's tragedy. Only Henrietta Stackpole could anticipate that the sudden wealth would merely feed the self-deception of her friend. She warns Isabel that she is not enough in touch with the toiling, suffering, sinning world and foretells that Isabel will be judged in terms of her fortune and not of her intrinsic self. In a world of extremes, where Madame Merle has a purely social existence, and where Isabel insists by contrast that she alone expresses her inmost self, Henrietta's advice displays a formidable critical intelligence:

. . . you must sometimes please other people . . . but there's another thing that's still more important—you must often *dis*please others . . . You think we can escape disagreeable duties by taking romantic views—that's your great illusion my dear. But we can't. You must be prepared on many occasions in life to please no one at all—not even yourself.

Had Isabel heeded this counsel, she would never have fallen in love with her concocted image of Gilbert Osmond; and had she even recalled it after the disastrous marriage, she would have abandoned her vicious husband. From the very outset, he decides that his wife has too many ideas of her own and that these must be sacrificed. Unfortunately for them both, she has even more than he first suspects, because during their courtship, 'she had made herself small, pretending there was less of her than there really was', like many a woman before and since. Those feminists who claim that James never ponders the injustice of a woman's situation pay little attention to the greatest chapter of his entire writing career, where he depicts Isabel's post-marital self-reckoning.

Osmond has accused his wife of harbouring sentiments worthy of a radical newspaper, but 'the real offence, as she ultimately perceived, was in having a mind of her own at all'. Her mind was supposed to be an extension of him, like a garden-plot added to a deer-park. As a consequence of his monstrous egotism, she is driven back into herself, to the point where covert observation becomes for her an instinctive form of self-defence. With his profound sensitivity, Ralph soon senses her spiritual agony, just as Henrietta is unsurprised to find her worst predictions vindicated. Yet Isabel is pained by the off-hand way in which Henrietta can advise the desertion of a husband. Again, it is a mark of Henrietta's intelligence that she should couple her belief in divorce with a staunch aversion to the extra-marital adventures counselled by such Europeans as the Countess Gemini. Henrietta's is the blunt honesty of the cities of the American West, which allow divorce and 'to which we must look in the future'. At the beginning of her time in Europe, Isabel had praised Henrietta as an emanation of the great democracy, but Ralph had complained that she smelt so much of the future that it almost knocked one down. In her refusal to take her friend's advice and abandon Osmond, Isabel displays that very trait against which James had warned in an early description of Isabel's penchant for 'keeping up the flag after the place has surrendered, a sort of behaviour so crooked as to be almost a dishonour to the flag'. This forecasts the final pain of a woman who takes the spirit of the Alamo too far, and continues to present a brave face to the world, long after her marriage has collapsed into mockery. James is too subtle to say whether he sees her return to Rome as an act of bravery or foolhardiness, but it is significant that he gives the last word on the matter to the lady of the future. 'Just you wait!'

Long before her final catastrophe, however, Isabel has already been guilty of keeping up a false front. It is made clear from the outset that her abiding love will be Ralph Touchett. Her refusal to admit her dire suffering to Ralph comes from love. When Warburton proposes to her, she considers confiding in her aunt, her female friend, her uncle, 'but she would have had to do herself violence to air this special secret to Ralph'. Later, on meeting Madame Merle, Isabel is troubled by the suspicion that there was something between her cousin and this glittering lady, but she suppresses her doubts with the steadfastness of a true lover: 'If it were something of importance, it should inspire respect; if it were not, it was not worth her curiosity', for she had a natural reluctance to peer into the unlighted corners of Ralph's life. By the time he arrives in Florence, a shambling and self-mocking convalescent, Isabel, after months of separation, comes to an awareness of her true feelings for him. She is moved by the incredulity and irony with which he contemplates his disabilities, and her manly instinct to protect is wedded to a womanly wish to be charmed. With his 'advantage in disadvantage', his capacity to turn real disabilities into fancied triumphs, he appeals to her deepest imagination:

Isabel had grown fond of his ugliness, his awkwardness had become dear to her. They had been sweetened by association: they struck her as the very terms on which it had been granted to him to be charming. He was so charming that her sense of his being ill had hitherto a sort of comfort in it; the state of his health had seemed not a limitation, but a kind of intellectual advantage; it absolved him from all professional and official emotions and left him the luxury of being exclusively personal. The personality so resulting was delightful; he had remained proof against the staleness of disease, he had had to be content to be deplorably ill, yet had somehow escaped being formally sick.

Ralph is man enough to bear his pain with a joke and a grin, yet his ailment has given him the sensibility of a complex woman, unlike the Goodwoods and

Warburtons who are too busy with the world to cultivate the life of the emotions. The passage quoted depicts the interpenetration of one mind by another very like it. The androgynous nature of an achieved love is seen by James as 'nothing less than an equal meeting of two souls', a meeting made possible only 'if both lovers somehow shared elements of the mystical feminine sensibility'.[17] In the increasingly poignant meetings between Ralph and Isabel, it is a sense of implicit but unavowed suffering which puts the seal on their developing feelings for one another.

Trapped in her desolate marriage in Rome, Isabel finds that a visit from the dying man made the blasted circle round which she walked more spacious and she ponders on his moral superiority to the man she *did* marry. Ralph 'made her feel the good of the world; he made her feel what might have been.' It seemed to her an act of devotion to conceal her misery from him, by endlessly finding work for her hands even as they talked. Ralph is not fooled, for his awareness of her unadmitted suffering is, if anything, even deeper than her divination of his.

Yet that very sensitivity which makes this love real to him is what finally prevents him from pressing his case. From the beginning, he had never dreamed that he could be loved and had permitted himself only 'the imagination of loving', on the condition of forbidding himself 'the riot of expression!' His early confessions of love to Isabel were made in a mode of self-protective irony, lest he expose himself to the indignity of embarrassing another even more than himself. His 'proposals' had all the parodic charm of caressed clichés: 'I care for nothing but you, dear cousin', to which Isabel always responded with a combination of nervous tact and collaborative mockery: 'If I could believe even that, I should be glad.' That exchange occurs soon after he has confessed that he keeps his innermost chamber eternally locked to outsiders. No sooner has this been said than Isabel wishes to enter; however dismal the quarters, 'she would have been glad to undertake to sweep them and set them in order'. The image of domesticity is as revealing as it is surprising in the hopeful woman who still has other aspirations in mind. It is no wonder that the newly-arrived Henrietta cannot accost Ralph without repeatedly accusing him of flirting with her best friend. He takes revenge by flirting with *her* and seems at once attracted and repelled by this bossy woman, who berates him for being 'too passive' in his attitude to Isabel.

Much later, when Henrietta insists on nursing the sick man on his journey from Rome to Gardencourt, the repulsion has been dissipated by her unaffected kindness. Now her masterly demeanour is simply charming 'and the great oddity was that the prospect pleased him; he was gratefully, luxuriously passive'. But in their early encounters at Gardencourt, it was Henrietta's probing intelligence which outmanoeuvred Ralph and compelled him to an unwitting declaration of love for her friend. Ralph, who had no desire to learn about Mr Goodwood of Boston, has just told Henrietta that he cannot invite him to Gardencourt:

'It's just as you please', Henrietta returned. 'I had no idea you were in love with her yourself'.

'Do you really believe that?' the young man asked with lifted eyebrows.

'That's the most natural speech I've ever heard you make! Of course I believe it', Miss Stackpole ingeniously said.

'Well', Ralph concluded, 'to prove to you that you're wrong I'll invite him'.

They both know, of course, that he is trying to prove it to himself. When the American industrialist fails in his suit, Ralph's 'poor Mr Goodwood!' sounds somewhat automatic an exclamation, for 'it failed exactly to express his thoughts which were taking another line'. When Warburton's suit fails, Ralph quite openly admits to Isabel that he is glad for himself, only to be crushed with embarrassment when Isabel in London refuses to allow him to accompany her to her inn, on the grounds of his weakness and fatigue. When people forget his ailment he is often incommoded, he says, but he is far more upset when someone like Isabel remembers it.

In his decisive conversation with his dying father, Ralph protests that he would only permit himself to love Isabel if he were well and she were not his cousin. But the old man asserts that it is more natural to marry someone you love than to stay single on false principles, a remark which, at that stage, applied with as much justice to Isabel as to Ralph. Mr Touchett is clearly worried by the sexual diminution of the younger generation, for when *he* was young, he wanted to do more than look at a beautiful woman. But now young men are full of 'scruples' and 'ideas', just like young ladies whom Ralph himself will later accuse of having 'too much conscience'. The worship of brainpower and abstract principle has, as Henrietta later admits, come between Americans and the rich potentialities of a life. In a masterly essay, William Bysshe Stein has traced the similarities between the writings of Henry Adams and the remarks of the dying Mr Touchett, lamenting the asexuality of the new generation of Americans.[18] The father's final acquiescence to Ralph's request is made with the prophetic reluctance of a man who knows that it may leave Isabel prey to fortune-hunters; but Ralph insists that 'it's just to do away with anything of that sort that I make my suggestion', for the bequest will leave her as free and independent as she wishes to be. But the weight of evidence suggests that Ralph never speaks his real motives, which the old man, with the insight of the dying, instantly divines. Ralph procures her the money not to make the woman he loves free, but to keep her single.

That Isabel was always aware of this is made clear in her last conversation with Ralph, as he prepares to die. The androgynous ideal is achieved, an interpenetration of minds between lovers who 'needn't speak to understand each other'. Ralph thought Isabel would come, but wasn't sure till he saw her before him—a state of mind identical to Isabel's own. He has always understood the secret pain of her marriage to Osmond, just as she inwardly knew the true source of Mr Touchett's bequest. 'I never thanked you—I never spoke—I never was what I should be!' cries Isabel, who would die with Ralph, if that could keep them one. In the past she has been upset by the suspicion that Ralph might intuit her suffering, but now that knowledge is a liberation which makes her happy for the first time in years and carries her beyond the pain of his death. She who was hated is now adored. The unconscious unity with which the lovers have acted all through the narrative survives even the death of

Ralph, for when Isabel wakes next morning, she knows that a spirit was standing by her bed.

This androgynous element in the two major characters of *The Portrait of a Lady* was remarked by James Herbert Morse in one of the earliest reviews in *Century Magazine*. He observed with approval how James infused his own personality into males and females alike, with the result that the book seemed a conscious challenge to the Victorian vice of excessive sexual differentiation between men and women. If a liberated author is one who greatly softens the differences between men and women, then this book has come close to achieving that feat: 'The men and women are almost equally quick-witted, curt and sharp. While each has a certain amount of individuality, the sharpness is one of the elements in common, preventing a complete different-iation.'[19]

It should be added that James never saw androgyny as an end in itself. Hostile critics have argued that his finest characters are too good for this world and that their 'refinement' all too often amounts to 'masochism'.[20] Arnold Kettle went so far as to suggest that 'their sensibility is an end in itself and not a response to the issues of life',[21] but the scathing portrait of Osmond should give the lie to that. Osmond *does* cultivate a sensibility for its own sake, but his attempt is a pathetic failure, as Ned Rosier notes on inspecting his vulgar bric-a-brac, for there is nothing more vulgar than a flaunted dread of vulgarity. Yet many feminist critics have endorsed Kettle's claim that James never protests against the values of his chosen circle of expatriates, for, so the argument goes, without those values, the very things which he finds inter-esting could not exist—the consciousness of the leisured woman and the sensitive man.[22] Patricia Stubbs has elaborated this charge by arguing that the only way a woman could break free of the pressures of that society was to follow the example of Hester Prynne and break out of society itself, but then they forfeit James's sympathy. She cites his satiric dismissal of Henrietta Stackpole's clear-cut and radical mind, 'without any of the moral dithering which James is precisely admires so much'.[23] But, in conspiring in the traditional misreading of Henrietta Stackpole, she does the author an injus-tice, for, although he mocks her from time to time, he also endows her with the only prescient intelligence in the book and makes her his sole spokesman for the future. To Henrietta alone does he pay the subtle tribute of a happy marriage; and, on this occasion, James reserves all his satire for Isabel:

Henrietta had, after all, confessed herself human and feminine . . . It was a disappoint-ment to find that she had personal susceptibilities, that she was subject to common passions, that her intimacy with Mr Bantling had not been completely original.

One wonders what she wanted of Henrietta, what triumphs of orgiastic androgyny would have made the relation sufficiently original. Her disapproval of this happy marriage shows just how much Isabel has yet to learn—unless, of course, she has now in the light of bitter experience come to disapprove of marriage as such. (This is virtually unthinkable, given Isabel's aversion to divorce.) In the marriage of Henrietta and Mr Bantling, James shows that an androgynous relationship is not an end but a beginning and that the sexes are at their best when they complement rather than contradict one another.

*   *   *

On the subject of the suffragettes, James said that they showed 'all the signs of the beginning of a great movement, in spite of the ease of ridiculing them for desiring martyrdom on such cheap terms'.[24] Like many males who commit themselves with some reservations to feminism, he discovered that his reservations were of far more interest to feminists than his commitment. These provided the basis for a slanted misreading of his two main books on the subject, *The Portrait of a Lady* and *The Bostonians*. The first is a great deal more feminist in its sympathy than the second, but, taken together, they form a valuable outline of the opportunities and excesses of a movement which James saw as the most important of his time. His critique of the impulse to a theatrical martyrdom is as valid a comment on today's feminists as it was on Isabel Archer, as are his warnings against those who take their radicalism so far as almost to wish the blacks back in bondage. His dismissal of the innate frivolity of those suffragettes who gave more thought to looking deliberately dowdy than most others do to looking handsome is even more applicable now than when he wrote it. But, above all this, the courage with which he used the words 'so-called' before the phrase 'womanly virtues' is the tersest illustration of his greatest achievement—to have challenged the dominance in literature of the manly hero and the womanly heroine, and to have protested that real men and women are a lot more baffling and interesting than that.

Henry James, History, and 'Story'

Charles Feidelson

I

In the midst of a rather tedious memoir of an expatriate American artist whose Roman palazzo he frequented in his early years abroad, James inserts a notable passage on what he calls the 'sense of Rome'.[1] He is playing on the word 'sense'. It refers both to a feeling for Rome—a spiritual impress that physical Rome itself, he says, left upon him and all his fellow-visitors—and also to the kind of meaning, and especially the kind of *intelligible* meaning, for which this shared feeling-for-Rome was the medium. The 'spirit of the place', the felt presence of a long human history impacted in the physical city and infusing the 'golden air', cancelled all individual pretensions to personal significance. It reduced everyone, in his own eyes and the eyes of everyone else, to an instrument in its universal 'orchestra', a celebrant of the meaning of Rome. Simultaneously, however, 'kept in order, kept in position before the spectacle', all revealed 'their essence and their type' to the one 'conscious individual' who preserved enough self-possession to watch them. The young Henry James 'had them all, . . . imaginatively, at his mercy'. They had shed their individual idiosyncrasies, 'their extravagance and their overflow', such as they might have exhibited in London or Paris or New York, 'cities in which the spirit of the place has long since . . . lost any advantage it may ever have practised over the spirit of the person'. But the imaginative observer was fully compensated by what Rome had conferred on them—absolute intelligibility. As mirrored in *romanitas*, 'they couldn't elude, impose or deceive', but only manifest their 'essences'.

James hastens to meet the charge that he is 'making a mere Rome of words . . . which was no Rome of reality'. He meets the charge by granting it and turning it to his own ends: 'no Rome of reality was concerned in our experience . . . the whole thing was a rare state of the imagination'. He is, of course, obviously claiming that in some way he and his friends 'really' experienced this state. but he wants to insist that it was a state in which 'reality', as he says, was not 'concerned'—reality simply did not exist for them as a factor to be reckoned with. And by the term 'reality', on this level, he clearly intends something other than what his critic would have meant—an objective or material world outside their imaginative experience. For that would have been easy enough to ignore. The 'reality' in question is a dimension of imaginative experience itself, one that can be *wholly* excluded only in a very '*rare* state of the

104

imagination'. This excluded dimension is what James glances at when he speaks of the 'extravagance and . . . overflow' of personality that London, Paris, and New York would have permitted or encouraged, an imaginative existence full of freedom and accident, of unique persons and mutually incommensurable worlds. A 'Rome of reality', in short, would have been a purely temporal Rome, for better or for worse. In the sublime Rome that James is attempting to render, on the other hand, time itself had put an end to time; all possible moments, persons, worlds had been rehearsed to infinity; and time had brought itself to rest in an eternal place. In this Rome the *genius loci* was nothing short of the total spirit of man come home to itself. It was a theoretical limit of imaginative experience such as James elsewhere sought to suggest through the 'grand style' of the Bay of Naples, 'with all accidents merged, all defects disowned, all experience outlived . . . gather[ing] itself up into the mere mute eloquence of what has just incalculably *been*'.[2] Small wonder that those who entered here could only submit the 'spirit of the person' to the spirit of the place, and also that they could seem to become transparent, wholly typified and intelligible, to that member of the company who still somehow had one foot in 'reality', who had kept enough of the 'spirit of the person' to derive some personal imaginative profit from his immersion in his eternal reservoir of intelligible forms.

But if Italy, and Rome especially, could be the scene of this kind of imaginative miracle, what these places in themselves often presented to James was another face of the matter—an all-inclusive, uninterpretable meaningfulness that baffled the narrative artist as much as it enticed him to become a fictional 'historian'. In his preface to *The Aspern Papers*, written not many years after his celebration of Rome, James notes that 'one must induce almost any "Italian subject" *to make believe* it gives up its secret'. For 'right and left, in Italy—before the great historic complexity at least—penetration fails.' Though 'we hang about in the golden air, . . . we exaggerate our gathered values only if we are eminently witless.' Potentially 'penetrable' subjects presumably belong more properly to those secular societies where experience is sufficiently temporalized and individualized to yield specific 'senses', however much these may be beclouded by the slipperiness of individual men, their liability to 'elude, impose or deceive' as they pursue their course in time. James is unaccustomedly forthright on this topic:

I delight in a palpable imaginable *visitable* past—in the nearer distances and the clearer mysteries, the marks and signs of a world we may reach over to as by making a long arm we grasp an object at the other end of our own table. The table is the one, the common expanse, and where we lean, so stretching, we find it firm and continuous.[3]

Thinking of James's fictional practice, we might say that the 'sense of Rome', the postulate of an overriding intelligibility in human affairs, was the most basic implication of the generally European settings of his best work, while for him *narrative* meaning, the particular 'sense' that is made by a personal 'story', depended precisely on his remaining at a considerable intellectual distance from the 'Roman' absolute of his theoretical geography. In these terms, Paris and London—if not those actual cities, the regions of experience that he associated with them—were the places most happily situated for the 'story-teller' that he always claimed to be. They were places with enough 'historic complexity' to light up intelligible essences in people and with enough modern indeterminacy to leave room for the display of significant personal 'extravagance'.

At the opposite end of his universe lay New York (or, more largely, America), his native place. Here, as James takes care to intimate, a 'sense' like that of Rome had obviously not been *lost*; nothing cognate to the Roman 'spirit of . . . place' had ever existed, no plenum of historic 'types' for personality to overflow. And one of the earliest writings of the young man in the Roman drawing-room, who was pleased to find all the other guests at the mercy of his imagination, had been a tale entitled 'A Most Extraordinary Case', which implies an imaginative situation equally extreme but diametrically opposed.[4] The story has to do with a man (a New Yorker) who is so profoundly unable to characterize himself, whether as scholar, as Civil War Officer, or as lover, much as he yearns to demonstrate a public identity, that he is already very ill as the story opens and soon brings it to an end with his death. The 'extraordinary' fate of Ferdinand Mason consists in a preclusion of any personal 'extravagance': in him, the 'spirit of the person' evaporates for lack of a capacity to image itself in the stuff of ordinary experience. It is unable to seize the time, to place itself in the process of imaginative 'reality'. Mason is a man with no 'story' except his growing knowledge of his failure to attain one.

This is not a distinguished piece of work, but it has a special interest because of some very acute comments of a privileged reader, William James, when it was first published.[5] More concerned with the author's extraordinary point of view than with the extraordinary fate of the hero, William took the story as an indication of what his brother was aiming at in all his literary experiments up to this point. He saw it as a kind of fiction that was bound to a radically 'elusive', barely intelligible subject-matter and therefore could be honestly presented only at the price of flaunting its own imperfect knowledge. William found this artistic posture somewhat unhealthy, and he urged a more 'articulate displaying' of the subject—at least a working assumption of intelligible stories to be told and of adequate knowledge in the teller. Nevertheless, the future radical empiricist had his own kind of commitment to the evanescence of experience, and this enabled him to describe the intent of stories like 'A Most Extraordinary Case' very effectively, if not wholly to approve. The aim, he said, was to render the scant traces, the brief 'orbits', of people who 'come out of space . . . and then . . . whirl again into the unknown, leaving us with little more than an impression of their reality and a feeling of baffled curiosity as to the mystery of the beginning and end of their being, and of that intimate segment of it which we have seen'. In this light, Mason's truncated career (which really has ended before it has begun), as well as Henry James's acceptance of the peculiar conditions of such a subject, had a certain validity: 'on the whole the scepticism and, as some people would say, impudence implied in your giving a story which is no story at all . . . has a deep justification in nature, for we know the beginning and end of nothing.'

What Henry James might have wanted to add to this analysis was some reference to the specifically American provenance of his 'scepticism'. Though Mason's story-of-no-story may well remind us of the more famous case of the Londoner, John Marcher, in 'The Beast in the Jungle', Mason's most immediate affinity is with the American scene of James's earliest artistic aspirations, as he later figured it in *A Small Boy and Others* and *Notes of a Son and Brother*.[6] That mid-nineteenth-century America falls nearly as far short of meaning-in-time as the accreted 'historic complexity' of Rome stands beyond any further story. And Henry James, small boy and youth, is as much a creature of it as anyone else. As in Rome, he has the special status of a man whose awareness is heightened because he knows of another world; here the alternative is deeply imprinted on his mind in the image of the Place Vendôme, remembered (or so he would have it) from when he was less than two years old.(SBO 53) But his youthful obsession with the 'sense and . . . image' of life can only serve as an inverted index to the absence of such things in an American world where human 'life or force' seems forever doomed to emerge as *'presence without type'*. (SBO 290, 224) He and his family, whose 'disconnectedness' from 'business' extends into a suspicion of all definitive social or personal undertakings, merely refine upon the basic anomaly of American experience at large: it is a 'void' in which significant external connections (and therewith the materials of 'story') await the self-creation of 'figures'.(SBO 189; NSB 66, 71) Self-creation *ex nihilo* is of course a great deal to ask of human beings, and James is ready to give them the benefit of the doubt—willing 'to rinse [his] mouth of the European aftertaste' so that he may 'do justice to whatever of the native bittersweet [may] offer itself in congruous vessels'.(NSB 305) To some extent, he does find American 'vessels'—in his family and in occasional persons who cross his path, in the human 'types' and the signs of 'constituted order' in Boston and Cambridge, even in the country as a whole during the 'intensified time' of the Civil War years.(NSB 367f., 304ff., 243, 427-429) But the aspiring artist always suspects that his program of 'projecting into the concrete . . . some show of . . . life' is foredoomed on American ground, where his art can succeed only to the extent that the country also 'projects' itself.(NSB 290f.) Given his premises he has little reason to look forward to more than a half-projection of people scarcely conscious of any need for self-projection (like Mason's doctor and rival, who glibly dubs him an 'extraordinary case') or, as in the case of Mason, someone tragically aware of his incapacity to project a 'figure' of any kind.

James's contrasting pictures of an inexpressible America and an all-expressive Rome are fantastical. But the very fact that they are blatantly overdrawn points toward something more interesting and more cogent than the nostalgic culture-hunger that also doubtless enters into them. As mythical countries of the mind, 'Rome' and 'America' embody a theoretical polarity, one that underlies James's notion of what narrative art could make of life in the nineteenth century and of what nineteenth-century life demanded of the story-teller.

His obvious addiction to such abstract polarities can be traced back to a prototypical human figure, the ideal personage whom he liked to call the 'man of imagination'.[7] The inherently problematical nature of this putative being is reflected in many aspects of James's familiar theory of the central consciousness in the novel as well as much of his fictional practice. The Jamesian 'man of imagination' is the denizen of 'experience', which is radically ambiguous, at once human and imaginative. Within his life and within his consciousness, two basic functions or dimensions of 'experience'—life and consciousness, man and imagination, existence and vision—are always laying claim to the whole of it, pursuing one another in a circle that can be described in various parallel sets of terms: imaginative *man* and *imaginative* man; the foreknowable world and the thinkable or desirable; the way events happen and the event of their apprehension. In James's most general terms, the conjunction of humanity and imagination, 'life and 'consciousness', in imaginative man yields two major (and still circular) modes of experience, the 'real' and the 'romantic'. 'Real' experience embraces the legible forms in which human life has imaged itself and thereby declared its 'sense' (in effect, the significant appearances presupposed by social fiction). 'Romantic' experience is the vision (clearly derived from the Romantic poets) of more human 'sense' than social reality itself has yet generated or displayed. James does not summon up these circular antinomies in order to seek some point of resolution. On the contrary, they themselves constitute the inmost structure both of his chosen subject-matter and of his own experience as man and writer (for he, the reflexive hero of his autobiography and prefaces, is avowedly one avatar of the 'man of imagination'). And this circularity that he fosters is essentially *hermeneutical*; the 'real' and the 'romantic' are correlative functions of experience-as-meaning. They are phases or modes of an ongoing process of interpretation in which the event and its comprehension, the imaginative datum and the image of it, endlessly subsume one another. More specifically, they are modes of meaning-as-*intelligibility*, opposite 'values'—one of James's favourite words—through which a prime human value, knowledge of the knowable, manifests itself.

'Rome' and 'America' add a final turn of the screw to this circular system, placing the 'romantic' and the 'real' in an even more problematical light. The 'real' mode of Jamesian 'experience' is just what America has *not* attained, and seemingly cannot attain, for lack of stable, publicly attested manners and institutions, or, failing those, reflexive habits of mind in individuals, which would give intelligible forms to the overflow of spontaneous life. America is a portent of the unreality of any 'real' sense in the modern world. The 'romantic', conversely, is just what Rome does not and cannot validate, for lack of common ground between personal life-intentions and the intelligible essences accreted there. These historical co-ordinates call the very 'sense' of the Jamesian question into question by undermining the terms in which he was wont to frame it. As regions of final knowledge and of the almost unknowable, a virtually completed past and an all but totally elusive present, they jeopardize any knowledge of the knowable in a much more fundamental way than does the problematical relation between the 'romantic' and the 'real' in itself.

Yet this very challenge may indicate the most compelling consideration behind his entire method. Why should he have postulated a 'man of imagination' at all? Partly, no doubt, because of his own temperamental requirements, about which he is frank enough in his autobiography. Because he is forever the outsider, unsuited for 'living' except mainly in the exercise of 'imagination', he can imagine the unmediated life of 'others', which he profoundly envies and wants to embrace in all its immediacy, only as an alternative mode of imaginative life. The 'man of imagination' is himself as the 'other', the 'other' as himself, the ambiguous answer to his childhood prayer 'to *be* other, other almost anyhow'.(SBO 175) Or again, taking the contrary line, as he often does in his prefaces, James implies that his literary problematics are his response to an abject confusion in the social world given to him—a confusion on the part of contemporary 'life', or of 'life' in general, so great that it amounts to a plea for imaginative salvation. In the face of a total chaos of 'values', there is still one guarantee of meaning: an imaginative ironism which at least elevates the confusions of life into a problematical system of 'real' and 'romantic' sense.(P 222-224)

By taking historical experience as the stage of meaning, and the 'Roman' and the 'American' condition as the Omega and Alpha of imaginative life in historical time—a cultural heritage beyond any further interpretation one can make of it, and a present existence almost devoid of any interpretative or interpretable function—James strains his circular scheme to the breaking point. But perhaps this final, almost disabling opposition is actually what generates the system. Perhaps James's postulate of 'experience', and of its hero, the 'man of imagination', is both an assertion and a defiance of fatal limits that he knows he can never overcome—limits inherent in the actual experience of his era, in the narrative art that he would bring to bear on it, and even in the exemplary artist-figure that he himself aspires to be.

*   *   *

Something like that helps to account for certain features of the Jamesian trip-to-Europe story—the basis of his last three major novels as well as his first major work, *Portrait of a Lady*—and it may warrant one more survey of some familiar materials. The initial movement of such a story is simple enough: it derives very directly from the felt situation of the young Henry James in a formless, almost prehistorical America dreaming of a Europe of consummate historical form. In the two books that most clearly carry out the pattern, the *Portrait* and *The Ambassadors*, the protagonists are also actuated, like James when he first went abroad on his own, by memories of earlier glimpses. The story gets under way as a fulfilment of the dream: James's fictional surrogates are afforded a chance to exist once more in a European world of 'types'. But the aim of the narrative is to enable them to realize a larger destiny. They are people with a vocation—exponents of imaginative life in historical time. In them, the extravagance and overflow of human personality, which Rome suppresses and America provides with nothing to be overflowed, is channelled into a paradigmatic effort to reveal and exercise a significant human existence.

James's recapitulatory habit, his continual return to the legend of his youth, was closely connected with the importance of recapitulation or return or re-interpretation in the legend itself. This motif is at the heart of the subject in *The Ambassadors*: Lambert Strether, whose first attempt to enact the Jamesian role was abortive, comes back at fifty-five (James's own approximate age) to renew the attempt. Moreover, both the youthful James and his later heroes, by returning to a cultural point of origin, making a journey into the historical past, are initiating their personal stories, embarking on their futures. The theme of return to historical sources is not uncommon in American literature, but James gives it a peculiar twist. In effect, the story cannot truly begin until the protagonist has found a viable beginning-point, and that is what he or she is seeking among the perfected forms of Europe. Not only Strether but also Isabel Archer, of the *Portrait*, first appears before us as a person who is conscious of having reached a point of departure by getting back to a historical setting that can serve as a personal *terminus a quo*—Strether amidst the antiquities of Chester, Isabel at Gardencourt. And Strether's conscious self-dedication to the pursuit of his story, whatever it may prove to be, is against the backdrop of Gloriani's Parisian garden, where 'names in the air . . . ghosts at the windows, . . . signs and tokens' bespeak 'survival, transmission, association, a strong, indifferent, persistent order'. Here he launches himself by delivering the speech to Little Bilham which was the starting-point of James's own process of working out the novel.

A different way in which these books are set in motion—and this, one must grant, is the only structure of 'story' to which James gives much explicit attention in his prefaces—is the 'bewilderment' (P 63f) of a primarily 'romantic' American in the face of a densely 'real' European society. Thus the 'romantic' imagination of Isabel Archer is intent on fulfilling itself in 'real' life but baffled by the really 'real' at every turn. Isabel shies away from and then wholly misreads the 'imagination of others', notably Madame Merle and Gilbert Osmond, who are creatures and practitioners of the 'real' and engaged in reading her in their own fashion. Similarly, Strether's 'romantic' interpretation of the affair between Madame de Vionnet and Chad Newsome, an interpretation that credits it with the maximum 'sense' he can conceive in a love-relation, involves a prolonged mystification of the more limited, wholly 'real' imaginative values embodied in their actual mode of life. In the *Portrait* the 'real' tends toward the moral corruption of Madame Merle and Osmond, and in *The Ambassadors* it tends toward the moral elevation of Madame de Vionnet, but in both novels, if we approach them from this angle, the story is directed toward the 'romantic' protagonist's eventual self-discovery within a 'real' order which has redefined 'romantic' experience while the 'romantic' principle was seeking to define itself in the materials of the 'real'. Strether at last knows what it is to be fully 'mixed up with the typical tale of Paris', while Isabel accedes to 'the truth of things, their mutual relations, their meaning, and for the most part their horror'. Yet in neither case is the 'romantic' habit finally discredited by its disillusionment. What remains intact, demonstrated by the story as a whole, is the genetic power of 'romantic' over-reaching, the power to initiate the cycle which will conclude with the power of the 'real' to subsume it once more.

All this, however, hinges on the special virtue that James imputes to his heroes in order for their experience to become 'real' or 'romantic'—that is, 'imaginative'—at all. Such characters as Isabel and Strether are in some way *elect*, people with a vocation. And their new starting-points—though these come to signify a good deal more—betoken their redemption from the threat to imaginative life inherent in American life, their rebirth in a Jamesian Byzantium. At its most elementary, the American doom (it amounts to that, though James never treats it heavy-handedly) is the fate of Isabel in Albany. Not wholly without antecedents, ensconced in her grandmother's house, and certainly not without an impulse to project herself as a 'figure', she nevertheless feels betrayed by an inadequate cultural vocabulary and is vainly seeking support in a 'history of German Thought' while the cosmos utters a 'cynical . . . appeal . . . to patience'. Strether's fate has been grimmer, and he is more significant in this respect. Not only is he much older but also, instead of New York, where the personal destiny need only struggle with the primeval American vacuity, Strether's habitat is New England, where the empty place of viable historical forms has been filled by an absolutistic moral idealism. Though New England thus has its 'types', especially female, they have long lost such relation as they may once have had to the meaning of life in time; they represent rigid moral postures around which the 'practices' of business life go on in total indifference to any informing ideas. What Strether must find in the European, particularly the Parisian, setting, therefore, is salvation from a simplistic American apriorism, which is even more threatening and no more meaningful than the American formlessness it fends off.

Strether perceives that he himself is deeply imbued with this habit of mind. Even while he is urging Little Bilham to 'live' imaginatively in time, a weary wisdom tells him that consciousness is forever arrested in the first life-mold that receives it. He strongly suspects that temporal meaning, the 'clock of . . . freedom', is no more than an 'illusion', albeit a supremely nourishing one. Paris, for him, is the possibility of a firmer faith. Because the 'persistent order' of Paris is a temporal product, not a supervenient abstraction but a historical creation, it can foster the individual 'liberty . . . intensity . . . variety' which the New England order subverts in its terror of the void. Paris is the ground for his half-scared hope that, having got back to the very station where he once allowed the train of time to leave him behind, he need not be stranded again.

On the other hand, Strether is always an outsider in Europe, even in Paris—and this not only by necessity but also by conviction. James himself quickly adopted this posture when he first settled in London, aiming at a cosmopolitanism which may have been fairly easy for him to carry off but which becomes extremely difficult when it reappears as the imputed vocation of his heroes. For them, Europe, though not dispiriting, is in its own way as suspect as America. Strether maintains to the end that despite his sacrificing at alien altars his loyalty to the American gods is fundamentally unchanged; and though his earlier American apriorism has in fact been modified almost beyond recognition, the special *need* that he brings from America—the need to transcend that very disposition in himself—leads him to make demands upon Paris that no Parisian would ever think of. What Strether wants is not merely an official sanction for the imaginative existence of individuals but a fully operative imaginative order, one that develops its own 'sense' through the new senses that it encourages imaginative men to confer upon it. Measured by that standard, as Strether repeatedly notices, Paris is wanting in seriousness: it is a world where the sacrosanct past gazes benignly but from a great distance upon a modern playground. Only Madame de Vionnet seems an exception, and that is a major reason why she fascinates him.

But in this regard the definitive situation is that of Isabel Archer, who by nature is much less prone to pin her faith to the actualities of Europe. Though uplifted by the sustaining medium of the successive versions of Europe through which she passes—rural England, London, Paris, Florence, Rome— she nevertheless adheres all the while to a primitive American resistance to form, which in her becomes the more refined conviction that nothing external can express her. If this is her great 'romantic' error, it is also, from another standpoint, a wholly appropriate response to the European actualities of the *Portrait*. More explicitly topical than *The Ambassadors*, the *Portrait* presents a Europe in dead water, a place where historical settings, however salubrious for the American imagination, remain fundamentally external to the life of individual spirits, even those long habituated to the European scene. Here 'types' range from those who have no notion of what to do with their type (like Lord Warburton) to those who resort to cynical exploitation of typology (like Madame Merle and Osmond). Against this background, Isabel's anti-nomianism, though she applies it mistakenly, is her means of redeeming herself from her redeemer—from a Europe which, instead of providing a ready remedy for American formlessness, turns out to be a world where the productive agency of historical time has come to halt just as surely as it has never existed in America.

What devolves upon characters like Isabel and Strether, then, is the task of inventing an experiential substitute for the temporal meaning, the stuff of 'story', that their historical circumstances at once negate and impel them to seek. Though it is a heavy charge for a very naïve woman in her twenties and a tired man in his mid-fifties, we come to admire them in large part because they do attempt something like that. In the case of Isabel Archer, the achievement is much less complete than Strether's—indeed, it is minimal—but she arrives at it against much greater odds. Her mainstay in Europe is her conviction of spontaneous selfhood—the one positive trait to be salvaged from an America that provides no qualifying terms for the self—yet by the same token her only concrete self is that of a vagrant dreamer contemplating the infinite field of attributes she might take on. As if this were not a sufficient handicap for a potential heroine of the imagination, James almost cruelly magnifies the coercive force, however specious, of the institutional structures and social personalities that confront her in Europe. In much of the book the predominant authorial tone is one of confident social authority, reflected formally in the novelistic 'architecture' which, as James says in his preface, he deliberately 'put up round' her 'while she stood . . . in perfect isolation'. (p. 48) Unlike Strether, moreover, Isabel does not have even the kind of symbolic mid-point between the American and Roman extremes that Paris provides in *The Ambassadors*; her trajectory from the loose, rambling house in Albany to the prison-walls of a Roman palazzo marks out the full range of the Jamesian antinomy without any mitigation.

As a result, the 'story' of which she is capable is mainly the story of a vocation deferred, negatively implied, and perhaps not consciously accepted by her until the final moments of the book. Isabel certainly lives her life from the beginning as if it were incumbent on her to make it a tale worth telling, 'planning out her development, desiring her perfection, observing her progress'. But she is always brought to a halt, notably in the crucial period before she agrees to marry Gilbert Osmond, by her awareness of a 'dusky, uncertain tract' that her imagination dares not enter. And her marriage to Osmond, who truly says that he is 'convention itself', is her device for evading the dark tract of her problematical destiny. Rather than shoulder the burden of 'experience', she allows herself to be externally typed, brought to an end; her imaginative life has merely moved from the American doom of total indeterminacy to a Roman doom—to be 'ground in the mill of the conventional'.

The alternative course, to which she finally gropes her way, is first wholly apparent in the 'extraordinary meditative vigil' of Chapter XLII, the passage James considered the 'best thing in the book'. In his preface, James treats of this high point as a 'supreme illustration' of his plan 'to place the centre of the subject in the young woman's own consciousness', and in this chapter for the first time he allows Isabel to become a consciousness almost as fully 'central', as prescriptive to the point of view, as the 'registers' of his later fiction. But the particular advantage of the central consciousness that is singled out by the preface is its capacity to render 'inward life' without sacrifice of the necessary eventfulness of a proper story: James maintains that Isabel's reverie 'throws the action further forward than twenty "incidents" might have done'. (p. 51, 56ff.) Even more paradoxically, we might say ˆhat the action is here 'thrown forward' by the intrinsic *reflexivity* of consciousness, which is heavily emphasized by the fact that this is the first occasion of very extended *retrospection* on Isabel's part. The forward movement of the story becomes a function of recollection, interpretation, re-presentation of what has already occurred. Isabel's former reliance on open-ended, spontaneous self-projection, her now confessedly inadequate American counterweight to Europe, is being supplanted by a more complex process: a re-imagining of images that cannot be imagined away. Conversely, the mere type-casting which was her terrible fate at the hands of Osmond is being supplanted by lived images of the re-presented past. Her recurrent picture of Madame Merle and Osmond in silent communion, while it refers to an external and conventional order that still imprisons her, in itself has the character of a chosen starting-point, an accepted premise which is already being modified—'thrown forward'—by her process of taking it up again.

Furthermore, this kind of temporal structure is obviously not limited to moments of meditation. Just as reflection can be action insofar as it reconstitutes what it receives from the past, action can be reflection insofar as it is informed by the past that it is always revising. The book concludes with two large-scale demonstrations of this principle. Isabel journeys across the continent back to Gardencourt, which is not only the place where the dying Ralph Touchett awaits her but also the given point of origin for her future, the place where her imaginative life can at last truly commence. Even more strikingly, her final return to Rome is a rapid re-enactment of the pilgrimage that brought her there before—but a return now to a Rome (for all the rigours that await her there) which is subject to interpretation, a further point of experiential departure that she can leave (though she *only* can leave) by not trying to leave it wholly behind.

By adumbrating a structure for meaningful life in time, a ground of significant 'story', the personal disaster of Isabel Archer finally takes on a genuinely tragic value. In *The Ambassadors*, where the theoretical availability of such a ground is quickly established, the dominant mood of the novel is comic rather than tragic. Though the book ends tragi-comically—'all comically, all tragically', as the text has it—for most of his story Strether proceeds in the essentially comic spirit of a man who finds himself in a place where he can take his stand. But of course the distinctive feature of this place consists in its being quite literally no *place*; it is a utopia of metamorphic experience where nothing stands still. Strether's vocation appears in his willingness, despite natural trepidations, to welcome the peculiar situation prepared for him by his creator. His true position, he recognizes, must always be some new variant of the 'false position' already detectable in his speech to Little Bilham, which locates him somewhere between the *a priori* and the *a posteriori*. He stands at a moving point where the 'moral scheme of . . . approved pattern' that he brought with him, and which James 'figure[s] by a clear green liquid . . . in a neat glass phial', is undergoing the transvaluations of experience, 'turn[ing] from green to red, or whatever, and . . . on its way to purple, to black, to yellow'. (p. 313ff.)

James speaks of this in terms strikingly similar to his comment on Isabel's reverie: Strether, he says, is '*thrown forward* . . . upon his lifelong trick of intense *reflexion*'. (p. 316) Like Isabel, but for the full span of his story, Strether is engaged in the paradoxically forward-moving action of interpretive retrospection. Increasingly, this activity becomes meta-experiential, a process of reflection on the terms of temporal experience itself:

. . . He passed back into the rooms, . . . and, while he circulated and rested, tried to recover the impression that they had made on him three months before, to catch again the voice in which they had seemed then to speak to him. That voice, he had to note, failed audibly to sound; which he took as the proof of all the change in himself. He had heard, as of old, only what he *could* then hear; what he could do now was to think of three months ago as a point in the far past. All voices had grown thicker and meant more things; they crowded on him as he moved about . . . But . . . freedom was what was most in the place and the hour; it was the freedom that most brought him round again to the youth of his own that he had long ago missed . . . The main truth of the actual appeal of everything was . . . that everything represented the substance of his loss, put it within reach, within touch, made it, to a degree it had never been, an affair of the senses. That was what it had become for him at his singular time, the youth he had long ago missed—a queer concrete presence, full of mystery, yet full of reality, which he could handle, taste, smell, the deep breathing of which he could positively hear.

What he had missed long ago in his youth was temporality itself; and the experience of time at work, overlaying the voice of a nearer past with new voices, restores his primal past to him in the present exercise of the temporal freedom which he then rejected.

Strether knows that he is neither of Woollett nor of Paris any more; the Paris he inhabits is now a 'mere symbol for more things than had been dreamt of in the philosophy of Woollett'—or in the philosophy of actual Paris, for that matter. (p. 316) The story he is living out is only his personal way of making sense of his personal time. Yet he does have, or hopes he has, the authority of a model that is virtually world-historical. Madame de Vionnet seems to him a living and wholly individual expression of a splendidly complete and impersonal historical tradition, a past to which he himself and contemporary Paris in general can have no more than a distant relation. And she has managed to evoke a prodigy of 'type' out of an unlicked cub of an American youth, who miraculously has shown a receptivity that no one could have foreseen. The process of Strether's own story, as he watches it develop, is concurrent with his preservation and fostering of this (to him) supreme story; if the latter should go wrong, he says, his time will be up—it will make him old. It is at the height of his confidence in himself and in the two lovers that he makes his solitary excursion into the French countryside, which is a conscious fulfilment of his wistful Bostonian preconceptions and re-presenting of his earliest French impressions in a milieu which simultaneously seems saturated with the ongoing concerns of a man 'engaged with others and in midstream of his drama'. Though not unaware that his days abroad and his years on earth are numbered, he devotes himself to a kind of lived poem in celebration of the uses of time.

The interruption of this private revel by his discovery of the wholly quotidian side of the love affair between Madame de Vionnet and Chad must certainly be read as a deflation of 'romantic' vision by 'real' circumstances. But there is another way in which one must read it. For in fact, Strether adjusts very quickly to his new data insofar as they merely consist of evidence of a 'real' sexual relationship and of the 'real' social lies employed to obscure it. What disturbs him more lastingly is the altered perspective on experience as a whole that is forced upon him even while he freely accepts these aspects of the affair. They bring its *contingency* into sudden prominence, just as the way his great discovery occurs is a startling demonstration of the contingency of his own process of experience. He has of course all along been very much aware of the threat *ab extra*, both to himself and to Madame de Vionnet and Chad, presented by the adamancy of Woollett, and also of the subtler threat inherent in the frivolous tendencies of the Parisian audience who are watching them. But what now comes home to him is the inner treachery of experience itself, the fragility of any value that lives in time.

This is the tragic shadow that falls across his comedy and brings it to a conclusion: a consciousness of the foredoomed passion, 'mature, abysmal, pitiful', that has driven an aging woman, now 'visibly less exempt from the touch of time', to a work which, 'however admirable, was nevertheless of the strict human order' and is now visibly disintegrating in her hands. The historical gulf that the idea of 'experience' has bracketed out begins to show itself once more. For Chad, however transformed, is still the potential ad-man, hankering for the mindless American present; and Madame de Vionnet, however 'natural and simple', is 'old, old, old' beyond her personal age, the sublime creation of factors 'beyond anything she could intend, . . . things from far back—tyrannies of history, facts of type'. To Strether's 'historic sense', in the very midst of his admiration, the destructive senselessness of sheer history—'the smell of revolution, . . . the smell of blood'—is in the air. To his sense of himself only one gesture remains—by exacting such vows as he can from Chad, to fortify his emblem of time redeemed, and thereupon to depart into the limbo on the other side of the story he has had.

★   ★   ★

In their different ways, *Portrait of a Lady* and *The Ambassadors* are instances of what James called 'the personal history of an imagination'. Or rather, they are stories about the necessity and the difficulty of living out that particular kind of story. Isabel eventually discovers the necessity through her suffering of the difficulty; Strether pays final tribute to the necessity as the difficulty overcomes him. In either case, the time of their personal experience is invested with the 'sense' of the imaginative enterprise running through it—which is precisely an attempt to make sense of human time.

That is all these heroes can accomplish. It is at once something less and something more than their author wants to claim for himself, the 'man of imagination' *par excellence*. As 'imaginative' beings, James's protagonists are quasi-artists, but James draws an important distinction between the 'privilege of the artist' and the 'privilege of the hero'. (p. 29, 96ff.) The privilege of the fictional hero is the capacity to *fail* as an artist and yet to remain a significant man. Indeed, the hero becomes an 'interesting and appealing and comparatively floundering *person*', and thus *has* a 'personal history', in the very degree that the artist in him is 'deluded, diverted, frustrated or vanquished'. (p. 96ff.) Though Isabel and Strether are worth telling about because they aspire toward an ideal form of 'story', the 'spirit of the person' lives in them because they never catch much more than a glimpse of that ideal. Their personal 'extravagance' is both the medium in which the ultimate human type, the artist-in-life, is adumbrated and an incalculable human energy that overflows it.

The privilege of the artist is to embody that type to such an extent that his life is wholly subsumed by his art. James finds that he cannot depict a *triumphant* artist-hero in his fiction, for the personal success of the artist fades into the 'triumph of what he produces'. (p. 96) His 'works' contain but supplant the 'personal history' of their maker. In his own case, meaning-in-time is fully manifested in the succession of his works, 'recording scroll[s] or engraved commemorative table[s]', the concrete presence of an interpreted past that is completely open to reinterpretation. (p. 4) But there is no fictional 'story' in such a case, which has already achieved the lineaments of the ideal story. The successful artist pays for his privilege by being a fictionally unrepresentable man.

James's prefaces, taken as a whole, are his ingenious device for representing the heroic significance of an artistic career without infringing on the fictional 'privilege of the hero'. Each of the prefaces, he insists, is the 'private history of . . . [a] *work*', the 'story of . . . [a] *story*'. He is not doing anything 'so subtle, if not so monstrous, . . . as to write the history of the growth of . . . [his own] imagination'. (p. 4, 313, 47) Instead—and this is a crucial difference for the kind of exemplary value that he *does* want to attribute to his development—he is tracing a more impersonal sequence, a 'tradition of behaviour' to which his works bear witness. (p. 347f.) They reveal not so much a 'personal history' as the 'continuity of an artist's endeavour, the growth of his whole operative consciousness', at the present end of which, 'addicted to "stories" and inclined to retrospect' he sits writing his prefaces, the ultimate product of his entire 'process of production'. (p. 4) Whereas ordinary human experience is inevitably episodic, and 'we are condemned . . . to abandon and outlive . . . many vital or social performances', his 'literary deeds' belong to a 'superior and more appreciable order', in which 'our behaviour and its fruits are essentially one and continuous and persistent and unquenchable'. (p. 347f.) And yet the very removal of his artistic continuity from the plane of ordinary experience makes it exemplary for that experience. There is a model for the 'whole conduct of life' in the artist's special ability to 'remount the stream' and 'to live back . . . into the finer reasons of things', to re-enter the 'chapter of experience' to which a given work is the present key. (p. 135, 76, 29) Equally exemplary is his right and duty of 'revision' (specifically defined as 'seeing . . . again'), the perpetuation of his 'tradition of behaviour' upon the higher ground to which the tradition itself has led. (p. 339) The prefaces offer themselves as the latest chapter of this Jamesian artistic continuum. 'Experience' here is 'pausing . . . to consult its notes' lest it be lost in the 'widening . . . circle' of itself, but in this very act the circle is widening further, the 'process of production' proceeding. (p. 3) James actually suggested in a letter to Howells that a preface to the prefaces was not beyond his imagination.

In his autobiography James is trying to describe an even wider circle of experience than the one marked out by his books and their prefaces, his works and their revisions. He imputes to his youthful self an instinct to live in such a fashion as ultimately to make possible this artistic process of self-recovery, which is also a self-extension. Still claiming the full privilege of the artist for himself, he confers on his younger self something of the privilege of the hero. In James's preface, the 'forces of expansion, . . . necessities of upspringing' of the original literary work are revived and once more contained on that distant occasion when the writer 'recover[s], from some good standpoint on the ground gained, the intimate history of the business'. (p. 42) In the autobiography, the present Master, 'seeing the whole content of memory and affection in each enacted and recovered moment, . . . in the vivid image and the very scene', is able to 'cherish the moment and evoke the image and repaint the scene' because ever since he was a Small Boy these have been 'the only terms in which life has treated [him] to experience'.(SBO 3) The Small Boy long before he was capable of 'works', and the Son and Brother while he was yet an apprentice, not only had artistic leanings but revered the universal 'idea of representation'. They believed in a 'gain of importance . . . on the part of the represented thing' over the 'thing of accident, of mere actuality, still unappropriated', and they practiced life as a continuous translation of data into representative images.(SBO 263) This was a halting process in an almost unimaginable America, and not much easier in an already over-represented Europe, but it was a mode of life predestined to be recaptured, preparing its own eventual artistic salvation in the midst of the young hero's delusion, diversion, frustration, and vanquishment.

The temporal structure affirmed by James's prefaces and autobiography is surely one of the most thoroughgoing instances of 'organicism' on record. Though large and loose, this seems the best word for the kind of internally developing significance or significant development that he is always trying to establish. The force of James's testimony in this respect is more than theoretical, for though the prefaces and autobiography are artistic 'representations', not documents, the 'organic' continuity that they represent clearly was an ever-present personal recourse for their author. In his answer to the 'melancholy outpouring' he received from Henry Adams apropos of *Notes of a Son and Brother*, James impatiently brushes aside all complaints about the ravages of time:

Of course we are lone survivors, of course the past that was our lives is at the bottom of an abyss—if the abyss *has* any bottom; of course, too, there's no use talking unless one particularly *wants* to. But the purpose, almost, of my printed divagations was to show you that one *can*, strange to say, still want to—or at least one can behave as if one did. Behold me therefore so behaving—and apparently capable of continuing to do so.[8]

Adams, forever scrutinizing public history for the meaning of his time, was already far gone in despair of finding any. It was a historical despair that James himself was forced to admit at the outbreak of war a few months later: '. . . to have to take it all now for what the treacherous years were all the while really making for and *meaning* is too tragic for any words.'[9] But for the most part James confronted the mounting disjunctions of nineteenth-century existence with the calm of one who had an assured alternative to a failing tradition. He was far from being oblivious to the fatal course of public history; even while he delighted in the complacent England of the 1870s, according to *The Middle*

Years, he was dogged by the 'question of how long', the gaps between inherited social forms and historical functions, between the coming era and intelligible forms of any kind.[10] Yet these conditions, his whole posture seems to say, are mere presuppositions, too obvious to be worth labouring ('of course . . . of course . . . of course'); the point is to fill the gaps with experiential models of the 'organic' temporal structure that history itself is rapidly forgetting.

In effect, James recognizes his historical epoch by a studied independence of history *per se*—even of literary history, for in the prefaces he makes only a few perfunctory attempts to place his novelistic method in relation to the general historical development of the novel. The often quoted passage about the 'house of fiction' is instructive in this regard. A vast heap of a place, its façade pierced by random windows 'of dissimilar shape and size, . . . broad or balconied or slit-like and low-browed', the house of fiction has no historical structure at all but is merely a *prima materia* through which these 'apertures' are driven by the 'need of the individual vision and . . . the pressure of the individual will'. (p. 46)

Precisely in such a passage, however, we can discern an idea of artistic experience—the encounter of an individual will with a pathless world—that gives a strange inflection to James's organicistic account of human time. While his use of the notion of organic development is subtle and powerful, there is certainly nothing very original in proposing this as a means of containing the discontinuities of modern existence. Equally familiar in itself is the 'organic' model of literary form that he frequently invokes in the prefaces—the ideal of a work in which the parts fully 'conspire and interdepend' to make a whole that answers to their 'true intelligible nature'—though James was the first to apply organicism so extensively to the technical form of the novel. (p. 151, 219) What *is* very distinctive is James's simultaneous insistence on an organic 'tradition of behaviour', to which all his works belong and to which they give access, and on something very different—the toilsome pursuit, exhilarating yet perpetually inconclusive, of those 'really "done" things' which alone will constitute an artistic past that is worth 'seeing again'. (p. 348)

In this perspective, the 'continuity of things', as to which the idea of organic development reassures him, can itself turn out to be far from reassuring. It is positively a 'terror', though an exciting one, to the artist at the beginning of his career. The formal principles of organic holism come on trial as he anxiously perceives that 'really, universally, relations end nowhere', that 'the exquisite problem of the artist is eternally . . . to draw, by a geometry of his own, the circle within which they shall happily *appear* to do so'. The 'circle' that his approach demands, which will round off a particular work (or, in the long run, his career as a whole), is not inherent in the nature of things; it is a tentative construct. From the standpoint of the advancing (as opposed to the retrospective) artist, the world of his imaginative experience is like a canvas on which he must somehow embroider a determinate figure despite the 'boundless number of its . . . perforations for the needle', which 'invite, . . . solicit, . . . persuade, . . . practice a thousand lures and deceits'. He has no guidance except the 'presumability *somewhere* of a convenient, . . . visibly-appointed stopping-place', a provisional goal which will be reached as much by steadfastly ignoring as by attending to possible 'continuities'. (p. 5f.)

The prime record of this *ad hoc* geometrizing or artistic dead reckoning lies in James's notebooks.[11] Absorbed in his 'world of creation' (n. 112) yet wholly conscious of his own absorption, he at once pursues the indeterminate but presumably determinable story before him and notes the uncertain process of his pursuit. The story of the emerging story is enacted in an incessant by-play: question, exclamations, hypotheses, indecisions, decisions, counter-decisions, self-encouragements, self-warnings, stand-stills, miraculous inspirations. Art here is seen as a constantly renewed gamble, a mixture of calculation and luck, aiming at the 'really "done"' in a milieu where nothing can ever be 'done' except provisionally—where, as James says at the end of his sketch for the *Portrait*, 'the *whole* of anything is never told', and 'unity' amounts to what conveniently 'groups together'. (n. 18)

Even within the large-scale temporal circle of the prefaces, the stories that James remembers about his stories are tales of dangers and treacheries, anxieties and blind confidence, unforseeable windfalls and forced sacrifices, 'difficulties' at every turn. Each 'work' is a focus of contradictory imperatives, for, as we are instructed at the outset, 'the art of representation bristles with questions the very terms of which are difficult to apply and to appreciate'. (p. 3) James's experiences with such questions in artistic practice—the 'thrilling ups and downs, . . . intricate ins and outs of the compositional problem'—display the artist in a situation closely analogous to the unstable life-situations of his fictional heroes. His 'tradition' always in the making and never securely made, he leads a life of 'adventure transposed'. (p. 319) The preface-writer himself is engaged in a tortuous 'appreciation' of the very terms of the questions. This is not so much a process of definition or analysis as an 'adventure' in a thicket of concepts—a half-systematic, half-fortuitous discovery of problematic relationships that multiply the more as the theorist moves among them. Like the story-writing of which it tells the story, a preface reaches its conclusion only by fiat or good fortune.

Far from deploring these uncertainties of his art, James rejoices in the 'transposed' privilege of the hero, the quasi-personal extravagance and over-flow, which he thus regains within his own realm. He delights to see himself as a courageous adventurer courting 'free difficulty' amid the perils of imaginative life, and perhaps even more as an almost Nietzschean trickster-god, a master of 'dissimulation' and 'insidious proceedings'. (p. 29f., 324, 224) The fact remains, however, that he puts a barely tolerable strain on his organicism when he begins to talk in this vein. James was probably quite aware of this; there was a side of him that could take great pleasure in it, even invite it, as one more bristling question. But it is hard to say whether he ever permitted himself to recognize how inevitably, and why, this problem ultimately lay in wait for him.

It is latent in his entire conception of the temporal meaning of his artistic career. When he treats of his 'process of production' in terms of the organic continuity of 'experience', he is equally conceiving of experience in terms of the specific kind of meaning vested in books, in written words. Retro-spectively, it is not difficult for him to regard the long line of his writings as if they were predestined works of an evolving nature, with himself as the immanent spirit still 'producing' even as it returns upon itself. Prospectively, however, he has usually found himself in the position of fashioning artefacts in a verbal medium that suggests no infinitely evolving vital order but reduces life to a discontinuous field of imaginative possibilities. The idea of organic continuity saves the day for him in a period that is losing its historical co-ordinates; but that idea is being invoked by a writer who in fact has even less meta-physical belief in an organic *telos* than historical faith in the soundness of his particular epoch—a writer whose creative career has been the repeated exercise of an essentially arbitrary will-to-form in a world without any appointed sequences. Nietzsche again comes to mind, and despite the huge distance between his lonely agonies and James's humane traditionalism, at this point there is a real affinity. The ultimate 'privilege of the artist' can turn out to be a dubious privilege, the exemplification of a life that has no story except what it recurrently wills into transient existence amid a thousand and one possible goals.

Lytton Strachey and the Prose of Empire

S.P. Rosenbaum

In his influential essay 'Two Faces of Edward' Richard Ellmann characterized the Edwardian years as a Janus period that faced forward to modernism and backward to Victorianism.[1] His description illuminates the first book of a writer who transformed the genre in which Ellmann himself wrote so well. Lytton Strachey's unpublished Edwardian dissertation on Warren Hastings, the first Governor General of India, is a defense of an eminent eighteenth-century imperialist written a decade or so before the biographies that so memorably depicted Victorian imperialists of one kind and another. The paradoxes of the dissertation were just the kind the author of *Eminent Victorians* came later to relish. In debunking the debunkers of Hastings the work looks forward to Strachey's ironic modern biographies, while its defense of imperialism belongs to the nineteenth century. During the time he was writing and revising it, however, Strachey was unable to resolve even into paradoxes the contradictions he encountered about the literariness of history and the nature of imperialism.

Strachey's dissertation began in 1901 as a long undergraduate essay at Cambridge for a prize it did not win. It was then expanded into a fellowship dissertation on Hastings's dealings with Cheyt Sing, the Rajah of Benares, and submitted it unsuccessfully to Trinity College in September, 1904. Strachey spent the next year expanding the dissertation to include Hastings's struggle with the wife and mother of the Vizier of Oude who controlled his treasury. The revised dissertation, now well over 100,000 words, was resubmitted under the title *Warren Hastings, Cheyt Sing, and the Begums of Oude*, at the end of August, 1905, but again it failed to win its author a Trinity fellowship. For the next five years Strachey worked desultorily at turning the dissertation into a book, while reviewing mainly for the *Spectator*. Then he abandoned his decade-old exercise in unironic imperial history.

No writing of Edwardian Bloomsbury's displays more distinctly the inter-related Victorian origins of the Group than Strachey's dissertation. His family had been importantly involved in Indian administration for four generations; the very name Lytton that he chose to use instead of Giles was a viceroy's. His father and his uncle, both knighted for their Indian work, had been known as 'the Strachey Raj'; there was no important office in the government of India that one or the other of them had not held, Uncle John claimed in his book on

Indian administration.[2] In another book Sir John Strachey had defended Hastings's war with the Rohillas, following on the book that his and the viceroy Lord Lytton's close friend Sir James Fitzjames Stephen had written on Nuncomar and Impey. ('Another episode in the great Warren Hastings story', his brother Leslie Stephen called it.[3]) As an implicit defense of his family's tradition of Indian imperial service, Strachey's dissertation thus continued the work of both his and Virginia Woolf's uncles.

Yet the writing of the dissertation was a dead-end for Strachey in form and content. During the Edwardian years Strachey's and Bloomsbury's attitudes markedly changed towards imperialism and the nationalism behind it that was leading to the First World War. Leonard Woolf's experiences in Ceylon and, to a lesser extent, J.M. Keynes's in the India Office disillusioned the Group about achievements of empire. Strachey's dissertation is also the least literary of his books. Little of it is inherently interesting as writing, even though a number of the figures he was dealing with were masters of English prose. Almost none of the rhetorical flair or iconoclastic wit to be found in his reviews of the time and especially in his other unpublished Cambridge writings is present in the dissertation.

In his undergraduate essay on Warren Hastings Strachey proposes to give a short, clear, factual account of three episodes in Hastings's controversial career as Governor General. Only when this has been done, he maintains, can the examination of motives begin. Yet Strachey never does examine Hastings's motives, even in his dissertation, which makes these writings very different from his later ones. His narrative is not just an account of the facts, however, for Strachey also justifies Hastings's actions as he goes along. No doubt is left as to the nobility of Hastings's intentions or the greatness of his achievements. He is 'perhaps the best-abused personage in history', 'the one great figure of his time' (a time that included the founders of the United States), and the man who saved the Empire. Because his aims are unquestioned, Hastings remains vaguely mysterious in all of Strachey's writings on him. At the end of the essay he is uninhibitedly idealized as a superhuman being: 'he never descended to a fault or even to a foible; he was perfection as a statesman, a husband, a friend; he soared.'[4] One waits here for an irony that never comes.

Most of Strachey's essay is spent on Hastings's involvement in the Rohilla War, his difficulties with Nuncomar, and the revolt of the Rajah of Benares. Added to these is an undesignated fourth part briefly treating Hastings's relations with the Vizier and Begums of Oude, and a last section on Hastings's impeachment. The Rohilla War and the Nuncomar affair were the subjects respectively of John Strachey's and Fitzjames Stephen's books; the last two became the subjects of Strachey's dissertation. In the essay these different episodes are treated for the most part in narrative or descriptive summaries, with pauses for arguments against the prevailing view of Hastings. While describing Hastings's dealings with the Begums of Oude, for example, Strachey raises the question of what is illegal in a time of anarchy and then comments, 'it may be possible for some persons to hesitate in answering this question. For Hastings it was not, and the result is that the English are still in

India'. The view of Hastings as a ruthless imperialist was popularized by
Macaulay in a famous essay based on James Mill's biased history of the British
in India. Strachey thought Macaulay's rhetoric 'blatant', but Macaulay left his
traces in the recurrent contrasts of Strachey's essay. Hastings's career is a flash
of notoriety followed by nearly absolute oblivion. English rule in India is a
balance of native institutions and English administrative methods. The incorruptible goodness of Hastings is opposed to the utter malignity of his enemy
Philip Francis. Hastings the man of deeds is arraigned by Edmund Burke, the
man of words. History itself splits into facts and motives.

That Macaulay was a more important precursor of Lytton Strachey's than,
say Pater, was shown in the pieces Strachey was writing around this time for
the New Liberal *Independent Review*. Yet there are also touches in the Warren
Hastings essay that anticipate Strachey's development away from Macaulay
into complex irony. The death of Hastings that Strachey closes his essay with
goes considerably beyond facts or motives.

He was eminently secret; and it is in keeping with the weird seclusion of his mind, that
he drew his last breath in private. As he sank back upon the cushions he took in his
hands a napkin and covered his face; the onlookers, moved by a common emotion, were
awed as in the presence of some appalling mystery; and indeed, even to us, the vision of
the women's fingers plucking so softly and delicately the handkerchief away, and
revealing with all the shock of inevitability the silent fixity of the face, seems to give, by
the very force of its intimate pettiness, a new and strange terrible image of Death itself.

'Warren Hastings' is a remarkable performance by a twenty-one year-old
undergraduate, and its hyperbolic finale prefigures the creative biography
Strachey would later write.

*   *   *

The dissertation on Warren Hastings offers little that is this imaginative.[5]
According to a draft preface, its object is to continue the research begun by Sir
James Stephen and Sir John Strachey by giving 'an accurate and complete
account of the relations of Warren Hastings with Cheyt Sing and the Begums of
Oude', these being episodes that figured most importantly in Hastings's
impeachment. Because the events are so controversial, Strachey says he has
had to include a great number of extracts from the records of the time in order
to achieve his dual purpose:

My aim has not been merely destructive; I have not simply attempted to expose the
shortcomings of Mill; I have attempted to write an account based upon the evidence of
contemporary records, of the actual conduct, the actual motives, and the actual policy
of Hastings in two important sections of his Indian career.[6]

By the time of *Eminent Victorians* Strachey presented his historical
intentions as neither imposing nor proposing but exposing.[7] The scope of his
dissertation was wider and more diffuse. His examiners complained of its
obscure style and poor organization.[8] The masses of quotations in text and

footnotes that Strachey needed to expose Mill and Macaulay interfere with the narrative that is asserting Hastings's innocence and greatness. In addition to its unassimilated evidence, the dissertation's two purposes do not cohere stylistically. Fairly straightforward accounts of what was happening are rather jarringly interspersed with elaborate characterizations, summaries, and denunciations.

The difficulties that Strachey had with the writing of his dissertation, the incongruities of its styles, resulted first of all from the extent and complexity of his material. But they were also a consequence, it appears from the introduction to his dissertation, of the various accounts of Warren Hastings's administration that he had to work with. This interesting introduction, which was published in 1980, appears to be a mid-Edwardian reworking by Strachey of the original preface when he was thinking of turning *Warren Hastings, Cheyt Sing, and the Begums of Oude* into a book. To see the introduction in the context of Strachey's development as a writer of history, we first need to have some idea of what he did in his two-part dissertation.

The seven chapters on Cheyt Sing making up the first submitted version of Strachey's dissertation treat the relations between the Rajah of Benares and Hastings's Bengal government that culminated in the insurrection and expulsion of Cheyt Sing in 1781. Strachey is at pains in the first chapter to show how the illegitimate Cheyt Sing and his father were not hereditary potentates but robbers, tax collectors, and land-holders who had only recently become rajahs. The prose in which Strachey undermines their status becomes periodic at times. Chapter Two discusses the dependence of Cheyt Sing on the sovereignty of the East India Company, the argument here being interrupted by tableaux that a recent critic of the dissertation found smacking of Macaulay.[9] In maintaining Cheyt Sing's dependence, Strachey also fiercely attacks James Mill's 'jumble of incoherent arguments, of unbridled insinuations, and of malignant perversions of fact' (Dissertation, I 49). The third and fourth chapters concern Cheyt Sing's relations with the English governing Council in Calcutta, which became fatally divided when Hastings lost majority control of it to the three new members from England, one of whom was Philip Francis.

The summary narrative becomes leaner, as Strachey covers the developing Maratha War, Cheyt Sing's shuffling evasion of demands for troops or money, and the machinations of Francis that ended with Hastings shooting him in a duel. Hastings had said of Francis, 'I judge of his public conduct by my experience of his private, which I have found to be void of truth and honour', and Strachey observes nicely, 'after such words as these, a recourse to arms seems, even in the twentieth century, almost natural' (Dissertation, I 123). The last three chapters of Part I are about the revolt of Cheyt Sing. Page-long single-spaced quotations of evidence are given as Strachey traces the dispute between the Rajah and the Governor-General over the money due the Company for the Maratha Wars. Hastings fined Cheyt Sing fifty lacs of current rupees or £500,000 in late eighteenth-century sterling.[10] The correspondence of Hastings and Cheyt Sing, his arrest, the subsequent insurrection and massacre, then Hastings's retreat from Benares are covered in Chapter Six; the quelling of the revolt and replacement of Cheyt Sing, and the treatment of his female relatives in Chapter Seven.

Strachey's narrative of Hastings's surprise withdrawal and the consequent rumours that British rule in India had ended is dramatically effective. His Latinate adjectives, parallel clauses, and rhetorical questions anticipate their ironical use in his mature style: the natives remembered 'the tumultuous flight of the great Governor. He had disappeared, he had fled into the night; and who could tell when he would return?' (Dissertation, I 197) The chapter following this narrative is interrupted by a lengthy defense of Hastings's treatment of Cheyt Sing's women that Mill had so criticized. Strachey hotly describes Mill's misrepresentations as, 'the most disgraceful, the most wantonly malignant, and the most monstrous' of all his accusations; a phrase of Hastings's about the Ranee not escaping an examination concerning her treasure is contorted by Mill 'into an abominable license for indiscriminate plundering. Never was so terrible a charge based upon so frivolous a foundation' (Dissertation, I 219-220). Compared with this, the peroration at the end of Part I on the vanquished weak and foolish Cheyt Sing, who nearly brought down the great Governor-General, is calm.

The first version of Strachey's fellowship dissertation ended here. Two contemporary reactions to it may be compared. The first is that of the economic historian William Cunningham, who examined the dissertation for Trinity College. Strachey wrote his mother that Cunningham's main objection was to his dissertation's lack of originality; Strachey's view of Hastings's administration had already been established by Fitzjames Stephen and Uncle John. Holroyd adds that Cunningham also criticized the separation of the Cheyt Sing affair from that of the Begums of Oude, which made it less controversially important than the events Sir James and Sir John had investigated.[11] This led to Strachey's expanding his work in a further attempt at a Trinity fellowship. The other reaction was from Leonard Woolf, who was soon to be practicing English imperialism as a colonial civil servant. He apparently read the dissertation before going to Ceylon and found it 'too enthralling and not enough like a dissertation'; had it been less graceful, more laboured in its points, Strachey would obviously have been given a fellowship.[12] Leonard Woolf is quite simply sardonic here, for the writing in *Warren Hastings and Cheyt Sing*, uneven as it is, has at times a polish that is often regarded as inimical to the transmission of scholarly truth.

*   *   *

Warren Hastings's relations with Cheyt Sing were closely connected with the Vizier and Begums of Oude which adjoined the territory of Benares in the North of India. This wealthy, maladministered district remained independent until England annexed it after the Mutiny in 1858. Hastings's troubles with Oude began with the new Vizier, Asuph-ud-dowla, and a conflict in the governing Council between Hastings's and the majority's policies toward the independence of the Nabob's government, which itself was divided by the conflict between him and his mother and grandmother who controlled Oude's treasure. The role of these Begums in Cheyt Sing's revolt exacerbated the conflicts. Finally Hastings imprisoned the Begum's eunuchs until he obtained the money owing to the East India Company and restored the Nabob's authority. For the managers of Hastings's impeachment in London after his return from India, this despoiling of the Begums was among his most outrageous crimes. Strachey's account of these matters in Part II of his dissertation, which is also divided into seven chapters, forms a parallel narrative to Part I. The first and second chapters concern the majority of the Council's policy toward Oude and Hastings's efforts to implement it, and the third deals with his reforms in a treaty with Asuph-ud-dowla, and his financial support for the war with Mysore that the English were fighting. Chapters Four and Five discuss the nature of the affidavits about the Begums' support of Cheyt Sing. The last two chapters are about the treatment of the Begums and their eunuchs by Hastings's agent and then the Governor General's triumphant visit to Lucknow, the capital of Oude, after the Vizier's authority had been restored. Hastings had not been able to guarantee good government there, however, and with this point *Warren Hastings, Cheyt Sing, and the Begums of Oude* ends. There is no conclusion.

Again there are large infusions of quotation from the records into the narrative, but Strachey's indignation with the accounts of Hastings's enemies is somewhat abated. (On the question of the affidavits collected by Hastings's supporter the Judge Sir Elijah Impey, Strachey quotes the censure of Macaulay from Fitzjames Stephen's book on Nuncomar and Impey.) Hastings remains remotely superior but the portrait of Asuph-ud-dowla in Part II is more detailed and sympathetic than that of Cheyt Sing in the first part—and also more like some of the minor characters in Strachey's later biographies. Beset by powerful women, the Vizier led a life 'of gluttony, of intoxication, of abominable vice' (Dissertation, II 6).

His vacillating will, his hatred of business, his utter lack of ambition, combined to make him the most incompetent of rulers, and the enormous corpulence of his bodily frame appeared to symbolize a temperament which had fallen through sloth into a nerveless and incorrigible decay.[13]

Strachey's somewhat wordy description and imprecise imagery is shown up by Macaulay's more muscular writing:

. . . Asuph-ud-Dowlah was one of the weakest and most vicious of even Eastern princes. His life was divided between torpid repose and the most odious forms of sensuality. In his court there was boundless waste, throughout his dominions wretchedness and disorder.[14]

If Strachey's early prose is inferior to Macaulay's mature style, his sympathetic view of the Nabob is more paradoxical in portraying him as also pathetically honest and faithful, particularly to Hastings at the crucial juncture of the Mysore War. Strachey delights in the conclusion that 'it would indeed be difficult to exaggerate the debt which the Company owed this incompetent debauchee'. (Dissertation, II 64-5).

★   ★   ★

Strachey failed once more to gain a fellowship with his expanded dissertation, which he had resubmitted at the beginning of September, 1905. Instead of the lack of originality, it was now the writing and extensively quoted extracts that were criticized.[15] Whether, in reworking his unsuccessful dissertation for a book, Strachey intended to revise his method of presenting evidence to refute Mill and Macaulay is unknown, but the introduction he apparently composed later for *Warren Hastings, Cheyt Sing, and the Begums of Oude* suggests that the problems of style and arrangement were connected with the various historical attacks on Hastings's Indian adminstration which Strachey was trying directly or indirectly to refute.

After saying he is going to give an accurate, complete account of Hastings's involvements with the Rajah and the Begums, Strachey actually spends most of the introduction criticizing the historical accounts of Hastings by Mill, Macaulay, and Burke.[16] His concern here is more literary, more historiographic, than historical. Strachey's interest in the nature of historical writing was a lifelong concern, beginning with a Cambridge paper entitled 'The Historian of the Future', in November, 1903, and ending with his late miniature portraits of six historians. In the Cambridge essay Strachey offers a theory of historical writing that antedates his dissertation and is therefore interesting to compare with the introduction he wrote afterwards. Writing just a month after publication of G.E. Moore's *Principia Ethica*, Strachey applies Moore's analysis of good to the meaning and value of history. As a means to good ends histories are of little value because history does not repeat itself, but as goods in themselves Strachey finds them to be of great potential value. History is about true past events concerning man in society, but it cannot apply a scientific method to individual minds; for them a totally different 'artistic method' is required. Though this is never defined, it can be surmised from the intrinsic value of history, which according to Strachey depends on two conditions, 'first, the interest of the facts narrated, and secondly, the beauty of the narration'. The great historians who fulfill these conditions—he instances Gibbon, Michelet, Tacitus, Thucydides, and Carlyle—are stars to be contemplated for their own sake, not candles to illuminate the arid workshops of future historians.[17]

History as an art belonged therefore in the realm of *Principia Ethica*'s Ideal. And it did not take Lytton Strachey or his Cambridge brothers in the Apostles very long to realize that the incompatibiliy of intrinsic and instrumental value was a vulgar error in the interpretation of Moore, one that some critics of Bloomsbury continue to make. (The argument that science cannot deal with individual minds was another kind of vulgar error prevalent in early modernism.) Yet when Strachey shortly afterwards became a future historian himself in his dissertation, he encountered serious difficulties, as we have seen, with the interest of his facts and the art of their narration—both his own and that of the predecessors he was attempting to refute. And when he came to write the introduction to *Warren Hastings, Cheyt Sing, and the Begums of Oude* he was mainly concerned with the imagination of Macaulay, the style of Mill, the rhetoric of Burke, not their particular historical misrepresentations.

No English historical figure had more great prose stylists opposing him than Warren Hastings did. Hastings himself was a powerful writer, as his great enemy Francis acknowledged. In a *Spectator* piece, 'The Prose Style of Men of Action', Strachey wrote of Hastings's 'swelling and romantic utterance' as conveying at times the mystery as well as the grandeur of the East.[18] Philip Francis—described in Strachey's introduction as a Miltonic toad crouching by the ear of his Eve, Burke (Introduction, 238)—is generally recognized now as the author of the Junius Letters—those masterpieces of political invective that defended the importance of public opinion. Leslie Stephen thought their satire inferior to Swift's and their rhetoric to Burke's, but the very comparisons imply their power.[19] Edmund Burke was the prime parliamentary mover in Hastings's impeachment. In his dissertation Strachey alludes to his oratorical description of Hastings as ' . . . the head, the chief, and captain-general in iniquity—one in whom all the frauds, all the peculations, all the tyranny in India are embodied, disciplined, and arranged'.[20] And in his introduction, Strachey describes Burke's utterances as standing out

from among the rest in virtue both of their hideous violence of language and their splendid elevation of thought. the scintillating wisdom, the passionate nobility, the gorgeous rhetoric, which characterize Burke's speeches against Hastings, have given them a place in literature which they would certainly have ill deserved if sanity, clarity, and accuracy were the sole tests of literary merit. (Introduction, 227).

In these antithetical characteristics lay Strachey's problem as a writer of history. More celebrated than Burke's speeches at Hastings's trial, however, were Richard Brinsley Sheridan's. The playwright turned politician created a sensation with his defense of the Begums; phrases such as 'their treasures were their treasons'[21] were remembered rather than involved explanations by Hastings and his defenders of the women's duplicity. Then there was Fox's oratory. Macaulay said the managers of Hastings's impeachment before the House of Lords 'contained an array of speakers such as perhaps had not appeared together since the great age of Athenian eloquence'.[22] To which must be added Macaulay's own eloquence, though not Mill's. James Mill's terrible prose was, nevertheless, another kind of rhetoric used against Hastings, according to Strachey. Its 'crabbed, cold, and dull' style, the opposite of Macaulay's, gives the false impression that Mill 'has sacrificed every grace of language and every audacity of thought for the sake of meticulous accuracy', when actually his style's dryness 'is nothing more than the cloak for a multitude of errors'. Fitzjames Stephen accused Mill of bad faith, and Strachey speculates on the psychology of a historian's mind that will produce such distortions (Introduction, 226, 230). Macaulay's 'Warren Hastings', on the other hand, is a masterpiece—but of imagination, not history. His

Hastings is a Satanic villain of romance, Strachey exaggeratedly claims, who vanishes under the light of impartial inquiry but will live in the memories of common readers 'until there arises a greater master of the art of writing, who will choose to invest the facts of Indian history with the glamour of literature, and make the truth more attractive than even fiction itself' (Introduction, 225-6).

Strachey's introduction to *Warren Hastings, Cheyt Sing, and the Begums of Oude* thus finds, particularly in the writings of Burke, Mill, and Macaulay, an opposition between truth and art—between the facts narrated and the beauty of their narration. It must have been a dismaying recognition for a young man with an elaborately developed prose style, an Apostolic passion for reality, and a strong family interest in imperial history. As a disciple of Moore's, Strachey cared too much for truth to accept, like some post-modern critics, the equation of history with fiction. He knew that 'in all history, the evidence must be "treated"', as he says in his introduction when describing the supposedly impartial style of Mill (Introduction, 230). This was the chief problem with the writing of his dissertation: he does not 'treat' his evidence enough; long quotations from the records remain unassimilated as he moves between explanation, narration, and refutation. Yet the great prose 'treatments' by Junius, Burke, Sheridan, Fox, Macaulay, and even to some degree Hastings himself were too unhistorically fictive.

Strachey did not go on very far with the revision of his dissertation after the introduction that is so preoccupied with the historical rhetoric. Eventually he would resolve this dilemma of the literariness of history, absorbing the influence of Macaulay and others while maintaining his belief in the importance of truth, by becoming an ironist and limiting his historical scope to biography. (The writings of two other opposed eighteenth century prose-writers of genius would help him here: the ironical history of Gibbon and the moralized biographies of Johnson, who was also a friend and correspondent of Hastings.) In ironical biography Strachey found the freedom to write descriptive and narrative prose about the past that was critical yet imaginative, even flamboyant, and whose elucidations of truth, unlike the historical misrepresentations of Hastings's great literary detractors, could be appreciated as belonging to the art of irony.

*   *   *

Beyond problems with the interest of the facts to be narrated and with beautiful narrations to be confuted, Strachey also had to contend in his dissertation with changing attitudes toward imperialism in the Edwardian period. These may also have interfered with the revisions of *Warren Hastings, Cheyt Sing, and the Begums of Oude* into a book. The Boer War had already disillusioned many in England about imperialism. Leonard Woolf, looking back from the late Twenties, saw 1905, the year Strachey resubmitted his dissertation, as the beginning of a new period of complete revolt against European imperialism, signalled by the Japanese defeat of the Russians.[23] The essentially capitalistic purposes of imperialism had already been analyzed by J.A. Hobson in his very influential *Imperialism*, which Strachey could have read as articles in the New Liberal *Speaker* as early as 1902. In his revised introduction, however, Strachey was still writing with unironic enthusiasm of 'those wise and wondrous actions, those portentous revolutions, which from the time of Clive to the time of Dalhousie, have gone to the making of our vast, our mysterious, our noble Empire of India!' (Introduction, 231). In 1907 Strachey reviewed the letters of his namesake and godfather Lord Lytton, who wrote minor verse under the name Owen Meredith, and defended him as a viceroy, though not as a poet; he identified himself with Lytton in describing the Viceroy's close friendship with Fitzjames Stephen, whom Strachey associated with Thoby Stephen, his dear friend who had died the year before.[24] The next year he praised so highly for the *Spectator* a book on Indian guides converted through English discipline from savage barbarian to noble virtue that James Strachey included it in the posthumous *Spectatorial Essays* as a reminder of how his brother remained under the ancestral spell of British India despite his later pacifism and anti-imperialism.[25] The review belongs to Kipling's India rather than Forster's.

Lytton Strachey's last word on Hastings appeared in the *Spectator* in 1910 as a review of selections from his state papers. It could almost serve as the absent conclusion to his dissertation. The opening quotation from Hastings is, in fact, the same one he used at the end of his revised introduction to the dissertation. Strachey again laments that 'for some mysterious reason one of the most enthralling and stupendous interludes in English history has been left untouched by English historians'. The biographies of Hastings are 'unscientific' (a word he would not have used in 'The Historian of the Future'); historians from Macaulay onwards have concentrated on personalities rather than 'the great movements of peoples and policies' (a criticism that would be made of Strachey's own biographies). Again Hastings's actions in Oude are defended but without quite so much insistence on the blamelessness of the Governor-General. Here are his last published words on Warren Hastings:

His severities towards the Begums' Ministers were the necessary result of his determination to secure peace and order to a vast number of human beings, and it is to his honour that, having the intelligence to understand what his duty was, he possessed no less the courage to perform it.[26]

This is what Strachey's defense of imperialism seems to come down to: the suppression of violence and confusion, for the sake of security and stability. He does not mention what the cost was in the freedom of those for whom the suppressing and preserving were supposedly being carried out. In Strachey's public Edwardian writings the behaviour of the British in India is justified by the need for peace rather than the usual motives of power or profit or even civilization.[27]

The ethical principles behind this justification are revealed in the Apostle and other Cambridge papers that Strachey was also writing around the time of his dissertation. They display the values concealed or implicit in the dissertation and published reviews—values which were leading to a basic shift in Strachey's attitude towards imperialism. Though he may never have been completely free from the historical romance of the British raj, his view of late Victorian and early modern imperialism became quite grim. How remote the admiration for the consequences of Hastings's actions is from the conclusion, half a dozen years later, to 'The End of General Gordon': 'At any rate, it had all ended very happily—in a glorious slaughter of 20,000 Arabs, a vast addition to the British Empire, and a step in the Peerage for Sir Evelyn Baring.'[28]

To be sure Hastings was not Baring or even Gordon, but it is tempting to speculate on what might have been. Had Strachey been less romantically a hero-worshipper when he wrote on Warren Hastings, had the consequences of imperialism been more revealed to him, had he been less trammelled by his own family's imperial history, then his treatment of Hastings might have developed some of the ironic comic and tragic paradoxes of history and human behaviour that so fascinated him in his later biographies. The verdict of P.J. Marshall's thorough modern investigation of Hastings's trial, for instance, is that although Francis, Burke, Sheridan and the other investigators of Hastings's impeachment deserved to lose their case, by most standards Hastings sacrificed justice to the needs of the East India Company in his dealings with both Cheyt Sing and the Begums of Oude. The conflict of the Company's despotism with the security of the native subjects was the central issue of the impeachment, according to Marshall, but the rhetoric of Sheridan and Burke considerably distorted Hastings's problems, while his justifications were oversimplified. The seven-year trial was a cruel ordeal for Hastings but it also did much damage to Burke. For all the bitterness of their opposition, however, both men had deep respect for native customs and culture, which is more than can be said of Mill and Macaulay with their utilitarian ignorance of Indian religion and literature.[29]

Strachey brings out none of these antinomies in his various accounts of Warren Hastings. The Governor-General's personality and character remain impenetrable throughout. (If Strachey had chosen a picture of Hastings as he did for his eminent Victorians, it ought to have been Lawrence's marvellously enigmatic portrait of Hastings in implacable old age.) A suggestion of how Strachey might have treated Hastings, if the time had not been out of joint, may be found perhaps in the book yet another Strachey wrote on India and imperialism. The Labour Cabinet Minister and writer John Strachey— Lytton's cousin, the son of the *Spectator*'s St Loe—carried this family tradition into the fifth generation with *The End of Empire*, first published in 1959. This is how he describes Hastings:

Brilliant, scholarly, brave, arbitrary, financially lax (sometimes even to his own disadvantage), loving India, conquering India, enriching India, despoiling India, this strange man stands out as the first, and perhaps the only, fascinating figure amongst the long, stiff line of Governor-Generals who came and went over the next hundred and seventy-five years.

He was impeached for all the wrong reasons; he could not have been anything but an imperialist in his time, and was in fact genuinely concerned with the welfare of the Indians.

What was unique in Hastings amongst Governor-Generals was not that he was a reformer, but that he was an intellectual. He was that rare and usually uncomfortable being, an intellectual functioning as a man of action . . . His repute rests, I think above all, on what he was not: on the fact that he was not an ordinary, straightforward, normal, hearty Englishman . . . He was far more sympathetic to his Indian contemporaries than the virtuous but frigid noblemen who succeeded him. In old age Hastings said that he had loved India a little better than his own country. It may well have been true. A man may stay to love what he comes to rape. Above all, he loved not only India, as many a stolid nineteenth- and twentieth-century sahib was to do; he loved Indians.[30]

The influence of Bloomsbury from Lytton Strachey and Leonard Woolf to E.M. Forster is not difficult to trace here.

'The Writing "I" Has Vanished': Virginia Woolf's Last Short Fictions

Susan Dick

In January of 1941, Virginia and Leonard Woolf were living at Monks House in the Sussex village of Rodmell. The previous September, their London house in Mecklenburgh Square had been badly damaged during an air raid and the following month their former house at 52 Tavistock Square (on which they continued to hold the lease) was destroyed by bombs. Since the fall of 1939, when because of the war they had begun to live permanently at Monks House, the Woolfs had spent some time each fortnight in London. Now, with their Mecklenburgh Square house uninhabitable, and with constant air raids on London and Sussex making travel extremely difficult, these visits became less frequent. They were, as Leonard Woolf later wrote, 'marooned' in the country.[1] And although country living had always given Virginia Woolf much pleasure, this steady diet of it left her feeling at times both bored and isolated.

She spent much of her time writing. *Pointz Hall*, the novel she had begun to write as a relief from the fact-bound biography of Roger Fry (published in July of 1940) was finished, as *Between the Acts*, on 26 February 1941. While working on her novel in January and February, she also wrote two reviews, 'Ellen Terry' and 'Mrs Thrale', and she continued to work on 'Anon' and 'The Reader', the opening chapters of an unfinished critical work, called tentatively, 'Reading at Random'. In March, she completed two works of short fiction and started a third.

The discussion that follows focuses on these short fictions. 'The Symbol' and 'The Watering Place', like the unfinished 'English Youth', were found among Virginia Woolf's papers after her death, on 28 March 1941. Richard Ellmann has reminded us that 'we cannot know completely the intricacies with which any mind negotiates with its surroundings to produce literature'.[2] As his own work so eloquently demonstrates, however, we can explore those 'surroundings' and speculate about the complex process of those negotiations. This is what I would like to do here. In June of 1940, Woolf reflected in her diary on the effect of the war on their lives. ' . . . the war—our waiting while the knives sharpen for the operation—has taken away the outer wall of security. No echo comes back. I have no surroundings.' (*DV* 299) Part of the 'surroundings' Woolf felt she had lost were her readers. Who, she wondered, would read *Roger Fry*, then about to be published, or indeed, *Pointz Hall*, still unfinished? '. . . the writing "I", has vanished', she had noted two weeks earlier. 'No audience. No echo. Thats part of one's death.' (*DV* 293) My interest is in the ways that Woolf's last short fictions may help us to understand both what this radical change in her surroundings meant to her and how she attempted to deal with it in her fiction. My discussion is meant to supplement those of others who have sought to illuminate some of Woolf's late writings by considering them within the context of the last months of her life.[3] As we shall see, the contrast between 'The Symbol', a deeply personal meditative piece, and 'The Watering Place' and 'English Youth', sketches based vigorously on observation, embodies the tension she felt throughout her life, and with special intensity now, between the impulse to introspection and the effort to balance, or, as now, fight that impulse by engaging herself in close observation of the scene around her.

★   ★   ★

Virginia Woolf makes no reference in her diary or her letters to 'The Symbol' or 'The Watering Place'. On the day that she recorded in her diary the completion of *Between the Acts*, 26 February 1941, she also transcribed a conversation, overheard in the ladies' lavatory at the Sussex Grill at Brighton, which she would repeat in 'The Watering Place' (*DV* 356-57). The holograph draft of this sketch, called 'The Ladies Lavatory', is found at the back of a writing book, where it follows a draft of 'The Symbol' (called there 'Sketches'). The typescript draft of 'The Symbol', which appears to be made up of pages from several drafts, is dated 1 March 1941. The typescript of 'The Watering Place' is undated (*CSF* 304). Since it is impossible to know which of these two typescripts preceded the other, I have followed the order of the holograph drafts in the discussion that follows.

The mountain village setting of 'The Symbol' is one Woolf had not used in her fiction before. In choosing it now, she was giving expression to a 'persistent vision' she had had for some time. On 22 June 1937, she wrote in her diary, 'I would like to write a dream story about the top of a mountain. Now why? About lying in the snow; about rings of colour; silence . . . and the solitude. I can't though. But shant I, one of these days, indulge myself in some short releases into that world?' (*DV* 95, Woolf's ellipsis). On 16 November 1938, in a diary passage beside which she wrote 'symbolical', she noted: 'There are very few mountain summit moments. I mean, looking out at peace from a height.' (*DV* 187) And after recording the completion of the earlier draft of *Between the Acts* on 23 November 1940, she anticipated what she would write next and concluded, 'then I shall brew some moments of high pressure. I think of taking my mountain top—that persistent vision—as a starting point' (*DV* 341).

While the association of the mountain-top with an expansive perspective that brings solitude and peace is familiar, Woolf's vision derived, I believe, from some particularly personal associations, as well. One cluster of these centres around her father, Leslie Stephen. During the last months of her life, she was thinking a great deal about her father. Indeed, her talks in February and March with Octavia Wilberforce, her friend and doctor, led Octavia to conclude that she was 'haunted' by her father, a conclusion Leonard Woolf confirmed.[4] When in November of 1940 she stopped writing 'A Sketch of the Past', she had been recalling life with her father at 22 Hyde Park Gate in the difficult years after her mother's death (*MB* 143ff). In December, she reread some of her parents' letters and found in their lives an enviable serenity. 'How serene and gay even their life reads to me', she wrote in her diary, 'no mud; no whirlpools . . . Nothing turbulent; nothing involved: no introspection'. (*DV* 345) She had drawn on her father's fame as a mountain climber in *To the Lighthouse* where Mr Ramsay (a character modelled on Leslie Stephen) casts himself in the role of the leader of a doomed expedition who knows he must die before morning 'now that the snow has begun to fall and the mountain-top is covered in mist' (*TL* 58). Her thoughts about her father when she wrote that scene and again now may have prompted her to recall Thomas Hardy's sonnet, 'The Schreckhorn (With Thoughts of Leslie Stephen)', in which Hardy sees the 'aloof' and 'looming' mountain as 'a guise' of Stephen, who had risked his life to be the first man to climb it.[5] The final lines of the sestet, in which Hardy asks if at the end of his life Stephen will be drawn to the mountain, may in particular have been in her mind. 'Will he', Hardy wonders, 'in old love, hitherward escape',

> And the eternal essence of his mind
> Enter this silent adamantine shape,
> And his low voicing haunt its slipping snows
> When dawn that calls the climber dyes them rose?[6]

As we shall see, the association of death with the mountain is present throughout Woolf's sketch.

Another work Woolf may have been remembering when she chose the setting of 'The Symbol' is the description Leonard Woolf wrote of her during their courtship and which he records having shown her. She appears in this as 'Aspasia' and is associated by Leonard with 'hills, standing very clear but distant against a cold blue sky; there is snow upon them which no sun has ever melted and no man has ever trodden'. 'Sometimes', he writes near the end of this piece, 'I think . . . she is made merely of the eternal snow and the rocks which form the hidden centre of reality. And then I swear that this cannot be true, that the sun in her comes from a heart'.[7] The comment, 'more on Aspasia', which appears in her 'Notes for Reading at Random', further suggests that Leonard's evocative portrait may have been in her mind at this time (*AR* 370).

Finally, the beautiful opening paragraph of 'The Symbol' may also originate partly in the snows that covered the downs that winter. In January she described Asheham down as 'red, purple, dove blue grey, with the cross so melodramatically against it. What is the phrase I always remember—or forget. Look your last on all things lovely'. A few lines later she added, 'And t'other side of the hill there'll be no rosy blue red snow' (*DV* 351-2). This elegiac mood, like this landscape, dominates 'The Symbol'.

There was a little dent on the top of the mountain like a crater on the moon. It was filled with snow, iridescent like a pigeon's breast, or dead white. There was a scurry of dry particles now and again, covering nothing. It was too high for breathing flesh or fur covered life. All the same the snow was iridescent one moment; and blood red; and pure white, according to the day. (*CSF* 282)

Like a camera scanning a broad vista, the narrator's eye moves from the top of the mountain, where there is nothing but snow and the changing reflections of light on snow, down to the village and the churchyard with the graves of mountain climbers, and finally to the 'lady' sitting on the balcony of a hotel writing a letter to her elder sister. The narrator's expansive perspective contracts to that of the woman on the balcony. We see the scene in front of her as she does, and then as she describes it in her letter.

In *The Waves* we never learn what 'the lady' of Elvedon who 'sits between the two long windows' is writing (*W* 12). By contrast, this unnamed woman, who brings that earlier figure to mind, is given a voice through both her narrated thoughts and her letter to her sister. Although a letter is public in the way that a diary is not, this particular letter has many of the qualities of a narrative written in the private voice. It is a deeply meditative letter in which the woman attempts to explain her present state of mind and, as part of her effort to do that, tells over scenes from the past. The epistolary format functions here rather as it did in Woolf's early biography of her sister, which was written as a letter to Vanessa Bell's young son, Julian.[8] The special bond between the correspondents leads the letter-writer to speak with both intimacy and candour.

The reader starts to overhear the letter just as the woman tries to articulate the significance of the mountain. ' "The mountain", the lady wrote, sitting on the balcony of the hotel, "is a symbol . . ." She paused' (*CSF* 282). Unlike the 'fin in a waste of waters' (*W* 134ff) which was a deeply personal symbol for Woolf (see eg *D*VIII 113), the mountain is a familiar, public symbol, an image (often) of a goal to be reached, if reached at all, only through supreme effort. The woman on the balcony, however, finds that this conventional reading does not capture what she sees in the mountain. 'We are always climbing to some height', she thinks, 'that was the cliché. But it did not represent what was in her mind's eye; after seeing through her glasses the virgin height' (*CSF* 283).

In the holograph draft, the limitations of 'the cliché' are elaborated. 'But that was unfitting', the woman thinks. 'The other thing that this peak represented was not at all a cliché: in fact it was something that far from running into ink spontaneously, remained almost unspeakable even to herself.' (Hol 3, *CSF* 305) In another passage omitted from the typescript draft, the woman does, however, attempt to find analogies for this 'unspeakable' symbol. After looking at the graves and reflecting (in a cancelled sentence) that 'The virgin peak has never been climbed', the woman thinks: 'It was a menace, something lying cleft in the mind like two parts of a broken dish: two numbers: two or two numbers which cannot be added: a problem that is insoluble.' (Hol 1, *CSF* 305). The image of the severed parts that cannot be united, recalling as it does the contrary image of the globe, which Woolf often used to represent a unified vision, also appears in the earliest draft of 'Anon'. Woolf is comparing our enjoyment of song with the instinct of self-preservation. 'Only when we put two and two together—two pencil strokes, two written words, two bricks [notes] do we overcome dissolution and set up some stake against oblivion.' (*AR* 403) This passage also echoes a comment Woolf made in a letter to Ethel Smyth on 12 January. Ethyl had invited Woolf to visit her, but Leonard had said he preferred she not go. 'I think its a bad thing that we're so inseparable', she wrote. 'But how, in this world of separation, dare one break it?' (*L*VI 460).

In the typescript draft of 'The Symbol' the failure to 'put two and two together' takes the less personal form of the scenes the woman watches from her balcony. These are 'Entertainments to pass the time; seldom leading to any conclusion, . . . There was something fantastic about them, airy inconclusive' (*CSF* 282). Embodying as they do the absence of closure, these scenes are among the 'Inconclusions' to which the cancelled title on the typescript draft of 'The Symbol' refers.

While the woman writes her letter, she also watches a party of young men prepare to climb the mountain, cross a crevasse as they ascend, and then, near the end of the sketch, suddenly disappear from sight as they fall to their deaths. Her comments on their progress interrupt the reminiscences she records in her letter of the time she spent on the Isle of Wight with her mother, who was dying slowly of cancer. Through these fragmented memories we piece together part of the woman's past: an engagement prolonged by a parent's illness, followed by a marriage which brought an end to dreams of adventure. '"I have always had a great desire to explore for myself", she tells her sister. "But of course, when the time came it seemed more sensible, considering our long engagement, to marry."' (*CSF* 283). In the typescript, Woolf does not include passages from the holograph in which the woman says a great deal more about her present state of mind, which is one of acute despondency.

In the holograph, the woman begins her recollections by trying to describe her mood:

Am I enjoying myself, she wrote, with what remained of the ink in her pen? [No?] to tell you the truth, I have practically no [emotions?] left. I am sitting on a balcony and at one o'clock the gong will sound . . . I have not cut my nails. I have not done my hair. When I read a book I cannot finish it. (Hol 3, *CSF* 305, corrected)

She then confesses to her sister (in both drafts) that she used to long for their mother's death, to see it as a 'symbol' of her freedom. She then continues, in the holograph:

What is it that makes me write all this? I should I know be entering as they say into your life. That is the only way in which we can escape . . . She looked at the mountain . . . There are people who say that's the way to make two and two come together. Am I writing nonsense? I am only trying to tell you what I am thinking on the balcony. I am aware just as they are of the desire to master the height. The most absurd dreams come to me. I think if I could get there, I should be happy to die. I think there, in the crater, which looks like one of the spots on the moon, I should find the answer. (Hol 4, *CSF* 306; Woolf's ellipses)

Woolf's preoccupation with her father is again suggested in the first part of the passage, for the woman's confession that she had longed for her mother to die recalls and, one suspects, vastly simplifies Woolf's own feelings in 1903 as Leslie Stephen died slowly of cancer. 'Altogether it was a time of mounting and almost unendurable distress', Quentin Bell writes. 'Why must he die? And if he must why can't he?' 'Such, roughly, were Virginia's sentiments', Bell concludes.[9] The woman's reflections in the typescript on the life of adventure she relinquished by marrying are not made with bitterness, and if they have an autobiographical basis, it may be in the quiet life Leonard imposed upon his wife whenever signs of illness appeared.

The process of association at work in the next part of the passage, in which the woman seeks to 'escape' by entering into her sister's life and thus uniting the severed parts, movingly anticipates a passage from Woolf's final diary entry: 'This windy corner. And Nessa is at Brighton, and I am imagining how it would be if we could infuse souls.' (DV 359) The latter part of the passage, with its echo of the lines from Othello which she had used in Mrs Dalloway—'If it were now to die 'twere now to be most happy' (MD 39, 203)—is, it seems, the mountain summit vision which she seeks, but cannot attain. This passage does not appear in the typescript draft where the woman's desire to escape from her present life takes the more mundane form of her complaints against the omnipresence of the mountain and the boredom of hotel and village life, a mood that reflects Woolf's own periodic irritation with her 'vegetable exist-ence' in Rodmell (LVI 483).

In the typescript, death comes not as the welcome conclusion to a moment of vision, as it is imagined in the holograph, but instead takes the form, as it was doing so often in the war and had in Woolf's own life, of sudden and absurd loss. 'The pen fell from her hand, and a drop of ink straggled in a zig zag line down the page. The young men had disappeared.' (CSF 284) Later that evening, after the bodies of the climbers have been brought back to the village, the woman returns to her unfinished letter. She tries to find words that will express the meaning of this event, but again although the 'old clichés will come in very handy', they prove inadequate. 'They died in an attempt to discover . . .' she writes, but cannot complete the sentence. The story ends with the final inconclusion: 'There seemed no fitting conclusion. And she added, "Love to the children", and her pet name.'

This story seems in both its versions to be a projection of Woolf's own state of mind. The woman on the balcony writing to her elder sister (unnamed in the typescript, but in the holograph named Rosamond, like one of the sisters in Woolf's early story), telling over scenes from the past and attempting to articulate her despondency in the present is as radically isolated as Woolf felt herself to be. The silence she felt around her in Rodmell becomes in 'The Symbol' the letter-writer's own silence, her inability to find words to express first what the mountain symbolizes and then what one can say about the deaths of the young men. By giving this woman a past but no future, and by not quoting the 'pet name' with which she signs her letter, Woolf takes her further into the silence already impinging upon her. In the end, we as readers imitate in a chilling way the role of the emergent reader as Woolf described it in her unfinished second chapter of 'Reading at Random'. 'He can pause; he can ponder; he can compare;' she wrote of the reader, 'he can draw back from the page and see behind it a man sitting alone in the centre of the labyrinth of words in a college room thinking of suicide . . . He can read directly what is on the page, or, drawing aside, can read what is not written . . . We are in a world where nothing is concluded.'[10] 'Inconclusions' may be, as in this figure, rich with possibilities; however, they may also be, as in 'The Symbol', menacing anticipations of the inability to put two and two together, of the dissolution that takes its final form in death.

*   *   *

In April of 1939, Woolf described in 'A Sketch of the Past' three 'exceptional moments' she had experienced as a child. 'Two of these moments ended in a state of despair', she recalled. 'The other ended, on the contrary, in a state of satisfaction.' (MB 71) Despair and satisfaction: two states of mind Woolf had moved between all her life. She recalled in her memoir that the satisfaction she experienced after the third 'shock' came from her ability 'through reason to provide an explanation' for the 'sledge-hammer blow'. She realizes now, she says, that it is the 'shock-receiving capacity' that makes her a writer.

I feel that I have had a blow; but it is not, as I thought as a child, simply a blow from an enemy hidden behind the cotton wool of daily life; it is or will become a revelation of some order; it is a token of some real thing behind appearances; and I make it real by putting it into words. It is only by putting it into words that I make it whole; this wholeness means that it has lost its power to hurt me; it gives me, perhaps because by doing so I take away the pain, a great delight to put the severed parts together. (MB 72)

I quote this lengthy passage because it seems to me central to a full reading of Woolf's last sketches. In her memoir she describes the powers she feared she was losing by the time she wrote 'The Symbol', a fear she expresses there, I believe, through her imaginary letter-writer, who fails to find the words she needs and who cannot put the 'severed parts together'. When the young climbers die, she seems bound by an emotional and verbal paralysis and can offer only the inadequate clichés of consolation. 'But words have been used too often', the narrator of Jacob's Room notes as she concludes her exuberant celebration of letters as the 'stays and props' that 'lace our days together and make of life a perfect globe' (91). The letter-writer in 'The Symbol', like Woolf herself in the last month of her life, has lost confidence in her power to find the words that hang 'sweet beneath the leaf' (JR 92). 'But shall I ever write again one of those sentences that gives me intense pleasure', she asked herself on 26 February, after recording the scene she would recreate in 'The Watering Place' (DV 357). And without this power, and the 'writing "I"' who had used it, the 'enemy' could no longer be subdued in language.

'The Symbol' expresses this loss of the 'writing "I"' with great poignancy. Woolf's determination to 'conquer this mood' (DV 358) which, as Susan

Kenney convincingly argues, is reflected in the revised ending of *Between the Acts*, is absent from this sketch. Not even the consolation of an heroic attempt, which strengthened Mr Ramsay's resolve as he imagined certain death, can mitigate the failure of the dead climbers. Woolf's own attempt not to be engulfed by 'this trough of despair' (*DV* 354) reasserts itself once more, however, movingly if obliquely, in 'The Watering Place'.

*   *   *

The rhythmical exchange between opposites that informed both Woolf's life and her works—the movement between fact and vision, being and nonbeing, effort and acquiescence, satisfaction and despair; the question is life solid or shifting; the rhythm of expanding and contracting perspectives—is embodied in the contrast between her last two complete short fictions. 'No: I intend no introspection', she wrote in her diary on 8 March 1941. 'I mark Henry James's sentence: Observe perpetually' (*DV* 357). 'The Watering Place' is, as I have already indicated, as firmly based on observation as 'The Symbol' is on introspection. The narrator places no self-reflective commentator in the scene she presents and she concerns herself only with what an observer might see and hear: the inhabitants of the seaside town whose 'shelly look' associates them with the fishy smell that permeates the town and with the shells that litter the beach; the restaurant and its customers, some of whose voices we overhear in the ladies' lavatory. None of the irritation and disgust found in the diary entry in which Woolf records this conversation and describes some other women as parasitical 'white slugs', is heard in the sketch. The 'common little tarts' she overheard in the lavatory are refined in her sketch into 'three young ladies', although their harsh voices remain unchanged. In her sketch, Woolf also omits her description of herself listening to them while she sat 'behind a thin door, p－－－ing as quietly as I could' (*DV* 357), a comic scene that remains unthinkable even in Woolf's late and unpublished fiction. Indeed, the lavatory setting, along with the punning title of the sketch, are unusual for Woolf and they underscore the contrast between 'The Watering Place' and 'The Symbol'.

Besides removing herself, as it were, from the lavatory in the sketch, Woolf also omitted in the typed version an extensive description in the holograph of the lavatory attendant. The 'lives of the obscure' had always fascinated Woolf and in 'The Ladies Lavatory' she tried to imagine how a lavatory attendant would write her memoirs.

When, in old age, they look back through the corridors of memory, their past must be different from any other. It must be cut up: disconnected. The door must be always opening: and shutting. They can have no settled relations with their kind. The memoirs of a lavatory attendant have never been written. (Hol 2, *CSF* 307)

At the end of the sketch, the narrator thinks of this woman's restless life again. 'She inhabits a fluctuating water world . . . constantly tossed up and down like a piece of sea weed. She has no continuity. The rush of water is always floating her up and down.' (Hol 4) This transformation of the lavatory attendant into an inhabitant of an underwater world echoes the change the narrator sees when the town, in the holograph a 'gross body' by day, becomes 'a fairy town' as it sinks down into the night (Hol 1), a simplicity in the final paragraph of the typescript draft:

> But at night the town looks quite ethereal. There is a white glow on the horizon. There are hoops and coronets in the street. The town has sunk down into the water. And the skeleton only is picked out in fairy lamps. (*CSF* 286)

★   ★   ★

As well as writing these two short fictions, Woolf was also considering in the last weeks of her life composing portraits of her friends. Late in February she proposed to Octavia Wilberforce that she write about Octavia's childhood. Woolf had first met Octavia Wilberforce, a doctor who shared a house in Brighton with the actress Elizabeth Robins, in 1928. In December of 1940, she began sending milk and cream from her farm in Henfield to the Woolfs and visiting them occasionally at Monks House.[11] A distant link between their families prompted Woolf to refer to Octavia as 'a cousin' when she wrote in January to Vita Sackville-West and in February to Ethel Smyth to announce teasingly that she had 'a new lover, a doctor, a Wilberforce, a cousin' (see *LVI* 462, 465, and *DV* 48 n5). Octavia told Woolf she was both bewildered and 'immensely flattered' that Woolf should want to write a sketch about her, but warned her that she would find her 'dull'.[12] Woolf disagreed. She admired in Octavia the combination of power and reticence, and envied Octavia's ability to do useful work. '. . . she's healing the sick by day, and controlling the fires by night', Woolf wrote on 13 March to Elizabeth Robins, who was then in America (*LVI* 479).

A letter Octavia wrote to Elizabeth Robins the following day fills in the background of Woolf's interest in 'Octavia's story' (*DV* 359) and gives us a moving picture of her mood at this time. Octavia had been to visit Woolf who told her, she reported, that 'she had been feeling desperate—depressed to the lowest depths, had just finished a story. Always felt like this—but specially useless just now. The village wouldn't even allow her to fire watch—could do nothing—whereas my life—'. Octavia praised Woolf's writing, pointing out that no one else could write as she did. 'And then suddenly we talk of Lavington and my childhood', Octavia wrote, 'she says she sees the background and the beauty and peace . . .'[13] A week later when they discussed the portrait again, Woolf told Octavia that her other biographies, *Orlando* and *Roger Fry*, were failures. She thought she would probably do Octavia 'more like Orlando'. Then she added, 'but I can't write, I've not the art . . . I'm buried down here—I've not the stimulation of seeing people. I can't settle to it.'[14]

In wanting to write 'Octavia's story' Woolf was trying to follow Leonard's advice that she 'think more about outside things',[15] and, as she told herself, 'avoid introspection'. Her interest also reflects a preoccupation with memory and the past which we find throughout her career and, as Lyndall Gordon has also noted,[16] especially in the works of this period: *Between the Acts*, her unfinished memoir, 'The Symbol', 'The Ladies Lavatory', and her unfinished history of English literature. Contemplation of the past, particularly the pasts of others whether real or imaginary, might make her think less about herself in a present that seemed to anticipate no future (see eg *DV* 299, *LVI* 475).

Three fragments of sketches—'English Youth' and 'Another Sixpence' in holograph, and a single untitled typescript page[17]—appear to be all that survive of Woolf's desire to 'englobe' Octavia's story, 'English youth in 1900' (*DV* 359). Some of the details in the typescript sketch are based on Octavia's letters to Woolf, but the central incident is one she must have recounted in conversation.[18] The child in the sketch, who like Octavia is much younger than her siblings, is told by her sister to say 'damn' in the middle of tea and she'll give her a sixpence. The little girl does so and is summoned by her father to his library for a spanking.

'Let down your drawers' he said. He raised his hand over her bare bottom. 'D' he said and struck her. A another stroke. M a third. She shrieked and tried to get down. But there was a fourth letter it seemed N.
That lesson in spelling was one of the few she ever had.

The presentation of the father as simultaneously punisher and instructor is certainly suggestive; unfortunately, the typescript ends soon after this scene.

* * *

When in November of 1940 Woolf turned from her story 'The Legacy' (which ends melodramatically with a husband's discovery that his wife's death was suicide) to her memoir, she noted the contrast between the two. 'Then dipped into my memoirs: too circuitous and unrelated: too many splutters: as it stands. A real life has no crisis: . . . All the same, I can weave a very thick pattern, one of these days, out of that pattern of detail.' (*DV* 335) Her life was, however, to have its crisis. Leonard Woolf, Quentin Bell, and others who have looked back over this period of Woolf's life have found it impossible to say just when she began to consider taking her own life. She makes no references to her decision in her diary and her last letters to her friends give no hint of it.[18] The letters written at the time by the people most closely involved—Leonard Woolf, Octavia Wilberforce, and Vanessa Bell—combine to give a vivid picture of Virginia Woolf's mood during these last weeks. The nervous strain that always accompanied the completion of a book, the lack of enough good food, the isolation of Rodmell, and the war, all contributed to her growing depression.

Woolf's belief that she would weave a pattern out of the details of her memoir and her assumption that she could discover a pattern behind the cotton wool of ordinary life (*MB* 72) took a sinister form now as she perceived a destructive pattern in her own life. She had been mad during the first war, she would be mad during this one. She spoke of this fear to Octavia Wilberforce,

whom Leonard insisted that she see as a doctor on 27 March. Octavia told her
the pattern could work to her advantage: she had recovered before, she would
recover this time. There was no one she wanted more to help, she told her, as
she urged her to take her advice and try to rest. It may have been during this
visit that Woolf asked her if there wasn't anything she might do for her,
perhaps catalogue her books, an offer Octavia later regretted not accepting.[20]

Vanessa Bell gave her similar advice and made a similar plea in her last letter
to her sister, written on 20 March, following a conversation in which, Vanessa
reported, Woolf talked about herself. Even after this conversation, Vanessa
later told Vita Sackville-West, the possibility that her sister would commit
suicide never occurred to her.[21] 'Both Leonard and I have always had
reputations for sense and honesty', Vanessa wrote, 'so you must believe in
us.'[22]

Virginia Woolf's inability to believe in them must have been one of the
terrifying symptoms of the madness she felt overtaking her. Octavia Wilberforce told Leonard that during Virginia Woolf's visit to her on the day of her
death 'she suddenly said "I've been so *very* happy with Leonard" with such
feeling and warmth in her face'.[23] But she seems now to have felt that she had
lost this happiness. The bond between herself and Leonard which she had not
dared to break in this 'world of separation' was weakening. 'We have been
perfectly happy until the last few weeks, when this horror began', she told
Vanessa in her last letter to her (*L*VI 485). And in her final letter to Leonard she
wrote, 'All I want to say is that until this disease came on we were perfectly
happy' (*L*VI 487). Although Woolf's insistence in these letters on her happiness with Leonard and on Leonard's goodness may have been meant in part
to save him from feeling or from being thought in any way responsible for her
death, it seems to me that her primary reason for saying this was her desire to
assure him that the division she felt had come between them in the last weeks of
her life was caused by her disease and not by any change in her love of him.
'Everything has gone from me', she wrote, 'but the certainty of your goodness'
(*L*VI 481). Like 'The Symbol', Woolf's suicide letters convey an overwhelming sense of loss and of isolation. 'But I feel that I have gone too far this
time to come back again', she told her sister. The letters also express a
profound love for the two people whose love had until now helped to sustain
her. From her point of view, her death was in part a final gesture of love, for it
would free Leonard from the burden of caring for her and would, she said,
allow him to work. For Leonard, however, who could not share her belief that
she would not recover this time, her death was, as he said, a 'terrible thing' that
left him not free, but bereft.[24]

In using lines from the ending of *The Waves* as his wife's epitaph—'Against
you will I fling myself, unvanquished and unyielding, O Death!'—Leonard
Woolf was not only affirming the strength of her determination to fight 'the
enemy', but also the seminal place this book had in her life. In the ninth section
of *The Waves*, Bernard describes a day when 'the rhythm stopped'. The self
who had always been there to say 'I will not consent' had, he says, disappeared.
'Now there is nothing. No fin breaks the waste of this immeasurable sea. Life

has destroyed me. No echo comes when I speak, no varied words. This is more truly death', he recalls having felt, 'than the death of friends, than the death of youth'. (*W* 201-2) Bernard recovers his self and goes on to fight 'the enemy' again. Woolf, however, did not. In her last short fictions she may have been attempting to recover that rhythm, to hear that echo again, but she could not do so. Her effort not to give in is truly heroic. When on 24 March she wondered if she could 'englobe' Octavia's story, she had already, it may be, written two suicide letters and perhaps even attempted to kill herself. But the 'writing "I" ' had vanished; narrowed to the desperate alternatives of death or madness, her choice must finally have seemed clear. One must hope that in the last moments of her life she achieved in some form the 'mountain summit vision' she had so persistently sought.

Strange Meetings:
Eliot, Pound, and Laforgue

A. Walton Litz

The notion of investigating once again the familiar subject of Jules Laforgue's impact on Eliot and Pound—and the relationship between the two 'influences'—came to me when an extremely gifted young woman from a French university attended one of my seminars on modern poetry. As I rehearsed the usual received ideas about Laforgue's place in English and American modernism I could hear her mutter something very like a line from Yeats: 'They say such different things at school.' In conversations with her I discovered just how remote the Laforgues of Eliot and Pound are from the poet of the established French tradition, and this led me to think again about the reshaping of Laforgue's style and sensibility.

In his 1948 lecture 'From Poe to Valéry' Eliot said that Baudelaire appropriated the personality of Poe, while Mallarmé was more interested in Poe's technique, and in a rough way we might apply this formula to the encounters of Eliot and Pound with Laforgue. When Eliot picked up a copy of Arthur Symons's *The Symbolist Movement in Literature* in December 1908, and turned to the short chapter on Laforgue, he found in the first paragraph this description by Gustave Kahn:

D'allures? . . . fort correctes, de hauts gibus, des cravates sobres, des vestons anglais, des pardessus clergymans, et de par les nécessités, un parapluie immuablement placé sous le bras.[1]

Elsewhere in the chapter Laforgue's art is characterized as 'an art of the nerves', an art 'of spiritual dislocation'—he is a 'metaphysical Pierrot' who 'composes love-poems hat in hand'.[2] Within a few months Eliot was to write 'Spleen', a little poem where all the Laforguean gestures are in place. It ends:

> And Life, a little bald and gray,
> Languid, fastidious, and bland,
> Waits, hat and gloves in hand,
> Punctilious of tie and suit
> (Somewhat impatient of delay)
> On the doorstep of the Absolute.[3]

Eliot later said that his first meeting with Laforgue 'affected the course of my life'—life, not poetry—and I take him quite literally.[4] It was the first and most important of those many encounters with a ghostly *alter ego* that are the signatures of Eliot's poetic life. When Eliot declared in his 1936 Dublin lecture on 'Tradition and the Practice of Poetry' that he was fortunate to have been in his formative phase when Yeats was at his weakest,[5] he could also have said that he was doubly fortunate at that time to meet a young poet of about his own age who could be a friend, not a magisterial model. In the uncollected *Egoist* essay 'Reflections on Contemporary Poetry' (July 1919) that immediately preceded, and even announced, 'Tradition and the Individual Talent', Eliot spoke of just such a strange meeting, and I am sure he was thinking of Laforgue. Later this essay sank into obscurity while 'Tradition and the Individual Talent' was canonized when Eliot made it the program piece of *Selected Essays 1917-1932*, but 'Reflections on Contemporary Poetry' tells us far more about Eliot's inner life. Free from any references to 'impersonality' or 'objectivity', it speaks in passionate terms of young poets as 'bearers of a tradition'. Studded with emotional terms ('intimate', 'lovers', 'a genuine affair', 'friendship'), it reveals the feelings screened away by the cool prose of 'Tradition and the Individual Talent', just as the unpublished and suppressed poems of 1915-1921 (I am thinking especially of 'The Death of Saint Narcissus' and 'Ode') uncover the anguished sensibility that was sublimated in the 'impersonal' quatrain poems. Here is Eliot recalling his experience of a decade before.

There is a kind of stimulus for a writer which is more important than the stimulus of admiring another writer. Admiration leads most often to limitation; we can seldom remain long unconscious of our imitating another, and the awareness of our debt naturally leads us to hatred of the object imitated. If we stand toward a writer in this other relation of which I speak we do not imitate him, and though we are quite as likely to be accused of it, we are quite unperturbed by the charge. This relation is a feeling of profound kinship, or rather of a peculiar personal intimacy . . . it is certainly a crisis; and when a young writer is seized with his first passion of this sort he may be changed, metamorphosed almost, within a few weeks even, from a bundle of second-hand sentiments into a person. The imperative intimacy arouses for the first time a real, an unshakeable confidence. That you possess this secret knowledge, this intimacy, with the dead man, that after few or many years or centuries you should have appeared, with this indubitable claim to distinction; who can penetrate at once the thick and dusty circumlocutions about his reputation, can call yourself alone his friend: it is something more than *encouragement* to you. It is a cause of development, like personal relations in life. Like personal intimacies in life, it may and probably will pass, but it will be ineffaceable.[6]

Eliot's intimacy with Laforgue did pass, as we shall see in a moment, but this 1919 essay makes it easy for us to agree with William Jay Smith that 'the ironic framework and often the actual words of much of Eliot's early poetry owe everything' to Laforgue.[7] I would only add that the style in this case *is* the man, and that the transformation was a total one: it would fade in time, as all youthful intimacies do fade, but it left ineffaceable traces behind.

Now to the spring of 1917, when Eliot—who thought he had 'dried up completely' and felt 'rather desperate'[8]—warmed himself back to verse by writing the poems in French that were collected in his second volume (and others that have never been published). In April 1917 Pound told Joyce that Eliot had 'burst out into scurrilous french',[9] and that description certainly applies to some of the new unpublished poems in the Berg Collection of the New York Public Library (with their references to pederasty and the old female smell), although at least one of the published poems—'Dans le Restaurant'—retains much of the introspective irony of the earlier Laforguean poems. In his criticism of 1917-1920 Eliot is eager to establish Laforgue and the French Symbolists as the modern equivalent of the 'school of Donne', but at the same time the Laforguean tone with its dying fall gradually disappears from his poetry. To the end of his life Eliot generously acknowledged his early debt to Laforgue, 'to whom I owe more than to any one poet in any language', but on the same page of *To Criticize the Critic* (1961) he says that 'I turn more often the pages of Mallarmé than those of Laforgue'.[10] The turning point had occurred by 1920, when Eliot contributed an essay on 'Modern Tendencies in Poetry' to the Indian journal *Shama'a*. Eager to explain the latest developments to readers in a country whose literature and culture had meant a great deal to him, Eliot is unusually direct in this essay. It is the best summary of his critical views at that time. And he has this to say of Laforgue, in what is virtually an exercise in self-portraiture:

When I discovered Jules Laforgue, ten years ago, he gave me the same revelation which I imagine he has given to other people before and since: that is, he showed how much more use poetry could make of contemporary ideas and feelings, of the emotional quality of contemporary ideas, than one had supposed. . . . It is easier for a young poet to understand and to profit by the work of another young poet, when it is good, than from the work of a mature poet. I am no longer of the opinion that Laforgue, at the stage which he had reached at his death, was a great poet; I can see sentimentalism, absorption in himself, lack of balance. But in Laforgue there was a young man who was generally intelligent, critical, interested in art, science and philosophy, and always himself: that is, every mental occupation has its own precise emotional state, which Laforgue was quick to discover and curious to analyse.[11]

To the later Eliot, as to many others, Laforgue was the quintessential poet of the adolescent imagination, and the process of growing up as a poet entailed leaving him behind, as part of an earlier self. In the Clark Lectures of 1924-25 and in his later reworkings of these, such as the *Listener* talks of 1929 and the 1933 Turnbull lectures at Johns Hopkins, Eliot describes Laforgue as if he were describing his own younger self: Laforgue's poetry expresses 'the disillusionment of immaturity', he is 'a young man of ardent feelings and a gift for abstract thinking' desperately trying (as the young Eliot did) to unite the two. By contrast, Valéry raises 'the music, the fluidity' of Laforgue to a higher intellectual order.[12]

Pound's love affair with Laforgue was quite different: more mature, more measured, and in some ways longer lasting. In 1948 Pound told Warren Ramsey that when he arrived in London in 1908 he was 'an extremely unsophisticated individual. Eliot was born with all that, Laforgue and so on. I had to acquire it'.[13] But this is not by any means the whole explanation of why Pound's interest in Laforgue had to wait until 1916-17. One of the assumptions of Imagism was that it went beyond and against Symbolism, counteracting the influence of all those poets enshrined in Symons's *The Symbolist Movement in Literature*. Writing to Dorothy Shakespear in January 1914, in response to a letter which asked rather plaintively what Symbolism was all about, Pound distinguished true Symbolism (the visionary poetry that he and Yeats were discussing at Stone Cottage) from what he called aesthetic Symbolism 'that Arthur Symons wrote a book about—the literary movement'.[14] So Pound was naturally suspicious of the writers praised by Symons, and his early comments on French poetry focus on the generation that came to maturity after 1900. Although he may have started reading Laforgue before 1914, on the advice of F.S. Flint, it seems more likely that Pound was led to Laforgue in 1914-16 as his friendship with Eliot deepened. In any event, it is in Pound's letters of late 1916 that Laforgue suddenly becomes part of the essential canon; and in 1917-18 Laforgue takes centre stage. Pound's version of a Pierrots poem appears in May 1917, followed in November by the essay 'Irony, Laforgue, and Some Satire' and in February 1918 by the *Little Review* 'A Study in French Poets'.[15] Then in July 1918 Pound publishes 'Our Tetrarchal Précieuse', his 'divagation' from Laforgue's moral tale 'Salomé', which I take to be his most penetrating assessment of Laforgue.[16]

My French student was scandalized by Pound's 'Pierrots', which opens:

> Your eyes! Since I lost their incandescence
> Flat calm engulphs my jibs,
> The shudder of *Vae soli* gurgles beneath my ribs.
>
> You should have seen me after the affray,
> I rushed about in the most agitated way
> Crying: My God, my God, what will she say?!
>
> My soul's antennae are prey to such perturbations,
> Wounded by your indirectness in these situations
> And your bundle of mundane complications.
>
> Your eyes put me up to it.
> I thought: Yes, divine, these eyes, but what exists
> Behind them? What's there? Her soul's an affair for oculists.[17]

To my French student the cadences were choppy, the lines disconcertingly end-stopped, the emphasis on the rhymes a kind of heavy-handed parody: Laforgue's 'lunar' quality had been destroyed. She much preferred William Jay Smith's elegant and accurate translation. But Pound's distortions are a form of interpretation. As almost always in his transactions with another poet in another language, Pound has seized on a few techniques, a few tricks of language, as the *virtu* of the poet. To make my point I turn to Pound's hitherto-unpublished 'translation' of Eliot's 'Dans le Restaurant', which must have been made immediately after the poem was written in 1917. It shows that Pound could never resist translating anything that came to hand; but it also reveals the turns of language and feeling that Pound drew from Laforgue.

The waiter idle and dilapidated
With nothing to do but scratch and lean over my shoulder
Says:
  'In my country the rain is colder
And the sun hotter and the ground more desiccated and desecrated'.

Voluminous and spuminous with a leguminous
and cannimaculated vest-front and pantfront
and a graveyperpulchafied yesterday's napkin in a loop over his elbow
(I hope he will not sputter into the soup)

'Down in a ditch under the willow trees
Where you go to get out of the rain
I tried in vain,
            I mean I was interrupted
She was all wet with the deluge and her calico skirt
stuck to her buttocks and belly,
I put my hand up and she giggled',
            You old cut-up,
'At the age of eight what can one do, sir,
      she was younger
Besides I'd no sooner got started than a big poodle
Came sniffing about and scared me pealess',

Your head is not flealess
now at any rate, go scrape the cheese off your pate
and dig the slush out of your crowsfeet,
take sixpence and get washed, God damn
            what a fate
You crapulous vapulous relic, you ambulating offence
  To have had an experience
so nearly parallel, with, . . .

            Go away,
I was about to say mine,
I shall dine
elsewhere in future,
            to cleanse this suture

Phlebas the Phenicien, fairest of men,
Straight and tall, having been born in a caul
Lost luck at forty, and lay drowned
Two long weeks in sea water, tossed of the streams under sea, carried of
currents
Forgetful of the gains
Forgetful of the long days of sea fare
Forgetful of mew's crying and the foam swept coast of Cornwall,
Borne back at last, after days
to the ports and stays of his young life,
A fair man, ports of his former seafare thither at last[18]

  I think it is significant that Pound cannot handle the mysteriously personal
Phlebas lyric, and finally breaks off with a series of crossed-out attempts (the
last three lines are cancelled on the typescript). In the main body of the poem,

however, he has anticipated the rhymes and diction of the third poem in the second half of *Hugh Selwyn Mauberley* ('The Age Demanded'), where Hugh Selwyn Mauberley's drift into solipsistic exclusion from 'the world of letters' is cast in a language that plays off exactly against Eliot's 'The Love Song of J. Alfred Prufrock' and Pound's own 'Pierrots' translation:

> Incapable of the least utterance of composition,
> Emendation, conversation of the 'better tradition',
> Refinement of medium, elimination of superfluities,
> August attraction or concentration.

Or:

> Amid the precipitation, down-float
> Of insubstantial manna,
> Lifting the faint susurrus
> Of his subjective hosannah.

Clearly, at this time Laforgue held for Pound a precise value as a poet whose language and irony 'closed the circle'. The phrase comes from Pound's August 1919 contribution to the *New Age*, part of his long series called 'Pastiche: The Regional', where he took the occasion of his 1919 journey to France (part of the time spent with Eliot) to meditate on what both of them had learned over the last ten years.[19] The 'circle' Pound had in mind was the course of nineteenth-century realism, and his July 1918 rendering of Laforgue's 'Salomé' is a commentary on that 'circle'. This version is filled with what William Jay Smith calls 'surrealist touches',[20] where Pound will deliberately (at least most of the time) play with the literal but wrong-headed similarities between two languages—as in his *Homage to Sextus Propertius*. But the main point is that Pound is not interested in Laforgue's 'moral'—he leaves out some crucial plot elements—but in the style, which he reads as a critical parody of late Flaubert and all the other lush elaborations of decayed nineteenth-century 'realism'. In his essay 'The Temptation of (St.) Flaubert' Paul Valéry observed that in the end realist writers

lavished a care and industry, a subtlety and virtuosity, quite admirable in themselves, on the description of the most ordinary and sometimes the most trivial of objects . . . their peasants and their *petits bourgeois* lived and moved in a world which they were as incapable of seeing as an illiterate man is of deciphering a page of print. If they spoke, their fatuous remarks and clichés were encased in a highly elaborate style composed of rare terms and studied rhythms whose very word was carefully weighed, betraying its self-regard and its desire to be noticed. Realism ended curiously enough by giving an impression of deliberate artifice.[21]

And it is exactly this artifice that Pound, with the help of Laforgue, is out to mock and destroy.

Pound's well-known term *logopoeia*, the 'dance of the intelligence among words and ideas', seems to have been invented in 1918 to describe Laforgue's work, and in introducing it Pound declared that the 'intelligence of Laforgue ran through the whole gamut of his time'.[22] Whatever its larger meanings, the word defines what Pound discovered in Laforgue in 1917-18, and it was this perception that prepared him for Joyce's *Ulysses*, which began to pass across his desk in instalments a few months later. Pound even calls 'Salomé' a 'purge'[23], a term he would soon apply to *Ulysses*. 'Poor humanity has not produced a *pure hero*', Laforgue once wrote, 'and all those that are cited to us in antiquity are creatures like ourselves who have been crystallized in legend . . . I'd like to know their daily lives.'[24] Very soon Pound was to encounter the daily life of a modern 'hero', Mr Leopold Bloom.

One question remains: after roughly 1920, when Laforgue had become for Eliot part of his past life, what did the French poet mean to Ezra Pound? *Hugh Selwyn Mauberley* may seem the end of the Laforguean strain in Pound's poetry, but in Canto 116 we find this mysterious passage:

> and Laforgue more than they thought in him,
> Spire [Andre] thanked me in proposito
> And I have learned more from Jules
>   (Jules Laforgue) since then
> deeps in him

Presumably this meditation resulted from Pound's conversations with Warren Ramsey in the late 1940s and early 1950s, when Ramsey was writing *Jules Laforgue and the Ironic Inheritance*, and from other talk of that time with Mrs Rudd Fleming, who was translating Laforgue. I would like to know more about those conversations.

'Sufficient Ground to Stand on': Pound, Williams, and American History

Carol H. Cantrell

This is a revised version of a paper presented at the Conference on Politics, Economics, and Literature at Hamilton College, April 1985. Many thanks to my colleague, Ward Swinson, for numerous useful conversations about Pound and history.

Critics of William Carlos Williams almost always refer—however grudgingly—to Ezra Pound; critics of Pound usually give Williams little notice. Though Pound's effect on Williams is emphatic, Williams seems to have left little trace on Pound's work.[1] Richard Avedon's well-known photograph of the two poets[2] is an unforgettable depiction of an unequal relationship: Pound stands, bare-chested, confident, amused; Williams, buttoned-up, sits strained and patient, listing slightly. Pound's hands rest on Williams' shoulders rather as though he is propping up a ventriloquist's dummy. Whether this image is husk or caricature of an old friendship, it catches the pattern of one-sided competition established in their youth.[3] 'Ezra, even then, used to assault me (as he still does) for my lack of education and reading', Williams remembered; nor did he forget a mock fencing match instigated by Pound when he nearly put out Williams' eye with a walking cane.[4] And when Pound dedicated a book of poems to his friend, he entitled it *Ripostes* (1912).[5]

The division between the two poets was nowhere so clearly marked as in their differing relationships to the country of their birth. 'I contended for bread, he for caviar', Williams wrote.[6] If Pound berated Williams for his provincialism, Williams responded that by running to Europe, Pound 'had not sufficient ground to stand on'[7]—a phrase Pound picked up and used in his late cantos.[8] Bread and caviar, provincial and expatriate, rooted man and exile— these are not only opposite but complementary choices. Pound himself suggested that he and Williams were 'two halves of what might have made a fairly decent poet'.[9]

In fact, the 'two halves' worked together for about twenty-five years on a problem that gripped them both: the problem of locating a usable American past for poetry. Here Williams was the one who led and the one who challenged. The variety of solutions he developed to the aesthetic problems posed by American materials were worked out in a version of American history which challenged Pound at least as much as Williams' aesthetics. That Pound was listening to Williams and learning from him is evident in his published writings; in fact, taken together, the two poets' writings about the United States reveal an intensely two-sided exchange lasting until World War II, typically manifesting itself in pairs of complementary works. Pound's social history of the US, *Indiscretions* (1918),[10] found its counterpart in Williams' *The Great American Novel* (1923);[11] Williams' analysis of American origins, *In the American Grain* (1925),[12] was answered by Pound's differing version of origins in the Jefferson-Adams-Van Buren cantos (1934).[13] While Williams examined 'The Writers of the American Revolution' (1936)[14] Pound described 'The Jefferson-Adams Letters as a Shrine and a Monument' (1937) of that same period.[15] Pound responded to Williams' opera about Washington,[16] father of his country, with his portrait of John Adams, 'pater patriae' (62/350) in the Adams cantos (1940);[17] and Williams used his epic, *Paterson* (1946-1958),[18] to rebuke and continue Pound's epic, the *Cantos* (1930-1969).

When in 1923 Pound reprinted his *Indiscretions* as part of a series published by Bill Bird, he included with it the note that 'the other MSS are considerably more interesting than this one of mine . . . which . . . may have a function, if only as a foil to Bill Williams' *The Great American Novel*'.[19] Both works are 'history of a personal sort, social history, well-documented and incomplete',[20] but there the resemblance between them ends. Read in relation to Williams' experimental novel, it is easy to see why Pound praised Williams' work at the expense of his own. Pound's work is derivative; steeped in the writings of Henry James about whom he had recently written several essays,[21] he distances himself from his thinly veiled family history and autobiography with convoluted sentences and multiple ironies. In contrast, Williams' Dadaist novel, one of whose characters is a car, is brash, direct, and funny. Pound depicts declining families with British antecedents, Williams a miscellany of immigrants and native populations. While Williams insists that 'Every word we get must be broken off from the European mass',[22] Pound tries with more ambivalence and less success to free himself from his U.S. ancestors. As he wrote in a 1917 letter to Williams:

You have the naive credulity of a Co. Clair immigrant. But I (der grosse Ich) have the virus, the bacillus, of the land in my blood, for nearly three bleating centuries.[23]

Williams' success in treating American materials was possible, Pound thought, because he did not have to be self-conscious about his native voice. As Pound wrote in 'Dr Williams' Position':

> He was able to observe national phenomena
> without necessity for constant
> vigilance over himself, there was no
> instinctive fear that if he forgot himself
> he might be like some really unpleasant Ralph Waldo.[24]

Pound seems never to have rid himself of this fear, as the self-conscious Americanisms which persist in his letters attest.

In contrast, the 'observant foreigner', as Pound called Williams, had, through dint of constant experimentation, observation, and interchange with American painters and photographers, developed a poetics capable of 'perceiving American vegetation and landscape directly'[25] and was able to move from his relatively successful *Great American Novel* to his masterly *In the American Grain*. In this book Williams' historiography and method of presentation parallels Pound's Malatesta cantos (8-11) which were published as he began work on *In the American Grain*.[26] Just as Pound had done tacitly in the Malatesta cantos,[27] so Williams identifies the link between poet and historian not in the production of belles-lettres but in the process of selecting and interpreting a culture's manifestations, especially its documents. In the short note which prefaces the book, Williams writes,

> In these studies I have sought to re-name
> the things seen, now lost in chaos of
> borrowed titles . . . In letters, in
> journals, reports of happenings I have
> recognized new contours suggested by old
> words so that new names were constituted.
> Thus, where I have found noteworthy
> stuff, bits of writing have been copied into
> the book for the taste of it . . .
> it has been my wish to draw from every source
> one thing, the strange phosphorus of the
> life, nameless under an old misappellation.[28]

With minor changes, this note could preface the Malatesta cantos as well. In Williams' search for primary documents, his interest in the flavour of the life they record, and in his desire to 're-name the things seen', he uses Pound's example for his own purposes. *In the American Grain* demonstrates that American documents provide at least as rich a quarry as European materials. Williams also used in his prose Pound's ideogramic method of producing an assessment of a culture through a juxtaposition of texts; so that, for example, 'The Destruction of Tenochtitlan' comments silently on the Puritans 'who would succeed in making everything like themselves'.[29] Williams' method of juxtaposing many textures of language allows him not only to cover a tremendous range but also to present a coherent picture of what had gone wrong in the New World. *In the American Grain* presents a repeated moment of origin, a repeated corruption of a New World, as an America of highly developed native cultures[30] is discovered and ravaged over and over again by Scandinavians, Italians, and Spanish explorers. In this story the British are just one of many groups; a reader is a third of the way through the book before the Puritans appear.

Pound was unflagging in his enthusiasm for *In the American Grain* and finally succeeded in getting it reissued by New Directions in 1939.[31] He also responded to it with a counter-version of U.S. history adumbrated within his

Eleven New Cantos, cantos 31-41 (1934), in the Jefferson cantos (31-33), the John Quincy Adams canto (34), and the Martin Van Buren canto (37). Pound following Williams following Pound quotes huge chunks of primary American documents in order to 'rename the thing seen'. Pound's differences with Williams, however, are apparent even in his choice of materials; his source for the Jefferson cantos, *The Writings of Thomas Jefferson*, was a gift from T.S. Eliot,[32] who for Williams represented all that was worst in the expatriates.[33] And indeed, the Jefferson cantos do orient toward Europe. Pound had already suggested (in 27/97) that the U.S. was in many ways the heir of the Renaissance, and the positioning of this group of cantos suggests that 'America in the age of Jefferson and Andrew Jackson was a metamorphosis of the culture that Pound has traced throughout the first thirty Cantos'.[34] Pound's New World, unlike Williams', begins with the wealth of the sensibilities of Jefferson and Adams, not with the destruction of native cultures by the conquistadors and others. Thus Pound's first American cantos, the Jefferson-Adams cantos, solve the problem of poetic voice by following Williams' treatment of American materials in *In the American Grain*, while they counter his location of American origins in various acts of violence with his location of origins in the sensibilities of two great men. At the same time, Pound's founding fathers, like Williams' indigenous populations, both provide a measure of what has been lost. For Pound, for example, this loss is suggested by the contrast between Jefferson's active concern for the precise use of language in translation and Van Buren's speech whose 'directions on all points would seem not / to have been its conspicuous feature' (37/186)—and Van Buren stands heroically above his contemporaries in his fight against the National Bank. Whereas for Williams the loss of the New World took place at each new moment of failed 'discovery' of it, for Pound the loss amounted to a corruption of a culture that had in fact flowered. The cause of this corruption, as the *Eleven New Cantos* emphasize, is the economics of greed and, more specifically, the manipulation of credit. As Pound presents it, the failure is less of the inner life of the imagination, as it is for Williams, than it is of the material conditions created by usury. Pound is leading up to the point that the lost American heritage, 'the heritage of Jefferson, Quincy Adams, old John Adams, Jackson, Van Buren, is HERE, NOW, *in the Italian peninsula* at the beginning of fascist second decennio, not in Massachusetts or Delaware'.[35]

Pound's blind regard for Mussolini virtually insured Williams' later rift with him, but in fact the period between 1928 and 1935 was a time when he and Williams praised one another and worked fairly closely together. Pound wrote his only full-length essay on Williams, 'Dr Williams' Position' (1928) during this time and Williams wrote in response, 'Nothing will ever be said of better understanding regarding my work than your article'.[36] Williams dedicated his *Voyage to Pagany* (1928) to Pound, and between 1931 and 1935 published three essays about him.[37] Williams had joined Pound in the ranks of Social Creditors, who argued that credit should be decentralized and withdrawn from private control. For Williams, but not for Pound, Social Credit represented a political solution that avoided the difficulties both of Fascism and Communism.[38]

It was in this period that Williams wrote his powerful essay 'The American Background: America and Alfred Stieglitz' (1934), which best embodies the collaborative effort between the two poets. The essay is founded on Williams' insight that a 'borrowed culture' 'push[ed] back a very necessary immediate knowledge of the land to be made theirs',[39] but from this point on, Williams' U.S. history is an amalgamation of his and Pound's and stresses the importance of Washington and Adams, the founding fathers who had become increasingly important to Williams and Pound respectively. Williams argues that the revolutionary culture persisted in Jackson and notes that 'as Ezra Pound has recently pointed out, it was Jackson who because of his basic culture was able first to smell out the growing fault'.[40] Yet Jackson's efforts ultimately failed, and Williams' analysis of why this is so is a synthesis of his and Pound's positions: a borrowed culture, a 'culture in effigy' was overwhelmed and drained of community by wealth; 'the actual, the necessity for dealing with a condition as it existed, seemed to become unnecessary because of the mystical powers represented by money'.[41] In this reading of the role of money, as well as in his definition of 'culture'—'It isn't a thing: it's an act . . . It is the act of lifting these things into an ordered and utilized whole which is culture'[42]—that Pound and Williams for the moment at least stand on the same ground.

The relatively submerged political, aesthetic, and personal countercurrents of division were nonetheless at work. During this period, Williams struggled unsuccessfully to write the libretto for an opera about George Washington with Tibor Serly. After eight years of the 'fiddling and fussing that went with it' Williams was 'just about . . . ready for the psychopathic ward'.[43] The collaboration ended several years later, though Williams completed the libretto, knowing, as he wrote to Pound, that 'the body of the libretto text has little if any literary merit'.[44] The libretto's major problem is its lack of drama in the conception of Washington.[45] Indeed, Williams virtually ignored the events of Washington's life, insisting that the music was more important than 'a preconceived notion of plodding fact—the mere historicity of events'.[46] Williams had been outraged when Serly had suggested that he, the author of *In the American Grain*, read up on Washington.[47] He was instead looking for a way to represent a collective spirit at the same time he was using Washington who 'created an imaginary republic' to express many of the frustrations he felt as a poet trying to do the same.[48] Williams was moving out of the documentary approach to history, trying to catch a more elusive collective imagination— beginning, in fact, to write what would become *Paterson* some years later.

Pound, on the other hand, ignored Washington[49] in favor of Jefferson and Adams, and burrowed ever more deeply into documentary material concerning them. While Williams was groping toward a use of texts at once more eclectic and musical than anything he or Pound had yet developed, Pound had become ever more committed to the excernment and distribution of certain revelatory texts all but lost in U.S. history. In 1936 Williams had written an essay on 'The Writers of the American Revolution',[50] which is mostly devoted to 'those who by their writing served as instigators and coadjutators of the military',[51] discussing pamphlets, letters, and literary texts was less important in themselves than in their relationship to historical events. Williams did not publish this essay, but whether Pound read it or not, it was a topic of compelling interest to him. When in 1937 he published his important essay on the same topic, 'The Jefferson-Adams Letters as a Shrine and a Monument', he began by tacitly redefining 'literary', denying that 'the life of a nation's letters is restricted mostly to second-rate fiction'. Pound argues that the high quality of the letters written by Jefferson and Adams provide a measure of the civilization which they themselves defined, that 'The Adams-Jefferson Letters ought to be in curricula, representing as they do "a life not split into bits"'.[52] These letters, as Pounds treats them, are ideograms which reveal far more about the founding of the nation than historical 'events' as they are traditionally conceived.

Once Pound was able to acquire *The Works of John Adams* (in 1938 or early 1939), he moved quickly to write the Adams cantos (62-71)[53]—eighty pages of material Pound culled from these ten volumes. By quoting at such length the words of a founding father and president popular neither with the public nor with historians, Pound was implicitly insisting on a re-reading of U.S. history which he thought had enormous contemporary relevance. Adams was unpopular in part because, as Pound emphasizes, he was 'for peace' (71/420), as Pound thought Roosevelt should be and was not;[54] furthermore, Adams was the antagonist of Hamilton, who was for Pound the chief defender and perpetrator of the monopoly on credit. But Adams was far more than a mere mouthpiece for Pound's political and economic theories. In numerous ways, from his family history[55] to his abrasive personality, Adams was for Pound what Williams wanted Washington to be for him—an alter ego. Most important for Pound, Adams gave him an American voice. Through the simple expedient of the documentary method—quoting and juxtaposing chunks of material from Adams' biography, diaries, letters, and public writings—Pound was able to comment indirectly on U.S. origins and contemporary affairs with no danger of sounding like 'a really unpleasant Ralph Waldo'. At the same time Adams was no more a ventriloquist's dummy than was Williams, and what Pound learned from him about voice and introspection helped prepare him to write the Pisan cantos.[56]

If Pound found in Adams an individual American voice, Williams was finally succeeding in developing a collective voice. *Paterson*, his epic poem written over a twenty-year period, became what the Washington opera had tried and failed to be, a poem about the mind of a culture, a city whose dreams are its citizens, who at the same time is identified with the poet. Conceived and written while Williams' anger against Pound's Fascist activities grew, *Paterson* is lined with Williams' struggle to give Pound his due while angrily rejecting what in Pound was inimical to him. With some violence, Williams implicitly rejects Pound's allegiance to texts in Book III by celebrating the burning of the library;[57] more complexly and explicitly, he inverts Pound's condemnation of usury by celebrating invention in a passage imitating the rhythms of Pound's usury canto.[58] At the same time, he retains his and Pound's Social Credit analysis of the nation's decline. Hamilton is, in *Paterson*, as he is in the Adams cantos, the prime villain in U.S. history; *Paterson* condemns him for his role as organizer of the Society of Useful Manufacturers, the organization monopolizing the falls outside Paterson and responsible for the degradation of the city.[59]

With *Paterson*, which both incorporates and attacks Pound, the series of complementary writings by the two poets ends, mostly because of the estrangement between them resulting from Pound's broadcasting over Rome radio. Their joint effort to address American origins in their poetry lasted as long as it did because it was rooted in a shared perception of the central importance of the poet in modern culture. For both, the acts of naming and making are at the heart of poetic activities, and at the heart of a culture. The task of naming for both begins with the recovery of essential history that has been lost or distorted. For Williams, the task is 'to re-name the thing seen', because inhabitants of the New World have tended to read the Old World into it, as when the Puritans misnamed as robins 'thrushes only vaguely resembling the rosy, daintier English bird'.[60] For Pound, history is obscure for more ominous reasons; he approvingly quotes Adams' observation that any 'unlimited sovereignty', whatever its form or residence

has never failed to destroy all records, memorials, all histories which it did not like, and to corrupt those it was cunning enough to preserve . . . (33/160)

The task of recovering U.S. history was of utmost urgency for both poets because of their shared sense that whatever had gone wrong was a human construction, not an inevitability. For both poets, human culture is an artifact; those who make it are responsible for the choices they make in the course of producing it. As Williams bitterly noted,

Pound's 'faults' as a poet all center around his rancor against the malignant stupidity of a generation which polluted our rivers and would then, brightly, give ten or twenty or any imaginable millions of dollars as a fund toward the perpetuation of *Beauty*—in the form of a bequest to the Metropolitan Museum of Art.[61]

Both poets persistently make the claim that one can measure the worth of a culture by its treatment of the arts, for this treatment is continuous with its other choices and reveals and furthers its values. For both Williams and Pound, the destruction of land and the corruption of the arts are functions of the same cultural predisposition.

Williams' *The Great American Novel* ends with a suggestive metaphor: the last chapter describes an American product which is 'our main speciality'—a fabric known as 'shoddy'. Shoddy is a thing, not an attribute; it is a cheap fabric made from wool rags broken down into a fibrous mass and blown into cotton warp and woof—'One washing and the wool is gone'.[62] It is the stuff which American culture makes and of which it is thus inevitably made. Both Williams and Pound use this word as a noun with much the same meaning. When Williams writes about Washington, he says that 'It was a country he pasted together—a good deal out of shoddy—to represent the thing we still labor to perfect'.[63] And Pound picks up the word in canto 81, in his description of Santayana's arrival in the U.S., describing him as 'at first disappointed in the shoddy' (81/519).

Thus the question both poets ask of U.S. history might be posed in terms of 'our main specialty'. Where did shoddy come from? Why has it been so successful? Perhaps the Social Credit answer was attractive to both poets because it seemed to them to address directly the question of how a culture comes systematically to erode quality in design and manufacture. Social Credit seems to provide an answer: it implies that a monopoly on credit dries up financial support for anything that is not immediately profitable, that a culture will produce only that which will 'sell and sell quickly', (45/229) as Pound put it. Thus in the writings of both poets in the early and mid-thirties, during the period of their most intense activities as Social Creditors, the Nineteenth Century Bank Wars are seen as all-important struggles to wrest control of credit from an oligarchy interested in profit at any cost. Somewhat later, in the Adams cantos and in *Paterson*, the focus shifts to the origins of the nation; the paradigmatic villain is Alexander Hamilton, who at the founding of the nation gave the power over credit to the few.

This virtually unison reading of the origin of 'shoddy' in U.S. history is, however, worked out within two rival yet complementary poetics. Williams sets for himself the paradoxical task of making a poetry out of various American poverties, including poverty of sense experience and of language. Like Washington, he 'pasted together' a vision of a nation, 'a good deal out of shoddy—to represent the thing we still labor to perfect'. He did this in part by using American materials, especially American speech and writing, and by making of one kind of poverty a virtue—to see without preconception, to treat every act of perception as though it had no precedent. His reward from the U.S. government can only be called shoddy: he received the dubious honour of being investigated as a sympathizer both of Fascism and of Communism.[64]

Pound's poetics, in contrast, rest on his faith in the plenitude within sources and origins,[65] whether the source be Homer or *The Works of John Adams*; translation is an affirmation of this plenitude. Unlike Williams, Pound locates American origins in a culture flowering in the words and acts of Jefferson and Adams. And Pound found in Adams' works an abundance that he did not anticipate, which he sorely needed. For by the time he wrote the Adams cantos, he was busy manufacturing ever more reductive versions of the world, one of which is his presentation of Confucian China (cantos 52-61, which immediately precedes the Adams cantos) as centuries of good guys and bad guys in predictable succession. In Adams, however, Pound found a man, not a set of formulas, a man remarkably like himself in many ways, 'who at certain points made us / at certain points saved us' (62/350). One of the last political acts of Pound's life was his breaking his long silence in the year of his death to write the brief introductory note to his *Selected Prose* in which he disavowed his 'pretentious attempt to expand a merely personal view into a universal law'. Adams and Jefferson both died on 4 July 1826. Pound, still thinking of origins, and perhaps of the friendship of two complementary Americans, dated this note 'Venice, 4th July, 1972'.[66]

D.H. Lawrence's Physical Religion: The Debt to Tylor, Frobenius, and Nuttall

Daniel J. Schneider

The more closely one examines the works that D.H. Lawrence sought out in his effort to develop his 'philosophy', the more one appreciates the use he made of the best scientific evidence available to him. His indebtedness to the anthropology of his time is a case in point. His realization that Western men and women 'live by the spirit of destruction and of putting apart', as he said in November of 1916, and that the egoistic mental or ideal consciousness fostered by Western civilization prevents all 'Unanimity of Purpose', was leading him to take a deep interest in primitive cultures and the 'primitive mind', as ethnologists called it—a mind that had not been poisoned by Christianity or by rationalism and capitalism. His reading of Nietzsche had initiated him into the wisdom of the ancient Greeks: the myth of eternal recurrence had become an essential part of Lawrence's conception of god-nature in its creative and destructive power. His reading of Jane Harrison's *Ancient Art and Ritual* had excited his interest in his kinship of art and religious yearning—the idea that both express 'the world-wide desire that the life of Nature which seemed dead should live again'. Harrison had introduced him to the ideas of Frazer. By 1915 he was reading *The Golden Bough* and *Totemism and Exogamy*. By 1916 he had read Edward B. Tylor's two-volume *Primitive Cultures* as well as Gilbert Murray's *The Four Stages of Greek Religion*. In 1918 he read Leo Frobenius's *The Voice of Africa*. And in 1923 he read Zelia Nuttall's *Fundamental Principles of New and Old World Civilizations*. All of these works were to influence his thinking, in particular his thought about animism, the religion that he declared in 1924 to be 'the only live one'[1]—'the vast old religion of the prehistoric world', a religion not of 'gods and goddesses' but of 'the elemental powers in the Universe, the complex vitalities of what we feebly call Nature'.[2] Lawrence's research into primitive cultures was really very extensive; but for my purposes here I shall confine my inquiry to three anthropologists who appear to have exerted considerable influence on his thought—Edward Tylor, Leo Frobenius, and Zelia Nuttall.

Half of Tylor's influential two-volume study is devoted to Animism, and while Frazer, Harrison, Murray, Eisler and others also influenced Lawrence's thinking about animism, Tylor's study is so comprehensive and so impressive

161

that it must be regarded as a major source of the knowledge Lawrence assimilated of animistic religion and of the ancient 'blood consciousness'. At least two ideas that became central in Lawrence's later thinking about religion are stressed in Tylor. The first is that the ancient religion was, to use Lawrence's words, a 'physical religion', essentially pantheistic (though not like the Wordsworthian pantheism understood by moderns). The second is that the ancient religion was essentially amoral and non-retributive.

In New Mexico, where Lawrence encountered 'a remnant of the most deeply religious race still living', Lawrence summarized the conception of that vast old religion:

There is no God, no conception of a god. All is god. But it is not the pantheism we are accustomed to, which expresses itself as 'God is everywhere, God is in everything'. In the oldest religion, everything was alive, not supernaturally but naturally alive. There were only deeper and deeper streams of life, vibrations of life more and more vast . . . It was a vast and pure religion, without idols or images, even mental ones. It is the oldest religion, a cosmic religion the same for all peoples, not broken up into specific gods or systems. It is the religion which precedes the god-concept, and is therefore greater and deeper than any god-religion.[3]

Lawrence's conception here of the 'oldest religion . . . the same for all peoples' corresponds strikingly with Tylor's assertion that animism was 'an ancient and world-wide philosophy' and 'the groundwork of the Philosophy of Religion, from that of savages up to that of civilised man'.[4] The idea that 'everything was alive' is seen clearly by Tylor as the logical implication of animism. Tylor observes: 'Among races within the limits of savagery, the general doctrine of souls is found worked out with remarkable breadth and consistency. The souls of animals are recognized by a natural extension from the theory of human souls; the souls of trees and plants follow in some vague partial way; and the souls of inanimate objects expand the general category to its extremest boundary.'[5] Tylor also points out that among the Indians of North America 'souls are, as it were, the shadows and animated images of the body, and it is by consequence of this principle that they believe everything to be animate in the universe'.[6] Thus there is firm support in anthropology for Lawrence's conclusion that the ancient religion was 'a physical religion'. According to Tylor, the 'later metaphysical notion of immateriality [of the soul] could scarcely have conveyed any meaning to a savage'.[7] For the savages of North America, 'there is always something actual and physical to ground an Indian fancy on!'[8] Thus, for example, Tylor observes, 'in the religion of Northern American Indians, the Heaven-god displays the gradual blending of the material sky itself with its personal deity'.[9]

Tylor also, like Lawrence, rejects the 'extreme pantheistic scheme' proposed by the ethnologist Schoolcraft, who argued that the Great Spirit of the North American Indians is 'a pantheistic soul of the Universe, inhabiting and animating all things, . . . existing in the world under every possible form, animate and inanimate'.[10] Tylor doubts that 'the Red Indian mind even in modern times really entertained this extreme pantheistic scheme'.[11] The 'principal figures' shaped by 'the theologic mind of the lower races', he says, 'belong to strict Nature-worship . . . They are Heaven and Earth, Rain and Thunder, Water and Sea, Fire and Sun and Moon, worshipped either directly for themselves or as animated by their special deities'.[12] In a passage like this, Lawrence perhaps felt he had all the evidence he needed to confirm his intuition that all of nature is alive and that the four elements of Greek philosophy—air, earth, fire, and water—'have ever been, and will ever be/for they are the elements of life, of poetry, and of perception'.[13] The savage mind, as ethnologists of his time called it, had absorbed that great fundamental truth.

The second idea that Lawrence would have found emphasized in Tylor's survey of the nature and meaning of Animism is that 'savage animism is almost devoid of that ethical element which to the educated modern mind is the very mainspring of practical religion'.[14] 'The lower animism is not immoral, it is unmoral.'[15] Savages do not, presumably, judge others; and indeed, in the savage conception of an afterlife, there is no idea of future moral retribution. As Tylor observes, there are 'several well-qualified ethnologists, who have, in more or less degree, denied a moral character to the future retribution as conceived in savage religion'.[16] Dr D.G. Brinton, for example, commenting on the native religions of America, says, 'nowhere . . . was any well-defined doctrine that moral turpitude was judged and punished in the next world. No contrast is discoverable between a place of torment and a realm of joy; at the worst but a negative castigation waited the liar, the coward, or the niggard'.[17] For the savage, there is a 'continuance of the soul in its new existence, like the present life, or idealized and exaggerated on its model: while on the cultivated side the doctrine of judgement and moral retribution prevails with paramount, though not indeed absolute sway'.[18]

It is hardly necessary to point out that Lawrence, in considering the 'rival theories of continuance and retribution',[19] cast his lot with the savages. In *Mornings in Mexico*, he celebrates the sanity of the ancient view, in language that recalls Brinton's remarks about the liar, the coward, and the niggard. Lawrence points out that, to the Indian, the world, with its opposing hostile and benign or destructive and creative forces—'the fangs of the rattlesnake, and . . . the soft eyes of fawn'—elicits only wonder or fear; there is 'no judgement'.[20] The mind of the Indian 'bows down before the creative mystery, even of the atrocious Apache warrior. It judges, not the good and the bad, but the lie and the true. The Apache warrior in all his atrocity, is true to his own creative mystery. And as such, he must be fought. But he cannot be called a *lie* on the face of the earth'.[21] For the Indian there are only three great commandments: 'Thou shalt acknowledge the wonder'; 'Thou shalt not be a coward'; and 'Thou shalt not lie'.[22] And as the Indian eschews moral judgement, so does that other proponent of the vast old religion, the Etruscan: 'The leopard and the deer, the lion and the bull, the cat and dove . . . do not represent good action or evil action. On the contrary, they represent the polarized activity of the divine cosmos, in its animal creation.'[23]

If Lawrence was indebted to Tylor for his conceptions of the ancient religion, he was indebted to the German ethnologist, Leo Frobenius, for a view

of the health and vigour of that religion. I have dealt with this in an article in the
D.H. Lawrence Review, but it is worth repeating a part of what I said, for
Frobenius's *The Voice of Africa* undoubtedly stirred Lawrence's thinking
about what he calls in Chapter X of *Aaron's Rod* the 'strange wisdom' of the
past. Frobenius stressed that there was a 'perfected system of the primeval
age'—indeed, a 'high-toned philosophy, which once girdled the world at its
earliest dawn'.[24] This 'great plan' he found not only in Yoruba but also in the
Etruscan civilization. These and other societies constituted, he thought, the
legendary Atlantis, before Phoenicia and Grecia succeeded them. Before they
were destroyed, they produced superb arts and crafts and 'awe-worthy sons of
the Gods'. Frobenius celebrates the health and vigour of the ancient religion,
and stresses that Europeanization of Africa has caused debasement and
decadence. If African culture was ever to regain its original vitality, it must
return to the inspiration of the past.

The strength of the ancient religion became sharply evident to Frobenius on
his expedition to the Sudan, when he encountered the Nupés, whose ancient
religion has been suppressed by the Muslim Fulbés and by Christian mission-
aries. Frobenius wanted to see the old god of the Nupés, but the tribal
members were afraid. 'We had the Dako-Boea here once, it is true', said a
chieftain, 'but the white folk came; they talked about Issa [Jesus] and then took
our Dako-Boea away and burnt him. Since that happened we have no longer
dared to speak of our Great Father.'[25] Frobenius persisted, however, and the
Nupés were elated to see that the white man actually wished to revive the old
customs. The great day came: the Dako-Boea, a mask several yards in height,
danced in the square, and Frobenius records that there were thousands of men
and women and children assembled to see it—people stirred by a 'profound
emotion'. 'When they once again see him, their hearts are stirred to the depths,
and they remember that he was their saviour, their strength, their sign and
tradition of old.' The Nupés 'gave themselves up to jollity and gladness, once
more inspired by the return of their ancient God.'[26]

Frobenius's moving account of the restoration of the ancient god might
easily have kindled Lawrence's imagination. The author of *The Plumed Serpent*
certainly recognized, with Frobenius, that a native population debased and
demoralized by European influences needed to develop a vital culture and
religion of its own. As the Mexicans in *The Plumed Serpent* have been
unmanned by Christianity, so the Africans subjected to Christian and Muslim
domination have lost their ancient greatness. Yet Frobenius saw in the south of
the Sudan 'people . . . more imbued with a sentiment of real religion than any I
know'.[27] The lesson announced at the beginning of *The Voice of Africa* is that
'the children of the Gods had gone under, because they failed to remember the
law their awe-worthy ancestry had bequeathed them . . . they no longer
obeyed the laws handed down to the sons of the Gods, their sires of bygone
days'.[28] The Lawrence who, writing *The Rainbow*, had begun his quest for the
sons of God, might well have rejoiced when he read those words. The sons of
God did exist; one has only to discover their scions in the twentieth century.

If Frobenius emphasized the health of the ancient religion, Zelia Nuttall's book, *Fundamental Principles of Old and New World Civilizations*, confirmed Lawrence's view that the polarized activity of the divine cosmos was a fundamental principle of the ancient religion. L.D. Clark, in *Dark Night of the Body*, has taken note of the 'wealth of Above-Below symbolism' that Nuttall found in early American cultures and the union of opposites in Quetzalcoatl, who is both male and female. As Lawrence says in *The Plumed Serpent*, he is Lord of the two ways, who stands between 'the day and the night', between 'increase' and 'destruction', between 'love' and 'strife'. Here I would only add to what Clark has noted.

'The native American races', says Nuttall, 'were evidently entirely under the dominion of the idea of duality, of the Above and Below and the life-producing union of both.'[29] She speculates that for the ancient Mexicans there were two cults: 'the first, the cult of the Above, of the blue Sky, was directed towards the sun and the planets and stars; the second, the cult of the Below, of the Nocturnal Heavens, was directed towards the Moon, Polaris and circumpolar constellations—also the stars and planets during the period of their disappearance and possibly in the same way the enigmatical "Black Sun" . . . which may have been the sun during its nightly stay in the house of the Underworld, whose door was the west.'[30] Lawrence evidently seized on the idea of the black sun. Quetzalcoatl, he says, has slept 'in the place of the west', 'in the cave which is called Dark Eye,/Behind the sun'.[31] Now he is resurrected. But he announces that he owes his being to the black sun: 'It is I, Quezatlcoatl, rearing up in you, rearing and reaching beyond the bright day, to the sun of darkness beyond, where is your home at last. Save for the dark sun at the back of the day-sun, save for the four dark arms in heavens, you were bone, and the stars were bone, and the moon an empty sea-shell on a dry beach, and the yellow sun an empty cup . . . Without me you are nothing. Just as I, without the sun that is back of the sun, am nothing.' Nuttall remarks that the Mexicans 'had conceived the idea of two suns, a young day sun, and an ancient night or black sun'.[32] Lawrence imagines the black sun, the ancient sun, as the female origin of all, 'that made the sun and the world, and will swallow it again like a draught of water'.[33] The black sun is both tomb and womb, both black and the sun, for it is the homogeneous oneness out of which all things come, an unconsciousness and a death, yet fecund with promise. Quetzalcoatl sleeps in the 'dark eye behind the sun'. His resurrection brings him into the light. Jesus, however, becomes 'bone' and returns to the dark because 'the greatest of the great suns spoke aloud from the back of the sun: I will take my Son to my bosom . . . I will dip [Jesus and his Mother] in the bath of forgetting and peace and renewal'.[34] Thus Jesus will return to the female origin, where he will be renewed. Such is the will of Nature—a will which combines death and life, the destructive and the creative process.

The spinning of the sun and the black sun resemble a wheel. In the Plaza scene in *The Plumed Serpent*, a man holds a banner on which is 'the yellow sun with a black centre, and between the four yellow rays, four black rays emerging, so that the sun looked like a wheel spinning with a dazzling motion'.[35] The four great rays, both light and dark, recall the four cardinal points and the four quarters; but more than this, 'the four dark arms in the heavens' recall the swastika, the basis of the great plan which according to Nuttall has 'governed the human race from its infancy'. These four arms, she says, represent the positions of the circumpolar constellations during the solstices and equinoxes. They figure the annual rotation of the heavens. Nuttall observes that the Deity was figured not only as a serpent but also as a wheel, 'which obviously symbolized centrical force, rotation, lordship over the four quarters, ie, universal rulership'.[36] And the wheel was imitated in the great dance called the Mitotiliztli. 'No one', Nuttall says, 'on reading the description of the most ancient and sacred of native dances can fail to recognize that it was an actual representation of axial rotation . . .' Lawrence used the wheel-dance in his depiction of the dance in the Plaza, adding a reverse direction of inner and outer wheels to suggest male and female, the opposition which is union.

The conception of duality which Nuttall emphasizes in her description of 'the fixed immutable laws governing the universe' has of course been developed by Lawrence as early as *The Trespasser*, in which the antagonism of sun and moon, fire and water, day and night, and male and female are extensively explored. It was also extensively developed in 'Study of Thomas Hardy' and 'The Crown', and indeed in all the works following 1912. So Nuttall's book must have confirmed Lawrence's view of the duality of the universe. He did obviously believe that a central philosophy had 'governed the human race from its infancy'. The very rhythms of life were creative and destructive, an everlasting to-and-fro between night and day, a waxing and waning of 'love' and 'strife'. Like Nuttall, he hoped to discover the 'fixed immutable laws governing the universe'—the elemental two principles by which men lived, and will continue to live. Like Frobenius, he looked back to an age in which consciousness has not been poisoned by Christianity or by rationalism, and men had 'the power to devote themselves unreservedly and unshakenly, without confusion and unsteadfastness, to a firm faith in the eternal laws of natural forces and family life, and the rightness of their convictions'.[37] Like Edward Tylor, he believed that he had discovered 'an ancient and world-like philosophy' that was the very 'groundwork of the Philosophy of Religion'. It was important for Lawrence to paint convincingly his picture of *homines religiosi* in the past—and today. He needed the support of anthropologists if he was to establish that there was, in the religious beliefs of the ancient peoples, a wisdom that was real and attainable—a wisdom that must be recovered if men and women are to create 'a new heaven and a new earth'.

Notes on a Late Poem by Stevens

Denis Donoghue

The poem is 'Of Mere Being'. Between its appearance in *Opus Posthumous* (1957) and *The Palm at the End of the Mind* (1967), 'In the bronze distance' (l. 3) became 'In the bronze decor', on the authority of a typescript (H-4205) in the Stevens collection at the Huntington Library:

> The palm at the end of the mind,
> Beyond the last thought, rises
> In the bronze decor,
>
> A gold-feathered bird
> Sings in the palm, without human meaning,
> Without human feeling, a foreign song.
>
> You know then that it is not the reason
> That makes us happy or unhappy.
> The bird sings. Its feathers shine.
>
> The palm stands on the edge of space.
> The wind moves slowly in the branches.
> The bird's fire-fangled feathers dangle down.

The textual change is regrettable, if only because 'bronze distance' sufficiently indicates the scene and 'bronze decor' prematurely makes a judgement upon it.

We have a poem of four stanzas—tercets—metrically so free that only the ghost of blank verse can be summoned to testify to the liberties Stevens has taken. No rule of prosodic law obtains, whether we count syllables, accents, or phrases. One line is divided from the next by virtue of the sentence which distributes its parts over the stanza. In the first stanza a parenthetical phrase— 'Beyond the last thought'—starts off a new line, and accommodates the main verb in a rhetorically stressed because grammatically isolated position at the end of the line. The third line ends the sentence. In the second stanza, the first line is given to the subject of the sentence and its compound adjective. The second begins with the verb, which may be transitive or intransitive, a decision postponed by two structurally identical adverbial phrases, one at the end of the second line, the other at the beginning of the third, at which point the question is resolved—it is transitive, there is an object, 'a foreign song'. In the third stanza, sentences continue to dominate the metre, the division between the first and second line emphasising the main noun, 'the reason'. The rhythm of this stanza differs from the norm established in the first two by having the sentence distributed over two rather than three lines, and by having the third line filled with two short and parallel sentences: 'The bird sings. Its feathers shine.' Finally, each line of the last stanza coincides with a complete sentence; the first two are syntactically identical, the third brings the stanza and the poem to an end with an elaborate flourish, the subject of the sentence being postponed to allow for alliterative splendours—'fire-fangled'. The verb plays the internal rhymes and the final alliterations—'fangled/dangle down'—with such bravado as to recall the early Stevens of 'A High Toned Old Christian Woman' and 'The Comedian as the Letter C'. Meanwhile the stanzas move along as if they were chapters in a novel, complete with titles: St.1: The Palm; St.2: The Bird; St.3: The Bird (continued); St.4: The Palm, the Wind, and the Bird.

The poem has been well read, notably by Harold Bloom in *Wallace Stevens: The Poems of Our Climate* (1977) and by James Guetti in *Word-Music* (1980). I shall refer to these, and also to an essay which Bloom quotes and endorses, Paul de Man's 'Intentional Structure of the Romantic Image', now reprinted in de Man's *The Rhetoric of Romanticism* (1984).

Stanza 1: As usual in Stevens, the palm denotes a celebration of being, 'mere' because it is blessedly first and fundamental, manifestation of a first principle. It also denotes the fulfilment of desire, as in the sequence-surge of 'Description without Place':

> It is an expectation, a desire,
> A palm that rises up beyond the sea.

It is surprising, I suppose, to find Stevens celebrating anything that is to be found or imagined 'at the end of the mind' and 'beyond the last thought'. Generally, nothing is allowed to escape the mind's governance. On this occasion Stevens means, I assume, literally one's last thought, one's mind facing death. In a certain mood, it is a consolation to know that life goes on in one's absence. But the status of the palm is a question. Guetti has argued that what he calls 'noncognitive images' are crucial in Stevens's poems because of the relation between 'effortful imaginative sequences and the last images that relieve us of them'. Many of Stevens's poems 'begin with the problematically intelligible', set out a problem, and worry it according to rational procedures; it is only 'at the end of that sequence and after the intelligible motive has been tried and tried again' that we are released from the haggling. It is as if, 'after exercising one faculty, we were then prepared to exercise another'. After the ratiocination, we are given the palm and the bird. We run out the string of intelligible processes, and are then given the boon of a somehow satisfying noncognitive image.

This strikes me as one of the most telling observations elicited by a reading of Stevens's poems. But Guetti doesn't question the character of these images, apart from calling them noncognitive. Besides, I am not sure that the palm is such an image. It might be better to call it an emblem, in keeping with a distinction which Yeats makes in 'Symbolism in Painting' between an image and an emblem. An image refers to a natural object, and if the associations of that object are sufficiently rich in the life of a culture or several cultures, it becomes a symbol. In either case, it assumes what Paul de Man calls 'the ontological priority of natural things'. It gets its meaning and its force from nature, and thereafter from the human presence in a world in its first character natural. An emblem has its meaning, as Yeats says, 'by a traditional and not by a natural right'; we come to the meaning by consulting literature and art, the lexicon of tradition. Nothing in nature gives the palm any special privilege; the privilege comes from Roman tournaments, the New Testament, Blake and Wordsworth and Stevens's earlier poems.

But even if we call Stevens's palm an emblem, we have not determined its status. If the palm is not as it is found in nature, by what mode of imagination has Stevens produced it? Guetti takes the palm as an unproblematic image, a happy release from intelligible but difficult issues. But it may turn out to be just as problematic, in another mode, as the ratiocination that has preceded it. I don't mean the obvious, that in 'Of Mere Being' no ratiocination has preceded the disclosure of the palm. The phrase 'at the end of the mind' may be taken as a summary of manifold intellections, as if in Stevens's earlier and far longer poems. The point of my calling the palm an emblem rather than an image or a symbol is that it renders the status of the word questionable.

Perhaps I can clarify the point by referring to a passage in Sartre's *The Psychology of Imagination*:

Every consciousness posits its object, but each does so in its own way. Perception, for instance, posits its object as existing. The image also includes an act of belief, or a positing action. This act can assume four forms and no more: it can posit the object as non-existent, or as absent, or as existing elsewhere; it can also 'neutralize' itself, that is, not posit its object as existing. Two of these acts are negations: the fourth corresponds to a suspension or neutralization of the proposition. The third, which is positive, assumes an implicit negation of the actual and present existence of the object. This act of positing is not superimposed on the image after it has been constituted. It is constitutive of the consciousness of the image.[1]

It hardly matters whether we assign Stevens's palm to Sartre's third or fourth category; in either case, an emblem is posited rather than an object perceived, and it is posited as not being. In another idiom we might say that it is allegorical. Or, a last shot at it, we might say that it issues from what Philip Wheelwright in *The Burning Fountain* calls 'Stylistic Imagination', 'which acts upon its object by distancing and stylizing it'.[2] In any of these vocabularies, the palm is at a remove from existence. This is not because Stevens has failed to make his palm particular—this palm, not that one—but because the schema of his poem has removed it from perception; it cannot be posited as already existing, any more than the bird on the golden bough in Yeats's 'Sailing to Byzantium' which, as Bloom rightly says, is implicitly alluded to in Stevens's next stanza. Yeats's bird sings to lords and ladies 'of what is past, or passing, or to come'. Stevens's bird sings a foreign song, just as the cry of the wind in the leaves of 'The Course of a Particular' is not in any sense a human cry; it is on the way to concerning no one at all. If it is song, its achievement of form and expression has to do with birds, not with us. Nightingales are not singing to us, though we write odes to them. The near-repetition of 'without human meaning/without human feeling' releases us from the question of meaning, mitigates its severity by calling it feeling, but the song is still foreign.

Stanza 3: If we were made happy or unhappy by 'the reason', it would be because we insisted on finding the causes of our happiness or unhappiness intelligible. We would insist on talking about them, like one of Stevens's long poems. We don't: it is not a question of talk, of objects amenable to our most elaborate discourse, but of looking, acknowledging, as we look at a gold-feathered bird and feel that the foreignness of its song doesn't matter, what matters is life, its continuity, its changingness, our sense of it as living. Reason doesn't come into the matter; because by definition it comes too late, it can't recognise the 'firstness' of any form of life, its categories are belated. Firstness is the first principle, call it mere being, according to which the bird sings and its feathers shine, and we are silently or at least undiscursively ready for these events. The readiness is nearly all enacted in the last stanza; three lines, each coinciding with a sentence, no enjambements, no complication of metre or syntax, three simple indicatives. 'The palm stands on the edge of space': a variant of the first line's 'at the end of the mind' but more yielding since it doesn't even raise a question of the mind. If the mind has ever been present, it has let go, backed off to the point at which it merely—but this is not quite 'merely'—records a fact, the palm and where it is. 'On the edge of space' is so barely visualised that the phrase, like the palm, must be taken as emblematic rather than referential. The locale is nominal, we are not meant to see anything but to posit a relation, which need not be other than notional. One of our capacities is being exercised, our ability to abstract and to linger upon the abstraction. 'The wind moves slowly in the branches': we have been through our Shelleyan years, and 'moves' is just a little livelier than 'stands'. 'The bird's fire-fangled feathers dangle down.' Bloom quotes from Stevens's 'Our Stars Come from Ireland', 'fitful-fangled darknesses / Made suddenly luminous'. It is hard to say 'fangled' without seeming to say 'newfangled', a risk congenial to Stevens who sometimes liked to think of himself as foppish and liked to entertain the thought of his foppishness only to see it perish. The word has long been close to 'fashion', another venue of novelty for the sake of novelty. It has also been close, as in Stevens, to 'feathers'. The OED has Greene's 'There was no Feather, no fangle, Gem, nor Jewell . . . left behinde'. It also gives an obsolete sense of the word, derived from German *fankel* meaning spark, and quotes Daniel in 1649: 'There may we find without the fangle which Fires the dry touch of Constitution'. The bird's fire-fangled feathers are Stevens's version of the phoenix, the diction flaming in a tradition which he is happy to share with Keats and Hopkins. Most of the associations of 'dangle' have been playful, as in hanging loose because you feel you don't need to exert yourself. It has often been used to describe the aristocrat's way of passing the time; though of course he, too, could dangle from a gallows. Stevens lounged with it, especially in 'A Lot of People Bathing in a Stream' which Bloom aptly quotes:

> We bathed in yellow-green and yellow-blue
> And in these comic colors dangled down.

When we assemble the line again, we have the phoenix still, but freed from its air of demented recurrence by turning into the amiable clown of life, who to be colourful and vivid doesn't need to assert himself. It is as if first things coincided with last things, the fantasia a merry-go-round.

I assume that 'Of Mere Being' is a poem about coping with one's soon-coming death and making the best of it and being decent and undismal about it. If, as Stevens says in 'A Mythology Reflects its Region', 'the image must be of the nature of its creator', in so far as it is, the creator should make it lively rather than inflict his misery on others. Hence the gorgeousness of the last line in 'Of Mere Being'.

We could leave the poem at this point, except that Bloom, the poem still much in and on his mind, quotes several of Paul de Man's sentences as if they somehow, without referring to Stevens, circumscribed not only this poem but Stevens's entire work. De Man has been commenting on a passage about origination in Hölderlin's 'Brot und Wein', and turning the comment into a vast generalization:

It is in the essence of language to be capable of origination, but of never achieving the absolute identity with itself that exists in the natural object. Poetic language can do nothing but originate anew over and over again; it is always constitutive, able to posit regardless of presence but, by the same token, unable to give a foundation to what it posits except as an intent of consciousness. The word is always a free presence to the mind, the means by which the permanence of natural entities can be put into question and thus negated time and again, in the endlessly widening spiral of the dialectic.[3]

Bloom receives this passage as if it were entirely convincing, but it seems to me to go into a wobble. At first, de Man appears to be saying that the trouble with language is that a word can't be identical with itself as a stone—that one over there, not the one beside it—can be identical with itself. Language can't give a foundation to what it posits except as an intent of consciousness. I interrupt this gloss to say that Stevens, among post-Romantic poets, was the one most content with that constraint; an intent of his consciousness was for him an entirely sufficient foundation for whatever he posited. He doesn't give the slightest sign that he thinks his 'gold-feathered bird' disabled by the fact that its sole foundation is the poet's intent of consciousness: on the contrary, he takes pride in that fact, and would not have it otherwise.

The wobble of de Man's passage is in the final sentence. It is bound to surprise many readers to find de Man saying that 'the word is always a free presence to the mind'. Elsewhere, he has insisted that it is not free, that one's sense of the free presence of a word in one's mind is a delusion, since the word is already inscribed there by the structure of the language one speaks. The ideological character of language is inescapable, even if we continuously engage in the deconstruction of whatever offers itself as 'our' language. But in any case, if consciousness and nature are absolutely separate, as Bloom takes de Man to say, then the linguistic act of putting into question 'the permanence of natural entities' is clearly futile. If that is what early Romantic poets thought they were doing, they were spitting against the wind. Bloom quotes de Man as saying that Rousseau and Wordsworth were 'the first modern writers to have put into question, in the language of poetry, the ontological priority of the sensory object'. I think Blake was nearer the truth of the matter when he accused Wordsworth of choosing not to do this; of taking dictation from Nature, by giving such credence to Memory; of granting too much audience to 'the speaking face of earth and heaven'. Besides, to put into question is not to negate; on the contrary, it is to establish the object yet again, on the ground of one's relation to it, however ironic or sceptical the relation may be.

The passage which Bloom quotes from de Man seems to me to be contradicted by several other passages, especially from de Man's later essays on anthropomorphism and prosopopoeia. I take prosopopoeia to be the trope which conjures or summons into presence—or into a semblance of presence—something which is absent. De Man regarded this trope, and not metaphor, as 'the master trope of poetic discourse'. Presumably in that discourse the distinction between image and emblem would persist, since the positing which results in an emblem makes a claim, to use de Man's phrase, 'not given in the nature of things', while the production of an image is precisely an appeal to the nature of things. But if the distinction persists, as I think it does, then further distinctions arise. De Man deals with prosopopoeia as if the only question in its vicinity were: will the ghost appear or not? Will the face of the absent one emerge from the abyss or not? But the form of these questions suppresses the many differences, of kind and of degree, between emanations which are summoned by such diverse acts of consciousness as perception, imagination, fancy, positing, abstraction, and so forth. As soon as we advert to this suppression, we see that one of the distinguishing marks of Stevens's poem is what I might call its excluded first. Guetti assumes that the poem excludes Stevens's normal ratiocination or takes it for granted and offers the reader three noncognitive images as if to release him from the chore of patiently borne ratiocination. Provoked by de Man's essay, I am inclined to see the poem preceded by one of the great forms of the poetic faculty, an act of image-making or image-recognition, an assent indeed to the nature of things in that respect. If 'the palm' arises from an act of positing and remains an emblem; if 'the reason' is discourse too belated to make a difference to one's happiness or unhappiness; then the missing factor, the vital X is the image. There are no images in 'Of Mere Being': again, this is not a defect but a choice, an 'intent of consciousness' on Stevens's part. But it doesn't give any warrant to the later passage which Bloom quotes from de Man's essay, where the theme is Wordsworth's imagination:

This 'imagination' has little in common with the faculty that produces natural images 'as flowers originate'. It marks instead a possibility for consciousness to exist entirely by and for itself, independently of all relationship with the outside world, without being moved by an intent aimed at a part of this world.

Again this would be more convincing if it referred to Blake rather than Wordsworth. Or to Stevens, who in many of his moods aspired to such a declaration of independence. But de Man isn't saying anything new. The consciousness he describes is what Yeats called reverie and characterized as taking the form of the gaze rather than the glance. Insofar as this consciousness would give itself any other employment than that of delighting in itself, it would have to be the one that Pater indicated by saying that all the arts constantly aspire towards the condition of music. If the matter were to be argued further, and on the issue of ontology as de Man in several contexts raised it, I would be inclined to describe the motive of such a consciousness as angelic, and call it vanity. But the present is not an occasion for severity.

Finally, I risk a mild conjecture. Suppose Stevens were reading Mallarmé's 'Don du poëme', the first five lines of which allude to—or at least could be eked out to allude to—his nightly work on the never-to-be-completed *Hérodiade*. In the morning, he has written something, perhaps a poem, not Hérodiade but a shard of it, and he brings it into the next room where his child and her mother are asleep and he offers it to the child as a gift:

> Je t'apporte l'enfant d'une nuit d'Idumée!
> Noire, à l'aile saignante et pâle, déplumée,
> Par le verre brûlé d'aromates et d'or,
> Par les carreaux glacés, hélas! mornes encor,
> L'aurore se jeta sur la lampe angélique.

Idumean or Edomite refers to the ancestry of Hérodiade. Otherwise the passage is fairly clear: I bring you [as a gift] the child of an Idumaean night! [It is] dark, its wing is bleeding and pale, [its feathers are] plucked. Through the window [as if] burned with spices and gold; through the icy panes, still dreary alas!; the dawn hurled itself on the angelic lamp.

The next passage is more difficult:

> Palmes! et quand elle a montré cette relique
> À ce père essayant un sourire ennemi,
> La solitude bleue et stérile a frémi.

Palms! And when it [the dawn] showed this relic to the father [who was] trying out a hostile smile, the blue and sterile solitude shuddered. The smile was hostile, presumably, because the poem was not the *Hérodiade* he wanted. Perhaps the palms can be explained as the shapes the dawn light threw upon the ceiling or even upon the lamp. In *The Poem Itself* Stanley Burnshaw says that 'perhaps *Palmes* simply occurred to Mallarmé and he retained it because he felt he had to—much as he introduced in another poem the word "pytx" because this pure invention struck him as being both right and necessary for his purposes'. Perhaps; but note that the word, if not at the end of the mind, is outside its syntax. Every other word in the passage implies a context, a narrative setting, Idumaean asking only to be explicated. *Palmes* is a transgression, breaking the narrative, or at least suspending it arbitrarily. It is one word, free of syntax, either above or below the otherwise rational narrative, but in any case apart from the sequence. What then does it mean?

Suppose Stevens were reading 'Don du poëme' and coming upon 'Palmes!' brooded not upon its meaning, or even a possible meaning, but upon its character of being beyond or apart from the official narrative. Might he not have placed the palms, for his own quite different purposes, beyond the category which meant more to him than any narrative, the category of mind? And reduced them to one, 'the palm', making it in every respect singular?

The Difficult Debut of Denis Johnston's 'Old Lady'

Joseph Ronsley

Having attended school in Edinburgh, and received his baccalaureate in law from Cambridge and an LLD from Harvard, Denis Johnston returned to Dublin in 1924. By 1925 he not only had an education and a profession, but a keen interest in the theatre as well. It was a good time to arrive in Dublin with this interest since the Abbey had only recently been released from a period of doldrums by the advent of a new playwright, Sean O'Casey, whose *Shadow of a Gunman* and *Juno and the Paycock* had appeared during the previous two years. O'Casey, in fact, was nearing the pinnacle of his success, which would come a year later with *The Plough and the Stars*. What was even more important for Johnston, however, was the flourishing existence of the Dublin Drama League which Lennox Robinson, with Yeats's backing, had begun at the Abbey in 1918. The Abbey proper was committed essentially to Irish plays, though it was beginning to make some exciting exceptions, and the Drama League was formed to provide both participants and audiences with a much desired exposure to foreign classical and modern, and avant garde, drama. The Drama League productions ran for only two evenings each week, being performed on the Abbey stage Sunday and Monday when the Abbey company itself did not use it. Johnston, whose proper occupation as a brand new lawyer trying to make his mark should have been the law—he was called to the English and Irish Bars in 1925—must have been spending an inordinate amount of time in theatre activities because he joined the Drama League before the end of 1924, and in the first year after his return to Dublin played three minor roles. It was not long until he was to leave the practise of law entirely. He later thought of the legal profession with affection, but according to his diaries at the time, he pursued his practise of the law primarily to satisfy his family, and from the beginning it only got in the way of his much keener interest in the theatre.

Johnston's education abroad, along with other related advantages, earned him the suspicions and actual enmity of many of his less fortunate and more provincial theatre colleagues at home. He was very much a part of the Anglo-Irish ascendency, the Greystones crowd. His social life, especially after he began going out with the actress Shelah Richards, included parties and balls, picnics and treasure hunts, automobiles, boats and sporting events. He was relatively affluent and well-dressed, able to travel abroad, which he did frequently, and generally had a cosmopolitan, and probably somewhat arrogant, air about him. But this beautiful life, especially the education and travel, provided him with experience in and taste for a world drama, and especially what was new in it. The Dublin Drama League, then, was a natural attraction for him.

He began by acting: in Benavente's *The School of Princesses* (during which he became reacquainted with Shelah Richards, one of the princesses and his future wife), Shaw's *Fanny's First Play* and *Major Barbara*, Euripides' *Cyclops*, Margaret Kennedy and Basil Dean's *The Constant Nymph*, Pirandello's *The Game as He Played It*, Strindberg's *The Father*, and Evreinov's *The Chief Thing*. *Cyclops* was a Drama League production performed outdoors in Lennox Robinson's Dalkey garden (next door to a much later residence of Johnston himself), and Johnston was described in the *Irish Statesman* for 7 August 1926 as 'a very picturesque Ulysses. He nearly trailed the robe of tragedy', said Walter Starkie the reviewer, 'and his dignified gestures were an echo from the tragic drama'. Another reviewer found him unforgettable as Cusins in the Irish première of *Major Barbara* (an ambiguous compliment to be sure!), but Johnston was never much of an actor, and never considered himself one, though he continued to act from time to time until he left the theatre for broadcasting in 1936.

The more successful aspect of his apprenticeship came in the form of directing. In 1928 he directed O'Neill's *The Fountain* for the Drama League and also his most famous production, a controversial, somewhat expressionistic *King Lear* for the Abbey proper. His interest in expressionism was also manifest in his productions of two expressionist plays, Kaiser's *From Morn to Midnight*, which he directed for a group founded by himself and Shelah Richards called The New Players, in 1927, and Toller's *Hoppla!* which he directed for the Drama League in 1929. C.P. Curran, reviewing *From Morn to Midnight*, conferred 'The honours of the evening' on 'Johnston for adventurous and successful production . . .' Some reviewers did not like the play itself, which is not surprising given, among other things, the mode strange to Dublin audiences, but Curran became a consistent supporter of Johnston's work. At least one other reviewer, writing for *Honesty* on 26 November 1927, clearly was enthusiastic over the new dramatic form: *From Morn to Midnight*, he said,

is one of the finest plays I have seen performed in Dublin, and whoever is responsible for the choice—I believe it was Mr. Denis Johnston—deserves heartiest congratulations for giving Dubliners an opportunity of seeing a drama of such exceptional power, clarity of ideas, and starkness of purpose. There is not one superfluous scene or word in *From Morn to Midnight*. It stands out against a background of recent dramatic offerings as a statue of Epstein would against a collection of china figures.

Toller's *Hoppla!*, which had a very large cast—26 actors named in the programme—like *From Morn to Midnight* had mixed reactions for the play itself but general praise for the director. J.W.G. writing in the *Irish Independent* on 11 March 1929 said:

The real burden of the play was borne by the producer, Mr. E.W. Tocher [Johnston's pseudonym during these years]. Toller is more than any of the moderns the producer's dramatist, and nobody sets them problems at once more difficult and more intriguing. Mr Tocher made an excellent shot at all of them, and, unlike some producers, he did not in arranging the trees, ignore the wood. Even in dull stretches of the play, he kept his company going at a pace that swept the audience breathlessly along.

The mixed reactions to the plays themselves along with general praise for the producer's artistic work which was fast contributing to his rising reputation, must have encouraged Johnston in his preparation, already under way, of the first real shock he was to inflict on his Dublin audience, in the form of his own first play.

1929, in addition to being the year that *Hoppla!* was produced, was the year of the Dublin Drama League's demise, and also the year of the première production of that first play, *The Old Lady Says 'No!'* The Drama League was no longer needed because this same 1928-29 season saw the beginning of Hilton Edwards' and Micheál MacLiammóir's Dublin Gate Theatre Company, which spent its first two seasons in the little Peacock Theatre leased from the Abbey. The Gate provided a more substantial entity to precisely the kind of drama to which the Drama League had been devoted, and later called itself 'the first permanent international theatre in Ireland'.[1] It did not so much compete with the Abbey as provide a highly desirable complementary dramatic repertoire. As Lennox Robinson said, the Drama League had prepared a path for the Gate, and since it was a money loser anyway, the Abbey 'gladly stepped aside to make room for the Edwards-MacLiammóir Company'.[2] Perhaps we should not be too quick, however, to say that the founding of the Gate did no harm to the Abbey. During the twenties some of the Drama League productions, as well as other foreign plays, found their way to the Abbey stage, and contributed to the theatre a special vitality. This vitality was lost when the Drama League disappeared, and the Abbey went back entirely to the production of traditional realistic Irish drama, though by the mid-thirties it was again producing the occasional foreign play.

The mode of *The Old Lady Says 'No!'* had its inspirational origins in Johnston's theatre-going during the frequent trips he made to London and the continent between 1924 and 1928, though it may even go back to Boston and New York during his Harvard days. Shaw was a major general influence on the young Johnston, and although *The Old Lady* betrays a wide range of sometimes subtle influences, including Strindberg's *A Dream Play*, Kaufman and Connelly's *Beggar on Horseback*, Capek's *The Land of Many Names*, O'Casey's *The Plough and the Stars*, and Joyce's *Ulysses*, it was during these years that Johnston made his first real acquaintance with expressionist drama, the Kaiser and Toller, for instance, that he himself would produce a little later. In March, 1926, he saw at the London Gate Theatre what he called in his diary 'an amazing production of *Masses and Man* by Toller, that opened my eyes', and at least on one occasion he attended the London Gate Theatre in the company of his friend Sean O'Casey, to see Kaiser's *From Morn to Midnight*. O'Casey probably also developed at this time his taste for the expressionism he shortly after incorporated into *The Silver Tassie*. By 1928 O'Casey's play had been rejected by the Abbey; the controversy surrounding this event is now famous.

By 1928, too, Johnston's expressionist, or quasi-expressionist, play had also been rejected by the Abbey, also with controversy but which is not so famous.

Johnston began writing the play in 1926, a little over a year after returning to Dublin, and submitted it to Lennox Robinson at the Abbey on 9 March 1927. My ambivalence in calling *The Old Lady Says 'No!'* an expressionist play is due to the fact that Johnston himself did not like to see it as such, at least in later years. He has referred to the 'expressionist tricks'[3] which the play incorporates, and has also said that the play 'is not an expressionist play and ought never to have been mistaken for one'.[4] A real distinction is being made here, with the play containing elements which are clearly expressionistic and also those which are clearly not, but the distinction does at times, as D.E.S. Maxwell says, seem a 'quibble'.[5] Johnston was evidently not so hostile to the expressionist tag early on, when the mode was seen as avant garde, but it appears no author likes to be so neatly categorized.

Expressionism generally implies an absence of specific time and place, and characters that are abstract types, unidentifiable as individual people. A major reason often given for *The Old Lady*'s absence from repertories outside Ireland is that it is too localized, that is, set in a very specific time and place which may not be familiar to non-Irish audiences. Moreover, while the general chorus of characters assume only marginally personal identities, the central characters are readily identifiable historic personages, readily identifiable again, that is, for an Irish audience. So in these respects the play is not an expressionist play, as Johnston says. But since most of the play's action represents, in a sense realistically, the surrealistic hallucinations of an actor's disoriented mind after he is 'accidentally' knocked unconscious, there is ample opportunity for use of the expressionist 'tricks' of which Johnston also speaks. Dramatic action as portrayal of disturbed dream allows for the elimination of normal restrictions on time, space and behaviour, for the use of special theatrical effects of music, light and shifting scenes which interrupt the dialogue or are interwoven with it, and for the loss or change of characters' identities as they become more abstract types or symbols. Johnston does eliminate the ponderous, humourless atmosphere characteristic of the German expressionists, providing in its place a remarkable combination of poetic beauty, savage satire, and hilarity, and there can be no doubt that surrealism and expressionism work very well together.

At any rate, these or other of the play's ingredients were considered unsuitable for the Abbey by the theatre's directors. There is, in fact, considerable controversy over the reasons for the play's rejection, and to what extent there was unanimity among the Abbey's directors in reaching the decision. It has always puzzled me a little that, given Yeats's dissatisfaction with the theatre's tendency toward realistic drama, he would not have been pleased with such an offering. Hilton Edwards has noted that 'Expressionism was a method of play-writing that borrowed much from the abstract forms of music; and it dealt with archetypes rather than with individual character'. Clearly this comment applies to many of Yeats's own most original plays. And Edwards continues with observations of factors that also should have pleased Yeats, that expressionism 'was significant in that it freed the theatre, for a time, from the

bonds of Realism . . . '[6] The Abbey's turn to the dramatic realism for which he
had so little taste was one of Yeats's great disappointments. So Yeats should
have welcomed this new direction. But Johnston recorded in his diary that it
was at the time he was playing in *The Constant Nymph* that Yeats arrived with
the manuscript of his play in hand, and over lunch opened the conversation
with, 'First of all I want to ask you, just what is this play about?'—a lot of
nerve, one might say, considering Yeats's own plays!

Following revision in compliance with suggestions by Yeats and Lennox
Robinson, mainly to shorten the play, the manuscript was rejected again, and
finally. This time Johnston records the following scene:

> Walking back from Sorrento with Mr Yeats he gave me what was probably the most
> incisive criticism this play has received. 'I liked your play', he said, 'but it has one or two
> faults. The first is, the scenes are too long'. He was silent for a time, while we both gazed
> with some signs of embarrassment at a cargo boat rounding Dalkey Island. 'Then', he
> added finally and after considerable thought, 'there are too many scenes'.

Johnston goes on with, 'Needless to say I was grateful for this opinion. To say
that the scenes are too long and that there are too many of them goes right to the
root of the matter. Why do it at all? And if it does mean anything, isn't it better
left unsaid'.[7] But Yeats did think enough of the play, or of the young Johnston,
to go over the manuscript carefully, inserting many marginal notes, and
Johnston felt suitably honoured at the pains taken by the great poet over his
work. On Yeats's direction, Johnston says in his diary, 'I cut it to one act and
one hour and ten minutes—for the audience they say can't stand more than a
little of this sort of stuff you know'. While the departure from realism must
have pleased Yeats, however, the nature of the non-realistic elements were
evidently outside either his understanding or his sensibilities, or simply his
liking. In fact, none of the three Abbey directors took kindly to expressionism.
Still, as both Harold Ferrar and Christine St Peter have pointed out, Yeats and
Lennox Robinson were responsible for the Drama League, and encouraged
the production of new plays many of which neither of them understood or
liked.[8]

Johnston's play opens with a pastiche of highly romantic eighteenth and
nineteenth-century Irish verse, the most sentimental passages strung together
for the fugitive Robert Emmet to speak to his beloved, Sarah Curran, as he
melodramatically takes his farewell following the collapse of the rising he led in
1803. Johnston's recollection indicates that Yeats's criticism of the play
generally consisted of suggestions to shorten and condense. Thus, where
Johnston had written for Emmet the following lines in romantic parody: 'I, the
poor hunted fox: broken, driven to the hills, lying panting in the bracken and
stealing out only when night creeps down from the east to cloak my
nakedness', Yeats suggested this be replaced by 'I am as homeless as the fox'.
Evidently his thinking was in the context of his own vigorous verse of the
twenties, and he missed Johnston's parody completely. Johnston ultimately
responded to Yeats's suggestions, that he shorten the scenes and reduce their
number, by lengthening them and adding some. 'All I knew or ever felt or

heard or experienced about Ireland', he wrote in his diary, 'I put into that play until when I had finished it again, I felt that never again would I be able to write another play as I had said everything there was to say'. But to his 'great surprise', he said later, Yeats 'was charmed' with the results, 'and promised me £50 if I would have the play presented elsewhere'.[9]

Actually, the offer of the £50, according to Johnston's diary, was made by Yeats at the same time he suggested there were too many scenes. Yeats, Johnston says, told him that the play would cost the Abbey £50 and would annoy the audience; he didn't care about the £50, but he didn't want to annoy the audience. Clearly, according to Johnston, this was a lie; Yeats minded very much losing the £50, but didn't mind at all annoying the audience. In fact, Yeats was quite willing to annoy his audiences as a general rule throughout his theatre career. But *The Old Lady*, Johnston says, is a 'vicious' attack on the figure of Cathleen ni Houlihan, and this must have offended both Yeats and Lady Gregory very much.[10] There can be no doubt that the parody of Cathleen ni Houlihan is vicious, evoking a kind of black humour. Curtis Canfield, an early admirer of Johnston's work, agrees that this might have been what put Yeats off. Johnston's satire, he wrote in 1936, while Yeats was still very much on the scene, concludes

from the illustration of the Old Flower Woman's character that Ireland herself is unworthy to be saved by sacrifice. William Butler Yeats's beatific vision of Kathleen ni Houlihan, the spirit of Ireland for whom Irishmen went smiling to death in the field or on the gallows, has changed here to a drunken hag who curses her son as he dies for her. It is a savage and bitter conception that strikes at the heart of sentimental idolatry, and is, of course, a complete inversion of Mr Yeats's view of Kathleen.[11]

More recently, Harold Ferrar has made some poignant comparisons with Johnston's Cathleen: 'O'Casey's Cathleen can be an "old snarly gob"', he says, 'and "a bitch at times", Joyce's "the old sow that eats her farrow", but neither can equal Johnston's acid satire which has turned "matchless Kathaleen" into a whore who propositions her son's murderer as her boy lies dying'.[12] The case for Johnston's view of Cathleen as unsavoury, in contrast with Yeats's, is clear. I myself am not so sure, however, that Yeats would have rejected the play on this ground, especially in his salty later years. I agree with Harold Ferrar when he suggests that Johnston's attitudes toward Ireland as represented in *The Old Lady Says 'No!'* are consistent with those of Synge and O'Casey, and that their presentation is a 'natural fruition', even an extension of their work.[13] All three playwrights loved Ireland, but their love was too profound to permit them a hypocritical stand that pretended their country lacked the short-comings and foibles, both disappointing and amusing, that must be involved in any large collection of human beings. Yeats's feelings were the same.

This aspect of the play had probably been building in Johnston's mind since the time of the 1916 Easter Rising, when at fourteen years old he had his home occupied by both British and rebel soldiers in turn. He describes his initiation into the human irregularities that permeate national and patriotic causes in his preface to the late play, *The Scythe and the Sunset*.[14] If anything, the satire on these lapses, while perhaps being no more virulent than O'Casey's, is more interspersed with an obviously celebratory love of country than that of either Synge or O'Casey. This aspect of the play, in fact, must have been recognized by the IRA at the time, though strangely enough they evidently missed the patriotic slurs that offended others. Johnston has said that the IRA sent representatives to the play's first production in order to determine the advisability of supression, but they found the play patriotic, and recommended it as one that all good nationalists should see.[15]

About the same time Yeats also rejected O'Casey's *Silver Tassie* for reasons that had nothing to do with lack of patriotism, but at least partly, perhaps, because of theatrical elements that could be seen to correspond with certain ones in *The Old Lady*. It should be remembered, too, that *The Old Lady* was revised considerably a second time, and to its benefit, after its final rejection by the Abbey's directors. So there are several possible reasons for Yeats's dissatisfaction with the play; considering the evidence I have seen, determining which one struck the vital note is a matter of speculation.

Johnston in later years felt, perhaps a little fancifully, that Yeats 'really hated the play', and had Johnston himself in mind as one of those artists that in renouncing their artistic heritage are 'base born products of base beds', but he himself considered Yeats, at least for the record, 'a manager of impeccable taste, with a very strict canon of what may or may not be done'.[16] Writing some thirty years after the first production of *The Old Lady Says 'No!'*, he says:

in my younger days at the Abbey and the Gate, we did have the immense figure of Yeats dominating the field in which we were working. We did not, as a rule, sit respectfully at his feet, or attempt to imitate him. Nor did we even agree with him on many of the matters at issue. But he was there—this great, intimidating figure, with a canon of literary good taste that we defied at our peril. Whatever O'Casey may say to the contrary, to have had a script parsed and caustically annotated by Yeats was an experience that no aspiring writer can profitably forget.[17]

In fact, he may have been writing here in order to establish a different record than he had already established nearly ten years earlier in an article he wrote on O'Casey. There he said, referring to the Abbey's rejection of *The Old Lady*:

. . . the more I study this the more I realize after this long lapse of years, what a danger Yeats was to any young playwright coming within his orbit.

This is not in any sense an attack on Yeats's good intentions. He was as genuinely anxious to encourage all of us as he was sincere in his belief that he was doing O'Casey a kindness by rejecting *The Silver Tassie* . . . If you wanted to have a soul of your own, it was necessary to give Yeats an extremely wide berth.[18]

Yeats very clearly had some interest in Johnston's first play, and did make suggestions for revision which Johnston followed, even though Johnston preferred to speak only of those he rejected, and all these revisions substantially improved the first versions of the play shown to him, and to Lennox Robinson who had been Johnston's friend and supporter almost from the beginning. In fact, it is interesting to speculate as to whether Yeats would not have accepted the play were it not for Lady Gregory's stronger objections.

Lady Gregory was almost certainly the 'heavy' in the matter. After the play's rejection Johnston was given the job of directing *King Lear*, quite clearly by Yeats and Robinson without consulting Lady Gregory. While there is good reason to believe Johnston got the job because of the interest Yeats and Robinson took in the fresh, modern work he had been doing with the Drama League, it has been strongly suggested by Lady Gregory herself that he received this appointment at least partially in compensation for the rejection of his play, though Johnston later claimed not to believe this. He felt, he said, there simply was not any other suitable person on hand, and claimed not to have been aware of any resentment over his appointment as director.[19] While Lady Gregory was ultimately pleased with the production of *King Lear* ('*Lear* last night wonderful' she said in her journal) as Yeats was not, her praise was almost entirely for the actors, ignoring the director.[20] There can really be no doubt about her resentment. She was sympathetic with Arthur 'Boss' Shields, a regular Abbey director who was offended because he was passed over in preference for Johnston, and she speaks during the rehearsal time of Johnston's appointment with considerable annoyance, saying that he 'has no connection with us', and that 'Starkie and I agree that we must assert ourselves in future and not let business be settled over our heads'.[21] Johnston had in fact considerable connection with the Drama League, which was in turn connected with the Abbey, but it is clear that Lady Gregory was not an enthusiast for expressionism, and that Johnston was not one of her favourites. She speaks only disparagingly of him in her diaries, and he notes, with pointed emphasis, that he 'was never invited to Gort'.[22]

It is quite clear, too, that Lady Gregory's objections to Johnston's play were the strongest among the Theatre's figures of power. Roger McHugh has suggested that her dislike of the play 'was partly due to a very limited critical capacity, largely caused by writing for an unsophisticated audience, and partly to a certain prudishness which is reflected in her bowdlerisation of the heroic tales'. She reacted similarly, he says, to *The Playboy of the Western World*, despite her vigorous defence of it.[23] Ann Saddlemyer rejects this assertion, however, describing it as a rather commonly held view, but one which is refuted by Lady Gregory's own life and work.[24] Johnston himself tells of an incident which

took place in a back apartment of the Standard Hotel, Harcourt Street, where she interviewed the abashed author soon after [the play's] rejection by the Abbey. The little play with which it opened—she told me—she liked very much indeed; but later on she felt that the whole thing became rather common—her actual word.[25]

He remarks later in his diary that 'It seems almost incredible that Lady G should have taken the opening melodrama . . . seriously rather than as satirical parody. But this is literally true'. He assumed she never really read the play, but simply glanced at the text. From Lady Gregory's 'appreciation' of the opening parody, without being aware that it was one, Johnston goes on to say that 'it will be seen that Lady Gregory was by no means unappreciative of the doubtful merits of this opus'.[26] Whether she was appreciative or not, it is clear from a passage in her diary that she read the play. She wrote on 14 August 1928:

I read the Emmet play and liked it—thought all the early part much better than before, and that as the author would be producing it, it would be possible. I got tired when half through, and thought it was being tired that made me feel it was going into jazz, and that if Yeats had liked it we might put it on . . . But Yeats said he hadn't read it since alterations, and last evening I read it straight through. I still like the beginning, it set the mind wandering through romantic historical alleys, but the later part seemed really bad—poor—not worth putting on our stage. But I didn't say so, nor read it badly. I gave it every chance. I do not think it should be produced at the Abbey. I am sorry, for the early part sent the mind wandering—(mine permanently it seems!).

Yeats had said 'I told G.B.S. the other day I perhaps ought not to judge plays but give place to someone else as I don't know much about impressionism', and he said 'There is nothing in it, in impressionism'.

I asked Yeats then, 'What is impressionism?' and he said 'No law'—and I said 'all jaw' and he said 'Just so'. And that certainly describes the play.[27]

Johnston's assertion that Lady Gregory missed the parody in the opening melodrama is thus confirmed, as is her dislike of expressionism, or as she says, 'impressionism', or 'jazz'. But she did read the play, and Yeats comes off with uncharacteristic humility in his misgivings over his own judgement.

The play which Johnston had submitted to the Abbey under the title, 'Shadowdance', was returned to him by Lennox Robinson, as everybody 'knows', with the words written across the title page, 'The old lady says No'. And whether the words were written by Robinson, by Mick Dolan as Johnston believed,[28] or by Yeats himself, which I think highly unlikely but which has been suggested by Tomás MacAnna,[29] they provided another suggested revision, though one made inadvertently, which the author accepted by spitefully changing the play's title when it went into production at the Gate. In the process Lady Gregory joins Sarah Curran and the vicious old flower woman who torments the hero throughout the play, as another avatar of Cathleen ni Houlihan, though admittedly she does so in an historic rather than dramatic context.

Ernest Blythe, a later and long-time director of the theatre, has a different version of the Abbey's rejection of Johnston's play, one that exonerates both Yeats and Lady Gregory from any charge of limited sensitivity or critical capacity, and that makes the decision simply a matter of business-like pragmatism. He writes in 1963:

Obviously it could well happen that the Abbey might fail to see the worth of an outstanding script submitted to it. It is safe to say, however, that it has not done so as yet, though in two or three cases an important play, which was ultimately performed in the Abbey, was, for varying reasons, returned to its author when first submitted . . . The only case in which the Abbey definitely failed to produce a play of high merit which had been submitted to it, was that of Denis Johnston's satirical fantasy, *The Old Lady Says 'No!'* Actually the quality of the play was appreciated, but it required a style of production outside the range of the Abbey producers of the time. It was returned to the author; but the Abbey gave a subsidy to Messrs Edwards and MacLiammoir to enable them to produce it in the Peacock Theatre in which their newly-founded Gate Theatre was then operating.[30]

Lady Gregory's diary contradicts Blythe's version. Moreover, having written, as he has said, 'a director's play', incorporating elements that he would like to direct,[31] and actually being himself a director at the time, Johnston could certainly have directed the play, and quite clearly had this in mind. Indeed, Lady Gregory mentioned in her diary that likelihood. In any case, I find it difficult to believe that the Abbey directors, with the Drama League at the peak of its activities, could not have found the human resources to produce the play had there been a will to do so.

There is controversy, too, over the size of the Abbey's subsidy to the Gate for the play's production. £50 is the amount supposedly offered, but both Johnston and MacLiammoir have said emphatically that the amount actually given was £15, and MacLiammoir goes on to say that 'The figure sounds incredible but it is correct, and it is correct too to say that we welcomed it'.[32] The amount given undoubtedly was £15, but this does not indicate a reneging on the part of the Abbey directors. Lady Gregory notes in her journal that Johnston 'has spoken to Hilton Edwards, who will put on his Robert Emmet play, we guaranteeing against loss up to £50'.[33] Johnston in his diary says the £15 figure was an arbitrary one he himself suggested to Lennox Robinson as a compromise to avoid all the accounting procedures which the Abbey was demanding otherwise, and which the Gate considered unreasonable. Thus, whether the contribution was made begrudgingly or graciously (and it is certain, according to her diary, that on Lady Gregory's part it was begrudgingly), the £15 actual subsidy does appear to be consistent with at least Lady Gregory's intentions, if not with Johnston's and the Gate's expectations.

So *The Old Lady* went to the infant Dublin Gate Theatre, which theatre, itself, Hilton Edwards has said, was brought to Dublin 'upon the flood-tide' of the expressionist movement.[34] In fact, it was Johnston's wife, Shelah Richards, who energetically persuaded Hilton Edwards to produce the play, using the promise of the £50 subsidy as part of the incentive. 'Owing to Shelah's condition' [she was pregnant], Johnston says in his diary, 'she was not able to take the part she deserved for all her good work—I would never have done anything to get it on myself I'm sure, but for her'. As it turned out Johnston had every reason to be happy with the unfolding of circumstances. Whatever he believed at the time, he later claimed to agree with Ernest Blythe's explanation for his play's rejection by the Abbey. Both O'Casey's *Silver Tassie* and his own *Old Lady*, he said in 1961 with fine hindsight, were works 'of a type quite outside the competence of the Abbey's directors at that time, and . . . if Mr O'Casey had been a little less huffy, his play—like mine—would have been presented considerably better elsewhere, and with no hard feelings'.[35] *The Old Lady Says 'No!'* became Johnston's most popular play in Ireland and Johnston became the Dublin Gate Theatre's first notable Irish playwright 'discovery'; essentially the same production, with MacLiammoir in the lead role, was revived periodically at the Gate for over forty years.

And in 1977, nearly fifty years after its première at the Gate, *The Old Lady* was presented at the Abbey.

I mentioned that a major benefit derived from Johnston's Drama League experience came in the form of directing. But while *The Old Lady* may have been a director's play, written to include elements that he himself would have liked to direct, it was Hilton Edwards who was to benefit from this aspect of the play, almost certainly for the best so far as the play itself was concerned. Through the surrealist effects so appropriate to its theme and plot the play also gave Micheál MacLiammóir's visual imagination a free play beyond what was possible in any other Irish play. The 'head injury' sustained by the leading actor accounts for the distortions of his own identity both as an actor and as the character he is portraying, Robert Emmet, and of his view of the world around him, again, his own world of the 1920s and the early nineteenth-century world of his character. When all these perceptions become tangled with each other the fanciful possibilities in dialogue, action, effects of sight and sound, the abstraction of music and dance, are infinite for any lively imagination, much less for the combined imaginations of Johnston, Edwards and MacLiammóir.

It is not my purpose here to go into another detailed analysis of the play itself, and MacLiammóir's account of his first introduction to the play, the casting, rehearsals and its première, while apparently a little romanticized, makes lively reading in his *All for Hecuba*, and is reprinted in *Denis Johnston: A Retrospective*.[36] But it is interesting to look at the play's reception in that first Dublin production.

The reception was mixed. Joseph Holloway, who never cared for Denis Johnston or any of his work, of course did not like the 'madhouse play' as he called it, but did consider that MacLiammóir 'looked very like "Emmet" and spoke many passages poetically and well'. (Johnston himself, I should mention, later considered that MacLiammóir was just the kind of bad actor the part called for.) But Holloway is rather confused in his assessment of the actress Meriel Moore. He says that 'Miss Moore had little to do, only speak a few lines of poetry musically from the balcony', and then goes on to say, 'I lost my programme. She who played "Kathleen" made her a very wretched, foul-mouthed creature indeed, that now and then recited lines of poetry from Yeats'. In fact, it is crucial that the same actress play Sarah Curran on the balcony in the opening melodramatic playlet and also the terrible old flower woman; both represent Cathleen, and Meriel Moore played both parts.

Holloway felt that 'It was a really great achievement for the Gate people to get such a chaos of absurdities over at all'. 'The first part', he says,

might be summed up as a jeer at patriotism served up in the crudest, brutal way. The production and acting saved it from boredom, but left me feeling that if produced anywhere else save the Gate (even at the Abbey) it would not have been tolerated by an audience. In the second part, the burlesque of a modern Sunday At-Home, with O'Casey with his cap on and strong language ever on his lips had amusing moments, but the language of 'Kathleen' and others in the pub-scene exceeded the bounds of good taste, and would only be tolerated by aged ladies with a grah for much hard talk. I noticed that a good deal of blasphemy was introduced into the speeches at times.

The actress Ria Mooney responded differently. Holloway reports that she exclaimed at the end of Act I: 'I am immensely intrigued by the piece and almost wept at times', which, says Holloway, 'was appreciation run riot'.[37]

More publicly, there was also a full range of opinion. In the *Evening Mail* we have, 'If "E.W. Tocher" intended merely to mystify his audience with his first play . . . he certainly went a long way towards success'.[38]

Mystery appears to have been a keynote in speaking of the play even before it opened. Thus in *The Daily Express*:

I wish to heaven I knew as much about *The Old Lady Says 'No!'*, a piece which is to be produced at Dublin Gate Theatre in a few weeks time. The author . . . is a member of one of the learned professions. I am not permitted to say which; he is also the husband of a Dublin actress; I am not permitted to say who; this is his first play; I am not permitted to say what it is about. Indeed, after half-an-hour's converse with the author the other day, I reluctantly concluded that he did not know himself. Perhaps I am uncharitable, however.

I strongly advise the Gate people, nevertheless, if they want to make a lot of money out of this play—is it a play, by the way?—to advertise it as 'The Mystery Play', by 'The Mystery Man of Dublin'.[39]

I don't believe it was advertised that way, but considering the repeated revivals and frequent full houses from the beginning, it must have been a money-maker for the Gate for a good long while. It played to 'packed houses', Johnston says in his diary, 'for the last fortnight of the Theatre's season at the Peacock'. He also notes, moreover, that the Abbey would have been better off without having made that £15 compromise, since the play more than paid its own way. As to the mystery itself, from the little I know of Dublin and Dubliners who are likely to attend the theatre, I doubt it could have remained a mystery for long.

The Daily Express seems to have made quite a saga of the production. After the foregoing preliminaries there was a review of the dress rehearsal:

Everything which has been traditionally reverenced in Ireland has been made the butt of withering sarcasm, and the play expresses the outlook of an Irishman whose only religious conviction is a belief in the real existence of hell.

No Irishman has ever written a play even remotely resembling this, and it is certainly an act of courage on the part of the directors of the Gate to present it on an Irish stage . . .

The production has been a task to test the mettle of Mr Hilton Edwards, and the dress rehearsal lasted from eight o'clock until one in the morning.[40]

And finally a review of the production itself:

I have seen [the play] again since I wrote about it last week, and I am satisfied that it is not a great play.

It is a daring experiment in which Mr Tocher displays much cleverness, but it sparkles with the borrowed tinsel of quotations. It is a play to see and discuss, but not one to admire or imitate.[41]

I suppose the reviewer's most devastating personal comment comes elsewhere, when he refers to Johnston as being 'well known in Dublin as a producer with advanced ideas . . .'[42]

A more positive, though not unqualified view was expressed by D.S. of the *Irish Independent*:

It is an extraordinary play; I disliked it intensely and admired it enormously. Certainly, it is new, stimulating, and sincere . . . Mr Tocher has a remarkable mastery of technique and a powerful imagination. He lashes the Irish people with his bitter satire not in a spirit of cheap cynicism or of righteous indignation, but with the cold impersonal detachment of the artist.[43]

At least here is the concession that the play is in fact a work of art.

The critic for whom Johnston himself quite naturally had the highest regard was Constantine Curran, who indeed wrote in the *Irish Statesman* what was probably the most intelligent and intellectually conceived review:

The force, comic, ironic and imaginative, with which E.W. Tocher illustrates and drives home the subject matter of his first play has not been paralleled since Synge nor has so richly equipped and modern a mind for many years occupied our stage. He has chosen the expressionist method and given it its first complete Irish application. It is a tempting fashion which leads too often into a blind alley. Applied to a human action it tends to rob the stage of its chief wealth, the diversity of human nature, by reducing it to merely typical, mechanical action. Mr Tocher avoids this danger since he handles only ideas and tendencies, staging, as I apprehend it, the various epiphanies of the spirit of Dublin.

That Johnston's play dealt extensively with ideas aligned him with Shaw and virtually no other Irish playwright, and later caused Robert Hogan to refer to Denis Johnston's 'Adult Theatre'. But Curran also deals with the moral concerns that troubled Joseph Holloway:

I have heard exception taken to the occasional use . . . of language drawn from the liturgy. It always seems to me doubtful how far a dramatist may, for his own purpose borrow the religious emotions inevitably and inextricably associated with such language. In the present play, packed as it is with literary echoes, I find it used in grave circumstances, following immediately upon the grotesque. It is the desperate prayer of a drowning intelligence, or else is used in simile. As to the whole intent of the play, it is plain enough. It is a brilliantly witty and powerful onslaught, not on sentimentality merely, but on that expression of it in which, to the writer's mind, Dublin lies.[44]

Curran's moral defence did not satisfy a Mr James O'Reilly, however, who was a fellow-contributor to *The Irish Statesman*. He writes in a letter to the Editor:

I am amazed and pained that such a play as 'The Old Lady Says "No!"' was not condemned by *The Irish Statesman*. It is a play that could not be produced in any theatre open to the public outside this country. The symbolic figure of Ireland is represented by, to quote C.P.C. [Curran], a 'foul-mouthed harridan'. Imagine Britannia represented on the London stage as a lecherous, dirty-tongued old drab, or the symbolic France in a similar guise at Paris. This, however, is a minor matter in comparison with another. Here in the capital city of this Christian country, while the hymns of the multitudes who gathered so splendidly to worship God seems still fading in the wind, a coterie of persons, directed, I understand, by a foreigner [Hilton Edwards], have seen fit to insult the theatre-going public with a blasphemous outrage. A crazy 'Robert Emmet' raves and rants on the stage the most sacred passages of Holy Writ, preceded and followed by shouts and ejaculations from the other members of the cast of 'bloody'

and 'bastard' and the like . . . My opinion . . . certainly will be scoffed at by those who
think their own standards of literary or artistic merit are above and outside the law of
God and the law of the land . . . but I give it here so that it may not be said that
professing Christians who contribute to this paper are cowed or silenced on such
occasions when protest is a matter of conscience and good citizenship.[45]

This letter received a response from Curran, which was in turn responded to by
O'Reilly. Meanwhile, a Mr Geoffrey Coulter had entered the fray against
O'Reilly in the letter columns, but we will not pursue the argument, other than
to note that Johnston records in his diary that, 'O'Reilly, the Oxford Catholic,
his beady eyes blazing with fanatical bitterness [accosted him] in the law
library with the news that he had arranged . . . to appeal [to] the Attorney
General to have [him] prosecuted'. The Attorney General evidently was not
interested.

The Old Lady Says 'No!', then, was controversial! Johnston even berates in
his diary his friend and supporter Con Curran, who he says became timid
under pressure. He also lists some individual reactions to the play:

My father and mother liked it because it was my play. Otherwise I don't believe they
would have, for a minute.

Sybil le Brocquy was thrilled. But when I said that the House didn't take it too badly
she said indignantly 'Oh if you had heard them around me!'

Sir Philip and Lady Hanson sat throughout the performance with closed eyes. When
asked about it at the end their only comment was 'If people must have nightmares, why
inflict them on us'.

Adelaide Richards [Shelah's mother] was deeply moved and enthusiastically mis-
quoted [in place of the beginning of the famous final speech 'Strumpet city in the
sunset'] 'Strumpet sitting in the sunset' for several days afterwards.

The Golf Hotel, Greystones, left in a body in the interval.

Ned Stephens explained the play to me at great length as a 'study in the breakdown of
a synthetic personality', psychologically very interesting.

Irene Haughy, the Poetess and her sister were door slammers.

Johnston himself wrote in his diary:

I saw it myself one night, but on one night only. It was too unbearably oppressive in
that little theatre where everything happens on top of one and there is no escape. I could
not bear the shocked and taut reactions of the audience all on tip-toe—the women who
tut-tutted and clicked their tongues from time to time, and the people who got up and
walked out, slamming the door behind them. It was indecent that such people should be
listening to my play—this play into which I had put everything and left back nothing,
where I had spoken the truth about everything in general and myself in particular as
never before. It was an indecent exposure before such turds. And the few who were my
friends and who could understand seemed so few and so far between. Oh it is no
pleasure to have one's play given its first production, and I laugh to myself when I think
of how long and how hard I have worked for this consumation. Yet one way and another
I am not sorry. I have said my say and have spoken the whole truth for once in my life.
And if I ever get another chance I shall do it again. For somehow, in spite of everything,
it was worth while.

Nearly ten years later, on 15 January 1938, Johnston saw a revival of *The Old
Lady* at the Gate. His attitude toward the society he had satirized in the play

was now more mellow in maturity, his youthful outrage somewhat cooled, and in his diary he is critical of his first play:

It is not a great play. It is a strong play, a young play, a terribly bitter and sincere play. It is a wild cry of rage—the wind and fury of outraged youth. And it is, I am proud to say, an utterly fearless play. But that is all that can be said for it. It is the tormented offspring of disillusionment and Civil War—even in its violent Fascist conclusions. It is full of intolerable technical experiments, some of which come off and some of which do not.

I do not believe he does the play justice here, and it is quite possible his condescension toward his youthful production on the little Peacock stage is the product of his new-found worldliness at the BBC.

Various critics have pointed out that aside from some of Yeats's plays, which were so eccentric as to be virtually outside the public venue, *The Old Lady* represents the first production of an Irish play that departed radically from the realistic peasant tradition of the Irish dramatic movement. In a sense, then, it opened up that movement at a time when the excitement of its traditional mode had run its course. Failure of the Abbey at the time to recognize the event provided the young Gate Theatre a special opportunity; the Irish theatre's vitality shifted from the Abbey to it, and remained there for at least the next couple of decades.

In May, 1930, ten months after *The Old Lady*'s première, Mary Manning in an article entitled 'In Dublin To-Day' published in *The Saturday Review of Literature* spoke, with perhaps a little exaggeration, of the doldrums of the Abbey in contrast with the energies of the Gate under Edwards' and MacLiammoir's direction. In that article she writes:

The Gate Theatre has justified its existence if only for its production of that remarkable first play, 'The Old Lady Says "No!"' [Johnston's] is undoubtedly one of the most fresh and original minds amongst the younger men . . . [He] has that deadly combination—a cruel and at times savage humour, accompanied by a penetrating insight into the follies and inconsistencies of the society he satirizes. At present he is too serious about being frivolous; however, when he has learnt a little tolerance and finds his own medium he will write something very good indeed. He is a giant in the making.[46]

Her prophecy turns out probably to have been overstated. It could be, and has been argued, that Johnston never did find 'his own medium'. Still, Curtis Canfield could write in 1936 that 'Denis Johnston, by virtue of these two rich and mature plays [*The Old Lady* and *The Moon in the Yellow River*], is the spearhead of the new Irish Drama'. Canfield, like Mary Manning, held great hope for what Johnston might do in the future, saying that 'In him, more than in any other Irish playwright of the present time, the hope of the literary drama lies'.[47] While Johnston's radical methods may not have revolutionized the work of Irish writers who followed him, Hilton Edwards wrote ten years after Canfield that 'It is no accident that in his early work he was as much influenced by Joyce as the later O'Casey seems to have been influenced by Denis Johnston'.[48] And in 1950, from MacLiammoir:

The modern names that come into the mind among those writers for the theatre who are innate rebels against the tyrannies, whether their rebellion had been successful or not, are Toller, Cocteau, Beckett, Brecht, Thornton Wilder, Johnston, O'Neill and Yeats . . . [49]

By the late thirties Johnston's interest shifted from the stage to broadcasting, but he wrote at least six or seven beautiful and important plays, each very different from the other in form and substance. I believe they should be placed among those plays constituting the Irish dramatic canon which the world most highly values.

His second play, *The Moon in the Yellow River*, in contrast with *The Old Lady*, was in the realistic mode, seemingly suitable and safe for the Abbey where it was produced in 1931. It later was produced by the Theatre Guild on Broadway, and became Johnston's best known play outside Ireland. Despite its more conventional form, it turned out to be just as controversial as *The Old Lady*. But that is another story.

In Search of Horatio's Identity (via Yeats)

R.W. Desai

In his lines,

> There are more things in heaven and earth, Horatio,
> Than are dreamt of in your philosophy,[1]

the emphasis on *your* that I believe every reader of the play imagines Hamlet to place is the point of divergence between the two men. In general, critical judgement of Horatio has regarded him as the opposite of Hamlet: he is not 'passion's slave' as Hamlet recognizes himself to be in his second meeting with the Ghost[2] and, at the play's end, he is a worthy narrator whom Hamlet designates to tell his story to the world.[3] If, for convenience, an attempt at categorization is made, it might be said that Hamlet as a believer in the Ghost stands for medieval man, while Horatio the sceptic stands for Renaissance man.

Interestingly enough, though Yeats saw Hamlet as a representative of the Renaissance in a passage that he wrote in 1921, 'Shakespeare himself foreshadowed a symbolic change, that is, a change in the whole temperament of the world, for though he called his Hamlet "fat" and even "scant of breath", he thrust between his fingers agile rapier and dagger',[4] seventeen years later he seems to have revised this view: 'Hamlet's hesitations are hesitations of thought, and are concerned with certain persons on whom his attention is fixed; outside that he is a mediaeval man of action'.[5] That the Yeatsian stance toward the supernatural would have been close to that of Hamlet, not Horatio, is indicated by the echoes from the ghost scenes in *Hamlet* that find a place in his *Fighting the Waves* and *The Herne's Egg*. In *Fighting the Waves* the Figure of Cuchulain mocks Emer for drawing a dagger to wound the Woman of the Sidhe, 'You think to wound her with a knife! She has an airy body, an invulnerable body',[6] a rebuke that echoes Marcellus's recognition of the Ghost's immunity to human assault:

> We do it wrong, being so majestical,
> To offer it the show of violence;
> For it is, as the air, invulnerable,
> And our vain blows malicious mockery.

In *The Herne's Egg* the soldiers of King Congal attack the Great Herne first with stones, then with swords. Mike, one of the soldiers, barks out orders which the king ratifies:

MIKE	Stones.
CONGAL	This man is right.
	Beat him to death with stones.
PAT	All those stones fell wide.
CORNEY	He has come down so low
	His legs are sweeping the grass.
MIKE	Swords.
CONGAL	This man is right.
	Cut him up with swords.
PAT	I have him within my reach.
CONGAL	No, no, he is here at my side.
CORNEY	His wing has touched my shoulder.
CONGAL	We missed him again and he
	Rises again and sinks
	Behind the wall of Tara.[7]

That Yeats had in mind recollections of the Ghost's second appearance in *Hamlet* is unmistakable:

HORATIO	. . . Stop it, Marcellus.
MARCELLUS	Shall I strike at it with my partisan?
HORATIO	Do, if it will not stand.
BARNARDO	'Tis here!
HORATIO	'Tis here!
MARCELLUS	'Tis gone!

For Yeats the supernatural asserts its hegemony over the natural. Reacting against the widespread dominance of Darwin and Huxley in his own time, Yeats declared, 'I am very religious, and deprived by Huxley and Tyndall, whom I detested, of the simple-minded religion of my childhood, I had made a new religion'.[8] Affinities between the ages of Victoria and Elizabeth I have often been remarked. The emergence of a new moneyed class, the change of patronage from one group to another, a loss of faith accompanied by astonishing vitality and individuality—these were some of the characteristics that marked both periods. Yeats's reactions to his own times, as we shall see later, are often reflections of his dualistic attitude to the Renaissance. The Yeats who could write in 'Reveries Over Childhood and Youth',

I began occasionally telling people that one should believe whatever had been believed in all countries and periods, and only reject any part of it after much evidence,[9]

would, of course, be on the side of Hamlet, who after the play-within-the-play declares to Horatio, 'O good Horatio, I'll take the ghost's word for a thousand pound'.

＊   ＊   ＊

But is the Horatio at the end the same as the Horatio we see throughout the play, or has his close contact with Hamlet effected a change in his outlook? Or, is the sceptical Horatio of the play's beginning a mask concealing the real

Horatio who is fully revealed at the play's end? After all, it is to Horatio that Hamlet confides some of his most profound thoughts ('There's a divinity that shapes our ends'; 'We defy augury. There is special providence in the fall of a sparrow') and, despite Horatio's disapproval of some of Hamlet's apparently morbid utterances in the graveyard, Hamlet's influence on his friend is evident at the end when the once stoical Horatio takes up the poisoned wine cup, an act seemingly inconsistent with an earlier Horatio whom Hamlet had described 'As one, in suff'ring all, that suffers nothing'.[10]

The Horatio who is about to attempt suicide is also very different from the man we see at the play's opening who is self-opinionated, even smugly complacent. His 'Tush, tush, 'twill not appear', and, 'Well, sit we down, / And let us hear Barnardo speak of this' are contemptuous and condescending, respectively. But Horatio is, of course, mistaken: the Ghost appears on the stroke of one and Barnardo has the satisfaction of being able to say, 'How now, Horatio? You tremble and look pale. / Is not this something more than fantasy?' Appropriately, the unbelieving Horatio, now forced to believe, who trembles and looks pale, will, at the play's end, receive from Hamlet the mandate to report his cause aright to those 'that look pale and tremble at this chance'. The implication is that having passed through the baptism of a soul-probing experience Horatio, in turn, is the instrument chosen to convince and convict 'the unsatisfied'. Having become enlightened himself through a process of gradual discovery, Horatio is now fit to recount Hamlet's story of an audience as incredulous as he himself was at the play's beginning.

That the Horatio of the play's beginning is imperceptive in dealing with issues that transcend the senses ('the sensible and true avouch / Of mine own eyes' is his criterion for belief) is evident from his feckless command to Barnardo to strike at the Ghost with his partisan, a command at once outrageous and even sacrilegious. Horatio's scholarship ('Thou art a scholar; speak to it, Horatio') does not seem to have equipped him with the sensibility to distinguish between the supernatural and the natural, the metaphysical and the physical. On the other hand, Marcellus, unsophisticated and unlearned, is, as noted above, penitent ('We do it wrong, being so majestical'), and his impression of the Ghost as 'majestical' is at odds with Horatio's disparaging description of the Ghost being 'a mote . . . to trouble the mind's eye', of having 'started like a guilty thing', and of being an 'erring spirit'. Whereas Horatio is only concerned about his inability to compel the Ghost to speak ('Stay! speak, speak! I charge thee, speak!'),[11] Marcellus admits the affront done to the Ghost's dignity and the absurdity of trying to circumscribe it by force or strategy ('For it is as the air, invulnerable, / And our vain blows malicious mockery').

In contrast to Horatio's disjunction with the Ghost, Hamlet's thinking at certain moments in the play suggests a distant echo of the Ghost's actions. Thus its appearance on the stroke of one, 'the bell then beating one', as Barnardo relates, its punctuality emphasized later by Marcellus's 'Thus twice before, and jump at this dead hour', is echoed in the last act of the play in Hamlet's observation to Horatio, 'And a man's life's no more than to say "one" ', followed shortly by his actually saying 'One' on his scoring the first hit against Laertes in the duelling match. The brevity of the Ghost's manumission, restricted to 'While one with moderate haste might tell a hundred' on its first appearance ('But soft, methinks I scent the morning air; / Brief let me be'), is matched by Hamlet's sense of the brevity of human existence. Whether 'one', or 'a hundred' makes no difference, even as Yorick, Alexander, and Caesar are companions in death and decay. One more example: the dying Hamlet tells Horatio, 'The potent poison quite o'ercrows my spirit' and is arrested in mid-speech, 'O, I could tell you -', a scene elliptically reminiscent of the Ghost being thwarted in its endeavour to speak by the cock's crow: ('It was about to speak when the cock crew.')

Horatio's ignorance of the rules of proper conduct in a realm beyond his philosophical ken is counterbalanced by Marcellus's piety and simple sincerity ('Some say that ever 'gainst that season comes / Wherein our Saviour's birth is celebrated'), which, as before, Horatio dismisses as one only half convinced ('So have I heard and do in part believe it'). Unsure of his ground, Horatio straddles two worlds—the old world of the emotions and the new world of the reason—and has a divided self. His belief is 'in part', his identity fragmented. 'A piece of him' is his response to Barnardo's query, 'Say—/ What, is Horatio there?' The fracturing of sensibility that came with the Renaissance, rendering 'the human mind inorganic', a phrase of Yeats to be looked at presently, is suggested in Horatio's inability to bring to a focus the various events—the double appearance of the Ghost and the preparations for war—of the opening scene. It is appropriate, therefore, that the scene should conclude with Horatio's lines,

> Let us impart what we have seen tonight
> Unto young Hamlet, for upon my life
> This spirit, dumb to us, will speak to him.

Contrasting with Horatio for whom 'truth' can only be grasped by the five senses, Hamlet intuits in his soul the truth of both friendship ('Since my dear soul was mistress of her choice / And could of men distinguish her election, / S'hath sealed thee for herself') and of guilt ('Even with the very comment of thy soul / Observe my uncle').

This distinction between the philosophy of the two men reaches its most obtuse angle of divergence in Hamlet's resistance to the restraint Horatio exercises over him at the Ghost's summons:

> I do not set my life at a pin's fee,
> And for my soul, what can it do to that,
> Being a thing immortal as itself?

For Hamlet the soul transcends the life of the body as well as the physical universe. At about the same time that *Hamlet* was first performed, John Davies' poem 'Of the Soul of Man and the Immortality Thereof' (1599) was published, certain stanzas of which parallel the clarity of insight the soul possesses, as expressed in Hamlet's philosophy, in contrast to the inadequacy of the senses:

> Since then the soul works by herself alone,
> Springs not from sense nor humours well agreeing,
> Her nature is peculiar and her own;
> She is a substance and a perfect being.
>
> But though this substance be the root of sense,
> Sense knows her not, which doth but bodies know;
> She is a spirit and a heavenly influence
> Which from the fountain of God's spirit doth flow.[12]

The senses can perceive only the corruption and decay of the human body: 'Dost thou think Alexander looked o' this fashion i' th' earth? . . . And smelt so? Pah!'; they cannot conjure an image of Alexander above and beyond the reductionism to which the flesh is subject. But the Hamlet of the last scene does visualise a timeless projection of himself to be rendered by Horatio ('. . . draw thy breath in pain, / To tell my story').

Though, as noted above in passing, Yeats saw the human mind becoming inorganic with the coming of the Renaissance, his attitude to this historical epoch was not unilateral but dualistic:

I detest the Renaissance because it made the human mind inorganic; I adore the Renaissance because it clarified form and created freedom.[13]

Out of a combination of, and interaction between, these diverse elements Yeats sees great art taking birth. In his poem 'The Statues' he traces the progression of a Hamlet consumed with intellectual curiosity arriving at philosophical wisdom, true knowledge, in the last act of the play. The Hamlet Yeats visualizes at this stage of the action is 'No Hamlet thin from eating flies, [but rather] a fat / Dreamer of the Middle Ages', a description that echoes Gertrude's description of her son as being 'fat and scant of breath'. For Yeats, Hamlet, though a Renaissance man, has his roots in the Middle Ages and can still arrive at true knowledge despite his being 'out of phase', a description that Yeats often found appropriate for the subjects of his scrutiny. 'Empty eyeballs knew / That knowledge increases unreality' is the insight Hamlet gains; likewise in modern Ireland,

> We Irish, born into that ancient sect
> But thrown upon this filthy modern tide
> And by its formless spawning fury wrecked,
> Climb to our proper dark . . .

*   *   *

Throughout the opening scenes of the play, then, Horatio's perception of the truth is faulty. Yet Hamlet relies upon him for confirmation of his uncle's guilt as revealed by *The Murder of Gonzago*, and Horatio has assured Hamlet before the play within the play starts that 'If he steal aught the whilst this play is playing / And 'scape detecting, I will pay the theft'. We recall, with a certain degree of uneasiness, that Horatio was clearly mistaken when he declared to Hamlet that the Ghost stayed 'while one with moderate haste might tell a hundred', for he was immediately corrected by both Marcellus and Barnardo. Again, two scenes later, at his next appearance on the battlements of the castle, his failure to hear the twelve strokes of the bell is amazing and, as before, he is corrected by Marcellus:

HAMLET	What hour now?
HORATIO	I think it lacks of twelve.
MARCELLUS	No, it is struck.
HORATIO	Indeed? I heard it not.

The seeming triviality of these details may cause us to dismiss them as inconsequential, yet surely Shakespeare included them not simply to create an air of verisimilitude but as pointers toward possible interpretation. If, as I have been suggesting, Horatio is a character pulled in opposite directions, endeavouring to conceal his emotion behind a mask of reason, at times the former asserts itself and reveals a surprisingly volatile Horatio. True, Hamlet in his appraisal of his friend envies those 'whose blood and judgement are so well co-meddled', but perhaps Hamlet's compliment is excessive, a likelihood to be examined more closely in the next section.

That despite his professed rationality Horatio can describe the symptoms of acrophobia so accurately ('Think of it. / The very place puts toys of desperation, / Without more motive, into every brain / That looks so many fathoms to the sea') suggests the presence of the irrational Horatio planting the idea of suicide in Hamlet's mind lurking beneath a veneer of sceptical modernity. Who, then, is the real Horatio? The Horatio of the phlegmatic humour, or the Horatio who can say, 'Here's yet some liquor left'? If Hamlet's occupation throughout the play is not so much a quest for Claudius' guilt as for his own identity ('Am I a coward?'; 'I do not know / Why yet I live to say "This thing's to do"'), his choice of Horatio as the man he will wear in his 'heart's core, ay, in my heart of heart' opens up several lines of inquiry that are worth pursuing. Hamlet's recognition of his own false self and true self is stated by him explicitly in his address to Laertes before the commencement of the duel:

Was't Hamlet wronged Laertes? Never Hamlet.
If Hamlet from himself be ta'en away,
And when he's not himself does wrong Laertes,
Then Hamlet does it not, Hamlet denies it.

Though these lines made Dr Johnson uncomfortable,[14] that Laertes can say while dying 'Exchange forgiveness with me, noble Hamlet' is indicative of the conviction Hamlet's apology carries. Likewise the needle of Horatio's identity oscillates between extremities, moving away at the play's end from the philosophy that Hamlet called 'your philosophy' at the play's beginning, and pointing toward a view he now shares with Hamlet.

At the play's beginning Horatio the rationalist had grappled with Hamlet the romantic, endeavouring to restrain him from following the Ghost ('Be ruled. You shall not go'); at the play's ending the roles are reversed: Hamlet grapples with Horatio, and wrests the wine cup from his grasp. As the action draws to a close Hamlet seems to become increasingly passive, a change often noted by commentators, while Claudius becomes active in his scheming. Fearful for Hamlet's safety in the face of the King's obvious treachery, Horatio cautions, 'You will lose this wager, my lord', but Hamlet's calm confidence ('I do not think so . . . I shall win at the odds') is well founded for he does indeed prove a better duellist than Laertes.

Earlier too, in the churchyard with Hamlet, Horatio is not quite in tune with the mood of the scene. As we have noted, his terse acquiescence ('E'en so'; 'E'en so, my lord') with Hamlet's observations suggests disapproval of Hamlet's interest in the minute particulars of death and decay. While Hamlet, with irony and wry humour, reflects upon 'the noble dust of Alexander . . . stopping a bunghole', Horatio's sturdy practicality will not permit him to encourage Hamlet in these speculations: ' 'Twere to consider too curiously, to consider so', is his rejoinder. Concerning the gravedigger, 'How absolute the knave is!' Hamlet had said to Horatio, and Hamlet is equally absolute in his careful questioning of the man ('How long will a man lie i' th' earth ere he rot?'). In this scene Hamlet's closest affinities are with the gravedigger who is Death's old retainer, and Yorick,[15] not Horatio. Hamlet refers to the gravedigger as 'this mad knave'; in turn the gravedigger refers to Hamlet as 'he that is mad, and sent into England', and then to Yorick's skull as 'A whoreson mad fellow's it was'. Horatio is outside this closed triangle of jesting and drollery with Death. Hamlet's very presence in the graveyard upon his return from sea raises questions: as Professor Bradbrook asks, 'Why does Hamlet visit the graveyard first on his return? To approach the tomb of his father?'[16]

Further, that Hamlet and the gravedigger, with Yorick in the wings, are in communion on a plane beyond Horatio's comprehension is suggested by the irony contained in the gravedigger blatantly refuting his own philosophy by his practice of desecrator. The answer he gives to his own riddle, 'What is he that builds stronger than either the mason, the shipwright, or the carpenter?' is, 'And when you are asked this question next, say "a gravemaker". The houses he makes lasts till doomsday'; yet he himself is busily (and shamelessly) engaged in breaking up these very houses and preparing them for new tenants.[17] The truth that even in death man's condition is not one of permanence is realised by Hamlet who sees Alexander's progress from death to earth as a process as ironic as the 'grinning' of Yorick's skull that Hamlet interrogates ('Where be your gibes now? your gambols? your songs?')

The 'sea-change' in Hamlet that takes place after his encounter with the pirates, often noted by twentieth-century commentators on the play as being indicative of an enlightened Hamlet, one who can now speak of a 'divinity that shapes our ends', had been anticipated by Yeats in 'The Death of Synge':

I saw *Hamlet* on Saturday night, except for the chief 'Ophelia' scenes, and missed these (for I had to be in the Abbey [Theatre]) without regret. Their pathos, as they are played, has always left me cold. I came back for Hamlet at the graveside: there my delight always begins anew. I feel in *Hamlet*, as so often in Shakespeare, that I am in the presence of a soul lingering on the storm-beaten threshold of sanctity. Has not that threshold always been terrible, even crime-haunted? Surely Shakespeare, in those last seeming idle years, was no quiet country gentleman, enjoying, as men like Dowden think, the temporal reward of an unvalued toil. Perhaps he sought for wisdom in itself at last, and not in its passionate shadows.[18]

The 'wisdom' that Yeats sees Shakespeare arriving at in the last years of his life has its counterpart in Hamlet's recognition in 'The Statues', glanced at briefly above, 'that / Mirror on mirror mirrored is all the show'. In Act V of the play Hamlet acknowledges to Horatio the mirror-like nature of his experience, 'But I am very sorry, good Horatio, / That to Laertes I forgot myself, / For by the image of my cause I see / The portraiture of his', a feature that Yeats had remarked as early as 1903:

In *Hamlet* . . . the murder of Hamlet's father and the sorrow of Hamlet are shadowed in the lives of Fortinbras and Ophelia and Laertes, whose fathers, too, have been killed.[19]

For Yeats, the Hamlet of the play's final phase is a man looking beyond this life to the one to come. When nearing the end of the cycle, at Phase 22, the kind of man Yeats celebrates attains 'what is called the "Emotion of Sanctity", and this emotion is described as a contact with life beyond death. It comes at the instant when synthesis is abandoned, when fate is accepted'.[20] The 'delight' Yeats experienced when he 'came back for Hamlet at the graveside' was not an emotion that Horatio would have shared.

*   *   *

But it is to Horatio's credit that he does not remain permanently outside of Hamlet's spiritual orbit. At the point in the play when immediately after the challenge delivered by Osric Hamlet says to Horatio, 'But thou wouldst not think how ill all's here about my heart: but it is no matter', we recognise the forging of a new link between them. The statement is suggestive of Hamlet's sense of total isolation, but also of the expectation that from Horatio will be forthcoming an understanding of his situation, the two possibilities not being mutually exclusive. In continuation of this line of development, Horatio moves from stoicism to a visionary intuition of the truth: 'Good night, sweet Prince, / And flights of angels sing thee to thy rest.' This farewell reveals a world view quite the opposite of that suggested by his one-time refusal to 'let belief take hold of him / Touching this dreaded sight, twice seen of us', as reported by Marcellus. That Horatio's prayer is for Hamlet's soul to be at 'rest' is perhaps dictated by a trembling fear of the possibility that Hamlet's soul after death, like that of his father, may not be at rest unless Horatio can carry out Hamlet's dying wish: 'Horatio, I am dead; / Thou livest; report me and my cause aright / To the unsatisfied.' Undoubtedly Horatio recalls at this juncture, as we do, Hamlet's assurance, 'Rest, rest, perturbèd spirit', in response to the Ghost's insistence upon his companions being sworn to silence.

In the light of Hamlet's soul being accompanied by flights of angels, it is

appropriate that in both of his encounters with the Ghost he should spontaneously call upon the angelic hosts to protect him: 'Angels and ministers of
grace defend us!' and 'Save me and hover o'er me with your wings, / You
heavenly guards!' This instinctive recognition of the presence of benevolent
powers was not a part of the early Horatio's world view; in both of his
encounters with the Ghost the direction his thoughts took was towards a
questioning of the Ghost's motives, not towards a need for divine grace. In his
second encounter, though conscious of the danger, his resolve is, 'I'll cross it,
though it blast me', an attitude which, though intrepid, is quite unlike
Hamlet's instinctive reactions.

If the early Horatio, more governed by reason than faith, can be regarded as
a representative of the transition from the medieval to the modern, as a type of
Renaissance man, his alliance with Hamlet at the play's end shows both men
yielding to the pull of the medieval over the modern, a reversal of the historical
change that was taking place in Shakespeare's own time. Is Shakespeare, then,
we may well ask, repudiating his own age and yearning for a time that has
passed? Is *Hamlet* an expression of such a nostalgia? Based on a Vision of God,
the sustaining faith and belief of the Middle Ages from around the fifteenth
century onwards gave place to what may be called a Vision of Man, continuing
in our own times up to say World War I after which, as Auden has said
somewhere, mankind has no more Vision but only television. Yeats sees
Shakespeare caught between the pull of the medieval and the modern; he
speaks of 'Dante who revealed God, and Shakespeare, who revealed man',[21]
and sees such tensions in the fabric of a civilisation as being conducive for the
release of great creative energy. 'I see in Shakespeare', Yeats writes in *A Vision*,
'a man in whom human personality, hitherto restrained by its dependence
upon Christendom or by its own need for self-control, burst like a shell.
Perhaps secular intellect, setting itself free after five hundred years of struggle,
has made him the greatest of dramatists.'[22] At the same time Yeats recognizes
that each age possesses its own absolute identity, reaching efflorescence
through an inner genetic compulsion, and then yielding to its successor. Seeing
all history as a form of 'play'—'As though God's death were but a play', the
Musicians sing in *The Resurrection*—Yeats asserts that each age has its own
system of beliefs whose validity is not disproved by succeeding ages. As an
example of this Nietzschean refusal to regard 'truth' as an objective and
absolute entity, Yeats turns to *Hamlet*:

The world is a drama where person follows person, and though the dialogue prepares
for all the entrances, that preparation is not the person's proof, nor is Polonius
disproved when Hamlet seems to kill him. Once the philosophy, nation or movement
has clearly shown its face, we know that its chief characteristic has not arisen out of any
proof, or even out of all the past, or out of the present tension of the drama, or out of any
visible cause whatever, but is unique, life in itself. There can be neither cause nor effect
when all things are co-eternal.[23]

Thus for Yeats the dichotomy between the philosophies of Hamlet, Polonius, and, by extension, Horatio, is neither a proof of the one nor a refutation

of the others; each possesses its own individuality within its time and place, the
Heideggerian notion of each age being constituted by its own historical
moment rather than by any transcendent essences.

*   *   *

Though we know almost nothing of Horatio's past, unlike that of say the Ghost
who was 'a goodly king' and whose custom it was to sleep every afternoon in his
orchard, it is in Hamlet's moving tribute to Horatio that we are given a glimpse
of the Horatio who belongs to the pre-play period, a man who possessed stoical
qualities. Nevertheless, this is Hamlet's impression of Horatio at a much later
stage in the action, and implicit in his description is an awareness of his own
impassioned temperament:

> for thou hast been
> As one, in suff'ring all, that suffers nothing;
> A man that Fortune's buffets and rewards
> Hast ta'en with equal thanks. And blest are those
> Whose blood and judgement are so well commeddled
> That they are not a pipe for Fortune's finger
> To sound what stop she please. Give me that man
> That is not passion's slave, and I will wear him
> In my heart's core, ay, in my heart of heart,
> As I do thee. Something too much of this -
> There is a play tonight before the King.

Overcome briefly by emotion ('Something too much of this'), Hamlet struggles
to regain self control, abruptly turning the conversation into another channel.
This moment in the drama can be regarded as a kind of Joycean epiphany, a
moment 'of fullness or of passion', 'the accession of a sudden joy', as Professor
Ellmann has shown, to be sought 'not among gods, but among men, in casual,
unostentatious, even unpleasant moments'.[24] From Hamlet's tribute we learn
that Horatio has experienced much suffering, has been battered by Fortune,
but also rewarded by her, and is now able to accept life as it comes, with neither
jubilation nor despair. An audience unaware of Horatio's conduct at the play's
ending might well endorse Hamlet's description of his friend, but as so often
happens in Shakespeare, no single view is permitted to crystallize. Other
characters in the drama of this period who are comparable to Hamlet's version
of Horatio are Webster's Bosola and Flamineo who, however, have not
attained to the philosophical serenity Hamlet attributes to Horatio. Similarly
the First Murderer in *Macbeth*, a malcontent, describes himself as 'one . . . /
Whom the vile blows and buffets of the world / Hath so incens'd, that I am
reckless what / I do, to spite the world'. Unlike Horatio, these men have turned
cynics.

Considerably older than Hamlet, Horatio has finally chosen the life of a
scholar at Wittenberg.[25] That his appearance in the court at Elsinore is a great
surprise to Hamlet is clear from Hamlet's thrice repeated question, with slight

variations, 'But what, in faith, make you from Wittenberg?' (1.2.164, 168, and 174), indicative of Hamlet's conviction that Horatio could have no conceivable interest in the court. For Hamlet, then, this very move of Horatio's from the University of Wittenberg to the court of Claudius is out of character, an enigma, a contradiction of Horatio's avowed stoicism and philosophical detachment. By implication it is clear that the sole reason for Horatio being in Claudius's court is his concern for Hamlet.[26] That Horatio has otherwise been leading the life of a recluse is suggested, much later in the play, in his thinking aloud, 'I do not know from what part of the world / I should be greeted, if not from Lord Hamlet'.

Yet beneath a phlegmatic exterior, even at the play's beginning, Horatio reveals an aspect of himself less rational than he would like his companions to believe exists. Reminding Marcellus and Barnardo that before the assassination of Julius Caesar 'the graves stood tenantless, and the sheeted dead / Did squeak and gibber in the Roman streets', Horatio, like Calphurnia, shows himself susceptible to portents, omens, dreams, though he admits this only when within the ambience of the Ghost's presence. Faced with Hamlet's resolve to follow the Ghost despite all warnings, Horatio suggests entrusting the matter to the will of Heaven ('Heaven will direct it'), but Marcellus's rejoinder, 'Nay, let's follow him', is the corrective, for individual responsibility cannot be jettisoned no matter how inexplicable events may seem.

The emergence of the 'real' Horatio at the play's end who attempts to die with Hamlet is, perhaps, the consequence of his close contact with Hamlet. Such an interpretation of Horatio is consistent with the overall disguise, or concealment, of identity prevalent in both *Hamlet* the play and Hamlet the character. Claudius sees himself as comparable to the harlot 'beautified with plast'ring art', Hamlet urges Gertrude to 'assume a virtue, if you have it not', Polonius actually conceals himself behind the arras, and Hamlet, chameleon-like, alters his identity in various ways ('Seems, madam? Nay, it is. I know not "seems". / 'Tis not alone my inky cloak . . .'; 'Lord Hamlet, with his doublet all unbrac'd, / No hat upon his head').

*   *   *

Is Hamlet, then, correct in his assessment of Horatio as one who 'is not passion's slave', or has Horatio moved away from that position towards a stance more human, less impassive? Is he really as perfectly balanced in his composition ('whose blood and judgement are so well commeddled') as Hamlet supposes, or is Horatio's own embarrassed repudiation of the Aristotelian ideal with which Hamlet invests him closer to the truth?

HAMLET	Horatio, thou are e'en as just a man
	As e'er my conversation coped withal.
HORATIO	O, my dear lord –
HAMLET	Nay, do not think I flatter.

As the play draws to a close, Hamlet, after his escape from the pirates, is, as has been often noted,[27] a changed man. Committing his future to the 'divinity that shapes our ends', he seems now to be riding in tandem with this divinity, taking advantage of every seeming coincidence as if it were by benevolent design ('Why, even in that was heaven ordinant. / I had my father's signet in my purse'), fulfilling at last Horatio's early wish, 'Heaven will direct it'.

Matching Hamlet's new mood in this scene is a Horatio less tight-lipped than he has ever been before, except when with Marcellus and Barnardo at the opening of the play. At Osric's expense Horatio even permits himself a few jokes ('His purse is empty already. All's golden words are spent'; 'I knew you must be edified by the margent ere you had done'; 'This lapwing runs away with the shell on his head'). Whereas the Horatio of the graveyard scene was simply Hamlet's sounding board, the Horatio of this scene is witty, urbane, matching Hamlet's wit with trenchant comment, meeting Hamlet on his own ground.

The Horatio of the play's last scene, like the other characters, is revealed in his true identity, his mask ripped off by the proximity of Hamlet's death and the treachery that has finally come out in the open. As Claudius and Laertes stand exposed in all their villainy, Horatio stands revealed as Hamlet's true ally and staunch companion, not a man who 'is not passion's slave' as Hamlet had erroneously supposed, but as one intensely human and loyal to the prince, his friend:

HORATIO   Never believe it.
             I am more an antique Roman than a Dane.
             Here's yet some liquor left.
HAMLET   As th' art a man,
             Give me the cup. Let go. By heaven, I'll ha't!

A final Yeatsian signpost that indicates the direction towards a plausible interpretation of the Hamlet-Horatio relationship is Yeats's dismissal of any discussion on the 'character' of Hamlet, Timon, or Antony as being irrelevant, even sacrilegious. For Yeats the bond between Timon and Flavius, Hamlet and Horatio, or Antony and Cleopatra transcends all other considerations and attains what he calls 'unmixed passion, the integrity of fire':

In writers of tragi-comedy (and Shakespeare is always a writer of tragi-comedy) there is indeed character, but we notice that it is in the moments of comedy that character is defined, in Hamlet's gaiety, let us say; while amid the great moments, when Timon orders his tomb, when Hamlet cries to Horatio 'Absent thee from felicity awhile', when Antony names 'Of many thousand kisses the poor last', all is lyricism, unmixed passion, 'the integrity of fire'.[28]

Following the Yeatsian pointer, it can be argued that in spite of Horatio's claim to being more an antique Roman than a Dane, it should be clear to us by this time that his intention to die with Hamlet is not so much Roman as romantic. The Roman act of self-immolation—and Shakespeare had recently completed *Julius Caesar*—was to protect oneself from degradation and ignominy, consequences that would not arise in Horatio's situation. Clearly, then, his wish to die with Hamlet is dictated by friendship, not self-esteem. That he desists from draining the poisoned wine cup at Hamlet's importunity, even as Hamlet had earlier considered suicide and rejected it, is suggestive of a congruence between the two men emerging at the play's conclusion. And as the Ghost had entrusted Hamlet with the responsibility of setting the time right, so does Hamlet rely upon Horatio to report his cause aright.[29]

Labour and Memory in the
Love Poetry of W.B. Yeats

Elizabeth Butler Cullingford

Yeats was, as he said himself, a romantic in all things. Early in his poetic career he decided that, although he might never marry in church, he would love one woman all his life. That one woman was Maud Gonne, whom he courted from the time of their first meeting in 1889 until in 1903 she unexpectedly married someone else. After her marriage proved a failure Yeats resumed his attentions, and persisted in his devotion until 1917, when he himself married Georgie Hyde-Lees. He continued, however, to write poems about Maud Gonne. There are three points about their long drawn out relationship that I wish to emphasize. The first is that, although Yeats and Maud Gonne were not lovers during the first phase of their courtship, they were nevertheless extraordinarily close. Several of his love poems, most notably 'Old Memory', 'Adam's Curse' and 'Among School Children', look back nostalgically to that time of closeness, which, although it was painfully inadequate at the time, came to seem paradisal in the light of subsequent events. The second important fact about their relationship was their so-called 'spiritual marriage'. While acknowledging Yeats as her spiritual husband, Maud Gonne refused to grant him physical consummation. This arrangement, one calculated to wreck the nerves of a far less sensitive man than Yeats, led him to appreciate the cruelty of Platonic/Christian dualism, with its devaluation of the body and exaltation of the soul. Finally, it is helpful to know that there was once a moment when Yeats felt that he could have won the hand of his hitherto resolutely inaccessible beloved, but found himself incapable of decisive action. It is with agony that he remembers this failure of potency in poems like 'The Cold Heaven' and 'The Tower'.

Yeats as a love-poet, then, is no celebrant of present happiness. His work begins in the frustrations of unsatisfied desire and passes directly to memories of lost or imperfectly achieved felicity. He would certainly have agreed with Sigmund Freud that 'something in the nature of the sexual instinct itself is unfavourable to the realisation of complete satisfaction'.[1] In a fallen world we are tortured by our longing for perfection, for beauty, for an ideal love: but the conditions of mortality—time, change, and death—render our ideals forever inaccessible.

Yeats, although his acceptance of Plato was fluctuating and ambiguous, nevertheless agreed with his argument that Memory is the origin of Eros or

Desire. It is only through a memory of the eternal perfection of the world of Ideal Forms experienced by the soul before its birth that a man can recognize and pursue the beautiful here on earth. Yeats wrote, 'I think that Plato symbolised by the word "memory" a relation to the timeless' (*A Vision* p. 54). Yet Yeats was more aware than Plato of the terrible cost exacted by this recollection of Paradise in the world of time. In his love poetry he explores the price in labour that poets, women, and lovers, all of whom are subject to Adam's curse, must pay as a part of their pursuit of remembered beauty.

Memory is a double-edged sword: while it permits us intermittent access to the world of pre-natal bliss, it also opens up sudden vistas onto our own more immediate past, flooding us with remorse, regret, self-pity, or the desire to judge and accuse others. It is through memory that we experience the passing of time: today's wrinkles are shocking only because memory tells us that there were none yesterday. Memory is not just a relation to the timeless: Yeats also calls it paradoxically, 'the ash / That chokes our fires that have begun to sink' (*Collected Plays* p. 18). Time will defeat and waste all our labour to be beautiful, or our labour to create beauty. In many of Yeats's poems, however, the faculty of imagination combines with memory to redeem labour, love, and beauty from the ravages of time.

In the poem 'Old Memory', written in 1903 after Maud Gonne's marriage to Major John MacBride, memory operates in two distinct modes: it is both the nostalgic evocation of painful personal loss, and the agent of possible imaginative recuperation in the present:

> O thought, fly to her when the end of day
> Awakens an old memory, and say,
> 'Your strength, that is so lofty and fierce and kind,
> It might call up a new age, calling to mind
> The queens that were imagined long ago,
> Is but half yours: he kneaded in the dough
> Through the long years of youth, and who would have thought
> It all, and more than it all, would come to naught,
> And that dear words meant nothing?' But enough,
> For when we have blamed the wind we can blame love;
> Or, if there needs be more, be nothing said
> That would be harsh for children that have strayed.
>
> (*Variorum Poems* p. 201)

The stimulus to this 'old' memory is 'the end of day', the twilight moment between light and darkness that is always conducive to Yeatsian reveries over the past. Yet the speaker's first words concern the efficacy of a fictive, 'imagined' past as a mythical model for the politics of the dawning future. The woman's fierce strength may awaken Irish racial memory of the great queens of the sagas, Maeve, Aoife, Emer; and thus

> . . . call up a new age, calling to mind
> The queens that were imagined long ago.
>
> (*Variorum Poems* p. 201)

In these lines Yeats fuses memory, imagination, and desire; his tribute to the woman who has deserted him has, therefore, a poetic timelessness and energy. When, however, he turns to their personal history, and remembers their former unity and co-operation, which she has cast aside, he encounters the temptations of self-pity and accusatory judgement:

> . . . he kneaded in the dough
> Through the long years of youth, and who would have thought
> It all, and more than all, would come to naught,
> And that dear words meant nothing?
>
> (*Variorum Poems* p. 201)

On the most obvious level this last line suggests the broken promises characteristic of every failed love affair. But Yeats is one to whom words are both 'dear' in the sense of 'beloved', and 'dear' in the sense of 'costly': the product of much hard labour. The failure of language is a failure that strikes at the root of his potency and self-confidence. The metaphor 'he kneaded in the dough' carries within it an implied gender reversal: baking is traditionally a female labour. While Maud Gonne is manlike, a strong and fierce ruler whose unreflecting power may change the world, the poet is feminized as a humble maidservant, who is not even permitted to share the loaf she has baked, whose labour is wasted. With the interjection 'But enough', however, Yeats rescues his poem from the temptations of maudlin self-pity, and rediscovers self-control in the magnanimity of forgiveness:

> For when we have blamed the wind we can blame love;
> Or, if there needs be more, be nothing said
> That would be harsh for children that have strayed.
>
> (*Variorum Poems* p. 201)

Suddenly the queen is metamorphosed into a wayward child, and the poet, in withholding easy condemnation, regains the dignity of one who has the power to control words, tempering the 'harshness' of his implied rebuke until it is gently appropriate to the irresponsibility of youth. While as poet and as lover he has laboured, she, like the wind that symbolizes unappeasable desire, has simply been: she is a natural, uncontrollable, unblameable force. In associating her with nature and with childhood, however, Yeats employs a familiar patriarchal rhetorical strategy which allows him to reassert his masculine authority: the woman is marginal to the world of culture, which is by definition the world of work.

The same contrast between the poet who labours and the woman who, like nature herself, merely is, is evident in 'He Tells of the Perfect Beauty':

> O cloud-pale eyelids, dream-dimmed eyes,
> The poets labouring all their days
> To build a perfect beauty in rhyme
> Are overthrown by a woman's gaze
> And by the unlabouring brood of the skies:

> And therefore my heart will bow, when dew
> Is dropping sleep, until God burn time,
> Before the unlabouring stars and you.
>
> *(Variorum Poems* p. 164)

In this poem the speaker's words are once again fruitless, poetic labour overthrown by the images of 'unlabouring' perfection embodied in the stars and in the beloved. The poet can only bow before a spontaneity of unified consciousness that his analytic intellect can never achieve. This over-simplified and patronising appreciation of feminine beauty, however, is significantly refined and corrected in a much greater poem, 'Adam's Curse', written just before Maud Gonne's marriage:

> We sat together at one summer's end,
> That beautiful mild woman, your close friend,
> And you and I, and talked of poetry.
>
> *(Variorum Poems* p. 204)

The mood of the poem is predominantly nostalgic and elegiac: we are at the end of summer, the end of day, the end of the affair. The phrase 'one summer's end' locates the whole poem in an indeterminate past: memory here comprises still earlier memories. The title, 'Adam's Curse', evokes a fallen world, a spoiled paradise; but it also carries with it its binary opposite, the unfallen world that teases us with its promise of perfection. In the Book of Genesis God tells Adam, 'In the sweat of thy face shall thou eat bread, till thou return unto the ground' (3:19), thus separating forever the concepts of work and pleasure. Eve's curse condemns the woman to a different kind of hard labour: 'I will greatly multiply thy sorrow and thy conception; in sorrow thou shalt bring forth children' (3:16). Yeats frequently draws an analogy between the poet's creation of a work of art and the woman's production of a child: at the end of the 'Introductory Rhymes' to his volume *Responsibilities* he begs his forefathers to pardon him,

> . . . that for a barren passion's sake,
> Although I have come close on forty-nine,
> I have no child, I have nothing but a book,
> Nothing but that to prove your blood and mine.
>
> *(Variorum Poems* p. 270)

In 'Adam's Curse' his definition of poetic labour is couched in terms of women's work:

> . . . A line will take us hours maybe;
> Yet if it does not seem a moment's thought,
> Our stitching and unstitching has been naught.
>
> *(Variorum Poems* p. 204)

Like Penelope at her loom the poet weaves and unweaves his lines, searching always for a perfection which, like that of the stars in 'He Tells of the Perfect Beauty', will appear to be 'unlabouring'. In so doing he becomes as marginal to society as the needlewoman he emulates. According to classical economic theory, imaginative labour is 'frivolous' because it produces no commodity.[2] If we accept this definition, the poet articulates not only the curse of the original Adam, but also that of Adam Smith: the poet is an unproductive labourer, an 'idler'. Yet Yeats sees that the people who thus stigmatize him, the 'bankers, schoolmasters, and clergymen' who belong to 'service' professions, also fall under the curse of Adam Smith: they 'produce' nothing tangible either. As if in deliberate defiance of utilitarian economics, Yeats, disciple of John Ruskin and William Morris, disengages men of letters from the middlemen of the middle classes and aligns them with those marginal figures whose toil produces genuinely Adamic sweat on the brow: with servants, paupers, and, through the 'stitching' metaphor, with the women whose labour generates that most valuable commodity of all: more labourers.

> Better go down upon your marrow-bones
> And scrub a kitchen pavement, or break stones
> Like an old pauper, in all kinds of weather;
> For to articulate sweet sounds together
> Is to work harder than all these.

> (*Variorum Poems* pp. 204-5)

Although he rescues artistic production from the charge of 'frivolity', however, Yeats was as yet unable to approach Morris's joyful vision of a world in which all labour is artistic: 'One day we shall win back Art, that is to say the pleasure of life; win back Art again to our daily labour.'[3] For the Yeats of 1902, Ruskin's definition of labour was more pertinent: 'Literally, [labour] is the quantity of "Lapse", loss, or failure of human life caused by any effort . . . It is the negative quantity, or quantity of de-feat, which has to be counted against every Fact, or Deed of men.'[4] The idea of labour as loss or defeat governs 'Adam's Curse', which in defining poets as 'martyrs' comes dangerously close to the self-pity we saw Yeats resisting in 'Old Memory'.

The 'beautiful mild woman', whose model was Maud Gonne's sister Kathleen, gently rebukes the speaker in reminding him that women, whose beauty is apparently as 'natural' as the poet wishes his lines to seem, are also subject to a curse:

> . . . To be born woman is to know -
> Although they do not talk of it at school -
> That we must labour to be beautiful.

> (*Variorum Poems* p. 205)

In 'Before the World Was Made' Yeats defends a seemingly 'idle' and 'frivolous' woman obsessed by mirrors and makeup as one who is seeking to embody remembered pre-natal perfection (*Variorum Poems* p. 531). His portrait of the 'beautiful mild woman', however, also hints at a female labour more fundamental than the heroic discipline of the looking-glass. The woman 'for whose sake / There's many a one shall find out all heartache / On finding that her voice is sweet and low', emerges as a domestic figure, destined for love, marriage, and childbirth. To the pain in which she labours to create her physical beauty will be added the pain in which she will labour to 'produce' a child. Her knowledge of this truth is, like poetic knowledge, intuitive: 'they do not talk of it at school' because the 'schoolmasters', who despise beauty as 'idle', have no access to such bodily wisdom. Women 'know' at birth what their destiny is because they participate in something that Yeats calls the 'Great Memory' and identifies with instinct (*Essays and Introductions* p. 28). The Great Memory, like Jung's collective unconscious, is a storehouse of images created by human experience throughout the millennia.[5] Yeats calls it 'that age-long memoried self, that shapes the elaborate shell of the mollusc and the child in the womb, that teaches the birds to make their nest' (*Autobiographies* p. 272). 'Anima Mundi' or the Great Memory is the opposite of Plato's world of Ideal Forms, which are *a priori*, 'self-born', and owe nothing to human experience, though human experience may copy them. In 'The Tower' Yeats cries 'in Plato's teeth' that it is out of human experience alone, out of 'Poet's imaginings', 'memories of love', and 'memories of the words of woman', that man creates Anima Mundi, a 'superhuman / Mirror-resembling dream' (*Variorum Poems* p. 415).

The instinctive wisdom of the 'beautiful mild woman' occupies a central position in 'Adam's Curse', but it is in fact a displacement, an opportunity for Yeats to defer consideration of what is really troubling him. While the speaker's attention appears to be focussed on her, she is still 'that' beautiful mild woman, held at arm's length by a demonstrative adjective. The real intimacy within the poem exists between the speaker and the silent 'you'. From the toil of the poet and the travail of the woman, the poem moves to the labour of the courtly lovers, who have abandoned instinct in favour of a highly artificial code:

> There have been lovers who thought love should be
> So much compounded of high courtesy
> That they would sigh and quote with learned looks
> Precedents out of beautiful old books.
>
> (*Variorum Poems* p. 205)

Maud Gonne, who refused to marry Yeats, had imposed upon him the 'courtly' discipline of what he later called 'that monstrous thing / Returned and yet unrequited love' (*Variorum Poems* p. 358). At first he attempted to accept this 'labour of love', but in 'Adam's Curse', he defines it as 'an idle trade enough'. The poet produces a poem, the woman beauty or a child, but courtly love is essentially sterile, it produces nothing. Its essence is condensed into Yeats's image of the moon, which seems romantically lovely, but actually has close affinities with Shelley's 'companionless' moon, the 'dying lady lean and pale' whose pallor is the result of 'weariness'.[6] Yeats's moon is

> . . . worn as if it had been a shell
> Washed by time's waters as they rose and fell
> About the stars and broke in days and years.
>
> (*Variorum Poems* p. 206)

This image of the passing of time and its erosion of beauty forces the speaker to confront his own defeat: the thought that

> . . . I strove
> To love you in the old high way of love;
> That it had all seemed happy, and yet we'd grown
> As weary-hearted as that hollow moon.
>
> (*Variorum Poems* p. 206)

Happiness, as usual, is located in the past tense: the poet contrasts remembered joy with present weariness, the barren 'hollow' 'shell' which is all that remains of past hopes.

Although memory reveals to us the extent of our defeats, its operation may also redeem them. George Santayana writes persuasively about this double function of the faculty of recollection:

As it is memory that enables us to feel that we are dying and to know that everything actual is in flux, so it is memory that opens to us an ideal immortality, unacceptable and meaningless to the old Adam, but genuine in its own way and undeniably true. It is an immortality in representation—a representation which envisages things in their truth as they have in their own day possessed themselves in reality.[7]

A poem that affirms the present truth of past experience is 'Friends', which, despite its title, is actually a love poem memorializing three women who have 'wrought' 'what joy is in my days'. Unlike 'Adam's Curse', 'Friends' moves toward the reconciliation of labour and pleasure. With his first subject, Lady Gregory, the poet emphasizes the 'delight' produced by shared intellectual work, the marriage of true minds that the poet and the aristocrat forged in their creation of an Irish National Theatre. With his second, Olivia Shakespear, who after many doubts, hesitations, and failures of potency on Yeats's part, finally relieved him of his long preserved virginity, the poem moves from the relation between 'mind and delighted mind' to bodily power:

> . . . her hand
> Had strength that could unbind . . .
> Youth's dreamy load.
>
> (*Variorum Poems* p. 315)

Without exploring the peculiarities of Yeats's sexual constitution, we may note his continued emphasis on the strong woman and the relatively impotent man, and also his strange use of the word 'hand'. Olivia Shakespear's 'manual labour' finally awakens him from dreamy sexual incompetence and permits his life and his creative work as a love poet to interpenetrate at last: she

> So changed me that I live
> Labouring in ecstasy.
>
> (*Variorum Poems* p. 315)

This phrase points back to 'Adam's Curse', where labour was anything but ecstatic, and forward to 'Among School Children', where 'labour is blossoming or dancing'. Here the word 'labouring' carries the strong sexual overtones of Donne's 'Elegy XIX':

> Come madam, come, all rest my powers defy
> Until I labour, I in labour lie.

The recollection of achieved sexuality permits pleasure in work, pleasure in work results in a poetic 'birth': Adam's curse is momentarily lifted.

The memory of consummation, however, immediately turns the speaker's thoughts to what was never consummated: to the woman who 'took' while the others 'gave'. Once again the temptation to self-pity is confronted and dismissed. Although he initially baulks at the thought of praising her, the poet's hesitation is no more than a rhetorical strategy that intensifies the impact of his subsequent tribute. As he begins to assess the effect she had upon him in the past, mechanically 'counting' his 'good and bad', we learn that the setting is, as usual, that twilight which is conducive to reverie. In contrast with the earlier poem, however, the poet is not drowsing at the end of the day: he lies wakeful in the hour before the dawn. When the memory of 'what she had' merges with the image of her present 'eagle look', the speaker is roused by an emotion so powerful that it supersedes all desire to blame, praise, or assess. This is not 'emotion recollected in tranquillity', but emotion created in passionate response to the labour of the mind. Whereas 'Adam's Curse' ended with the weary 'hollow moon', 'Friends' climaxes with an orgasmic experience:

> . . . up from my heart's root
> So great a sweetness flows
> I shake from head to foot.
>
> (*Variorum Poems* p. 316)

Past and present combine to produce not reflection, but physical release: memory is used, as T.S. Eliot said, for 'liberation'.

Yeats arranged his poems in *Responsibilities* so that 'Friends' was immediately followed by 'The Cold Heaven', in which the speaker is once again physically 'shaken' by what seems to be an immediate experience of his past love: this time a bitter rather than a sweet one:

> Suddenly I saw the cold and rook-delighting heaven
> That seemed as though ice burned and was but the more ice.
>
> (*Variorum Poems* p. 316)

Memory has moved out of the twilight toward the complete clarity of visionary revelation. The bright cold sky, which combines the fire and ice found in the lowest circles of Dante's *Inferno*, 'suddenly' obliterates the trivial present. The poet experiences one of those terrifying moments when remorse (which exists only as a function of memory) strips away the defences we have erected against the knowledge of our own inadequacies and failures.

> And thereupon imagination and heart were driven
> So wild that every casual thought of that and this
> Vanished, and left but memories, that should be out of season
> With the hot blood of youth, of love crossed long ago.
>
> *(Variorum Poems* p. 316)

Memory has the power to destroy the regular and rhythmic patterns of time, in which emotions are experienced at the appropriate season. In thus 'disturbing' linear time, memory asserts the timelessness or eternity of the psyche. William Earle writes that 'My present act of remembering is not identical with my past act of experiencing; but the '*I*' which then experienced and now recalls must be one and the same, or its past acts would not be 'its' now . . . The self then in its core is atemporal, while its various acts are enacted in time. Time differentiates only the acts, not the self which acts'.[8]

Although one of Yeats's most cherished beliefs was in the immortality of the soul and the atemporality of what he called the 'ultimate self', such proof as 'The Cold Heaven' affords brings agony, not consolation. The logical world of 'sense and reason' has no power to assuage the speaker's conviction of his own eternal guilt:

> And I took all the blame, out of all sense and reason,
> Until I cried and trembled and rocked to and fro
> Riddled with light.
>
> *(Variorum Poems* p. 316)

Any 'sensible' or 'reasonable' assessment of Yeats's relations with Maud Gonne would probably arrive at the biographical conclusion that he was a man more sinned against than sinning. Poetic revelation, however, has greater imaginative truth than reason. In 'The Tower' Yeats confronts the same terrible memory:

> Does the imagination dwell the most
> Upon a woman won or woman lost?
> If on the lost, admit you turned aside
> From a great labyrinth out of pride,
> Cowardice, some silly over-subtle thought
> Or anything called conscience once;
> And that if memory recur, the sun's
> Under eclipse and the day blotted out.
>
> *(Variorum Poems* pp. 413-14)

Here memory 'eclipses' the daylight, while in 'The Cold Heaven' light destroys the quotidian world: the metaphors are opposed but the intended apocalyptic effect is the same. The poet is 'riddled with light' as one might be 'riddled with bullets', a trope suggesting the approach and inevitability of death. He wonders in terror if his ghost will be stripped, as he is stripped now, of everything except the paradoxical consciousness that his punishment is logically 'unjust' and yet imaginatively appropriate:

> is it sent
> Out naked on the roads, as the books say, and stricken
> By the injustice of the skies for punishment?
>
> (*Variorum Poems* p. 316)

The wakeful anguish of memory in 'The Cold Heaven' appears involuntary, while the nocturnal recollections of 'Broken Dreams' are deliberatly conjured by the speaker. This poem's project is the redemption from time, through the combined action of memory and imagination, of the image of his beloved, which the passing years have blurred and distorted:

> There is grey in your hair.
> Young men no longer suddenly catch their breath
> When you are passing.
>
> (*Variorum Poems* p. 355)

An 'old gaffer', however, remembers what the young men can never have seen: Maud Gonne in all the transient bloom of her youth and beauty. Like Plato, Yeats identifies the beautiful with the good, and Maud Gonne's earthly loveliness is seen as a portion of eternal, heavenly loveliness. Her beauty is so close to divine beauty that it has the power to recover the 'old gaffer' on his bed of death: but being mortal, it is subject to two tragic conditions. It causes 'all heart's ache' to herself and others, it is 'burdensome', as the 'beautiful mild woman' from 'Adam's Curse' has already told us; and it is necessarily evanescent:

> Your beauty can but leave among us
> Vague memories, nothing but memories.
>
> (*Variorum Poems* p. 356)

A young man begs:

> . . . Tell me of that lady
> The poet stubborn with his passion sang us
> When age might well have chilled his blood.
>
> (*Variorum Poems* p. 356)

All that the poet can offer in response are 'vague memories, nothing but memories', which conjure up not the living past, but an 'image of air'. 'Stubborn passion' weakens into 'rambling talk'. Yet at the centre of the poem Yeats suddenly moves from the fallibility of individual human memory, and the feebleness of mere words in the face of time, toward a different order of certainty:

> But in the grave all, all, shall be renewed.
> The certainty that I shall see that lady
> Leaning or standing or walking
> In the first loveliness of womanhood
> And with the fervour of my youthful eyes
> Has set me muttering like a fool.
>
> (*Variorum Poems* p. 356)

This stanza may appear to be a celebration of Plato's Ideal or Absolute Beauty, in which Maud Gonne's transient flesh has briefly participated and which will persist eternally when the human body, which Plato terms a 'mass of perishable rubbish'[9] has returned to the dust. But Plato's kind of immortality is too abstract, and too doctrinaire in its rigorous separation of soul from body, for Yeats to accept. After death he will see not an Ideal Form, but 'that' particular lady, exactly as she was. He therefore stresses, most movingly and most un-Platonically, her only blemish, which is part of her unique attraction for him. Her 'small hands' were 'not beautiful', but he begs her to

> . . . Leave unchanged
> The hands that I have kissed
> For old sake's sake.
>
> (*Variorum Poems* p. 357)

Yeats was evolving a philosophical justification for his belief in immortality: a justification founded upon memory. In his philosophical testament, *A Vision*, he posits an immortal self that moves from incarnation to incarnation remembering, albeit unconsciously, all it has ever been or known. This 'ultimate self', which he calls our Daimon, is constituted out of four memories:

> His *Body of Fate*, the series of events forced upon him from without, is shaped out of the *Daimon's* memory of events of his past incarnations; his *Mask* or object of desire or idea of the good, out of its memory of the moments of exaltation in his past lives; his *Will* or normal ego out of its memory of all the events of his present life, whether consciously remembered or not; his *Creative Mind* from its memory of ideas—or universals—displayed by actual men in past lives, or their spirits between lives.
>
> (*A Vision* p. 83)

Yeats's emphasis upon memory is part of his attempt to define reality as determined by the unique, individual soul, rather than by some external divine principle. The Daimon 'contains within it, co-existing in its eternal moment, all the events of our life, all that we have known of other lives, or that it can discover within itself of other *Daimons*' (*A Vision* p. 192). Although the Daimon is timeless, we who live in time cannot apprehend the nature of its eternity. The poet's labour, therefore, is to lift what he calls 'the curtain / Of distorting days' and reveal the permanence guaranteed and even created by memory. Just as the woman's 'burdensome beauty' effects the physical resurrection of the 'old gaffer', the poet's toil is directed toward an imaginative resurrection of her vanished loveliness.

In 'Among School Children' Yeats continues his debate with Plato, and comes to the climax of his discussion of love, memory, labour, and imaginative redemption from time. The tone of the first stanza is relatively cheerful:

> I walk through the long schoolroom questioning;
> A kind old nun in a white hood replies;
> The children learn to cipher and to sing,
> To study reading-books and history,

To cut and sew, be neat in everything
In the best modern way—the children's eyes
In momentary wonder stare upon
A sixty-year-old smiling public man.

(Variorum Poems p. 443)

Yet Yeats's original notebook entry, 'Topic for a poem', is tragically pessimistic:

School children and the thought that . . . [life] will waste them perhaps that no possible life can fulfil our dreams or even their teacher's hope. Bring in the old thought that life prepares for what never happens.[10]

There is, therefore, a tension at the poem's inception between the 'best' that education has to offer and the knowledge that the best is not good enough. Reading the first stanza with 'Adam's Curse' in mind we may infer that one of the things not talked of even in this excellent school is the doctrine that 'we must labour to be beautiful'. The 'kind old nun' in her colourless and concealing hood has renounced both beauty and sexuality: her labour is doomed to sterility because the children cannot possibly 'fulfil . . . their teacher's hope'. The voluntary celibacy of the 'kind old nun' is linguistically connected with the comical impotence of the 'sixty-year old smiling public man', later defined as 'a comfortable kind of old scarecrow'. Between these two kind, smiling, comfortable old people stand the children, who have not yet attained their sexual and physical maturity, who are at the stage before 'meagre girlhood' puts on 'burdensome beauty'. Their childish, undeveloped bodies and curious, distant stares suddenly catapult the speaker out of his carefully maintained objective pose into a highly subjective reverie, whose focus is the opposite of the 'neat', friendly, and hygienic daytime scene before his eyes: 'I dream of a Ledean body, bent / Above a sinking fire'. 'Dream', 'memory', and 'desire' are intertwined in this twilight evocation of a maturely beautiful Helen absorbed in re-creating a cruel scene from her childhood. So vivid is her memory of 'a harsh reproof, or trivial event / That changed some childish day to tragedy' that the poet, who says in his own *Reveries Over Childhood and Youth* that he can 'remember little of childhood but its pain' (*Autobiographies* p. 11), experiences a miraculous sympathetic union with his beloved:

It seemed that our two natures blent
Into a sphere from youthful sympathy
Or else, to alter Plato's parable,
Into the yolk and white of the one shell.

(Variorum Poems p. 443)

The woman's remembered past transforms the present into an eternal moment: the sphere in Yeats symbolises the timeless realm of pure being. Aristophanes' famous speech in the *Symposium* tells how Zeus divided rebellious and spherical mankind into two halves 'like eggs which are cut with a hair', and how the separated halves strove desperately to reunite. Love, according to Aristophanes, is 'simply the name for the desire and pursuit of the whole', and Eros is the product of memory, for without memory mankind would not be tormented by its longing for a lost unity and completeness. In 'Among School Children' the memory of Maud Gonne combines with the sight of the little girls in the classroom to generate in the speaker a powerful outburst of grief and desire:

> And thereupon my heart is driven wild:
> She stands before me as a living child.
>
> (*Variorum Poems* p. 444)

As in 'The Cold Heaven', memory breaks through the composure proper to comfortable old age, and abolishes the distance between past and present. This imagined child, whom Yeats never saw, is in fact as vividly and dramatically evoked as the old woman whose 'present image floats into the mind'.

There has been considerable debate about whether the lines that describe her, 'hollow of cheek as though it drank the wind / And took a mess of shadows for its meat', suggest anorexic glamour or the ravages of time.[12] The latter explanation is preferable. The 'hollow' cheek, like the hollow moon of 'Adam's Curse', suggests the barrenness attendant upon the loss of 'spherical' unity; the wind is Yeats's traditional image for unfulfilled desire; and the phrase 'took a mess of shadows for its meat' suggests the story of Esau, who because he was very hungry sold his birthright for a 'mess of pottage'. This woman has received nothing in exchange for her birthright: like the prisoners of Plato's Cave in *The Republic* she has mistaken 'shadows' for substance. Further evidence that the image is one of ruin is offered by the conjunction '*and* I, though never of Ledean kind / Had pretty plumage once'. The connective syntax suggests that both poet and lady have lost their 'pretty plumage': both are now 'scarecrows' in comparison with the imagined 'living child'.

In using the word 'plumage' Yeats alludes again to Plato, who in the *Phaedrus* speaks of 'the soul's plumage'.[13] (The specificity of reference is not surprising, since Yeats was re-reading Plato in 1926, the year of the composition of 'Among School Children'. Plato imagines the soul as a winged charioteer driving a team of two horses, one of which is docile and virtuous, while the other, who symbolises appetite, is wild and unruly. The souls set out to view absolute beauty, the realm of the eternal forms; but many miss the vision because of the uncontrollable behaviour of their bad horse, lose their feathers and their wings, and sink down into the incarnate state, which Plato considers debased. In the drafts of his poem Yeats refers directly to 'the soul's horses';[14] in the finished work only the loss of plumage remains.

In the *Phaedrus* Plato pays a 'tribute to memory', which alone can rescue man from his fallen state: under the form of time it becomes Eros or love of beauty, which enables the soul of the philosopher to 'regain its wings' through recollection of the heavenly vision.[15] In the *Symposium* Plato removes Eros still further from what we would consider 'erotic' love: Diotoma tells Socrates that the object of love is not beauty but 'to procreate and bring forth its beauty', because 'love is love of immortality as well as of the good'.[16] In the fifth stanza of 'Among School Children' Yeats considers both procreation and recollection, 'altering' Plato once again.

> What youthful mother, a shape upon her lap
> Honey of generation had betrayed,
> And that must sleep, shriek, struggle to escape
> As recollection or the drug decide,
> Would think her son, did she but see that shape
> With sixty or more winters on its head,
> A compensation for the pang of his birth,
> Or the uncertainty of his setting forth?
>
> (*Variorum Poems* p. 444)

The procreation of which Diotima speaks is purely spiritual; Yeats brings it down to earth. 'Honey of generation' refers to the sweetness of sex, which has 'betrayed' the child into leaving his blissful Wordsworthian pre-natal state for the 'uncertainty' of mortal existence. The soul—or the baby—will resist insofar as it remembers a better world than this: it 'must sleep, shriek, struggle to escape / As recollection or the drug decide'. 'The drug' of Lethean oblivion reconciles the soul to life: but it is a life of pain. The mother, like Eve, must bring forth her children in sorrow, must 'labour' in childbirth. The son will know what may be the greater pain of disappointing his mother's hopes.[17] At the end of his account of his childhood Yeats wrote:

When I think of all the books I have read, and of the wise words I have heard spoken, and of the anxiety I have given to parents and grandparents, and of the hopes that I have had, all life weighed in the scales of my own life seems to me a preparation for something that never happens.

(*Autobiographies* p. 106)

This is not what Plato meant by procreating and bringing forth in beauty. Neither, however, do those whose procreation is spiritual, the philosophers or lovers of wisdom, succeed in growing wings again, as Plato thought they would. In the sixth stanza Yeats treats them all, including Plato himself, with derision.

> Plato thought nature but a spume that plays
> Upon a ghostly paradigm of things;
> Solider Aristotle played the taws
> Upon the bottom of a king of kings;
> World-famous golden-thighed Pythagoras
> Fingered upon a fiddle-stick or strings
> What a star sang and careless Muses heard:
> Old clothes upon old sticks to scare a bird.
>
> (*Variorum Poems* p. 445)

According to his own prescription Plato has despised the living beauty of the child in favour of abstraction, 'a ghostly paradigm of things'. 'Solider' Aristotle has 'bruised' the body of the young Alexander. Pythagoras has reduced the spontaneous music of the 'unlabouring' stars and 'careless' Muses to a rigid mathematical formula. These laborious pursuits lead to something even worse than the loss of the soul's plumage: the philosophers become lifeless, empty, bodiless images, 'old clothes upon old sticks to scare a bird', that drive away those still blessed with feathers.

Yeats sees Plato's teaching as having had an enormous and destructive influence over the way we all experience love. In the *Phaedrus* Plato describes how

in selecting his love from among the possessors of beauty each man follows his own bent, and, treating his beloved as if he were himself a god, he fashions and adorns an image, metaphorically speaking, and makes it the object of his honour and workshop.[18]

Or as Yeats puts it: 'Both nuns and mothers worship images'. This worship is a cruel labour: instead of breaking stones as in 'Adam's Curse', it breaks hearts. Those images of unreachable perfection, which inspire the 'passion' of the lover, the 'piety' of the nun, and the 'affection' of the mother, may symbolize heavenly glory, but they lead to despair. Being 'self-born' they know no labour, and therefore 'mock' the fruitless enterprise of their terrestrial worshippers, who must toil only to create a beauty which will fade and perish. The Western world is intellectual heir to this Platonic dualism, which informs all our assumptions about the superiority of soul to body, of wisdom to ignorance, of heaven to earth. Love is doomed to failure and disappointment because it seeks what might ideally be, rather than what is.

Being himself old and unfeathered Yeats does not have the power to banish those baleful 'Presences' that remind him constantly of the beauty he had lost and prompt the pain of unfulfilled and unfulfillable desire. But in a mood of defiance characteristic of a man who could entitle a poem '*News* for the Delphic Oracle' he decides at least to tell them something. What he fashions in the last stanza is of course itself an image, but an image of a Paradise in which the dualism caused by the Fall has been healed: in which the labour that creates beauty is no longer Adam's curse but a joyful affirmation of life and spontaneous happiness. William Morris, supreme advocate of this kind of labour, had asserted the human right to take pleasure in the body:

To feel mere life a pleasure; to enjoy the moving one's limbs and exercising one's bodily powers; to play, as it were, with sun and wind and rain; to rejoice in satisfying the due bodily appetites of a human animal without fear of degradation or sense of wrong-doing: yes, and therewithal to be well-formed, straight-limbed, strongly knit, expressive of countenance—to be, in a word, beautiful—that also I claim. If we cannot have this claim satisfied, we are but poor creatures after all; and I claim it in the teeth of those terrible doctrines of asceticism, which, born of the despair of the oppressed and degraded, have been for so many years used as instruments for the continuation of that oppression and degradation.[19]

Following Morris, Yeats wrote that the 'Unity of Being Dante compared to a perfectly proportioned human body' was his Christ (*Essays and Introductions* p. 518). Evoking in *A Vision* the humanist ideal of the Renaissance he argued that at Phase 15, the Phase of greatest perfection, 'The ascetic, who had a thousand years before attained his transfiguration upon the golden ground of Byzantine mosaic, had turned not into an athlete but into that unlabouring form the athlete dreamed of: the second Adam had become the first' (*A Vision* pp. 291-2). The second Adam, the suffering Christ whose image has inspired the asceticism of nuns, is replaced by the effortless 'unlabouring' bodily beauty of Michaelangelo's 'half awakened Adam', an Adam as yet uncursed. 'Among School Children' ends with an evocation of this state:

> Labour is blossoming or dancing where
> The body is not bruised to pleasure soul,
> Nor beauty born out of its own despair,
> Nor blear-eyed wisdom out of midnight oil.
> O chestnut-tree, great-rooted blossomer,
> Are you the leaf, the blossom or the bole?
> O body swayed to music, O brightening glance,
> How can we know the dancer from the dance?
>
> (*Variorum Poems* pp. 445-6)

This justly famous stanza once more cries in Plato's teeth that nature is *not* a spume that plays upon a ghostly paradigm of things. The firmly rooted chestnut tree resists all attempts at abstract categorization, while the 'paradigm' or form of the dance exists only when it is embodied in the limbs of the dancer. This organic unity, is, like the sphere, a reality that transcends the Platonic Forms. Only in time does our experience fall into antinomies like 'body' and 'soul'. Platonic dualism is a true representation of human experience, but it does not correspond to the ultimate reality, a place 'where' body is not bruised to pleasure soul (as it was in Yeats's 'spiritual marriage') because body and soul are one.

Like Morris, Yeats offers a Utopian vision of labour both as painless procreation ('blossoming') and as a joyful art of the body ('dancing'). His emphasis is on process rather than product, becoming rather than being: in contrast with the 'marble or . . . bronze repose' of the images, he chooses to celebrate the most fragile and transitory of natural things, the blossom; and the most active and necessarily evanescent of artistic forms, the dance. His symbolic evocation of unalienated labour partakes not of heavenly but of earthly glory, which is defined as a fusion of work and play.

W.B. Yeats and That High Horse

Jon Stallworthy

The case for the Prosecution has been forcefully summed up by Seamus Heaney: 'All through his life, of course, and ever since his death, Yeats has been continually rebuked for the waywardness of his beliefs, the remoteness of his behaviour and the eccentricity of his terms of reference. Fairies first of all. Then Renaissance courts in Tuscany and Big Houses in Galway. Then Phases of the Moon and Great Wheels. What, says the reliable citizen, is the sense of all this?'[1] The Defence might be expected to plead guilty and enter a plea of 'diminished responsibility' on the grounds that the accused was of a category defined by Shakespeare—'The lunatic, the lover, and the poet'—but no, the case for the Defence involves a forceful counter-claim: that Yeats was a major poet. And what, says the reliable citizen, is a major poet? Dante, Milton, and Blake, the Defence replies, are by common consent accorded the rank and status of major poets. Their cosmological, theological, and political beliefs are then rehearsed to the greater bafflement of the reliable citizen, and the Prosecution is forced to concede that what the jury may rightly regard as wayward beliefs, remote behaviour, and eccentric terms of reference, do not necessarily disqualify one from holding the rank and status of major poet. But can these be qualifications? On the contrary, they are irrelevant to the question (though not, obviously, to the poet). A major poet has a larger imagination than a lesser poet and, with it, apprehends the Universe. He receives and he transmits a coherent vision of the world as revealed to him in his time and place. It is possible—indeed, it is usual—for a later reader to deny the *objective* truth of elements of that vision, whilst remaining utterly convinced of its *subjective* truth. The authority of the utterance leaves no room for doubt that the poet saw and heard and felt what he says he saw and heard and felt. His truth is the truth of the imagination, and if he is a major poet that truth will be proclaimed by the organic unity manifest in the multiplicity of his works, the whole greater than the sum of its parts. A lesser poet may write poems as great as all but the greatest of the major poet, but the difference between them will appear when their *Collected Poems* are compared.

This is not to say that the *oeuvre* of the major poet will be free of contradictions. Blake, indeed, asserted that 'Without Contraries is no Progression' and his work derives much of its energy from such structural polarities as innocence and experience, liberty and tyranny. Yeats was another such, by force of temperament and example. His intensive study of Blake's Prophetic Books from 1889 to 1893 brought him to an understanding not only

220

of his master but himself. No doubt it was an echo from Blake's anvil that, he wrote,

one day when I was twenty-three or twenty-four . . . seemed to form in my head, without my willing it, much as sentences form when we are half-asleep: 'Hammer your thoughts into unity'. For days I could think of nothing else, and for years I tested all I did by that sentence. I had three interests: interest in a form of literature, in a form of philosophy, and a belief in nationality. None of these seemed to have anything to do with the other, but gradually my love of literature and my belief in nationality came together . . . Now all three are, I think, one, or rather all three are a discrete expression of a single conviction.[2]

It is, of course, one thing for a poet to assert the unity of his thoughts, and quite another for his reader to find it in his works. In 1919, when Yeats made that assertion, he had been two years married and his wife's 'communicators' were guiding his hammer in the ultimate unification of his thoughts, the 'system' of *A Vision*. Five years earlier, however, in dedicating his *Reveries over Childhood and Youth* 'To those few people mainly personal friends who have read all that I have written', he had implied how he wanted to be read.

If, like many readers of Yeats, one is unaware of the nature of his enterprise, what will be one's experience of reading 'Under Ben Bulben', say, out of context or in an anthology? Without notes—and it is surely significant that the poet himself offers none on this poem—such a reader will make little of the first three sections and, of the last three, perhaps only the general sense of the exhortation to 'Irish poets' before he comes to the lapidary statements at its close. Here, in a literal as well as a figurative sense, one is on firm ground:

> Under bare Ben Bulben's head
> In Drumcliff churchyard Yeats is laid.
> An ancestor was rector there
> Long years ago, a church stands near,
> By the road an ancient cross.

The poet has recalled his imagination from its tour of Egypt, Greece, Italian 'Gardens where a soul's at ease', the Romantic English and French landscapes of 'Calvert and Wilson, Blake and Claude'; and has finally returned to 'that valley his fathers called their home'. In that familiar landscape, he orders the erection of a tombstone 'quarried near the spot' and, bearing an epitaph revised so that it may apply equally to horsemen living and horseman dead.[3] Drumcliff churchyard may be seen as a symbolic crossroads, for there the Sligo-Lissadell road that carries its 'hard-riding country gentlemen' intersects at right angles the route of the 'fierce horsemen' of the Sidhe who ride 'from mountain to mountain', from Knocknarea to Ben Bulben.

If the puzzled but purposeful reader of that poem follows its road to its source, he will find himself—in both the 1933 *Collected Poems* and Richard Finneran's 1983 new edition—at 'Crossways', a group of poems so called, Yeats wrote, because in them he 'tried many pathways'. As the sad shepherd of pastoral tradition, he wandered between a 'gentle valley' and the seashore. As an Indian, he 'passed along the water's edge below the humid trees', and as an

old fisherman rode in a cart 'That carried the take to Sligo town to be sold'. Our
purposeful reader will find himself on even more familiar ground if he is
reading the 1957 Variorum Edition that, following the arrangement of the 1949
two-volume edition, opens with 'The Wanderings of Oisin'.

Here I have to say that, grateful as I am for the improved texts and expanded
notes of Finneran's edition, I wish he had followed the 1949 edition in its
integration of longer with shorter poems, an *aesthetic* arrangement chosen by
Yeats, I believe, in preference to that proposed (for *commercial* reasons) by the
publishers of his 1933 *Collected Poems*. There are two schools of thought here,
and I think each must in honesty concede that the bibliographical evidence is
inconclusive. But what is gained or lost by moving the long poems—so
carefully integrated with shorter poems in Yeats's individual volumes—to a
separate section at the end of the *Collected Poems*? I can see no gain, but only
innumerable broken connections.

The purposeful reader of the *Collected Poems*, who begins where I believe
Yeats wanted us to begin, will find Oisin, the pagan poet, telling St Patrick how
(in a valley where, later, a poet's tombstone would stand near an ancient cross)
he found

> on the dove-grey edge of the sea
> A pearl-pale, high-born lady, who rode
> On a horse with bridle of findrinny . . . .

In this characteristically indeterminate zone of the early poems, between shore
and water, day and night, the high-born lady lures the poet on to her high
horse:

> And then I mounted and she bound me
> With her triumphing arms around me,
> And whispering to herself enwound me . . . .

She the active, he the passive partner, they visit islands of 'Vain gaiety, vain
battle, vain repose', until the magnetic force of recollection draws him home to
his valley. There, leaning from his horse to help two men who '*fell* with their
burden', Oisin himself '*fell* on the path . . . and [he said] my years three
hundred *fell* on me'.[4] Asking St Patrick where his former companions are to be
found, he learns they are in Hell,

> Watching the blessèd ones move far off, and the smile on God's face,
> Between them a gateway of brass, and the howl of the angels who *fell*.[4]

Oisin rejects the Saint's call to penance that might, in due course, place him
with the blessèd ones *on high* and, loyal to his friends, elects to join them *below*.

Shortly after giving the typescript of *The Wanderings of Oisin and Other
Poems* to its publisher, Yeats wrote in a letter: 'I have noticed some things
about my poetry I did not know before : . . . that it is almost all a flight into
fairyland from the real world, and a summons to that flight. The Chorus to the
"Stolen Child" sums it up—that it is not the poetry of insight and knowledge,
but of longing and complaint—the cry of the heart against necessity. I hope

some day to alter that and write poetry of insight and knowledge.'[5] He might also have noticed another and related movement which, with its counter-movement, is the subject of this essay. Though the speaker in 'Crossways' and 'The Rose' is often aware of things above him—heavy boughs, Autumn, stars—there is usually an accompanying sense of oppressive weight, and poem after poem enacts a spatial descent, ending in water and reflected in the dying fall of its music. Earth and water are the dominant elements of the Yeatsian universe at this time. A descent from the one to the other is undertaken by his ancient heroes—Cuchulain fighting with 'the invulnerable tide', Fergus ruling 'the white breast of the dim sea'—and by the poet himself 'in a field by the river . . . full of tears' or contemplating flight to 'The Lake Isle of Innisfree'. This last, quintessential expression of Yeats's early imagination, opens with an up-beat echo of the Prodigal Son, 'I will arise and go now', and the resolution to *build* a small cabin and *raise* nine bean-rows. But the dream of activity is no sooner articulated than it yields to indolent passivity:

> And I shall have some peace there, for peace comes dropping slow,
> Dropping from the veils of the morning to where the cricket sings:
> There midnight's all a glimmer, and noon a purple glow,
> And evening full of the linnet's wings.

He longs for peace to drop with the dew that drops and glistens in so many of the early poems, a descent twice repeated in the stanza's temporal movement from morning to midnight, noon to evening. The third stanza's opening echo of the first sounds almost self-hypnotic, an impression reinforced by the lullingly alliterative 'lake water lapping with low sounds by the shore'. And the resolution to *arise* is now countered even more swiftly by the descending movement initiated by those 'low sounds' that lead to 'the deep heart's core'.

Deep and *low*, drop (with its variants *drip* and *droop*) and *fall*, *down* and *under*, *sad/ness* and *sorrow* reappear from poem to poem, like sombre threads reinforcing the subtextual metaphor of 'woven woods' and 'the deep woods woven shade'. The reader enters a tapestry world of low-lit, low-lying places: island and lake, valley and seashore, paced by a Romantic Solitary and the mainly mythic inhabitants of his imagination. In *The Wind among the Reeds*, the reeds that grow between land and water conspire with the wind of inspiration to speak of the Beloved that increasingly dominates that imagination. The twilight falls still further and the Poet's world contracts as he bids her

> cover the pale blossoms of your breast
> With your dim heavy hair,
> And trouble with a sigh for all things longing for rest
> The odorous twilight there.

Poem after poem speaks of *his* longing to hide himself under her loosened hair and closes, in a final gesture of abasement, with the worshipper's eyes fixed upon the Beloved's feet.

In 1902, John Quinn introduced Yeats to the works of Nietzsche, and soon the poet was writing to Lady Gregory: 'I have not read anything with so much excitement since I got to love Morris's stories which have the same curious astringent joy.'[6] Nietzsche's celebration of the hero who, by living dangerously, discovers heroic joy had a dramatic effect on 'a man whom Sorrow named his friend'. Shortly afterwards he tells Lady Gregory: 'My work has got far more masculine. It has more salt in it.'[7] A new posture, a new tone are immediately apparent in the poems of *In the Seven Woods*, a book whose very title indicates a more specific landscape. The title-poem, juxtaposing noble past and ignoble present, the Hill of Tara and 'new commonness . . . about the streets', ends with the poet's eyes no longer cast *down*, but *up*lifted to the constellation Sagittarius,

> that Great Archer
> Who but awaits His hour to shoot, still hangs
> A cloudy quiver over Pairc-na-lee.

The long poem that in the first (Cuala Press) edition followed this, 'The Old Age of Queen Maeve', opens with its narrator-poet glancing up at a latticed window (behind which he evidently hopes Maud Gonne is listening) as he sings of Maeve 'In her high house at Cruachan'. Once again, time past is contrasted with time present:

> Though now in her old age, in her young age
> She had been beautiful in that old way
> That's all but gone; for the proud heart is gone,
> And the fool heart of the counting-house fears all
> But soft beauty and indolent desire.

The '*high* house' of the fearless '*High* Queen' of '*high* Cruachan' has given place to the counting-house that 'fears all . . . '. The spatial terms of the younger poet's relationship, first, with his landscape and, then with his Beloved have now been extended to define his view of a once heroic society 'fallen from its high estate' to a base materialism. The 'old way', however, is said to be 'all *but* gone', a crucial qualification preparing for the introduction of the one exception to the general 'falling off', the lady behind the lattice: 'For there is no high story about queens / In any ancient book but tells of you.' Like the previous poem, this high story ends on a rising note, an updraught of wish-fulfilment, as in another world the lovers are united:

> They had vanished;
> But out of the dark air over her head there came
> A murmur of soft words and meeting lips.

Shattered by Maud Gonne's marriage in 1903, Yeats directed his energies into plays and 'Theatre business, management of men'. Those five years turned the private poet into a public man and when, in 1908-9, he returned to poetry it was without his former coat 'Covered with embroideries / Out of old mythologies'. In the 1949 edition, the last poem of *In the Seven Woods*, 'The Happy Townland', was followed by *The Shadowy Waters*, on which Yeats had worked from 1899 to 1906. Another dream of flight into Tir-na-nOg, the

Country of the Young, it ends with Forgael 'gathering Dectora's hair about him' on the deck of the otherwise deserted ship. Yeats effects another masterly transition when he begins *The Green Helmet and Other Poems* with 'His Dream' of a gaudy ship carrying a figure in a shroud. The face of the corpse is never revealed, but given the poems' similarity of setting, it seems reasonable to suppose that this is a sequel to 'A Dream of Death' and 'He Wishes His Beloved were Dead'. Such an interpretation is supported by the subject of the poems that follow: 'A Woman Homer Sung', 'Words', and 'No Second Troy'. This last offers a striking demonstration of the poet's development during his years in the theatre. Statement is now dramatically disguised as question:

> Why should I blame her that she filled my days
> With misery, or that she would of late
> Have taught to ignorant men most violent ways,
> Or hurled the little streets upon the great,
> Had they but courage equal to desire?

One sentence contains Yeats's private and public charges against Maud Gonne, and implies that her behaviour towards him was as unnatural as her desire to disrupt the social order by hurling the little (and *low*) *up-on* the great (and *high*). Gone, however, is the note of lachrymose complaint and, far from descending towards water, the poem rises—through the trajectory of its repeated questions—towards fire. The 'high and solitary' lady is found guilty, but acquitted on the grounds that her heroic nobleness and beauty, which are 'not natural in an age like this', place her beyond its jurisdiction. The speaker we had assumed to be putting the case for the Prosecution sums up for the Defence with an echo of Dryden's ode, 'Alexander's Feast', brilliantly turned to his own purpose: 'Why, what could she have done, being what she is? / Was there another Troy for her to burn?'

The poet exalts his beloved, but without abasing himself: indeed, by association, he shares in her exaltation, a strategy repeated in the book's later poems about Coole. He appears again as advocate, with a series of loaded questions, in the lines 'Upon a House Shaken by the Land Agitation':

> How should the world be luckier if this house,
> Where passion and precision have been one
> Time out of mind, became too ruinous
> To breed the lidless eye that loves the sun?

The connection between Lady Gregory's high house and Queen Maeve's is made clear in the image of the eagle's nest, where—according to folk lore—the King of the Birds learns to meet the gaze of his great rival, the sun. In 1907, Yeats had visited 'Urbino's windy hill' with Lady Gregory and her son, and in this and subsequent poems he transfers to her and her little 'court' an ideal of aristocratic excellence acquired from Castiglione's celebration of life in Urbino's ducal palace, *The Courtier*. This influence now blends with that of Nietszche, the laughter of whose heroes is audible behind 'the laughing eagle thoughts that grow / Where wings have memories of wings'. Yeats's voice, too, takes wing on its updraught of interrogation, as he asks how could those bred in lower 'nests' acquire the aquiline 'gifts that govern men' and, over and above these, 'gradual Time's last gift, a written speech / Wrought of *high* laughter, loveliness and ease?'. Ostensibly he refers, with the deference expected of a Renaissance poet to his patron, to Lady Gregory's 'written speech', but if literature is to be regarded as the highest achievement of civilization, then his own place is at her side. 'The Fiddler of Dooney' is moving up in the world.

The 'Responsibilities' of his next book are those of poet and aristocrat, each out of tune with a middle class moved only by the music of the cash-register. It is a sombre book, but the years following its publication removed many of Yeats's reasons for regret and bitterness. In the wake of the 1916 Easter Rising, he came round to Maud Gonne's opinion that 'tragic dignity has returned to Ireland', and a year later marked the end of his estrangement from his country by returning himself. With a gesture symbolic of his new commitment, he renamed and refurbished Ballylee Castle on Lady Gregory's demesne. He had written of his Norman Tower in *The Celtic Twilight*, associating it with Raftery, 'the greatest poet in Ireland',[8] and it is tempting to see a vision of his return in an essay written in 1906, 'A Tower on the Appenines'. This opens like a letter or a diary: 'The other day I was walking towards Urbino', but soon the documentary mode changes to something more mysterious:

I was alone amid a visionary, fantastic, impossible scenery. It was sunset and the stormy clouds hung upon mountain after mountain, and far off on one great summit a cloud darker than the rest glimmered with lightning. Away south upon another mountain a mediaeval tower, with no building near nor any sign of life, rose into the clouds. I saw suddenly, in the mind's eye an old man, erect and a little gaunt, standing in the door of the tower, while about him broke a windy light. He was a poet who had at last, because he had done so much for the word's sake, come to share in the dignity of the saint. He had hidden nothing of himself, but he had taken care of 'that dignity . . . the perfection of form . . . this lofty and severe quality . . . this virtue'. And though he had but sought it for the word's sake, or for a woman's praise, it had come at last into his body and his mind.[9]

The description of that landscape as 'visionary, fantastic, impossible' prepares for the dramatic shift of focus from the distant tower, with no sign of life near it, to what the *mind's eye* sees: the poet/saint, erect as his tower, haloed with inspirational illumination. 'He has in his ears well-instructed voices, and seeming-solid sights are before his eyes . . . as this were Delphi or Eleusis'. It may be that, walking towards Urbino and Lady Gregory, Yeats's imagination brought into a single constellation court and Duchess, Coole and its lady, tower and poet. And never was his utterance more Delphic than when, a decade before he moved into Thoor Ballylee with a wife whose supernatural communicators were revealing the sustance of *A Vision*, he wrote of 'well-instructed voices' in the ears of that old poet he was to become.

With Yeats's marriage in 1917, the happiness it brought, and the excitement of revelation, he began to rebuild his life as he rebuilt his Tower. 'The perfection of form' he had sought ever since an earlier internal voice told him to hammer his thoughts into unity, seemed at last within his grasp.

The Wild Swans at Coole begins in the familiar landscape where *Responsibilities* had ended. The title-poem opens at the water's edge in another autumnal twilight. Remembering the white birds of 'The Rose', 'buoyed out on the foam of the sea', the reader prepares for another dying fall, and consequently shares something of the poet's surprise and exaltation when the swans 'All suddenly mount'. If we have already read 'Baile and Aillin' in what I take to be its proper position, we know why he sees them as 'lover by lover' and we know whom he has in mind—the lovers of that poem, turned into swans, and 'linked by a gold chain each to each'—as his imagination soars into the poem's final question:

> But now they drift on the still water,
> Mysterious, beautiful;
> Among what rushes will they build
> By what lake's edge or pool
> Delight men's eyes when I awake some day
> To find they have flown away?

While Yeats's fortunes were rising, Lady Gregory's were falling. In January 1918, her only son was killed in action on the Italian Front and, five months later, her poet composed his elegy 'In Memory of Major Robert Gregory'. Continuing the wheeling climb of the swans, he climbs his own winding stair for the first time in his *Collected Poems*, and for the first time calls up the dead: Lionel Johnson, John Synge, George Pollexfen, and then 'my dear friend's dear son', the new friend over whose presumed meeting with the old 'in shades of underground' he vicariously presides. Despite Yeats's grief for Robert Gregory, his own happier circumstances are not concealed: 'all things the delighted eye now sees / Were loved by him.' With his marriage, delight enters his life and his poems; an emotion transferred to Gregory the solitary hero of 'An Irish Airman Foresees his Death'—'A lonely impulse of delight / Drove to this tumult in the clouds'—and related to the emotion ascribed to Gregory the solitary artist in the elegy 'Shepherd and Goatherd'. The Goatherd says:

> He had often played his pipes among my hills,
> And when he played it was their loneliness,
> The exultation of their stone, that cried
> Under his fingers.

In this, the earliest and most conventional of Yeats's three 'collected' poems on the death of his friend,[10] their common grief has brought together the Goatherd from the hills and the Shepherd from the valleys. The Shepherd reports that the dead man's mother 'goes about her house erect', the epithet used to describe the poet in 'The Tower in the Appenines', whose 'lofty and severe quality' is echoed in the description of the 'austere, sweet, lofty pipe tunes' left by her son. 'Erect' and 'lofty' are adjectives of altitude, variants of Yeats's favourite 'high', used originally of kings, queens, and heroes, but extended increasingly to artists as he came to see the artist as hero. At his elegy's consolatory close, Gregory is likened by the Shepherd to a bird that has taken to the air from water, following the flight of the wild swans. The thought of his soul's celestial ascent 'journeying / To his own dayspring' is offered with

another consolatory thought, an associated image of terrestrial ascent, 'to wife
and mother, / And children when they spring up shoulder-high'.

Gregory, I believe, climbs again in Yeats's imagination, dressed as 'The
Fisherman':

> Although I see him still,
> The freckled man who goes
> To a grey place on a hill
> In grey Connemara clothes
> At dawn to cast his flies,
> It's long since I began
> To call up to the eyes
> This wise and simple man.

The Irish Airman had said: 'Those that I fight I do not hate, / Those that I
guard I do not love'; and those cadences recur as the poet meditates on 'The
living men that I hate, / The dead men that I loved'. Those that he hates are
held responsible for 'The beating down of the wise / And great Art beaten
down'. As so often, the placing of the adverbs *up* and *down* reinforces the
movement of the poem. The image of the Fisherman had been called *up* only to
be eclipsed by bitter memories of those who beat *down*, but these are in turn
eclipsed as affirmation triumphs over negation. The Fisherman reappears,
climbing *up*, and the poet makes a resolution fulfilled by his poem: that for this
man—and, by implication, for others like him, as yet unborn—he will write a
poem 'cold / And passionate as the dawn'.

When Yeats's *Collected Poems* are read in what I take to be their intended
sequence, his images may be seen to develop and unfold in a process of natural
growth. Tree and tower, for example, with which *Michael Robartes and the
Dancer* ended, reappear at the start of *The Tower*. But now, seeing 'That is no
country for old men', he turns from 'The Young / In one another's arms, birds
in the trees' to utter a prayer not for his infant daughter but his elderly self. He
has come up in the world since the days when he so often sang under the
boughs and, envisaging his continuing ascent to a higher realm, depicts
himself as a golden bird 'set upon a golden bough'. Present reality, however,
drags him back to earth and indignity: 'Decrepit age that has tied to me / As to a
dog's tail'. No sooner is he *down* than his imagination struggles to *rise*,
remembering his boyhood when he 'climbed Ben Bulben's back'. Now he
climbs to the battlement of his tower and, as if its winding stair were rooted in
the grave, once again calls up the dead. Reverie prompts resolution:

> It is time that I wrote my will;
> I choose upstanding men
> That climb the streams until
> The fountain leap, and at dawn
> Drop their cast at the side
> Of dripping stone . . .

His terrestial ascent is to be continued, his celestial ascent ('being dead, we
rise') reflected, in the activities of such Ascendancy figures as his Fisherman.

Lady Gregory's decision, in 1927, to sell Coole prompted Yeats's (reached the day after he learnt of hers) to leave Thoor Ballylee.[11] Neither went at once, but both were forced to accept that an era was drawing to its end. The poet finally severed his connection with the Tower in 1929 and, in that year, wrote the first half of an elegiac diptych that shows a further elaboration of the structural pattern I have been considering.

The reader of the *Collected Poems* who comes to 'Coole Park, 1929' will know how to interpret the symbolic values of the landscape presented with such seeming simplicity:

> I meditate upon a swallow's flight,
> Upon an aged woman and her house,
> A sycamore and lime-tree lost in night
> Although that western cloud is luminous,
> Great works constructed there in nature's spite
> For scholars and for poets after us,
> Thoughts long knitted into a single thought,
> A dance-like glory that those walls begot.

It is twilight again; not only a Celtic Twilight, but the Twilight of the West. A high house is about to be lost in the night that has already engulfed its attendant trees. However, the fact that 'Great works constructed there' are for those who will come *after* the speaker, the aged figure in his landscape (and, incidentally, his reader), indicates that they will survive the descending night; this by virtue of their radiant unity, 'A dance-like glory that those walls begot'. The generative verb picks up, with beautiful tact, the dynastic associations of the word 'house' and implicates Lady Gregory in the birth of its offspring. The 'swallows' are now identified as the architects of culture and society, to whose diverse energies she gave direction. But, as in 'The Second Coming' the falcon could no longer hear the falconer, swallows no longer circle round the mistress of Coole. Synge and two of Lady Gregory's nephews, John Shawe-Taylor and Hugh Lane, are dead and, in the last stanza, the poet's eye drops from 'the dreaming air' to 'a shapeless mound' of earth suggestive of a grave, enacting the gesture of respect enjoined upon those who come after:

> dedicate—eyes bent upon the ground,
> Back turned upon the brightness of the sun
> And all the sensuality of the shade—
> A moment's memory to that laurelled head.

The second panel of the diptych, 'Coole Park and Ballylee, 1931', depicts a second symbolic landscape related to the first by their connecting stream. To its racing waters—so much more active than the placid lake-water of Yeats's earlier landscape—the reader's eye is directed, as they rise and fall:

>   drop,
> Run underground, rise in a rocky place
> In Coole demesne, and there to finish up
> Spread to a lake and drop into a hole.

The second stanza brings the reader ashore in the landscape—and the season—of 'The Wild Swans at Coole', preparing him for the 'sudden thunder of the mounting swan', that draws the poet's eye from earth to sky. But the swan follows the swallows out of the picture; the exalting moment and movement pass; and at this mid-point in the poem the reader is brought back to earth. Instead of the thunder of the swan we hear the sound of Lady Gregory's stick upon the floor, as she moves, slowly and painfully, among art-works of a happier past. As the poet who has lost his tower observes the 'last inheritor' of a house and gardens that 'glorified / Marriages, alliances and families', he associates himself with her: 'We shift about—all that great glory spent—/Like some poor Arab tribesman and his tent.' But no sooner has he chronicled the decline of ancestral glory, than his recollection of their shared 'dance-like glory' initiates a counter-movement:

> We were the last romantics—chose for theme
> Traditional sanctity and loveliness;
> Whatever's written in what poets name
> The book of the people; whatever most can bless
> The mind of man or elevate a rhyme;
> But all is changed, that high horse riderless,
> Though mounted in that saddle Homer rode,
> Where the swan drifts upon a darkening flood.

His proud boast rises on the wings of its verbs—'bless' and 'elevate'—to be countered in turn by an echo of 'Easter 1916': 'All changed, changed utterly'. However, there can be no mistaking the clear inference of the closing lines: that 'the last romantics' rode in Homer's saddle. The high horse Pegasus may now be riderless and the high swan vanishing upon the tidal darkness threatening Coole, but there remains the possibility that these symbols of the exalted imagination may survive and, some day, be recalled to earth. Such a conclusion is reinforced by the overall movement of these linked poems: from *air* to *earth*, swallows to broken stone; and then from *water* and *earth* into the *air* again with Pegasus and swan.,

A similar progression is discernable in the structure of *A Full Moon in March*, where songs from the roads—they speak of marching and riding—lead to 'Supernatural Songs' more elevated both in diction and in altitude. These culminate in the hermit's-eye view from Meru, the sacred mountain, that sees man

> Ravening through century after century,
> Ravening, raging, and uprooting that he may come
> Into the desolation of reality:
> Egypt and Greece, good-bye, and good-bye, Rome!

The implications of that vision are developed in the yet more sibylline utterance that follows when the poet calls on his *alter ego*, Old Rocky Face, to observe 'The gyres! the gyres!' The buoyancy in the mountain hermit's farewell to Egypt and Greece and Rome anticipates the one word that comes from Old Rocky Face's cavern: 'Rejoice!' He understands that the fall of one

civilization is occasioned by the rise of the next, a perception extended by
'Lapis Lazuli': 'All things fall and are built again, / And those that build them
again are gay.' Those that build the civilizations, restoring the ravages of the
sword, are revealed as the artists, whose instinct is to build in joy, to celebrate
and consecrate. Yeats's great poem enacts its theme, as in homage to the
unknown sculptor of the mountain of lapis lazuli, he remakes it in his own
medium. The Chinamen 'climb'—to their re-maker's 'delight'—and, when at
last 'One asks for mournful melodies', we understand that the musician's
accomplished fingers are playing such a piece as we have ourselves been
hearing.

The gaiety that is the theme of that poem finds further expression in the little
song that follows, called 'Imitated from the Japanese':

> A most astonishing thing—
> Seventy years have I lived;
> (Hurrah for the flowers of Spring
> For Spring is here again.)

Yeats's quest for wisdom has led him from sorrow by autumnal shores to a
joyful Spring among the mountains. A related structural movement of ascent
predominates in these *New Poems*: 'The Lady's Third Song', 'An Acre of
Grass', 'Beautiful Lofty Things', 'To Dorothy Wellesley'. Now, however,
aware that height needs depth as fair needs foul, he counterpoints these poems
with such *descending* movements as those of the songs of Lover and Chambermaid. Similarly, two voices counterpoint each other: that of the Archpoet,
speaking for the most part in elevated iambic pentameters, and that of the
ballad-maker, speaking with the swifter rhythms and 'lower' diction of the
street.

It seems that in 1939 Yeats drew up a List of Contents, which was
overlooked by his literary executors when they came to publish his *Last
Poems*.[12] The alternative arrangement destroyed the movement of the
intended coda to the *Collected Poems*, but Finneran reconstructs it in his New
Edition, and a striking improvement it is. *New Poems* had ended with Yeats's
answer to the question asked of Shelley by his ghostly alter-ego—'Are you
Content?'—and that poem should be followed by the voice of the same ghost
speaking now from the grave, in 'Under Ben Bulben'. Recognising that, we
hear in the repeated imperative, 'Swear', an echo of the ghost of Hamlet's
father on the battlements of Elsinore. We recognize the sages seen in 'Demon
and Beast', and 'those horsemen' of the Sidhe often encountered since their
first appearance in that first poem in Yeats's first book, 'The Wanderings of
Oisin':

> Now they ride the wintry dawn
> Where Ben Bulben sets the scene.
> Here's the gist of what they mean.

His explanation brings him round to the role of the artist in civilizations seen
from the heights of Meru—Egypt and Greece—and in Rome's Sistine Chapel,

as described in 'Michael Robartes and the Dancer'. When he addresses himself specifically to Irish poets, all the figures commended to their attention have been celebrated in his own earlier poems. And when, at the last, he turns to Drumcliff, he returns to the churchyard and cross, rector and horse of 'Are you Content?'

'Three Songs to the One Burden' were intended to follow 'Under Ben Bulben'; and that burden—*From mountain to mountain ride the fierce horsemen*—should bring the reader to 'The Black Tower', where 'old bones upon the mountain shake'. Poem is thus matched with poem as in the earlier mosaic books, and the movements of ascent and descent are no less carefully composed. The most pronounced upsurge occurs in 'The Statues', whose seer-speaker extends the theme of 'Under Ben Bulben'—'Measurement began our might'—into the proud claim of 'The Municipal Gallery Revisited'. By analogy with the Greek sculptors, who are credited with putting *down* the Persians at the battle of Salamis, the artists of the Irish Renaissance are credited with the triumph of Easter 1916. They introduced into the imagination of Patrick Pearse the figure and the spirit of Cuchulain, summoned / called *up* to his side in the heroic defence of the Post Office. His vision of that Easter *Rising* prompts the poet's closing prophecy of his people's ascent:

> We Irish, born into that ancient sect
> But thrown upon this filthy modern tide
> And by its formless spawning fury wrecked
> Climb to our proper dark, that we may trace
> The lineaments of a plummet-measured face.

Shipwrecked, they climb from shores fouled by the blood-dimmed levelling tide to heights of form and true proportion prepared by their artists.

As if in ironic commentary on the Archpoet's oracular ascent from past to future, the voice of the ballad-maker now sends 'News for the Delphic Oracle' from Tir-na-nOg, the country beyond time. He reports that his *dramatis personae*—from Oisin and Niamh to Pythagoras—are disporting themselves (and presumably the poet with them) in endless love-making. The poem's movement follows their descent,

> Down the mountain walls
> From where Pan's cavern is
> Intolerable music falls . . .

to where, in a timeless tide far removed from its 'filthy modern' counterpart, 'nymphs and satyrs / Copulate in the foam'. In 'Long-Legged Fly', the Archpoet returns to his dominant theme with instructions as to what must be done 'That civilization may not *sink*' (my italics): warrior, lover, and artist must fulfill their destinies as, successively, its saviour, destroyer, and creator. The sequence implies a clear progression—up, down, and up again—with Michaelangelo, up on his scaffolding, at the highest point. The maker of civilization, who remakes its ideal images (in this case, its image of perfect sexuality), stands higher than the hero in Yeats's pantheon. The artist is the ultimate hero.

As he designed the end of his *Collected Poems*, he was to descend from his scaffolding, from the 'high stilts' of Malachi Stilt-Jack, to the final retrospection of 'The Circus Animals' Desertion'. That unsparingly ironic review brings his reader full circle, down from the mountains to 'the sweepings of a street': 'I must lie down where all the ladders start, / In the foul rag-and-bone shop of the heart.' And the heart—not for the first time—was to have the last word, in 'Politics'. The warrior-poet of the first poem of Yeats's first book had been 'starved for the bosom of his faery bride', and now we hear the 'old man young', about to set sail for the Country of the Young, speaking to himself:

> And maybe what they say is true
> Of war and war's alarms,
> But O that I were young again
> And held her in my arms!

No poet in the English Language has had a grander view of the poet's task, and none has hammered his thoughts and his language—the *high* and the *low*—into a greater unity.

'What Can I But Enumerate Old Themes'

Peter Kuch

It seems customary, when charting the development of Yeats's style, to use *The Green Helmet* and *Responsibilities* to distinguish between an 'early' and a 'middle' style. It also seems customary to relate the stylistic development to the poet's life. *The Green Helmet* and *Responsibilities* are rightly said to disclose a maturing poet, a man of the world whose matter and manner have been tempered by self-criticism, disappointment and conflict. The poetry, for the most part, is rightly said to be tougher, more colloquial and direct, and to be in the main a more honest confrontation with the public world than the dream-laden verse of 'Crossways', 'The Rose' and *The Wind Among the Reeds*, or the transitional poetry of *In the Seven Woods*. The events commonly thought to have contributed to this maturation include: the 'lightning'[1] marriage of Maud Gonne to John MacBride in February 1903; the literary association with Synge, the *Playboy* controversy, and Yeats's work in the theatre; his reading of Nietzsche and Castiglione; his deepening friendship with Lady Gregory in which, as he says, nothing came 'between mind and delighted mind',[2] and his growing identification with an aristocracy of taste that aligned itself with Renaissance Italy; the American lecture and theatre tours; the publication of the *Collected Works* by A.H. Bullen in 1908; the enthusiastic tutelege of Ezra Pound, who attempted to propel him into modernity; the Lane controversy, and his public estrangement from an emerging Catholic middle class he considered myopically devoted to material self-advancement and the creation of a Holy Republic; and, towards the end of the period covering the years 1902 to 1916, his consorting with mediums and his research into spiritualism. Each event, at its own time and in its own way, it is argued, remade the poetry and the poet.

Yeats himself often speculated about the interplay between circumstance, the self and style. There are a number of poems and several passages in the letters and the autobiographical writings that seek to relate one to the other before announcing fresh intentions or describing new points of departure. Most accounts of Yeats's artistic development use at least two or three of these, though none seems to have attempted to use them all. But if all the passages are arranged chronologically, they collectively disclose something different from what each appears to assert individually. There is the 15 May 1903 letter to John Quinn in which Yeats disparages his recent book, *Ideas of Good and Evil*,

234

as 'too lyrical, too full of aspirations after remoter things, too full of desires', and announces his intention to write in a style that is vital and direct: 'Whatever I do from this out will, I think, be more creative. I will express myself . . . by that sort of thought that leads straight to action, straight to some sort of craft.'[3] Then there is the April 1904 letter to George Russell (AE) about *New Songs*, an anthology of young poets' work that Yeats himself would probably have preferred to entitle *Old Tunes*. 'Some of the poems', he assured his friend,

I will probably underrate . . . because the dominant mood in many of them is one I have fought in myself and put down. In my *Land of Heart's Desire*, and in some of my lyric verse of that time, there is an exaggeration of sentiment and sentimental beauty which I have come to think unmanly. . . . We possess nothing but the will and we must never let the children of vague desires breathe upon it nor the waters of sentiment rust the terrible mirror of its blade. . . . Let us have no emotions, however abstract, in which there is not an athletic joy.[4]

It is customary to remark the presence of Nietzsche, whom Yeats began to read with excited attention in 1902, and to speculate about the extent of his influence.

The Preface to *Poems 1899-1905* contains another passage that is often cited by those intent on charting the development of the poet's style:

Some of my friends . . . do not understand why I have not been content with lyric writing. But one can only do what one wants to do, and to me drama—and I think it has been the same with other writers—has been the search for more of manful energy, more of cheerful acceptance of whatever arises out of the logic of events, and for clean outline, instead of those outlines of lyric poetry that are blurred with desire and vague regret.[5]

Then there is the 1906 repudiation of the early poetry as 'full of decorative landscape and of still life';[6] and the diary entry for 12 March 1909; 'it was only when Synge began to write that I saw that our movement would have to give up the deliberate creation of a kind of Holy City in the imagination . . . and . . . be content to express the individual'.[7] Another passage that is often cited is the one labelled 'First Principles' in a diary note dated Christmas 1912:

Not to find one's art by the analysis of language or amid the circumstances of dreams but to live a passionate life, and to express the emotions that find one thus in simple rhythmical language. The words should be the swift natural words that suggest the circumstances out of which they rose.[8]

Finally, it seems customary to complete a survey of Yeats's stylistic development from 1902 to 1916 with a discussion of 'A Coat'. In this poem, first published in May 1914, Yeats not only distanced himself from the young Irish poets of the day, particularly those who had contributed to *New Songs*, but he also appeared publicly to repudiate his own poetry.

> I made my song a coat
> Covered with embroideries
> Out of old mythologies
> From heel to throat;
> But the fools caught it,
> Wore it in the world's eyes
> As though they'd wrought it.
> Song, let them take it,
> For there's more enterprise
> In walking naked.[9]

Nakedness is customarily taken to symbolize a poetry that is tough, colloquial, direct, and that is an honest attempt to explore the complexities of the interaction between the self and the public world, the dream and the actual.

Once they have been arranged in chronological order, these declarations of intent reveal a common preoccupation. The poetry written after each statement is made is consistently characterized as aspiring after the remote, as feminine, decorative, blurred, and as being drawn from the private world of dream. In contrast, the poetry that is about to be written is consistently characterized as being directed toward action, whether engaging the public world or celebrating manful energy; as drawing its diction from the language of common speech; and as being the apparently spontaneous utterance of a passionate, individual life. Thus each declaration, whether it comes from 1903, or 1914, or anytime in between, announces a similar programme. The poetry that has been written and the poetry that is about to be written are described using the same pairs of opposites: vague as opposed to clear; feminine as opposed to masculine; the decorative as opposed to the naked; and, perhaps the most persistent, the dream as opposed to the actual.

The similarities between the various statements Yeats made about his style should make critics cautious about using them to plot his artistic development. That development was more varied and more complex than his own statements about it. The changes and the lack of change that characterize the years from 1902 to 1916 resist the neat dialectic of Yeats's own prescriptions and the orderly formulation of any calendar of artistically significant events. The similarities also emphasize the persistence of his stylistic intentions. Not only did he persistently seek a quality such as simplicity, but he seems to have come to have felt that the simplicity he had achieved was essentially a new type of complexity. Pruning his style served to stimulate it to such an extent that he needed to prune it again in order to keep it fruitful. For example, despite his declared intent in 'A Coat', Yeats did not go 'naked' after May 1914. His mature work is replete with mythologies that have been used to furnish 'embroideries' for poetry. Perhaps the most elaborate are those used for *A Vision* and its associated poetry. But even then we find Yeats declaring: 'I can now, if I have the energy, find the simplicity I have sought in vain. I need no longer write poems like "The Phases of the Moon" nor "Ego Dominus Tuus"'.[10] Yeats never limited himself to his own prescriptions. He not only knew the value of coats, but he also knew that with style today's nudity might be tomorrow's ornateness.

The similarities between the various statements Yeats made about his style also point to the tensions that persist throughout his poetry. These tensions are part of that dialectic of vagueness and clarity, femininity and masculinity, ornateness and nudity, the dream and the actual that he reverted to when he came to talk about his stylistic intentions. As possible attitudes, they belong as much to his subject matter as to his manner. But a preoccupation with charting the development of Yeats's style, particularly with reference to his life, seems to have prevented critics from exploring the thematic affinities between the early and the middle poetry posited by the similarities between his statements of intention. When Yeats asked in 'The Circus Animals' Desertion', 'What can I but enumerate old themes?',[11] he seems to have addressed his rhetorical question as much to himself as to his readers. The word 'but' expresses both a sense of compulsion—the 'old themes' will eventually prove irresistible; and a sense of hopeful resignation—the 'old themes' will probably prove as fruitful as they have in the past.

Yeats's willingness to risk a fresh inspiration on an old theme can be seen clearly in the 'prose sketch' for 'Among School Children'.

Topic for poem—School children, and the thought that [life] will waste them perhaps that no possible life can fulfil our dreams or even their teachers' hope. *Bring in the old thought* that life prepares us for what never happens.[12]

This 'prose sketch' is from a manuscript book begun at Oxford on 7 April 1921. The earliest occurrence of this 'old thought' in Yeats's writing is, to my knowledge, some twelve years before in a Journal entry dated 16 September 1909 in which Yeats records his reaction to Lady Gregory's wondering where she will be when her grandson first goes to public school.

Two days ago Lady Gregory said, when they spoke of her grandchild's going to Harrow in 1921, 'Where will his grandmother be then?' I thought of this house, slowly perfecting itself and the life within it in ever-increasing intensity of labour, and then of its probably sinking away through courteous incompetence, or rather sheer weakness of will, for ability has not failed in young Gregory. And I said to myself: *Why is life a perpetual preparation for something that never happens?*[13]

Though Yeats did not include Lady Gregory in his poem, he did make his 'old thought' about life being a 'perpetual preparation for something that never happens' one of its main themes. The more he listens to the 'kind old nun' from Waterford explain the progressive methods of her convent school, and the more he observes the students themselves, the more he realizes that his own life, and probably theirs, has not been, and probably will not be, lived according to the curriculum. Is it the case, he then asks himself at the conclusion to the poem, that what is being prepared for will not happen, and that what happens cannot be prepared for as every preparation is itself a performance? Finally, it should be pointed out that Yeats wrote the 'prose sketch' for 'Among School Children' in 1921, which was the year that Richard Gregory first went to Harrow. So when he decided to 'bring in the old thought', he may well have been recalling his reaction to Lady Gregory's question when she was confronted with the date that her grandson would begin his public school education.

The theme to which Yeats perhaps most persistently returned in the years of his stylistic development from 'Crossways' to *Responsibilities* was the theme of the conflict between the world and the dream. The first poem in *Crossways*, like the first poem in *The Green Helmet*, takes as its theme the conflict between the public world and the private dream and the ambiguous nature of dreams. The speaker of 'The Song of the Happy Shepherd' admonishes himself and his audience to turn away from a world obsessed with empiricism, scientific discovery and an education system that reduces poetry to dead fact and enter the world of dream. But the world of dream is treacherous, and so the invitation is accompanied by several cautions. The listener is warned not to 'worship dusty deeds' and not to

> hunger fiercely after truth,
> Lest all thy toiling only breeds
> New dreams, new dreams . . .

He is assured that 'there is no truth saving in thine own heart', but he is also advised that if he merely listens to himself, his speeches, even though they will comfort and beguile him for a time, will eventually turn on themselves and die. Instead, the listener is directed to song, presumably a metaphor for poetry, and the dream.

> Sing, then, for this is also sooth . . .
>
> Dream, Dream, for this is also sooth.

Through poetry, the dreamer will be able to engage and exhaust the dream and so free himself from its power. The final section of the poem, where the speaker uses the personal pronoun to assert his intentions, reveals that he wishes to sing his song to the dead and the living because he is equally aware of their presence:

> I must be gone: there is a grave
> Where daffodil and lily wave,
> And I would please the hapless faun,
> Buried under the sleepy ground,
> With mirthful songs before the dawn.
> His shouting days with mirth were crowned;
> And still I dream he treads the lawn,
> Walking ghostly in the dew,
> Pierced by my glad singing through,
> My songs of old earth's dreamy youth:
> But ah! she dreams not now; dream thou!
> For fair are poppies on the brow:
> Dream, dream, for this is also sooth.[14]

The word 'pierced' seems ambiguous. It may mean that the songs which he wants to sing to please the hapless faun, presumably a symbol for the Arcadian past, are sharply effective; or it may mean that his intention to please the hapless faun goes awry and his songs wound the very past he is attempting to revive. The possibility that the dreamer can mortally wound the dream, a possibility that Yeats was to re-encounter in his reading of Nietzsche, is further suggested by the image of the 'poppies'. 'The Song of the Happy Shepherd' thus explores some of the dilemmas confronting the dreamer in terms of his search for happiness, his conflicts with the public world, and the ambiguous nature of his dream.

In 'His Dream', the opening poem of *The Green Helmet*, Yeats re-engaged several of these themes. As a preface to the poem, he placed the following immediately beneath the title:

A few days ago I dreamed that I was steering a very gay and elaborate ship upon some narrow water with many people upon its banks, and that there was a figure upon a bed in the middle of the ship. The people were pointing to the figure and questioning, and in my dream I sang verses which faded as I awoke, all but this fragmentary thought, 'We call it, it has such dignity of limb, by the sweet name of Death'. I have made my poem out of my dream and the sentiment of my dream, and can almost say, as Blake did, 'The Authors are in Eternity'.

> I swayed upon the gaudy stern
> The butt-end of a steering-oar,
> And saw wherever I could turn
> A crowd upon a shore.
>
> And though I would have hushed the crowd,
> There was no mother's son but said,
> 'What is the figure in a shroud
> Upon a gaudy bed?'
>
> And after running at the brim
> Cried out upon that thing beneath
> – It had such dignity of limb -
> By the sweet name of Death.
>
> Though I'd my finger on my lip,
> What could I but take up the song?
> And running crowd and gaudy ship
> Cried out the whole night long,
>
> Crying amid the glittering sea,
> Naming it with ecstatic breath,
> Because it had such dignity,
> By the sweet name of Death.[15]

The poem, which was originally entitled 'A Dream', was first used to introduce a set of eight poems with the common title of 'Nicolas Flamel and his wife Pernella'. The other seven, in order of composition and with their final titles, were: 'Reconciliation' (September 1908); 'No Second Troy' (December 1908); 'Words' (22 January 1909); 'King and No King' (7 December 1909); 'A Woman Homer Sung' (5-15 April 1910); 'Peace' (May 1910) and 'Against Unworthy Praise' (11 May 1910). All eight poems were addressed to Maud Gonne, and all examine various aspects of their relationship.

In a draft of his *Autobiography*, Yeats says that he first spoke to Maud Gonne about emulting the mystic devotion of Nicolas Flamel and his wife Pernella

when Maud Gonne was initiated into the Golden Dawn. She was initiated on 16
November 1891, but did not remain long nor progress beyond the Outer
order.[16] The title for this set of poems then may have been intended to direct
the reader to those few months in 1891 when, as Yeats says, 'she had come [to]
have need of me, as it seemed, and I had no doubt that need would become
love, that it was already coming so'.[17] Her need, as the *Autobiography*
emphasizes, was mainly caused by the recent death of her three-year old girl, a
child she assured Yeats she had 'adopted', but who was in fact the love-child of
her relationship with Lucien Millevoye, a French newspaper editor and ardent
Boulangist. For several weeks after the child's death she wrote Yeats letters of
'wild sorrow', but then she decided to leave Millevoye and France to be with
Yeats in Dublin. As he recounted in his *Autobiography*:

She returned to Ireland in the same ship with Parnell's body, arriving at Kingstown a
little after six in the morning. I met her on the pier and went with her to her hotel, where
we breakfasted. She was dressed in extravagantly deep mourning, for Parnell, people
thought, thinking her very theatrical. We spoke of the child's death. She had built a
memorial chapel, using some of her capital. 'What did money matter to her now?' From
another I learned later on that she had the body embalmed. That day and on later days
she went over again the details of the death . . . [18]

Perhaps the extravagant, theatrical mourning of Maud Gonne (which would
explain the repeated used of the word 'gaudy' in the poem); the public
misconception that she was honouring Parnell; and the clamorous, running
crowds that sought to dignify Parnell's destruction with the sweet name of
'Death' coalesced in Yeats's mind to evoke the characters and the setting of the
poem. If these associations did inform the poem, then the lines

> Though I'd my finger on my lip
> What could I but take up the song?

may refer to Yeats's own conventional tribute to Parnell entitled 'Mourn—and
then Onward!' which he rushed into print in the *United Ireland* the day the boat
docked.[19] If these speculations are correct, then even though the authors of the
poem, as Yeats claimed, were in eternity, their sources were in the somewhat
more mundane locations of Dun Laoghaire and Paris.

There are at least two major affinities between this poem and 'The Song of
the Happy Shepherd', even though the poems were written some twenty-three
years apart. In both poems the speaker represents himself as standing in a
privileged relation to the dead. The speaker in the 'Shepherd' poem claims that
the faun is affected by his songs; the speaker of the 'Dream' poem depicts
himself as the steersman of a funeral ship, a role that sets him apart from the
running, clamorous crowd. In both poems 'the dead', whether it is the buried
faun or the shrouded figure, seem to symbolize some heroic past to which the
speaker claims privileged access. But in both poems the speaker unequivocally
admits that his position of privilege does not mean that he is in control. The
speaker of the 'Shepherd' poem acknowledges that he is obliged to sing his
songs before sunrise; the speaker of the 'Dream' poem finds that he cannot

hush the crowd. Though he is repelled by their clamorous desire to dignify what is pervasively showy and tasteless, he admits: 'What could I but take up the song?'

Between the publication of *The Wanderings of Oisin* in 1889 and *Responsibilities* in 1916, Yeats persistently returned to the theme of the conflict between the world and the dream. The poems that best demonstrate this are the ones derived from Irish mythology, particularly the Fenian cycle.

'The Madness of King Goll' from 'Crossways' depicts the tragedy of a hero whose mind has not been sufficiently robust to accommodate the actuality of his own dreams and the expectations of his subjects. He believes his battle prowess to be so great that he can readily expel the pirates who are threatening his kingdom, but he does not take into account the psychic forces that will be unleashed by the combat. At the height of the fighting, he falls victim to a type of battle-fever and goes insane. Reduced from powerful champion to itinerant madman, he travels aimlessly through the arcadian landscape of his former kingdom searching for a poet or a musician to quench 'the whirling and the wandering fire' that now seems to burn constantly in his head. For a time his own music had given him relief, but the strings of the old harp he had used to accompany himself have broken and so he must search for someone else to sing to him to dampen the fires of his madness. King Goll's harp thus parallels the 'echo-harbouring shell' of 'The Song of the Happy Shepherd', which could reword

> in melodious guile
> Thy fretful words a little while,
> Till they shall singing fade in ruth
> And die a pearly brotherhood;[20]

The poem contains a number of paradoxes which emphasize that King Goll is a dreamer who has become deluded by the very dreams that had driven him to win his reputation. In the opening verse, the permanence of his reign of peace is praised by aged poets 'with fading heads'. In the second verse the plea for help is delivered by herdsmen from an inland valley who claim that pirates, who presumably conduct most of their raids along the coast, are driving off the herds of swine. And in the fifth and sixth verses the mad King's description of the rural delights of the country and the slumbering peace of the town are at odds with the refrain he chants:

> They will not hush, the leaves a-flutter round me, the beach leaves old.[21]

These paradoxes suggest that King Goll, both as sane ruler and insane wanderer, is deluded by the same dreams that have impelled him to action. As a legendary figure, King Goll, or the 'Ajax of the Fenians' as Douglas Hyde called him, is a particularly apt symbol for this type of partial-sightedness. Originally called Aedh mac Morna, he became known as Goll (or the blind) Mac Morna after losing an eye in the battle of Castleknock, which he won after killing Cumhail, the father of Finn.

In 'Fergus and the Druid', which was eventually incorporated in 'The

Rose', Yeats again returned to the theme of the conflict between the world and the dream. In this poem Fergus discovers that he cannot fulfil his present private dreams of kingship or achieve esoteric wisdom. Neither can he match the wisdom of his advisers nor meet the expectations of his subjects. His final speech to the Druid in which he claims that his previous lives have been successful, particularly 'A King sitting upon a chair of gold', is undercut by his prior admission that

> A King is but a foolish labourer
> Who wastes his blood to be another's dream.[22]

Other poems that depict similar conflicts in 'The Rose' are 'Cuchulain's Fight with the Sea' and 'Who Goes with Fergus'. The latter, which particularly appealed to Joyce, ironically juxtaposes Fergus' dream against his performance. Fergus was a victim and a failed protector of young love. He was forced to surrender his kingdom to Conchubar when his consuming passion for Nessa made him unfit to rule. Much later he offered to protect Deirdre, who had eloped with Naoise to avoid marriage to Conchubar, but he was deceitfully separated from them when they returned so that they could be murdered by Conchubar's soldiers. When Fergus discovered their bodies he burnt Emain Macha and ravaged Ulster. In Yeats's poem he is presented as an heroic champion who apparently

> rules the brazen cars,
> And rules the shadows of the wood,
> And the white breast of the dim sea
> And all dishevelled wandering stars.

The assurance given in the poem that the young lovers need

> no more turn aside and brood
> Upon love's bitter mystery;[23]

is thus ironic. Fergus, so weakened by love that he had to surrender his own throne, was not able to control his own enchantment or fulfil his dream of protecting the lives and love of Deirdre and Naoise.

In *The Wind Among the Reeds*, the personal dream is brought into conflict with both the supernatural and the public worlds. Niamh, in 'The Hosting of the Sidhe', the opening poem of the book, warns that

> if any gaze on our rushing band,
> We come between him and the deed of his hand,
> We come between him and the hope of his heart.[24]

That these words are spoken by Niamh should alert the reader to the possibility that this intervention could be both beneficent and malign. It was Niamh who carried off Oisin to Tir na nOg, the Land of the Ever Young. But Niamh was also Cuchulain's sweetheart. She was eventually supplanted by one of the daughters of the evil wizard Calatin, who assumed her shape and lured Cuchulain to his death by placing him under gesea to fight the phantom army created by the evil magic of one of her sisters. In two other poems from *The*

Wind Among the Reeds, 'The Host of the Air' and 'The Song of Wandering Aengus', the Sidhe come between the dreamer and his dreams to rob him of the object of his dreams. However, Niamh's warning that the dream may become a form of enchantment that forever tantalizes the dreamer is partly countered by the speaker of 'The Hosting of the Sidhe' who asks whether there is any source of dreams better than the Sidhe. 'And where is there hope or deed as fair?' In pursuing his dream, the dreamer may have to risk the paralysis of enchantment.

The other legendary figure named in 'The Hosting of the Sidhe' is Caoilte. Caoilte, one of the few Fenians to survive the battle of Gabhra, became the poet of the vanished splendour of the Golden age of the Red Branch. Toward the end of his life, he tried to acquaint Saint Patrick and his disciples with the heroic past, but they were either unsympathetic or hostile. As the celebrant of a vanished golden age, compelled to live in an alien world, Caoilte is a later version of the 'Shepherd' of the 'Crossways' poem. He also serves to introduce poems like 'He Remembers Forgotten Beauty' and 'The Secret Rose' in which personae speak about their attempts to evoke the heroic past. The structure of 'The Secret Rose' recalls the structure of 'The Song of the Happy Shepherd' in that both poems are brought to a close by the speaker asserting his personal identification with the heroic past.

'The Grey Rock' in *Responsibilities* is also spoken by someone whose celebration of the heroic past has set him at odds with most of his contemporaries, though in this poem Yeats explicitly identifies himself as the speaker. His remarks are addressed to his companions at the Cheshire Cheese, a pub in London where the Rhymers' Club had met in the early 1890's. The poem is offered both as a salute to the more recalcitrant of the Rhymers—Dowson and Johnson—and as proof that Yeats himself had kept faith with the programme for poetry he had devised in their company, despite his disappointment in love and despite his fellow Irishmen's preference for 'sword strokes' rather than 'lover's music'. 'The Grey Rock' thus challenges the reader to discover the affinities between the poetry of *Responsibilities* and the poetry of the nineties. As the speaker of 'The Song of the Happy Shepherd' had dismissed a contemporary preoccupation with 'warring kings', so the speaker of 'The Grey Rock', who identifies himself as 'Yeats', dismisses a contemporary preoccupation with 'sword strokes', and determines to tell a story of frustrated love. As the speaker of 'The Song of the Happy Shepherd' had asserted that 'fair are poppies on the brow', so the speaker of 'The Grey Rock' determines to tell a story about passions that have 'more life in them than death', even though he suspects the Rhymers will think that this is implausible.

Yeats sets his story at the time of the Danish invasions, but draws his characters from the mythological cycle. The choice of the mythological cycle, rather than say the Fenian cycle, parallels the Shepherd's determination to sing of 'old earth's dreamy youth'.[25] As Douglas Hyde has pointed out, the mythological tales deal with the first settlement of Ireland. 'The whole of their creations are thrown back, even by the Irish annalists themselves, into the dim cloud-land of the unplumbed past. . . . There is over . . . all a shadowy sense of vagueness, vastness, uncertainty.'[26] So, by using characters drawn from the mythological cycle and setting his story at the time of the Danish invasions, Yeats is able to re-explore the relationships between the dream and the actual posited in 'The Song of the Happy Shepherd', 'He Remembers Forgotten Beauty', and 'The Secret Rose'.

Yeats opens his story with the gods gathered at Slievenamon, glutted with food and drunk on wine provided by the legendary smith Goban. Their revels are broken into by Aoife, a woman of the Sidhe. She wants them to come with her to dig up the body of her faithless human lover, who has been killed in a battle between the Irish and the Danes. Aoife tells the gods that when she saw her lover was determined to fight she gave him a pin that made him invisible. But in the heat of the battle, after inflicting heavy losses on the Danes, he discarded the pin so he could fight alongside the King of Ireland's son, the courageous Murrough. Both have been killed. Aoife protests bitterly to the gods:

> I'd promised him two hundred years,
> And when for all I'd done or said -
> And these immortal eyes shed tears -
> He claimed his country's need was most,
> I'd saved his life, yet for the sake
> Of a new friend he has turned a ghost.
> What does he care if my heart break?
> I call for spade and horse and hound
> That we may harry him . . . [27]

The gods respond to her urgent call by drenching her with the wine of forgetfulness.

> And she with Goban's wine adrip,
> No more remembering what had been,
> Stared at the gods with laughing lip.[28]

The poem thus images in mythological terms one of the dilemmas of the dreamer. Aoife's compulsion to disinter the body of her lover enacts the dreamer's compulsion to possess and control the object of his dream—even after that dream has failed. But the gods, who are unmoved by tales of unrequited passion for mortals, refuse to yield the dream to Aoife. Instead, they drench her with the wine of forgetfulness, which both expunges the dream from her mind and restores the divine perspective.

But as the poem itself indicates, the gods also parallel the Rhymers, their drunkenness elevating to an epic scale the drunkenness of Dowson and Johnson (who are named in the poem). Their dousing of Aoife with wine represents their strategy for covering the debris of their own collapsed dreams. Dowson died of dissipation and drink after breaking his heart, as Yeats explained with studied quaintness in 'The Tragic Generation', 'for the daughter of the keeper of an Italian-eating house'.[29] Of Johnson, Yeats wrote:

He drank a great deal too much, and, though nothing could, it seemed, disturb his calm or unsteady his hand or foot, his doctrine, after a certain number of glasses, would become more ascetic, more contemptuous of all that we call human life. I have heard him, after four or five glasses of wine, praise some Church Father who freed himself from sexual passion by a surgical operation, and deny with scorn, and much historical evidence, that a gelded man lost anything of intellectual power.[30]

Goban's wine thus symbolizes the drunkenness of sublimation or the eradicating power of dissipation. As Yeats wrote elsewhere, largely with Dowson and Johnson in mind:

> What portion in the world can the artist have
> Who has awakened from the common dream
> But dissipation and despair?[31]

Like Aoife, Yeats could have allowed himself to be doused by Goban's wine as he agonized about Maud Gonne and John MacBride. But instead of allowing his broken dreams to drive him into dissipation and despair, Yeats moulded and remoulded them into his own type of poetry.

In 'The Grey Rock', the hunger of the immortal Aoife for her mortal lover is compared with the hunger of the mortal Florence Farr for immortal love.

> *I knew a woman none could please,*
> *Because she dreamed when but a child*
> *Of men and woman made like these;*
> *And after, when her blood ran wild,*
> *Had ravelled her own story out,*
> *And said, 'In two or three years*
> *I needs must marry some poor lout',*
> *And having said it burst in tears.*[32]

The plight of Florence Farr dramatizes another of the dreamer's dilemmas; the dreamer who dreams a dream that is so far removed from the actual that it can never be realized seems doomed to suffer despair. And this despair will transform whatever is achieved into a parody of the heart's desire. Perhaps Yeats, despite his disclaimer at the beginning of the poem, intended the story of Florence Farr to be a cautionary tale for his own benefit. Perhaps he sensed that one of the possible consequences of deifying Maud Gonne was that he might so fall victim to his dream of her that all other women would come to seem common. This section of the poem thus re-explores one of the main themes of 'The Hosting of the Sidhe'—the dreamer who empties his 'heart of its mortal dream' to follow the Sidhe may discover that they have 'come between him and the hope of his heart'.[33]

The responsible attitude to dreams, Yeats implies in 'The Three Beggars', a poem placed toward the middle of *Responsibilities*, is the attitude of the old crane of Gort. His nonchalance and detachment are contrasted against the belligerence of the old beggars who quarrel about their own 'exorbitant dreams' instead of trying to answer King Guaire's riddle and so win the prize that would enable them to realize their dreams. The beggars eventually fall asleep, but the old crane remains standing.

'Maybe I shall be lucky yet,
Now they are silent', said the crane.
'Though to my feathers in the wet
I've stood as I were made of stone
And seen the rubbish run about,
It's certain there are trout somewhere
And maybe I shall take a trout
If but I do not seem to care'.[34]

In terms of *The Green Helmet* and *Responsibilities*, 'The Three Beggars' completes the mythological treatment of the dreamer's dilemma announced by 'The Madness of King Goll'. In all ten poems the dreamer fails to achieve his dream. Most of these failures are tragic. King Goll goes insane. Fergus, in his own words, has 'grown nothing, knowing all'.[35] Cuchulain goes mad and fights the sea. Niamh and Caoilte are drawn into the enthralled, destructive company of the Sidhe. Aengus himself admits to being condemned to wander perpetually 'through hollow lands and hilly lands' (hardly an ideal landscape) in search of his dream. Cuchulain goes mad for love of Fand, until he is cured by a Druid drink of forgetfulness; while Aoife, embittered and vengeful, has to be drenched with the wine of forgetfulness. In all the poems the dreamer is in conflict with the public world or the supernatural world, and in many of them the supernatural world comes between the dreamer and the dream to rob him of the object of his dream. Finally, all the poems explore the ambiguity of dreams. They show that while dreams can be revelatory, they can also delude; and they show that while dreams can partake of the supernatural, which can be malefic or beneficent, they can also be merely solipsistic. They also show that while dreams can stimulate action, they can imprison the dreamer in reverie. The speaker of 'Under the Moon' asserts that

To dream of women whose beauty was folded in dismay,
Even in an old story, is a burden not to be born.[36]

And in 'The Circus Animals' Desertion' Yeats implied that all his early mythological poems explored 'themes of the embittered heart'.[37] For Yeats then, the mythological poems like the 'songs' sung by the 'Happy Shepherd', seem to have functioned ambiguously. They 'pierced' in that they were sharply effective for exploring the dreamer's dilemmas, but they also 'pierced' in that they punctured the enchantment of the heroic past even as they evoked it.

Some of the love poetry that Yeats wrote between 'Crossways' and *Responsibilities* also demonstrates his persistent attraction to old themes. For example, the theme first introduced in 'The Rose of the World' and 'The Sorrow of Love' that Maud Gonne was a reincarnation of the same destructive beauty which had once incarnated in Helen of Troy, is explored further in 'A Woman Homer Sung' and 'No Second Troy' in *The Green Helmet* and 'When Helen Lived' in *Responsibilities*. The most obvious affinities are between 'The Rose of the World', first published in 1892, and 'No Second Troy', first published in 1910. The closing rhetorical question of the latter—'was there another Troy for her to burn?'[38]—brings into intense focus the opening statement of the former:

> For these red lips, with all their mournful pride,
> Mournful that no new wonder may betide,
> Troy passed away in one high funeral gleam . . . [39]

In both poems 'Troy' is used to symbolize the heroic past. In 'The Rose of the World' it is contrasted with the mundane present; in 'No Second Troy' it is ironically juxtaposed against the mock-heroic present. In both poems Maud Gonne is represented as aloof, as caught up in solitary self-absorption that removes her from the confused jostle and jumble of the temporal. In 'The Rose of the World' her 'lonely beauty' is said to transcend the age:

> We and the labouring world are passing by:
> Amid men's souls, that waver and give place
> Like the pale waters in their wintry race,
> Under the passing stars, foam of the sky,
> Lives on this lonely face.[40]

In 'No Second Troy' she is said to be the embodiment of a beauty

> That is not natural in an age like this,
> Being high and solitary and most stern?[41]

The word 'high' has affinities with the spatial image of the face living on under the passing stars, while 'solitary' echoes 'lonely'. In both poems Maud Gonne's preternatural beauty is represented as being charged with a haughty sexuality. In 'The Rose of the World' this is imaged as 'those red lips, with all their mournful pride', while in 'No Second Troy' it is imaged as 'beauty like a tightened bow'. In both poems Yeats advances the idea that this haughty sexuality, and the brooding sense of tragic inevitability that it engenders, make Maud Gonne restless. In 'The Rose of the World' she is said to have 'wandering feet' and to be 'mournful' that she cannot witness any new wonders. In 'No Second Troy' the speaker asks:

> What could have made her peaceful with a mind
> That nobleness made simple as a fire . . . [42]

Finally, in both poems Maud Gonne is shown to be inexorably driven to arousing destructive passions. It is as if she is partially aware of herself playing the lead role in a tragedy she has never seen or acted in before. And though she strongly suspects the outcome of the plot, she finds the role allotted to her, and her own performance of it, irresistably enticing.

Another theme that Yeats explores and re-explores in his poetry is his fear that Maud Gonne may repudiate the image of herself that he is creating in his poetry with the result that he might lose her and the love that he has been able to generate through his poems. This fear is the main theme of 'He Wishes for the Cloths of Heaven', first published in 1899; 'Old Memory', first published in 1904; and 'Reconciliation', first published in 1910. Yeats wrote all three poems as if he were speaking directly to Maud Gonne. He turns all three on the paradox that though he seems to have been impoverished he has actually become enriched. In the first poem he compensates for his apparent poverty—he cannot afford the expensively embroidered cloths of heaven— with the richness of his compliment. Though he can only afford to use his dreams as a cloth, these dreams, it is implied by the plea to 'tread softly', are as delicate and as beautiful as the cloths of heaven. In 'Old Memory' the loss of Maud Gonne and the apparent waste of his youth and the ineffectualness of his poetry are set against his claim that at least half her strength has come from his conception of her. This is the strength, he reminds her,

> . . . that is so lofty and fierce and kind,
> It might call up a new age, calling to mind
> The queens that were imagined long ago . . . [43]

Though she has gone (the poem was written a year after she had unexpectedly married John MacBride) she can never really be separate as he will still retain that part of her which his poetry has created. 'Reconciliation' (written the year after Maud Gonne separated from John MacBride) affirms the main possibilities suggested in 'Old Memory'. The new age that might have been announced by his poetic celebration of her beauty has, in her absence, come to pass. 'The world', he tells her, 'now lives as long ago'. The 'day' that Yeats refers to in the second line was the one on which he received the letter announcing her marriage.

> Some may have blamed you that you took away
> The verses that could move you on the day
> When, the ears being deafened, the sight of the eyes blind
> With lightning, you went from me, and I could find
> Nothing to make a song about but kings,
> Helmets, and swords, and half-forgotten things
> That were like memories of you—but now
> We'll out, for the world lives as long ago;
> And while we're in our laughing, weeping fit,
> Hurl helmets, crowns, and swords into the pit.
> But, dear, cling close to me; since you were gone,
> My barren thoughts have chilled me to the bone.[44]

From his impoverishment of 'barren thoughts' and apparently rich songs about 'kings, Helmets, and swords, and half-forgotten things', Yeats affirms that they can advance to a rich reconcilition in a world seemingly sympathetic to their mood.

Finally, all three poems conclude with a plea, though each of the pleas is different. 'He Wishes for the Clothes of Heaven' ends with the plea: 'tread softly because you tread on my dreams'. 'Old Memory' closes with the plea that if anything additional to the poem needs to be said it should be said in the manner that a parent would speak to a wayward child if he didn't wish to alienate that child. 'Reconciliation' ends with the plea to cling close to him so that he will not feel the barrenness of his thoughts.

Maud Gonne in youth and age is another theme that Yeats returns to in 'The

Rose', *In the Seven Woods*, and *The Green Helmet*. In 'When You are Old', which was first published in 1892, Yeats invites her to take down the book of his poetry in her old age and rediscover her beauty and his love for her.

> When you are old and grey and full of sleep,
> And nodding by the fire, take down this book,
> And slowly read, and dream of the soft look
> Your eyes had once, and of their shadows deep;[45]

By the time he came to publish 'The Folly of Being Comforted' in 1902, Maud Gonne, as Lady Gregory observed, had begun to have 'threads of grey' in her hair, and 'little shadows come about her eyes'. Hoping that she would realize she was getting old, and that this realization would make her turn to him, Lady Gregory advised him to be patient. But he replied that Time would not soften her, and that even if she did turn to him, it would be an ambiguous consolation.

> Heart cries, 'No,
> I have not a crumb of comfort, not a grain.
> Time can but make her beauty over again:
> Because of that great nobleness of hers
> The fire that stirs about her, when she stirs,
> Burns but more clearly. O she had not these ways
> When all the wild summer was in her gaze'.
>
> O heart! O heart! if she'd but turn her head,
> You'd know the folly of being comforted.[46]

The poem, 'Peace', which was first published in 1910, brings these bitter/sweet assertions into question. Time has indeed affected Maud Gonne, but not in the way that Lady Gregory had hoped or that Yeats himself had asserted. She has retained her great nobleness, but she has also retained the softness and charm that he had praised eighteen years before in 'When You are Old'. And time and the realization that she is getting old have not drawn her to him, but neither have they driven her away. They have brought, not the folly of being comforted, nor the wistful reveries of old age, but peace.

> Ah, that Time could touch a form
> That could show what Homer's age
> Bred to be a hero's wage.
> 'Were not all her life but storm,
> Would not painters paint a form
> Of such noble lines', I said,
> 'Such a delicate high head,
> All that sternness amid charm,
> All that sweetness amid strength?'
> Ah, but peace that comes at length,
> Came when Time had touched her form.[47]

Thus the three poems, 'When You are Old', 'The Folly of Being Comforted', and 'Peace' may be said to comprise a trilogy on the theme of the expectations of youth and age.

Finally, a major recurrent theme of the love poems from 'The Rose' to

Responsibilities is Yeats's sense of the myth-making power of his own poetry. Early in his relationship with Maud Gonne, he came to realize that though he could enchant the public with his images of her, they left her largely unmoved. An early expression of his dilemma can be found in the draft of a lyric written some time in 1897.

> O my beloved you only are
>   not moved by my songs
> Which you only understand
> You only know that it is
>   of you I sing when I tell
>   of the swan on the water
>   or the eagle in the heavens
>   or the faun in the wood.
> Others weep, but your eyes
>   are dry.[48]

This draft could almost have served as the 'prose sketch' for the poem entitled 'Words'—though there is no evidence that it did.

> I had this thought a while ago,
> 'My darling cannot understand
> What I have done, or what would do
> In this blind bitter land'.
>
> And I grew weary of the sun
> Until my thoughts cleared up again,
> Remembering that the best I have done
> Was done to make it plain;
>
> That every year I have cried, 'At length
> My darling understands it all
> Because I have come into my strength,
> And words obey my call';
>
> That she had done so who can say
> What would have shaken from the sieve?
> I might have thrown poor words away
> And been content to live.[49]

The sense that he is in a 'blind, bitter land', and the realization that he is fashioning rich poems from the poor words of disappointment can be found in 'He thinks of those who have Spoken Evil of his Beloved', which was published in 1898 and eventually included in *The Wind Among the Reeds*. The poem announces a theme that is re-explored in two poems in *Responsibilities*—'Against Unworthy Praise' and 'A Woman Homer Sung'.

Yeats opens his poem, 'He Thinks of those who have Spoken Evil of His Beloved', with an invitation to Maud Gonne to assume a richly sensuous pose.

> Half close your eyelids, loosen your hair,
> And dream about the great and their pride;
> They have spoken against you everywhere,
> But weigh this song with the great and their pride;
> I made it out of a mouthful of air,
> Their children's children shall say they have lied.[50]

The poem works by repeated addition and subtraction until the final sum is greater than the original proposition. Having been invited to dream about the rich and the great, Maud Gonne is abruptly reminded that they are maligning her. Yet, immediately, she is invited to weigh his poetic defence of her against their pride, only then to be informed that this poetic defence has been made out of the seeming weightlessness of 'a mouthful of air'. But, the final line assures her, the poem will outlast the slander of the great and their pride for at least two generations because the grandchildren of the slanderers will believe the poem rather than the slander.

'Against Unworthy Praise', which was first published in 1910, uses a similar method to develop a similar theme. An image is advanced, and then withdrawn, only to have the withdrawal revealed as a strategic advance that has in fact carried the expression of the emotion beyond its original point. As with the earlier poem, there is a similar contempt for the public that is maligning her; there is a similar identification of his poetry with the apparently inconsequential; and there is a similar conviction that together they will triumph.

> O heart, be at peace, because
> Nor knave nor dolt can break
> What's not for their applause,
> Being for a woman's sake.
> Enough if the work has seemed,
> So did she your strength renew,
> A dream that a lion had dreamed
> Till the wilderness cried aloud,
> A secret between you two,
> Between the proud and the proud.
>
> What, still you would have their praise!
> But here's a haughtier text,
> The labyrinth of her days
> That her own strangeness perplexed;
> And how what her dreaming gave
> Earned slander, ingratitude,
> From self-same dolt and knave;
> Aye, and worse wrong than these.
> Yet she, singing upon her road,
> Half lion, half child, is at peace.[51]

The poem returns us to some of the dilemmas of the dreamer. Maud Gonne's dreams were powerfully conceived and yet they did not earn her worthwhile praise. The labyrinth of her own life has been further complicated by her own unexpected actions. But her dreams have been powerful enough to enable her to inspire him, and enable her to gain peace. His poetry and her peace are far greater accomplishments than the reward of unworthy praise. It is enough, the poem asserts, 'if the work had seemed'.

This power of seeming, a power derived from a dream so powerful that should a lion dream it the wilderness would cry aloud, is triumphantly affirmed in 'A Woman Homer Sung'.

If any man drew near
When I was young,
I thought, 'He holds her dear',
And shook with hate and fear.
But O! 'twas bitter wrong
If he could pass her by
With an indifferent eye.

Whereon I wrote and wrought,
And now, being grey,
I dream that I have brought
To such a pitch my thought
That coming time can say,
'He shadowed in a glass
What thing her body was'.

For she had fiery blood
When I was young,
And trod so sweetly proud
As 'twere upon a cloud,
A woman Homer sung,
That life and letters seem
But an heroic dream.[52]

What he dreams the coming times will say he has achieved is immediately surpassed as 'clouds' are beyond 'shadows' and as 'fiery blood' is beyond 'the thing her body was'. The juxtaposition of 'but' and 'heroic dream' in the final line secures the status of this dream-bred-dream by acknowledging its limitations. Though everything seems a dream next to her actuality, the perception of that actuality has been partially formed from dreams. Dreams generate dreams. As the Speaker of 'Song of the Happy Shepherd' had asserted: 'words alone are certain good' and 'dream, dream, for this is also sooth'.

In 1932, when he was revising his work for another collected edition, Yeats wrote:

I spend my days correcting proofs. I have just finished the first volume, all my lyric poetry, and am greatly astonished at myself. As it is all speech rather than writing, I keep saying, what man is this who . . . says the same thing in so many different ways.[53]

While Yeats's imaginative and stylistic development were a good deal more complex that his own prescriptive accounts of them, his constant attraction to 'old themes', and his persistent boldness in bringing in 'the old thought', should not be overlooked.

Yeats's Stream of Consciousness

Terence Diggory

The new value assigned to the condition of indeterminacy in current critical discussion extends even to literary history, last bastion of positivism. That bastion was undermined in its foundation by the disjunction of the two perspectives from which any historical moment may be viewed: the perspective, on the one hand, of what came before; on the other hand, of what came after. Thus, to Marjorie Perloff, reading in the light of Allen Ginsberg, Frank O'Hara and Ed Dorn, Yeats appears as the opponent of the 'poetics of indeterminacy' promoted by the experiments of Ezra Pound. On the other hand, to Balachandra Rajan, reading in the light of a late romanticism defined by its radical commitment to Mutability, Yeats appears 'as a poet of indeterminacy more fundamental than Eliot or Pound amid all the apparent chaos of their fragments'.[1] Ironically, though they both march under the most contemporary of standards, both Perloff and Rajan read Yeats in the light of an older criticism that claimed Yeats as champion. Both attend to what is 'fundamental' rather than 'apparent', to use Rajan's terms.

For traditional formalist criticism, what was 'fundamental' was a scholastic notion of form, available to the intellect rather than the senses. Though Rajan replaces the traditional reconciling function of form with a radical indeterminacy, the new principle operates on the same plane as the old, as a 'view of reality' more than, or rather than, a style. In the rare moments when he deigns to focus on style, as in his comments on 'the dislocation of syntax' in 'An Acre of Grass' (1938), the acuteness of Rajan's analysis testifies that only a contempt for style as epiphenomenal could allow him to generalize misleadingly that Yeats's style 'remains stubbornly consecutive'.[2] Perloff has more respect for style, yet the persistence of the traditional notion of 'spatial form' in her view of Yeats largely cancels the benefit that might accrue from that respect.

In 'Spatial Form in the Poetry of Yeats: The Two Lissadell Poems' (1967), Perloff argued that spatial form was demanded by Yeats's replacement of a 'sequential reasoning structure' by 'a shifting . . . succession of phantasms . . . as called up by the imagination'—here Perloff uses the *OED*'s definition of 'phantasmagoria'.[3] Since the 'shifting succession' in itself appeared formless, structure must reemerge as 'a unified pattern' achieved through the 'reconciliation' of the phantasms or images, a point that 'Yeats understood', Perloff concluded, but that 'later poets such as Pound and Williams have not always grasped'.[4] In *The Poetics of Indeterminacy* (1981), Perloff re-evaluates Pound and Williams by setting them outside Yeats's tradition, which Perloff identifies with Symbolism. To grant the legitimacy of the alternative aesthetic, Perloff must waive her previous demand for 'unified pattern', and accept the 'shifting succession of phantasms' on its own terms. She must accept the condition 'that the symbolic evocations generated by words on the page are no longer grounded in a coherent discourse, so that it becomes impossible to decide which of these associations are relevant and which are not'.[5] Such 'undecidability' is synonomous with the 'indeterminacy' from which Perloff's new poetics takes its name.

My concern is not that Perloff has re-evaluated Pound's and Williams's relative position to Yeats. In the light of contemporary poetry, she has learned to read the younger modernists differently, and no one has done a better job of expounding what that method of reading entails. Because I am persuaded by Perloff's exposition, however, I believe that a corresponding reassessment of our method of reading Yeats is in order. If 'phantasmagoric succession' can produce satisfactory poetry in the absence of 'unified pattern', as Perloff maintains in her defense of the 'poetics of indeterminacy', then the two principles are independent of one another. In Perloff's approach to Yeats, however, as in the approach of the formalist critics who instructed Perloff, these two principles compose a hierarchical rather than a complementary relationship. The succession is 'grounded' in the pattern, and thus in fact loses the quality of succession. This allows Perloff to argue, in her earlier study, that sometime after 1920 Yeats's aesthetic shifted 'from sequential to spatial form',[6] rather than from one type of sequence to another.

A reading of Yeats that is more internally consistent will also show a greater consistency with Pound's version of modernism. In my view, Williams, whom Perloff pairs with Pound, more radically represents the 'Other Tradition' that Perloff seeks to delineate.[7] Yeats's relationship to Pound, which I will take as my starting point, demonstrates how nearly akin 'High Modernism' and the 'Other Tradition' can appear. In place of Williams, I will pair Pound with Joyce, as Yeats himself tended to do. Perloff attempts to dissociate Pound and Joyce on the grounds that *Ulysses* is rigidly structured on a 'unified pattern', precisely that condition of the Symbolist legacy which the 'poetics of indeterminacy' rejects.[8] But here again, Perloff seems to operate on the formalist premise that a work that employs such pattern will stand or fall on the basis of the pattern alone. On the contrary, I will argue, the complementary principle of 'phantasmagoric succession' retains its interest independent of 'spatial form', and was in fact the chief interest shared by Yeats, Pound and Joyce. Interestingly, Joyce's characteristic expression of that principle finds its way—by the back door, as it were—into Perloff's discussion of Pound. To emphasize Pound's contemporary relevance, Perloff compares her analysis of the *Cantos* to Leo Steinberg's description of Rauschenberg's collages, but to find his analogy, Steinberg looks back to the literary technique of 'internal monologue'.[9] After comparing Joyce's technique of 'interior monologue' or 'stream of consciousness' with the 'phantasmagoric succession' of Yeats's poetry, I will close by considering how far the independence Yeats grants to the principle of succession opens his work to indeterminacy.

*   *   *

The text on which Perloff bases her distinction of Yeats and Pound is Yeats's introduction to *The Oxford Book of Modern Verse* (1936).[10] Clearly dissatisfied with the *Cantos*, Yeats claims that Pound's work exhibits 'more style than form', and he draws a careful distinction between those two principles: 'Style and its opposite can alternate, but form must be full, sphere-like, single.' No doubt recognizing an emblem of 'spatial form' in Yeats's image of the sphere, Perloff argues that few 'contemporary poets' or 'their readers' would subscribe to that notion today,[11] but she fails to attend to what Yeats has to say about style. If form is what Perloff had previously recognized as the 'unified pattern' in Yeats's work, style is the 'shifting succession of phantasms'. Where form is synchronic, spatial, style is diachronic, subject to alternation over time. The complementarity Yeats grants to these principles must be recognized if Yeats's specific criticisms of Pound are to be understood. It is a question of balance rather than of preference for one principle over the other.

In fact, Yeats's chief criticism of Pound is that he pushed imbalance, 'more style than form', to the extreme of excluding form altogether, as the word 'merely' implies when Yeats observes, 'Like other readers I discover at present merely exquisite or grotesque fragments' in the *Cantos*. Perloff is right, therefore, that Yeats would condemn the exclusion of form that she seeks to justify. Caught up in the logic of exclusion, however, she mistakenly identifies Yeats exclusively with form, and misreads the following statement as a blanket condemnation: 'He [Pound] hopes to give the impression that all is living, that there are no edges, no convexities, nothing to check the flow.' Perloff protests, 'Yeats's negatives have become the positives of a later generation of poets . . . who want precisely to convey the "living flow" of experience'.[12] So did Yeats, who recognized also the legitimate role of fragments in conveying that experience.

In the opening entry of *Estrangement*, the collection of diary extracts published in 1926, Yeats defended his decision to preserve the diary form: 'To keep these notes natural and useful to me I must keep one note from leading on to another, that I may not surrender myself to literature. Every note must come as a casual thought, then it will be my life.'[13] In his introduction to *The Oxford Book of Modern Verse*, however, Yeats protests the *exclusive* reliance on fragments in the *Cantos*, because it *removes* 'the "living flow" of experience': 'There is no transmission through time, we pass without comment from ancient Greece to modern England, from modern England to medieval China; the symphony, the pattern, is timeless, flux eternal and therefore without movement.' A sense of time was essential to a sense of life, in Yeats's view, but a sense of 'flux', such as Pound produced, did not guarantee a sense of time. What was lacking was some check to the flow, which, for Yeats, would function not as a dam, bringing the flow to a halt, but as a regulator. If the flow is to be discernible, it must be measurable.

In Yeats's view, Pound represented the sort of extremism in which opposites meet, in which flux becomes stasis. In the *Cantos*, Pound's pursuit of extreme flux, his aesthetic radicalism, met his pursuit of extreme stasis, his political radicalism. Where many critics would dismiss the *Cantos* for excessive self-indulgence, Yeats warned against a 'loss of self-control, common among uneducated revolutionists', by which he implied that Pound set too little value in the self, rather than too much. He was like those other revolutionists of 'Easter, 1916' (1916), who made 'a stone of the heart' by sacrificing themselves to a cause.[14] In that poem's most memorable passage, Yeats corrects the imbalance by setting the stone in the midst of 'the living stream', not to reconcile opposites, but to produce the energy generated by their tension. The loss of that tension is what Yeats laments when he describes the extremism of the literary avant-garde in the first edition of *A Vision* (1925). After defining the literature he has in mind by naming Pound, Eliot, Joyce and Pirandello, Yeats describes how their art, lacking the ballast of 'the personal dream', rocks crazily back and forth between 'myth' and 'fact': 'It is as though myth and fact, united until the exhaustion of the Renaissance, have now fallen so far apart that man understands for the first time the rigidity of fact, and calls up, by that very recognition, myth—the *Mask*—which now but gropes its way out of the mind's dark but will shortly pursue and terrify.'[15] A fascinating study might be made of the correlation between the opposing pairs that Yeats associates with Pound: myth and fact, and form and style.

While myth was still groping its way, the rigidity of fact was the quality in modern literature that Yeats found most distressing. He took it as the sign of a naturalistic tendency that he traced back to nineteenth-century prose fiction, as distinct from the romantic poetry of that century. In the spirit of Yeats's distinction, it seems appropriate to turn now from the poet Ezra Pound to a novelist, James Joyce, as the object of Yeats's critical attention. *A Vision* has already provided evidence that Pound and Joyce were connected in Yeats's mind. A short time later, in his introduction to a book on Bishop Berkeley (1931), Yeats again linked Pound and Joyce, this time in the company of another novelist, Marcel Proust: 'The romantic movement with its turbulent heroism, its self-assertion, is over, superseded by a new naturalism that leaves man helpless before the contents of his own mind. One thinks of Joyce's *Anna Livia Plurabelle*, Pound's *Cantos*, works of an heroic sincerity, the man, his active faculties in suspense, one finger beating time to a bell sounding and echoing in the depths of his own mind; of Proust who, still fascinated by Stendhal's fixed framework, seems about to close his eyes and gaze upon the pattern under his lids.'[16]

In reading this passage, as in the case of Yeats's discussion of Pound in *The Oxford Book of Modern Verse*, we need to remain alert to the subtlety of Yeats's discriminations and of his own position in their midst. Yeats is usually held to have exhibited romantic 'self-assertion' in abundance, yet Berkeley's eighteenth century provided Yeats with a position from which to criticize even romanticism. A few paragraphs later, he boasts that his 'ancestors never accepted the anarchic subjectivity of the nineteenth century'. Insufficient 'self-assertion', on the other hand, is the weakness of naturalism, whose objectivity appears to Yeats as mere passivity. Nevertheless, Yeats's distinction of romanticism and naturalism attributes a kind of heroism to both movements. Richard Ellmann, our most knowledgeable guide to the relation between Yeats and Joyce, went so far as to detect in the image of the sounding bell in this passage an admiration for the lyrical quality of Joyce's prose.[17]

Such evidence suggests a greater respect for naturalism than we would expect to find in Yeats. The explanation for his attitude seems to lie in his desire to distinguish the 'new naturalism' from the old, typically represented in Yeats's work at this period, by the figure of Stendhal. Proust's transition, as Yeats describes it, from 'Stendhal's fixed framework' to 'the pattern under his lids' rehearses what was to be a crucial movement in the argument of Yeats's introduction to *The Oxford Book of Modern Verse*: 'Nature, steel-bound or stone-built in the nineteenth century, became a flux where man drowned or swam; the moment had come for some poet to cry "the flux is in my own mind".'[18] If naturalism in general was characterized by the passive reception of images that presented themselves to the mind, it made a difference whether those images were felt to come from 'the sensual scene',[19] or from the mind itself. The latter impression offered the hope that the mind would reassert its authority over images.

By 1936, when Yeats published his Oxford anthology, he had ceased to look to the novelists for fulfilment of that hope. Having lost faith in Pound as well, he was forced to wish on the much dimmer stars of W.J. Turner and Dorothy Wellesley. Earlier, however, the situation appeared brighter. In 1918, when Yeats read the first chapters of *Ulysses* in the *Little Review*, he responded to Joyce's technique with evident excitement: 'It is an entirely new thing—neither what the eye sees nor the ear hears, but what the rambling mind thinks and imagines from moment to moment. He [Joyce] has certainly surpassed in intensity any novelist of our time.'[20] Commenting on this passage, Richard Ellmann has conjectured that 'the separation of the mind from the senses may have troubled' Yeats, and that the 'rambling' of the mind would have seemed a betrayal of Yeats's commitment to 'the conscious mind's intelligible structure'.[21] But in reaction to the 'old' naturalism of the nineteenth century, Yeats sought 'the invention of images more powerful than sense', and in reaction to Victorian rationalism, he sought the liberation of the mind from 'a mechanical sequence of ideas', a liberation that might well be expressed in 'rambling'.[22]

The essay from which I have just been quoting is 'Certain Noble Plays of Japan' (1916), Yeats's manifesto for a new anti-naturalistic theatre that set 'the world as we know it' at a distance. The goal was to 'enable us to pass for a few moments into a deep of the mind that had hitherto been too subtle for our habitation'.[23] At the close of 'Certain Noble Plays', Yeats celebrates that 'technical sincerity' that became manifest 'when heroism returned to our age', in the art of Walter Pater, Puvis de Chavannes, Mallarmé and Verlaine. Reading *Ulysses* in the midst of renewed enthusiasm for such an art, Yeats naturally welcomed Joyce's stream-of-consciousness technique as another entry into 'the deeps of the mind'. By the time of his essay on Berkeley, his reading in modern philosophy had convinced him that Joyce's technique might be only a manifestation of a new realism, but his praise for 'heroic sincerity' lingers as an echo of his earlier hope.

Thus, the dates represented by 'Certain Noble Plays of Japan' and 'Bishop Berkeley', 1916 and 1931, may serve to delimit the period in which the stylistic experiments of Pound and Joyce are likely to have meant the most to Yeats. Pound's use of ellipses in 'La Fraisne' (1908) 'to capture his hero's incoherence', as Richard Ellmann phrases it,[24] came before Yeats was prepared to absorb the lesson. In his late work, on the other hand, although Ellmann claims that Yeats finally 'acknowledged the domain of incoherence' in his use of the refrain in 'What Then?' (1937),[25] the repetition of the refrain contributes more to the 'sphere-like' form that Yeats now sought to reassert against a line that threatened to unravel. In contrast, interruption that is not dictated by a formal pattern, such as the refrain, can draw attention to the line: 'No, no, not night but death' ('Easter 1916'); 'No, no, not said, but cried it out' ('Under Saturn'); 'No, not in boyhood when with rod and fly . . .' ('The Tower').[26] All drawn from Yeats's two volumes of the 1920s, *Michael Robartes and the Dancer* and *The Tower*, these are extreme examples of that 'progress by digressions' in which, according to Hugh Kenner, Yeats prepared the way for 'progress by ellipses', exemplified by Pound.[27] In his volumes of the 1920s, however, Yeats himself was making dramatic use of ellipses:

> Wind shrieked—and where are they?
>   ('Nineteen Hundred and Nineteen')

> Hanrahan rose in frenzy there
> And followed up those baying creatures towards -
> O towards I have forgotten what—enough!
>   ('The Tower')

> And I though never of Ledaean kind
> Had pretty plumage once—enough of that . . .
>   ('Among School Children')[28]

Although it can be revealing, the notion of ellipsis threatens to obscure the degree of disjunction in Yeats's style. More conservative in matters of syntax than his younger contemporaries, Yeats never produced an extended passage in which ellipsis functions as the norm. He preferred to work by dislocation and fragmentation, as William E. Baker has observed. Despite his use of different techniques, however, Yeats could achieve effects very similar to those of the other modernist writers. As Baker notes, 'fragmentation could develop out of excessive elaboration', as the multiplication of the parts places them at an increasing distance from their centre. More specifically, elaboration could produce a tone like that of 'interior monologue' in the modern novel.[29] Once again, Joyce may offer a more useful standard than Pound for measuring Yeats's modernity.

Through the study of interior monologue, narrative theory has gone further than the criticism of poetry in identifying features beyond the level of grammar that distinguish discontinuous style. According to Dorrit Cohn, Joyce shares with his immediate predecessors in fictional monologue a peculiar semantic application of a feature that, grammatically, signals dialogue. 'I' and 'you' refer to the same person.[30] Cohn expands the implications of this peculiarity by way of Jan Mukařovskí's postulation of 'different semantic contexts' coexisting in the mind of the speaker of monologue.[31] For Cohn, these 'contexts' become different 'voices', 'vying for simultaneous linguistic expression' but 'forced by the temporal dimension of language to wait and take their turns'. Such competition produces 'various discontinuous speech patterns [that] distance monologue from dialogue even before the laws of communicative language are broken in any single sentence'.

For Yeats, who preferred not to break those laws, there remained, then, a number of stylistic devices that would serve to 'break up the logical processes of thought', as Yeats found the modernist avant-garde to be doing.[32] The elaboration of sentence elements could stretch the bonds of syntax to the breaking point, if not beyond. Pronoun shifts could split the unity of the speaking subject. In other ways, too, abrupt shifts in the 'angle of vision', as Marjorie Perloff calls it,[33] could represent the jostling of those several 'voices' seeking simultaneous expression within a single mind. Unlike the technique of ellipsis, however, these other devices of the stream of consciousness cannot be demonstrated satisfactorily through a series of brief quotations. Rather than being exhibited in isolation, they need to be examined in their cumulative operation over the course of an entire poem.

As my test case, I have chosen 'Among School Children' (1927), in part because previous criticism of that poem has already done much of my work for me. I could not hope to produce a better summary of the poem's main effects than the account provided by Cleanth Brooks: 'The dramatic method is that of an apparently rambling and whimsical meditation which meanders toward no goal in particular. One item of reflection suggests another until, at the end of the poem, the stream of consciousness has flowed with all the seeming purposelessness of a real stream to a point far from its source, casually floating on its surface references to Leda, Plato, the ugly duckling, and a host of personal reminiscences.'[34] True to his formalist principles, however, Brooks proceeds to subordinate these effects to 'the unifying principle of the organization which *is* the poem'.[35] If we release style from its subordination to form, what, then, is the poem?

★   ★   ★

'Among School Children' belongs to a series of poems that Hugh Kenner has characterized as 'the major performances that distinguish his last twenty years'.[36] Extending from 'In Memory of Major Robert Gregory' (1918) to 'Coole Park and Ballylee, 1931' (1932), the series coincides almost exactly with the period I have already defined as that of Yeats's greatest interest in the stylistic experiments of Pound and Joyce. In terms of syntax, what distinguishes these poems for Kenner is the elaboration of a single sentence over an entire stanza. Typically, the sentence unwinds in such a 'labyrinth of predications' that it would produce 'congested prose'. Therefore, Kenner hypothesizes, 'the sentence needs the stanza, the measured lines set off by the rhymes and the off-rhymes, to guide an enquiring mind, an entrusting voice'.

What Kenner is observing in his distinction of sentence and stanza is Yeats's distinction between style and form in *The Oxford Book of Modern Verse*. Unfortunately, Kenner's theoretical framework has room for form alone, so he concludes that the prominence of this type of stanza in Yeats's late work indicates that the poet has abandoned his earlier ideal of lines that would 'seem a moment's thought' ('Adam's Curse'),[37] and has determined instead to become 'the poet-mage of resolute concatenated statement'. Neglecting the disjunction that must occur *between* stanzas the more 'resolute' each stanza in itself becomes, Kenner also forgets that, within each stanza, the resolution of the form is balanced against unusually irresolute syntax. Twisting through its 'labyrinth of predications', the sentence is a perfect medium for conveying the momentary quality of thought, with the important difference that Yeats had directed his thought to the external world in the period of 'Adam's Curse' (1902), whereas in the later period thought floats up from 'the deeps of the mind'. In the first case, thought can be expressed in something approximating natural speech; in the second case, the medium of thought will be the never-spoken 'interior monologue'.

According to the manuscript evidence, Yeats began work on 'Among School Children' with stanza 5,[38] which reads as follows in its final version:

> What youthful mother, a shape upon her lap
> Honey of generation had betrayed,
> And that must sleep, shriek, struggle to escape
> As recollection or the drug decide,
> Would think her son, did she but see that shape
> With sixty or more winters on its head,
> A compensation for the pang of his birth,
> Or the uncertainty of his setting forth?

The 'uncertainty' stated as a theme in the final line has been present in the style throughout, not only in the signals of the interrogative mode, but also, more significantly, in the indeterminate relation between each new sentence element and those that precede it.

Critics have debated, for instance, whether the 'honey of generation' of line 2 betrayed the 'mother' or the 'shape' of line 1.[39] The manuscript evidence and Yeats's own note agree that the 'shape' was intended, but disagree about how firmly Yeats wanted his intention to guide a reading of the poem.[40] If, indeed, we read lines 2 through 4 as a description of the betrayal of the soul by the process of generation, as Yeats's note recommends, we resolve a syntactical ambiguity only to enlarge the ambiguity of point of view. The stanza begins by establishing the point of view of the mother, but then develops the point of view of the child, returning to the mother only at line 5. No sooner does the unity of the subject seem to resolve itself, however, than the object divides, doubling a 'son' with the 'shape' already introduced. That doubling persists in the alternation of the neuter and masculine pronoun ('its head'; 'his birth')—or is this rather a persistence of the divided point of view? And does the latter division persist further in the alternation of 'pang', the mother's physical suffering, and 'uncertainty', the child's mental suffering?

From the context of the poem as a whole, we know that the subject of the thoughts represented in stanza 5 is in fact the child now grown up to be 'that shape / With sixty or more winters on its head'. The larger context offers no 'controlling' point of view, however. Between stanzas as well as within stanzas, the perspective repeatedly shifts, and, in the absence of logical connectors, the shifts continue to take us by surprise. At the poem's opening, we meet Senator Yeats inspecting a model classroom, where he seems content to be 'A sixty-year-old smiling public man'. After that last line of the first stanza, the announcement that opens the next stanza, 'I dream of a Ledaean body', abruptly shifts the scene from the public into the private world, that of Yeats's mind. Not only the scene, but also the point of view has changed. The image of 'A sixty-year-old smiling public man' was what the children stared at, not the man himself, though we now adopt his perspective as we enter his mind. In fact, although the first word of the poem is 'I', ever since the third line the point of view has been occupied by someone else: first the nun who conducts the Senator; then the school children; then a woman with a 'Ledaean body', whose point of view is especially valued for its ability to 'blend' with Yeats's own.

As in stanza 5, so on a larger scale, the poem's alternation of point of view is complemented by a splitting of the object of contemplation. The 'Ledaean body' of the opening of stanza 2 is usually identified as Maud Gonne, as she appeared when Yeats first fell in love with her. But the presence of the school children helps Yeats imagine a still younger Maud whom he never knew. In fashioning her image, Yeats employs not only the form of the children but their power of imagination as well: he tries to 'wonder' how Maud would have looked, just as the children in stanza 1 had stared at the visiting Senator 'in momentary wonder', and created an image that Yeats knows to be as fictional as his image of the younger Maud. Fictional or not, in the last line of stanza 3, 'She stands before me as a living child', only to be replaced abruptly in the first line of the following stanza, when 'Her present image floats into the mind'.

Unlike that of the child Maud, this new image emerges without Yeats's conscious co-operation. Representing Maud as Yeats knows her in old age, the new image presumably has more ground in reality than does the image it supplants. However, Yeats blurs the distinction between image and reality by personalizing the fiction ('she') and de-personalizing the acquaintance ('image'). This would seem to prepare for the contrast of 'son' and 'shape' in stanza 5. Once again, though, Yeats makes the transition between stanzas as abrupt as possible by willing a premature termination to his reverie:

> - enough of that,
> Better to smile on all that smile, and show
> There is a comfortable kind of old scarecrow.

This shift to the imperative mood conceals what might otherwise be the clearest shift of point of view in the entire poem. The subject of the imperative is an implied 'you' ('you were better to smile'), supplanting Yeats's previous use of the first person. As Dorrit Cohn found in fictional monologue, so in Yeats's verse monologue, the semantic equation of 'I' and 'you' signals an internal debate. Significantly, Robert Langbaum explicitly excludes such debate from the verse tradition of the dramatic monologue.[41]

In reading the first five stanzas of 'Among School Children', I have sought to emphasize Yeats's debt to the prose tradition by highlighting effects of contiguity, the principle that Roman Jakobson identifed with prose in contrast to poetry.[42] To link Yeats's practice to prose more concretely, we can compare a passage from the second ('Nestor') episode of Joyce's *Ulysses*. The episode shows another poet, Stephen Dedalus, 'among school children', teaching a class in Mr Deasy's school. In this passage, the class has just gone out to play hockey, but one student, Sargent, has remained behind for help with his mathematics:

> In long shaky strokes Sargent copied the data. Waiting always for a word of help his hand moved faithfully the unsteady symbols, a faint hue of shame flickering behind his dull skin. *Amor matris*: subjective and objective genitive. With her weak blood and wheysour milk she had fed him and hid from sight of others his swaddlingbands.
>
> Like him was I, these sloping shoulders, this gracelessness. My childhood bends beside me. Too far for me to lay a hand there once or lightly. Mine is far and his secret as our eyes. Secrets, silent, stony sit in the dark palaces of both our hearts: secrets weary of their tyranny: tyrants, willing to be dethroned.[43]

Yeats would have read this passage in the *Little Review* for April 1918. The letter from which I have already quoted Yeats's praise of Joyce's new work was written in June. These circumstances make it tempting to claim that the theme of the originating stanza 5 of 'Among School Children' was directly influenced by Joyce's linking of child and disappointed mother. (Stephen is haunted by his refusal to kneel and pray at his mother's death bed.) However, a year before Joyce's instalment appeared in *The Little Review*, Yeats had already treated the theme, as scholars have long noted, in *At the Hawk's Well*, the first of his plays in the new style announced in 'Certain Noble Plays of Japan'. The lines that anticipate 'Among School Children' are chanted by the chorus before the entrance of the play's main characters:

> What were his life soon done!
> Would he lose by that or win?
> A mother that saw her son
> Doubled over a speckled shin,
> Cross-grained with ninety years,
> Would cry, 'How little worth
> Were all my hopes and fears
> And the hard pain of his birth!'[44]

Comparison of this passage with stanza 5 of 'Among School Children' reveals how radical was the stylistic shift from the 'natural speech' of Yeats's middle period to what I have called the 'interior monologue' of the late work. To the extent, therefore, that 'Among School Children' reflects Yeats's contact with

Joyce, the evidence is more likely to reside in style than in theme. But the point of contact itself may well have been at the level of the mental process that Joyce's style was designed to represent.

Although, in his essay on Berkeley, Yeats appears to condemn the stream-of-consciousness technique for suspending the mind's active faculties, in his writing of the preceding decade, it is remarkable how frequently Yeats portrays the mind in a passive state. In the first edition of *A Vision*, Yeats clearly has Joyce in mind when he describes a new style of writing built on 'associated ideas or words that seem to drift into the mind by chance', but only a few pages later, Yeats employs the style himself: 'that Gainsborough face floats up.'[45] Six months after the publication of *A Vision*, Yeats was writing 'Among School Children', where 'Her present image floats into the mind', in marked contrast, as I have already noted, to the deliberate effort that had been required to evoke the childhood image. Granting the significance of Yeats's immersion in occult studies, I would argue nevertheless that the stream-of-consciousness technique also made a contribution to much of what we think of as 'phantasmagoric' in the poems of this period, whenever, as in 'Meditations in Time of Civil War' (1923), 'Monstrous familiar images swim to the mind's eye'.[46] The esoteric quality of the images, 'familiar' only in the demonological sense, appears to have justified the process that produced them, in Yeats's view. His chief objection to the process was its use as a vehicle for 'the vulgarity of a single Dublin day'.[47]

Like the childhood image in 'Among School Children', the image of mother and child in *At the Hawk's Well* is evoked by an effort of will, announced in the play's first line: 'I call to the eye of the mind.' In contrast, in both *Ulysses* and 'Among School Children', the image of the mother seems to 'float into the mind' by unconscious association with the child already present in the scene. The sense of wilfulness in *At the Hawk's Well* is reinforced by the orderly procession of equal sentence units. Although they include some subordination, the potentially digressive effect of that construction is held strongly in check by its assimilation to the repetitive form of the verse. That form is of course entirely lacking in *Ulysses*, and it is countered by the flow of the syntax in 'Among School Children'. The process of association that weaves those texts is infinitely convoluted, though the convolutions receive different expressive treatment, staccato for Joyce, legato for Yeats.

The convolutions continue their winding course through the remaining stanzas of 'Among School Children', until, in the famous last lines, the images of tree and dancer suddenly emerge:

> O chestnut tree, great rooted blossomer,
> Are you the leaf, the blossom or the bole?
> O body swayed to music, O brightening glance,
> How can we know the dancer from the dance?

Their emergence, as sudden as in the line 'She stands before me as a living child', is driven by the progress by disjunction that has been at work throughout the poem, but the images themselves have traditionally been read as an assimilation of all disjunction into a transcendent (Kermode), or at least ironic (Brooks) unity. Moreover, the traditional reading has regarded the image of unity, which such reading constructs from the *two* images offered by the poem, as the proper concern of the reader, whereas the mental process from which the image emerges is a private concern of the artist, additionally of interest only to the critic who seeks a fuller understanding of the image.[48] In contrast, the approach to Yeats that I have outlined suggests that the indeterminacy of process in itself makes a significant contribution to any reader's experience of the quality of Yeats's best poetry. The force of that indeterminacy affects even the icon of unity that the conclusion of 'Among School Children' seems to display with unshakeable faith.

Critics have generally agreed that the final lines of 'Among School Children' function as rhetorical questions. To formalist critics, that function requires that the local grammatical structure be read in the service of a larger figurative meaning, just as they would read style in the service of form, in Yeats's terms. By application of this principle, questions that appear to challenge unity may be translated as assertions of unity. Posing the distinction of dancer and dance as a question suggests that the distinction cannot, and should not, be made. An alternative approach, called 'rhetorical' by its leading exponent, Paul de Man, treats grammar and rhetoric as independent forces, opposed to each other rather than hierarchically integrated. For this approach, it is impossible to determine whether Yeats's question is rhetorical or literal.[49] Although the rhetorical question is acknowledged as a figure of unity, the grammatical question is given full weight by recognizing that it may indeed be important to be able to distinguish the dancer from the dance. As Yeats understood the aesthetic of the Japanese Noh, 'the interest is not in the human form but in the rhythm to which it moves'.[50]

While de Man, in the spirit of this quotation (not cited by him), tends to split Yeats's figure in favour of the abstract dance, Michael Gallagher, applying a rhetorical method developed independently, favours the dancer.[51] In opposing the unity of the figural reading, the literal reading comes to oppose its own unity, and thus becomes figural. Gallagher's view, too, finds support in Yeats's prose, for instance in Yeats's sympathetic citation of an experience recorded by Synge in *The Aran Islands* (1907). Wandering in a dream-like state, Synge felt himself captured by mysterious music to the point where, 'my breath and my thoughts and every impulse of my body became a form of the dance, till I could not distinguish between the instrument or the rhythm and my own person or consciousness'. But the sacrifice of self proved intolerable: 'Then with a shock, the ecstasy turned to agony and rage. I struggled to free myself . . .'[52]

The 'struggle' depicted here, and the 'shriek' that joins it in the next sentence, appear to echo the plight of the soul 'that must sleep, shriek, struggle to escape' at the moment of birth in 'Among School Children'. However, the contrast of the two struggles, Synge's against the dissolution of the body, the infant's against the acquisition of the body, points to a final indeterminacy that is especially characteristic of Yeats: the problem of locating the self. Gallagher poses the problem as the opposition between the worldly, lowercase self and the transcendent Self of Yeats's late essays on Indian philosophy. De Man poses the problem in terms of Yeats's 'Dialogue of Self and Soul' (1933).[53] Such dualism is too tidy, however, to do justice to the problem as a felt experience. Yeats needed the multiplicity of the stream-of-consciousness technique to achieve the texture of 'Among School Children', with its frequent shifts in point of view and its division of a single subject into 'his' and 'its', 'son' and 'shape', or even son and mother.

Recognition of the related principles of rhetorical and psychical indeterminacy qualifies Yeats as a 'truly modern poet', according to Paul de Man in his essay 'Lyric and Modernity'. 'Modern poetry is described by Yeats', in de Man's reading, 'as the conscious expression of a conflict within the function of language as representation and within the conception of language as the act of an autonomous self'.[54] Basing this judgement on the same text cited by Marjorie Perloff, Yeats's introduction to *The Oxford Book of Modern Verse*, de Man accepts Yeats's argument that he is more modern than Pound, the reverse of Perloff's argument. However, rather than entering into a debate over the relative position of two writers in the progress of literary history, de Man seeks to call into question such a linear notion of history altogether. The indeterminacy that, for Perloff, distinguishes the contemporary sensibility from such unfashionable modes as Symbolism, is, for de Man, a necessary consequence of the conditions of literature. What de Man means by 'modernity' is simply a thorough awareness of those conditions, an awareness that is theoretically possible in any historical period.

In contrast to the conventional 'genetic' model of literary history, in which 'the son understands the father and takes his work a step further',[55] de Man proposes an alternative model by way of a brief analysis of Mallarmé's relationship to Baudelaire. I find de Man's analysis a useful model for the claims I would want to make about Yeats's relationship to Pound and Joyce. That relationship was much too complex to be adequately explained as the simple transmission of 'influence'. Its complexity has led to endless critical debate, in the case of Pound, and to almost total neglect, in the case of Joyce. Certainly, a good deal of wilful blindness on Yeats's part was involved, but that blindness was not unproductive. It allowed Yeats to oppose what he saw as a naturalistic tendency in Joyce and Pound, while at the same time he responded to the figural potential of their style. Just as he transformed grammatical questions into rhetorical questions, Yeats directed the stream-of-consciousness technique away from its representational function and gave it a whole new emphasis, though not a radically different structure.

What can be said of Yeats's relationship to Pound and Joyce must be said also, however, of Yeats's relationship to de Man, in whom Yeats would have recognized a continuation of the same intellectual tendency whose first glimmerings were evident in Pound and Joyce. De Man's model of literary history, with its continual interchange of the literal and figural elements of language, or what de Man in 'Lyric and Modernity' calls the representational and the allegorical, would have seemed to Yeats just as timeless, ahistorical, as the interchange of ancient Greece and modern England in the *Cantos*. To prevent time from degenerating into mere flux, it has to be set in opposition to the timeless; the stream requires the stone in its midst. Genuine historical change requires the origination of what has never existed through some power of creativity, the mysterious Thirteenth Cycle of *A Vision* (2nd edition, 1937), 'which is in every man and called by every man his freedom'.[56]

For Yeats, unlike the formalist critics, this timeless principle is no more a determining or determinate force than the principle it opposes. If Yeats's expression of the temporal principle links him to later developments in literature, his understanding of the timeless principle links him to his romantic heritage, particularly to Shelley. At this point, we rejoin Balachandra Rajan's argument about the indeterminacy of 'the ultimate reality', Eternity, conceived as 'the abyss which receives and creates' the 'stream' of Time, in Yeats's reading of Shelley.[57] In *Prometheus Unbound*, to which Yeats returned in a late attempt (1932) to settle persistent doubts, 'Eternity' is the name claimed by Demogorgon, whose meaning Yeats struggled to explicate. He concluded, however, that Shelley's admission of that power into his poem 'made his plot incoherent, its interpretation impossible'.[58]

Yeats: The Masker and the Masks

James Flannery

There can be no other cultural institution (except perhaps the whorehouse) which has supplied so many terms of colloquial abuse as the theatre. As Jonas Barish writes in *The Anti-Theatrical Prejudice*:

Most epithets derived from the arts are laudatory when applied to the other arts or to life. If one describes a landscape as 'poetic', or a man's struggle with adversity as 'epic', or a woman's beauty as 'lyric', one is using a term of praise . . . Similarly, terms like musical, symphonic, graphic, sculptural (or *sculpturesque*) are nearly always eulogistic.

But with infrequent exceptions, terms borrowed from the theatre—*theatrical, operatic, melodramatic, stagey*, etc—tend to be hostile or belittling. And so too do a wide range of expressions drawn from theatrical activity expressly to convey disapproval: *acting, play acting, playing up to, putting on an act, putting on a performance, making a scene, making a spectacle of oneself, playing to the gallery*, and so forth. Nor are such terms confined to English. The French speak cuttingly of those who *jouent la comédie*, or dismissingly of an action that it was merely *du théâtre*. One does not, in Italian, if one is behaving well, *fare la commedia* or *fare il pulcinello*, nor does one in German, *sich in Szene setzen* or *sich in den Vordergrund spielen*.[1]

These pejorative expressions embody, in current idioms, the vestiges of a prejudice against the theatre that goes back as far in European history as the theatre itself can be traced. Think of Socrates famous expulsion of the poets in Plato's *Republic* on the grounds that by assuming a *persona*, that is, by donning the mask or fictional character of someone else, the poet would be distracted from purusing his own proper role in life or, worse, would instruct his audience in dangerously volatile emotions that could undermine the controlling effect of reason.[2] The Greek word for actor, *hypokrites*, originally meant an interpreter of oracles, the actor as priest, but 2,500 years of semantic mutation have successfully defrocked him, exposing all shamans as charlatans and all masks as masquerades or false faces. Call someone (a politican, say) an actor today and one is implying that he is a hypocrite.

How surprising and salutory, then, for anyone with a positive feeling for theatre to encounter the figure of W.B. Yeats, who borrowed from the theory and practice of acting some of the cardinal doctrines of his life and art. A shy, dreaming and physically awkward youth, as a young man Yeats literally transformed his personality through an histrionic process equivalent to acting. Style and personality 'deliberately adopted and therefore a mask' became, as with Oscar Wilde, a means of shielding himself from the vulgarity of the world. The adoption of a mask was also a means of disengaging himself from and dominating those whom he wished to influence.[3] Criticized by his boyhood friend George ('AE') Russell for wearing a top hat at the Dublin Horse Show, Yeats defended himself: 'I read in that book which I still think the wisest of all books, *Wilhelm Meister* by Goethe: "The POOR are; the rich are enabled also to seem." I was then shy and awkward, and I set myself to acquire this technique of seeming!'[4] Elegant clothes and a ceremonial manner became part of the Yeatsian *persona*—no small reason why, to this day, many, particularly in Ireland, think of him as an aristocratic *poseur*.

In the United States, there is considerable interest today in what some social critics have called a performative culture. What they mean by this is a theatricalized approach to life in which, through a process of role-playing, people try to project the most favourable possible image of themselves. Everyone, it seems, is interested in the techniques of 'Performance': car dealers, stock brokers, business executives, psychodrama counsellors, sex therapists, television producers and war games players. When every issue is made to bear the mark of a performative structure from nuclear politics to school prayers to abortion to tax reform, a remarkable resonance is set up in the minds of a population that has already accepted as normal the devices of melodrama through the forms of soap opera and popular film. What occurs (has occurred) is that it becomes impossible—and, moreover, unnecessary in the eyes of some—to separate authentic from simulated behaviour.[5]

This cynical attitude is reinforced in the writing of the influential sociologist Erving Goffman for whom, following ancient tradition, the equation of theatricality with inauthenticity, the deception of mere appearance, is a paradigm for life as an individual and social activity. In Goffman's theatre of everyday life we all, regularly—daily—perform a series of little acts consisting of conventionalized signs, gestures and dialogues which serve to project an image and which enable us to slip smoothly past each other without any real threat to the fragile identity hiding beneath our masks. So obsessed are we with defensive tactics, with acts of deception designed to counter inevitable acts of deception on the part of others, that we forget what we were defending in the first place. But that doesn't matter, for in Goffman's theory the best way to protect the fragile self is to deny that there is such a thing at all. Like Ibsen's image in *Peer Gynt* of the self as an onion, peel it, layer upon layer, and in the centre there is ultimately nothing.[6]

There could be nothing further from these ideas and attitudes than Yeats's mature doctrine of the mask, which involved not only a careful consideration of effect but of the effort of the psyche to produce that effect. Yeats instinctively understood a theatrical truism that Goffman and, indeed, many theatre practitioners and scholars fail to perceive, namely that the art of acting is not based upon a binary system in which the actor as performer either a) loses himself in a role; or b) cleverly manipulates the role as a masker. The former model confirms the suspicion that actors have no selves; the latter that it all is a form of deception and hypocrisy. Instead, what we ought to consider is a triadic model in which, besides the actor and role, always present, even in the most representational forms, is a third factor, the person or self as actor. John

Top left: Dick, aged five. Top right: the undergraduate. Left: in Paris, 1945. Photos: courtesy the Ellmann family.

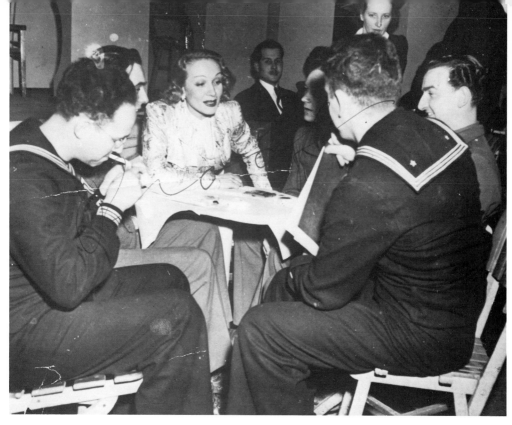

Above: Dick (left) with Marlene Dietrich, Noel Coward and Lon Myers at the opening of the Paris Stage Door Canteen in April 1945. Below: Dick, with his children (left to right) Maud, Lucy and Stephen. Photos: courtesy the Ellmann family.

Dick and Mary, 11 September 1959. Photo: Al Phillips of *Chicago's American*.

On Howth Hill, Ireland. Photo: Peter Harding, courtesy Seán O Mórdha.

New York, 1980. This and the following photos are all by Virginia Schendler.

In his office in Oxford, 1982.

In the gateway of New College, Oxford, early 1983.

Oxford, April 1987.

Gielgud the actor may play quite a different Hamlet from Laurence Olivier. But in neither case does Gielgud or Olivier, the human beings who brush their teeth in the morning, entirely disappear. In that case, the method (i.e. the Stanislavsky system of psycho-physical action) would indeed be madness.[7]

My point is that social roles, like theatre roles, are plural: none of us plays only one role in life any more than on stage and, like stage roles, each social role has different performance requirements. My skills as a lecturer are as little use to me the gardener as my directorial skills are when, God help me, I climb Knocknarla with my fourteen year old son. The important thing is that I, the continuing masker, am not simply satisfied in doing my own thing, but that I learn how to adopt the most appropriate and effective mask for each of the roles I am called upon to play. To do this I must, as any acting teacher realises, start with an understanding of my primary identity as stamped upon me from birth. This biological, psychological and physiological self is incapable of being changed, but within a knowledge of that identity, I am capable of playing an infinite number of variations upon my personal identity theme, from political right to left, from a closed, opaque person to someone almost raw in openness and vulnerability. These observations would suggest that the variations of one's identity theme are at least as important as the theme itself; in fact, such variations constitute nothing less than a transformation of the self.[8]

This brings us back to Yeats for whom the adoption of pose and mask had much deeper significance than either self-protection or personal advancement. In contrast to Goffman, for whom appearance is the only reality and who accepts the impossibility of achieving a unified personality, Yeats struggled to make a virtue out of the war of 'incompatibles' that perpetually raged within his mind. Within the confines of a restrained, austere form, 'something hard and cold . . . which is the opposite of all that I am in daily life', his teeming, fantastic inner life was given fuller rein to develop and express itself.[9] Reality, for Yeats, existed fully neither in the self nor mask, or 'anti-self', as he sometimes called it, but in the product born of their dialectical struggle. Moreover, Yeats discovered a positive moral virtue in the histrionic process of trying to become his own antithesis—his ideal self, as it were—by living according to a theatrical model of role identification:

If we cannot imagine ourselves as different from what we are and assume that second self, we cannot impose a discipline upon ourselves, though we accept one from others. Active virtue as distinguished from the passive acceptance of a current code is therefore theatrical, consciously dramatic, the wearing of a mask. It is the condition of arduous full life.[10]

                                *   *   *

Yeats applied these ideas to virtually every aspect of his involvement in the theatre. He sought for a style of acting, speech and stage décor that, in effect, was a giant mask and, like his personal mask, exhibited a formal austerity on the surface only to expose a more passionate internal life. No fanatic slave to his own theories, Yeats wore many masks throughout his life: as poet, playwright, critic, theatre manager, mythologist, philosopher, politician and mystic avatar. Instead of being victimized by circumstances, particularly the circumstances of revolutionary Ireland with its clash of personality upon personality, masking provided him with an intellectual and emotional distance from life that, as both man and artist, was immensely liberating.[11]

Just as he had transformed himself, so Yeats sought to inspire and challenge his fellow countrymen to seek an equivalent transformation in their personal and social lives. The problems of colonial and post-colonial Ireland were, he believed, part of much greater problems exhibited in Western culture as a whole. Above all else in modern life he despised that view known to those he termed 'the sentimentalists'—those so-called 'practical men and who believe in position, in a marriage bell, and whose understanding of happiness is to be so busy whether at work or at play that all is forgotten but the momentary aim'.[12] The acceptance of this essentially materialistic code had made men timid and passive in the face of life's deeper, existential struggles. Like Brecht, Yeats's hatred of realism as a dramatic form was that it reflected and reinforced the same code by drawing people into 'a vast play of circumstances' from which there was no apparent escape. To put it in histrionic terms, realism depleted energy, evoking depression rather than exhilaration, because it limited the expressive powers of the actor.[13] It provided, in effect, no models of a higher being, no heroic masks of individuation with which the audience might identify and ultimately introject into their own personalities.

Yeats drew a clear distinction between the reductive theatre of realism and the dramatic art he hoped to foster at the Abbey Theatre. As he once wrote, 'A wise theatre might make a training in strong and beautiful life the fashion'.[14] Describing in 1910 the improvised comedy of a troupe of Sicilian actors, Yeats said that in their work one experienced 'life leaping like a fountain'. Because they were used to inventing not only their actions but the plays themselves, the art of the Sicilians had 'a joyous spontaneity' based upon an understanding of their own instincts. In conventional theatre actors appeared to do 'nothing right unless taught to do it, intonation by intonation, movement by movement'. The Sicilians, however, made one feel that they were 'showing their whole natures. They had confidence in themselves; they poured themselves out; you felt they went home exhausted because they expressed themselves so completely'.[15]

Years later Yeats recalled in *A Vision* the effect made upon him by the Sicilian players in describing the existential freedom of individuals who were destined to function within antithetical, or lunary subjective phases—phases one to fifteen—on the Greet Wheel of Life. Such individuals, in order to complete their personalities sought a mask as unlike as possible to their empirical selves which would provide them with an image of what they wished to become. By striving to become that mask, defined by Yeats as 'A form created by passion to unite us to ourselves', they achieved 'a deeper being' in which the entire personality was expressed as 'a union of qualities'.[16] Elsewhere, Yeats defined this total realization of personality as 'Unity of Being', and, again drawing upon his theatrical experience, said that it emanated not from the brain only but from 'the entire hopes, memories and sensations of the body'.[17] In contrast, the primary mask of solar man who inhabited the dark objective phases of sixteen to twenty-eight on the Great Wheel was enforced from without. This created what Yeats termed 'character', meaning 'a union of qualities and their limitations'. While the lunar phases were 'revelatory' because through the mask the being attained self-knowledge, the solar phases offered 'concealment' as the being gradually grew so other-directed that it was concerned only with 'objects that have no relation to its unity but a relation to the unity of Society or of material things'.[18]

As complex and confusing as *A Vision* may appear at times, it functions most clearly and effectively when read as a study of the drives and forces that operate in defining the individual personality. We would do well to remember that no human being belongs exclusively to lunar or solar phases of the Great Wheel, thus leaving a considerable amount of room for individual choice, change and growth. At the same time, in Yeats's model the subject is never completely free from the primordial field of tensions that define it; thus the subject is not entirely an independent agent in the individuating process. Put more simply—and truly—none of us choose our parents, hence our genetic make-up. Nor do we always choose those moments when we are called upon to make critical decisions that define our ultimate destinies. We are, in effect, subjects of both choice and chance, improvisational performers who at one and the same time act out two mutually inclusive roles, that of witness and participant, in the fluctuating play of life.

All of these ideas demonstrate how fully theatrical was Yeats's understanding of life. But to a man of the theatre they take on special meaning when one examines their practical application in the training of Yeatsian actors and the staging of his plays.

*　　*　　*

'Passion' was a term of very special significance to Yeats. Essentially, it sums up his concept of the combined intellectual and emotional qualities required by the actor of tragedy.

Yeats compared the actor of passion with the character actor, borrowing the latter term from common theatre usage. The character actor is one who builds up his part mainly by observation, adapting his voice, body and manner in small details so as to enable him to play a variety of roles. (Note the direct parallel of Yeats's description of other-directed objective man in *A Vision*.) By contrast, the actor of passion, or emotional actor as Yeats sometimes called him, creates his roles not through observation or by employing 'reason' but out of his own 'personality' and 'instinct'.[19] Thus, like a great athlete, singer, dancer or even political leader, he appears to display 'some one quality of soul again and again'.[20] (And note the continued echo of the terms used to describe the existentially liberated Sicilian actors, as well as Yeats's re-amplification of concepts used in *A Vision* to describe subjective man, the man who functions out of knowledge of his primary identity.)

At first hearing we might think that Yeats, by defining the character-actor as one who functions in an objective rather than subjective mode, is setting up another polarity to reinforce his dislike of theatrical realism. But as previously noted, *A Vision* does not categorize men as being exclusively subjective or objective. Nor, as Richard Ellmann observes, was Yeats himself so completely divided as he liked to pretend.[21] Our understanding of what he truly had in mind becomes clearer if we imagine both the actor of passion and character actor as wearing actual theatre masks. Let me try to explain this by talking out of personal experience about some of the concepts and techniques employed in the contemporary theatre to train actors through the use of masks.

Étienne Decroux, the father of modern mime and the teacher of, among many major artists, Marcel Marceau and Jean-Louis Barrault, once said: 'The most technical art of all is the art that succeeds in making a faithful portrait of the soul.'[22] Decroux's pupil, the great teacher Jacques LeCoq, has devoted his life to the study of the mask as a means of giving expression to what he calls the 'soul state'.[23] In LeCoq's terminology, the equivalent of the Yeatsian actor of passion is the wearer of the neutral mask. The neutral mask is just that—a mask, usually white, without any personal expression, which, in its perfect geometrical proportion, resembles the facial physiognomy of fifth century pieces of classical Greek sculpture. Something surprising occurs, however, when students put on neutral masks for the first time. Suddenly the masks lose their neutrality as the tics, mannerisms and muscular tensions that we carry with us as part of our inherited or acquired personal armature become all too clearly evident. Unless corrected, these aspects of our personal physiognomy will continue to show through in every role we attempt to play. One can draw an analogy between the actor's body and a blank painter's canvas. Put smudges on the canvas and, no matter what colours are applied, the smudges will continue to spoil the effect.

Training in neutral mask techniques therefore involves a rigorous physical discipline so as to attain, for each individual, a perfect physical alignment equivalent to the geometrical purity of the mask. Yeats would have particularly appreciated this, for he developed an extraordinary sensitivity to the ways in which 'the divine architecture of the body' reflects the total integrated personality. 'An exciting personality', he once wrote, 'whether the hero of a play or the maker of poems, will display the greatest volume of personal energy and this energy must seem to come out of the body as out of the mind'.[24]

An unmasked actor can, of course, give the impression of changing the direction of his gaze with a simple movement of his eyes. But this is not the case with the masked actor, for the audience cannot usually see his eyes. This occasions the use of a masking technique in which the actor thinks of his entire head as a giant eye. Thus, to animate the mask, the full bodily energy of the actor must be employed. One of the results of this approach to actor training is that, as Jean-Louis Barrault writes: 'Far from limiting expression, the mask makes us discover new instincts, and serves as a springboard for expression by the whole body. I have dreamed of a modern tragedy, treating a present-day subject and played in masks. It is the only case where total nudity would be acceptable.'[25] Think of the freedom associated with donning masks in Mardi Gras festivities. Or of the randy comedians with bloated phalluses in the plays of Aristophanes. Without a mask they are simply vulgar. With a mask—a full body mask, really—they embody that glorious combination of the sacred and profane that is the key to ancient Greek comedy.[26] As it is to the Japanese Noh and Kabuki. And to the performance of Yeats.

Another aspect of neutral mask training involves a discipline of the mind that gradually opens the personality to a flood of images and feelings from deep within the psyche. As the body and mask are neutral, so the mind must also become a *tabula rasa* that can freely respond to long-buried instincts from our childhood experience when, with an undifferentiated consciousness, we understood our own natures as whole both in and of themselves and in relation to the world. One of the things we, in fact, tell actors who wear neutral masks for the first time is that the mask knows nothing, but because of its emptiness has the perpetual curiosity of a child. It is amazing what effect this image can have upon the psyche. I have seen students wearing a neutral mask explore a plain wooden box for half an hour, finding in it an infinitesimal range of microscopic sensory details. Often, when they are finished, they think that only minutes have passed, so focused, intense and deep are their powers of concentration.

On rare occasions, that concentration reaches an almost transcendent state. In this trance-like state the actor seems to be possessed by another spirit. The external world vanishes and the habitual personality is transformed into a vessel through which thoughts, emotions and images pass that are so mysterious, so profoundly archetypal that the performer scarcely knows from whence they have come. It is as if behind the mask a secret identity is revealed for the first time. Yeats talks about a similar trance-like condition as essential to the creative process of writing, a process he equated, in many respects, with the visionary state of the magus or seer.[27]

It is no wonder that masks have always played a vital role in magical rites, particularly those liminal rites of passage or change that occur in association with birth, puberty, warrior initiation, marriage, exorcism, birth and death. As the anthropologist David Napier writes in *Masks, Transformation and Paradox*, the use of masks in these transitional states illustrates an attempt to confront a central paradox of human existence, that 'mutability is a precondition of personality rather than an aberration'.[28] Yeats was no stranger to such ideas. Indeed, he rejoiced in the struggle of life as continual change—continual destruction and rebirth. As he once wrote in an almost gleeful espousal of masking as the only rational response to this condition:

All happiness depends on the energy to assume the energy of some other life, on a re-birth as something not one's self, something created in a moment and perpetually renewed; in playing a game like that of a child where one loses the infinite pain of self-realization, in a grotesque or solemn painted face put on that one may hide from the terror of judgement.[29]

And again he wrote of the precious joy found in the impermanent lovely things of life:

The poet must not seek for what is still and fixed, . . . but be content to find his pleasure in all that is forever passing away that it may come again, in the beauty of woman, in the fragile flowers of spring, in momentary heroic passion, in whatever is most fleeting, most impassioned, for its own perfection.[30]

Yeats never formally studied acting. Yet he possessed a naturally histrionic temperament which was exercised and developed not only through his involvement with the theatre but his lifelong involvement in the experiential as well as intellectual discipline of magic. Many of the ceremonies of the Order of the Golden Dawn, the magical society to which he belonged from 1890 to 1922, involved exercises not unlike those a student of acting might undertake. One of the basic premises of the Golden Dawn was that the psyche of man contains archetypal images emanating from the supernatural world. This unconscious level of the mind is called the Astral Light or Anima Mundi and is similar to Jung's idea of the 'collective unconscious'.[31] In a process similar to a training in neutral masks, the method of ceremonial magic employed by the Golden Dawn was intended to enable the Adept to discipline his Will and Imagination so as to achieve a transcendent state in which his Holy Guardian Angel, or inner Daimon, was summoned to consciousness, thereby giving him direct access to the Anima Mundi. In order to contact specific astral forces from the collective unconscious the Adept often wore masks representing those forces.[32] Thus the mask becomes an outward manifestation of his own most inward being—an idea that, as we shall see, is directly connected with Yeats's theatrical practice.

As we have observed, Yeats sought to identify with his higher self, or opposite, by deliberately creating a new *persona*. Through a series of visionary experiences Yeats came to believe that this opposite, or mask, instead of being the conscious product of his own mind, might be a spirit or Daimon with a soul of its own. This meant that, as Richard Ellmann observed, the conflict between self and anti-self which Yeats had previously viewed as internal and psychological might, in reality, be external, that is a conflict between the living and the dead, this world and the next. In this way Yeats received a supernatural sanction for his pose; the doctrine of the mask became the cosmic personal and historical drama of *A Vision*.[33]

★　　★　　★

Now nothing could further demarcate Yeats from the swirling facade of signifying masks that passes for identity in today's performative culture than his belief in masking as a source of supernatural wisdom and power. And this also separates Yeats from such great maskers in the modern theatre as Alfred Jarry, Bertolt Brecht and Luigi Pirandello, all of whom raised profound questions about the reality of a continuous self. Yeats scarcely ignored such ontological questions. Nor as an artist, particularly an artist of the theatre, could he afford to do so and expect to communicate spiritual truths to a sceptical modern audience. Yeats's dilemma was how to combine both subjective and objective perceptions of reality within the one dramatic medium. It is by examining the distinctions between the technique and effect of character versus neutral masking that we can better understand how Yeats resolved this problem.

We have seen that one of the purposes of training in neutral masks is to enable the actor to achieve such perfect mental and physical control that the accidental whims of his personality no longer interfere with his creative process.[34] Creating a character, then, is not primarily a matter of inspiration but rather involves the exercise of conscious mental and physical choices in conjunction with inspiration. Character masks often involve two or more contrary expressions: for instance, a furious grimace with the lips along with manic laughter in the eyes and forehead. In theatrical practice, a character mask is animated by first studying it to determine its expressive qualities and then donning it in front of a mirror to determine how various angles of the body, particularly movements of the spine, can articulate those qualities. With the neutral mask it is rare that mirrors are utilized or that the actor is concerned with changing his physical expression. As a result, the spine remains erect and feelings appear to flow from within outward.

Neutral masks provide a vital training mechanism for the actor, but in actual performance character masking is far more widely utilized. This is true in Yeats's theatre as well. In fact, he employed a greater variety of character masks than any of the maskers in the modern theatre: satiric masks for spiritually incomplete and dehumanized characters; heroic masks that embody man's quest for nobility and a god-like transcendence; masks that personify dream states and the dialectical nature of the personality; and masks that represent frozen persona—false selves—behind which we sense a terrifying insecurity and cosmic *angst*.[35] Only for disembodied characters emanating from the supernatural world (the Angel in the *Hour Glass*, the two ghost figures in *The Dreaming of the Bones* and Fand, the glittering seductress of Cuchulain in *The Only Jealousy of Emer*) are neutral masks appropriate. But the real point I am making is that character masks in Yeats's theatre contain all of the psychic values associated with the neutral mask. They therefore function as did Yeats's own *persona*, on two levels at once, subjective and objective, thereby reflecting both the conscious and unconscious mind activated to their highest power.

The plain fact is that, for all his protestations against the theatre of realism, Yeats was a master of realistic dramaturgy. This is easily seen in plays such as *The Words Upon the Window Pane* which, in its vivid depiction of a group of seedy participants at a *seance* held in a Dublin tenement once inhabited by Jonathan Swift, could more than hold its own with any mystery drama created by Alfred Hitchcock. One of the fascinations of the play is the *tour de force* of the actress playing the medium who, in a trance state, must, in effect, don five masks as she portrays the various characters, including Swift, whom she summons to consciousness. But, successful as it may be when measured by the standards of conventional theatre, this is not typical of Yeats's style. His grasp of realism is more normally exhibited in an infinitely subtle but exact rendering

of the shifting psychological patterns of the mind. The aim of Yeats's theatre is
to evoke an equivalent to what Islamic scholar Henry Corbin calls 'the
imaginal', an out of the ordinary perception that brings with it an order of
being no less real than physical reality.[36] His method is not to ignore physical
reality but rather to distil and shape it through a pattern of images and rhythms
that corresponds to a dialectic between inner and outer reality.

In Yeats's own words what he sought was 'the theatre's anti-self—a mysterious art of dearly loved things, doing its work by suggestion, not by direct
statement, a complexity of rhythm, colour, gesture, not space-invading like
the intellect, but a memory and a prophecy'.[37] A puzzling statement, perhaps,
unless one has experienced the 'poetry in space' of the Japanese Noh, Chinese
Opera or Indian Kathakali, all of which employ masks, symbolic gestures and
hieroglyphic design images so as to lift the action to a metaphysical level where
pure essence rather than appearance is revealed. Each of these Oriental forms
of total theatres is based upon the aesthetic and psychological premise that the
greater the degree of artifice—that is, the greater the displacement from iconic
(or realistic) imagery—the more intellectually and imaginatively rich is the
response it evokes. Such displacement occurs through a variety of presentational conventions that acknowledge the artificial, or fictive, aspects of theatre:
that is, by having male actors play female roles; by employing masks and
elaborately decorated costumes that make no attempt to hide the human figure
of the actor beneath; by breaking the continuity of extraordinarily complex
physical routines so that a stage manager can matter-of-factly adjust the belt of
the performer or wipe his perspiring face; and by focusing the attention of the
audience almost entirely on the capacity of a highly trained body and voice to
create a world of its own. All of these conventions openly acknowledge and
celebrate the human dimension of the theatrical experience. All involve a far
more immediate identification with the actual life of people onstage and in the
audience than representational forms that, by direct imitation, attempt to
create an illusion of real life.

The presentational forms I am describing are also generous in their effect;
the very absence of all but the most essential scenic elements and properties
impels the audience to complete the action with their own presence. Another
generosity occurs in the act of restoring to us, for the time of the performance
and sometimes with lingering effect, a precious child-like state of undifferentiated consciousness in which literally anything is possible.

'The theatre's anti-self.' Another puzzlement, perhaps, until we recognize
that, like the forms of theatre we have just described, Yeats's intention was not
to escape from life but to enhance it by conceiving of existence dialectically,
that is, by insisting upon a relation between reality and the dream which makes
the latter no mere abstraction but a driving force in life. 'All art', he wrote in
1908, 'is the endeavour to condense as out of the flying vapour of the world an
image of human perfection, and for its own not for the art's sake.'[38]

Yeats argued that in order to live a full life, to realize one's total being as a
man and artist, it is necessary to see and understand mankind in every possible
circumstance, in every possible situation. 'Only when we have put ourselves in

all the possible positions of life, from the most miserable to those that are so lofty that we can only speak of them in symbols and in mysteries will entire wisdom be possible.'[39] Functioning out of this belief Yeats plunged himself into an astonishing range of activities that would have exhausted the combined energy of several average men. Some of his exercises were undoubtedly reckless, silly, even somewhat aberrational—at least by normal standards. Who in their right mind could condone much less tolerate a twenty-five year obsession with a woman like Maud Gonne? Or a flirtation with fascism? Or engenic breeding? Or believe that an operation equivalent to a vasectomy could restore his waning sexual powers? Yet, as Elizabeth Cullingford asserts, although he occasionally followed wayward impulses, Yeats always returned to a central core of values by which he lived a sane and productive life.[40]

No one was more critical of his errors of judgement than Yeats. And often he criticized himself in public. For every myth that he constructed Yeats deconstructed another. Thus *Purgatory* is not, as often thought, an *apologia* for fascism but, instead, a bitter attack on the outrageous folly of living a life according to rigidly inhuman, philosophical, religious and political abstractions. *The Unicorn from the Stars*, *The Dreaming of the Bones* and *The Herne's Egg* provide a critique of the romantic myth of martyrdom in the fanatic cause of Irish freedom as embodied in his own *Cathleen ni Houlihan*. And what is the Cuchulain Cycle but ultimately a deconstruction of Yeats's vision of Ireland's heroic destiny in the modern world? For, as Yeats wrote: Cuchulain should 'earn deliverance from the wheel of becoming by participation in the higher self, after which he should offer his spiritual history to the world; instead, he condemns himself to a career of violent and meaningless action, and this is responsible for the developing tragedy of his life'.[41]

For every truth Yeats presented a countertruth. Like all advocates of the unconscious, he was a sturdy rationalist who recognized man's divided nature. Yet throughout his life he powerfully resisted the logocentric tradition of Western thought and its tendency to separate reason and imagination, soul and body, the transcendentally divine and the imminently temporal. What he advanced, instead, was a dialectical way of thinking in which opposites are balanced in a pattern of perpetually creative conflict, contradiction and confluence. In this regard his mind was quintessentially Irish, for as Richard Kearney argues, the Irish inevitably prefer the logic of *both/and*, or the Joycean 'two thinks at a time' to the reductive categorical logic of *either/or*.[42]

As Yeats saw life in dialectical terms, always his endeavour as a lyric poet, dramatist and man of the theatre was to remain in touch with and yet preserve an appropriate balance between these antithetical extremes. As he declared in 1913:

Great art, great poetic drama is the utmost of nobility and the utmost of reality. The passions and drama fall into two groups commonly, the group where nobility predominates and the group where reality predominates. If there is too much of the first all becomes sentimental, too much of the second all becomes sordid. Nobility struggles with reality, the eagle and the snake.[43]

Yeats's twenty-six plays reflect, each with its own stylistic form and substance, the movement of the individual towards the achievement of complete personality: that is, psychic wholeness and differentiation from others together with a clarification of the many selves involved in coming to that wholeness. As such, his plays reflect Yeats's own lifelong process of redefinition and transformation through the doctrine of the mask. Some characters succeed and some fail in their quest for wholeness just as, in each phase of *A Vision*, distinctions are clearly drawn between True and False Masks that are appropriate for individual fulfilment. How well we achieve our life's purpose and destiny depends upon the masks we choose to adopt or discard. If, as Harold Bloom alleges, Yeats was a fatalist without a redeeming faith in mankind,[44] is it not hard to believe that he would have created a system posited upon the possibility of change for individual human beings and the world—or that it even mattered?

Yeats was, I believe, one of the few modern artists with a positive vision for mankind. His ideal was an open democratic society in which everyone works for the good of all, with access to the greatest number of possibilities. This ideal is what lay behind his battles on behalf of Synge, O'Casey and the social realists of the Irish dramatic movement. To Yeats, intellectual freedom and psychic fulfilment are necessary components of political and economic liberation. And all are necessary for the creation of his life's ambition, 'a great community where the finest minds and Sean the Fool think the same thing though not the same thought on it'.[45]

As he challenged himself, so Yeats challenged his fellow Irishmen to rid themselves of sentimentality, of intellectual solopsism and of petty factionalism and sectarianism so as to create 'a new character, a new pose' rooted in what was best in the living and historical Irish tradition.[46] Yeats's own art—'a memory and a prophecy', as he called it[47]—attempts to bridge the gap between tradition and the radical subversion of that tradition. Though increasingly ironic in his judgements of himself and others, his work, unlike many modernist and postmodernist exemplars, never involves a philosophical cop-out that relieves the writer of responsibility for his position. Yeats may have deconstructed his own myths, but it was only to reconstruct them in new forms. Even in battling his father, he loved and supported him both emotionally and financially, accepting in the end how much he owed him for his own convictions. In the same way, he gave of himself to an Ireland with which he was in almost constant combat.

Yeats's overall poetic and dramatic *oeuvre* coheres within a dialectical framework of assertion and counter-assertion. Despite its seeming contradictions and ambiguities, his work adds up to a meaning, even though the particular meaning may vary in parts as different people respond to it. This is a result of the fact that his *grand narrative* is made up of all the specific little narratives of his individual poems and one act plays. It is also because his art, particularly in its theatrical context, functions as a kind of mask or screen upon which each of us can project archetypes drawn from the depths of our own being.

As Seamus Deane has remarked in an exceptionally fine analysis of his importance as a dramatist, the formalistic aspects of Yeats's theatre have profound political and cultural intent: 'They are not esoteric in the sense that they are at some considerable remove from the public domain. They are aristocratic only in the sense that they wish to replace the very idea of a collective public with the idea of a national community in which individuality, not individualism, would be the primary element.'[48] Deane goes on to argue that by rejecting the Yeatsian forms of drama, the theatre of Ireland 'has joined with the dull reaction of the thirties, both right and left wing, against all that [is] important and innovative in the modern arts. Yeats is a more profoundly political dramatist than O'Casey, [and] it is in his plays that we find a search for the new form of feeling that would renovate our national consciousness'.[49]

Yeats's *persona* provided him with a unified, self-confident self which made him appear far more authoritarian, far more privileged than, in fact, he really was. Austin Clarke once told me that 'Living in the same country as Yeats was like being in the shadow of a great oak tree'. So obsessive, so overwhelming, so insistent are Yeats's demands on us to become that most difficult of things, our truest and best selves, that it is hard for us not to be engulfed by him. Like the heroes of his ritualistic plays, Yeats himself has to be slain before his ideas and spirit can be reborn within our own consciousness. That psychological process of introjection has yet to occur, particularly in Ireland. And so we continue to resist Yeats, failing to read him whole, failing to see his life and work for the lovely, generous gift that it really was. In rejecting Yeats we really reject, I think, the discovery of our own *personae*—those masks by which we are enabled, in a profoundly theatrical act of regeneration, to become our own authentic selves.

'Yours Affly, Dobbs': George Yeats to Her Husband, Winter 1931-32

Ann Saddlemyer

'I am delighted', Richard Ellmann replied when I excitedly reported the state of my research toward the biography of George Yeats. For he above all others had written warmly, sympathetically and most fully of this remarkable woman who had contributed so much to perfection of the life and of the work during the twenty-three 23 years of Yeats's marriage. Typically, as I recounted my adventures and voiced yet more questions, he offered advice, gentle warnings, most of all, encouragement. While Mary sat loyally nearby, her occasional remarks offering fresh insight, we laughed over some of the problems yet unsolved and puzzled out further implications. He told me with pleasure of the programme on Wilde, broadcast the night before in Dublin. We spoke of friends in common, work being done. Then, just before I left, with that courtesy, courage and honesty that marked both his scholarship and his nature, he tapped out, 'If and when, my papers are going to America. You will find them of interest'. Thirty-six hours later, he was dead. That hour round the dining room table with Dick and Mary was both a privilege and a benediction.

'You are much the best letter writer I know, or have known,—your letters have so much unrestrained animation, so much natural joyousness', W.B. Yeats once responded to his wife. Approximately 150 letters from George to W.B. Yeats dating from 1920 through 1938 have so far been discovered. Given WBY's haphazard approach to preservation of his correspondence and GY's reluctance to publicize her own private life it is remarkable that such a record of their relationship exists, especially if we consider that it was George who determined as much as she could what would remain of her own papers. Apparently she preserved most of WBY's letters to her; fortunately towards the end of her life her son persuaded her not to destroy her letters to Willy.

As his secretary (often the only one who could read his writing) and business manager, George frequently wrote brief business missives; many of these have not survived. There were of course many lengthy periods when they were not apart. But when they were separated, they missed each other's companionship, and George did her best to keep Willy informed of domestic details, local Dublin gossip, and her own many activities with the Cuala Industries, the Abbey Theatre, and the Dublin Drama League. The letters published here, covering the final year of Lady Gregory's life when WBY spent most of his time at Coole, reveal the many facets of their shared life and responsibilities, not the least of which was George's ability to keep the windows of their world open for her interested husband. For although WBY had resigned from the Senate in 1928 he was still actively involved in Irish affairs, including the formation of the Irish Academy of Letters; and there was always Abbey Theatre business to attend to. Typically, the first of these letters deals with WBY's public engagements and her own suggestions to smooth the way; the last, just weeks before Lady Gregory's death, speaks of the small details of home and community that were so important to them both.

Unless otherwise indicated, all of the following letters were written from 42 Fitzwilliam Square, the upper flat of Bethel Solomon's house, in which the Yeatses lived from 1928 to 1932. Most of them are typed with manuscript additions. Except for a few inspired guesses, which I have retained, George, unlike her husband, was an impeccable speller; obvious typing errors have been silently corrected, but her idiosyncratic punctuation has been preserved.

I

WBY's first radio broadcast would take place from the Belfast offices of the BBC on 8 September 1931. The Abbey Theatre company toured the United States and Canada from October 1931 to April 1932. Shan F. Bullock was a novelist, poet and short story writer, and one of the early members of the Irish Academy of Letters; Lennox Robinson, playwright, fiction writer and essayist, was producer-director and general mainstay of the Abbey Theatre, Michael Yeats's godfather and for many years one of GY's closest friends; John H. Perrin was business manager of the Abbey Theatre until replaced by Eric Gorman in 1932. During Horse Show week Cuala was always represented in the Royal Dublin Society exhibition hall. Jack B. Yeats, who was a frequent visitor at Coole, did not always agree with his brother politically, but he and his wife Cottie kept on friendly if somewhat distant family terms.

42, Fitzwilliam Square,
Dublin.
Phone 61831.

Friday [31 July 1931]

My dear William,

DID you get a letter I forwarded to you last Tuesday from the BBC, Belfast? I sent it straight on to you without opening it (I concluded it was BBC as it had a Belfast postmark). Mr Bullock rang up from Belfast today terribly anxious for an answer. I thought it better to arrange at once as he had to fix up his programmes seven weeks ahead. The arrangements are that you are to broadcast a 'talk' about your version of Oedipus the King, referring to the fact that it is to be broadcast from Belfast a week later (Sept. 15) and that the players are going to America, making a sort of 'farewell' windup to the 'talk'. (This for publicity for the Abbey) At 8.40 you are to do fifteen minutes readings from your own poetry. I asked

Bullock if you could do the readings with commentary, and he said you could do anything you liked! He also said that he proposed to add five guineas to the fee originally arranged as you were to broadcast the 'talk' as well as the readings! So you will get thirtyfive guineas . . . .

I think you must write him at once 'to confirm' these arrangements—you might perhaps say you will be glad of the opportunity of meeting him again! (He told me on the phone that he had met you in the Abbey years ago when the Ulster players were there . . .

By law it is necessary for you to send a copy of your 'talk' to be vetted. I have written to Mr Bullock to ask him to write to you at Coole IF HE WANTS THE COPY BEFORE FRIDAY NEXT. I think it will be time enough when you get to Dublin. You could dicate it. You'll have to keep closely to the fifteen minutes in both cases—you can try the 'talk' out on me.

I asked him if it would be possible to have a try-out on the microphone before you actually do the thing, and he said it could easily be arranged & very much approved of the idea. As your two doings are to be radiated from the London centres and you havent broadcasted before I think a try-out might be an advantage—you wont be able to tiger up and down the room as you usually do when you speak!

Heaven knows what Bullock's initials are . . . I couldnt get hold of Lennox or Perrin to ask and had to write at once to confirm the telephone conversation. I made a squiggle which looked faintly like S T but not enough so as to be traceable. B.B.C. Belfast.

Please let me know when you come up and by what train, for Horse show starts on Tuesday and my hands will be very full!

                                                              George.
Met Jack today. He says he has never seen you in such good health!

II

George H. Tulloch of Craig, Gardner and Associates, a well-known Dublin firm of chartered accountants, had been in charge of the Abbey Theatre's financial records since 1923; Peggy was one of the two household maids; Michael Yeats was ten years old and a day student at Mount Temple School in Palmerston Park. While at Coole WBY was completing the series 'Words for Music Perhaps'; the line GY quotes is from an early draft of 'Old Tom Again', which WBY instantly acknowledged was wrong and revised it to 'Though fantastic men suppose'.

                                                     October 15 [1931]
My dear William, do you know that you pocketed without even opening a letter from dear Mr O'Donovan (the income tax inspector) addressed to ME, pocketted it in the inner pocket of your dark brown coat? I found it today because I was feeling that Peggy had nothing to do and so might

mend the lining which I had remembered was torn. Now that letter came
when you were up for the Abbey farewell dance! I have taken all the
blame on myself—except to Tulloch who is dealing with our claim now for
reasons too long and complicated to go into—reasons forced on by that
pocketted letter, incidentally.

I suppose you wont have contrite heart because you didnt mean to
pocket the letter, didnt know you pocketted the letter, and so on, like
Michael who used to refuse to apologise for accidentally kicking people on
the grounds 'I didnt do it on purpose'.

Incidentally, Michael got a star for another 'composition', and has been
told that he is a very good 'goal' (hockey).

Hope the lamps arrived, also writing paper, loose leaf, etc.

I like that poem—but I'm not sure if I've misread the fourth line. You
might re-write it to me.

> 'Though man's bitter heart suppose?'

G.

III

Yeats had written an introduction for Joseph Hone and Mario Rossi's book on
Bishop Berkeley, which was published by Faber and Faber in October 1931;
the letters of William Drennan, eighteenth century nationalist and poet, edited
by D.A. Chart, were published by Her Majesty's Stationery Office in Belfast in
1931; Margaret Gatty, nineteenth century author of books for children whose
five-volume series *Parables from Nature* (1855-71) were internationally renow-
ned, was also editor of a children's journal, *Aunt Judy's Magazine*. The
government, under the leadership of William T. Cosgrave's beleaguered
Cumann na nGaedheal Party, had recently pushed through the Constitutional
Amendment Bill to set up the Military Tribunal to try political offences; Mrs
O'Higgins was the widow of Kevin O'Higgins who, one of the ablest Ministers
in the Cosgrave administration, had been assassinated in July 1927; Thomas
Jepson O'Connell (whose address, WBY replied, was 21 Trafalgar Terrace),
former general secretary of the Irish National Teachers Organisation, was
Leader of the Labour Party from 1927 to 1932 and served in the Senate until
1944. For three months Dublin and London newspapers carried details of a
case being heard in Dublin's High Court concerning the suit of two London
hairdressers, Antonio Apicella and Matteo Constantino, against café proprietor Emilio Scala, also of London, claiming a share of the first prize in the Irish
Hospitals Sweepstake on the Grand National.

October 16 [1931]

My dear Willy

I post you under separate cover the Berkeley which arrived this
morning—Its a nice handsome looking book, and it is most self-sacrificing
of me to post it on to you at once instead of keeping it to look over the

week-end. However I'm amusing myself with the Drennan Letters which
came four days ago, and which are decidedly not of handsome appearance.
Paper like the paper of Dail reports, a hideous navy-blue cover made of
that slightly bumpy material which makes a mousey noise when scratched
with the fingernail. The letters themselves are both 'amusing and
instructive' as I was told on being given Mrs Gatty's 'Parables from
Nature' as a school prize. No, that's hardly fair on the Letters—they're
amusing and interesting, at least to me who knows very little of that part
of history. I've asked the stationery Office Belfast to post a copy to Lady
G. You can read'em from her copy.

Great excitement in Dublin over the Coercion bill. I met Mrs O'Higgins
twice—she told me a very interesting thing which I cannot tell you in a
letter. I was not able to find O'Connell's address. It is probably in your
address book. IF IT IS NOT 24 Trafalgar Terrace Monkstown will you
please write to her and tell her the correct address. I told her the number
in T. Terrace from my imperfect memory. Her address is Knockbeg,
Cowper Gardens, Rathmines. In the meantime she is writing a non-
commital letter asking him to come and see her, a letter which can be
returned through the dead letter office.

Jack and Cottie are keeping themselves to themselves at the moment
. . . although on Saturday when Anne and Michael and I were returning
home we saw him in the distance and the children said with one voice 'he
is crossing the road to speak to us!'

Have you been reading the Scala sweepstake case? The morning papers
did not give as full an account as the evening ones. One very pet thing
was Mrs Apicella's evidence about the seance that Scala held to enquire of
the spirits whether he held a winning ticket. 'He kept on calling on
Rasputin, and I thought he said rice pudding and he got so angry he
wanted to turn me out of the room'.

When I have [not] been prancing in the evenings I've been going to bed
at 8.30 or 9 every evening (surrounded with base fiction) and I feel very
much better for it.

Yours affly

George.

IV

While the Abbey players were on their American tour, the Directors instituted
an occasional series of performances entitled 'Mainly ballet: The Abbey
Directors' Sunday Entertainments'. The Abbey School of Ballet had been
established in 1927 when Yeats persuaded Ninette de Valois, a native of
County Wicklow who had danced with Diaghilev and was later to found the
Sadler's Wells Ballet, to become its Director; she sent over her most promising
students as teachers and occasionally performed herself, while arranging the
choreography for most of WBY's dance plays during this period. His dance

play *The Dreaming of the Bones*, written in 1917 and published in 1919, had never been produced at the Abbey. GY, who spoke four languages fluently, regularly attended the monthly meetings of the French Society, and came to know the French Minister to the Irish Free State, Charles Alphand and his family, well; 'the Lodge' refers to the residence of the Governor General, James MacNeill, who was a staunch supporter of the Abbey. 'Dobbs' was GY's childhood nickname, which WBY frequently used.

October 26 [1931]

My dear William,

Here are two very important questions which you must answer, and answer at once.

  I. Will you be able to produce 'The Dreaming of the Bones' (for Sunday Nov 29)

 II. Are you coming up to see Miss de Valois when she comes over the first week of November?

These two things are inseparable . . . IF YOU DO NOT FEEL THAT YOU CAN COME TO DUBLIN YOU MUST LET ME KNOW AT ONCE. I think you are probably feeling that you cannot leave Coole, but I must know quite definitely. If you do not think that you can come up to produce 'Dreaming of the Bones' I must see Miss de Valois, and must also try to work up some people to go to the Ballet.—the Lodge, the Alphands etc.

If you are not coming up for the first week of November I want to know in order that I may arrange to come to Coole. I want to be in Dublin for November 18th for a meeting of the French Society. You make things a little difficult by not writing any sort of plans. If you cannot make 'plans', I think you must say so in order that I may know what to do about a number of problems that I find difficult.

I want a definite answer about my problems I and II.

Please do not think that I am 'feeling neglected'—your own phrase!

Dobbs.

V

Walter Starkie, Professor of Romance Languages at Trinity College, was the government appointee to the Abbey Theatre Board of Directors; Sara Patrick (daughter of Ben Iden Payne), the school's first ballet teacher, was being replaced by Nesta Brooking. Both the Yeatses were avid readers of mystery novels; according to Ninette de Valois, WBY insisted that the plot include a love interest. The extensive Abbey Theatre tour (seventy-nine centres) had been arranged by Bronson Albery of Wyndham Theatres Limited; Maureen Delany had first performed with the 'second company' when the theatre last visited America in 1914 and remained one of the Abbey's most popular comic actors until her death in 1961.

Thursday [29 October 1931]

My dear William

I have just wired to you 'Valois arrives November seven performance postponed until December six'. She is bringing over the new ballet mistress and I dont think the ballet could be got into trim—granted the change of teacher etc. in time for the 29th Nov. I rang up Perrin and he entirely agreed. I did not know until yesterday that Miss de Valois was not arriving until the 7th.

If you will come up on the 9th (she arrives on 7th and probably will be busy all Sunday going through things with Miss Patrick) I will fix up a meeting for Tuesday 10th with you and Walter and her.

Unless I hear to the contrary I shall expect you by the first train on Monday November 9th and shall meet you at Broadstone.

I didnt send the Berkeley because after I had written to you I glanced at the end of it and found that the last thirty odd pages had been bound with a different book altogether! I returned the copy to Faber and asked them to post you another. It was an 'advance copy' so they may have had to wait for the general edition. Do you remember how we once bought a crime fiction because of its name and when opening it at home found a ghastly sentimental novel within the cover 'The Eternal Love' or something similar, whereas the cover said 'Murder at Keyes'.

I hear that all 'the girls' in the Abbey Company were most terribly seasick on their journey over and that poor Delany lost nearly two stone—this is not of course strictly true, but let us hope there is some truth in the statement! Their first month has had to be completely altered as regards performances as some of the places they were going to have 'diseases' and are therefore 'in quarantine'. However the Albery people got out new advertisements etc and made new bookings.

Yours affly

Dobbs.

VI

Performers remaining in Dublin were those not on permanent contract or who had recently graduated from the Abbey School of Acting: W. O'Gorman (who remained a member of the company until 1945) did perform the role of the Young Man, John Stephenson (who had for some years performed at the Abbey, earning Joseph Holloway's admiration for his clear speaking and singing voice) was the Stranger and Joseph O'Neill (a newcomer) the Singer, but Hilda Lynch (who does not seem to have joined the company) lost out as Young Woman, danced by Ninette de Valois' newly appointed teacher, Nesta Brooking ('only her dancing power has to be considered', WBY had replied, approving of the rest of GY's casting). The play was produced by Dossie Wright, theatre electrician and occasional actor since the Abbey's early days. Yeats's one-act play *The Cat and the Moon* had been performed on 21 September 1931.

[30 or 31 October 1931]

My dear William

If you want a rehearsal or more than one rehearsal while you are in Dublin from November 9th, please wire by return stating your ideas about the cast. These people are all very busy and must have notice. To say nothing of the fact that you may not agree to my suggestions!

Young Man O'Gorman (Lame Beggar, in Cat and Moon)

Young woman Hilda Lynch

Stranger Stephenson

First Musician O'Neill (1st. Mus. in Cat)

Hilda Lynch may not do, but was v. good in school of acting. Might be given a try-out anyway.

I suggest O'Gorman for the Young Man rather than Stephenson because O'Gorman speaks well but with a terrific natural accent! And as he was 'in the Post Office' in the play . . . etc . . .

Do do something about it all! No letter this morning

G.

Parts are all typed.

VII

A.P. Watt was WBY's literary agent. Dermod O'Brien, artist, was President of the Royal Hibernian Academy and of the Dublin United Arts Club. Denis Johnston, a member of the Dublin Drama League and later to become one of Ireland's most under-rated playwrights, had achieved notoriety with the 1929 Gate Theatre production of *The Old Lady Says 'No!'*; in recompense for rejecting the play, the Abbey directors invited him to direct *King Lear*, and in April 1931 produced his play *The Moon in the Yellow River*. Perhaps because of its earlier manifestation as a morgue, the Abbey Theatre had always been considered haunted; in an October 1927 letter to Olivia Shakespear WBY reported the disturbing events surrounding the production of his *Oedipus at Colonus*.

Sunday [1 November 1931]

My dear Willy

I have posted to you by the same post a large envelope marked immediate.

You will see that the claim is (Gt. Britain) for 467 pounds odd. This (minus agents' fee) will help very much in the 1931-32 year—what with Cuala and London Macmillan whose account for this year is £104 . . .

(Watt's commission not deducted). So I want it sent off immediately! And, do get it registered! When I say 'immediately', I only mean that I want it sent off by the first convenient post; I dont mean that I want you to walk to Gort in order to send it off after the usual messenger has left.

Posts are so inconsequent that I dont know whether you will get this letter first or the large envelope first.

As you know, I dont want to get an 'advance' from Macmillan this year, because I want to have the cash from the Collected Edition kept beautifully isolated.

Various newses—which I will keep until you arrive—from U.S.A. In Dublin, Dossie Wright has a new daughter; Mr and Mrs Dermod O'Brien went to the Arts Ball as '<u>Fig Leaves</u>'!; Denis Johnston went down to the Abbey to ask permission to stay there for Hallowe'en night to lay the ghost. Now for God's sake keep this last piece of news to yourself and dont impart it to Lady G. I havent heard yet what happened, if anything happened etc. If you repeat this I shall never write you a letter to Coole containing anything frivolous or serious. Perrin rang me up yesterday (Saturday) to say Denis was in the office asking if he could stay all night in the Abbey and Starkie was away, and he (Perrin) did not feel that he could give permission on his own. So I said I was sure that if you were in Dublin that you would give permission subject to Denis seeing that the premises were securely locked up on his departure from the Theatre. His father is, in any case, a Free State Judge, and one does not suspect Denis of republican or communist tendencies!

I may get a letter from you tomorrow (Monday) saying that you come up on the 9th -

Yours affly

G.

VIII

WBY reported on 1 November, 'I have just finished a beautiful and exciting second part to my commentary on the Swift play'. *The Words upon the Window-pane* had been produced at the Abbey 17 November 1930; both parts of the commentary, destined for his volume *Wheels and Butterflies*, were first published in Seumas O'Sullivan's *The Dublin Magazine* October-December 1931 and January-March 1932. Seumas O'Sullivan was the pen name of the poet, essayist and editor James Starkey, who was married to the artist Estella Solomons; but 'the Starkies' referred to are more likely Walter Starkie, Director of the Theatre, and his wife. Padraic Colum, prolific author who with his wife the critic Mary Maguire Colum were at this time spending most of their time in France, had been one of the founding members of the Irish literary movement; they frequently returned to Dublin.

Tuesday, Nov.3 [1931]

My dear William

Delighted to hear about the second part to the Swift. I am very excited to hear it. For Heaven's sake dont forget to bring it up with you. You can read it to me, and dictate it.

The lamp of course consumes lamp oil, paraffin. What in Heaven's name else could it consume?! Its very form shouts paraffin oil; you could surely not have imagined that it demanded Sanctuary oil, or olive oil?

I think I wrote to you that Denis had asked permission to make vigil at the Abbey Halloween night? He and Perrin stayed together, Perrin frankly admits that he slept—like Peter in the Garden of Gethsemane—Denis watched, found nothing to watch, and at the witching hour of three aroused the sleeping Perrin in order that they might adjourn to the gas ring and cook eggs and bacon . . .

I have asked the Starkies and Colum to dine on Friday (13th). Starkie will be away until then—I shall fix up a meeting of you and Miss de Valois on <u>Tuesday</u> Other arrangements depend on my hearing from you . . . I hate bothering you about the Dreaming of the Bones, but if it is to be done it must be got going—anyway, have you thought out who is going to shake dem bones when you is gone back to Coole? ('bones' is a name negroes give to dice—shaking the 'bones' . . . very low)

Yours affly

George.

IX

Fighting the Waves, Yeats's ballet-drama based on *The Only Jealousy of Emer*, was produced at the Abbey Theatre on 13 August 1929 with music by George Antheil, masks designed by Hildo van Krop, curtain and costumes by Dorothy Travers Smith (Mrs Lennox Robinson) and choreography by Ninette de Valois, who danced the part of Fand. His newly-written introduction was published in *The Dublin Magazine* April-June 1932. In the published version the lines preceding 'Only a Caesar could do what I want . . .' (Section II) lament that there is no literary school which would substitute 'positive desires for the negative passion of a national movement beaten down into party politics'. Section III includes the discussion of Latin, the grammar as corrected by GY. 'The world's greatest sweepstake draw', the Irish Hospitals' Sweepstake on the Manchester November Handicap, began on 18th November and continued for two days; GY usually bought a ticket.

November 18 1931

My dear Willy

I send you the copy of introd: to Fighting the Waves which I want you to correct and return to me . . . (envelope and stamps enclosed). One of the 'see back's' has been completely crossed out but the subsequent pages—i.e. p.4 'I would have Caesar compel' etc is unexplained without a former line or two? I have also queried in blue pencil, p.4. '<u>knows that it</u> /would/ <u>be Latin</u>' should not that 'would' be '<u>should</u>'?

Let me have it back soon that I may send it to Starkey. The streets resound with newsboys shouting the first stop press of the Sweepstake draw. I was a fool not to buy a ticket and so share in the excitement!

In haste for post

Love G.

X

The November 24th issue of *The Irish Press* carried a lengthy memorial article on the novelist and Republican politician Robert Erskine Childers, who had been executed 24 November 1922 by a Free State Firing squad. Maud Gonne, from whom WBY had been estranged over political differences, had spoken on 21 November at a meeting of The People's Rights Association protesting treatment of prisoners arrested under the Constitution Act; a meeting for the same purpose arranged for the following day had been proclaimed by the Minister for Justice. Anne Yeats, now twelve years old, was a boarder at Hillcourt School, Glenageary, run by the Misses Phyllis and Gladys Palmer. GY, who was at least as well read as her husband in phenomenological literature, had persuaded WBY to write *The Words Upon the Window-pane*, based on their many experiences at seances and the conclusions in *A Vision*.

Nov. 24 [1931]

My dear William

For some reason or other I thought I'd sort out all your letters to me this morning—all undated—and among them I found one written from the Savile Club about your waking to the sound of two volleys—'Childers is dead'—Then the post came with a letter from Dulce Philpotts (who was Dulce Childers) then I saw—an hour later—the Irish Press notice. Dulce wrote to me about nothing at all, but it just happens that she wrote on the very day, Nov.22, that we last met, when she was in Dublin before Childers was shot. That was all only the sort of coincidence that so frequently happens—one sees a new word in some book, meets it again three or four times within twentyfour hours; the 'dramatisation' perhaps of which you write in that Part II of the 'Windowpane'.

Maud has been terrifically busy! She got in a meeting that had been banned twentyfour hours earlier than the banned one . . .

Anne has been in profound disgrace at school for not working; she wrote to me 'Miss Palmer blew me up and made me go to late prep: every day last week. I think the results were good for I got 8 out of 10 for arithmetic, 14 out of 15 for Geometry, 10 out of 10 for French, 12 out of 15 for Algebra, but dont think I shall be much higher in the class because I didnt work at the other subjects'.

I sent off the 'Windowpane' and 'Fighting the Waves' commentaries to

Starkey. I think that the reason I did not very much like Part II
Windowpane is that your argument—the dramatisation of the secondary
and tertiary personalities of the medium, seem so close to the old psychical
research theory of the 'subconscious' or at least that I cannot personally
understand what you mean except in those terms. If I had to interpret that
'commentary' I could not say that any 'spirit' were present at any seance,
that spirits were present at a seance only as impersonations created by a
medium out of material in a world record just as wireless photography or
television are created; that all communicating spirits are mere
dramatisations of that record; that all spirits in fact are not, so far as
psychic communications are concerned, spirits at all, are only memory. I
say 'memory' deliberately, because 'memory' is so large a part of all
psychic phenomena. I dont remember any case in which a spirit
(communicating through a medium) had during the latter part of his life
or during any part of his life been cut off from that every day faculty of
memory. Those people who were wounded in the head during war—they
dont come—the insane dont come???—the spirits who tell us about their
houses, their horse racing, their whiskeys and sodas, their children, their
aunts and God knows whatnots, their suicides, were all mainly
preoccupied during their lives with those things. Have we any record of a
spirit communicating who had been at any period of his life been so
physically or mentally incapacitated that memory, even 'subconscious'
memory, had been obliterated?

Apologies for this diatribe—it all comes out of an idea I had lately that
small nations have long memories, big nations have short memories, small
nations make Empires.

Yours affly

G.

XI

Excited by GY's letter, WBY sent two commentaries, and briefly contemplated incorporating her comments and his response in his introduction.
Oliver St. John Gogarty, poet, wit, surgeon and fellow Senator, was one of
WBY's life-long friends; American-born Molly Childers, who shared her late
husband's Republican fervour, was still active in the Fianna Fail party;
Dorothy Devoy was the Abbey Theatre costumes mistress. Suzanne Alphand,
daughter of the French Minister, whose engagement to Michael E. Fitzgerald
('well known in Irish legal and hunting circles') had recently been announced,
spoke to the French Society in the Russell Hotel on 25 November on
'L'Irlande vue par les Francais'; Michael and Anne Yeats, who had been to
school in Switzerland, were encouraged by their mother to keep up their
French; Anne Gregory was Lady Gregory's granddaughter, Margaret her
daughter-in-law. WBY had indicated that Lady Gregory was expecting GY to
return to Coole with him.

Friday [27 November 1931]

My dear Willy

Your two letters came this morning; I havent had time to digest the two commentaries as Michael's school is having a sale tomorrow and he has the sweet stall . . . so I have had to make fudge and make it all up into pretty little parcels! Tonight I dine with the Gogartys—on Tuesday I go to tea with Mrs Erskine Childers!-!

The rehearsals seem to be going well. On Tuesday morning I have an assignation with Miss Devoy to look out dresses. I'll tell Dossie that you come up on Friday so that he can arrange for dress rehearsal

I've asked the Alphands and one or two others to come and return with us after the performance for supper. Hope you wont find this too tiring Michael has developed a passion for Suzanne Alphand—he heard her 'conference' at the French Society and never took his eyes off her for a moment. Afterwards he said 'She's very like Anne Gregory but I think she's even prettier. She is pretty'. And later on 'I dont wonder she's engaged, she wouldnt be difficult to engage'.!

About Coole; do you think Lady Gregory is well enough to stand the strain of a visitor? In any case I hope you have not forgotten that you told me she is using Margaret's room and that I should feel very upset if I found I had been put into that room.

I am afraid that she may find my coming adds to her burdens.

Love

G.

XII

John Smyth Crone, medical doctor, editor of *Irish Book Lover* (1909-1924) and *Concise Dictionary of Irish Biography* (1928), was president of the Irish Literary Society, London 1918-1925; WBY was to speak at the Society's dinner, which finally took place in April (see no. XXII). Lough Cutra near Coole was the home of Lady Gregory's daughter-in-law and her second husband Guy Gough; Lennox Robinson was in charge of the American tour; Rupert Gordon was the son of WBY's Aunt Fanny and Samuel Gordon; GY was especially fond of Rupert's sister Ruth.

Dec. 15 or 20 [1931]

My dear Willy

I enclose an income tax form which I want you to sign in the two places marked in blue pencil and return, in stamped envelope.

I send also a letter from Dr Crone. Its a pity he says February or March—

Lennox writes 'I am convinced that W.B. and Tulloch think I am blueing all the proceeds—I wish there was half a chance of doing so' (He

is feeling poor) 'the money question is still stringent but will straighten
out soon'. He has evidently had a pretty bad time with his back.

I wired to the impertinent person whose letter I enclose—'Harry Watts'
to say 'regret cannot give permission Yeats'.

We had a good drive up, lunched at Athlone, and arrived in Dublin at
four. (We didnt leave Lough Cutra until well after 10.30 -)

This letter is all new paragraphs because it is all information—the
unfinished play will reach you by registered parcel post as it is in one of
the old loose leaf books. It was really very pet and nice of you to be up
when I was going yesterday, thankyou. I found Michael very well,
bursting to tell all his doings during the week—the plot of the play at the
French Society—the lion cubs at the zoo and the charms of Rupert . . .
(your cousin) the conversation he had with someone at the French Society
'I didnt know him, he was French, and I dont think he knew me, I like
talking to people I dont know' . . . A thrilling cinema (gunmen) and a star
for composition! Two mice caught in his cupboard, his crocusses all much
bigger, thank goodness painting classes were over for the term, how many
hours until Anne returned from school on Friday, what was a moon's
nebula (that stumped me,) kippers for breakfast twice, no chicken since I
went away, and so on ad infinitum. Very pleased with his book—he writes
to thank for it himself, but probably not until Wednesday or Thursday as
he has two late days at school—Tuesday and possible Wed: also.

Yours affly
G.

XIII

Anne Yeats was already exhibiting exceptional artistic talent, regularly gaining
honours standard and first place in various competitions.

Tuesday [22 December 1931]

My dear Willy

I've just written an awful scrawl to Lady Gregory but I cant compose a
proper 'roofer' being too tired to think. That unfortunate Anne came
home ill (better today) with a terrific temp: and throat, and it was only.
certain yesterday that she was NOT developing diptheria! We had to have
three different lots of swabs tried out at the laboratory . . . anyway, its
just a very bad sceptic throat. The doc thought the temp. was too high for
diptheria, but had to make sure. She'll be in bed for Xmas poor child but
I hope she['ll] be well enough by then to enjoy presents. Her temp. was
down today to just under 101. She really is unlucky.

Write and tell the news, such as it is.

Yours affly
G.

Please write to her about her 'linotype' and dont forget to read the
inscription on the back of the calendar! She wrote it before getting ill, but
in bed so writing is atrocious! A lino-type is <u>cut</u> in linoleum—she cut it
herself but did not print it herself

XIV

Peggy was one of the household maids. The Gate Theatre, run by Hilton
Edwards and Micheál MacLiammóir, produced Padraic Colum's play *Mogu of
the Desert* on 29 December 1931, with setting and costumes designed by
MacLiammóir; Ashley Duke's *Jew Suss* had been produced in October; Orson
Welles performed in both plays. GY, who had been an art student, also had
considerable musical training. The 1902 two-volume edition of Walter Pater's
Marius the Epicurean is in the Yeatses' library.

January 2 1932
My dear Willy, very distressed to hear you had such a bad cold. I hope
you are quite well again???? Anne managed to get a cold in her head in
spite of extreme precautions and so had to return to bed again after being
up for one hour, two hours and three hours on three consecutive days!
She is better tonight and her temp. is lower than this morning. Michael
extremely well. He and I went to see Colum's 'Mogu of the Desert' last
night. (I left Peggy in charge of Anne) Colum was there. He and his wife
had to come to Dublin on some other business for a week, or so he said,
and they arrived last night. It was a bad performance, the music was quite
intolerable, it turned the play into something approaching light opera
although there was not a great deal of it. The music should have been
flute only, the songs almost spoken. No difference was made between the
dressing of the Romans and that of the Persians, nor was their acting
different so one lost a most necessary sense of balance in the first act and in
the 3rd. Hilton Edwards played Mogu as he played the jew in Jew Suss,
the women were atrocious, the scenery and lighting excellent, the dresses
and colours ditto; Colum said to me as we were going out 'I dont
recognise my play'. (They had cut an essential part of the second act, he
told me)
    Poor Anne is missing everything—children's parties, pantomimes etc—
its rotten luck for her.
    A very queer thing happened on the day after Christmas (Boxing Day)
the telephone rang about 5 to nine. I answered it but instead of a reply I
heard Italian opera being sung; I seized a chair and sat and listened.
Presently, when I. Op. had ceased, a voice said 'this is 2 RN' then an
announcement of a pantomime that was to be broadcast. Then a sort of
preliminary song and the telephone suddenly cut off! I have been trying to
find out what could have happened to make my telephone wire cut in on a
broadcast, but so far without success.

I havent seen anyone except Colum and relations so havent any gossip.
Nor have I been to see anything but Colum's play. Nor have I read
anything but detective stories and some of Burns' verses (to Anne who had
learnt some at school and liked 'em) or the encyclopedia—to answer
Michael's intolerable questions, and 'Marius' in bed for tranquility of
mind, and that one excellent detective story which I got Peggy to post to
you when I heard you had a cold!

Various people have telephoned. The Gogartys, who at one time asked
me round time and time again have not uttered. Either something queer
happened about that night at the Abbey on Dec. 6 or they are in Galway?

I posted on to you a letter from the Spectator—it had an English stamp
but had not been through the post—which was left here this afternoon.
Had you received from them the letter they mention having addressed to
the Kildare St Club?

When you write tell me facts, how you are, how Lady Gregory is, did
you get a new bed-coat sent to you from Horton's (Grafton St) is there
anything you need?

Dobbs.

XV

In 1932 Elizabeth ('Lolly') Yeats of the Cuala Press published *The Wild Bird's
Nest*, poems from the Irish by Frank O'Connor, novelist, short story writer
and translator, who later became a Director of the Abbey Theatre and, in 1941,
a Director of the Press. Tom Graham was an eye and ear surgeon. The
embroidery division of Cuala Industries had been under GYs management
since Lily Yeats's illness in 1923; in addition to Lily Yeats, Sara Hyland and
May Courtney worked in embroidery from designs contributed by a great
many Irish artists including Cottie (Mrs Jack B.) Yeats, AE and occasionally
GY herself. No play by Walter Starkie appears to have been produced at the
Abbey, unless he had a hand in the production of Pirandello's *Six Characters in
Search of an Author* in 1934.

Jan.4 1932

My dear Willy, alas, Anne's illness put O'Connor out of my head, and
your letter today reminded me of my deficiencies. I have posted his poems
to him today with an explanatory letter.

Anne is still in bed—she had two days of a normal temp. and was lively
and active and up for two or three hours each day—got a slight cold and
returned to temperatures and headaches and post-nasal nuisances. Tom
Graham came in this evening and punctured her right anterrim (he shoved
in cocaine first). When it was all over he said in a most casual way 'I think
that's worth a shilling isnt it?' Anne obviously didnt know what to answer.
He shoved his hand into his pocket 'I hope I've got one!' Brought it out
with a shilling. All of course carefully pre-arranged, I'm sure he does it

with all his young patients, but Anne who had got over three pounds for
Xmas presents is treasuring that shilling as no other shilling was ever
treasured! I hope that the cleaning out of the anterrim will have stopped
what ever was the origin of the sceptic poisoning.

Cuala is wound up—the embroidery I mean. I have paid all the bills
except the overdraft at the Bank which could not be cleared up until, after
Jan 2 (Xmas and Bank holdiays etc) Sara Hyland and May Courtney have
decided to try and carry on as a 'Mendery and dressmaking establishment'
They pay their rent to Lolly, and bear their proportion of telephone. As
they said to me—'the only other expense is our wages and our firing' and
as May has 10/- a week from the Carnegie Libraries—she is librarian of
the Carnegie library at Dundrum—and Sara gets some similar sum or
perhaps more from organising Irish classes—they are prepared to do work
at a very much lower rate than in the days when they were under the
control of 'Cuala'. They undertake 'mending'—rates sixpence upwards—
etc. They are going to issue a printed circular shortly. They will acts as
agents for Lily's embroidered pictures, banners, Stations of the Cross, etc.
I think it is a courageous idea and I am doing everything I can to
circulated the idea. It is easy to do propaganda when propaganda is
altruistic! Lily sold her first 'Customs House' last Friday. She will now
have the job of doing another for exhibition.

Walter rang up today about that translation of his, I said you were at
Coole, he said shall I send the first act to Mr Yeats at Coole, and I said
yes! Later the Irish Press rang up to enquire for Lady Gregory. I said that
I had seen her recently and that she was well.

Yours affly
Dobbs.

XVI

In January GY took the children for a holiday to Killarney, while WBY paid a
brief visit to Dublin to see the dentist, James E. Hogan.

[Killarney]
Thursday [21 January 1932]

My dear Willy,

Hope you arrived safely back to Coole and had not too bad a time with
Hogan?

We had an excellent journey—arrived in gales, storms and floods! No
front rooms overlooking the lake could be used because the wind so
terrific. The next morning dead calm, some sun, floods vanishing. Today a
summer's day, and the lake dead smooth and transparent and the children
have gone off with an old boatman for a 'grand tour' which is to take 3-4
hours! We had a long drive yesterday (outside car) all round the Muckross

estate up to Torca Mountain etc. Anne has done a quite excellent sketch from the covered in verandah, and proposes to start another tomorrow so as to get two done! She is getting back her colour and energy.

No news—we shall be back in Dublin on Monday evening and A. returns to school on Tuesday.

Love

George.

XVII

The Most Unfortunate Day of My Life by Maria Edgeworth was published in 1931 by Cobden-Sanderson of London with illustrations by Irish artist Norah McGuinness, who had in 1927 illustrated WBY's *Stories of Red Hanrahan and the Secret Rose*. Both GY and WBY were fond of animals, especially cats.

Jan. 25 1932 (Monday)

My dear Willy

I see, on going through my letters tonight, that you have paid £2.7.0 to Pigott's; a sum I paid in 1930 and for which I have the receipt. I will reclaim your £2.7.0 and refund it to you.

Anne has returned from Killarney looking pink and well and fatter. We had amazing summer weather; arrived in tremendous storm and flood, drove on Wednesday all round the middle and lower lakes going, on part of the road, through floods so deep that the foot rest of the outside car almost touched the water. Swans swam over what the hotel had once hoped to make a tennis lawn! We had the hotel entirely to ourselves. As it was not 'the season' the Manager and his daughter were able to entertain in the house all their dogs—ages 3 months to five years, species varied— and a regally colossal black cat. During the season the proprietors of the hotel ban animals, and the animals are banished to the stables. Such is German discipline—the manager is a German—that the animals, or so I was told, understand that from Whitsun until September 15 they must cease to be house dogs and cats. I doubt very much that the cat would permit this code to be imposed upon him, he did not seem at all obedient. He was a very determined cat. Cobden Sanderson has just published a forgotten and unprinted fragment of Maria Edgeworth's. It is called 'The Most Unfortunate Day of My Life' Printed in fine type on handsome paper it seems an incomparable piece of style—of its own kind—the grandfather and grandmother of all the Virginia Woolf's and Stella Bensons and of all those modern novelists who seem to write with the astonished eyes of an imaginary child.

I had hoped, when I arrived home this evening, to find a letter from you.

Yours affly

George.

XVIII

WBY had been sent an advance copy of *Pigeon Irish* by Francis ('Harry')
Stuart, Iseult Gonne's husband. A third sister, Miss Eileen Palmer, took in
boarders for Hillcourt School. Joseph Hone, biographer, translator and editor
(who would become WBY's first official biographer) was collaborating on
Swift; or, the Egoist with Italian philosopher and scholar Mario Rossi, who had
recently visited Coole. Walter Starkie, the government appointee to the Abbey
Board of Directors, had made headlines in 1928 when he disagreed with the
decision to reject O'Casey's play *The Silver Tassie*. A scratch company under
the direction of Dossie Wright continued to keep the Abbey open during the
American tour: *Family Failing* by William Boyle had first been produced in
March 1912; *Queer Ones*, a curtain-raiser by Con O'Leary, in October 1919;
Frolie Mulhern first began performing in 1930, while Gertrude Quinn was
only an occasional actor with the company. The novel sent by well-known
hostess and republican sympathizer Hazel Lavery was probably by one of her
protegées; her husband's portrait of her as a romantic Cathleen ni Houlihan
decorated Irish banknotes from 1928 to 1977. Michael Yeats attended
Baymount School as a boarder under Headmaster W.L. Scott until he enrolled
in St Columba's in September 1935.

Feb 1 [1932]

My dear Willy

Glad to get yours this morning—and glad that you like Harry Stuart's new
novel.

Anne was here yesterday and looks very much better in spite of a septic toe
(on her other <u>foot</u>, the one which did not have its big toenail removed!) She is
evidently having a happy time and, so far, is finding herself very popular! In
fact everything is beautiful in the garden, even maths, for which she got five
out of ten. This may not seem much to <u>you</u> but her last term was frequently
nought out of ten! She is still being crowed and cooed over by the Miss Palmers
and matron and cossetted by the 'dormitory' although to my eyes she now
looks quite well!

I dined with Joe Hone last Thursday—he rang up to say he was in Dublin
and he had had Rossi's introductory chapter to his book on Ireland and would I
come and dine at the K[ildare] St. Club so that he could hear the latest news of
you and Lady G. So I dined, and not only had Joe no other diner but no one else
was dining or sitting, so we had those two vast rooms to ourselves. Joe
discoursed at length on religion, death and so on. I am afraid the poor man
thinks he hasnt very long to live. If you feel inclined you might write to him St
Ann's Hydro, Blarney and ask him about his book on Swift.

I saw Walter on Thursday also—he came in very late to a committee of the
French Drama League and stayed on afterwards to gossip. He had heard
nothing about the Abbey since the meeting you and he had. I handed him the
letter from Tulloch (which he had not seen) that I found lying around in your

bedroom. Poor Walter does so feel that he is a cardboard and cottonwool director and does so like to be consulted!

'Family Failing'—I never saw it before last Friday, a lifeless production about lifeless people. 'Queer Ones' a lifeless prod: also. Not Dossie's strong point, production? A sprinkling of people on Friday night, most of them looked like friends' friends. I didnt even agree with the casting. Frolie Mulhern would have been far better than Gertie Quinn (I think that's her name) and O'Gorman (who played your cat and moon and dreaming of the bones) had been done nothing with. He needs stimulus and obviously hadnt got it. Peter Nolan and Tom Moran, old Abbey people, were half asleep too. NO, NO!

I am posting you on a novel sent you by Lady Lavery. She enclosed a letter, it came today. I smelt the novel between the unwrapping and the re-wrapping, and I dont think you need bring it home when you come. I posted to you also a letter from the B.B.C.

Now the B.B.C. is important, and you must come up in good time to dictate your piece. I think in any case that you should come up before your dash to London. I think you should come up in two or three weeks time for a week. I want to take you out to Baymount when I go to see Mr Scott about Michael (he goes there in May)

Yours G.

XIX

On 16 February WBY went up to Dublin to vote in the general election which defeated Cosgrave's government and brought in Fianna Fail under the leadership of Eamonn de Valera, thereby causing some doubts as to the future of The Abbey Theatre's subsidy and WBY's plans to establish an Irish Academy of Letters. The possible replacements for Walter Starkie as government-appointed Director were playwright T.C. Murray, soon to retire as headmaster of the Model School, Inchicore, Co Dublin, playwright and critic F.J.H. O'Donnell, and Norman Reddin, a lawyer who had been associated with the Irish Theatre (1914-1920) and who, with his brother and mother, were strong supporters of the Dublin literary scene; both O'Donnell and Reddin had in recent years debated the role of the theatre with Yeats at Dublin Literary Society meetings, while Murray was known to be very conservative in his views. In the event, the government nominee was Dr Richard Hayes, who had been jailed for his part in the 1916 Rising, was a TD in the first Dail, and although he became Film Censor in 1940 remained on the Board until his death in 1958; meanwhile WBY appointed Starkie an ordinary shareholding member of the Board. WBY had for some time been trying to persuade Lady Gregory to accept Denis Johnston as a Director of the Abbey Theatre. Former Abbey actress Sara Allgood was performing in a touring production of *The Chocolate Soldier* at the Gaiety Theatre; Lennox Robinson and designer Dorothy ('Dolly') Travers Smith had married just before leaving on the American tour.

Feb 29 1932

(No 2 Letter) P R I V A T E

My dear Willy

Starkie has just gone. He entirely agrees that the Irish Academy should be independent of Government, in fact he thinks it is the only way in which the Academy could be made a success. I know he tends to agree with everything anyone says but he spoke with real passion about it. He made various suggestions about the Abbey which I think very sound, but they must be talked about, not written.

He is evidently anxious about his position, as Abbey Director. The Gate Theatre have been spreading rumours that now Fianna Fail is in Starkie will be booted out and Murray or F.Hugh O'Donnell put in, or Norman Reddin. I do not imagine that the directors of the Abbey would stand an 'imposed' government director? Starkie asked me if I thought he ought to resign before the problem arose. I told him that I would write to you. I do very much wish that I could see you to talk over a few of these things now that the political situation is clearer. If you think that you cannot come to Dublin again before you go to London, I wonder if you could come to Galway for a night—I would make an excuse to go there . . . a friend . . . because I dont think Lady G. ought to have the burden of a visitor. I really do believe that this is the moment to start things off, and the few people I have seen since you went away all say the same thing—we are tired of politics, we want an intellectual movement politics are the death of passion and passion is the food of the intellect.

*Please do agree that either you come up, or we have an assignation in Galway! I have marked this letter PRIVATE.

Incidentally, the fact that Denis Johnston is now a director of the Gate marks him off the list as a possible director of the Abbey! The Gate, is either playing for the Abbey Audience or playing for a subsidy from the new government (this is not Starkie's gossip) They announced at the party to Sally that they were going, in future to specialise in Irish plays.

Anne was home yesterday—she celebrated her birthday—was enchanted with her mahogany chest of drawers, a present from you and me. It is a nice thing, with charming handles and nice wood. I got it on the Quays.

It is most horribly cold, north-east wind, the kitchen is the only really warm room. I envy Lennox and Dolly in Florida! Dolly writes that New Orleans is worth it all, by which I imagine that she means worth all the train journeys and horrible cities. Lennox writes very cheerfully and sends me a story of Edith Wharton's which he says I wont like but he does! They are both evidently feeling warm and pussy in sunlight.

Yours ever George.

(Among the directors of the Gate Theatre are—Longford, Denis Johnston, F.H. O'Donnell, Norman Reddin—)

XX

American monologuist Ruth Draper, who was performing at the Gaiety
Theatre, appeared at the Abbey in the Directors' special Sunday evening
series. The Peacock Theatre, designed by architect and occasional Abbey actor
Michael Scott, was built in 1927 and housed the Abbey School of Acting and
School of Ballet; it was frequently let to other groups and had been the home of
the Gate Theatre from 1928 to 1930 until they secured their own premises.
Joseph Holloway, avid theatre-goer and persistent diarist who had been the
original architect for the Abbey Theatre, appears to have forgone the Sunday
night performance, attending a Gaiety performance instead. WBY had asked
GY to arrange for Lady Gregory's doctor to send some pain-killing drugs to
Coole; until now Lady Gregory had refused all medication, fearing that she
would not remain alert. Francis Hackett, novelist, historian, and former
literary critic for *The New Republic*, was living with his wife, the Danish
novelist Signe Toksvig, in a cottage in County Wicklow.

March 2 [1932]

My dear Willy

I have just seen Perrin about the arrangements for Sunday night. Miss
Draper's manager was at the Abbey this morning to make arrangements
. . . Perrin tooted him around and showed him the Peacock and so on!
Prices of back stall and front gallery seats are being raised, postcards are
being printed to circularise. Free list entirely suspended, I told Perrin that
the Abbey Directors (and wives) would pay for their seats so that there
should be no question about free lists . . . my joy that Holloway will have
to pay!

I wrote to Slattery again this morning—I wrote the day after you left
but got no answer. I think he will answer the letter I wrote him this
morning, it was extremely tactful . . . he would perhaps send a
prescription himself . . .

Starkie has buzzed off to England, will be back on Thursday, returns to
England on Saturday . . .

Miss Draper lunches at 1.30 on Sunday and asked me if I would mind
asking Francis Hackett to lunch as she had meant to go to Wicklow to see
him on Sunday until she got our invitation. So I wrote to him.

I sent on your letter to Anne, crossing out the 'almost' and commenting
in a letter of my own the fact that you had dated your letter March 8 . . .
I told her that you had asked to me to read it to 'see if it was legible', and
that I hoped she would be as amused as I was to see that you lived always
a week or two behind time or in advance of time. (She wont mind the date
because she will remember that you came to Dublin a week too early
once!)

Here is what Michael's present headmistress says about him: 'I never
knew so nice a little boy, he is so solemn and yet merry, so innocent, but
he's clever'. Its like an epitaph on an eighteenth century tomb.

I want you to stay here until Tuesday, because I want you to see
Starkie. I have excellent reasons for wanting you to see Starkie, which I
will tell you when I see you on Saturday. I shall of course meet you at the
station.

Yours ever affly

Dobbs.

XXI

WBY was preparing *Words for Music Perhaps and other Poems* for his sister
'Lolly' Yeats at the Cuala Press; Dr Slattery had been asked to send more
medication to Lady Gregory; a speech to the Irish Literary Society in London
on 3 April prevented WBY from accepting the date suggested for his BBC
broadcast. Lady Longford's comedy, *Queens and Emperors*, received its first
performance at the Gate Theatre on 15 March; C.P. 'Con' Curran was a
lecturer at St Enda's School, and as 'Honor Lavelle', his wife had acted with
the Abbey before joining the Theatre of Ireland. Mrs Cooper may be the
widow of Major Brian Cooper, whose *Let the Credit Go*, the first detective play
at the Abbey, had been performed in September 1930. 'My Friend's Book',
WBY's article on AE's *Song and its Fountains*, appeared in *The Spectator* on 9
April.

March 19 [1932]

My dear Willy

Many thanks for the registered envelope with poems . . . I will type the
MSS part—Lolly isnt ready yet, she had a big order for prints from
Boston which have kept the press busy.

I hope you got the two boxes of tablets? What a nuisance about the
BBC. I do hope they can fit you in later. By the way, you have got it
firmly in your head that April 3 is a SUNDAY?

I went last night to The Gate to see Christine Longford's play. I had to
stay to the end because the Longfords were sitting rather close and the
theatre was not full enough to cover departure! The Currans skeddaddled
after the end of the second act, but they were sitting further back . . .

Tomorrow Anne is bringing four children from her school (Mrs
Cooper's niece among them) for a picnic and home for tea. A long
day—we start at 11 and they leave at 5.30! Anne would I think have liked
to have the full day which is 10.30 to 7.30, but I told her firmly that it
was too long . . . I hope to heaven it will be fine.

I asked you in a letter if I was to send the Russell article direct to the
Spectator, and as you didnt reply I have done so, asking them to send the
proof direct to you at Coole.

Yours ever

George.

XXII

WBY's programme, 'Poems about Women', was broadcast on the BBC on the evening of 10 April; his letters home reported on meetings with Bernard Shaw who agreed to co-sign the invitations and announcement concerning the Irish Academy of Letters, with T. Sturge Moore and Shri Purohit Swami over the latter's *An Indian Monk*, and most intriguing of all, with the High Commissioner over the Irish government's quarrel with England concerning the Oath of Allegiance. Lennox and Dolly Robinson had returned from the United States by mid-March. Dr John Larchet, composer and Professor of Music at University College Dublin, was Director of Music at the Abbey Theatre from 1907 until 1934. Jack Yeats regularly exhibited at the Hibernian Academy spring show.

April 12 [1932]

My dear Willy

Your news is very interesting! Dolly and I listened to your broadcast—the machine was working badly and your voice was unrecognisable, so I couldnt judge of it at all. I thought it was too slow, so very much slower than you lecture or read. We went on to the Abbey for the ballet etc. Just missed Dreaming of the Bones, but I was told that it went very much better than the last time. Larchet had altered the music for songs a little. There was a good house, not packed, but good. Ballet <u>very</u> much better than last time.

No news. I went to the opening of the Hibernian Academy yesterday—the usual crowd, and four lovely Jack pictures, two especially so.

Anne is beginning to walk about but not much yet. The toe, however, doesnt hurt her, so she can manage to amuse herself quite a lot.

This is a terribly dull letter, cant help it!

Yours ever
George.

Lady Gregory died on 22 May 1932, while WBY was in Dublin briefly on business, and the long connection with Coole was ended.

Joyce as Letter Writer

Richard Ellmann

RTE, Features Radio. Talk broadcast 28 April 1984.

Letter writing imposes its small ceremonies even upon those who disdain the medium. An audience of one requires confrontation too, and even a perfunctory message discloses a little, with what candour, modesty, or self-esteem its writer ranks himself in the world. Some accompanying hint of his appraisal of that world is bound to appear in the way he asserts or beseeches a tie with his correspondent, the degree of familiarity he takes for granted, the extent to which he solicits action or approbation, the alacrity and tenacity with which he joins issue. He may present himself in various guises: as machine, badger, deer, spider, bird. Whatever his mode, if he is a practising writer, his assembling of words can never be totally negligent. Once enslaved by language, forever enslaved.

James Joyce did not regard the letter, or its brazen sister, the postcard, as a literary form of any consequence. But almost every day he burdened postmen in different parts of his hemisphere with his sedulous correspondence. At letter's length he felt comfortable, and wrote sparely and to the point. His letters adopt a stance which at first may appear the reverse of that in his books. His creative works are humorous, lyrical, daring. These qualities appear from time to time in his correspondence, but his prevailing tenor is wry, terse, pressed-down. 'I am in double-trouble, mental and material', he writes, and says in another letter, 'My spiritual bark is on the rocks'. In both of these the statement has a sweep and finality which, paradoxically, imply that all may not be lost. His summaries of his condition are sometimes more epigrammatic: 'My mouth is full of decayed teeth, and my soul of decayed ambitions.' And sometimes he relents a little to joke, 'Well, as Mr Pater beautifully says, I have reached the low-water mark in Xmases this year time'. He is fond of deflating his life into a vista of ludicrous confusion. As Joyce writes later of Shem, 'Oh, the lowness of him was beneath all up to that sunk to'. In an early letter he wrote that he could not enter society except as a vagabond, and there is perhaps always a submerged pleasure in his not being an upstanding British subject.

The sense of contradiction between his works and his letters is illusory. The attitude of resignation is not so far removed from that of confidence as it first appears. It contains, in fact, a pre-emptory note: underneath themes which are favourites of Joyce from beginning to end, the meticulous exposition of his penury, his physical weakness, or his discouragement, there is the conviction that he expresses rarely because he holds it so unshakeably, that his needs are trivial when weighed with his desserts. The letters simultaneously plead and berate. He tells his brother, 'Do not delay so long executing my requests, as I waste a lot of ink'. He demands patronage rather than charity. Joyce's conviction of merit was justified in the event, yet he was imbued with it long before there were publications or even manuscripts to confirm it. Confidence in his powers may be said to have antedated their manifestation. Because of this confidence he has little patience with those who fail to pay tribute to his talent, and is likely to shift suddenly from supplicant to renunciant. He is regularly on the verge of scorning the help he requires. Though his gestures of renunciation, and threats of gestures, might argue that Joyce was, as he called Ibsen, 'an ego-ark', they must somehow be reconciled with his other qualities.

Joyce was gregarious, filial, fraternal, uxorious, paternal, in varying degrees, and surrounded himself with relatives and friends. His letters to his son, Giorgio, and his daughter, Lucia, demonstrate his talent, when they were in the dumps, for finding miseries of his own equivalent to theirs, with which he proposed to cheer them up. He needed to return from hours of isolation, it would seem, and to feel that a few people were in rapport with him.

Joyce's lifelong reluctance to comment publicly on his work gives unusual value to his letters as evocations of his mental scenery. They do not, however, offer more than fragments of self-analysis, and we must relate them ourselves. Certain expressions appear often enough to claim special notice. Among them the word 'artist' had origins in his early life. If A Portrait of the Artist may be said to plead for anything, it is for the continuity of the artistic temperament almost from infancy. He apparently first articulated this vocation soon after he passed from childhood to adolescence. The words 'artist' and 'puberty' had in fact a relation that is several times hinted at in his letters. As early as the age of fourteen, Joyce said, he began to go to brothels, initially with a strong sense of guilt. The Church urged him to master these impulses, but he found himself unable, and at heart unwilling to do so. At confession he could find comfort and pardon, but not sanction. He was unwilling to give up either the spiritual idealism which has sustained him as a child or the erotic drive which was agitating his adolescence. If debauchery was a part of his character, and he sometimes said it was, then it must be justified. The word 'artist', which in the late nineteenth century had been invested with a secular awe, offered a profession which would protect all his soul, instead of only its idealistic side, and might yet give it a profane sanctity. He thought of it as denoting something solid, unitary, and radiant, compounding into a new purity the errant flesh and the moral nature.

In early youth, Joyce began to formulate the relation of art and the spiritual self into an aesthetic, as his letters testify. This aesthetic would vindicate him by establishing the primacy of the poet over the priest through a system rival to that of theology. The artist was to be shown as devoted to integrating human experience on a level higher than the priest's, and without external or supernatural authority to make his work easier. This conscious definition of the principles of his art finds an accompaniment in his letters in Joyce's reiterated insistence that his own behaviour has been defensible, and even praiseworthy. He tells his brother that his struggle with conventions 'was not entered into by me so much as a protest against these conventions, as with the intention of living in conformity with my moral nature'. He granted contemptuously, 'There are some people in Ireland who would call my moral nature oblique, people who think that the whole duty of Man consists of paying one's debts'. He is not less but more moral than other people. Although Joyce does not bother to mention his moral nature often, his awareness of it lies behind most of his letters. It enables him to assert to Grant Richards, '*Dubliners* is a chapter of the moral history of my country'. It underlies his criticism of other writers, such as Thomas Hardy. He writes his brother in December 1906, to complain of a book of Hardy's stories called *Life's Little Ironies*, and says:

One story is about a lawyer on the circuit, who seduces a servant, then receives letters from her so beautifully written that he decides to marry her. The letters are actually written by the servant's mistress, who is in love with the lawyer. After the marriage, servant is accompanied to London by mistress. Husband says fondly, 'Now dear J.K.S., will you write a little note to my sister, dear A.B.X., and send her a piece of the wedding cake? One of those nice little letters you know so well how to write, Love'. Exit of servant-wife. She goes out and sits at a table somewhere and I suppose writes something like this: 'Dear Ms X, I enclose a piece of the wedding cake'. Enter husband-lawyer, genial. Genially he says, 'Well, Love, how have you written?' And then the whole discovery is found out. Servant-wife blows her nose in the letter, and lawyer confronts the mistress. She confesses. Then they talk a page or so of copybook talk, as distinguished from servant's ditto. She weeps, but he is stern. Is this as near as Thomas Hardy can get to life, I wonder? Oh, my poor fledglings! Poor Corley! Poor Ignatius Gallaher! What is wrong with these English writers is that they always keep beating about the bush.

In discountenancing Hardy, Joyce was attacking not only a kind of fiction, but a way of seeing, or failing to see. Hardy appeared to him to lack the directness which he had taught himself by accepting nothing because it had been accepted before. As a result, the characterisation in Hardy's stories was a false one based upon conventional ideas of class. Joyce, living with a servant girl himself, was particularly entitled to detect the improbability here. He rejected, as well, the whole idiom as 'copybook talk'. For Joyce, Hardy had lacked the courage to break through, and so was already dated, the moral fault breeding a literary one.

Joyce did conceive of himself as a hero, but thought it advisable not to say so explicitly. He thought of himself also as in some ways a martyr, but as usual his way of saying so is by seeming to repudiate the idea. Referring to this Christ-like resemblance, he wrote his brother, 'I must get rid of some of those Jewish bowels I have in me yet'. And in another letter he said, 'I am not likely to die of bashfulness, but neither am I prepared to be crucified to attest the perfection of my art.' The figure pleased him, and a year later he remarked once more, 'I have written quite enough, and before I do any more in that line I must see some reason why. I am not a literary Jesus Christ'. But three disavowals of the crown are less convincing than one. Whatever he might say in the cold mutton of letters, Joyce was fascinated by the Christ-like analogies of the artist, and developed them fully in *A Portrait of the Artist*.

A powerful sacrificial feeling sustained him as he fought for a literary foothold around southern Europe, staving off mosquitos in Pola, instilling an alien tongue in Triestines, cashing cheques for other people in Rome. But he undercut it with modesty by jokingly, or grimly, calling attention to his defects and failures. This mixture permeates his letters, and is somewhat explained by them. Joyce often appeared to be cold and aloof, but in his own view these qualities were less fundamental than others. He thought of himself most fondly as fragile and vulnerable. Once this part of his self-portrait becomes visible, other elements take shape around it. The enigma of a manner, which he speaks of in the first draft of *A Portrait* as consciously fabricating, is seen as an attempt at self-protection: 'Can you not see the simplicity which is at the back of all my disguises? We all wear masks', he writes to Nora Barnacle. And he is pleased, at least temporarily, when she pierces his magnificent poses, and recognises him to be an imposter.

Joyce liked to think of himself as weak, and of others as stronger than he. The letters to Nora Barnacle-Joyce, which make this position plain, are psychologically the most important that he wrote. They move gradually towards self-surrender, as if it were a kind of *Ultima Thule*. At first their tone is jaunty, with some of that Don Juanism that he attributed to the young Shakespeare. But within a month of the beginning of their courtship, the tone is solemnised. She must become his mistress, to be sure, but he seems more occupied with something else, as she becomes his fellow conspirator against the established order. 'My mind rejects the whole present social order and Christianity, home, the recognised virtues, classes of life, and religious doctrines', he writes to her in August 1904. His intransigence to the world is related to his submission to her. Their elopement must not be sportive, but agonised, a sign and portent of his future work. He was aware that to his father, and to many of his friends, the relationship with Nora Barnacle was a misalliance, though he pretended to be impervious to their criticism. 'Their least word', he told her, 'tumbles my heart about like a bird in a storm.' Yet like Heine, as he says, and like others he does not trouble to name, he had the courage to see that the world was wrong about this as about other things. By virtue of being poor and in love with him, Nora became the banned sweetheart of a banned artist: 'It seemed to me that I was fighting a battle with every religious and social force in Ireland for you, and that I had nothing to rely on but myself.' Chambermaid and prodigal son might make a match of it; obliquity was the state they might share like pleasures of the bed.

Joyce's affection for Nora Barnacle developed rapidly, though she complained it lagged behind her own. He was already unconsciously altering his role in the affair from active to passive. 'Allow me, dearest Nora', he wrote her, 'to tell you how much I desire that you should share any happiness that may be mine, and to assure you of my great respect for that love of yours which it is my wish to deserve and to answer.' The word 'love' was one that mustered up all his doubts, doubts of his own sincerity, doubts of the emotion itself. 'To talk of spiritual love', he informs Stanislaus, 'was lying drivel', though in a few years he used the phrase without irony. But as he said, he was deeply impressed by the unqualified feeling Nora Barnacle had for him, and the fact she expressed it without the coyness he had come to expect in girls of his age. 'I never could speak to the girls I used to meet at houses', he wrote her later. 'Their false manners checked me at once.'

Stephen Dedalus represents Shakespeare as equally shy. If Nora was untutored she was equally unspoiled, a simple, honourable soul, and one incapable of any of the deceits which passed for current morality. It was very important for him, knowing with what intricate devices he met most people, to have in her someone he could trust. His reserve, his sense of watching his own dignity, are involved in almost all his other relationships. With Harriet Weaver, his patron, for example, he seems to want not only to act politely towards her, but to see himself as meeting the English Protestant middle-class with adequate decorum. A certain gentleness comes through regardless, but almost against his will. With Nora there was the possibility available to him nowhere else of complete self-revelation, a great relief to a suspicious man. He came to feel that she was more than a wife or mistress; she must triple as a symbol of Ireland, and a more genuine one than Yeats's Maud Gonne. In her he saw, as he said, 'the beauty and the doom of the race of which I am a child', and he asked her, 'Oh, take me into your soul of souls, and then I will become indeed the poet of my race'.

This yielding of himself was not achieved without difficulty. Joyce had to pass through stages of amusement, perplexity, boredom, and even distrust. The last was, of course, the most serious. In 1909, on his first trip back to Dublin, he was led mistakenly to believe that Nora had been faithless to him during a period which he held sacred, the early months of their love. In a few days he was undeceived, and felt guilty for having so misjudged her. His first letters were filled with remorse: 'What a worthless fellow I am'. But gradually he tried to turn the incident to advantage by ushering her into a greater intimacy. His letters became a turbulent mixture of erotic imagery and apologies for it, the apologies being accompanied by equally extreme flights of adoration. His relationship with her had to counter-balance all his rifts with other people. Had they become partners in spiritual love, they must now share an onanistic complicity, agitating each other to sexual climax by means of their letters. In this way Joyce renewed the conspiritorial and passionate under-standing that they had had when they first left Ireland together. The atmos-phere is not one of Catholic guilt, but it is certainly not one of pagan insouciance either. He feels compelled to set images of purity against images of impurity. He dwells upon the association of the sexual and excretory organs, then fears she will consider him corrupt, although he has found learned sanction in Spinoza. Yet he also wants corruption to be a part of their love as well as incorruption. 'Are you too, then, like me', he asks hopefully, 'one moment high as the stars, the next lower than the lowest wretches?' They must share in shame, shamelessness, and unashamedness. Yet the letters rebuke obvious labels by their ulterior purpose; besides the immediate physical goal, Joyce wishes to anatomise and reconstitute and crystalize the emotion of love.

He goes further still, like Richard Rowan in *Exiles*: he wishes to possess his wife's soul, and have her possess his in utter nakedness, to know someone else beyond love and hate, beyond vanity and remorse, beyond human possibility almost, is his extravagant desire.

The hints and declarations in these letters enable us to see Joyce a little as he saw himself. While he considered that rebellion had been for him the beginning of wisdom, a kind of birth of consciousness, he did not regard himself primarily as a rebel. His dominant image of himself was one of delicacy and fragility, of perpetual ill-health and ill-luck, of a tenor among basses. It led him to imagine himself as like a deer or a bird or a woman, or like a Gandhian Christ. He reacted against varieties of power by juxtaposing the strong with the weak, Boylan with Bloom, or the Ondt with the Gracehoper. Then his wit challenged the powerful masculine energies until they had lost their strength. He wished to protect the lyrical centre of his work by acknowledging with laughter all the absurdities of human conduct through which it must draw its breath. He counters a possible contempt for his almost effeminate delicacy by examining in the fullest and liveliest way its inescapably comic embodiment. Where other writers, like Wells, appear always to be thrusting, Joyce characterized himself more nearly by the parry. Each of his works concludes in a lyrical assertion which is made possible by the undermining of maleness by comedy, as if brute force had to be overcome by subtler devices. In *Finnegans Wake* the Crimean War is reduced to a scatalogical joke, the Battle of Waterloo to an extravaganza in a waxworks museum, and the World War to a prize fight. In *Ulysses* the Cyclops is defeated; in *A Portrait* Ireland is left. Joyce's distaste for war, crime, and brutality relate to this preference for all that is not for the bully. His work is not conceived as a blow in the face but, these letters help us to perceive, as a matrical envelopment. But this appraisal of Joyce which his letters sponsor is not entirely satisfactory; his disclaimers of masculinity, his assumption of feminine weakness, were secondary manifestations. After all, strong men have hidden themselves among women before.

His succession of mewing exhortations always sprang from initial decisions inflexibly pursued. He cared for his daughter with a solicitude that could be called feminine, but his delicate coaxing and joking were directed to twist her mind back to sanity like a resistent piece of iron. Though he lived in discouragement like a bad climate, and sporadically thought of not finishing his books, he needle-and-threaded each one to its conclusion. As if adjusting himself to his pliant, jointless body, which was basically tough and wiry, he imagined himself in the state of being malleable and passive, and commenced to live there, like a second residence.

The mixture of such qualities as pride and plaintiveness, the flashes of candour amidst stretches of tortuous reticence, or confessions that are off the point, lent his spare self-portraiture in these letters an interest quite different from that to be found in the shaped nuances of Henry James, or the open-collared eloquence of D.H. Lawrence. An urge to the immoderate is always there, but at various distances from the surface. Read in this light, these letters, the best of them, are among the most interesting, and insinuating, ever written.

Joyce and Mythology

Terry Eagleton

The distinction between myth and history is sometimes thought to correspond roughly to one between pre-industrial and industrial society, or country and city. It seems plausible to assume some kind of relation between the closed, cyclical structures of mythological thought and the traditionalist, repetitive, season-based life and labour of pre-industrial society. Conversely, there would seem a tempting analogy between the linear, evolutionary, open-ended nature of the 'historical' and the typical life-rhythms of urban industrialism, where what matters is dynamic development rather than cyclical recurrence, future-oriented action rather than the ritual invocation of sacred origins. With the gradual emergence of urban civilisation, along with the increasing penetration of industrial capitalist techniques into agrarian society itself, the static world of myth is invaded by a restless narrativity which (as in the fiction of Defoe) knows no 'natural' closure, could carry on endlessly if it wished, and treats each 'accumulation' of narrative as the opportunity for yet more accumulation in the manner of the canny entrepreneurs who are often enough its thematic content.

One has only to compare the work of Yeats and Joyce to see how beautifully this contrast doesn't work. For both are of course deeply mythological writers, despite the fact that the former inhabits a traditionalist aristocratic countryside and the latter's milieu is intensively urban and petty-bourgeois. Does the shared mythologising of the two then lie somehow in their Irishness? It has certainly been claimed that the so-called 'Irish imagination' broods typically upon great cyclical recurrences and eternal returns, eliding sequential time for an eternal now in which all battles are the same battle, all conquerors the same conqueror, all acts of rebellion expressions of an unbroken continuity of resistance. If colonialism tends to deprive those it subjugates not only of their land, language and culture but of their very history—if the history of an oppressed people dwindles to a reflex of the history of their rulers—then it is arguable that the mythological imagination of Ireland, if one can talk in such terms, is itself a markedly historical phenomenon. A people robbed of their sense of agency and autonomy, unable to decipher the social institutions around them as expressions of their own life-practice, may tend quite reasonably to read their collective experience through the deterministic optic of mythology, with its sense of human life as shaped by the mighty forces of some process quite hidden to consciousness. Myth is in this sense less some regrettable primitive irrationalism than a kind of historical truth. The Belfast republican song 'The men behind the wire', which speaks of Margaret Thatcher as Oliver Cromwell, is not simply a shoddy historical inaccuracy. And it is surely true that Yeats's celebrated gyres have been far too little examined by literary critics (many of them hailing from the colonialist or post-colonialist heartland) in the context of the tragic course of Irish political history.

Even so, crypto-Jungian talk of racial imaginations is enough to make any good materialist nervous; and I want therefore in this essay to suggest some rather more historical reasons for the role of mythology in Joyce, though still doubtless too generalised and speculative for a conventional empiricist criticism. Joyce shares the mythologising habit of mind, of course, not only with his pseudo-aristocratic compatriot but with artistic modernism in general, which evinces a remarkable re-emergence of myth all the way from Stravinsky to T.S. Eliot. Suppressed by the varieties of Victorian rationalism and positivism during the era of classical or liberal capitalism, myth makes its dramatic re-entry into modern European culture, with Nietzsche as its lonely heroic precursor, on the threshold of that capitalism's gradual mutation into 'higher' corporate and monopoly forms in the early decades of the twentieth century. If a relatively uncoordinated *lassez-faire* capitalism is now moving into more rationalised, systemic modes, then there is something peculiarly apposite about the rebirth of myth—itself, as we have learnt from Lévi-Strauss, a highly organised 'rational' system—as a central imaginative means of coming to terms with this new kind of social experience. Such mythical thought, for one thing, belongs with a radical rethinking of the whole category of the autonomous human subject—a rethinking which involves Ferdinand de Saussure as much as Wyndham Lewis, Freud and Martin Heidegger as much as D.H. Lawrence and Virginia Woolf. For it is really no longer possible to pretend, given the transition from market to monopoly capitalism, that the old strenuously individualist ego, the self-determining humanist subject of classical liberal thought, is any longer an adequate model for the subject's phenomenological experience of itself under these changed social conditions. The modern subject, like the mythical one, is much less some sharply individuated source of its own actions and master of its own destiny than a kind of obedient function of a broader controlling structure, which now appears more and more to do its thinking and acting for it. It is no accident that so-called 'structuralism' has its roots in the period of modernism and monopoly capital—that this period witnesses a turning away on all sides from the classical 'philosophy of the subject' of Kant, Hegel and the early Marx, troubledly conscious as it is of the human subject as constituted to its roots by forces and systems not only beyond its individual dominance but utterly opaque to its routine consciousness. Whether one names such implacable forces Language or Being, Capital or the Unconscious, Tradition or the *élan vital*, Archetypes or the Destiny of the West, their effect is to open a well-nigh unspannable gulf between the waking life of the old befeathered ego and the real determinants of its identity, which are always covert and inscrutable. And if the subject is accordingly fractured and dismantled, then the objective world which it confronts is now quite impossible to interpret as its own spontaneous self-expression. What stands over against this anguished, divided subject is an autonomously self-regulating world which appears on the one hand wholly rationalised, eminently logical in its minutest operations, but blankly disconnected from and indifferent to the rational projects of individuals themselves. This immense, enclosed, self-determining artefact of a world, resistant as it is to human purpose, then rapidly takes on all the appearances of a 'second nature', erasing its own source in human action to seem as self-evidently 'given' and immovably solid as those rocks, rivers and trees which are the very stuff of mythology.

If mythology is a matter of cyclical recurrence, then the recurrence which matters most in the world of monopoly capitalism is the eternal return of the commodity. Capitalism indeed has a history; but the dynamic of that history, as Marx ironically noted, is the perpetual recreation of its own 'eternal' structure. Each act of commodity exchange is at once unique, differential, and a mere replaying of the same old story, as the true differences of 'use value' are submerged in that abstract logic of identity and equivalence which is 'exchange value'. The epitome of the commodity, as Walter Benjamin recognised in his great study of Baudelaire,[1] is the cult of fashion, in which the familiar returns with a slight variation, the very old and the very new are caught up together in a curious logic of identity-within-difference. The paradox of modernism, then, is that its exhilarated sense of new historical and technological possibilities (Futurism, Constructivism, Surrealism) finds itself constantly taken up into a static, quasi-mythological world in which all dynamic process seems frozen and arrested. One result of this is a new form of interplay between chance and necessity. From one viewpoint, every apparently contingent bit of experience is now secretly, remorselessly controlled by some underlying text or structure (the Homeric text, in the case of *Ulysses*), of which it seems no more than the momentary manipulated product. Reality is coded to its very roots, as the mere ephemeral working out of some deeper logic invisible to the naked eye, and randomness accordingly banished. Yet these determining 'deep structures' are now so thoroughly abstract and formalistic that they seem, contradictorily, to stand at an immense distance from the realm of sensuous immediacy, superbly autonomous of the chance combinations of matter they throw up. This is surely the case with *Finnegans Wake*, a text which appears to offer a minimum of mediation between its local, idiosyncratic units of signification and the mighty Viconian cycles which generate and enclose them. It is not difficult to perceive a similar dislocation of abstract structure and perversely idiosyncratic unit in Saussure's celebrated distinction between *langue*—the formal, universal categories of language itself—and the apparently random, unformalisable nature of ordinary speech or *parole*.

In a strange reversal or regression of historical time, capitalism's 'higher' stages would seem to return it as a system to the pre-industrial world it has left behind—a closed, cyclical, deterministic, naturalised sphere of which myth is one appropriate reflection. Indeed such a conjuncture of the most primitive and most sophisticated is a stock formula of modernism, whether in the shape of Eliot's ideal poet, the role of 'archaic' materials in art and psychoanalysis, or the uncanny double-process by which Baudelaire in Benjamin's reading of him continually finds himself geologically excavating the old in his restless hunt for the new. This 'neverchanging everchanging' world as *Ulysses* has it, is one in which space seems at once fragmentary and homogeneous; and this, once more, is the appropriate space of the commodity, whose 'novelty' is the outcome of a massive levelling and equalizing of all things to a common, recurrent identity. The allegorical signifier, Benjamin remarks, returns in the modern epoch as the commodity; and we might say that it is as the mythological signifier that it returns in the work of James Joyce.

In such conditions, however, mythology becomes not only an appropriate way of experiencing the world, but a convenient way of trying to make sense of it. For Walter Benjamin, allegory arises when immanent meaning seems to have been struck from social reality, and the allegorist is thus set free to pick among the symbolic rubble and create new, arbitrary, shocking correspondences or 'constellations' of his own from these now blank and exhausted bits of a once meaningful totality.[2] The steady loss of immanent meaning clears the way for new, marvellously subtle totalisations; but these will always be dogged by a sense of their own gratuitousness, since as Benjamin comments the allegorical signifier can be made to mean absolutely anything at all. Something of this kind is surely at work in modernist mythologising, which in a world now depleted of significance can furnish just those ordering, totalising, reductive schemas necessary to elicit unity out of chaos. If mythology must here take over something of the traditional role of historical understanding and explanation, it is because that historical form of thought is now itself part of the symbolic rubble, as the classical concepts of 'progress', 'evolution', 'total history' and the rest come to look increasingly shabby and discredited in the aftermath of imperialist world war. Such diachronic models, as Lévi-Strauss will later claim in his celebrated contention with Jean-Paul Sartre, are themselves no more than modern myths, and must now yield ground to a more stabilising, sychronic form of understanding.[3] Yet if myth for T.S. Eliot elicits some *given* pattern in reality, one incomparably deeper than the mere comings-and-goings of historical events, this is precisely not the case for Lévi-Strauss or for a modernist like Joyce, whose texts are comically aware of the essential arbitrariness of the allegorical signifier, and who knows that a day in Dublin must be *made* to mean the wanderings of Odysseus, wrenched into it by hermeneutical violence rather than rest on the guarantee of some immanent set of correspondences.

If 'form' and 'content' have come alarmingly adrift from one another in the society of the commodity, then this, as Marx saw, is a contradiction internal to the commodity form itself, resolutely indifferent to the concrete content of its own 'use value' as it is. What gets eternally reproduced in capitalist society is the abstract form of commodity exchange itself, which will seize upon any old content in the manner of *Ulysses*'s cavalier appropriation of the Homeric narrative. The early decades of the twentieth century witness a search for ever more abstract, highly formalised models of social explanation, from structural linguistics and psychoanalysis to Wittgenstein's *Tractatus* and certain currents of anthropology; but these are in tension with an anxious turning back to 'the things themselves', whether in Husserlian phenomenology or in that pursuit of the 'lived' and particularized which sweeps from German *Lebensphilosophie* to re-emerge somewhere in the doctrines of *Scrutiny*. Perhaps, then, mythology can provide the missing mediations between the over-formalised on the one hand the excessively individuated on the other—between that which threatens to evade language in its abstract universalism, and that which offers to slip through the net of discourse in its very ineffable particularity. Myth, to this extent, would then figure as the return of the old Romantic symbolic systems, a reinvention of those Hegelian 'concrete universals' in which every sensuous particular is secretly inscribed by a universal law, and any place, time or identity pregnant with the burden of the cosmic whole. If this can be achieved, then a history in crisis might once more be rendered stable and meaningful, reconstructed as a set of hierarchical levels and correspondences.

In this light, a novel like *Ulysses*, in which any apparently random particular opens out microcosmically into some portentous universal, might be said to be standard Hegelian stuff. Yet to say no more than this would surely be to overlook the enormous irony with which all of this is actually accomplished— the way in which this remorseless totalizing gestures to its own flagrant artifice in its very pokerfaced exhaustiveness. The sweated Flaubertian labour necessary to bring off such a *tour de force* points in effect to the fictive or impossible nature of this whole enterprise, and contains, indeed, the seeds of its own dissolution. The paradox is that if a world of symbolic correspondences is to be constructed, some kind of mechanism or switch-gear will be necessary whereby any one element of the world can become a signifier of another, and a harmonious, self-sealing unity thus created. Yet there is clearly no natural stopping place to this play of allegorical signification, this endless metamorphosis whereby anything can be magically converted into anything else. The symbolic system, in short, contains the forces of its own deconstruction— which is to say, in a different idiom, that it operates very much by the logic of that commodity form which is responsible in part for the chaotic fragmentation it hopes to transcend. It is the commodity form above all which ceaselessly transforms any one quality, object or identity into any other, at once effecting a spuriously stable identity between them *and* generating an unstable, open-ended flux which outruns all such imposed symmetry. If the experience of a day in Dublin can be rendered 'meaningful' by being placed in allegorical correspondence to a classical text, could not the same be done equally, indifferently, for a day in Barnsley or the Bronx? The textual strategies which lend an unwonted centrality to a particular time and place, ridding it of its randomness and contingency, do so only to return the whole of that contingency to it—for these strategies are abstract, formalized and universal enough to render all specific realities idly interchangeable. In this sense the compliment which Joyce pays to Ireland, in inscribing it so triumphantly on the international map, is of a distinctly backhanded sort. In order to 'privilege' and intensify the experience of a particular time and place, you can no longer rely on any structure which is always elsewhere. But to do this involves assuming a certain levelling or equivalence between the two realms, and this is itself enough to rob both of them of their uniqueness. The project, in short, is self-defeating and self-deconstructive, and the irony of *Ulysses* is the signifier of this truth. What appears to be 'symbolism' is in fact 'allegory'; the allegorical signifier, which is always arbitrary and polyvalent, merely *disguises* itself as immanent symbolic meaning, but not quite thoroughly enough for us to fall for it.

Ulysses is thus among other things a satire on older, now discredited modes of sense-making, turning the straight-faced pedantry of its own modes of signification against themselves. And the novel is precisely at its most radical and scandalous in this calculated assault on the bourgeois myth of immanent meaning, on which a whole élitist, stabilized bourgeois culture depends.[4] But the greatest irony of all is that, in order to pulverise this myth, *Ulysses* (as, in its own way, the *Wake*) turns the forms of bourgeois *economy* against the patterns of bourgeois *culture*. If the later holds to hierarchy, distinctiveness, privilege, individual difference, the former casually undermines all this in that great confounding, commingling and 'indifferencing' of all particular identities which is the movement of exchange value. *Ulysses* thus 'progresses by its bad side', as Marx commented of history itself—it being part of the emancipatory nature of capitalism for Marx to transgress all frontiers, dismantle all jealously demarcated 'sacred' spaces, travesty all holiness and melt all solidity into air. What Walter Benjamin calls 'mechanical reproduction' has just the same ambivalence—on the one hand the very dynamic of capitalist technology itself, but on the other hand a revolutionary opportunity to tear objects away from their sacred origins, 'refunctioning' them (as Brecht would have said) for new productive uses.[5] Mechanical production is for Benjamin the enemy of 'auratic' art, which intimidates by its serene classical distance, its aura of sacred origins; and *Ulysses* is the type of all anti-auratic texts, profaning, travestying and refunctioning the 'sacred' scripture of a Homer, breaking down distinctions between past and present, high and low, authenticity and derivitiveness with all of the demotic vulgarity of the commodity itself. Franco Moretti has pointed out how ruthlessly *Ulysses* 'commodifies' discourse itself, reducing the whole bourgeois ideology of 'unique style' to a ceaseless circulation of 'packaged' codes and idioms without metalinguistic privilege, a polyphony of scrupulously faked verbal formalisations implacably hostile to the 'personal voice' of literary bourgeois Man.[6] But this extreme reification of language is then exactly what licenses Joyce's 'Bakhtinian' radicalism, his dialogical, carnivalesque impacting of one idiom on another with scant regard for the 'transcendental signifier' whose role would be somehow to unify and homogenize this Rabelaisian babble of tongues. The true Circe is both commodity and allegorical signifier, 'bad' and 'good' sides of history together—just as in the *Wake* a profoundly political subversion of fixed meaning comes about through a polymorphous signifier which must always level and equalise significances in order to permutate them in scandalous new ways. The mechanism of exchange is here the pun or multiple sign itself, within whose inner space, as with the commodity form, the most strikingly disparate meanings can indifferently combine.

It might be easier in the light of this ambivalence to understand why *Ulysses* should have been received at once as sterile, petrified waste land and exuberant affirmation. For this is simply another way of talking about the 'bad' and 'good' sides of commodification, focusing either on the degrading, levelling, emptying operations of the commodity form or on the riotous possibilities which it thereby liberates. If *Ulysses* is a deeply unsettling text for an orthodox culture which has nevertheless done a good job in recuperating it, it is in part because it neither simply disowns or espouses the logic of orthodox society, but rather inserts itself craftily into a fissure or contradiction which runs through the very heart of that social order. The contradiction is one between the realm of *meaning*—the symbolic order in which rigorous discrimination is the order of the day—and the realm of economic reproduction, which that symbolic order exists to legitimate but which threatens in its very routine processes to confound all unique identity. *Ulysses* marks the historic point at which capital begins to penetrate into the spheres of culture and ideology themselves, reorganising these sacrosanct territories in accordance with a new and alien logic. To put the matter in classical Marxist terms: *Ulysses* and (even more outrageously) the *Wake* lift a protean dissolution of all reality from the 'base' into the 'superstructure', thus passing the great circuit of desire which is capitalist productivity through the realms of language, meaning and value, and consequently eroding the classical distinction between bourgeois 'civil society' (the privatised terrain of appetite, possessiveness and economic production) and bourgeois 'culture', the high-minded, harmonious stability of which is supposed precisely to mask and mystify the former set of practices.

If anywhere is everywhere, then you can scribble away in Trieste without ever having left Dublin. Modernism, as Raymond Williams has argued, is among other things a running battle between a new form of rootless, for-malized, cosmopolitan consciousness and the older, more parochial national formations from which this new consciousness has defiantly broken loose.[6] The vibrant modernist international centres of Paris, Berlin, London and New York are the cultural nodes of a now thoroughly global capitalism, which is in the process of leaving behind, and reorganizing from a distance, the national enclaves in which capitalist production earlier flourished. Ireland or Britain will come to figure as no more than random regional instances of an abstract, autonomous international capitalist network, whose operations traverse par-ticular cultures as indifferently as 'deep structures' cut across distinct literary texts, languages or individual egos. The deracinated condition of the moder-nist exiles and emigrés is one of the real material conditions for the emergence of a newly formalizing, systematizing thought, one which having spurned the ambiguous comforts of a motherland can now cast a bleak, analytic eye, from its 'transcendental' vantage-point somewhere in Paris or Berlin or London, on all such specific historical heritages, discerning the underlying universal logics by which they are governed. The modernists, as Sean Golden has suggested,[7] were never hamstrung by those vested emotional interests in a specific national culture which mark a more provincial art; instead, they could approach such indigenous traditions from the outside, estrange and appropriate them for their own devious ends, roam in the manner of a Joyce, Pound or Eliot across the whole span of European culture in grand liberation from the oedipal constraints of a motherland. If this powerfully estranging perspective on traditional pieties is one source of modernism's radical force, it also reveals well enough its complicity with the 'bad' side of international monopoly capitalism, which is quite as nation-blind as the *Cantos* or *The Waste Land* and has scant respect for regional particularity. To spring like Joyce from a chronically backward colonial society was to this extent to turn political oppression to artistic advantage: if you had little enough rich national heritage in the first place, having been systematically deprived of it by the British, then you were already a kind of non-place and non-identity and could thus be catapulted from margins to centre, offering a kind of ironic paradigm of the fate that would now befall even the most advanced national capitalist formations in the era of international capitalism. In this sense also, the pre-industrial—Ireland's status as a stagnant, actively underdeveloped enclave—enters into a dramatic new correspondence with the most developed, as 'primitive' and sophisticated once more interchange and commingle in the modernist sensibility. If Dublin now becomes the capital of the world, if a traditional, smallish, agriculturally-based city rather than the more obvious metropolitan centres is now somehow the paradigm, then it is for one reason because the life-rhythms of such a parochial spot, with its settled routines, recurrent habits and sense of inert enclosure, are coming to seem exemplary of the shrunken, self-sustaining, repetitive world of international monopoly capitalism itself. The closed circuits of the one reflect, microcosmically, those of the other. Colonialism and modernism are able to become strange bedfellows, not least because the liberal realist concepts with which modernism makes a break were never as obvious and acceptable on the colonized margins as they were in the metropolitan centres. For the subdued subjects of empire, the individual is less the vigorously self-fashioning agent of its own historical destiny than empty, powerless, without a name; and there can be none of the great realists' confidence in the authority of linear time, which is always rightly perceived as on the side of Caesar. Confronted with a barren reality, the colonial subject is likely to retreat into the kind of internal dream and fantasy which we find in the so-called 'magic realism' of the post-colonial societies today, and which lend themselves culturally speaking much more obviously to modernism than to the realism of the imperial nations. In these and other ways, there is a kind of secret compact between modernism and the colonial experience, of which Joyce is perhaps our major exemplar. If the traditional national languages are now giving way to new global semiotic systems, cherished national literary heritages yielding ground to *avant garde* techniques which are portable across national frontiers, then who better placed to speak this new non-speech than one already disinherited in his own tongue, one who already, perforce, speaks the language of the foreigner?

The Joycean future, then, lies not so much with young Romantic intellectuals still oedipally enthralled to national traditions which at once fascinate and repel, but to faceless advertising agents of mixed nationhood and little domestic stability who can be at home anywhere because anywhere is everywhere. But if Leopold Bloom is in this sense the 'good' side of international capitalism, with its impatience of all sectarian chauvinism and parochialism, its democratic scorn for the hieratic and esoteric, his vague humanitarian creed of universal brotherhood also bears witness to the impotent, abstract universalism of the bourgeois 'public sphere'. Bloom is at once sunk in gross particularism and too abstractly cosmopolitan, reproducing in his own person the contradiction of form and content which pertains to the commodities he peddles. He is also a striking instance of what Walter Benjamin would call the impoverishment of experience in urban industrialism—the kind of figure who, like Benjamin's Baudelaire, fences constantly with sense stimuli at the surface levels of consciousness so that they no longer deposit those deep unconscious traces which go to make up Proustian memory or historical tradition. For Joyce, tradition is just the nightmare from which modernism is rebelliously awakening; and the radicalism of *Ulysses* is in this sense at one with Marx's scorn for the compulsive repetitions of history in *The Eighteenth Brumaire of Louis Bonaparte*, or Benjamin's iconoclastic rejection of the classical and auratic for the closeness and 'now' of mechanical reproduction. Yet Marx, Benjamin and Freud were also aware that, without true remembrance, we are bound to do no more than compulsively repeat—that tradition, as Benjamin puts it, has in every epoch to be wrestled away from a conformity which would overpower it.[8] The modernist opposition of 'tradition' and the 'now' is finally barren; for the past is what we are made of, then the only instruments we possess for awakening from the nightmare of history are those handed to us by history itself.

The exuberant, experimentalist, anti-traditional side of early European modernism belongs to an historical moment at which it was still possible to believe in the emancipatory force of technology—a moment at which that technology was still exhilaratingly novel, and at which the enthusiasm for it, as with the Futurists and Surrealists, was caught up in complex ways with a bracing sense of the still open possibility of radical social change. It is this current which passes from Mayakovsky and Joyce to Brecht and the socialist *avant garde* of the Weimar republic. The dead weight of inbred, exhausted national traditions, indeed the very structures of the old-fashioned nation state itself, are about to be thrown off by new international styles and techniques, in architecture or political organisation, fiction or economic production, and the *émigré* modernist artist is at the hub of this cultural revolution. Early modernism predates the century's most virulent outbreak of nationalism, which was to demonstrate that international monopoly capitalism, far from leaving national lineages behind it, is able to exploit them for its own ideological ends at points of severe political crisis, once again drawing the old and the new, the primitive and the sophisticated, into unexpected constellations. It is precisely such a constellation of the archaic and the *avant garde* which characterizes the facism of the 1930s, as the sensuous particularity of blood and soil become coupled to global imperialist expansion. In this context, the wandering Jew is part of a mythology considerably more sinister than the brave new cosmopolitan world of Leopold Bloom. Later than Joyce, and perhaps only to that degree wiser, we know that the old world, if cast off too prematurely in the name of the future, will only return with a vengeance.

Mr Leopold Bloom and the Lost Vermeer

Mary T. Reynolds

'Martha, Mary. I saw that picture somewhere, I forget now, old master or faked for money'. (*U*.78; VP 5. 289).[1]

'Somewhere', indeed.

Mr Bloom is describing a painting he could not possibly have seen, Johannes Vermeer's 'Christ in the House of Martha and Mary'. It was discovered in Scotland in 1901, and was briefly exhibited in London before being returned to Edinburgh where it has ever since remained.[2] Joyce himself never saw the painting, and must have gotten his knowledge of it from a photograph. No photograph of the painting appeared in print as early as June 16, 1904; the lines in Ulysses are, in fact, the earliest evidence we have of Joyce's well-known admiration for Vermeer.

★   ★   ★

The painting is among the earliest of Vermeer's known works; de Vries dated it to 1654-55, on the basis of suggestions that had been made for the source of some of the figures.[3] There are three life-size figures, grouped around a table. Christ sits in an armchair on the right; Martha holds a basket of bread, and bends over the table to listen. Christ, the left side of his face painted in profile, points with his right hand to Mary who is seated at his feet, gazing upward; she leans on her right elbow, holding her hand under her chin. The eyes of Martha, looking downward to Christ, are hidden. The design of the carpet on which Mary is seated resembles closely a carpet in one of Vermeer's later paintings, 'Girl asleep at a Table'. At the lower left of the picture is a small bench, on which appears a signature, V Meer with the V and M intertwined. This signature, which was also used in two later paintings by Vermeer, became known for the first time when this painting was discovered in 1901.

'Christ in the House of Martha and Mary' demonstrates strikingly the originality of the young Vermeer. The first impression of a viewer—as Leopold Bloom's description shows—is somewhat different from the biblical story; both women are listening eagerly to Christ, and the three faces show no hint of the reproof which traditionally forms the burden of the anecdote. One critic contrasts it with 'the iconographic practices of his contemporaries', alleging that Vermeer was aware of the tradition but that he excluded the narrative

context and provided 'visual information [which] neutralizes the judgement
that is the point of the original story. His Martha is, if anything, even more
raptly, radiantly attentive than Mary . . . the values embraced in this painting
are . . . predicated on a refusal of moral judgement'.[4] Without arguing for the
critical validity of this viewpoint, it can be admitted as a description of
dramatic values that form one aspect of the painter's treatment of the biblical
story, and as a feature that distinguishes Vermeer's 'Martha and Mary' from
paintings by Rubens and others.

The painting is dominated by primary colours, red, yellow and blue, with
strong lighting and a broad style of brushwork quite different from Vermeer's
later work. Christ's robe is purple and blue; Martha's dress is yellow, with a
red border and white sleeves while Mary's dress in a slatey blue with red trim.
The women wear head scarfs, or caps, Mary's in red and white, Martha's in
light yellow. The colour yellow, which with blue was his favourite, appears in
this painting in different shades, in the tablecloth, in the faces of the three
figures, and in Martha's basket.[5]

*   *   *

Vermeer's 'Christ in the House of Martha and Mary' was lost for almost two
centuries; indeed, little has been known about the painter himself until the last
decade. He was unequalled in his extraordinary combination of domestic
tranquility with traditional Dutch realism; but he painted with conscious
intention, at a leisurely pace that was determined, apparently, by his unhur-
ried study of formal aesthetic problems. Consequently his artistic production
was small, and even now only thirty or so works can definitely be assigned to
him.

However his work did not go unappreciated. During his life high prices were
paid for his paintings, and after his death in 1675, at the age of 43, there was a
50-year period in which his paintings sold well. But he died in poverty, leaving
an accumulation of debts. The year of his death was a period of economic crisis
in Holland, and his widow, Catharina (she was left with eleven living children),
was declared bankrupt by the High Court of Delft. After this Vermeer
vanished into oblivion until the middle of the nineteenth century.

'Christ in the House of Martha and Mary' was bought for £8 by a furniture
dealer, from a family in Bristol. It disappeared until April 1901, when it was
briefly exhibited in the Bond Street gallery of Forbes and Paterson, in London.
In the catalogue of the exhibition W.A. Coats appears as the owner, and in the
1904 catalogue of the Collection of W.A. Coats, in Skalmorlie Castle, Scotland,
the painting is listed as No 37. In 1927 it was given to the National Gallery in
Edinburgh by the two sons of W.A. Coats, in memory of their father, and it has
since remained there.[6]

*   *   *

We turn now to the function of the Vermeer painting in the novel. It comes
into the thoughts of Leopold Bloom in the fifth episode, the chapter called

'Lotus Eaters'. It is a brief paragraph, which follows upon the revelation that Bloom has involved himself in a clandestine correspondence with a woman name Martha Clifford; he writes to her, and asks, in response, sexually suggestive letters, one of which he has just received and read—its text is given in full. Thoughts of this escapade link the name of Martha, in Bloom's mind, to a long-ago encounter with 'two sluts in the Coombe' (the Coombe was the run-down slum around St Patrick's Cathedral in central Dublin), in the rain, drunkenly singing an obscene rhyme, 'O, Mairy lost the pin of her drawers'. The last line, 'To keep it up', brings in the painting of two women, Martha and Mary, listening to Christ:

Martha, Mary. I saw that picture somewhere I forget now old master or faked for money. He is sitting in their house, talking. Mysterious. Also the two sluts in the Coombe would listen.

To keep it up.

Nice kind of evening feeling. No more wandering about. Just loll there: quiet dusk: let everything rip. Forget. Tell about places you have been, strange customs. The other one, jar on her head, was getting the supper: fruit, olives, lovely cool water out of a well, stonecold like the hole in the wall at Ashtown. Must carry a paper goblet next time I go to the trottingmatches. She listens with big dark soft eyes. Tell her: more and more: all. Then a sigh: silence. Long long long rest.
(*U.* 78; VP 5.289-299)

Critics, in the few instances where this paragraph has been mentioned, have attached it to the Biblical story of Martha and Mary without comment; a few have noted that the two names are the names of the two women in Bloom's life, Marion (Mary) or Molly Bloom, his wife, and Martha Clifford, his secret correspondent.[7] There is also, of course, a third woman, Bloom's fifteen year old daughter, Milly, very much in his thoughts.

In *Ulysses* a recurring motif centers on the linked names: after the reference to the painting, the phrase 'Martha, Mary' comes into Bloom's mind at three other places in the novel. Two of these have a direct connection with the primary occurrence.

In the 'Aeolus' chapter Bloom is found in the newspaper office, watching 'a stately figure' enter to speak to the editor, Ruttledge. The episode's 'headline' tells us that this is William Brayden, Esquire. Red Murray, a pressman, whispers to Bloom, 'Don't you think his face is like Our Saviour?' Murray's question recalls the Vermeer painting, for Bloom's thoughts make a complicated connection between Mario the tenor (Mary), and the opera, *Martha*, in which he sang.

Our Saviour: beardframed oval face: talking in the dusk Mary, Martha. Steered by an umbrella sword to the footlights: Mario the tenor.
  – Or like Mario, Mr Bloom said.
  Yes, Red Murray agreed. But Mario was said to be the picture of Our Saviour.
  Jesus Mario with rougy cheeks, doublet and spindle legs. Hand on his heart. In *Martha*.

Co-me thou lost one,
Co-me thou dear one. (*U* 116; VP 7.52-60)

In the 'Nausicaa' chapter, when Bloom is enticed by Gerty MacDowell on the beach in the early evening, he remembers the obscene rhyme, 'O Mairy lost the pin of her drawers'. Because he is thinking of the enticements of female clothing, he muses, 'Fashion part of their charm. Just changes when you're on the track of the secret', and now he recalls the painting and makes an exception:

Except the east: Mary, Martha: now as then.
(*U* 362; VP 13.805-806)

Presumably Bloom's exception refers to the unseductive robes of the two women in Vermeer's painting.

Joyce manages to work the name of Martha into *Ulysses* a total of 28 times; sometimes it is Martha Clifford, sometimes it is Flotow's opera *Martha*. In the 'Cyclops' chapter one of the prolonged interpolations includes a catalogue of 'All saints and martyrs, virgins and confessors'; here Joyce places 'S. Martha of Bethany' (in the Biblical story the house of Martha and Mary was in Bethany), and 'S. Mary of Egypt'. S. Marion Calpens is also in this list. (*U* 333; VP 12.1709-1710)

In the 'Circe' chapter Bloom's guilt-ridden hallucinations produce a comment from 'Bello', his torturer, 'Martha and Mary will be a little chilly at first, in such delicate thighcasing . . . ' again referring to seductive female clothing. (*U* 524; VP 15.2892)

The name of Mary comes into the novel 49 times, in great variety. In Molly Bloom's soliloquy she thinks of 'that slut, that Mary we had' (*U* 724; VP 18.56), who has been identified earlier in the 'Circe' chapter, when Bloom's hallucinations call up a vision of Mary Driscoll, scullerymaid, 'that slut', to whom he made tentative advances. (*U* 452; VP 15.859-893) But Bloom insists that she enticed him. No other occurrence of the name (other than the three connected with the Vermeer painting) seems to have any relevance for the Martha/Mary motif.

Yet it is obvious that the function of the Vermeer painting in the novel is to anchor Joyce's ornamental motif. The biblical anecdote, with its moral of Mary choosing the better part and Christ reproving Martha for being 'busy about many things', does not enter into Joyce's novel. The suggestion has been made that the two women represent the active and the contemplative life, the biblical story being relevant 'because it shows stasis rewarded. Jesus defended Mary, who sat idly by and listened to the Master while her sister Martha bustled about serving the meal. So, too will the indolent, supine Molly Bloom effortlessly retain the devotion of her husband and vanquish the enterprising Martha Clifford, just as Bloom will Boylan'.[8] But, granting that stasis is rewarded in *Ulysses*, the association of Molly Bloom and Martha Clifford with the women in *Luke* 10:38 cannot be supported within the text of the novel. The names alone, but not the characterizations, form the motif.

What, then, is the function of the Martha/Mary pattern in *Ulysses*? I believe that it is Joyce's reinterpretation of the biblical story, a new and different version that came directly from his interpretation of the Vermeer painting. It is one of Joyce's small, complex, obliquely rendered constructions that invite the reader to look for a larger meaning only to confound his search. The allusion to the biblical pair is a deliberately false clue, inviting explication that comes only to a dead end.

Joyce has fictionalized a great painting, as he has fictionalized countless literary and musical works; Vermeer joins Shakespeare, Dante, Mozart and others who have taken up residence in the mind of Leopold Bloom. The presence of Vermeer's painting in the novel illuminates the sensibility of Joyce's unheroic hero. Recurrent allusions to the painting combine with other fragmentary patterns to register Bloom's exceptional openness to emotional impressions. His recall of the Vermeer painting is the true focus of the pattern, and everything else is secondary and incidental: not pointless, not merely ornamental, but on a subordinate and collateral level in the complex characterization of Joyce's protagonist.

Let us look, therefore, at the circumstances in which the description of the painting entered the text of the novel. Bloom could not have seen it; Joyce himself could have seen only a photograph. Did Homer nod? Or was it a deliberate anachronism?

*   *   *

Ulysses was written between 1914 and late 1921 or early 1922. Joyce began with an extremely simple rough draft, little more than a synopsis of the narrative action, and enlarged this as he wrote the individual chapters. These were not written in sequence, but when the chance of publishing the book in serial form arose Joyce held himself to a schedule. Claude Sykes agreed to type the drafts for publication in the *Little Review* in America, and *The Egoist* in England. Joyce sent his manuscript of the first chapter to Sykes in November 1917, and the first episode was published in the *Little Review* in March 1918.[9]

Joyce's habit of composition was based on continuous revision, additions and changes being made right down to the date, almost to the moment, of going to press. Thus we have, for each of the chapters of *Ulysses*, significant and extensive revisions at every stage: typescripts, fair copy manuscripts, annotated sheets of chapters in serial form, galley proofs, and page proofs. By no means all of these materials have survived; but those that have often present in a meaningful pattern the sequence of Joyce's composition of a small design such as the one involving the Vermeer painting.

The 'Lotus Eaters' episode, the book's fifth chapter which contains the primary allusion to the lost Vermeer, was published in the *Little Review* in July 1918, having been finished apparently in April. The magazine had been under attack since serialization began, and this fifth episode brought to a head the conflict of Margaret Anderson and Jane Heap, publishers of the *Little Review*, with the New York censorship. Previous issues had been confiscated and burned; now the Society for the Prevention of Vice forced a trial that began on February 14, 1921. The editors were convicted; they paid a $50 fine and ceased publication of *Ulysses*.[10]

Joyce had, of course, hoped that serialization would help him to find a publisher for the book; the adverse verdict filled him with despair. Sylvia Beach, the American proprietor of a Paris bookshop, Shakespeare and Company, now offered to publish *Ulysses* in an edition of a thousand copies, on a subscription basis. She found typists for the later episodes, and Joyce began to rework the five early chapters that had been serialized. From 1919 to 1921 the book was, with infinite pains, developed into the intricate work that finally achieved publication on February 2, 1922.[11]

The 'Lotus Eaters' chapter is, unfortunately, one of the episodes for which few documents survive—only a few sheets of galley proofs (the 'placards' of Sylvia Beach's French printer, Darantière) and page proofs. There is no first draft, and no manuscript except the Rosenbach manuscript of the entire novel which is now believed to be, at least in the section where the Vermeer painting allusion appears (and elsewhere in large part), a fair copy made by Joyce long after publication, specifically for sale to a collector. There is no typescript.[12]

Despite these and other gaps in direct transmission of the text, the changes Joyce made—at whatever stage—are interesting and significant. The text of the Vermeer painting paragraph is identical in the *Little Review* and the Rosenbach manuscript.[13] Two emendations which are not present in the Rosenbach manuscript are, first, the phrase 'old master or faked for money', and second, 'jar on her head'. These are additions to the primary allusion, in the Lotus Eaters episode.

No changes appear in 'Aeolus', the seventh chapter, which we know was being typed in mid-May 1918. But in the 'Nausicaa' chapter the emendation that ties the paragraph to the Vermeer painting is not in the Rosenbach MS, nor in the galley proofs (placards); the words 'except the east: Mary, Martha: now as then' were added at some point between galleys and page proofs—the document carrying the revision is not extant.

In summary, the allusion to the lost Vermeer was in Joyce's mind at the earliest stage of writing. He placed it in the 'Lotus Eaters' chapter, early in the novel, and the intention to use it as a motif was also part of his original plan, as evidenced by the presence of a related allusion in two later episodes, 'Aeolus' and 'Nausicaa'. With the placement of a fourth, more casual, reference in the 'Cyclops' chapters the Vermeer painting became an indicator of Bloom's sensibility: a small, discrete, complex construction that added significantly to the characterization of Joyce's protagonist.

We must therefore consider more specifically the role played by Bloom's description of this painting; and I will then conclude with a review of the evidence—which is slight and problematical—relating to Joyce's acquaintance with Vermeer, and with 'Christ in the House of Martha and Mary'.

*   *   *

Christ in the House of Martha and Mary has been the subject of a great many paintings; had he been interested merely in the biblical anecdote, Joyce could have used Rubens, El Greco, Tintoretto, or any one of a large number. It is most unlikely that he made a deliberate search, but it is altogether likely that he took the Vermeer painting as a deliberate choice. Vermeer's originality of treatment and his skill in rendering domestic interiors offered a scene well-suited to capture the interest of a Dublin Odysseus; Mr Bloom's description of the painting hits upon those aspects that seem to be uniquely applicable to the Vermeer.[14] If this was his deliberate choice, then the pattern that Joyce wove into his novel encourages an imaginative extension from this small piece of reality into a wide and echoing mythic entity. Fabrication, invention, fantasy announce their presence; everything in Joyce's little construction both is and is not. Bloom's words bring into being an imaginative mythic reality precisely because they are inaccurate in one aspect, while at the same time they are, in another aspect, shrewdly in conformity with truth.

Of course it is Joyce, the author, who is pulling the strings to manipulate his lay-figure. Leopold Bloom has become so real to the readers of Ulysses that we frequently have to remind ourselves that he is an invention of the author; the pattern of the Vermeer painting is one of several in which the reader becomes convinced that he is in close contact with the imagination of James Joyce. When Bloom's mind connects the Vermeer painting with the opera Martha and with his clandestine correspondent it might be (as Bloom himself says) coincidence, but then the voice of the book itself comes up with the echoing resonance of 'S. Martha of Bethany', and the reader's perception of the very real and well-known Vermeer painting moves irresistibly into an entirely fictional world. This is the special magic of Ulysses.

Lenehan, an unsympathetic witness, makes a surprising comment: 'There's a touch of the artist about old Bloom.' (U 232; VP 10.582-583) Bloom has a great fund of intellectual curiosity that has led him to explore scientific and philosophical questions for which he has really no background. The effect is often comic, mingling absurdity with provocative hints, disquietingly astute and penetrating observations. Bloom has also made an effort with literature, and here he is indeed a comic figure as he daydreams of writing for a magazine or as he seeks earnestly in the works of Shakespeare for a solution to the problems of life. Bloom's silent reflections run parallel to those of Stephen Dedalus, apprentice artist, who is the other protagonist of the novel, their silent monologues (in 'Proteus' and 'Lestrygonians' especially) treat identical themes, and this may be the reason why he is not allowed any serious literary perception or ability.

In music it is a different matter. As the day goes on, evidence accumulates that Bloom is sensitive and discriminating in his understanding of music. Although untutored, he is in some sense musically competent. He is a careful listener with a good ear; he knows at once that the piano has been tuned, he appreciates a competent performer, and though he does not use the term 'absolute pitch' he describes this phenomenon. 'Nice touch', he says. 'Must be Cowley. Musical. Knows whatever note you play.' And the accuracy of his observation is soon confirmed, when 'Father' Cowley hears Simon Dedalus begin to play and remonstrates, ' "No, Simon. Play it in the original. One flat". The keys, obedient, rose higher'.[15] (U 267; VP 11.603)

It is in character, then, for Mr Bloom to recognize the equivalent of perfect pitch in human communication. One is born with perfect pitch; it cannot be learned. On the human level he defines it as the instinctive response of one person to another, a quality that he associates with Molly, his erring wife. Thus he notes that she understood the Italian boy who played the hurdy-gurdy, 'without understanding a word of his language. With look to look: songs without words . . . She knew he meant the monkey was sick . . . Gift of nature'. (U 281; VP 11.1093-1094)

Bloom has many deficiencies and weak points, most of these on the intellectual level of musicology; Stephen Dedalus, on the other hand, is most comfortable in the intellectual approach to music. In the mechanics of music Bloom's formulations seem knowledgeable and to the point. He rates above any mechanical instrument, 'the human voice, two tiny silky chords. Wonderful, more than all the others'. (U 272; VP 11.791-792)

Bloom's interest in music, though untrained, has led him to an understanding of the theoretical basis of harmony. 'Numbers it is. All music when you come to think . . . Vibrations: chords those are. One plus two plus six is seven.' (U 274; VP 11.830-832) From this choice of words it is clear that Bloom recognizes intuitively the construction of a musical seventh: unison plus second plus sixth. He calls this 'musemathematics'. (U 274; VP 11.834) His observations are original and to the point. When he thinks of girls learning to play the piano, playing scales up and down, he imagines the sound as 'two together nextdoor neighbours' (U 274; VP 11.842-843), a statement so comparable to Stephen Dedalus's description of rhymes as 'two men dressed the same, looking the same, two by two', (U 136; VP 7.715-716) that it must surely be Joyce's deliberate parallelism.

Music, then, despite many ironic qualifications, seems to be Bloom's aesthetic métier. What about pictorial art?

His accurate description of the Vermeer painting is just the kind of straightforward observation that is typical of his response to music. He also says, 'Old Master or faked for money'. This comment, which points so strongly to Vermeer as creator of the painting in Bloom's mind, can be interpreted as something he has read about the painting; or it can be read as an indication of interest in the marketplace value of art. The latter interpretation fits well with Bloom's observations about literature, for he wonders during the day how much a writer might be paid for a story. In music too, his mind is never far away from the pecuniary value of musical talent; he is proud of his wife's ability as a concert singer, interested in what she might earn by making a tour.

Like a harmonic in musical phrasing, these ironic intrusions devalue Bloom's pronouncements on aesthetic matters. But the solid reality of his discriminating sensibility remains, and grows as one progresses through the novel. Joyce has used the Vermeer painting to make Mr Bloom a most uncommon common man, or as Joyce himself put it, an all-round man.[16]

*   *   *

We come finally to the tantalizing question of whether Joyce's construction is a deliberate anachronism or accidental. Where and when did Joyce himself become acquainted with Vermeer's 'Christ in the House of Martha and Mary'?

Certainly the painting was never shown in Dublin. The National Gallery of Scotland confirms that after its brief showing in London in 1901, the painting never left Scotland. The National Gallery of Ireland acquired the Rubens painting of the same subject, also in 1901, as part of the Henry Barron Bequest. The Board meeting at which the Committee decided to accept the bequest was on Friday, February 21, 1901, a date very close to the date of the Vermeer exhibit in London.[17]

The Dublin press seems to have ignored both the Rubens acquisition and the newly discovered Vermeer; there is no mention of either in the *Irish Times*, the *Irish Independent*, or the *Freemans Journal* between February 22 and March 31, 1901. The Irish papers in this period devoted almost no space to the arts or to literature. The *Irish Times* on March 2, 1901 published a list of recent acquisitions by the National Gallery with no mention of the Rubens, presumably because it had not yet been exhibited. The National Gallery has no record of the date on which the Rubens was first displayed.

The Rubens painting of 'Christ in the House of Martha and Mary', which Joyce almost certainly did see, and which therefore Leopold Bloom might have seen, is a small panel only 25 1/4 x 24. Rubens depicts the biblical story more overtly than Vermeer. Martha stands to the right of Christ, clearly reproaching her sister, and the countenance of Christ shows him reproving Martha as he points to Mary. There is fruit in the picture, but here is no figure of a woman with a jar on her head, nor does this detail appear in any of the other interpretations of the theme that I have seen; and the dinner is being prepared not by Martha but by a man who is seen through a doorway. The composition does not correspond to Bloom's description.

There is only one contemporary account, so far as I have been able to discover, of the Vermeer painting; but this one might have been seen by Joyce, and therefore also by Mr Bloom. The *Athenaeum* (London), on March 30, 1901, carried a short noice with the title, 'The Newly Discovered Vermeer'.[18] Based on the printed notice by D.S. MacColl, which the Forbes and Paterson gallery printed for this exhibition, the *Athenaeum* article describes the canvas with a critical account of the place of this painting in Vermeer's development. '. . . the real strength of the work lies in its genuine Dutch genre feeling, its vigorous homely characterization. Nonetheless, we cannot doubt that Vermeer was right in giving up the attempt at a dramatic art and devoting himself, as he did subsequently, to motives which required no great psychological imagination.' Nothing is said of the painting's history except that it is a most important work, 'recently discovered in a private collection'.

Is it possible that Joyce saw this notice in the *Athenaeum*? There is no direct evidence that he did. Joyce had just turned 20, in March 1901; he had written (a year earlier) an essay on a famous painting; he had published an article on

Ibsen in the *Fortnightly Review*;[19] and he had had some correspondence with Ibsen, with William Archer who had translated Ibsen, and with W.L. Courtney, editor of the *Fortnightly*. The National Library subscribed to the *Athenaeum*, and Joyce may have begun to read it at this time. He had also made his first visit to London, in May 1900, with the money he received for the Ibsen article. All these circumstances are, of course, purely speculative in regard to his knowledge of the Vermeer painting.

One must also ask whether Joyce at this period had any interest in painting. His brother Stanislaus, who did have some such interest, makes no mention of discussions or visits to the National Gallery; yet Stanislaus's diary does show a specific interest in Velasquez[20] (who also produced a painting of 'Christ in the House of Martha and Mary'), and there is sound evidence that Joyce himself did visit the Dublin museum.

In September 1899, his first year in college and the same period in which he wrote the Ibsen article, Joyce wrote an essay on Mihály Munkacsy's trilogy of paintings on the Passion of Christ. The essay is focused on Munkacsy's 'Ecce Homo', which was on view at the Royal Hibernian Academy, and the young Joyce gives a detailed description of the artist's portrayal of the highly dramatic scene. He is most impressed by ' the sense of life, the realistic illusion', and he was obviously drawn to the picture because it is, as he writes, 'intensely, silently dramatic, waiting but the touch of the wizard wand to break out into reality, life and conflict'. Joyce says that the artist in choosing to avoid the portrayal of Mary as a Madonna and John as an evangelist, and preferring 'to make Mary a mother and John a man', has elected 'the finer and subtler treatment'. He compares the drama of Munkacsy's picture with the didactic treatment of Christ by Horace Van Ruith, whose paintings had been exhibited in London at the Royal Academy from 1888 to 1899.[21]

A still more telling remark is found in the concluding sentence of a 1903 book review by Joyce, in which he praises a monograph by Alfred Ainger on George Crabbe, 'one of the most neglected of English writers'. Crabbe, says Joyce, 'except for a few passages wherein the world of opinion is divided, is an example of sane judgement and sober skill, and . . . has set forth the lives of villagers with appreciation and fidelity, and *with an occasional splendour reminiscent of the Dutchmen*'[22]

At the time of this review Joyce was writing chapters of his first novel, *Stephen Hero*, which has been called a 'First draft' of *A Portrait of the Artist as a Young Man*. In *A Portrait* there is only one slight reference to pictorial art; it comes into Stephen's discussion of aesthetics, using the portrait of the 'Mona Lisa' as an example. Joyce tells his friend Lynch that he has a book at home in which he sets down questions for his theory of esthetic (*sic*) (*P* 214). This notebook, we now know, contains notes for *Stephen Hero*, chapter by chapter, and there is one sole reference to painting, which reads, 'Christ and Leonardo: exoteric and esoteric'.[23] The notebook contains the early essay, 'A Portrait of the Artist as a Young Man', (which was rejected by the new journal, *Dana*), followed by Joyce's notes as he began to enlarge the essay into a novel. In a later notebook Joyce mentions Leonardo's notebooks.

Joyce's 'Epiphanies', fragments that he later worked into his novels, include one that suggests a painting; it is a girl standing, reading, and the paragraph ends, 'What is the lesson that she reads . . . Who knows how deeply meditative, how reminiscent is this comeliness of Raffaello?'[24] The epiphanies were written between 1900 and 1903.

In *Stephen Hero* some of these fragmentary references to painting emerge, predictably in the same context of the youthful protagonist's discussions of aesthetics. Stephen is presented as no dilettante but a serious young man who read avidly in his effort 'to pierce to the significant heart of everything', and who was vividly moved by 'the rude scrawls and the portable gods of men whose legacy Leonardo and Michelangelo inherit'. (*SH* 33) Stephen writes an essay that is clearly taken from Joyce's own essays, and tries to get it accepted by the College Literary Society. But his essay is censored by the Jesuit head of the College, and in the course of an argument with him Stephen compares Aquinas's definition of the beautiful to 'A Dutch painter's representation of a plate of onions'. (*SH* 95)

Slight though these instances may be, they do offer clues to an otherwise unsuspected interest in painting, and specifically to an early acquaintance by Joyce with the Dutch school that includes Vermeer. There are later indications as well. In a letter to his wife's uncle, Michael Healy, in 1927, Joyce wrote incisively his impressions of the inhabitants of Amsterdam: 'To see 600 of them in a Square eating silvery raw herrings by moonlight is a sight for Rembrandt.'[25] In this same summer he bought a reproduction of Vermeer's 'View of Delft', which thenceforth hung in his Paris flat.[26] 'View of Delft' is Vermeer's most popular picture. It would be fruitless to search for reasons why Joyce bought it, and critics have dismissed the purchase as an indication that Joyce had no serious interest in pictorial art. But the purchase does register a specific interest in Vermeer.

In conclusion, we return to the additions Joyce made to his initial paragraph. The text is identical in the Rosenbach MS and in the *Little Review*, a simple description of the composition with Bloom's personal reactions. Where did Joyce get the comment he allows Bloom to insert in the first sentence—'old master or faked for money'—? and what is the source of the descriptive addition, 'jar on her head'? (We can assume that the insertions which do not refer to the painting—'stonecold like the hole in the wall at Ashtown. Must carry a paper goblet next time I go to the trottingmatches', come as a simple extension of Bloom's free association with 'water out of the well'.)

The *Little Review* text was written in Zurich, before 1918.[27] We do not have any indication of date of insertion of the revisions, but we know they were made after Joyce had moved to Paris in 1919. He must have seen a photograph of the painting in Zurich, if he did not see it earlier in Trieste; Bloom's description is too accurate to be merely random. It seems likely that at some time after the original text was written, Joyce read—probably for the first time—some account of the history of the painting that led him to add Bloom's remark about possible forgery. These are, of course, numerous possible accounts that Joyce might have read in Paris, in magazines or books. But we have no evidence of such reading; to the contrary, the lists of books and periodicals in his library show no titles at all (though there are many about music) in the field of pictorial art.[28] Richard Ellmann was right when he described Joyce's purchase of Vermeer's *View of Delft* as 'a rare concession to the pictorial arts'.[29]

One likely source, however, is the eleventh edition of the *Encyclopaedia Britannica*, which we now know to have been used by Joyce several times when he was looking for persuasive detail. The *Britannica* entry appears under Meer, Jan Van Der, and it emphasizes the problem of ascription and authenticity that is implied in Bloom's comment. 'For almost two centuries Van der Meer was almost completely forgotten, and his pictures were sold under the names and forged signatures of the more popular De Hooch, Metsu, Ter Borch, and even of Rembrandt.'[30] The article describes 'Christ in the House of Martha and Mary', and also 'the luminous and masterly "View of Delft"', and specifies the location of both. Vermeer's artistic development and painting styles are discussed, but not in the terms of the *Athenaeum* article about 'Christ in the House of Martha and Mary'. In short, the *only* item in the *Britannica* account that relates to Joyce's *Ulysses* pattern is the mention of forgery; and this was a late addition to the manuscript.

Joyce's revision of Bloom's description of the painting to include 'jar on her head' for Martha must, I think, be accounted another purposefully false clue: a late addition, obviously inserted after he had seen the Vermeer, it has the effect of diminishing Bloom's credibility as observer and critic. The first-sentence insertion makes it clear that Bloom has not seen the painting recently; 'jar on the head' is an almost ludicrously inappropriate addition. The effect must be deliberate.

★   ★   ★

Robert Martin Adams saw in Joyce's wilful use of tonal shifts a degree of artifice, and a heightened presence of the artificer in his work, that signals two related effects: first, the presence of a Joycean mind and imagination in the consciousness of Mr Bloom; and second, a perspective on the novel that produces another voice which is not a narratorial voice but a more complex construction that Adams called 'the mind of Joyce-over-the-novel'.[31] It is a strategy that is demonstrably present in Dante's *Divine Comedy*, where it contributes to the poem's complexity a challenging resonance. It can be called the voice of the book itself. The materials of construction are insistent motifs, parallels, parodies, fugitive bits of detail, literary and historical allusions. In Joyce's *Ulysses* the result is an extraordinary fusion of intellect with art, a massive work of art dominated by mind.

The Vermeer painting and the motif built around it must, then, be reckoned an intentional anachronism. Joyce was an obsessively precise writer. When he gave Mr Bloom an appreciative familiarity with first-class pictorial art it is only to be expected that he would hedge this about with ironic qualifications. The little episode is drawn partly from his own life; but it was James Joyce who bought the 'View of Delft', and Bloom who had in his bedroom the oak-framed picture, 'The Bath of the Nymph', which he acquired as a giveaway with the Easter number of *Photo Bits*. (*U* 64-65; VP 4.370) Bloom describes this picture as 'splendid masterpiece in art colours', but these words are a quotation from *Photo Bits*, not the words of Bloom.

We get a brief and different glimpse of Bloom in his description of the Vermeer painting and his reaction to it: a response that is not be to judged primarily on its quality of critical acumen or educated taste. It is best approached, perhaps, on a level of simple humanity. There is in it an element of Joyce's own life: he did see the painting, the terms of description are Joyce's; but its use in 'Lotus Eaters' also fits Bloom's role as Odysseus. The presence of a great picture in the mind of an uneducated Dubliner, in June 1904, with all the comic or ironic overtones, offers a sympathetic prospect; as Ellmann says, Joyce makes the future of man appear less sinister.[32] The discovery of pattern in the use of Vermeer's painting once more enlarges our sense of the scope of Joyce's creative imagination.

'There's a Medium in All Things': Joycean Readings

Fritz Senn

The starting point of this purely intratextual study is a misappropriation of a Joycean line. James Joyce misappropriated constantly—his own life and that of his family and friends, the *Odyssey*, the Mass, newspapers, Irish history, songs: they were transformed into something they had not been before. Criticism documents such mistreatments, changes that have also become themes *in* the works. In *A Portrait* we hear two verses of a song, and then read instantly after: 'That was his song'. *His* song is a misappropriation, one defective line, 'O, the geen[1] wothe botheth' (P 72)[2], supplanting two of the original. The new creation is less than its prototype, but also positively surpasses it. Stephen's very first utterance in the book suggests a 'green rose' in the face of botanical probability; it has engendered several non-words or, according to subjective evaluation, neologisms. The pattern, imperfection and innovation, that is set seems to be representative for the budding artist as a young child under inspection, as well as for the cunning artist who contrives all of this behind the scenes, showing his fingernails. In *Ulysses* we observe how 'metempsychosis', an ancient term for the soul's serial appropriation of new physical residences, is assimilated to something like 'Met him pike hoses'. The result is both mollifyingly inadequate and resourcefully creative; the distortion comes to pass as a word made out of letters on a page being metamorphosed into a string of sounds. When a printed text is appropriated by the speaking voice there are innovative gains, but also deformations and losses.

In the same game spirit, new theories appropriate above all creative works, notably Joyce's later ones. This too had been anticipated. Shakespeare was 'made in Germany', as Stephen Dedalus claims when he, Irishman, theorises about a British poet, 'as the champion French polisher of Italian scandals' (U9.766). In brilliant non-concern for his audience, Stephen Dedalus sets forth a nucleus of Shakespearean adoptions and posits a psychological need for them. If such adaptations (borrowings, assimilations, influences, etc.) succeed they become Culture or Art. For his lecture in the library Stephen has already misdirected a former thought of his own: 'Now your best French polish' (U9.315). French polish has been misapplied and extended. An artist (or critic) appropriates what looks profitable—forced grist to his strategic mill. What has gone before, the past, literature, is adapted, usurped, exploited, plagiarised. There is a huge tradition at hand.

If the beginning of *Ulysses* is not the morning of creation, but—in Richard Ellmann's characterisation[3]—'the morning after', it is also 'ages after'. The morning is young but the world is as old as Ecclesiastes found it thousands of years ago. Much has already happened, must have preceded (to be called up or misappropriated by Mulligan). Everything, almost, has been said before: Buck Mulligan's Ballad of Joking Jesus ('Three times a day, after meals', U1.610), or Stephen's idea of Hamlet, still relatively new ('No, no, . . . I'm not equal to Thomas Aquinas . . .', U1.545), history may be 'a tale like any other too often heard' (U2.45); it can turn into a nightmare. In *A Portrait of the Artist as a Young Man* Stephen fears his soul might be affected by 'a false homage to a symbol behind which are massed twenty centuries of authority and veneration' (P243). Stephen's mind is full of 'the accumulation of the past' (U17.777), and so is Joyce's. A Church had to be founded and all its institutions and ceremonies, a priest has to be educated and grow old and lose his way, disease has to do its deadly work, a boy has to become 'impressionable' before James Joyce's earliest prose story starts with its accumulated past trailing behind it, a story whose *first* sentence retrospectively reads 'There was no hope for him this time'.

If now in microscopic narrowing we extract one word from the twenty centuries of authority and veneration that are *'massed'* in Stephen's phrasing and find it gratuitously appropriate, we may indulge in misuse and readerly usurpation. As etymology—the accumulated lore of linguistic misappropriation—would tell us, *massed* (from a Greek word *massein*, to knead) has nothing to do with the *Mass*, which is derived from its final words: *'Ite, missa est'*, except that by accident the two words have developed into identical shapes and that, as it happens, the Mass is one of the central acts of the Church, part of the impact that has been massed against James Joyce and against a fictitious, conglomerate, counterpart, Stephen Dedalus. The opening words of the Mass are, again, misapplied by a mimicking Buck Mulligan in the first spoken words of *Ulysses*. The first chapter has a strong theological flavour which may encourage us to exploit even narrowly denoted words from their primary context, like 'a dull green mass of liquid' (U1.108). Mass and mass[4] tend to fuse and interfere with each other.

A mass of evidence has been accumulated in this introduction to pave the artful way to a concordant deflection of one Joycean word. In an imaginary court room scene Leopold Bloom, accused, defends himself by pleading:

There's a medium in all things. Play cricket. (U15.878)

What he seems to enlist for his own defence is Horace's well-known *est modus in rebus*, usually rendered as 'there's a measure in all things' (or 'a mean'), towards the end of his First *Satire* (I,106), which is continued: *'Sunt certi denique fines, quos ultra citraque nequit consistere rectum'* ('there are fixed bounds, beyond and short of which right can find no place').[5] This appeal to moderation and propriety is strange in a chapter like 'Circe' whose trade mark is excess, which stridently oversteps traditional limits of verisimilitude, sanity, individual psychology, proportion or, as was once thought, good taste—this in a book which seemed to defy all classical canons.[6] A medium in all things: Bloom is himself a kind of medium: in the midst of things, Joyce's principal mean to whatever ends, somewhat average ('*l'homme moyen sensuel*' he was once called), a mediator. In classical grammar *medium* is a voice of the verb that is reflexive or reciprocal; if we consider Bloom in 'Circe' to be thinking (or speaking) to himself, then this would be the medium voice, in which much of Joyce's works seems to be implicitly written.[7]

For present strategies the term 'medium', by nature rich in meaning, is misappropriated in a different, more modern, way that the 20th century has evolved when it recognised the importance of the media, usually plural, as mass communication. Joyce put his main *Ulysses* characters into what we now call media: talking, writing, advertising, photography, teaching, lecturing, singing (their range was more restricted than it has become since, and the media of then did not yet know they were media). He pre-integrated television into *Finnegans Wake*. For the purposes of this article the word is used simply to introduce the two modes in which Joyce's works have to be experienced, as the arrangement of letters on a surface (as we read them through our eyes), or else as spoken aloud by the human (or recorded) voice. These are specific applications of the ineluctable modalities of the visible and of the audible, *nebeneinander* and *nacheinander* in terms of German philosophers, whose opposition the 'Proteus' chapter immediately brings to attention in its opening paragraphs and in many throwaway details ('you see: I hear', U3.24).

Joyce himself had an ear finely attuned for the way people speak and also a sense for what happens when speech becomes public and pompous or when it is transformed into writing, or the medium of print. His books are full of what Dubliners can do extremely well, speak, talk. The same works are paradoxically also very pointedly configurations of letters and symbols, contrived into some elaborate order on paper, with title, pagination, with margins we really need for our notes: they invite concordances. Joyce is extreme either way— both in the vocabulary of his works, their skill in capturing speech, and in the nature of the same works as graphic artefacts, signs on paper. There is both *more* sound and *more* writing.

So it is visible letters against audible voices, and the consequential implications. 'Reading' can mean both. The significant disposition of letters is convertible into sound. The same text can be apprehended through the eyes or through the ears, but it will no longer be the *same* text. The truisms that will follow simply spell out a few effective changes. In practice the opposition between ocular reading and aural listening is lopsided, not symmetrical. We normally are in charge of our own silent reading, determine speed and halts, repetition and retrospection.[8] When a text is read to us, a passive element comes in; all of the options are present. Choices have, actively, been made for us already; we may not even notice the alternatives that have been excluded— tacitly. The text our eyes encounter has yet to be processed in the mind; the sound that reaches our ears has—up to a significant point—already been processed by the speaker. This discriminating speaker's own preferences and defaults become the restrictive basis for our own.

Joyce's works, we are often told, have to be read out aloud, preferably by a
Dublin voice, to come into their own, to be better appreciated, or understood.
This stereotype view is justified: what pedantic reading might overlook—the
tonality, the animation, humour, dynamics, immediacy, resonances: the sheer
pleasure—can be brought alive. Hearing 'Cyclops' or 'Anna Livia Plurabelle'
is—can be—a great experience, a necessary supplementation to silent reading
in the closet. Reading *Ulysses* aloud, moreover, is doing auditory justice to its
changing voices as they are heralded by Malachi Mulligan. His first utterance is
'intoned'; his next words are 'called out [up[9]] coarsely', then 'said sternly', he
returns to 'a preacher's tone'—a broad vocal range is proclaimed all within half
a page ('wheedling, rasping' etc. voices are soon to follow). The quality of his
voices is meticulously recorded. 'Circe' later parodies this manner in bizarre
excess. Mulligan is the protovocaliser of *Ulysses*.

The observations in this essay merely point out and particularise that there is
a medium in both kinds of reading. We become aware of the handicaps when
no live voice is available to give sensuous expression to phrases on the page, or
conversely, when in lecturing we can only use our voices and have no text for
close reading. It makes a difference. Confusingly enough, language does not
always make a clear distinction between seeing and hearing: terms like
'reading' or 'expression' pertain to either area of interpretation, as though they
were identical.

Hearing a text spoken provokes disagreement. We naturally and vehemen-
tly disagree (as we will about the direction of a play), disagree about tone and
emphases, about the distribution of voices. More specifically, is it allowed to
leave anything out in the reading, as happens in a play where stage directions,
obviously, are not part of what we hear? In a play, the persons speaking or
acting do not and cannot indicate their identities in the way the printed version
has to. When a play is being read aloud, the speakers' voices may determine
their identity and their names might not have to be announced each time. In
Joyce's 'Circe' with its dramatic semblance, however, they would be read
scrupulously, as would the apparent stage directions. Possibly a parenthetical
remark like '(*excitedly*)' could be audibly imparted and excitement manifested
directly through the voice, but even a perfect actress could not easily convey
the tenor of an instruction like '*richly*', (U15.1462). Circean parenthetical
passages probably have to be read out aloud since beyond stage-management
they display their own exuberant artificial existence. They have a penchant to
become clownish actors in their own wrong.

It is not always necessary to be told who is speaking, or that something *is*
being spoken, when the situation makes it sufficiently clear. Since only Bloom
and Molly are present in the first bedroom scene a question like '- Do you want
the blind up?' (U4.255) needs no attribution to Bloom, nor does Molly Bloom's
line: '—She got the things'. Neither would a 'said' be needed for Molly's
command, but the Dublin reading leaves out what Joyce put in, so that all we
hear is:

Hurry up with that tea. I'm parched. (U4.263)[10]

There is no ambiguity, yet the author has divided the two sentences by an interpolated 'she said'. In a recital the 'correct', though dispensable, alternative would be:

Hurry up with that tea, **she said**. I'm parched.

This appropriately preserves the pause in between. As information the interjected 'she said' is nearly superfluous, it serves—rhetorically or metrically—to determine the rhythm, it adds stress and poise. If, however, the interjection is spoken by a different voice (a narrative one, reproduced above in **bold** type), the original unit is broken up and the 'said' phrase, which our eyes hardly take note of, is given dramatic and slightly distractive prominence. The kind of prominence that an interposed clause has when Bloom answers 'Who are the letters for' and slowly looks through the mail in his hand:

A letter for me from Milly, he said carefully, and a card to you. And a letter for you. (U4.251)

He does in fact, as we may or may not pick up on a first reading, speak with great care, in an order chosen with deliberate postponement.

how to pronounce (U7.151)

There are gains and losses. The spoken voice reveals by accentuation, it overacts at times, and it conceals. Imagine *hearing* the end of Sirens, where an 'unseeing stripling' saw 'not bronze . . . not gold', nor any other person among those present. The paragraph ends:

Hee hee hee hee. He did not see. (U11.1283)

A performer might decide on what quality to give the four 'Hee's', whether to make them similar to, or distinct from, 'he'—more pronoun or more laughter? At any rate, after so much echoing negation of seeing, we go on to *hear* (quotations only heard can, unfortunately, not be suitably spelled, the correct verbal appearance shown in print, with the give-away '*sea*', is a falsification):

Seabloom, greaseabloom viewed last words (U11.1281)

The ear would probably interpret a contrast between the unseeing piano tuner and Bloom who is seen ('*see* Bloom'), or sees and 'views' words. Perversely we hear 'see' but we see 'sea'. The letters we see on the page line up to a homophone; ocular reading might overlook (aurally miss) sight in favour of the visible ocean ('greaseabloom' can be recognised as echo; earlier in the chapter the composite grew out of 'O greasy eyes' and 'greasy nose', U11.169ff.). In a reading voice 'greasy' might emerge from 'grease'; the eye would also pick on a phantom of maritime flowering, a duplicated 'sea-bloom'; the voice would suggest it, if at all, very remotely. The instant associations offered here need not coincide with that of any one reader or listener, but the associations, the inherent priorities, will differ with the medium. The readings are complementary and, in part, may occlude each other. When we combine them, both follow the text with our eyes and listen to a recording, having it both ways, the problem may become the strain of simultaneous multimedial overload. No one reading—eye or ear or stereographonic—is 'better' in itself than any other.

'Transvocalisation', a rendering by means of the human voice, resembles ordinary translation into other languages with its inevitable reductions. The French version of the 'Sirens' passage changes the direction of the light in order to match '*luit*' with the pronoun: '*Lui lui lui lui. Pour lui rien ne luit . . .*' Some echo is then provided: '*Leux Bloom, huileuxbloom lisait ces dernières paroles*'.[11] The phonemic orchestration typical for 'Sirens' is achieved by '*lui—luit—leux—huileux—lisait*'; however, both 'see' and 'sea' have disappeared, greasiness is foregrounded. '*Leux*' looks like a sound compromise between '*lui(t)*' and '*huileux*', not an independent semantic vehicle. The medium of French imposes its own conditions.

That is oratory (U7.879)

Joyce himself translated some of his written words into his voice. Oddly enough he singled out from *Ulysses* not some of its best-known, representative features, but a passage that he had appropriated, at least in part, from an actual speech delivered in court by a real barrister, John F. Taylor.[12] He selected what already posed as language spoken aloud; it is paraded, in the chapter, as a rhetorical showpiece, 'the finest display of oratory' (U7.792), with stage directions supplied: where the speaker 'lifted his voice' (U7.860), Joyce naturally elevated his own. Yet the selection included parts that are narrative, silent; Joyce gives them different volume and tone. He speaks a paragraph of Stephen's internal quotation from Saint Augustine ('It was revealed to me . . . ' U7.842) in a low key, monotonous patter reminiscent of church litany, but hard to absorb. He also pronounces one of the editorial headlines, whose existence is in imitative print: 'FROM THE FATHERS'. The translating voice can make suitable distinctions.

The seventh chapter in which this takes place, homerically termed 'Aeolus', is one in which the two linguistic modes—speech and writing (or print)—mingle prominently, an episode of inter-section, where the two main characters, and many minor ones, converge. 'Aeolus' is the first of several chapters of crossroads, confusion and interaction. On the one hand the chapter features mainly conversation, speech, talk that may have deteriorated to mere wind, inflation ('gassing, windbag')—air set in motion by vocal organs. Some of it is highly volatile, transient, sufficient for the moment of utterance ('sufficient for the day', U7.726). Whether one of Lenehan's unheeded witticisms or momentous historical occasions—'the tribune's words, howled and scattered to the four winds'—such sound fades into 'Dead noise' (U7.881). The treasury of skills that have been handed down from antiquity, the Art of Rhetoric, serves to make the words entrusted to the air more efficient and less evanescent and forgettable.

But then the chapter takes place in the composing room and the editorial offices of a newspaper, where idle sound is fixed into permanent print. The daily paper transcribes, for example, events at a funeral into a report, to be retained for posterity: 'This morning the remains of the late Mr Patrick Dignam.' Such a phrasing, fabled routinely by professional 'daughters of memory' (as at U2.7) or by communicative chance, will become a record, what the world has a chance to remember ever after, once personal defective memories have died down. The 'Aeolus' episode makes the quality of letters conspicuous by visibly appearing, partly, in the guise of the medium it describes. It shows two kinds of type; the habitual story line in plain characters is disrupted by intrusive phrases, set off from the rest, in capitals that stick out in the semblance of 'headlines'. They are attributable to a kind of supereditorial agency that thereby draws attention to itself and to the medium as an event in print, movable letters. Typography, a standardised manner of writing, manifests itself. Type is not only mentioned ('in leaded', U.145) but exhibited or advertised. Advertisement in the narrower sense has been made possible by its application: design, placement, pictures, visual means to catch the eye.

The bipolarity, the pointedly double nature, is conjugated throughout the chapter. Leaden letters are arranged and distributed. Newspaper bombast is turned from print into sound and commented; when print is voiced, particularly in mocking exaggeration, it can be ridiculous. Famous speeches are repeated or reconstructed. Stephen, speaking as he goes along, improvises a sketch; the newspaper editor wants to usurp it for print: 'That's copy' (U7.1009). It therefore needs a title to conform to the requirements of the printing press. Titles hardly occur in daily speech.

Taylor's oration, the one selected by Joyce for the recording, includes a speech within a speech, what an Egyptian high priest might have spoken to 'the youthful Moses' (U7.833), who was to change history. The rhetorical focus on Moses is ironic. According to scripture, Moses was 'not eloquent'; he admitted 'I am slow of speech, and of a slow tongue' (Ex.4:10). The climax of Taylor's speech, on which it comes to rest, are 'the tables of the law, graven in the language of the outlaw' that Moses brought down from the mountain, the first instance of writing, divine writing, in which the law has been fixed for all times, irrespective of the lapses of human tongues and the obtuseness of human ears. The chapter appropriately includes the inception of writing as well as, antithetically, the first words uttered among humans, according to Lenehan's facetious and anachronistic version: 'Madam I'm Adam'. (Structurally this primeval salutation is a perfect form, a palindrome, which makes sense only in writing: speech cannot be inverted acoustically, sound technically reversed does not mirror itself; what we hear is only a rhyme.) This sort of superficial, perhaps irreverent, quipping or vacuity that abounds in the chapter—and has mainly social and perhaps entertainment value—contrasts with 'the breath of life' put into Adam which induced the joke in the first place (U7.680). Spoken words are short-lived; at the other extreme of the scale is the divine utterance, to 'have spoken with the Eternal' (U7.865), and those of Virgil, Dante or Shakespeare that are evoked in the chapter. In counterpoint also there is the supreme, ideal, perennial chronicle: 'Akasic records of all that

ever anywhere wherever was' (U7.882). Akasic records in theosophical doctrine retain everything, no matter how trivial, for all eternity. In small scale
reproduction, *Ulysses* may have been designed as an Akasic document in which
even a damp night in Fumbally's lane (U7.927), noises like the clanking of
printing presses, or an unassigned 'Ha' (U7.758) await their own minuscule
immortality.

Reading aloud a chapter like 'Aeolus' which is so full of voices (and voice
directions: 'cried—shouted—whispered—crowed in high treble', in rapid
succession, U7.359ff.) poses its specific problems beyond the already familiar
ones of stress or register. How does one voice the headlines? They might be
allotted to a separate voice that would indicate their distinct substance and
derivation. Even then the empty space surrounding print has to be reduced to
the silence of pauses, not differentiated, except possibly in length, from other,
ordinary, pauses, the ones actually occurring: 'Pause. J.J. O'Molloy took out
his cigarettecase' (U7.760). Vocally interpolated *no speech* in a narrative can
denote actual silence, or else editorial manipulation (blank space). Above all it
is visual appearance of the headlines, what we see first, that does not
transvocalise. Capital letters, peculiarities of typography, are simply not to be
heard; graduations of sound volume do not suffice.

Nor are other particularities to be heard. The ingredients of the headline
'HOUSE OF KEY(E)S' do not come across: we would hear 'keys' and
perhaps, if informed, the Manx 'House of Keys', but hardly the advertisement
for Alexander Keyes. Typographically speaking, the parenthesis that signals a
homophonous alternative remains acoustically unmarked. To our eyes the
parenthesis reveals a semantic flutter that no ear could catch; that is to say, a
very Joycean trait finds no vocal expression. And how, even with most skilful
articulation, can a line of purely graphic representation be put into sound, a
headline that consists of three questions marks: '???'(U7.512)?

Well, the voice, yes: gramophone

Mechanical voices are heard in 'Aeolus': trams, printing presses, doors:
'Everything speaks in its own way' (U7.177). 'The telephone whirred'. Bloom
as 'A DISTANT VOICE' interrupts a demonstration of a clever journalist who
cabled information to New York by graphic, letter-coded, superimposition. If
the invention of a 'DISTANT' (*tele*) 'VOICE' (*phone*) had been available at the
time, all the tele*graphic* ingenuity that is being extolled would not have been
necessary. The 'Aeolus' chapter, one of communication (by tram, mail service,
newspaper distribution, and other) achieved or failed,[13] thematically introduces the bridging of distances by the voice, telephone, and by writing, the
telegram. The scene of action are the offices of the *Evening Telegraph*, in local
phrasing 'tell a graphic lie' (U16.1232). Graphic and phonic lies abound; a
graphic one is 'Stephen Dedalus B.A.' or 'L. Bloom' (to say nothing of
M'Intosh) in the evening edition of the *Telegraph*; or a curiosity to show like:
'Nother dying come home father' (U3.199).

In Glasnevin cemetery Bloom reads words graven into stone. Inscriptions perpetuate names, dates, perhaps a person's occupation or the world's evaluation. But how could you remember everybody, asks Bloom. 'Eyes, walk, voice'.[14] Lapidary letters cannot capture what is most individual and unique: glances, movement, vibrations. But there is something:

Well, the voice, yes: gramophone. Have a gramophone in every grave or keep it in the house . . . Remind you of the voice like the photograph reminds you of the face (U6.962-7)

An invention that turns sound into a kind of writing, that conserves fleeting moments, can overcome the mortality of the human voice. Gramophone as a word labels the anomaly: the composite fuses writing (*gram[m]o*) with voice (*phone*: 'phonograph' is an alternative); the invention is a series of medial transformations: a live voice is graven into the surface of a disk, from whose grooves the sound can be resurrected as vibrations of the air, which in turn are translatable into letters, which for us will be spoken again. The human voice can be written *as* voice and aural memory is made possible: 'After dinner on a Sunday. Put on poor old greatgrandfather'. But before the departed ancestor is put on, in Bloom's imaginative evocation, the machine might assert itself:

Kraahraark!

The onomatopoetic signal is, ironically, hard to voice with the sort of accuracy the letters are devised to project. Bloom is empirically aware of the conditions and mischances that the relatively new medium entails by its nature, disturbing scratchy noises that interfere with the message. (Joyce's own reading of the Aeolus passage is now nearly inaudible, the recording, a mechanical copy, enunciates mainly that the writing of the voice has worn badly in time.) The medium intrudes. It also shapes the message itself and evolves its own code. Phatic contact is established first.

Hellohellohello

The telephone adapted this fairly recent salutation, originally used for unexpected meetings,[15] to its novel situation of non-meetings. After the repeated 'hello' spoken into vacancy, Grandfather falls back on what he might say in a real, face to face, encounter:

amawfullyglad

He may or may not be 'awfully glad' (he does not seem to be), but he uses one of the available formulas. The run-on word, a hurried congestion, makes us aware that the logical, grammatical word divisions of the writing convention need not coincide with pauses in actual speech.[16] Another noise then intrudes (which might also translate the kind of pause-filling sounds we make):

kraark

Then the message is partially repeated, not so much for emphasis or to prevent misunderstanding (as in Bloom's phone call), perhaps, as out of embarrassment. The medium has an effect on human psychology. When Greatgrandfather addresses posterity[17] he may not feel at ease:

awfullygladaseeagain

Again the words are rushed into one long unit. The almost habitual 'see again' shows that no convention is yet at hand to speak to people that are remote in both space and time and definitely not visible. No-one would take the phrase literally, of course, or perhaps even notice a discrepancy: To say 'awfully glad to be heard again' would sound oddly pedantic and would be equally untrue. Any stereotype, no matter how inadequate, would serve the purpose. The message, in essence, is nothing but indirect contact: 'I am speaking to you'. The communication may well terminate now. There is nothing to follow but repetition and more interference. A new noise seems to reproduce the misadventure of a scraping needle, sound without vowels:

hellohello amawf krpthsth.

As in farewell, the gramophone draws again attention to itself and its inadequacies. The imaginary appearance of Greatgrandfather addressing invisible ancestors by technical contrivance shows Bloom's shrewd common sense observation. Not only does the medium display its own restrictions, it also determines situations and speech forms. A gramophone recording does not present a slice of life, random, average, but turns the act of recording into an artificial event of heightened self-consciousness. The gramophone message in itself,[18] consisting of repetition with modification and odd novelties thrown in (all in need of interpretation), formally imitates features of Joyce's works.

Bloom 'envisioning' (typically there does not seem to be a word for aural imagination!) dead Greatgrandfather's staged after-dinner declamation prefigures analogous scenes in 'Circe' where they take on a life of their own and where the late Paddy Dignam, for one, makes statements to his survivors, including 'My master's voice' (U15.1247). There too a gramophone is heard. In Circean fashion it is treated like a person:

> THE GRAMOPHONE
> Jerusalem!
> Open your gates and sing
> Hosanna . . . (U15.2170)

True to its mechanical nature, it soon changes its tune, 'drowning' a more human voice:

Whorusalaminyourhighhohhh . . . (*the disc rasps gratingly against the needle*) (U15.2211)

The THREE WHORES then echo and squawk: 'Ahhkkk!' The gramophone's intrinsic voice seems to be an *Ahhkkk* or *Kraak* noise. Everything speaks his own way. This time the noise interference is also semantic: 'Whorusalamin . . .' combines the song theme with 'whore'. The wording makes the gramophone's utterance almost coincide with the next stage

identification, as though the voice saying 'Whorusalamin . . .' were to chime
with the exclamation of the whores. Voices overlap.

Voicing 'Circe' consists in reading out everything, stage directions included
('*richly*', above), especially when they take over narrative functions. Even the
purely spoken parts are not unproblematic. At one point, the VOICE OF ALL
THE DAMNED says:

Htengier Tnetopinmo Dog Drol eht rof, Aiulella! (U15.4708)

This is laborious to enunciate, and even harder to 'understand', especially if
said by many voices[19] ('ALL' the damned cannot be enlisted anyway). The eye
has little trouble spelling out a message in reverse (which will be visible a few
lines later: 'Alleluia, for the Lord God Omnipotent reigneth!'). The unaided
ear would hardly make sense out of a strange conglomerate of sounds. We
cannot hear backwards; phonetically, *eht* does not mirror *the*. But even if,
listening, we were to recognise the inversion, we would never pick up—as the
eye might—that '*God/Dog*' is positioned exactly in the centre, flanked by 18
letters each side. This optical fact need not be of significance (though
'Dooooooooooog!' and its inversion 'Goooooooooood!' will be highlighted[20]
right afterwards), but it makes a certain kind of structural or numerical
interpretation possible. The inversion of letters and their spatial disposition
have a literary and an occult tradition, which has become possible precisely
because letters are transferable objects.

Voicing 'Ithaca' and 'Penelope'

The 'Ithaca' chapter is visibly distinct from all others, broken into paragraphs with many blank spaces between the segments, paired usually as
question and answer. If it is to be read aloud, a level, dead pan voice, detached,
neutral, would conform best. There are no outward and visible signs of
emphasis: music, literature, prostitution, exposed corporation emergency
dustbuckets, the Roman Catholic Church—all seem to be given equal stress.
The result of a non-commital voice would be monotony and somnolence. A
certain amount of dramatic misrepresentation (vocal differentiation and accentuation, perhaps assigning different tones to questions and answers, and
whatever a histrionic repertoire might contribute) would no doubt be felt
acceptable.

The patent visuality of the chapter would not transvocalise too well. How
would one distinguish words from ciphers, show in a single paragraph the
variable whatness of signifiers like 'five thousand six hundred and sixtyfour'
against '6617' or 'MCMIV' (U17.95ff.)? An acrostic, intrinsically spatial, is
not easily put into sound: 'Poets oft have sung in rhyme / Of music sweet . . .'
(U17.412). The reciting voice would indicate the spaces between the sections,
naturally, as pauses, but how would those pauses be distinguished from the
final full stop which substitutes for an answer? The voice can hardly make a
distinction between a pause—silence—that represents nothing, empty space,
and one that expresses a full stop. It will moreover, not do justice to the extra

size of the famous, inaudible, full stop that brings the chapter to a visible[21] close.

We cannot put the blatant, large full stop at the end of 'Ithaca' into sound, but ironically in a recital of the 'Penelope' chapter the full stops that are graphically absent *are* being read. This by the sheer need of a speaker to stop for breath. The non-stop flow of 'Penelope', its best known feature, must break into pieces, the stream of consciousness becomes a succession of gulps. The chapter, of course, invites translation into a Dublin voice. Molly Bloom's monologue has become a set piece for one woman readings, or stagings, usually with a gutsy Irish brogue and an endearing lilt. Words come alive, vibrations, humour, pathos are put across in ways that the perusal of a text in the closet could never achieve. Such readings belong to the great aural pleasures available. The emotional gains are not nullified by the platitude that a spoken interior monologue is a contradiction in terms: it externalises interiority, turns it into its opposite, it speaks the unspoken. The implicit misrepresentations are worth some scrutiny simply because they spotlight essential dynamics.

Some of the decisions for a reading of 'Penelope' are those any director of a play would have to take. How to voice the abbreviated 'H H' in 'give something to H H the pope for a penance' (U18.121)—as 'aitch aitch', Irish 'haitch haitch'—or fully as 'His Holiness'? More generally, should the voice be a quiet, meditative, muted, even, flow, as would befit Molly's situation in bed, or should emotions be acted out, as on a stage, for dramatic effect? Will an actress move about, raise her voice, shout, scream, cry, climax? Decisions involve a temporal dimension. The monologue is in a continuous present, late at night, all is NOW. Memories are in the past tense; when a scene of long ago is called up,

the one and only time we were in the box . . . a fast play about adultery that idiot in the gallery hissing the woman adulteress he shouted
    (U18.1110-9)

this can all be part of the same low key monologue, a recollection of a former event in the present. If the voice is dramatised to a hiss, and if the man's shouting 'The woman adulteress!!!' is actually shouted (as Molly would never shout it right now), then we seem to be transported into the past, all becomes THEN. When a memory of 'Love's Old Sweet Song' breaks in and 'comes loves sweet soooooooooooong' in the performance is 'let out full' (as Molly imagines it will be: 'when I get in front of the footlights again', U18.877), we have actually moved into that future that is mentally rehearsed; in her bed she does not sing. The tone and volume of voice can correlate to tense, change tenses, take us into the past, which is brought alive as it was then, or else imaginatively ahead in times to come. In other words, which *time* should the reading voice prefer? The written text offers the option; the spoken voice favours one over the other.

And how to speak the famous last cadences? The orchestra increasing its volume for the finale, a crescendo of YESses—an affirmative, all-embracing, orgiastic, climax? This would also pay homage to one of the text's prototypes, the closing aria of Claudio Monteverdi's *Il Ritorno d'Ulisse in Patria*, in which

Penelope and Ulisse join in a string of yesses (drawn out in operatic repetition): *'Sì, sì, vita! Sì, sì, core, sì, sì!'*[22] Or is the end a somnolescent fade-out, a breath before unconsciousness takes over, a return to that first sleepy soft grunt 'Mn' (U4.57), hardly audible, *de*voiced again? Or else we might prefer a casual, distanced, almost indifferent 'yes, I will, yes' (in line with 'as well him as another'), or some other alternative? Various endings are possible and to be considered as potentialities of the text. The mind can superimpose them. The speaking voice by choosing one tends to drown out all the others, the roads not taken.

Most important is the change of the process of understanding itself. Having the last chapter spoken to us means that uncertainties in our own reading have been eliminated, along with alternative decisions, and meaning has been predetermined. In ocular reading the linear, unmarked, unscanned, unpunctuated, succession is continuous and chancy exploration. As we go along we constantly surmise, create mini-contexts, test provisional views. We overshoot and have to turn back, change the strategy. Progress is characterized by course corrections, adaptations, retracing, reaccentuation. The continuous string of words has to be dissected into significant phases among ghostly configurations that may prove to be erroneous. The task requires Odyssean resilience. Here is Molly imagining a seduction scene (and suppose that you come across this passage for the first time on the printed page and take it in, as in practice we may not notice we have to, phase by phase):

unless I paid some nicelooking boy to do it . . . a young boy would like me Id confuse him a little alone with him (U18.84)

We know, right away, that 'like' is not a verb, not (as theoretically it might be) a preposition after a pause. What no voice would bring out is the unorthodox spelling of 'Id' without its apostrophe; but no reader is sidetracked towards a Latin pronoun (though in *Finnegans Wake* we would no longer be quite as certain). Eye reading is constant, habitual, mainly unconscious, translation.

if I were

If I were *what*? But no, this phrase points backward. It is a close, not the new opening we might have thought; with a different intonation. Gears have to be changed:

alone with him if I were Id let him see my garters the new ones and make him turn red looking

Where or what is he looking? No, the sequel reveals that *she* is

looking at him seduce him I know what boys feel with that down

For another brief moment we may wonder what boys feel with *what* down where, until we mentally convert a possible preposition (compare 'down on bathingsuits', U18.9) into a harmless noun:

with that down on their cheek

We then know Molly is thinking how young boys are:

doing that frigging drawing out the thing

In a setting of seduction—with 'doing that frigging'—'the thing' that is drawn out might be disturbingly suggestive, also in view of the sort of reputation that Molly has been given long before her actual appearance. Again misconceptions are cleared away as we move on:

drawing out the thing by the hour question and answer . . . (U18.85ff)

If we have gone astray, the postponed 'by the hour' takes us back to the main road and changes both 'drawing out' and 'the thing'. A first reading will not always, and not automatically, and not inevitably *at once*, determine the syntactic drift. Semantic dislocation is part of the experience of finding one's unpredictable way. A vocal translation will save us from such error-prone straying and give clear and meaningful direction, without hinting at potential wrong turnings. We gain a lot in clarity, the way is smooth, obstacles have been removed, there is far less exertion.

keep turning and turning (U18.408)

Reading 'Penelope', in particular, is an exercise in weaving, pursuing uncertain threads, interlacing them into provisional patterns. Lack of overt guidance makes the procedure a constant retexturing, a matter of undoings and new adjustments. Misreadings are abandoned textures, though they may be readmitted, epiphenomenally or self-reflexively: 'drawing out the thing by the hour', for example, would serve to portray the chapter, or all of *Ulysses*, or our own probing activity. A Joycean reading is often the delayed readmission of former semantic rejects: the winner of the day's race is 'Throwaway', something, the name suggests, to be got rid of, which, against expectation or probability, has come back.

No typographical signs guide us through the monologue; but a reading voice gives guidance. It has eliminated the hesitation, the puzzling at cross roads, wrong tracks, dead ends, and the need for unweavings. A fine voice makes the text come alive; we are carried along with the current. The wayward stream of consciousness has become a smooth channel. A commodious high road has replaced the jungle or the labyrinth. The labyrinth was recognised early on as an instructive metaphor for the works that featured someone named Stephen Dedalus, who evokes the 'old artificer' at the end of the novel, which in a Latin epigraph acknowledged Ovid's *Metamorphoses*, a forerunner of cunningly wrought *Ulysses*. Ovid's description of the labyrinth in design and construction has affinities with a text in which readers have to find their way. Daedalus, famous for his skills, *'ponit opus'* [does not work], and *'turbatque notas'* [confounds the marks of distinction] *'et lumina flexum ducit in errorem'* [leads eyes into (erroneous) wanderings] *'variarum ambage viarum'* [by the intricacy of various passages] (*Metamorphoses* VIII: 159-61). What perplexes in reading is the lack of '*notas*'—no punctuation or typographical pointers; eyes are misdirected. James Joyce, cunning artificer, '*turbat notas*', infuriated his early readers, as their reviews document. Frequently the *Notas* are now supplied from outside (Ariadne's thread[23] is the analogy), or by the reciting voice which imperceptibly lures us onto the approved path, away from ambiguous and devious windings.

By way of illustration Ovid introduces the river Maeander as a simile: The labyrinth is 'not otherwise than watery Maeander playing in the field—'*non secus ac liquidus Maeandros in arvis ludit*' . . . It plays, '*et ambiguo lapsu refluitque fluitque*' [and with doubtful (ambiguous) course flows back and forth]; '*occurrens sibi venturas aspicit undas*' [meeting itself, seeing its own waves coming] '*et nunc ad fontes, nunc ad mare versus apertum incertas exercet aquas*' [it sends[24] its uncertain waters now towards their source, now towards the open sea] (*Met* VIII:162-6). Directions keep changing, backwards and forwards (Ovid in imitation puts '*refluit*' before '*fluit*'), as though in prediction of the meandering stream of consciousness with its turnings, especially of Molly's '*lapsus*' (smooth motion or falling), or in prediction of the unforeseen turns of reading. Courses are uncertain: ambiguous ('*amgage, ambiguo*'), they demand going or acting about, around (*ambi, agere*). The Maeander digression is figurative, a comparison: Just so ('*ita*'), Ovid goes on: Daedalus '*implet innumeras errore vias*' [filled the paths with winding passages]. Joyce did this almost literally. The winding passages become reading 'errors' in our explorative groping. The builder of the labyrinth himself scarcely was able to find his way back to the entrance, such, Ovid summarises, was the deceptiveness of the construction: '*tanta est fallacia tecti*'. (*Met* VIII,166-8).[25] The maze is puzzling, the structure fallacious, readings fallible. Errings and wanderings can be called odysseys.

Daedalus knew his construction and succeeded, though barely, in finding his way out; but others did not. For Molly Bloom herself her meandering thoughts are clear at each single instant of her weaving; as the originator of the monologue, she knows what she means as her memory flows forward and backward; she knows the implied grammatical subject of each of her phrases as they take shape:

and did you whatever way he put it I forget no father (U18.111)

This would have to be transcripted, in Circean mode, by instructive differentiation (and would correspondingly be acted out by a reading voice); for example:

PRIEST: 'And did you . . .?'
MOLLY (*thinking*): whatever way he put it, I forget. (*aloud*): 'No, father . . .'

In linear reading there is, to begin with, a string of letters, with a '*fallacia texti*' that might possibly resolve itself to 'I forget no father' (a vague recall of 'a brother is as easily forgotten as an umbrella', 9.975, might help such an error along)—a reading we instantly abandon as we go further along the winding passage. The phantom configuration 'I forget no father', tested and instantly thrown out, is an erroneous weaving whose threads will be retextured to the much more satisfactory script given above. The signifiers are fallacious for the readers on a first encounter. It is hard to imagine a novice reader who would not, on occasion, rush into error.

when I used to go to Father Corrigan he touched me (U18.107);

The continuation—'father'—puts the preceding three words into a more decorous context, a context, again, that the dramatising voice would have set up from the start (maybe by a confessional whisper). Father Corrigan caught in tactile transgression is recognised as a misapprehension, a hermeneutic risk; but even when displaced by a better accou t, it is still part of devious lateral meanings (all the more so since Molly seems to pursue a similar dark winding soon afterwards: 'I wouldnt mind feeling it neither would he' (U18.114). Once the text is prepared and pruned, the right turnings marked, wrong ways closed for traffic, the procedure becomes plain sailing, more of a guided tour. Daedalus, cunning artificer, has given way to a no nonsense architect.

The chapter's lack of overt differentiation is in tune with the characterisation of the heroine as 'prudent indifferent *Weib*'.[26] A 'Penelope' chapter that is pre-edited for us also changes Molly's character and nature. She becomes more simple-minded, easier to master, to chart, she becomes domitable, the one thing which Joyce seems at pains not to make her (though some readers may). Molly Bloom, as well as Homer's Penelope, is smart, alert—'*periphrôn*' (*Od* 1:329 *et passim*). The prefix *peri-* indicates that something is going on all around; Penelope is someone who thinks 'on all sides', is circumspect. Circumspection is what we need in deciphering a text.

The notion of a slow, step by step, circumspect worrying about ambiguities, as exercised here, falsifies 'the' reading process as much as do all others. Sequential analysis is not the norm to measure alternative procedures against; it merely serves to magnify mental predicaments in slow motion. The 'usyslessly unreadable Blue Book of Eccles' (FW 179.26) *is* unreadable, unpronounceable (there exist two rival accentuations of the title—*U*lysses and U*ly*sses), unrecitable, untranslatable. No one modality (visible or audible) can do it full justice. *Ulysses* is also defined by the specific inadequacies of its transmediations; they are, like home without Plumtree's Potted Meat, incomplete. The handicap approach to Joyce may be supplementarily revealing.

At times a right decision may not be evident even in retrospection:

Boylan talking about the shape of my foot he noticed at once even before he was introduced when I was in the DBC with Poldy laughing and trying to listen (U18.246-8)

Boylan noticed Molly's foot when she and Poldy were in the same DBC café: who, of the three, was laughing and who was 'trying to listen'? In Homeric, inflected, Greek, identifying the subject of 'laughing' would be no problem. Translators, when using finite verbs for dangling participles or gerunds, are forced to determine the antecedents; in this case they offer different scenarios.[27] In a chapter like 'Circe', the problem would have been resolved too; its expositional mode would have identified the person laughing and trying to listen. In this respect, 'Circe' is in pointed contrast to 'Penelope': it over-differentiates, assigns voices and actions; it signals all shifts as on a stage, spells out WHO (even if there is no logical WHO) is doing WHAT; it separates speech from the rest. Again translations into other languages tend to determine the correct grouping and leave out disconcerting illicit affairs between words, analogous to the vocal differentiation in reading a text aloud. Such attempts *de*Penelopise 'Penelope'. As we do anyway: we stop, scan, punctuate, pull apart, dissect, underline. Conversely we tend to *Circefy* the chapter when we clarify vocal identities, roles, or intonation, and the shifts that the lettered text in its visibly dead pan way leaves undecided. We always read—or recite—against the grain: the separative activities of understanding require it. Reading 'Penelope' aloud with histrionic abandon, and with stress on its musical dimension, again would *Sirenise* the chapter. Most of our abstract writing about 'Penelope' *Ithacises* it, as do our sedate analyses: certain aspects are singled out, extracted and reassembled, usually in the orderly manner that the chapter takes conspicuous efforts to defy.

*   *   *

The handicap approach to Joyce—by revelatory failures. Two main modes have been pitted against each other. They help us to see/hear that sound is sound, letters are letters, and never quite compatible, never quite congruous with the dynamics of a literary work. Whatever we call reading is conforming to each chapter's or work's programmed modality *and* in essential ways going against it. In more positive terms, we apply medial parallax, turn each text also into what it pointedly is not. Perhaps literary texts are distinguished from others by their inability to be left unchanged. We paraphrase and heterophrase and antiphrase. *Finnegans Wake*, as always, remains the extreme challenge to mental reprocessing. It manifests itself as a configuration of letters or an orchestration of sound and on occasion comments on their collusion and opposition.

What can't be coded can be decorded if an ear aye sieze what no eye ere grieved for. (FW 482.34)

Tantalisingly, this seems to be about coding and decoding by the imperfect means of the ear and the eye. Synesthetically, if 'an ear aye sieze', the ear misses a lot: it 'sees' and it 'seizes' something, but *sieze* is also neither seeing nor seizing. Spelling (which fusses about *seize* against *sieze*) is important to the eye which does not acknowledge in 'ear eye' and 'eye ere' the faulty contaminations that hearing might prompt: 'ear-eye' and a reciprocal 'eye ear'. But it is through eye-ear that we approach the *Wake*: the senses combine and encode divergent messages. Non-perception enters the game: proverbially, 'What the eye can't see the heart can't grieve for' (U15.1998); there is a heart in 'de*cord*ed'. In German, something can *ergreifen* ('ere grieve'), (seize, touch, move) the heart. In German *greifen* corresponds to 'seize', composites like 'begreifen' are used for 'comprehend, seize mentally'. What the senses cannot comprehend the heart may reach for. Or else: 'Eye hath not seen, nor ear heard, neither have entered into the heart of man, the things which God hath prepared for them that love him' (I Cor. 9). What can't be cured must be injured (as in P88) or endured, in grief. In trying to decode, or de-*cord* the various strands, we use ear, eye and tactile groping and perhaps the intuition that is granted to the heart. A lot of sense perception has to be mustered in order still not to understand, not to *com*prehend, a passage whose gist has been misappropriated to insinuate what we have come to learn anyway, that neither ear nor eye are sufficient means to reach a Protean end. The charming air and rhythm of the *Wake* sentence tempers resignation with vague homely comfort, an easement that probably affects us more through the ears by sound than through our scrutinising eyes, more through the spell of language than its spelling.

Apologetic Bloom is right. There *is* a medium in all things.

Transition Years: James Joyce and Modernist Art

Alison Armstrong

There's a genial young poetriarch Euge
Who hollers with heartiness huge:
    Let sick souls sob for solace
    So the *jeunes* joy with Jolas!
Book your berths! *Apres mot, le déluge.*

(Joyce to Eugene Jolas, 1933)[1]

In the relationship between literary art and the visual arts, various collaborations developed among editors and critics, some of whom were also poets, to promote new ideas at the heart of modernist sensibility. *transition*, arriving relatively late in the era of manifestoes, was a long-lived publication with an editorial stance which favoured no single '-ism'. Its polemics embraced a number of means for achieving new art.

Edited by Eugene Jolas from 1927 to 1938 in Paris and New York (with a two-year hiatus in the early 30s), *transition* was, as Stuart Gilbert wrote in 1949, '. . . no "little magazine" . . . but a big one in every sense'. It explored 'the interest in the problems of a language aspiring to transcend the norms of speech and to retrieve the poetic form of its beginning'.[2]

James Joyce and Gertrude Stein were perhaps the most controversial and important writers in *transition*. Samuel Beckett, Hart Crane, Kay Boyle, Jean (Hans) Arp, Louis Aragon, Franz Kafka, and Dylan Thomas are but a few others who exemplify the quality and diversity of the better literary offerings. Contributors other than 'creative writers' included art critics Carl Einstein, Carola Giedion-Welcker, and Herbert Read; architects Le Corbusier and Siegfried Giedion; composers Aaron Copland and Edgar Varese; photographers Brassai, Cartier-Bresson, and Man Ray; sculptor Alexander Calder; painters Wassily Kandinsky, Paul Klee, Jean Miro, Pablo Picasso.

In his 1938 retrospective statement, Jolas (who had capitalised the magazine's name in 1932) speculated:

The great period of transition through which humanity seems destined to pass so painfully into the . . . new era is surely not ended. I believe it is not impossible . . . that the review *Transition* may, for future generations, constitute an important record of . . . its earlier manifestations.[3]

We are now in that era, the 'post-Modern era', which in literature is commonly thought to have begun with the end of World War II while others consider 1939 the end of Modernism—the year of *Finnegans Wake*'s publication as well as of the beginning of the war. Perhaps Jolas's statement still applies; we may still be in a painful transition phase, awaiting that new era which the next *fin de siècle*, the end of a millenium, may bring: a healing synthesis of aesthetics and ethics. However, the climate of post-Modernism is mannerist; it concerns itself with the present and, especially in painting, architecture and decorative arts, plays with motifs from past eras—including the era of modernism. Literary art now plays upon its modernist heritage of *formal* innovation and seems less concerned with language itself as an artistic medium. Modernists were concerned with transforming the world with their art of the future; post-Moderns have lost the spiritual and aesthetic drive and are more concerned with wittily commenting upon the state of the world (which includes their artistic heritage) than with changing it. The freedom of art was won by modernists in those transition years—in which the exile seemed a pre-condition for fulfilment of the imagination, in which mobility in time and space was newly enhanced by the Machine, in which the imaginative leap from man's 'primal' psychic roots to his outwardly sophisticated civilization was made with the aid of discoveries in physics and psychoanalysis.

Like many of his contemporaries, Jolas felt a need to redefine human experience in relation to the external realities of a newly mechanized and alienating society. The plastic arts and music seemed to be outstripping innovation in linguistic art. Writers were demanding the right to be freed from outworn assumptions as were painters and other artists. The scientific community, responsible for the fast-moving new Machine Age, also produced psychoanalysis and modern physics whose discoveries helped artists to redefine 'reality'; or perhaps helped to prepare an audience receptive to parallel 'discoveries' in the arts. Einstein's theories of relativity and the new concept of an expanding universe—in conjunction with consciousness of the 'shrinking world' of the Machine Age—appealed to the imagination.

As Jolas says in *The Language of Night*,[4] he became interested in both Freudian psychoanalysis and Surrealism, which derived its main tenet, that creativity springs directly from the Unconscious, from their misprision of Freud's *The Interpretation of Dreams* and *Psychopathology of Everyday Life*. Although Jolas nearly joined Breton's clique, he ultimately disagreed with the movement, yet published their work from time to time. While Surrealism was a fusion of the rational and irrational—a third element—Jolas was more interested in a direct expression of unconscious experience.

One reason for Jolas's success as an editor was his ability to keep *transition* free of submersion in any single -ism. He maintained his aesthetic independence and developed the revolutionary stance of the review in which he could expound his own new terminology: New Magic, mantic, paramyth, orphic creation, hypnologue, and vertical (later called vertigral) tri-lingual syllabic verse.

Jolas's concern for a new language was motivated by 'the profound disquietude in which the sensitive man of our age lives. He has trusted to pure reason too long'.[5] He found many on both sides of the Atlantic who shared his *mal du siècle*. Since one of his aims was to make contemporary experimental literature available to readers 'in a language that Americans can understand', he and his wife, Maria MacDonald Jolas, along with assistant editor Elliot Paul (and later James Johnson Sweeney) found much of their time consumed by translating as well as by their general editorial duties. Jolas himself contributed over fifty critical and poetic pieces in the interest of defining the 'Euramerican mind'.

Most Americans involved in the ferment of artistic innovation found that they preferred to work and 'grow up' artistically in Europe. By maintaining the cosmopolitan nature of his review, Jolas ensured a continuous dialogue between the American and European audiences. However, for all the intercontinental talk it is doubtful whether a truly Euramerican mind ever developed to the extent he envisaged. Most 'Euramericans'—such as Ezra Pound, Djuna Barnes, Kay Boyle, Ernest Hemingway, Sylvia Beach, and Gertrude Stein—were already within the fold, not necessarily of *transition* but of its audience.

Attacks, rejections, and misunderstandings inevitably arose between *transition* and some of the other little magazines. Wyndham Lewis's *The Enemy* was an early annoyance. In January, 1927, the British Lewis had published the first issue in which he put forward an attack upon Joyce in an essay, 'The Revolutionary Simpleton', at a time when Joyce had been trying to get a magazine upon which to rely for serial publication. But negotiation with *transition* had begun the previous month and, with two successful readings, an agreement was reached that *transition* would re-print fragments that had appeared in *transatlantic review*, *Le Navire d'Argent*, and *Criterion*. Some who had previously helped Joyce turned against 'Work in Progress'. Ezra Pound and Harriet Shaw Weaver (editor of the *Egoist*) thought that Joyce was wasting his genius. With regard to *transition*, Pound politely stated that if he had known about its imminent appearance he would not have brought out *The Exile* review in 1928. But Pound missed his chance with Joyce's new work and a literary 'scoop', for although he had asked Joyce for a typescript in November, 1926, his response, in the form of a private letter, was: 'Nothing short of divine vision or a new cure for the clapp can possibly be worth all the circumambient peripherization'.[6]

But Lewis and Pound were not concerned, as were Jolas and Joyce and a number of others, with the nature of time nor with a 'language of night' which would reproduce the unconscious experience which knows no chronological time. In holding to the Jungian and Husserlian idea that all mental events are as real as 'objective' reality, Jolas put forward his philosophical beliefs which had mystical elements. In 'Frontierless Decade', he reiterates his aims after ten years of editing:

[*transition*] encouraged a new style . . . by postulating a metamorphosis of reality. *Transition* progressed from an experimental into a constructive phase by associating the mutation of language with the new discoveries related to the expansion of consciousness (night-mind) and the intercontinental, social amalgamations occuring today. It was the first to relate this problem to the reconstruction of myth. It asked for a linguistic reformation, not out of esthetic caprice, but because such a reformation was actually taking place . . . (*t.*, No 27, 7)

But the magazine had only a little longer to live and the 'constructive phase' was cut short by overwhelming social and political events that would lead to another World War which would cause most of the innovators to flee Paris.

Transition, which fostered 'mystic union with the Logos', was an ideal means of circulation for Joyce's new work. As French critic Marcel Brion called it, '*la maison de Joyce*' devoted more pages to Joyce's work than to any other author's. Despite interruptions caused by Joyce's many eye operations as well as by his perpetual additions and corrections on galley proofs (some of which had to be specially set up in large type)[7] Joyce and Jolas maintained a close friendship.[8]

The effect which 'Work in Progress' had on its first generation of readers resulted in praise, insightful commentary, imitation, and mockery. Those who understood *transition*'s aims welcomed it as the highest achievement in the quest for new language. Stuart Gilbert, one of Joyce's best hand-picked critics, helped explain the technique in 'Functions of Words'.

> . . . pictures, like words handled in a certain way . . . are emotive signs. The 'Revolution of the Word' is a movement to explore this secondary, non-utilitarian function of language, to treat the *aura*, the 'light vapour which floats above the expression of the thought', as material for art . . . for a super-reality . . . words are treated as plastic media . . . applying a spirit which may breathe new life into the dry bones of modern literature. (*t.*, No 18, 203-5)

Just as Freudian psychoanalytic discoveries resulted from the technique of free association by making the unconscious conscious, so did modernist art aspire 'to make an invisible reality visible—to discover a visual language capable of capturing the spiritual spheres beyond the world of phenomena', as Carola Giedion-Welcker explained in her book on Arp. 'The new art asserted the *inner image* . . . to be grasped by unprecedented methods . . . this double orientation toward the organic form and the abstract articulation . . . was to define the basic directions of modern art.'[9] The use of visual analogues of the inner image is essential, too, in modernist poetic prose.

'Work in Progress' utilized this 'double orientation' by paradoxically removing us from and reimmersing us in universal 'primal' experiences through a cyclic organic form and linguistic constructions highly conducive to unconscious association with visual and auditory imagery. We must approach this text with open eyes and minds in the light of conscious wide-awake reading (be Joyce's 'ideal reader' with the 'ideal insomnia') and turn toward an image-filled world in which the dimensions of time and space, and all sensory perceptions, shift and interact in a 'continuous present tense integument' (Joyce's allusion to a term used by both Freud and Gertrude Stein, *Finnegans Wake* 186.1).

Regardless of aesthetic or political squabbles, the exiles of the transition years had in common an awareness that putting time and space (and, for Americans, a favourable exchange rate) between the artist and his or her origins had a freeing effect which released unconscious associations and created new social ones. No one knew this condition of exile better than Joyce who had flown the nets of British imperialism, Roman catholicism, and Irish nationalism. Regarding his Irishness, he said:

It is my revolt against the English conventions, literary and otherwise, that is the main source of my talent . . . I have great difficulty in coming to any understanding with the English. I don't understand them no more than they understand me . . . I don't write in English.[10]

Joyce seemed to feel that an Irishman is, by nature, an exile even in his own country, for he must use 'the conquerer's language'; in his thought, speech, and in most of his literature it is a source of perpetual tension. As Stephen Dedalus expresses it in *Ulysses* (in reaction to the Englishman Haines), 'My soul frets in the shadow of his language'.

Italo Svevo, Joyce's Triestine friend whom Joyce encouraged to overcome a thwarted writing career, once expressed dismay at the use of the term exile: 'Exiled? People who return to their own country?'

'But don't you remember', Joyce replied, 'how the prodigal was received by his brother in his father's house? It is dangerous to leave one's country, but still more dangerous to go back . . .'[11]

Despite the negative rebellious impulses which motivated Joyce, the cosmopolitan multilingual nature of exile positively helped to prepare the artist, and his audience, for experimentation. Joyce stated that the language of 'Work in Progress' was musical and continually revised for the sake of sound and rhythm, conflating many languages into rhythms derived from Irish-English speech patterns.

'A work of art consists of two elements, the inner and the outer',[12] Kandinsky wrote in explaining the elements of painting in synaesthetic terms. 'Inner and outer'—akin to other distinction such as 'content and form', 'spiritual and material', and 'sense and senses'[13]—point to another distinction which Jolas pointed out at Joyce's urging, the duality of inner voices:

Friedrich Schlegel . . . called attention to the fact . . . that 'there is an inner dualism not only in our dreams, but also in our waking state so that we really think in twos . . . ' I think it is about time to pension off the term 'interior monologue' and give the process its proper designation: interior duologue. (*t.*, No 22, 126)

Not only is there a particularly strong interdependence in Joyce's writing between outer form and inner content (Beckett's statement that it *is* that something which it is 'about' makes this point[14]) but the interior duologue is shown in forms of doubling in *Finnegans Wake*. Every prominent character is either dual or multiple. The sons are twins within the Earwicker family *and* recall every pair of warring brothers in myth and history (e.g. Cain and Abel, Jacob and Esau); the parents are a pair with complementary roles (Adam/Eve, culture/nature) and have equivalents in natural forms (river/hill, stem/stone); the daughter Issy/Iseult has her double in a narcissist-sister mirror image, is a youthful version of her mother (as Nuvoletta), is multiplied in the twenty-eight Raynbow Girls, and doubled by association with Swift's two Esthers (Stella and Vanessa). The relationship between the sons (Shem and Shaun—the penman and the post, Mutt and Jute, Ondt and Gracehoper, et al.) and their father HCE is symbolized by the white and yolk of the cosmic egg which is also Humpty Dumpty who fell from a wall, as did Tim Finnegan . . . and so on.

The element of free association (the psychoanalytic technique that reveals the patient's own inner logic and leads the analyst—who 'reads' the text of the patient's life-story) is clearly part of Joyce's technique by which he reconstructs a *realistic* model of unconscious 'organization' in which all ages and events of historical experience are conflated into a dense nightmare of dreaming back. As readers, we 'analyze' the dream-text in terms of the outer reality; as analysts, we must collaborate in the process of the apparently compulsive free associations in order to comprehend the method in the madness.

Joyce accomplished what Paul Ricouer and others have called 'the verbal icon' which has three traits: 'fusion of sense and the senses, density of language that has become "stuff", virtuality of the experience articulated by this non-referential language.'[15]

Jolas also attempted to use language to reproduce the reality of subjective life. But his writing was qualitatively different from Joyce's. Theorizing about the sort of 'night language' that would most directly convey what he imagined, Jolas claimed:

I invented poem-phonemes in an attempt to approximate the incantatory grammar of inner experience. I invented a new poetic form I called *hypnologues* that tried to give a verbal replica of the experiences between waking and sleeping . . . I took the dream material . . . immediately after waking and integrated it into the rhythmic structure of poems or prose-tales by the union of unfamiliar words, or by phantasmatic world-components, or by the use of authentic dream words.[16]

Here are two examples of the prose-poem styles, the *hypnologue* and the *paramyth*:

A hat upon the beach it was frivering so much it much it was were it not missouring down a word a telegram and never and and her hair floated flat in roseys and in trontelles so loney before a god and and she was tears so tears was she tears . . . [17]

and,

Alone in the wilderness I shall not bleed to death. I am waiting to move in the spell of my wishes. Alone I brew my magic. New world, miraculous humanity of my mind, I kneel before you, dusty refugee in my century's shambles.[18]

The *hypnologue* sounds similar to the repetitious style of Gertrude Stein; the second resembles the incantatory tone of egoism of Stephen's diary at the end of Joyce's *A Portrait*. But, the results show, Jolas was not working out of true inner impulse so much as from external theory. Subsequently, he did not produce literary art of any intrinsic merit. If it survives, it is as an historical curiosity. Jolas's true service to literary art was as an editor.

Joyce, who was artistically successful, keeps his reader in a condition of re-reading. He compresses more 'meaning' potential into his words than can be absorbed in a casual first reading. He simultaneously stretches the capacities of sight and hearing so that we keep returning to pick up and 'foreground' what we could not at first focus upon. Just as the structure of the entire book is 'doublends jined', so is our reading process cyclical; this is as true within the serialised fragments as it is with the book as a whole.

In 1929 some of the most important critical essays in *transition* that dealt with Joyce's 'Work in Progress' were published by Sylvia Beach's bookshop, Shakespeare and Co., with Joyce's supervision. The collection was given the wakese title *Our Exagmination Round His Factification for Incamination of 'Work in Progress'*. Dougald McMillan has pointed out that Joyce was operating from behind the scenes to overcome hostility in the hope of preparing a wider audience for the completed work:

Joyce seems to have had four major concerns in mind: to make specified answers to hostile critics, to present the public with an outline of the structural principles of the work, to establish that 'Work in Progress' was a development within literary tradition and not a flaunting of it, and to provide an explanation and justification of the linguistic innovations.[19]

The Irish writer Thomas McGreevy stated that Joyce's style was 'not a reaction from realism but the carrying on of realism to the point where it breaks . . . into fantasy, into the verbal materials of which realism, unknown to the realist, partly consisted'.[20]

Many of its first generation of readers expected that when 'Work in Progress' had achieved final form all obscurities magically would become clarified. The myth of 'the key' to *Finnegans Wake* still lures some critics. But it is the continual process of discovery, expanded into communal re-readings of the *Wake*, which itself is a key—to conscious experience of a model of the unconscious. Readers engage in 'factification' to give substance to a passage which they can then 'exagmine'. Thus reading is both mystery and revelation; Joyce's language of night—as does dream language and imagery—tells by showing that which it also conceals. And, like a dream, the *Wake* has both manifest and latent contents.

Joyce, as Shem the Penman 'self exiled in upon his ego', has as his subject not only his life but the racial memory of the western world. His method is the condensation and repetition characteristic of unconscious processes which know no time other than the continuous present. Who the dreamer of the *Wake* is has never been agreed upon. It may be Humphrey Chimpden Earwicker, publican and Everyman; or Leopold Bloom of *Ulysses* as he lies head to toe in bed beside Molly. But it is not a private dream of Joyce's, for it becomes our dream, too, as we read. It is the nightmare of history come alive. The title may be a command: Finnegans, wake! The uncreated conscience of his race—conscience in the sense of knowing-with—is forged by Joyce/Stephen/Shem in these pages which use Vico's notion of cyclical history as a 'trellis'. We are still an audience-in-progress who must recall the early responses to 'Work in Progress' of nearly sixty years ago which opened the three-hundred year period during which Joyce wanted to keep the critics busy.

Imagine the twelve deaferended dumbbawls of the whowl abovebeugled to be the contonuation through regeneration of the urutteration of the word in pregross. (*FW* 284.18-22)

As the following comparison shows, Joyce continued to develop his text after its *transition* debut. This was published in February 1928:

At maturing daily gloryaims! A flink dab was frankily at the manual arith sure enough which was the bekase he knowed from his cradle no boy better why his fingures were giving him whatfor to fife with. (*t.*, No 11, 7)

By 1939, published as a section of 'The Maths Lesson' in Book II of *Finnegans Wake*, it had grown:

At maturing daily gloryaims!²* A flink dab for a freck dive and a stern poise for a swift pounce was frankily at the manual arith sure enough which was the bekase he knowed from his cradle, no bird better, why his fingures were giving him whatfor to fife with.
. . . .
²*Lawdy Dawdy Simpers. (*FW* 282.6-12; 35)

This section gained, in addition to footnotes, right and left marginalia. The footnotes are in the voice of sister Issy while the marginalia bicker in the voices of Shem and Shaun.

Jolas periodically restated the importance to *transition* of Joyce's new work:

By publishing and defending *Work in Progress* . . . *transition* established a basis for a literary insurrection . . . [Joyce's work] will, I am very sure, continue to baffle the non-visionary minds . . . . (*t.*, No 19-20, 14)

The above mentioned insurrection had been given substance and impetus by a manifesto; the 'Revolution of the Word Proclamation' had appeared in No 16-17 with twelve statements parenthetically supported by quotations from William Blake added by Joyce's friend Stuart Gilbert. It insisted upon the already established autonomy of the creative writer. The following proclamations are descriptive of Joyce's attitude toward his art. (However, as he never signed petitions, Joyce declined to put his signature to this list.)

  6 The literary creator has the right to disintegrate the primal matter of words imposed on him by text-books and dictionaries.
10 Time is a tyranny to be abolished.
11 The writer expresses, he does not communicate.
12 The plain reader be damned.

While Jolas's tendency, as with many other 'innovators' of the word, was toward automatic outpourings and uncrafted reproductions of individual fantasy which relied heavily upon simple word-combining ('clingmourned') or made up words ('frivering'), Joyce was a highly conscious craftsman who constructed a model of unconscious inner reality. As Dougald McMillan observes, Joyce made use of the unconscious 'as a technique of presentation and not as a source of material to be presented'.[21]

Although Jolas recognized that Joyce's methods were unlike his own or those of the Surrealists and others whom he published, he continued to defend and explain Joyce's intentions:

History being, in his earlier words, 'a nightmare', Mr Joyce gives us a multidimensional idea of Time in sleep. His conception of Time is born out of his deep sense of race parallelism. It has relations with the newest discoveries of physical science as well as with oneiromantic experiments . . . He incorporates continually into his work with living folklore and mythology gathered in his travels . . . His verbs transmute the quotidian gesture . . . man's primal language. 'This book', he sometimes says, 'is being written by the people I have met or known'. (*t.*, No 27, 272)

Joyce defied history by making it the subject of his art. He makes an historical event out of his rebuttal of chronology; he awakens by means of a dream.

As 'post-Moderns', we stand where Picasso and Stein, Duchamp and Eisenstein, Schoenberg and Einstein, Joyce and Wittgenstein have left us. The Modernists expanded our perceptions by the 'evolution of the senses' and, as Jolas put it, helped to 'disintegrate the philistine notion of a pragmatic world'.[22] James Joyce in particular demonstrated that the language of the unconscious is poetic and bridges the gap, found in ordinary language, between sense and sensation, between meaning and gestural form. What we read and recognize anew in Joyce's work is the *déjà dit et déjà vu*, the already said, the already seen. He made up nothing, for all his tale-telling, with the exception of this advertising copy:

> Buy a book in brown paper
> From Faber and Faber
> To hear Annie Liffie trip, tumble and caper.
> Sevensinns in her singthings,
> Plurabells on her prose,
> Sheashell ebb music wayriver she flows.
>
> Humptydump Dublin squeaks through his norse;
> Humptydump Dublin hath a horriple vorse.
> But for all his kinks english plus his irismanx brogues
> Humptydump Dublin's *granddada* of all rogues.[23]

(*t.*, No 21, 18)

'All That Fall': Samuel Beckett and the Bible

Vivian Mercier

The National Library of Ireland Richard Irvine Best Lecture, given at the Royal Irish Academy, 11 December, 1986.

I should begin by explaining that I don't propose to engage in a minute analysis of Beckett's radio play, *All That Fall* (BBC, January 1957), which might be described as Ireland's sardonic answer to Dylan Thomas's *Under Milk Wood* (BBC, January 1954). The phrase is quoted in my title to remind us of a passage where Beckett, for once, makes it clear to his audience that he is quoting from the Bible. His work, as we shall see, is full of hidden biblical quotations, but this most emphatically isn't one of them. Just to make conversation, Mr Rooney of *All That Fall* asks his wife:

Who is the preacher to-morrow? The incumbent?

MRS ROONEY: No.
MR ROONEY: Thank God for that. Who?
MRS ROONEY: Hardy . . .
MR ROONEY: Has he announced the text?
MRS ROONEY: 'The Lord upholdeth all that fall and raiseth up all those that be bowed down'. (*Silence. They join in wild laughter* . . .)[1]

Except for the omission of a comma after 'fall', this is an exact quotation from the 145th Psalm, verse 14, according to the King James version. (In the Douay version, the fourteenth verse of Psalm One Hundred and forty-*four* is translated more succinctly and a little more intelligibly as 'The Lord lifteth up all that fall; and setteth up all that are cast down'). It is very likely that Beckett quoted this verse from memory, as he often does quote the Bible. How do we know he is in the habit of quoting from memory? Paradoxically, because his memory is sometimes at fault. In *How It Is* he mentions 'the sky whence cometh our help', a misquotation from the first verse of Psalm 121 in the King James Bible, which reads, 'I will lift up my eyes unto the hills, from whence cometh my help'.

To return to the passage in *All That Fall*, let us assume that Beckett is quoting from memory and ask ourselves what inferences we can draw from that assumption. On the one hand, we might argue that Beckett was required to learn some or all of the psalm by heart while at school. Verses 15 and 16 of Psalm 145 are in fact more familiar to me than verse 14:

The eyes of all wait upon thee; and thou givest them their meat in due season.
Thou openest thine hand, and satisfiest the desire of every living thing.

Though Beckett may not have known it, the Vulgate Latin of these two verses is incorporated almost word for word into one of the graces recited every day in the Dining Hall of Trinity College, Dublin:

> Oculi omnium in te sperant, Domine;
> tu das eis escam eorum in tempore opportuno.
> Aperis tu manum tuam,
> et imples omne animal benedictione tua.

After he moved into College rooms in 1926, Beckett must often have heard these words. The fact that he was entitled to free Commons every night as a Foundation Scholar may even have convinced him of their literal truth. On the other hand, if nobody had compelled him to learn the passage by heart, then the fact that verse 14 implanted itself spontaneously in Beckett's memory encourages profounder speculation. After all, these are among the most comforting and reassuring words in the whole English Bible. We can hardly deny the thought that this sentence once held deep meaning for Samuel Beckett. At the very least, its rhythm must have enchanted his ear. Listen to it: the first clause contains four iambic feet with an internal rhyme—'The Lord upholdeth *all* that *fall*'; the second clause is a complete line of Miltonic blank verse, 'and raiseth up all those that be bowed down'. The last two syllables, with their assonance 'bowed down', may be read as a spondee, and 'those' assonates with 'hold' in the first line.

It was by no accident, in any case, that Beckett chose it as the title of what is surely his most deeply pessimistic play: almost everything that happens in *All That Fall* directly contradicts the psalmist's blessed assurance. Maddy and Dan Rooney's life-experience seems to deny at every turn the existence of a merciful God. Yet they are not unbelievers: as far as we know, they attend their church every Sunday, no matter how boring the incumbent's sermons may be. The use of this very word 'incumbent' proves that they are members of the Church of Ireland, although the word is more familiar to English Anglicans than to Irish ones; in Ireland, we would be more apt to say 'the rector' or, if there were no rector, 'the curate'. In writing 'the incumbent', Beckett may be having his little joke, since the imagery of the word suggests a clergyman lying in or on his parish. The point is that the Rooneys are definitely not Presbyterians, their theology is not Calvinist. It is true that there are Calvinist elements in the Thirty-nine Articles, but Anglican theology envisages a far more merciful God than Calvin's. Even dotty old Miss Fitt seems aware of this when she helps Mrs Rooney up the steps at Boghill (ie Foxrock) railway station: 'Well', she says, 'I suppose it is the Protestant thing to do'. It would be more natural, of course, to say it is the Christian thing to do, but Beckett is having his joke again. Miss Fitt, although she worships in the same church as Mrs Rooney, is an ultra-Protestant. When Mrs Rooney reminds her that 'Last Sunday we worshipped together. We knelt side by side at the same altar. We drank from the same chalice', she emphasises the ritual, High Church side of Anglicanism. Miss Fitt, on the other hand, being so Low Church as to resemble a Quaker, is shocked by this reminder: 'Oh but in church, Mrs Rooney, in church I am alone with my Maker. Are not you?' This attitude of Miss Fitt's is a logical outcome of the history of Protestantism, which began with secessions of minority groups from the universal Catholic Church. Once the process of splitting off has begun, there is no logical end short of One Man One Church or, in Miss Fitt's case, One Woman One Church. The next step after that is One Man No Church. As Professor Augustine Martin has pointed out, this step has been taken very easily by several Irish Protestant writers—Synge for example—without much apparent soul-searching, whereas an Irish Catholic author's parting from his faith may well provide material for one or more autobiographical novels in the tradition of *A Portrait of the Artist as a Young Man*.[2] Brian Moore seems to need constant reassurance that his hard-won unbelief remains unshaken: see, for example, that remarkable novel *Cold Heaven*.

Beckett, on his own admission, felt no symptoms of withdrawal. As he told Tom Driver: 'The family was Protestant, but for me it was only irksome and I let it go'.[3] The only hint of anguish about breaking with the faith learned quite literally at his mother's knee is to be found in the 'wild laughter' attributed to the Rooneys. There is surely no more blasphemous moment in any Beckett work, except Hamm's cry in *Endgame*, after a moment of silent prayer: 'The bastard! He doesn't exist!' That is black humour, if you like, but Beckett would have expected that an Irish audience, Catholic or Protestant, would react to it first of all as blasphemy: any subsequent laughter, however loud, would sound uneasy. Every blasphemer, obviously, must once have been a true believer: there is no thrill—at least for an intelligent person—in breaking a prohibition one has never felt threatened by. The harshness of the blasphemy is perhaps a measure of one's sense of loss or of having been deceived by what one trusted most.

Before leaving *All That Fall*, let us look for a moment at the *hidden* biblical allusions in the play. Mr Tyler, one of those who overtake Mrs Rooney on her weary way to the railway station, finds that the back tire of his bicycle has got flat again. Mrs Rooney hears him muttering, and with her usual politeness says, 'I beg your pardon?' 'Nothing, Mrs Rooney, nothing, I was merely cursing, under my breath, God and man, under my breath, and the wet Saturday afternoon of my conception'. The reference here is to the Book of Job, chapter 3, verse 3: 'Let the day perish wherein I was born, and the night in which it was said, There is a man child conceived.' Tyler's response to his flat tire seems a little excessive: Job's bitter cry was torn from him not only because he had lost all his children and all his wealth but because he had been smitten with 'sore boils from the sole of his foot unto his crown'. Furthermore, despite the urging of his wife, Job did *not* curse God at any time. By the way, this was not Beckett's first allusion to a text beloved by pessimists. In the fourth chapter of *Murphy*, Neary is in dire need of a drink; the following dialogue occurs:

'But by Mooney's clock', said Wylie, 'the sad news is two-thirty-three'.

Neary leaned against the Pillar railings and cursed, first the day in which he was born, then—in a bold flash-back—the night in which he was conceived.

'There, there,' said Wylie. 'Needle knows no holy hour'.

'Needle' Wiley then brings Neary to 'an underground café close by', where they circumvent the licensing laws by drinking two large coffees ordered by Wylie, who specifies 'Three star'. Was this subterfuge the origin of Irish Coffee?

There is yet another type of Biblical allusion to be found in *All That Fall*, perhaps not quite so carefully concealed as the quotation from Job. Here, Mrs Rooney surprisingly ventures into the arena of textual scholarship. 'It wasn't an ass's colt at all, you know', she says to her husband, apparently apropos of nothing. 'I asked the Regius Professor.' After a pause, Mr Rooney gives a safe answer: 'He should know'. Mrs Rooney goes on, 'Yes, it was a hinny, he rode into Jerusalem or wherever it was on a hinny. (*Pause.*) That must mean something. (*Pause.*) It's like the sparrows, than many of which we are of more value, they weren't sparrows at all'. Mr Rooney accuses her of exaggerating the number of sparrows, but Maddy is quoting accurately from St Matthew, 10:31: 'Fear ye not therefore, ye are of more value than many sparrows'. Christ's entry into Jerusalem 'sitting on an ass's colt' is described in these exact words in St John's Gospel; in St Matthew the King James has 'a colt the foal of an ass'; in the other two gospels the animal is described simply as a 'colt'. The Regius Professor mentioned is presumably the Regius Professor of Divinity at Trinity College, Dublin, but whether Beckett had any particular holder of that office in mind is a question which might lead us into a morass of pedantry.

We have had perhaps enough for the moment about Beckett's accuracy and ingenuity in the quoting of Scripture. Let us ask: What sort of education made this possible? *A Portrait of the Artist* has made millions of readers aware of the thoroughness of James Joyce's Catholic education under the Jesuits, but Beckett's Anglican training was, in its own way, almost as thorough. I say 'in its own way' because there was one extraordinary gap in it—an almost total absence of theology. This was certainly true of my own education, which I believe to have resembled Beckett's very closely. Nobody ever told us who Luther and Calvin *were*, let alone discussed how their teachings differed from each other. More surprisingly, perhaps, we learned very little about the points of dogma that separated our Church from Roman Catholicism. I heard rumours of a book called *Roman Claims* that was sometimes set for examinations in Religious Knowledge, but to this day I have never seen a copy. I can find nothing to disagree with in the following passage from a recent review by George Steiner:

The very anti-intellectuality, the abstentions from philosophical rigour and abstraction which have, since the end of the seventeenth century, afforded the life of the Churches in England their enviable civility, mutual tolerance and low-key presence, may, under today's exactions, prove a fatal virtue. So very little in contemporary Anglican thought or practice seems equipped to face, on comparable terms, either the summons of atheism and agnosticism or the temptations of dogma.[4]

This may be the true explanation of the Irish Anglican's readiness to abandon his faith, already mentioned.

What did we learn, then? First of all, the habit of involuntary public worship. At Portora Royal School, Enniskillen, where Beckett spent three-and-a-half years as a boarder (1920-23) and I spent eight (1928-36), we were subjected to a thoroughly Evangelical regime. Until recently, the Headmaster was always a Church of Ireland clergyman: throughout Beckett's and my time there, he was the Rev E.G. Seale. Every weekday morning, Seale read prayers and a passage from the Bible at Assembly. He or some other master read prayers and Scripture again at the end of homework preparation for bedtime. The roll-call of boarders before breakfast was performed with care by the master on duty, but the prayer that followed was usually brief and hasty. On Sunday mornings the Church of Ireland boarders paraded to St Macartan's Cathedral, wearing Harrow-style straw boaters if the weather was clement. On Sunday evenings in summer, we walked to church again in the nearby country parish of Rossory; during the rest of the year, Sunday evening service was in the dining hall, usually conducted by the Headmaster. Occasionally there would be a missionary sermon by an ordained 'old boy', who was already labouring in the vineyard, whether with the Church Missionary Society in the British Empire, or in the slums of Belfast. We used the *Public Schools Hymnal*, bound in the school colours—the British Royal Arms in yellow on a black ground. The biographical notes told us that Henry Francis Lyte, author of 'Abide with me' and other fine hymns, was educated at Portora and Trinity. We liked the many hymns at these evening services, and naturally we sang Lyte's *fortissimo*.

All this 'gentility and church-going'—to quote yet again from *All That Fall*—was less important for Beckett's development as a writer than the almost daily teaching of Holy Scripture as a regular school subject up to the Fourth or Fifth Form. In a Protestant School, the Old Testament of course received at least as much attention as the New. We learned some of the Psalms and some of the prophecies of Isaiah by heart, as well as passages from the Gospels and from the Epistles of St Paul. The Acts of the Apostles made a particularly strong impression because of the thrilling adventures by land and sea, and especially the conversion of St Paul. When I heard of the publication of Beckett's first volume of fiction, *More Pricks Than Kicks*, later banned by the Irish Censorship Board, I recognised the allusion in the title at once. When a light from heaven shines round about the future Apostle on the road to Damascus, he hears a voice saying, 'Saul, Saul, why persecutest thou me?' Saul, not yet christened Paul, answers the question with another, 'Who art thou, Lord?' In the King James version, the Lord replies, 'I am Jesus whom thou persecutest: it is hard for thee to kick against the pricks'. The Douay version, more readily intelligible, has 'It is hard for thee to kick against the goad'. In a Scripture class at Portora, normally taught by a layman, the image of the ox kicking against the goad would have been explained, like other archaic allusions or words, but, as I have said, theological explanations were rare. Of course there were other Protestants in these classes besides members of the Church of Ireland—

Presbyterians, Methodists, perhaps an occasional Quaker or Baptist—whose doctrine might disagree on this or that point. I have a feeling, however, that the basic principle underlying this practice was the widely accepted Protestant Evangelical doctrine of the 'sufficiency' of Holy Scripture. If one already possessed the necessary faith, the Bible contained all the teaching necessary to attain salvation. The Hibernian Bible Society prided itself on distributing Bibles, whether in Irish or English, that were printed 'without note or comment'. The assumption was that if Catholics read these Bibles, or had someone read them aloud, in their own language, they would almost automatically be converted to Protestantism.

Since Beckett did not enter Portora until he was almost fourteen, he must have picked up much of his familiarity with the Bible earlier: in church, in Sunday School, and in Scripture classes at the other Protestant schools he attended. All I am suggesting is that his biblical knowledge when he left Portora at seventeen was roughly the same as mine at that age. One of the peculiarities of Bible teaching at Portora was that we took examinations set by our teachers rather than those approved by the Church of Ireland Diocese of Clogher. I assume this was another ecumenical gesture to the boys of other Protestant denominations attending the school. Beckett, however, must have taken examinations in the Diocese of Dublin at some stage before he went to Portora. Otherwise, he would hardly have been inspired to write the following humorously incongruous passage in *More Pricks Than Kicks*:

He had underlined, as quite a callow boy, a phrase in Hardy's *Tess*, won by dint of cogging in the Synod: *When grief ceases to be speculative, sleep sees her opportunity.*

'Cogging' is a word used all over Ireland for copying or cheating, but what is 'the Synod'? I read it as shorthand for an annual examination in religious knowledge inaugurated by the Board of Education of the General Synod of the Church of Ireland over a century ago, which I often heard mentioned as 'the Synod exam'. Indeed, I took it once in the Diocese of Ossory while I was briefly at school in Abbeyleix. My prize was a prayerbook. No doubt there were different prizes as well as different examinations according to age, but I'm prepared to bet that no amount of cogging would ever have won Thomas Hardy's notorious *Tess of the D'Urbervilles* as a prize in *any* diocese of the Church of Ireland, however enlightened, to this very day!

Many Bibles, especially nowadays, do of course include much more than the text 'without note or comment'. Estragon, in *Waiting for Godot*, does not seem to remember the Gospels, but he does remember 'the maps of the Holy Land. Coloured they were. Very pretty. The Dead Sea was pale blue. The very look of it made me thirsty. That's where we'll go, I used to say, that's where we'll go for our honeymoon. We'll swim. We'll be happy'. Besides maps, one may find a concordance, a subject-index, and other 'helps'. A widely circulated Oxford edition of the King James includes a 'Dictionary of Scripture Proper Names'. In it, the meaning of the name Shuah is given as 'depression'. This may help to explain why Beckett named the central character of *More Pricks Than Kicks* Belacqua Shuah: Belacqua, from Dante's *Purgatorio*, was famous for indolence and procrastination; the name Shuah emphasizes another characteristic of the unhappy anti-hero.

The passage just quoted from *Waiting for Godot* forms part of the longest and best-known Biblical allusion in Beckett's work: that concerning the fate of the two thieves crucified with Jesus. Vladimir says, 'One of the thieves was saved . . . It's a reasonable percentage'. Later it occurs to him that 'of the four Evangelists only one speaks of a thief being saved . . . One out of four. Of the other three two don't mention any thieves at all and the third says that both of them abused him'. It's odd that so many of the commentators on what some believe to be a crux in the play accept Vladimir's statement as gospel truth. St Luke is indeed the only Evangelist to mention the penitent thief, but St Matthew *and* St Mark state that both the thieves abused Jesus. St John alone does not identify the two men crucified with the Saviour as thieves. Curiously, the King James translation of St Luke uses the word 'malefactors' rather than 'thieves', but this does nothing to validate the account given by Vladimir, who goes on to say that 'Everybody' believes St Luke. 'It's the only version they know.' On which Estragon's comment is, 'People are bloody ignorant apes'. I wouldn't dream of calling Mr Beckett a bloody ignorant ape; some of his commentators, however—myself included—might pay heed to Estragon now and again.

One thing at least is certain: the presence of the discussion of the two thieves so early in the play has encouraged many people to read *Waiting for Godot* as some sort of Christian parable. Vladimir and Estragon (or Didi and Gogo, as they call each other) may be waiting for god, or at any rate for some kind of salvation. I myself have argued that Godot does arrive, in both acts, disguised as Pozzo: Didi and Gogo fail to recognise him, just as, Christians believe, the Jews failed to recognise the Messiah. The cruelty and uncharitableness of Pozzo, however, make this theory hard to defend. A more plausible hypothesis might be that Lucky is the Messiah; he is a man of sorrows and acquainted with grief, a true Suffering Servant. Pozzo, his cruel or indifferent master, reminds one at times of Herod and at other times of Pontius Pilate. The 'country road' on which the play is set might be the road to Calvary, though the rope around Lucky's neck suggests hanging rather than crucifixion. If this is so, Didi and Gogo are the two thieves. They think seriously of hanging themselves in both acts. Vladimir, who once says, 'suppose we repented', is thus obviously the penitent thief. I don't expect this interpretation to be accepted; frankly, I don't quite believe in it myself. I am just putting it forward as an example of how the simple yet universal elements and relationships in *Waiting for Godot* can be interpreted as symbols of so many truths, both human and divine. Beckett told Colin Duckworth, who edited the French text of *Waiting for Godot* for use in English schools and universities, that 'Christianity is a mythology with which I am perfectly familiar, so I naturally use it'.[5] Be that as it may, he has never again used it with quite the subtlety and ingenuity displayed in *Waiting for Godot*.

In *Happy Days*, I see—and hear—Beckett making a different, though still subtle, use of his Protestant heritage. It seems to me significant that this play, like *All That Fall* and *Krapp's Last Tape*—but *un*like most of his other dramatic works—was written first in English. Winnie and Willie of *Happy Days* are just as clearly a Foxrock couple as the Rooneys in *All That Fall*: the difference is that they are more normal—or at any rate they manage to conform better outwardly to a rather Anglicized suburban stereotype. Far from being grotesques like the Rooneys, they are well-preserved for their respective ages, and try to keep well-groomed under most trying conditions. Because of some tremendous catastrophe, the world has ceased to turn and time can no longer be measured by the alternation of day and night, yet just before the final curtain Willie manages to appear '*dressed to kill—top hat, morning coat, striped trousers, etc, white gloves in hand*', much as he must have looked on his wedding day. In the heat of perpetual noon, such punctilio reminds us of the legendary Englishmen who used always to dress for dinner, even in the tropics. Winnie's fortitude is less concerned with externals, though she is anxious that her hat should be at a becoming angle even when she has lost her hand-mirror. Her religious training has clearly been Anglican: she concludes her brief prayers with the formulas 'For Jesus Christ sake Amen' and 'World without end Amen'. She remembers sitting on the knees of 'Charlie Hunter', who afterwards became a bishop. She proclaims 'another heavenly day' and constantly speaks of 'Many mercies'. If we have read Newman's *Idea of a University*, however, we may begin to feel that her relentless optimism—so unlike Mrs Rooney's encircling gloom—is more appropriate to a pagan Stoic than to a Christian. Nevertheless, one can't help admiring what Belacqua Shuah calls 'The grand old family Huguenot guts'. Although Beckett's mother, unlike my own, did not attend Alexandra School and College in Dublin, I can't help feeling that Winnie did. Despite her lady-like speech, she is not above dropping into the slang of her generation occasionally. 'Come on, dear', she says to Willie, 'put a bit of jizz into it . . . ' If it were not for one recurrent biblical allusion, we might lose patience ultimately with Winnie's apparent shallowness. It is very important to her that Willie should be there within earshot, even though he does not always hear and often does not answer her, perhaps for days on end. As long as this is true, she can say to herself, 'Something of this is being heard, I am not merely talking to myself, that is in the wilderness, a thing I could never bear to do—for any length of time'. Over and over again the word 'wilderness' recurs in a similar context, in phrases like 'such wilderness'. The reference is primarily to the description of John the Baptist, in the third chapter of St Matthew's Gospel, as 'The voice of one crying in the wilderness'; this in turn echoes a passage in the fortieth chapter of Isaiah: 'The voice of him that crieth in the wilderness . . . ' *Vox clamantis in deserto* is the Latin version of both passsges, but the King James often prefers the resounding Anglo-Saxon word 'wilderness' to the Latin word 'desert'. If Willie has died or gone away, Winnie will be left alone, buried in a heap of sand, with nothing but sand around her; all the vegetation has burned up long ago.

The audible conclusions of Winnie's otherwise silent prayers remind us that Beckett was of course familiar with the *Book of Common Prayer*, though in quoting from the Psalms, for instance, he always prefers the wording of the King James rather than the somewhat different translations in the prayer-book. As for the *Irish Church Hymnal*, there is an extraordinary passage in, of all places, *The Unnamable*, where the reader is suddenly confronted with the opening lines of four well-known Anglican hymns. The Unnamable in this novel constantly denies that he has ever existed, maintaining that what appears to be his own interior monologue or stream of consciousness is actually spoken by other people: 'That's one of Mahood's favourite tricks', he says, 'to produce ostensibly independent testimony in support of my historical existence.' His alleged parents relate instalments of the Unnamable's alleged life-story:

The instalment over, all joined in a hymn, Safe in the arms of Jesus, for example, or Jesus lover of my soul, let me to thy bosom fly, for example.

I first read this passage in French, before it was translated by the author, and I vividly remember how incongruous it seemed to read *Jésus amant de mon âme* instead of the words familiar since childhood. Yes, I suppose *amant* is the absolutely correct translation of 'lover', but one is used to reading the word in a quite different context in French. The two other hymns referred to were 'Gentle Jesus, meek and mild', a children's hymn by Charles Wesley—Also the author of 'Jesu, lover of my soul'—and another that Beckett seriously misquotes. He remembers the first two lines as 'Jesus, my one, my all, hear me when I call'; actually they run thus:

> Jesu, my Lord, my God, my All,
> Hear me, blest Saviour, when I call . . .[6]

Yet again, such errors may be taken as evidence that the other hymns were quoted, almost correctly, from memory.

Once we know the kind of upbringing and the kind of education Beckett received, his knowledge of the Bible and other religious texts ceases to be surprising; it would be pointless to continue adding further examples. The questions we need to ask *now* are twofold. First of all, *why* did Beckett make so much use of Christianity rather than of some other 'mythology' with which he was perfectly familiar? Secondly *what effect*, in the widest possible sense, has Christianity had on his development as a writer?

As might be expected, all Beckett's most significant references to Christianity focus upon the Passion of Christ, the pivotal scene of the Christian drama, where God sacrifices Himself as Man, for Man. There is one scene yet more dramatic, namely the Resurrection; to that, however, Beckett pays no heed at all: one assumes that he does not believe in it. The Crucifixion he accepts as an historical fact: it is in keeping with his sense of man's inhumanity to man. But whenever the Crucifixion is mentioned, Beckett is making an implied or explicit comparison between the suffering of Christ and the suffering of man. A classic example of explicit comparison is this passage from *Waiting for Godot*:

VLADIMIR:	But you can't go barefoot!
ESTRAGON:	Christ did.
VLADIMIR:	Christ! What has Christ got to do with it? You're not going to compare yourself to Christ!
ESTRAGON:	All my life I've compared myself to him.
VLADIMIR:	But where he lived it was warm, it was dry!
ESTRAGON:	Yes. And they crucified quick.

Silence.

God's suffering in human form can never equal Man's, according to Beckett, because it has a self-imposed limit: three days after the Crucifixion, it will all be over. But consider the case of Molloy:

. . . my progress . . . from the slow and painful progress it had always been . . . was changed, saving your presence, to a veritable calvary, with no limit to its stations and no hope of crucifixion, though I say it myself, and no Simon . . .

Although he speaks on the same page of 'the immemorial expiation', it is likely that Molloy does not believe in life after death: the idea of suicide attracts him momentarily from time to time. 'But I never succumbed', he says. An eternity of torment would almost necessarily guarantee that Man's sufferings were greater than Christ's; Molloy, however, suggests that his prolonged suffering on earth is at least equal to that of the Saviour; note his deprecatory 'saving your presence': Molloy, though alone in his room, knows that Christ is always with us. I must leave any further discussion of comparative suffering to the theologians. The subject is, however, fundamental to Beckett's thinking about the human condition. As an artist, his first premise is that life on earth consists chiefly of suffering, a view which, as we all know, has been held by many Christians, both Catholic and Protestant. Beckett's most concise statement of this belief will be found in *Endgame*. Hamm, after being told that his mother is dead, asks whether his father is dead too. Clov, his servant, answers: 'Doesn't look like it'. Hamm next asks: 'What's he doing?' 'He's crying', comes the answer. 'Then he's living', says Hamm. Beckett has never quite accepted Descartes' axiom, 'I think, therefore I am'. Here, he offers an alternative: 'I cry, therefore I am'. To drive home the point, Hamm asks Clov one more question: 'Did you ever have an instant of happiness?' 'Not to my knowledge', answers Clov.

To my mind, however, the aspect of Beckett's works that has been most powerfully affected by his religious training is his style. A century from now he may well be regarded as the last—or nearly the last—great writer in English to model his style on the King James Bible. There is always the possibility, of course, that literary people will continue to deplore the aesthetic quality—or lack of it—shown by such well-intentioned translations as *The New English Bible, The New American Bible*, and *The Jerusalem Bible*. It is interesting to compare the versions of the 'all that fall' passage in these three Bibles, only the first-named of which is Protestant. An ecumenical touch is provided by the fact that all three now locate it in the 145th Psalm. First, *The New English*:

the LORD holds up those who stumble
and straightens backs which are bent.

Next, the *New American*:

The LORD lifts up all who are falling
and raises up all who are bowed down.

I must preface the quotation from the *Jerusalem* with a reminder that this is the most determinedly scholarly of the translations; also, its ecumenism, in the Old Testament, is naturally first directed to Judaism:

Only stumble, and Yahweh at once supports you, if others bow you down, he will raise you up.[7]

Far be it from me to comment on these three 'modern' translations, but it is not inconceivable that they may eventually provoke cries of 'Back to King James', 'Back to Douay'. In fact, to some degree they already have done so. My present task, however, is not to convince anyone that Beckett is the *last* in a great English prose tradition, but to show that he belongs in that tradition at all.

James Knowlson remarks in his brilliant foreword to *The Beckett Country*,

I have heard some Beckett scholars speak of a marked vein of lyricism in his writing about nature, while others have disputed whether one can speak of lyricism in the case of a writer who so drastically and so self-consciously deflates his own descriptive effects.

I have never had the pleasure of discussing the matter with Professor Knowlson, but he may count me among those who recognise this lyricism, and not merely in descriptive passages; what's more, this lyricism can often be compared with the poetry of the Old Testament. Before offering some examples, let me quote Professor Knowlson once more:

. . . although Beckett self-consciously manipulates fiction within the tradition of Sterne and Diderot and is also acutely conscious of and struggles with the unreliability of language . . ., none the less a form of stark yet moving lyricism remains, as his prose strives above all to 'sing'—a term that Beckett has used to me several times, half apologetically, as being the only term that he could find appropriate to what he was trying to achieve in his prose.[8]

Armed with the magic word 'sing', I began to turn the pages of Beckett's trilogy in search of inspiration. He that seeketh findeth, as the Bible says. There, in the middle of the famous sucking-stones passage in *Molloy*, I found this:

. . . one day suddenly it dawned on me . . . that I might perhaps achieve my purpose without increasing the number of my pockets, or reducing the number of my stones, but simply by sacrificing the principle of trim. The meaning of this illumination, which suddenly began to sing within me, like a verse of Isaiah, or of Jeremiah, I did not penetrate at once . . .

Why did the illumination *sing like a verse of Isaiah, or of Jeremiah*? One's first thought might be that the illumination or revelation was in some sense a prophecy, whose meaning, especially the word 'trim', did not reveal itself without some interpretation. But then, why use the word 'sing' in referring to a verse from either of these Old Testament prophets? Because, of course, these prophets' words *are poetry* in the original Hebrew, and are printed as such in most contemporary translations of the Bible. Furthermore, they are so printed in my 1947 edition of the Latin Vulgate. The hallmark of ancient Hebrew poetry is its paired parallel structure, often so well imitated by the King James translators, even though they may not have consciously recognised it. Robert Lowth, Anglican Bishop of London in the late 18th century, seems to have been the first English-speaking scholar to perceive this underlying principle, which naturally also characterises the Psalms and certain songs that occur in the historical books. Of these last, the most powerful is surely David's lamentation over Saul and Jonathan:

> The beauty of Israel is slain upon thy high places:
> how are the mighty fallen!
> Tell it not in Gath,
> publish it not in the streets of Askelon;
> lest the daughters of the Philistines rejoice,
> lest the daughters of the uncircumcised triumph . . .
> How are the mighty fallen,
> and the weapons of war perished.

One can hardly fail to notice the same parallelism in the 'all that fall' verse, though the *New English Bible* pretty well destroys it.

When one starts looking for this parallel structure in Beckett's work, one soon finds that it was there almost from the beginning, and that it gives a lyrical quality to narrative passages at least as often as to descriptive ones. Listen to the conclusion of the first chapter of *Murphy*, published in 1938:

> The rock got faster and faster,
> shorter and shorter,
> the iridescence was gone,
> the cry in the mew was gone,
> soon his body would be quiet.
> Most things under the moon got slower and slower and then stopped,
> a rock got faster and faster and then stopped.
> Soon his body would be quiet,
> soon he would be free.

I have written out this last passage as verse so as to emphasise the parallelisms, but sometimes the subject-matter and the language are enough to supply the biblical ring without much parallelism. Take this sentence from *Lessness*, a work I don't particularly admire, published in 1970: 'He will curse God again as in the blessed days face to the open sky the passing deluge.' Take it and roll it on your tongue while you consider its implications: God and Man together again, believing in each other, blaming each other, afflicting each other. Not happy days exactly, but blessed days, and certainly happier than those after the recent greatly exaggerated death of God, when Man suddenly found it hard to believe in his own existence, as Bishop Berkeley said he would.

It is in ending a chapter or a work that Beckett uses this biblical lyricism most freely. *That Time*, a short play from 1976, is lyrical—or perhaps I should say elegiac—almost throughout, and particularly the final speech:

not a sound/only the old breath/and the leaves turning/and then suddenly this dust/ whole place suddenly full of dust/when you opened your eyes/from floor to ceiling/ nothing only dust/and not a sound only what was it it said/come and gone/was that it something like that/come and gone/come and gone no one/come and gone in no time/gone in no time

Though Listener, the protagonist, is still alive on stage—'*Breath audible*' is the stage direction—this is his own recorded voice describing perhaps the first moments in the grave; his life, viewed from the perspective of eternity, has 'come and gone in no time'. Reassured by this prophetic voice that his few times of happiness and his many times of suffering will soon be over, Listener manages a smile—'*toothless for preference*' says the stage direction—as the curtain falls.

It may be objected that some of the passages I have quoted don't sound very like the Bible, but that is a matter of the choice of vocabulary: the point is to keep listening for the underlying rhythms and the parallel structure. Try this for yourself on Beckett's latest works—*Company*, for example,—and I think you will find that you understand them better and appreciate them more. I have only one more quotation, the conclusion of *The Unnamable*, perhaps the most often quoted passage in all Beckett's works. Some readers hear it as a description of Beckett's literary method; others as a rambling, almost meaningless example of so-called automatic writing. What I want you to hear is a skilfully ordered rhythmic sequence that comes to a natural close, even though the words deny the possibility of an ending:

. . . you must go on, I can't go on, you must go on, I'll go on, you must say words, as long as there are any, until they find me, until they say me, strange pain, strange sin, you must go on, perhaps it's done already, perhaps they have said me already, perhaps they have carried me to the threshold of my story, before the door that opens on my story, that would surprise me, if it opens, it will be I, it will be the silence, where I am, I don't know, I'll never know, in the silence you don't know, you must go on, I can't go on, I'll go on.

We began with a verse from a psalm; we end with what almost sounds like a mystic's meditation. I haven't said all there is to be said about Samuel Beckett and the Bible, but maybe this will be enough to be going on with.

Postscript

I first met Dick Ellmann in Dublin in 1946, just after his arrival to work on Yeats, on the eve of my departure for the U.S. From that day onwards, the history of our friendship largely consists of innumerable acts of kindness on his part. His secure place in the American academic world enabled him to help me in all sorts of ways: in fact, he arranged for me to succeed him at Northwestern

University, but I had to turn down the offer because of illness in my family. When his wife in turn became seriously ill, I felt even closer to him, but inevitably we saw less of each other because of our responsibilities. I am surprised to find how many letters I have from him, but we had completely lost touch recently; his death was a great shock to me. What did I ever do for him? Never enough, certainly, but my review of the first edition of *The Identity of Yeats* greatly pleased him, I remember.

Beckett's Recent Acivities: The Liveliness of Dead Imagination

Daniel Albright

It is clear that the first half of the 1980s has been one of Beckett's periods of great creative activity, comparable to the late 1940s and the early 1960s. He has also managed to get his name into the newspapers because of his threat of a lawsuit against a performance of *Endgame* (Cambridge, Massachusetts, Winter, 1984), a performance that disobeyed the stage directions in every conceivable way—instead of a stage wholly empty save for a chair, two windows, and a door, the Cambridge production presented the play inside a cross-section of forty-foot high concrete tunnel, around which Clov scrambled acrobatically by means of a complicated system of ladders; and instead of Beckett's specified cast of red-faced and white-faced actors, the Cambridge production used two black actors from its repertory company, speaking sometimes with the intonations of American black dialect.

In order to placate Beckett the company added a programme note in which Beckett said that this production was merely a parody of his play—this leads to many speculations about what comments the great playwrights of the past might have stapled onto playbills of recent productions, for example what Shakespeare might have said about a *King Lear* in which Lear enters in a helicopter, or about a Hamlet who plays with a slinky and spray-paints graffiti on the castle walls. In Beckett's attempts to restrain this exuberant staging of his play, and in Beckett's prose fiction of the 1980s—*Company, Ill Seen Ill Said, Worstward Ho*—there is a common theme, the suppression of creative impulse down to the bare minimum. The spectacle of a great writer working against creativity, cultivating what he calls 'dead imagination' is, I think, worth our attention. In this paper I will try to describe some of the consequences of this preference for dead imagination. Let me begin by rehearsing something of the evolution of Beckett's theory of imagination, of the imagination's process of disaffiliating itself from the outer world, as it is presented in a recently published book called *Disjecta*, an anthology of his early writings edited by Ruby Cohn.

Disjecta is a handy volume. It brings together a number of famous texts, such as Beckett's essay on Joyce's *Finnegans Wake*, long inconveniently located for students, and a number of newspaper reviews and unpublished manuscripts little known even to specialists. If this miscellany may be said to have a central theme, it is Beckett's assault on mimesis, his desire for an art not contingent on the objective world—for in Beckett's view, a vase of flowers and a painting of a vase of flowers have nothing whatever to do with one another, not the faintest connection. In his descriptions of Joyce, of modern painters, even of William Butler Yeats, Beckett continually discovers a central involution of contentlessness, an imitation not of objects but of the invisibility, the fleetingness of objects. For Beckett, the phenomenal world continually recedes from the observer who would grasp it, and art must constitute itself in the gap between subject and object (p. 70). We may find it difficult to adjust to a style of writing that seeks to deny the usual satisfactions of fiction: a secure, precise field of action occupied by amiable or engrossing characters whose feelings and ideas are recognizably similar to our own. All that is absent from Beckett's project.

Disjecta also contains some of Beckett's earliest experiments in writing non-mimetic fiction. Jean du Chas in 'Le Concentrisme' (about 1930) is so brittle and affected, literary, as to be almost post-human: he has no trace of social life, and 'his indifference and unconsciousness scarcely agreed with the sacrosanct tradition of the cave and fear and ignorance and solidarity huddled under the thunder' (p. 38, my translation). A picturesque sunset repells him, and a childhood bout with fever teaches him to associate light itself with heat and disgust. Here is one of the earliest versions of the Beckett hero, the man who turns away from sensuous reality in order to entertain himself with the faintest traces of ideas and feelings, the self-evacuator.

More interesting still are the excerpts from *Dream of Fair to Middling Women* (1932), in which each of the characters is linked with a note of the chromatic scale. Here Beckett contrasts his own practice with that of Balzac and his 'chloroformed world': whereas Balzac's characters centre themselves, behave complacently according to type, real people are always altering, 'strain[ing] away from themselves', modulating into new identities (pp. 46-47). This trial novel revels in its inability to find a melody, a form of integration of its themes and characters: 'The music comes to pieces. The notes fly about all over the place, a cyclone of electrons' (p. 45). In the final excerpt Beckett takes Beethoven as a hero of the art of dispersal, an art verging on chaos, subatomic gas, and it is clear that Beckett wants to do with words what Beethoven did with notes. Music is, of course, the least referential art, the least susceptible to mimesis; it is easy to see why Beckett hoped to write a novel in the form of an atonal sonata, or the dreams of a deaf ear.

Change the premise from characters-as-tones to characters-as-pebbles and you have *Malone Dies* (*Malone meurt*, 1948); in both cases the elements of fiction have been reduced from imitations of men to neutral counters artfully or randomly permuted. It is all part of Beckett's search for a novel that does not copy, that erects itself not out of second-hand objects from a soiled world but out of its own private thingliness. It is an art at once overabstract and overconcrete: overabstract because the venue of the novel is infinitely removed from earth, on a different ecliptic altogether, and overconcrete because the special molecules of fiction possess amazing ontological prestige—they are not *about* something, they *are* something, as Beckett remarks of passages from *Finnegans Wake*.

Disjecta also sketches a theory of an anti-symbolist art. In the 'German Letter of 1937' Beckett again praises Beethoven for his ability to suggest abysses of silence beneath 'paths of sound suspended in giddy heights'; Beckett goes on to posit an art less noisy, chattering, interpretable than the usual sort:

For in the forest of symbols, which aren't any, the little birds of interpretation, which isn't any, are never silent. (p.172)[1]

Symbolism was an art movement originally designed to resist the discursive, the prosaic, to edge toward silence; but Beckett finds that the symbolic method hinders the symbolists from attaining their goal—the blank page desired by Mallarmé. The true art of silence, the art that tears aside the verbal surface to peer at what is underneath, must rid itself of symbols and their clamour for clarification. Beckett's essay *Proust* (1931) shows Beckett's debt to the symbolist method, according to which a whole village can be baked into a cookie; but it is possible that he also learned from Proust a certain revulsion against symbols, a hatred of the overmeaningful that is a countertheme throughout Proust's novel. In *Swann's Way* Proust describes the relief of dissociating the pain of a toothache from various symbolic equivalents, and his reeling disgust at his inability to empty the smell of the staircase varnish from its evocations of private sorrow. It has long been noted that Beckett's novels skirt autobiography at every turn; but perhaps his purpose is not to evoke his youth but to desymbolize it, anaesthetize it, neutralize it into music or a pebble collection. The symbol must be reduced to 'autosymbolism' (*Proust*, p. 60); its tentacles must let go of the world, and instead clutch and defend the thing in its isolation.

*   *   *

A fiction purged of mimesis and symbol alike would seem to deny itself every resource. What is left for Beckett to do? Beckett's chief mode of self-entertainment has been to refine the procedures through which a text can reflect its lack of content, the central absence.

For the last twenty years or so, almost everything Beckett has written concerns either a rotunda or a desert wanderer. Now a rotunda, even if it looks from above like a zero, is not nothing; nor does it lack symbolic evocativeness, for it reminds us of home or temple or asylum or crypt or columbarium. Indeed the rotunda and the desert wanderer are extreme stylizations of the human condition: we are always in hiding or in flight. Because of this sense of severe simplification of our state, we tend to look for allegory in Beckett's recent work; but we are defeated, precisely because the elements are so excessively suggestive that they suggest nothing at all. A rotunda may suggest the comfort of shelter or the marble chill of death. Schoenberg was fond of saying that his music was not atonal but pantonal; Beckett ingeniously reverses the curriculum, moves from pansignificance to insignificance. Some scientists believe that the universe is expanding so quickly that it will never be able to collapse and regenerate itself, and therefore in the distant future it will thin itself into better and better approximations of unbeing; this is just what happens in Beckett's recent fiction, which keeps distending into ever wider and feebler meanings.

Furthermore, the images of rotunda and wanderer are easily combined, colluded, as if motion and rest, birth and death, were indistinguishable. Beckett's earliest rotundas, like that in *Imagination Dead Imagine* (*Imagination morte imaginez*, 1965), were snug white edifices about three feet in diameter, stuffed with two white imperceptibly animate bodies. In *The Lost Ones* (*Le Dépeupleur*, 1970), the universe of discourse consists of a rotunda fifty metres in circumference, filled with 200 residents who shuffle about or climb ladders to nowhere or are still. In *Ill Seen Ill Said* (*Mal vu mal dit*, 1981), the female protagonist can appear inside or outside her vaguely circular cabin in various frozen iconic postures—she does not have to cross the intervening ground, for time and space in this text are jumpy, discontinuous. She brings flowers to a stone monolith, and herself often seems a monolith, a 'Memnon' (p. 35). She is so surrounded by stone that she seems infected by it. In *Worstward Ho* (1983), we are bemused by the spectacle of a pair of figures walking across a void:

Say better worse now all gone save trunks from now. Nothing from pelves down. From napes up. Topless baseless hind-trunks. Legless plodding on. Left right unreceding on. (p. 43)

Beckett seems to crave an image which is simultaneously a person and a place, flesh and stone, aperture and closure, motion and rest, construction and wreck. It would be hard to improve on *Worstward Ho*'s image of a fragment of Ozymandias plodding leglessly across a void; a visible oxymoron. The method of a novel from the middle of Beckett's career, *The Unnamable* (*L'Innommable*, 1949-50) is to deny reference semantically, by a stategy of perpetual contradiction of every proposition; the method of *Worstward Ho* is to deny reference imagistically, by constructing a lapsed and incoherent thing, by displaying its deformity, its blight, its muteness from every angle, by letting it vanish into thinglessness. Figures of speech from Beckett's earlier work are promoted to events: Malone in *Malone Dies* compared himself to a dwindling heap of sand (p. 222); and recently Beckett's gaze has been fixed on the image of a desert walker who is turning into a heap of sand, at one with the desert through which he walks, a single plenum or vacuum without quality or attribute or distinguishing mark.

*   *   *

All Strange Away (1976) begins with a sentence that was also used as the title of *Imagination Dead Imagine*; and since Beckett has been long labouring to kill imagination in order to sunder art from outer reality, we might ask what distinguishes a dead imagination from a live one. A dead imagination, it seems, is too weak and incompetent to elaborate its images; it simply grasps some dull premise—a rotunda crammed with bodies, or a doll with its feet sewn together (*Ping*), or some clockwork searchers stumbling around in a cage (*The Lost Ones*). Then the dead imagination regards this *donné* from several angles, lets the automaton conclude its gesture and come to a halt, and at last abandons its image. A dead imagination, then, is a device less for forming images than for getting rid of them. There is another possibility, however: that a dead imagination, since it is unable to seize and hold even a sketchy, boring, or farfetched image, is a faculty that continually tinkers with, alters, erases, redraws its images; because it can never find an image that satisfies it, it is endowed, zombie-fashion, with a febrile parody of life, positing images in a long agony of mutation. This is why a dead imagination can sometimes seem strangely active, alert.

Thus the dead imagination in *All Strange Away* (printed in *Rockaby and Other Short Pieces*) invents a man sitting in a small cubicle, wonders where the light comes from, decides to show the man lighting one match after another for eternity, finds that unattractive, pronounces that the light simply comes from an unspecified source, decides to decorate the cubicle with pin-up pictures of a naked girl named Emma, describes how the man rubs up against them, decides that it would be more diverting to posit a woman in the cubicle looking at pictures of a naked man named Emmo, and so on. After each change in the premise we are told that it always was the new way, that there never were matches, or that the protagonist never was a man; the whole history of the premise is revised. A dead imagination helplessly drifts from image to image, unable to credit any of them, to declare that a particular image is solid and satisfying. Things that move get nowhere, while things that rest keep shifting queasily; in this manner change and stasis are one.

Another symptom of the dead or moribund imagination lies in the imaginer's inability to conceive himself as a coherent entity. From *Watt* (1942-45) on, Beckett's artist-figures have tried in vain to understand the provenance of images and voices, the mechanisms by which material comes into one's head and is elaborated and transcribed. In Beckett's last long work, *How It Is* (*Comment c'est*, 1961), the protagonist crawls with a sack of canned fish through a whole world of mud, but through the mud he sees—by means of a second pair of eyes—glimpses of what seem to be scenes from Beckett's childhood. Of course the protagonist doubts that the scenes are memories or that they have any relation to his life. He assumes that these images, his faint cries, will somehow be recorded; and so he hypothesizes generations of auditors and scribes, dynasties of Krims and Krams, perched over his prone body in the mud, living only to listen and record. Of course, according to Beckett's doctrines, a work of art and its ostensible models or references in the physical world are in a state of total unrelatedness; and so the protagonist of *How It Is* endlessly multiplies figments of relation, figments that complicate, attenuate, and discredit any connection between the imagination's seizures and the world of experience. The text as it appears on paper, the images in the

artist's head, and the artist's personal engagement with the world of experience, all dwell in separate and hostile zones of being. Therefore Beckett does
not wish to speak of a single man who dwells in all three zones, a single artist
who sometimes takes bracing walks in the countryside and sometimes invents
fictions and sometimes writes them down; Beckett prefers to personify a
separate entity in each zone, and to refuse to suggest how intercourse among
them is possible.

Most of Beckett's recent works embody this fracturing of the artist. The
initial premise of *Company* (1980) consists of a hearer lying supine in the dark
and a voice telling him homely stories about a life, not necessarily the hearer's
life—stories about a little boy asking his mother how far away the sky is, or
about the decomposition of a hedgehog put in a box, or about an old man
listening to his footfalls on a country road. Eventually we are told of a third
entity, the deviser who devised both hearer and voice. The deviser starts to
wonder about himself—is he too lying supine in the dark?—but eventually
decides that he is crawling about on all fours, a posture helpful for
dinstinguishing himself from the hearer. Of course, the more the deviser keeps
trying to construe his own position and identity, the more the reader is forced
to posit a fourth entity, someone to devise the deviser; as in *How it is*, there is
no limit to endless multiplication of chimeras when one tries to work out the
relations among unrelatable things. By the end of *Company* the deviser and the
hearer seem to grow more and more intimate, congruent, and it begins to
appear that the hearer may have invented the deviser, instead of vice versa; but
the hypothesis that the figments are one and the same is no more compelling
than the hypothesis that discriminates them. The human subject is, as always
in Beckett's works, amazingly unstable, and the personage in *Company* finds it
possible to entertain himself with the companionable ghosts of his own
plurality—the most available company. In *Endgame* Hamm speaks of 'the
solitary child who turns himself into children, two, three, so as to be together,
and whisper together, in the dark' (p. 70); and I think that the playgoer who
enjoys *Endgame* might find *Company* an attractive work.

Worstward Ho also presents the creative process as divided beyond any hope
for integration; but here it is a division, not among human agents, but among
statues. The dim void on which the text dwells is interrupted by three sets of
effaced, almost featureless figures: a standing figure, a pair of desert plodders
hand in hand, and, to perceive them, a solitary head with downcast eyes.
Having presented this tableau, the narrator does what he can to worsen it, that
is, to improve it: the standing figure is demoted to a kneeling figure, the pair of
plodders are parted and (as we have already seen) made to lose their heads and
legs, the subjective head is hewn down until it is only a slab from eye to eye,
foreheadless, jawless. The passage in which Beckett starts to perform surgery
on the standing figure (number one, in his enumeration) is one of his most
hilarious:

First one. First try fail better one. Something there badly not wrong. Not that as it is
it is not bad. The no face bad. The no hands bad. The no ---. Enough. A pox on bad.

Mere bad. Way for worse. Pending worse. First worse. Mere worse. Pending worse still. Add a ---. Add? Never. Bow it down. Be it bowed down. Deep down. Head in hat gone. More back gone. (pp. 21-22)

Picasso said that he spent all his life learning how to paint like a child; it seems that Beckett, possessing the most remarkable literary equipment of his age, has spent a lifetime learning how to write like a mental defective, in a toothless, broken-jawed, goggling idiom, maniacal and compulsive, what someone might say as he pounded a puppet with a hammer. In its way, this style is a triumph of diction. It is a kind of verbal gravel.

★   ★   ★

In the midst of *Worstward Ho* we are told that the purpose of language is not to figure forth or embody the pictures in the author's mind, but instead to obscure them: 'Less seen and seeing when with words than when not . . . Stare by words dimmed. Shades dimmed. Void dimmed. Dim dimmed' (p. 40). Beckett's language, then, is chiefly a tool for unconstruing images; a usage very proper to a non-mimetic art. In his drama, however, the backdrop, the actors, their clothes, are presented not through language, with all its immense powers of veiling, breaking, dissolving, but as physical properties; he cannot simply unsay his tableau and expect it to go away without ever having been. Another relation between images and words must be found. Or is it possible that Beckett's theatre, is, after all, a kind of mimesis?

Is there any human situation or ceremony to which Beckett's plays seem to allude or correspond? They have been called rituals, but I can see in them little that resembles a sacrament or a rite of passage; they have been called the ravings of lunatics, but the lunatics I have known have raved in quite a different fashion. What is it that sets them apart from standard patterns of human behaviour?

For one thing, the message conveyed by the spectacle, by the images, is often quite different from that conveyed by the words. When we go to a performance of *Happy Days* (1961), we are first surprised to see a woman buried to her waist in earth; we are then surprised to see how tranquilly, how placidly she abides her condition: 'Another heavenly day' (p. 8). This calculated irrelevance of language to the visual images is mutually discrediting; this jangle, this inconsistency, cannot be palliated by any strategy of interpretation.

Beckett, as I mentioned, has offered strenuous objections to Joanne Akalaitas' version (at the American Repertory Theater, Cambridge, Massachusetts) of *Endgame* (*Fin de Partie*, 1957). One may wonder whether, according to Beckett's philosophy of art, the author is permitted to object to any director's whim; after all, if there is no relation between 'real life' and the images suggested in a drama, there is no possibility of inadequacy of those images—there is nothing for them to be adequate to. One may also wonder whether, in a collaborative art form such as drama, an author may arrogate to himself the role of perpetual occult director and producer. And yet, I think Beckett was right to protest, for Ms Akalaitas managed, in the course of an impressive production, to destroy the central aesthetic effect of Beckett's play.

In Ms Akalaitas' version *Endgame* is set in a post-nuclear subway tunnel, where people huddle in abandoned cars or industrial drums because they are the only forms of shelter left. Amid flickers and short-circuits, concrete walls and iron trestles crumble into dust. Hamm, it seems, is blind from the explosion; Clov's legs are bad because of radiation burns. It is clear what Ms Akalaitas has done: she has asked herself, In what sort of real world would the behaviour described in *Endgame* make sense? There are not many possibilities—an abandoned colony on a watery airless planet, as Venus was once supposed?—and Ms Akalaitas has chosen the most sensible. If the play were a mimesis, it would be mimetic of just such a radioactive wilderness, which no spring would ever refresh.

But it is not a mimesis. Ms Akalaitas has imparted to the drama of man's inability to sustain himself a *double entendre* of atomic devastation, when scarcely a *demi-entendre* is intended. This is why Beckett prefers his directors to reduce his meanings, not to multiply them. The madman of Hamm's memory, who looked out at the rising corn and the sails of the herring fleet and saw nothing but ashes (p. 44), is not a keen prophet of political catastrophe; he is a madman. (In the new production, Philip Glass embellishes this famous speech with a bass fiddle's practice scales, similar to the repetitive figures played by the violinist Einstein in Glass' opera *Einstein on the Beach*. There is a story that Nero set Rome on fire as a stage setting for a musical spectacle—Rome burned so that Nero might fiddle; and Glass is expert at catching this sense of psychotically casual holocaust.)

The new *Endgame* usefully alters our sense of Beckett's relation to Shakespeare. We think of Hamm as a modern Lear, still more forked, skewered, than the original; but Ben Halley Jr.'s performance has nothing of tragic dignity. Mr Halley sometimes resembles Ray Charles, smiling at nowhere over his piano playing; sometimes a preacher, haranging by rote; sometimes a pouty queen demanding an admirer's attention ('Kiss me!'). There is little continuity. W.H. Auden once said that Iago, when in the company of other characters, ought to be played as a consummate actor, but in soliloquy he ought to be played with every technical fault of the poor actor (*The Dyer's Hand*, p. 258); for Iago's goal is annihilation, and he is nothing in himself except a bundle of random histrionic gestures. Mr Halley seems to have extended this theory of portraying a zero man—and that is just what Hamm is—to an entire evening's entertainment.

But Hamm is not Iago, just as he is not exactly Lear. Imagine the island of *The Tempest* if Prospero became too indolent and moody to go back home: Ariel has long since vanished and Caliban—wondering why he pays any attention at all to his master's harsh whims—has pretty much usurped authority. Prospero still dreams, though his bad health occupies most of his thoughts, and his magic has dwindled to a few boring tales of prowess to which no one will listen unless offered a bribe. *Endgame* is a kind of sequel to *The Tempest*—Hamm even says, 'Our revels now are ended' (p. 56), quoting

Prospero's speech about the scenery that dissolves, leaving not a rack behind. Clov is the Caliban of an impoverished island, and Hamm is a sour blind Prospero, his staff broken, his book drowned, a Prospero of dead imagination. Ms Akalaitas and her stage crew went to immense trouble to construct an elaborately detailed locus of deprivation, but this very urge for specificity betrays the drama; what the play wants is not a precise image but imageless-ness.

Endgame must, above all, not make sense; any rationalization of the actions illustrated in the play must seem flimsy; there must be a tension between the familiar sort of discourse spoken by the characters and the preposterous *donné*—that is, a tension between language and spectacle. The dialogue must not seem a response to the situation, but a continuous aberration from it.

In his 'Essay on the Origin of Languages' (1749-55) Rousseau suggested that gesticulation and pantomime are opposite habits: primitive man, more conscious of things than of words, was able to use his body to figure forth meaning in a direct and telling manner; while modern Europeans simply flail about with their limbs as they talk, relying on their verbal skills to convey meaning. I find in this notion a clue about the quality of spectacle in Beckett's plays: in post-modern Europe language has sophisticated into inconsequence, while the ability to sketch meaningful gesture, pantomime, has remained lost; and so the characters shamble about and stike each other and yelp in the hope that such acts will constitute some significant expression of their state; but it is all gesticulation in Rousseau's sense, superfluous, pointless, a gesticulation in the absence of any system of meaning that it might reinforce. As the Unnamable says (p. 367), when you burn someone alive, you don't have to teach him to shriek and rush about in all directions, he'll do it without being told how.

And yet it is true that Beckett's spectacle does manifest a certain sense of design—and it is hard to understand what patterned gesticulation might be. To explain this design we must turn elsewhere. There is a clue, I think, at the end of *Molloy* (1947-48), when Moran claims that he is the only man on earth who understands that bees dance, 'not as men dance to amuse themselves', but to impart information to other bees about the location of food—by means of complicated figures in air, variations of humming, a whole system of signs (p. 168). Beckett's plays often seem to be such noisy dumb-shows, as if a hive tried to enact meaningful signs after everyone had forgotten the code. Johann Gottfried Herder, in his 'Essay on the Origin of Language' (1772), seems to suggest that language refines itself out of the instinctual behaviour of animals: the spider spins its web to organize its world, while men, with their duller sensory apparatus covering a far wider spectrum of reality, are forced to think and talk. The characters in Beckett's plays sometimes seem to be losing species, regressing to the subhuman, trying to rehearse the figures of instinct but botching the job. For example, in *What Where* (1983) a set of four characters enact a rigidly determined sequence of interrogation and torture, the torturer in one module always becoming the victim in the next. This design serves no purpose, gratifies no desire; it is simply obedience to a compulsion, like the courtship dances of the ptarmigan.

*   *   *

The users of the concept of dead imagination seem to extend far beyond the plays and fiction of Samuel Beckett. There has arisen a popular school of criticism that might be called applied Beckett, for it treats the imaginations even of such men as Homer, Goethe, and Tolstoy as essentially dead, helpless, convulsive, able only to embody in their work the structures of power that prevailed in their age. This school of deconstructionism has produced some of the most enjoyable and penetrating criticism of recent years. Perhaps there is some danger that, if we murder the imaginations of all the great writers of history, we may have to murder our own imaginations as well—and it may turn out that literary critics need imagination, even if Sophocles, Flaubert, Beckett can dispense with it. Yet it is important that we understand that the literary imagination is not something celestial or uncanny, beyond the bounds of speculation, but instead something that can be studied, analyzed, described. I like to think that Beckett has done to imagination what an entomologist does to an insect: killed it, examined it with a microscope, so that we all can come to a clearer comprehension of just what imagination is.

The Fatal Circle: Composition and Direction of *Come and Go*

Dougald McMillan

Epigraph: They are like birds, beautiful birds, he said that.
(Jocelyn Herbert, Author's Interview, 1979)

Come and Go evolved in three stages.[1] Manuscripts and typescripts of two closely related but distinct versions preceded the composition of *Come and Go* itself. The first attempt was an undated holograph on three sheets of typing paper entitled 'Good Heavens' (Reading University Library, MS 1227/7/16/4). In a second undated typescript of five pages designated (almost certainly provisionally) as 'Viola, Poppy, Rose' (Reading University Library MS 1227/7/16/5), Beckett condensed and altered this original version. Both these versions were identified by Beckett as 'before *Come and Go*' at the time he gave them to Reading University Library. Finally, in three typescript versions Beckett revised the play into its present form.

From the outset Beckett envisioned a play using the archetypal configuration of three women who reveal confidences to show the human condition bounded by love and death in the face of divine indifference. The structure was from the first based on a series of conversations by all three, the exit of one of them, and shared confidence between the remaining two about the absent friend.

Beginning with this concept, Beckett worked consistently to condense the original dialogue and action of a short but still relatively conventional play into only 127 words—a form so concentrated that it required him to revive the word 'dramaticule' to describe it.

In 'Good Heavens' the themes of love and death are stated much more explicitly than in the final play. The structure in this earliest stage was also more elaborate than in later versions. Beckett made no effort in 'Good Heavens' to develop the conversations among all three. He merely numbered them 1 to 3 indicating 'Conversation ABC'. In his first attempt Beckett devoted his attention exclusively to the conversations between only two characters. Focusing on feminine concern for external appearance, each of these sections was to have presented three revelations: two explaining looks of well-being and a contrasting third explaining a look of ill-health.

Each section opens with a compliment by one of the women ('A' in II, 'C' in IV, etc) on how well a second, 'B', looks and a request to reveal the secret of her beauty. The compliment is met with a surprised 'Oh!' followed by an unheard, whispered confession. The responses to the confessions allow the audience to infer that a secret love is the cause of beauty and freshness. Following the revelation of B, A responds to a similar compliment by her with an 'Oh!' and her whispered confession. The theme of the third whispered confidence—illness or diminished capacity—is foreshadowed in what we learn of each of the secret lovers. A's lover is recently 'discharged', presumably from a hospital. B's lover has apparently been bedridden but is now 'up'. C's lover is a former croquet champion who has lost his title.

To complete the triad of whispered revelations, A next asks B her opinion of the appearance of the absent C and whispers into her ear the announcement of C's impending death and unawareness of it. In this version there is no ambiguity about the 'appalling' revelation, and it is much less climactic than in *Come and Go*. By telling B that C is 'condemned' in Section II, A adumbrates the revelation which she will whisper two lines later. C has an unspecified disease of 'the worst kind' and has only 'three months' to live. In Scene IV C asks B, 'How do you think A is looking?' 'Shocking', she replies. The manuscript breaks off at this point, before A's malady is specified. Even in this fragmentary form, however, it it evident that Beckett's plan called for revelations that A and B also suffer from terminal illnesses like C.

Originally, the three revelations of section II were met with different explicatives of surprise expressing obliquely the themes of confidences, 'You don't tell me'; health, 'Well!'; and rejection and disbelief of tragic circumstances, 'No!' In the fourth section, the expressions of surprise, 'Heaven!' and 'Good Heavens!' achieved a cumulative effect. To preserve and intensify this effect, Beckett made emendations and insertions at section II in a very heavy marker to make 'Good Heavens!' the uniform response following each of the whispered revelations. In the same pen he wrote the phrase as the title at the top of page one. This change placed emphasis on the implied questioning of Providence—an emphasis Beckett was to retain but balance with other elements and render more subtly in his final version.

In this first version there is more extensive treatment of elements which Beckett was to integrate with greater economy as he condensed his play into a 'dramaticule'. In 'Good Heavens' there is a heavy undercurrent of sexual *double entendre*. Words and phrases which could be taken as references to semen and erection are prominent. 'I was about to ask you how you do it', B says to A. A tells her secret and adds '*Nostorum nostorium*' (the remedy of remedies) to which A replies, 'I did not know he had been discharged'. With a 'complacent laugh', B assures her, 'Oh very much so, very much so indeed'. When C asks B, 'Have you been putting something on your skin?' she tells her secret and volunteers, 'No cream to touch it'. C then says, 'I didn't know he was up'. B responds with another 'complacent laugh' and the same phrase used earlier by C, 'Oh very much so . . . Very much so indeed'.

Although B's confession to C involves a lover, her initial confidence to A concerns a place. She too gives a complacent laugh and the assertion 'Very much so', but they come in response to A's question, 'Is that place going still?'

The ensuing dialogue suggests that the place is a beauty or health clinic or perhaps a place that accommodates trysts. This mention of the place (which Beckett retained and expanded in his second version) reflects his concern with location. If they are frequently left undefined to preserve multiple suggestions, the places in which Beckett's characters find themselves imply their predicament. Neither 'Good Heavens' nor the second version contain a set description, and in *Come and Go* the set is deliberately vague. Coming just after the reference to someone 'discharged', this textual reference to the place 'going still' gives a sense of location to the condition depicted. It indicates that while some may be released from institutions of recuperation, the unwittingly futile attempt to preserve waning vitality will bring others to such places.

The exchange concerning place has sexual undertones:

B   I am told it has gone up.
A   Gone up? You mean the fee?
B   Yes.
A   Yes that is so.
B   And at the same time gone down.
A   Gone down? You mean the . . . er the . . . er
B   Yes.
A   Not in my experience.

The association of the three women with natural beauty and freshness Beckett was to achieve in the later versions through the names of the characters, setting, costume, and allusionary tableau is presented in 'Good Heavens' through the dialogue. The name of C's sister, 'Mrs Flower', is repeated three times in four short lines and again six lines later. A, B, and C are told by their companions that they look 'wonderful', 'fresh', 'young', 'radiant'.

'Viola, Poppy, Rose'

The second stage of composition is represented by an undated five page typescript headed, 'Viola, Poppy, Rose' (Reading University Library MS 1227/7/16/5-6). In this version Beckett began to develop the visual component so important in *Come and Go*. He gave the characters names associated with flowers and the visual spectrum. He provided no description of costume or set, but the few stage directions imply a configuration of three women seated side by side. While still concentrating on the revelatory even sections, he made a first attempt to deal with the scenes in which all three women converse. The typescript opens with Scene I. In it Poppy reads from chapter seven of a mildly pornographic novel the account of Hermione who, rising from her bath, examines and caresses her body in 'an ecstasy of anticipation'. She is awaited by her hairy legged lover Aubrey who 'stretches out before her, finishing his cigar and looking at obscene postcards'. References to previous passages indicate that the women have obviously been reading the novel aloud together on previous occasions. There is also naturalistic differentiation of character in this scene. Poppy is innocent and naïve, reading the sentence 'Hermione rose at last' as 'Her my own rose at last', and always quoting the text unquestioningly for confirmation of her opinions. Viola displays a salacious interest in the details of the descriptions, which leads her to question physical possibilities and complain of 'slipshod writing'. Rose avoids these two extremes. She simply wants to get on with the story. She corrects Poppy's mispronunciation but dismisses Viola's objections cautioning her, 'Purism can go too far' and urging Poppy to 'proceed'.

Though there is more naturalism than usual in his plays—providing an immediate reason for the three women to be assembled and psychological differentiation of character—Beckett's attention was in this scene as much focused on the visual elements as upon naturalistic depiction. The three women side by side, Poppy in the centre opening the book on her lap, and the description of Hermione rising from 'the steaming sweet-smelling foam' hands on her bosom and flanks suggests Botticelli's 'Birth of Venus' in the Uffizi in Florence. The painting depicts not only Venus herself, but the wind goddess to her right blowing flowers and the feminine figure of Spring awaiting her on the left. Beckett's version is ironic. This birth of love depicts a carnal *naïveté* rather than the graceful sensuous innocence of Botticelli's painting. And from the opening line, 'How mild it is for August', we know that Spring is past and that it is Autumn that awaits.

A scheme at the bottom of page two shows the pattern of the women's changing position on the bench.

I   V.R.P.
II   V.R.
III   V.R.P.
IV   P.R.
V   V.R.P.
VI   V.P.
VII   V.R.P.

The normal pattern of the spectrum, violet to red with rose in the middle, begins and ends the play, and also recurs at III and V when the trio is united after the exits of one of the members. The order of the appearances of the two characters who share confidences is also that of the spectrum. Both extremes interact with rose-violet first, then poppy. And then the extremes meet.

In this version Beckett began the process of reducing the number of confidences in Sections II, IV, and VI from three in 'Good Heavens' to one in *Come and Go*. Each of the even numbered sections is in two parts. The first presents the vitalizing power of love with the question about beauty secrets followed by the confession of a lover who confers health. The second presents the imminence of death with the question about the unhealthy appearance of the absent woman followed by a reference to a grieving husband. In this version the repeated question about the appearance of the absent woman is illustrated by an allusion to Blake's poem, 'Rose thou art sick', which links love and death. Poppy asks, 'How do you think Rose is looking?' Vi replies, 'Sick'. For Blake, love is an unrecognised disease.

O Rose thou are sick
The invisible worm
That flies in the night
In the howling storm

Has found out they bed
Of crimson joy
And his dark secret love
Does thy life destroy.

Although they do not know it, Poppy, Rose, and Violet are like Blake's rose, part of the natural process which begins with sexual attraction, then engenders life and vitality for a while, but finally leads to death.

Come and Go

In *Come and Go* Beckett retained almost all of the elements present in his first two versions but incorporated them with maximum theatrical economy. While achieving formal concentration, he achieved greater integration of themes and changed the tone of the play. In contrast to the drafts which preceded it, *Come and Go* is a more poignant expression of the themes of love, death, and divine indifference. In it Beckett greatly reduced the dialogue using the title, names of the characters, structure of the exchanges, and the visual elements to convey what was conveyed more discursively in the earlier versions.

The acknowledgement of love as a part of the sexual process which initiates both life and death presented earlier in the undercurrent of broad *double entendre* and in allusions to Blake and Botticelli is indicated only by the recognisable but unobtrusive sexual pun in the first word of the title. The abridgement of their lives is indicated by the new truncated names of the characters.

The change in names also made the association with the spectrum more apparent. Changing Rose to Florence and Poppy to Ruby, allowed for a less restrictive association of the women with faded flowers. While some of the original association is maintained in the names Flo and Vi and in the 'dull' colours of their dresses, only the name Flo has primary floral associations. And even it does not evoke the image of a specific plant.

After sending the text to Faber for the British first edition but before sending it to Grove Press for the American edition, Beckett made his own French translation of the play. *Va et vient* and the Grove Press edition of *Come and Go* both begin with additional dialogue establishing the name of the characters. In the Grove edition the play opens with 'Ru', which calls attention first to colour, the 'Flo', with its floral associations, and finally six lines later 'Vi', which combines both, completes the spectrum. The motif of the spectrum is underscored visually by the costumes designated in the notes, Vi in a violet dress, Flo in yellow, and Ru in red. With only the repetition of their names and their costuming, Beckett represents in Ru, Flo and Vi the gamut of the extremes of human existence. This suggestion was strengthened by the exchange of places on the bench. The second version began and ended with Violet, Rose, and Poppy seated in the same position on the bench—the normal order of the spectrum from violet to red. In the final version the order at the beginning, Flo Vi Ru, presents a condensed spectrum with then normal centre outside and the extremes brought together. This order is inverted at the end. Although it is unnoticed by the characters who say they are unable to perceive change visually, there has been a progression from red to violet, and from love to death—from one extreme of the human condition to the other.

The less restrictive emphasis on the women as flowers achieved by the change in names also allowed Beckett to use costuming and set design to associate the women with birds. The notes of the final version specify that the figures are 'as much alike as possible apart from colour'. They are seated on a 'bench-like seat without back just long enough to accommodate them'. And 'it should not be clear what they are sitting on'. They simply 'appear and disappear quickly and silently'. They 'are not seen to go off or come back on stage'. (This is in direct contrast to Poppy's 'laborious' exit after excusing herself in the second version.) While there is no overt or latent textural reference to them as birds, these silent, unannounced exits and returns to a minimal perch are like those of birds. They are still ephemeral natural creatures, but there is greater emphasis on an absolute sense of presence and absence than on the failing vitality of faded flowers.

The most extensive changes from the first two versions involve the structure of the interspersed conversations. The multiple revelations in the even sections of the first two versions had created the ironic juxtaposition of a state of complacent unawareness engendered by love and the appalling recognition of death. In the final version, Beckett reserved the treatment of love for odd sections focusing attention in the even sections exclusively on the revelation of death. By eliminating all specific references to illness, Beckett made death at once more abstract and more ominous. It becomes only a whispered secret, the details too awesome to articulate aloud. And in the final version the element of surprise is reserved until the whispered secret itself. In the second version, when asked about the appearance of the absent friend, the women declare themselves 'shocked', 'appalled', 'aghast'. In the final version their answers emphasize their inability to see the appearance of death: 'I see little change', 'She seems much the same', 'One sees little in this light'. Only after the confidence do they register amazement.

The reaction to the revelation of death is also more extreme in this version than in the earlier ones. Instead of the 'Good Heavens' of the first version and 'Heavens' of the second, the women say only 'Oh!' As Beckett's notes point out, their 'Ohs' are 'very different'. Individual reaction to the great secret varies in the details of expression; ultimately, however, the response is the same—an inarticulate expression of surprise, dismay, and helplessness.

While condensing treatment of the theme of death into the even sections, Beckett also condensed the treatment of the theme of love in the odd sections. He abandoned entirely his long prosaic first attempt at a conversation among all three characters. The dialogue of the four odd sections is in the final version as stychomythic as in the even sections. He also established a formal balance in length between the even and odd sections. The opening and closing conversations each have an equal number of lines and silences as the even sections (eight) and the two medial sections, one half that number.

In contrast to the even sections, each of which is complete in itself, these odd sections form one long, continued dialogue about love interrupted by the three exits and three revelations of death. Beginning with Ru's 'Let us not speak' and culminating in Vi's, 'Can we not speak of the old days? Of what came after?'; the dialogue of the even sections provides the play with a developing action dramatizing its central subject an unspoken recognition. The continuous structure and formal balance of the odd sections also emphasize unspoken recognition. In the odd sections, the women say they will dream of love, not speak of it, but the word itself is highlighted. Coming as the final word of a long interrupted sentence at the exact centre of the play, the word 'Love' is given special prominence. In the even sections the women do whisper of death, but the word itself remains unspoken in the play.

The picture of love in the final version is less ironic than in the earlier versions. Just as he had removed the specific references to illness in dealing with death, Beckett removed references to specific loved ones. The secret lovers no longer create a delusion of well-being, and there is no longer the disturbing contrast between them and the grieving husbands. The mention of rings at the end implies husbands, but of them we find out nothing. Only the passing of love is certain. If the husbands are alive they will grieve over the loss of their wives, if they are already dead, they will have been the source of grief.

This new concentration of the themes of love and death in the odd and even sections created a circular plot. As the secret of death that is still to come is revealed in the three even sections, the odd sections turn toward memories of love which is already gone. To strengthen the sense of circularity, Beckett introduced the central emblem of the wedding rings. Two allusions to archetypal configurations of three female figures, one at the opening of the play and one at the conclusion, also give the play a circular structure. The question, 'When did we three last meet?' echoing the words of the weird sisters in *Macbeth*, introduces suggestions of an ominous destiny unperceived by those who will experience it. This verbal allusion is balanced at the end by a visual allusion. The concluding tableau of crossed arms and interlocking hands recalls the intertwined arms familiar in western art depicting the 'Three Graces'. The lines of Beckett's diagram for this tableau echo the lines of Botticelli's 'Three Graces' as closely as the opening line echoes *Macbeth*, so the play comes full circle to an image of feminine beauty and freshness with which the natural cycle of love and death begins.

The dialogue added in *Va et vient* and the American edition also creates awareness of this cycle. At the opening Vi calls the names of Ru and Flo, and they answer 'yes', affirming their presence together. This is echoed at the conclusion of the play when Flo addresses her two companions, but this time the response is not 'yes' but silence, suggesting that, if not immediately at least ultimately, there will be absence. The conclusion of the play contains both ending and beginning.

These larger structural changes create a balance and integration between odd sections dealing with the knowledge of love and even sections dealing with knowledge of death. They also create an implied three part progression of recognition of bitter truths extending beyond the events presented. In this version the truth of love's passing has already been experienced and accepted; the truth of approaching death is revealed in the present and is appalling; the truth of Divine indifference should be evident but awaits recognition.

Beckett made smaller changes in the responses of the women which integrated the theme of providence more explicitly as part of this progression. In the first two versions the references to 'Heaven' in the responses to both the revelation of secret love and of death contained an ironic allusion to Divine providence. When Beckett changed the response to a simple 'Oh!' that suggestion was removed. In *Come and Go* Beckett retained the allusion to providence not in the responses to the secret of death but as part of the questioning about knowledge of the condition.

He introduced two balanced sets of negative questions and statements which unite the question of recognition of the condition and the role of providence in allowing it to exist. After her initial 'Oh!' each of the characters asks a question.

Ru: Does she not know? (Section II)
Vi: Has she not been told? (Section IV)
Flo: Does she not realise? (Section VI)

Cast in the negative, these questions imply a positive response. The ominous secret should be known. Each of these questions is followed by an answer, also in the negative, which implicitly expands the nature of the revelation:

God grant not! (Section II)
God forbid! (Section IV)
Please God not! (Section VI)

Idiomatically, the references to God are only a means of intensification. Literally, they point to the fact that the common fate is one which God might have prevented or possibly even enjoys. There is a growing note of imprecation in the series implying at least the possible awareness of a metaphysical condition as well as a physical one. In the final version the role of providence thus becomes a third potentially more awesome revelation in the future to complement those concerning love experienced in the past and death confided in the present.

Berlin Production

In 1978 Beckett assisted Walter Asmus in directing *Kommen und Gehen* at the Schiller Theatre. His notebook for this production (Reading University Library MS 1730) is only six pages of notes and diagrams without systematic headings. There are no references to lines of dialogue at all. The notebook is about equally divided between the physical appearance of the characters and the structure of the exchange of dialogue and position on the bench. Their German names, Lo, Mei, and Su contain no suggestions of flowers or extremes of the spectrum. Only 'Mei', English May, has prominent secondary suggestions of Spring. In translating them Elmar Tophoven had given precedence to finding familiar shortened names and to the pattern of changing vowel sounds. In notes on the costuming Beckett compensated for that fact:

Lo	Mei	Su
Red Hat	Violet Hat	Yellow Hat
Yellow Dress	Red Dress	Violet Dress
Violet Shoes	Yellow Shoes	Red Shoes

While still associated primarily with one part of it, each of the characters now represents visibly the full range of the spectrum. Some of the contrast between Viola and Poppy as extremes in the second version is reinforced in the interaction of Mei (Vi) and Lo (Ru). Here too their opposed tendencies are emphasized. In his one indication of emotional dynamics Beckett notes that Mei raises her hands 'in irritation'—after her question, 'May we not speak of the old days?'—a reaction against Lo's, 'Let us not speak', which met her question opening the conversation.

The note on costuming also allows for overtones of both flowers and birds but the stronger suggestion is to birds with ruffled plumage which make quick, silent exits:

Hats: flimsy, broadbrimmed, beflowered—ribboned—feathered to stir in draught
Dress: loose, light for suave effect
        If ventilator(s) then screens L and R
Shoes: genre ballerina, exits silent

Except for the notes on costuming, the notebook is almost exclusively devoted to pointing out structural patterns.

Just as they change places on the bench, the three women change roles as initiators of dialogue or responders in a mathematically formal pattern. The principles are spelled out on page three.

1 When 3 each in turn opens and responds
2 When 3 together always central opens
3 Opener always one to go
4 When 2 always responder [of previous section] opens (confides) to non-responder

In a cyclical pattern of coming and going, each respondent succeeds in turn to the central, active role of opener and confider and then becomes the absent subject of the whispered confidence of impending death. (As a note points out, the pattern is broken at the end of the play when Ru has the last line because Flo is holding two left hands and is thus the only one who could feel and comment on the wedding rings.) Their positions on the bench correspond to the succession of roles. When the central figure exits, her vacant seat is filled by the former respondent as she moves closer to the new respondent to deliver her confidence. Although it is inherent in the text, Beckett made two schematic diagrams with arrows indicating the direction of movement in the exchange of seats. The exits of the central figures alternate right, left, right. Each exit is balanced by a counter movement in the opposite direction as the respondent takes her place.

Such a balanced system might go on and on like *Play*, and Beckett contemplated a repetition like that in *Play*. He wrote out a 'continuation' of the pattern through a replica of the original play which would exhaust the possibilites of confidences 'Lo to Su re Mei' etc. Since the even sections are identical except for the change of speakers, this alternative could easily have been implemented. But in a note, he rejected the idea as 'mathematically desirable' but 'logically unacceptable' and 'impossible'.

The notebook contains one indication of detailed stage actions, the directions for the joining hands. In Berlin *Come and Go* concluded in a broad gesture recapitulating the major structural elements: interconnected confidences and destinies, and falling hopes. The women do not simply join hands, rather their hands are 'raised all six together at first' then joined: 'in air at top of gesture'. And finally the hands 'sink gently plumb together'. Although they are not indicated in the notebook, a series of smaller gestures at each of the whispered confidences prepares for this final gesture. As the confider raises her fingers to her lips as designated in the text, the listener raises her hand to her throat and then together both hands drop slowly.

The Consolation of Art: Oscar Wilde and Dante

Dominic Manganiello

> His gilded shrine lies open to the air;
> And cunning sculptor's hands have carven there
> The calm white brow, as calm as earliest morn,
> The eyes that flashed with passionate love and scorn,
> The lips that sang of Heaven and of Hell,
> The almond-face which Giotto drew so well,
> The weary face of Dante . . .

'Ravenna'

The works and life of Dante exercised a considerable fascination in Victorian times. Carlyle, Arnold, and Rossetti, to name a few, all felt compelled to eulogize the writer who was, in Ruskin's words, 'the central man of all the world'.[1] Wilde was no exception to this trend. His mother used to boast about having Dante as a noble ancestor, or so she liked to believe. To those who remained skeptical she cited her maiden name, Elgee, thought to be a corruption of Alighieri, as corroborating evidence.[2] Although Wilde did not draw directly on this putative genealogy, he did claim an artistic kinship with the Italian poet: 'Those who have the artistic temperament go into exile with Dante and learn how salt is the bread of others and how steep their stairs'.[3] Given Wilde's own experience of social ostracism towards the end of his life, it might be tempting to view this affinity as having occurred to the Victorian writer only then. This would be misleading, however, for the figure of Dante cast his shadow over Wilde's imagination from the outset of the latter's literary career.

Two early poems articulate this shared sense of exile. 'Ravenna', winner of the Newdigate Prize in 1878, exalts a Christlike Dante 'bound with crown of thorns' who offered ignobly at the hands of his countrymen:

> Alas! my Dante! thou hast known the pain
> Of meaner lives,—the exile's galling chain,
> How steep the stairs within kings' houses are,
> And all the petty miseries which mar
> Man's nobler nature with the sense of wrong.[4]

Despite the grief which marked Dante's earthly existence, Wilde commemorates his burial place in this ancient Italian city and grants the 'mightiest exile' some spiritual consolation in death: 'Thy soul walks now beside thy Beatrice'.

In the later poem, 'At Verona', published in 1881, something similar occurs. Wilde repeats in the opening of the sonnet the key image of trudging up steep stairs:

> How steep the stairs within kings' houses are
>   For exile-wearied feet as mine to tread,
>   And O how salt and bitter is the bread
> Which falls from this Hound's table,—better far
> That I had died in the red ways of war,
>   Or that the gate of Florence bare my head,
>   Than to live thus, by all things comraded
> Which seeks the essence of my soul to mar.[5]

The octave recalls Cacciaguida's dark prophecy in *Paradiso* XVII about Dante's banishment from Florence to Verona, where he would live under the auspices of Can Grande (the Hound) Scaligeri:[6] 'Thou shalt make trial of how salt doth taste another's bread, and how hard the path to descend and mount upon another's stair.' But Wilde's persona, unlike Dante the pilgrim, regrets not having died in battle, and not having suffered the stigma of returning to Florence as a penitent.[7] These calamities, he claims, would have been preferable to living in misery in Verona as a lonely exile 'comraded' by all things that thwart the possibility of transcendence. At this point the temptation to despair seems irresistible.

Accordingly, the voice of despair is heard in the first part of the sestet:

> 'Curse God and die: what better hope than this?
>   He hath forgotten thee in all the bliss
>   Of his gold city, and eternal day' -

The suggestion that God could apparently forget the plight of his servant momentarily links Wilde's Dante with Job. The note of gloom is especially acute since the voice denies not only hope but also the symbolical nature of Dante's suffering and exile. That is, it denies Wilde's pilgrim figure, who has experienced alienation and the loss of community, the possibility of making the archetypal journey from Verona or the earthly city to his true home among the community of the blessed in the New Jerusalem or 'gold city'.[8] It seems, then, that for the time being this Victorian Dante can only take his place among those in *Inferno* VII who wilfully live in sadness.

The experience of sorrow, however, cannot be accounted for as simply as that. While in prison, Wilde learned how better to appreciate its complex nature. In *De Profundis*, for instance, Wilde remarked that when he first read the *Divine Comedy* in Oxford he thought Dante, who says 'sorrow re-married us to God' in *Purgatorio* XXIII. 81, had been unnecessarily harsh to those who were enamoured of melancholy. In retrospect, he concluded, 'I had no idea that some day this would become to me one of the greatest temptations of my life'.[9] He now realized that gloom was an ally of hopelessness, whereas sorrow had come from 'the hands of Love' so that the human soul could attain perfection.[10]

Dante—indistinguishable from Wilde in this context—achieves a similar understanding of pain in the final lines of 'At Verona':

> Nay peace: behind my prison's blinded bars
> I do possess what none can take away
> My love, and all the glory of the stars.

The operative word is indeed 'peace' since it points to the New Jerusalem, *visio pacis*, his soul's health, peace of mind, the city of God, all of which the voice of dejection had insisted was out of reach. The crowning vision of his art enables the speaker, like Dante the pilgrim, to overcome bitterness in adversity, his 'prison's blinded bars', and to transform a potential human tragedy into a divine comedy.

Wilde could testify from personal experience on behalf of art's power to alleviate sorrow. While visiting the great prison in Lincoln, Nebraska during his American lecture tour in 1882, he was surprised to find an inmate there reading the *Divine Comedy*: 'Strange and beautiful it seemed to me that the sorrow of a single Florentine in exile should, hundreds of years afterwards, lighten the sorrow of some common prisoner in a modern gaol'.[11] Thirteen years later in Reading Gaol, Wilde, broken by his own sorrow, also took to reading the whole of Dante.[12] As he confessed to Frank Harris,

Surely like Dante I have written on my face the fact that I have been in hell. Only Dante never imagined any hell like an English prison; in his lowest circle people could move about; could see each other, and hear each other groan. There was some change, some human companionship in misery.[13]

This sense of confinement in a personal hell is captured in a typical passage from 'The Ballad of Reading Gaol'.

> So they kept us close till nigh on noon,
>   And then they rang the bell,
> And the warders with their jingling keys
>   Opened each listening cell,
> And down the iron stair we tramped,
>   Each from his separate Hell.[14]

In his 'Apologia', however, Wilde had asserted that such external fetters could be shattered:

> I burst the bars,
> Stood face to face with Beauty, known indeed
> The Lové which moves the Sun and all the stars![15]

In signalling the triumph of the imagination over life's degradations, or what might be called the consolation of poetry,[16] Wilde underwrites the salvific quality of Dante's vision of Love at the end of the *Paradiso*.

Still, Wilde's total vision is not as consistently divine as was Dante's. In 'Vita Nuova', for example, Wilde contemplates once more his pain-filled life as he

stands fishing by the sea. In one final attempt to haul in some panacea for his
melancholy, he casts his torn nets into a sea of troubles

> When lo! a sudden glory! and I saw
> The argent splendour of white limbs ascend
> And in that joy forgot my tortured past.[17]

Dante's 'new life' began when he enjoyed a 'mirabile visione' of Beatrice in
heaven, whereas Wilde's marvellous vision refers to the birth of Aphrodite
from the sea.[18] He deliberately displaces Dante-like spiritual love with pagan,
sensual love.

By suggesting a more earthly kind of ecstasy or beatitude than is found in *La
Vita Nuova*, Wilde in this instance follows the so-called 'fleshly school of
poetry' established by Dante Gabriel Rossetti.[19] Images of the latter's 'Blessed
Damozel', such as the mystic eyes, the long ivory throat, and the loosened
shadowy hair, abound in Wilde's poems, especially those with Italian titles.
'La Belle Donna Della Mia Mente' is one such poem, but more pertinent to the
Dantescan context is 'Madonna Mia'. In the octave of the sonnet, Wilde
describes the physical qualities of 'A lily-girl, not made for this world's pain'.
The description ends with the familiar image of the white throat 'Through
whose wan marble creeps one purple vein'. This attention to meticulous detail
which governs the sensual impulse is sublimated in the sestet:

> Yet, though my lips shall praise her without cease,
>   Even to kiss her feet I am not bold,
>   Being o'ershadowed by the wings of awe,
> Like Dante, when he stood with Beatrice
>   Beneath the flaming Lion's breast, and saw
>   The seventh Crystal, and the Stair of Gold.[20]

The poet likens his awe to that experienced by Dante in the seventh heaven
(Saturn) beneath the constellation Leo when he beholds with Beatrice a vision
of a golden ladder on which countless splendours arise and descend wheeling
like birds in flight.[21] Like Dante, Wilde now shies away from sensual contact
in order to embrace the ultimate vision. Earthly passion yields to heavenly
contemplation or, as Wilde puts it in 'Amor Intellectualis',[22] 'The seven-fold
vision of the Florentine' leads to the love of minds. The Victorian poet remains
characteristically torn between the love that imparadises the mind and the love
that awakens the sensual body.

The tensions that arise from these competing visions are also evident in
'Flower of Love', a lament about the limits of the human condition: 'had I not
been made of common clay / I had climbed the higher heights unclimbed yet,
seen the fuller air, the larger day.'[23] If it had not been for mortal finitude, the
poet continues,

> I had trod the road which Dante treading saw the
>   suns of seven circles shine,
> Ay! perchance had seen the heavens opening, as
>   they opened to the Florentine.

And the mighty nations would have crowned me,
who am crownless now and without name,
And some orient dawn had found me kneeling on
the threshold of the House of Fame.[24]

Wilde now argues, as opposed to his previous poems, that the 'wildness' of his
wasted passion has prevented him from undertaking a pilgrimage like Dante's
and from gazing at the beatific vision. His passion has likewise cost him his
reputation and a place in Chaucer's House of Fame. In other words, the poet,
unlike Dante, cannot hope to return to his baptismal font and there place on his
own head the laurel wreath for, he affirms, 'I have found the lover's crown of
myrtle better than the poet's crown of bays'.[25] The rose petals of youth, though
withered, have enabled him to live his poems instead, to turn from art to life.

   This last image of the rose reminds us of the well-known declaration about
art in 'The Decay of Lying':

Remote from reality and with her eyes turned away from the shadows of the cave, Art
reveals her own perfection, and the wondering crowd that watches the opening of the
marvellous many-petalled rose fancies that it is its own history that is being told to it, its
own spirit that is finding expression in a new form. But it is not so. The highest art
rejects the burden of the human spirit, and gains more from a new medium or a fresh
material than she does from any enthusiasm for art, or from any lofty passion, or from
any great awakening of the human consciousness. She develops purely on her own
lines.[26]

The concept that life imitates art involves a modification of Plato's cave
analogy. In Plato's epistemology man moves from the shadows of the cave to
the light in a supernal world of forms. This movement from the realm of the
tangible to the realm of the intelligible implies that life is an imperfect imitation
of some ideal world. For Wilde, however, this ideal world is earthly not
celestial, and can be located in Art itself. This world of Art is compared, or so it
seems, to Dante's 'many-petalled rose' in *Paradiso* XXXI, an image of
communal infinity, of divine as opposed to human love. But Wilde, as Richard
Ellmann points out, denies the image its transcendent origin: 'when Wilde
speaks of the "highest" art he associates it with a change of technique, not of
content or aspiration.'[27] A reader can become another Dante when he opens
the *Divine Comedy* and can be transported into the heaven of poetical thought,
a world which is timeless and universal and therefore more real than the reality
offered to the senses, as Wilde has Gilbert argue in 'The Critic as Artist',
whereas life can only cheat us with 'shadows'.[28]

   The theory that art derives from itself alone distorts Dante's views on the
subject as well as Plato's. In *Inferno* XI, for instance, Dante has Virgil employ
the language of filiation to explain that 'Art is God's grandchild' ('arte a Dio
quasi è nipote') since it follows (imitates) nature which in turn follows
(imitates) the Supreme Artifex. Dante's vision of the multifoliate rose, then, is
not remote from reality, or a form of 'lying' as Wilde would have it, but rather a
shadowy preface to the reality of the vision contained in God's Book.[29] The
shadowy beings that populate the page, moreover, remind the poet that his

verbal power is derivative, that words are shades not solid things: *Imago* not *Verbum*. A striking illustration of this point occurs when Statius, on attempting to embrace the knees of his hero Virgil, remembers he is a soul rather than a body: 'Now you can understand the quantity of love that warms me towards you, so that I forget our vanity, and treat the shadows like the solid things.'[30]

Wilde exposes the dangers of mistaking the world of shadows for reality in *The Picture of Dorian Gray*. For Plato, too, language was a moving shadow of reality. Since the reality the word signified was itself transient, the word was the shadow of a shadow.[31] Dorian, on the other hand, posits a radically different linguistic epistemology: 'Words! Mere words! . . . They seemed to be able to give a plastic form to formless things . . . Was there anything as real as words?' He confuses signification with an identity between sign and object. Language, rather than corresponding to that which is spoken about, creates reality instead: 'If one doesn't talk about a thing, it has never happened. It is simply expression, as Harry says, that gives reality to things.' This new *dico* principle ('I speak, therefore it is') usurps the power of the primal Word and allows Lord Henry to make disciples such as Dorian into 'his own creation', a verbal icon or 'echo' of himself. As Lady Henry says, 'I always hear Harry's views from his friends. It is the only way I get to know them'. Dorian's mentor believes that the world of images is indeed the world of reality: 'the mere shapes and patterns of things becom[e], as it were, refined, and gain . . . a kind of symbolical value, as though they were themselves patterns of some other and more perfect form whose shadow they made real.'[32] Confusing the two worlds results in what might be called a linguistic or intellectual narcissism.

The reification of language leads inevitably to a reification of persons. Each of the main characters—Dorian, Basil, Lord Henry—treats the other as if he were an *objet d'art*.[33] Dorian is furthermore infatuated with Sybil Vane, the Shakespearian actress, because she gives 'substance to the shadows of art'. However, when Sybil tells him 'I know nothing but shadows and I thought them real. You taught me what reality really is' by way of explaining her decision to leave the stage, Dorian retorts bitterly,

Without your art you are nothing. I would have made you famous, splendid, magnificent. The world would have worshipped you, and you would have borne my name.[34]

Dorian's frustration stems from his inability to imitate Lord Henry by recreating Sybil in his own image and likeness. The dread of losing one's subjectivity or identity makes each character manoeuvre the other into precisely the same position as a way of dealing with the threat.

This threat is exacerbated by another: 'petrification'. Wilde applies the myth of Medusa to Dorian's strange story of beauty changed to ugliness, of fascination changed to horror. Time has stopped for him because he has bartered his soul away for eternal youth, but the marks of sin displayed by the image of his corrupt soul on the canvas continue to 'petrify' him: 'Time being dead . . . dragged a hideous future from its grave, and showed it to him. He stared at it. Its very horror made him stone.'[35] But Dorian is a modern day

Narcissus as well as Medusa; he is both enamoured and terrified of his own image. In effect, he exchanges his 'original self' for a reflection becoming, in Blake's phrase, 'idolatrous to his own shadow'.[36] His narcissitic idolatry, as witnessed also in his desire to have the world worship his creation Sybil Vane, matches the 'curious artistic idolatry' of Basil who fears he has put too much of himself in his painting of Dorian.

Wilde's application of the Medusa myth in *The Picture of Dorian Gray* corresponds in this important respect to Dante's in the *Divine Comedy*. As John Freccero has shown,[37] idolatry is precisely the threat Dante the pilgrim confronts in *Inferno* IX. In the fiction of the poem Medusa is no mythological character but the poet's own creation which he has become enamoured of. Images and words that are exclusively self-referential constitute an 'infernal' art, the worshipping of the man-made sign for its own sake. When Dante reaches Mount Purgatory, therefore, Beatrice chides him for his former sensual fascination and idolatry: 'I see thy mind turned to stone and, stonelike, such in hue that the light of my word dazes thee.'[38] Dante's intellect is petrified because up to now it has been unable to point beyond itself, to give way to transcendence in the person of Beatrice, the light that imparadises the mind.

In Wilde's novel, Lord Henry persists in a similar kind of interpretive or intellectual obtuseness. He believes to the end that Dorian has remained unscarred by the pursuit of beauty for its own sake despite the evidence to the contrary, and repeats his disciple's fatal wish: 'To get back my youth I would do anything in the world.' He exalts, moreover, Dorian's narcissistic perspective on life and art: 'I am so glad that you have never done anything, never carved a statue, or painted a picture, or produced anything outside of yourself.' The final, devastating irony occurs when Wilde has Lord Henry quote scripture: 'what does it profit a man if he gain the whole world and lose his own soul?' This is the central moral subtext of Dorian's Faustian adventures, but Lord Henry is blind to its implications and proceeds to register his disbelief in the soul.[39] This blindness to things unseen renders Lord Henry, like Dante in *Inferno* IX, 'petrified into absolute insensibility'.[40]

Basil, on the other hand, emerges from the world of shadows to the light of revelation. He invites Dorian to renounce his idolatry by reciting the prayer, 'Though your sins be as scarlet, yet I will make them white as snow'; that is, he offers Dorian the possibility of counter-transformation through the mercy of the divine Artist in whose image his soul was originally fashioned. The soul is, as Dante's metaphor implied, God's child since there exists a spiritual resemblance between the two.[41] From this point of view Wilde locates art in the tradition of what Jacques Maritain called 'transcendental realism'.[42] Basil achieves a vision that recalls the one enjoyed by Dante when he moved from seeing his own image in a clear fount in *Purgatorio* XXX to seeing 'our image' ('nostra effige') in the God-man at the end of the *Paradiso*. Dorian, however, resists transcendence, the image of God in man ('the divinest thing in us' as he had earlier defined conscience), by killing Basil, the voice of that conscience. 'By suicide', according to Richard Ellmann,[43] 'Dorian becomes aestheticism's first martyr', a 'saint Narcissus' embodying the contradictory impulses of self-denial and self-indulgence rather than a 'transhumanized' Narcissus like Dante.[44]

At first glance *The Picture of Dorian Gray* invites the tragic conclusion that one cannot go to Art for everything, as Gilbert asserts in 'The Critic as Artist', without suffering the consequences. For this reason Dorian claims repeatedly that he has been poisoned by a book Lord Henry gives him.[45] Art from this perspective gathers its ephemeral leaves into a flower whose name is narcissus. Contrariwise, when Basil urges Dorian to abide by divine rather than human words, Wilde, like Dante, suggests that art can point beyond itself and be glossed by another text which is bound together by Love and which opens into a marvellous many-petalled rose.[46] Art can articulate the constant aspiration of the soul's journey, but it cannot substitute for the reality of its experience. If Plato 'stirred in the soul of man the desire to know the connection between Beauty and Truth',[47] then Dante inspired Wilde to envisage the possibility of standing face to face before them.[48]

Wilde considered Dante 'the supreme modern poet' because he had explored 'all the complexities of the modern soul'.[49] In his own poetry and prose fiction Wilde's exploration of spiritual states was no less complex and no less modern.

Wilde's Criticism:
Theory and Practice

Jonathan Culler

In 'The Critic as Artist as Wilde', Richard Ellmann writes,

In protesting the independence of criticism, Wilde sounds like an ancestral Northrop Frye or Roland Barthes. These portentous comparisons do indeed claim virtue by association, and such claims may be broadened. André Gide found Nietzsche less exciting because he had read Wilde, and Thomas Mann in one of his last essays remarks almost with chagrin on how many of Nietzsche's aphorisms might have been expressed by Wilde, and how many of Wilde's by Nietzsche. What I think can be urged for Wilde, then, is that for his own reasons and in his own way he laid the basis for many critical positions which are still debated in much the same terms, and which we like to attribute to more ponderous names.[1]

Professor Ellmann's assessment invites the expert on contemporary criticism to read Wilde so as to discover a precursor of today's most innovative critics. The invitation is doubly tempting: first, because Wilde's coruscating wit makes him a pleasure to read, whatever one's purpose, and second because reading Wilde in this pursuit would be an exception to the rule of source hunting, which so often takes one into massive and dreary tomes forgotten in a library. But if one goes to work on Wilde the critic, in the hope of declaring him the true precursor of today's literary theory, one is brought up short by René Wellek's assessment in the fourth volume of his *History of Modern Criticism*. Wellek devotes eight pages to Wilde as critic—a fairly generous allotment— but his judgement is severe: the 'myth or legend' of Wilde as

the martyr of aestheticism, the scapegoat of a society enraged by the worship of beauty and art for art's sake . . . gives to Wilde's ideas on art and literature a historical position which they may not deserve in a history of criticism, apart from the personality and the pitiful fate of the man. Obviously Wilde's ideas are anything but new and can be easily traced to their sources in Pater, Swinburne, Arnold, Gautier, Baudelaire, and Poe.[2]

Wilde, then, may be something of a trap for the proponent of contemporary criticism. Even if not given to paranoia, the modern theorist may be excused for wondering whether Wilde is dangled before him as a piece of bait, a richly befeathered and nattily striped lure, to which he would rise, only to find that he had been taken. The wit and resonance of Wilde's critical aphorisms tempt one to seize the opportunity to declare him the true precursor of today's literary theory, but if one does so one finds, too late, that one has thereby declared contemporary literary theory blatantly unoriginal: anticipated by a Victorian dandy who got all his ideas from others.

If one sets these suspicions aside, however, and undertakes to read Wilde's criticism so as to see what happens when Wilde turns from the radical aphorisms of his dialogues, 'The Decay of Lying' and 'The Critic as Artist', to essays on particular authors or works, one finds a different sort of surprise: Wilde, it turns out, was not only a good critic; quite remarkably, he was a very *sound* critic. The criteria he invokes, the standards he applies, are, if not unexceptionable, at the very least right-minded. His character Gilbert, an unsound man, may urge that poetry should aspire to the condition of music, but here is Wilde on Swinburne: 'It has been said of him, and with truth, that he is a master of language, but with still greater truth it may be said that Language is his master. Words seem to dominate him. Alliteration tyrannises over him. Mere sound often becomes his lord. He is so eloquent that whatever he touches becomes unreal.'[3] Quoting some lines from 'A Word with the Wind' –

> Be the sunshine bared or veiled, the sky superb or shrouded,
>   Still the waters, lax and languid, chafed and foiled,
> Keen and thwarted, pale and patient, clothed with fire or clouded
>   Vex their heart in vain, or sleep like serpents coiled.

– he writes, 'Verse of this kind may be justly praised for the sustained strength and vigour of its metrical scheme. Its purely technical excellence is extraordinary. But is it more than an oratorical *tour de force*? Does it really convey much? Does it charm? Could we return to it again and again with renewed pleasure? We think not. It seems to us empty'.[4] The tone of this judgement, the very idea of condemning something as an oratorical *tour de force*, seems quite out of keeping with the principles articulated in the dialogues.

Here is Wilde contrasting Dostoevsky with Turgenev and Tolstoy, seeking, it might appear, to see the object as it truly is: 'he has qualities which are distinctly and absolutely his own, such as a fierce intensity of passion and concentration of impulse, a power of dealing with the deepest mysteries of psychology and the most hidden springs of life, a realism that is pitiless in its fidelity and terrible because it is true.'[5] No suggestion here that, as 'The Decay of Lying' would have it, 'To art's subject matter we should be more or less indifferent. We should, at any rate, have no preferences, no prejudices, no partisan feeling of any kind'.[6]

One could quote other exemplary judgements. This is good criticism, but it is interesting precisely because the powerful aphorisms of the dialogues seem not to have affected it. Nor have they necessarily affected Wilde's remarks on criticism itself. Reviewing Walter Pater's *Appreciations*, he concludes, 'Certainly the real secret of Wordsworth has never been better expressed. After having read and re-read Mr Pater's essay—for it requires re-reading—one returns to the poet's work with a new sense of joy and wonder and with something of eager and impassioned expectation. And perhaps this might roughly be taken as the test or touchstone of the finest criticism'.[7] This seems positively to seek the response, 'How true, how true! How different from those arrogant modern critics who tout criticism as creation, misreading, and so on'.

Now of course the aphorisms are not presented as the principles Wilde follows in his own critical writing, but the lack of apparent fit between the aphorisms and critical practice does pose an interesting problem and lead one to ask about the significance of this discrepancy. In particular, is there a connection between this discrepancy and the celebration of Wilde as the precursor of contemporary critical theory? A suspicious reader could certainly imagine an affirmative answer. Wilde produced brilliant and suggestive theoretical formulations but these are not involved in his sound assessments of literary works. His theoretical formulae are therefore not principles to be relentlessly applied but *wit*. To take Wilde as precursor and model, then, is to suggest a view of modern literary theory as failed wit: jokes that didn't come off, weren't clever enough, or have gone sour through excessive application.

The strange relationship between theory and practice in Wilde's criticism would indeed enable it to be put to this use; these aphorisms made comfortable by the fact that they are outrageous proposals with no consequences could be held up as a model to contemporary theory, which might then to be said to err in taking its jokes and paradoxes seriously. But the important question to pursue is why these aphorisms do not become imaginative resources in Wilde's writings about particular works, as similar axioms do for modern criticism. The answer I would offer helps one to define the relationship between Wilde and contemporary literary theory.

Theorists are given to general statements of the form 'X is really Y' or 'X always does Y', and these statements are open to two interpretations. Either they purport to describe a crucial feature about a given class X, or they define a new class composed only of those old X's which fit the new definition (the only genuine X's are those which do Y). 'Art never expresses anything but itself',[8] one of Wilde's more modern maxims, can be a proposition about art in general, telling us that all the things we call art will prove, when rightly viewed, to have this crucial property. But it can also be taken to stipulate that something only counts as art if it has this property and that some of what we now think of as art is not in fact art. Thus, while the first interpretation preserves a single class and urges is to consider whether, ultimately, these works do not in fact express nothing but their own nature as art, the second interpretation leads us to distinguish two classes: what is truly art according to the new definition and what fails to measure up to the new stipulation.

I would suggest, generalizing wildly, that by and large when radical contemporary theorists make a claim about the nature of language, the nature of writing, the nature of literature, the nature of interpretation, it is a claim of the first kind. If one of them were to say 'Art never expresses anything but itself' that would be part of a theory with methodological consequences, enjoining us to try to interpret works in this way and to treat anything the work seemed to be saying about the world as a way of expressing or commenting upon its own nature as work of art. But when this statement appears in Wilde it is a statement of the second kind, a way of claiming that what does not fit this definition is not true art. Indeed, it is swiftly followed by the further principle that 'All bad art comes from returning to life and nature'. Wilde's aphorism gives us two classes: good art which fits the definition and bad art which doesn't.

Take a second example: the claim in contemporary critical theory that interpretation is always a historical act—an act which can never free itself from its own historical limitations and which can never therefore be other than a misreading. This is a redefinition which directs attention to certain aspects of all acts of interpretation, both the immensely scrupulous and the irreverently anachronistic. It preserves a single class and makes a claim about that class. But when Wilde talks about the perpetual re-writing of history he speaks of it as a duty—'The one duty we owe to history is to re-write it'[9]—as though there were a considerable possibility of not re-writing it. His aphorism would seem to yield two classes, accounts that re-write and accounts that do not, rather than redefining a single class. To see the object as it is not isn't, according to Wilde, writers' and critics' fate but their *duty*; and 'The Decay of Lying' is specifically about the loss literature suffers when talented youth 'falls into careless habits of accuracy'.[10] Once again, Wilde's principles produce two categories: admirable writing that lies and degenerate writing that is accurate.

Now it might seem that theoretical principles of this sort, which divide works into two classes, are precisely the kind that the critic would apply in his critical practice. Doubtless of lesser minds this is true, but Wilde's is too complex a sensibility to be satisfied with rating works according to these crude criteria and rejecting those which imitate nature, are sincere, are not self-reflexive, and so on. Theoretical generalizations of the first sort, which redefine an entire domain, prove immensely fruitful for criticism by focusing attention in a different way and reordering interpretive priorities; whereas principles of the second kind make possible only a rather blatant evaluative application, a separation of good from bad in terms of a particular theoretical principle. A Leavis attempt to separate works into those which are 'for' life and those which are not is imaginatively much less productive than, for instance, the New Criticism's claim that the language of poetry is the language of paradox. This, I suggest, is why Wilde would not put his theoretical principles into practice. They would make him an *obvious* critic.

But to think of Wilde in this way—as producing aphorisms whose evaluative force is such that he cannot allow them to energize his criticism—is perhaps to give him too little credit. One of his most interesting theoretical moments comes in his reformulation of the story of tropological origins told by Vico and Rousseau. According to Vivian's essay, 'The Decay of Lying: A Protest', civilization originates with the first liar, 'who first, without ever having gone out to the rude chase, told the wondering cavemen at sunset how he had dragged the Megatherium from the purple darkness of its jasper cave, or slain the Mammoth in single combat and brought back its gilded tusks'.[11] This liar is 'the true founder of social intercourse', the 'lost reader', and Vivian, who praises lying, who calls us to do our duty and revive the art of lying and concludes with a vision of the splendid civilization that will result if we heed his call, is casting himself in the role of the lost leader: 'Society must sooner or later return to its lost leader, the cultured and fascinating liar.'[12] If he is to occupy the role to which he aspires through his essay, Vivian must tell lies, as must Wilde. Perhaps, then, the function of Wilde's sober critical judgements is to show us that his startling aphorisms are lies and thus qualify him as the lost leader. Lest this conclusion seem a bit of fanciful wit or an easy rhetorical turn, let me point out that in fact Wilde calculated correctly. It is precisely the brilliance of his lies that causes us to treat him as precursor of modern critical theory or, as Richard Ellmann puts with greater accuracy, neatly sidestepping the question of whether Wilde's aphorisms serve as his critical principles, as one who 'for his own reasons and in his own way . . . laid the basis for many critical positions which are still debated in much the same terms'.[13]

Playing in Earnest

Thomas R. Whitaker

I The Action of Farce

'For me', says Gwendolen Fairfax to her nervous suitor, 'you have always had an irresistible fascination.' And why? 'We live, as I hope you know, Mr Worthing, in an age of ideals. The fact is constantly mentioned in the more expensive monthly magazines, and has reached the provincial pulpits, I am told; and my ideal has always been to love some one of the name of Ernest.' That, of course, is from Wilde's masterpiece of 1895. Almost eighty years later Stoppard's *Travesties* has Old Carr recall or imagine another Gwendolen who gave the same assurance to Tristan Tzara in Zurich about 1917, but with a different explanation. 'As you know', she says, 'I have been helping Mr Joyce with his new book, which I am convinced is a work of genius, and I am determined to secure for him the universal recognition he deserves.' On learning that Tzara edited 'a magazine of all that is newest and best in literature', she knew she was 'destined' to love him.

Victorian high seriousness is out; devotion to the avant-garde is in. But ideals propagated by journalism can still serve a pragmatic young lady as masks for erotic impulse, personal vanity, or social power. In both plays the mask-wearing invites satirical judgement but the absurdity of the situation disarms us. Our criticial animus yields to delight. Even if we wanted to assess the degrees of disingenuousness, self-deception, and folly in Gwendolen Fairfax and Gwendolen Carr, we'd be hard put to do so. They are not real persons, not even rounded characters whose motives we might plumb. These mask-wearers are themselves playfully earnest masks that we must wear, directly as actors or indirectly as members of an audience, when we share in the performance of these plays.

Any performance discloses meanings that often remain hidden from readers of the script as a literary work. In the theatre we don't confine our attention to characters and events, or to the verbal shaping of an imagined world. We respond to theatrical figures, to actors who are playing roles for us, and who invite us to enter into that role-playing. Their styles may vary from the sympathetic inhabiting of a character to the ironic wearing of a grotesque or brittle mask. Their rhythms may range from the *lento* of Maeterlinck to the *allegro* of Wilde or the frequent *prestissimo* of Stoppard. They may relate to us through a shared solitude, as in Chekhov, a sardonic commentary, as in Brecht, or a farcical mugging, as occasionally in Shakespeare and Molière.

Always, however, the figures on stage are unstable compounds of player and role, and we attend at least peripherally to the complex shape of the playing in which they invite us to engage. That playing both actualizes and supplements what's implied by the script. And its dominant meanings, though often ignored by dramatic commentaries, are undeniably central whenever a script is mediated by a community of performance.

We may take account of such mediation by reading scripts from directorial points of view, analyzing performances, studying acting styles and audience expectations, or reflecting more generally on role-playing. We may focus on one playwright (as in J.L. Styan's *Chekhov in Performance*), on versions of one play (as in Marvin Rosenberg's *The Masks of King Lear*), on historical periods (as in Peter Holland's *The Ornament of Action* or Judith Milhous and Robert Hume's *Producible Interpretation*), or on yet broader questions of playing (as in Michael Goldman's *The Actor's Freedom* or Bruce Wilshire's *Role Playing and Identity*). I want here to examine some traits of the communities of performance implied by four related scripts: *The Importance of Being Earnest*, *Travesties*, and two earlier responses to Wilde—Shaw's *You Never Can Tell* and Orton's *What the Butler Saw*. Each is in some sense a 'serious farce', and the actions in which they ask us to engage can shed some light on the peculiarities of that omniverous modern genre.

Shaw wrote *You Never Can Tell* soon after reviewing *The Importance of Being Earnest* and partly in reaction against what he took to be its intellectual frothiness and lack of earnest feeling. He seems to have tried to free Wilde's title from self-irony without lapsing into the solemn or sentimental. Orton read Wilde's play when in secondary school—aloud, and with relish, to his sister Leonie. He began *What the Butler Saw* much later, in 1966, at least partly in revisionary homage to a precursor whom he had come to think insufficiently tough-minded. That was also the year in which Stoppard's first playful responses to Wilde appeared—*Rosencrantz and Guildenstern Are Dead* and *Lord Malquist and Mr Moon*, which gave us Wilde mediated through Beckett and Joyce. Shortly after Orton's play was posthumously produced in 1969, it helped to determine the shape of Stoppard's *Jumpers*. And in 1974 these Wildean permutations came to a whirlwind climax in *Travesties*, which also reached out to incorporate some Shavian political and emotional dialectics.

These plays all belong to a rich modern tradition or tangle of traditions that has raised farce to a master genre, able to subsume not only burlesque, satire, comedy of manners, and romantic comedy but also the didactic, the pathetic, and even the tragic. Though earlier playwrights could mix up the genres, there seems never to have been such a flood of mingled levity and gravity as that which has resulted in such works as Jarry's *King Ubu*, Chekhov's *The Cherry Orchard*, Synge's *The Playboy of the Western World*, Pirandello's *Six Characters in Search of an Author*, Brecht's *Threepenny Opera*, Beckett's *Waiting for Godot*, Ionesco's *The Chairs*, Durrenmatt's *The Visit*, Pinter's *The Birthday Party*, and the satirical *commedia dell'arte* of Dario Fo. And there have been similar outpourings in film and fiction, from Chaplin to Truffaut and Allen, and from Faulkner and West to Heller, Nabokov, Pynchon, and Grass. David Lodge's metaromance, *Small World*, is a recent addition to the group of seriously farcical narratives. And perhaps we can glimpse on the theatrical horizon a metafarce called *The Importance of Being Absurd* in which yet another Gwendolen will explain her fascination:

'We live', she might say, 'in an age that won't take anything just in earnest or just in fun. Ten years before Wilde wrote his "trivial play for serious people", Nietzsche had said we must learn to laugh if we are hell-bent on remaining pessimists. Ten years after Wilde's play, Freud showed that every joke is serious as well as playful. Since then the psychologists have told us that farce enacts our secret desires and guilts, anthropologists have told us that the saturnalia and carnival are safety-valves for repressive societies, and historians of drama have traced our passion through what John Styan calls Dark Comedy, Walter Kaiser calls the Grotesque, and Martin Esslin calls the Absurd. Call it what you like. My ideal—for this is still an age of ideals—must be to love someone like *you*, whether your name is Alec or Buster or Charlie or Didi or Gogo or Hamm or Hulot or Humbert or Krapp or Quilty or Woody or Yossarian or Zero.'

Though understanding our passion, this glibly eclectic Gwendolen couldn't help us very much in our attempt to describe specific communities of serious farce. Nor could the academic definitions that suggest, in their categorical rigour, that a 'community' of farce would be a contradiction of terms. One critic has said that the spirit of farce 'delights in taboo-violation' but 'avoids implied moral comment or criticism' and 'tends to debar empathy for the victim'. Another has said that farce is 'a destroyer and detractor', a 'negating force'. According to another, it 'emphasizes quirks and eccentricities of behaviour and tends to exclude such worthwhile human emotions as tenderness, sensitivity, sympathy, and compassion'. Yet another has called its principal motor the 'impulse to attack': 'in farce hostility enjoys itself'. And yet another has said that farce 'enacts something like a primitive superego punishment for the characters' libidinal release in the form of a maniacal plot which both arranges libidinal gratification and punishes them for it'.[1] Those definitions point to important elements in many farces, including some by Feydeau and Orton, but they have little bearing on the work of Wilde, Shaw, or Stoppard. Certainly they can't explain why so many modern farces do incorporate moral comment, social criticism, and even tenderness and compassion. Perhaps that narrowness of definition has encouraged the tendency to slight the importance of farce even in discussions of Dark Comedy, the Grotesque, and the Absurd. (In *The Theatre of the Absurd*, for example, Esslin pays attention to *commedia dell'arte*, the music hall, and the silent film, but 'farce' doesn't appear in his index.) In any event, if we define farce in terms of a staged world of madness, a blocking of our humane feelings, and an acting out of secret cravings and hostilities, we simply ignore the fact that, like every kind of play, a farce is an art-work created and interpreted by a community.

More helpful, therefore, are some statements by writers who never lost sight of the artistic and social impulses in the theatre. 'In a sense', said Stark Young, 'all drama moves toward the condition of farce. That is because the theatre's very essence consists in the heightening of its material. Heightening that is free, fluent, almost abstract, unless it has the restrictions of character and rational measure, floats off into farce; which is closer to poetic drama and serious tragedy than to plain everyday prose realism.' W.B. Yeats would have agreed. 'What attracts me to drama', he once said, 'is that it is, in the most obvious way, what all the arts are upon a last analysis. A farce and a tragedy are alike in this, that they are a moment of intense life.' They focus 'an energy, an eddy of life purified from everything but itself'. On two occasions—when writing *The Player Queen* and *The Herne's Egg*—Yeats took abortive verse tragedies and translated them into farcical modes. Near the end of his life, bringing farce, comedy, and tragedy together once more, he elucidated that 'energy' or 'eddy of life' which is their common reason for being. 'The arts', he said, 'are all the bridal chambers of joy. No tragedy is legitimate unless it leads some great character to his final joy.' He heard 'dance music' in Hamlet's last speech; and in the last moments of Cleopatra, Lear, and Oedipus he also read signs of the 'energy' that Blake called 'eternal delight'.[2]

Yeats understood that the play's actors and spectators must participate in that delight. The poem 'Lapis Lazuli' imagines Hamlet and Lear as actors on the stage of history, the choric spectators as figures in a work of art, and all as sharing in the 'gaiety' of the artist. Their script is a tragedy, but their real play is a transcendent comedy. The distinction in 'Lapis Lazuli' between the tragic heroes on the stage of history and the musical Chinamen observing from within the virtual eternity of art and nature recalls the distinction between the Apollonian heroes and the Dionysian satyr chorus made by Nietzsche in *The Birth of Tragedy Out of the Spirit of Music*. The 'metaphysical joy in the tragic', said Nietzsche, translates the 'instinctive unconscious Dionysian wisdom' of the chorus into the language of images. The hero as a manifestation of the will is annihilated, but 'the eternal life of the will is not affected by his annihilation'. Tragedy as Nietzsche understood it enables us to share an 'eternal life' of which 'music is the immediate idea'. Indeed, he proposed a *'mystery doctrine of tragedy*: the fundamental knowledge of the oneness of everything existent, the conception of individuation as the primal cause of evil, and of art as the joyous hope that the spell of individuation may be broken in augury of a restored oneness'.[3]

Though the young Nietzsche insisted that the Greek chorus derived from the satyr play, he believed farce to be a sign of decadence. Wagner's music-drama was for him 'the gradual awakening of the Dionysian spirit' in the Alexandrian modern world. He later turned against his own Wagnerizing, however, and began to praise Bizet and Offenbach. 'What is good is light', he then could say; 'whatever is divine moves on tender feet'. And his Zarathustra declared: 'Come, let us kill the spirit of gravity'.[4] As Morton Gurewitch has argued, we may therefore understand farce in a somewhat Nietzschean spirit, though against the letter of *The Birth of Tragedy*, as 'our only source of Dionysian comedy'.[5] I would go further. In what Gurewitch calls sexual, psychic, social, and metaphysical farce, we can often find the Dionysian spirit struggling to awaken from the nightmare of our modern Alexandrianism. That is one reason for the persistent effort of farce to encompass the serious. There it enacts what the later Nietzsche might have called the 'mystery doctrine of farce'. Against our psychological and social alienation, our objectifying know-ledge and chronic doubt, and our suicidal technology, it continues the joyous hope that the spell of individuation may be broken and oneness may be restored.

In order to understand that power of farce, we must recognize that its negative elements are balanced, contained, and transmuted by its artistic and social form. In the Plautine tradition, from *The Menaechmi* through Shake-speare's *The Comedy of Errors* to the sexual farces of Georges Feydeau and Orton's *What the Butler Saw*, the imitation of madness, confusion, and frenzy tends to occur within quite rational dramatic designs. *The Comedy of Errors* develops with rigour the permutations and combinations of error made possible by its premise of not one but two sets of twins. This is also true within the British, Irish, and French tradition of the short farce, from John Maddison Morton's *Box and Cox* to Ionesco and Beckett. *Waiting for Godot* explores its bog of uncertainty within a most symmetrical pattern of paradoxical doublets, reversals, and repetitions. In farce, moreover, every reduction in sympathy for the characters as victims is balanced by our heightened identification with the actors who play those characters, or with the characters themselves as players of their own life-roles. Farce tends to replace the centre of gravity in the world; it plays with a centre of levity in our shared playing. It doesn't block our social feelings but redirects them into the action of performance. Having invited us to identify with a player or a character-as-player, it can then easily lead us on to a new kind of pathos, as in Chaplin's films, or toss us back and forth between levity and gravity, as in the plays of Beckett, Ionesco, or Dürrenmatt. That is also why, in the version of *The Comedy of Errors* developed at the Goodman Theatre in 1983 with the Flying Karamazov Brothers and the Vaudeville Nouveau, Shakespeare's design of oppositions, mirrorings, reversals, and symmetries could be so exuberantly and appropriately translated into the troupe's own juggling, doubling, disguises, and acrobatics.

These formal strategies of farce lead to a single end. As Stuart Baker has argued in *Georges Feydeau and the Aesthetics of Farce*, this genre 'makes a game of reality', and its devotion to laughter is not 'an invitation to anarchy' but 'the key to a unifying principle'.[6] We see and feel the often hostile and confusing appearances of the world as a brisk and even frenzied game of music and masking in which we all participate. The design of that game, I would add, suggests that our ideas, our social roles, and even our cherished personalities may be no more than changeable masks for the rigorously playful mind that moves through us. A farce therefore willingly abandons rounded characters, individualized speech, and realistic action. It prefers the heightened rhythmic and rhetorical forms of a single style of playing, a blend of the conventional and the idiosyncratic that we may experience as the given and yet surprising gait of our shared mind. As a game in which we may see ourselves as changeable masks for that mind, a farce also prefers to concoct its plot from bits and pieces of those old stories about masters and servants who change places, lovers who are disguised, families who are dispersed and reunited, antagonists who are blood brothers or even twins, and opposites of all kinds that finally disclose their unity. Farce delights in burlesquing those premises of melodrama and romance partly because they express its own deep desire to break the spell of individuation and alienation that holds us in thrall.

This is quite clear in Morton's short farce of 1847, *Box and Cox*, which became in 1867 the musical farce *Cox and Box*, by F.C. Burnand and Arthur Sullivan, W.S. Gilbert's future collaborator, and which seems to have bequeathed some of its motifs and devices to Wilde, Beckett, Ionesco, and Stoppard. In this play Box the printer, who works by night, and Cox the hatter, who works by day, accidentally discover (as do Mr and Mrs Martin in Ionesco's *The Bald Soprano*) that they have been renting the same room and sleeping in the same bed.[7] Quarreling about their rights to the room, they soon discover that they have both been engaged to the same woman, the formidable widow Penelope Ann, a proprietress of bathing machines, whom they now both wish to escape. Box has already given her the slip by faking suicide and therefore enjoys a condition of life-in-death that Cox much envies. They quarrel over whose proposal to Penelope Ann is now valid (somewhat as Wilde's Gwendolen and Cecily will quarrel over their proposals to Ernest), but each man here wishes to pass the lady on to the other. Deciding to dice for her hand, they throw only sixes. Tossing coins, they can throw (rather like Stoppard's Rosencrantz and Guildenstern) only a steady run of 'heads'. On learning that Penelope Ann has apparently drowned and left her property to her intended, they suddenly take up all their arguments in reverse. The apparent arrival of Penelope Ann at their rooming-house leads to yet another reversal as they join forces to stave off her entry. But another letter suddenly announces her 'immediate union' with Mr Knox—whose name, as often in Beckett's work, suggests an endless series of rhyming characters neither dead nor alive. And the dénouement weds Box and Cox as firmly and enigmatically as Beckett's Didi and Gogo or Hamm and Clov will be wed. As they are about to embrace, Box stops, seizes Cox's hand, and looks eagerly in his face. 'You'll excuse the apparent insanity of the remark', he says, 'but the more I gaze on your features, the more I'm convinced that you're my long-lost brother'. 'The very observation I was going to make to you!' replies Cox. 'Ah—tell me—in mercy tell me—' says Box, 'have you such a thing as a strawberry mark on your left arm?' 'No!' exclaims Cox. Whereupon Box exclaims: 'Then it is he!' And with this demonstration that true brothers require neither birth-marks nor other evidence of consanguinity, they rush into each other's arms.[8]

The stylization of this farce—its repetitive pattern of speech and counter-speech, violent reversals, and puppet-like gesticulations—ensures, according to one critic, that the interest of the audience is 'strategic, rather than empathetic'.[9] But if we don't respond seriously to the loves and fears of this Tweedledum and Tweedledee, surely we do participate with empathy in the playing out of their absurd duet to its harmonious close. And the play then reverberates, amid our laughter, with feelings of unity that we can indeed take quite seriously—just as we can warmly assent to Dromio of Ephesus (and the

actor who plays him) when at the end of *The Comedy of Errors* he says to
Dromio of Syracuse, 'Methinks you are my glass, and not my brother', and
then, dismissing all concern for seniority or superiority, ends our game of
mirrors with this couplet:

> We came into the world like brother and brother:
> And now let's go hand in hand, not one before another.

Antagonisms, differences in rank, characters, actors, spectators—what are
they but different masks of a playful mind?

The greatest of the late nineteenth-century British farceurs, W.S. Gilbert,
who helped to pass the tradition on to Wilde and Shaw by way of *Engaged* and
the Savoy operas, knew very well that in farce the musically scored dissonances
must lead to a final consonance. We may recall that opera of 1878, *H.M.S.
Pinafore*, in which Little Buttercup finally reveals that when she was young
and charming she had practiced baby-farming, and nursed two tender babes,
one of low condition, the other of a patrician—but she mixed those children
up. 'Then I am to understand', exclaims Sir Joseph, 'that Captain Corcoran
and Ralph were exchanged in the childhood's happy hour—that Ralph is really
the Captain, and the Captain is Ralph?'[10] Precisely so: hierarchy is now
reversed, individuality is negated, and three loving pairs can be happily
united. With that the tradition of farce was well on its way to Miss Prism's
mixing up of a baby and the manuscript of a sentimental novel, John
Worthing's discovery that he is Algernon Moncrieff's brother Ernest, and the
union of three more loving pairs. And that led in turn to the discovery by
Shaw's Clandon children that their father is Mr Crampton, the discovery by
Orton's Geraldine Barclay and Nicholas Bennett that they are the twin
children of the Prentices, and the mixing up by Stoppard's Gwendolen and
Cecily of Joyce's manuscript for an episode of *Ulysses* (that in which Mrs
Purefoy's baby and modern prose come to simultaneous birth) and Lenin's
manuscript for a revolutionary tract.

II The Truths of Masks

Each of these four plays is a rhythmic or musical masking, a game of doublings,
oppositions, analogies, and reunifications that revises the tradition and reinter-
prets some serious aspect of the modern world. *The Importance of Being Earnest*
finds our social and intellectual life to be a changing construct of masks. *You
Never Can Tell*, putting those masks in a more historical context, discloses
behind them a common heart. *What the Butler Saw* puts them in a psychological context and discloses behind them a polymorphous sexuality. And *Travesties* asks us to recognize the earnest, arch, or Dionysiac masks that we project
into politics, art, and history the protean mind of a single but multiform
player. That sequence outlines what I've called the mystery doctrine of farce.

Though the first production of *The Importance of Being Earnest* depicted a
society with which the audience was intimately acquainted,[11] its revisionary

artifice would have been quite evident. The witty rakes, imperious aunt, and adroit young ladies suggest not only Restoration comedy but also such earlier Wilde plays as *Lady Windermere's Fan* and *An Ideal Husband*. The burlesque mechanics of the well-made play are shared with French vaudeville and English farcical comedy. The absurd amatory and gustatory obsessions, the blend of romantic idealism and crass self-interest, and such details as Algy's Bunburying and Jack's wearing of mourning for someone who hasn't died are clearly reminiscent of Gilbert's *Engaged*, a play that also required of its actors 'the most perfect earnestness and gravity'.[12] And the precisely choreographed debates and duets recall the Savoy operas.[13]

In summarizing the tradition of wit from its own perspective, *The Importance of Being Earnest* no longer confines its epigrams to a witty Lord Darlington or Lord Goring, as in earlier Wilde plays. Now the entire script consists of the modulations of a single voice, whose shrewd absurdities and knowing non-sequiturs effectively turn all the characters into paradoxical and semi-transparent masks. That's why it is so hard to say just who is being deliberately witty. If the often childish Algy is a self-conscious wit, so is his laconic manservant Lane . . . or is he? And can Lady Bracknell really be, as critics often assume, the unconscious butt of her own satirical remarks? Gwendolen often seems yet more oblivious of her own wit, but she can wield a verbal rapier quite skilfully in her duel with Cecily. And Cecily amply demonstrates, there and in her earlier chats with her 'Ernest', an ironic subtlety that seems to belie her innocence. Even Prism and Chasuble, those versions of the pedant and senex of comic tradition, speak witty truths that may or may not be beyond their understanding. 'The good ended happily, and the bad unhappily', says Prism. 'That is what Fiction means.' Is she really 'unconscious of the humour' of that remark, as one commentator assures us?[14] The question can hardly be answered. As Stoppard seems to have known when he revised those lines for the Player in *Rosencrantz and Guildenstern Are Dead*, their real speaker is the playfulness that articulates our shared game. Such quite pervasive masking is further complicated, of course, by Jack's and Algy's claims to be 'Ernest' and by the final revelation of Jack's identity as Ernest. But because that revelation rests on a farcical coincidence, Jack's assertion that he must always have been speaking the truth just gives another spin to the whirligig of trivial seriousness and serious triviality.

This game of masks leads us dancingly through patterned oppositions and complementarities toward a hidden consanguinity and a triple marriage. Algy's opening volley with Lane prepares us for the more complex contest with Jack—in which the self-consciously trivial seeker of truth engages the self-deceptively serious 'Ernest'. The sophisticated Gwendolen and the innocent Cecily (each of whom shares to some degree her counterpart's dominant trait) will expand this pattern and prepare us for a double courtship, with Lady Bracknell and Jack ironically paired as blocking parental figures. These symmetrical possibilities are developed in Act II when Algy now poses as Ernest, Cecily now receives a proposal, and the young ladies move to a stylized Gilbertian confrontation. After the simultaneous exposure of Jack's deception and Algy's, the young ladies momentarily pit themselves against the men. The action now moves through increasingly echoing speeches toward the moment in Act III when the men enter whistling 'some dreadful popular air from a British Opera' and the ladies then simultaneously speak their common mind, with Gwendolen beating time. This sequence is almost as operatic in conception as the finales of Gilbert and Sullivan's The Yeoman of the Guard or Mozart and da Ponte's Cosi Fan Tutte. When Lady Bracknell arrives, there are two announcements of each of the two engagements, whereupon the blocking parental figures reach a stalemate that can be broken only by the arrival of Prism—an arrival that is both ordered and fortuitous. Jack then discovers that he has always been Ernest and that—though Prism is not his mother, as he thinks for a moment—Algy is indeed his brother, Lady Bracknell his aunt, and Gwendolen his cousin. The young couples embrace; and when Prism and Chasuble join them in doing so, our stage picture seems all in the family.

What's the meaning of our musical masking? According to John Russell Taylor the plot is there only 'to hold up a glittering display of epigrams'. According to Eric Bentley the epigrams are 'serious relief' in 'ironic counterpoint with the absurdities of the action'. According to Morton Gurewitch the farce neutralizes the satire 'so that our mental delight in detecting idiocy is subordinated to the joys of unreason'.[15] But in performance the play is not so disjunctive or double-minded as those comments suggest. There are integral connections between our game of masks and the running critique of a moneyed, fashionable, and intellectually pretentious society. Speaking from within what Lady Bracknell calls 'an age of surfaces', these masks embody both the superficiality that is criticized and the self-conscious act of criticism. The play gives us a heightened model of our usual follies and insincerities and also of a critical awareness that itself can know only surfaces. For Wilde, we should recall, even the 'truths of metaphysics are the truths of masks'.[16] We must therefore choose between wearing an unconscious or hypocritical social mask, which may seem serious but is really trivial, and wearing a self-conscious artistic mask, which may seem trivial but involves a serious insight into our world of appearances. If the alternative to one kind of mask is another, should we complain of nihilism? Certainly we must recognize that appearances in this play constitute a screen that hides what can never be known in itself. but the musical masking in which we participate should also lead us to a complementary recognition. Through its music the play is breaking the spell of a deceptive individuation and inviting us into a sprightly community of performance where appetites and aggressions have been transformed into the shared miming of muffin-eating, cake-serving, and scintillating conversation, and where each absurd and witty mask can be worn with profit and delight by us all. Like Bunbury, the alienated individual has been exploded, at least for the moment, and we glimpse the ordered freedom and gaiety of a hidden identity that plays through us. Both the social criticism and the farcical music of The Importance of Being Earnest point toward that immanent end.

III   The Wisdom of the Heart

The revisionary artifice of *You Never Can Tell* is also quite evident, though more problematic in its coherence. It seems novel to begin a play in a dentist's office, though in fact Labiche had used that setting in 1874 for *The Gladiator's Thirty Millions*, but the seaside hotel of the remaining Acts is almost *de rigueur* in the farcical comedy that Shaw aimed to 'humanize'.[17] The typical masks of that genre here gain some new traits: a sharper intellect, a fuller awareness of their moment in social history, and reservoirs of untapped, repressed, injured, or generous feeling. The dentist Valentine is a boyish version of the volatile hero bent on sexual conquest. Gloria Clandon, the 'feminine prig', discovers behind her mask as 'New Woman' an emotional vulnerability and power. Both Mrs Clandon, the bluestocking who has written extensively on modern manners and morals, and Mr Crampton, her curmudgeonly former husband, are concealing emotional wounds. And the comic waiter, whom the younger Clandons call William, dispenses the balm of a perceptive and melodious equanimity. (William is an English waiter of Norman ancestry, a kind of Shavian natural aristocrat, but his generous waiterly manners are pure Irish.) This scheme of masks overlaps with another that is drawn from the English pantomime. Crampton recalls Pantaloon; Valentine and Gloria recall the young lovers; and Mrs Clandon's old socialist friend, McComas, recalls the learned doctor. More boldly, and by Act IV more explicitly, the Clandon twins Dolly and Philip are stylized as an asexual Harlequin and Columbine. And William's son Bohun, the intimidating Q.C., enters in a grotesque mask as a pragmatic *deus ex machina*.[18] Shaw may not have known the Italian *commedia dell'arte* scenarios except in their corrupted music-hall form, but there is one such scenario called 'The Dentist' in which Arlecchino tricks Pantalone into letting him pull four sound teeth. (George Fitzmaurice, an admirer of the music hall, may have based his grotesque farce *The Toothache* on some Dublin version of that skit.) It seems appropriate that Valentine's gagging and gassing of Crampton in order to pull a broken tooth painlessly is a replay of the old trick with humanizing reversals.[19]

This eclectic style gains coherence partly through the unmistakably Shavian voice that expresses the paradoxical life of each farcical but feeling mask, but also through an insistent response to *The Importance of Being Earnest*. In January, 1895, when reviewing *An Ideal Husband*, Shaw had praised Wilde as 'our only thorough playwright. He plays with everything: with wit, with philosophy, with drama, with actors and audience, with the whole theatre'. That aim was surely Shaw's own. But a month later he objected to *The Importance of Being Earnest* as being an updated farcical comedy of the 'seventies that relied on 'inhuman' Gilbertisms and mechanical humour. He wanted 'to be moved to laughter, not to be tickled or bustled into it'. He thought the play's devices 'could only have been raised from the farcical plane by making them occur to characters who had . . . obtained some hold on our sympathy'.[20] By August he had begun a play of the kind he thought Wilde should have written; and if we attend a performance of *You Never Can Tell* with *The Importance of Being Earnest* rather fresh in our memory, we can watch many of Wilde's meanings being transformed into Shaw's.

'Come, old boy', says Wilde's Algy when he's trying to learn the identity of Cecily, 'you had much better have the thing out at once'. 'My dear Algy', retorts Jack, 'you talk exactly as if you were a dentist'. Shaw's Valentine, of course, talks like the 'five-shilling dentist' he is—even though Phil Clandon thinks 'dentist' an 'ugly word'. Valentine specializes in having the thing out, which Dolly tells Crampton is very like plucking from the memory a rooted sorrow. Dental therapy in this play is one metaphor for the healing process of farce. Valentine also echoes Lady Bracknell's demand that Jack produce at least one parent before the season is over: 'in a seaside resort', he tells Dolly and Phil, 'there's one thing you must have before anybody can afford to be seen going about with you; and that's a father, alive or dead'. Through him our masking already signals the desire for a family reunion. Gloria, who has a more intellectual version of Gwendolen's pretentiousness, soon uses this Wildean argument herself, saying to her mother that a 'woman who does not know who her father was cannot accept' an offer of marriage. But her effort to learn her father's identity collapses when it turns out—with a wink at Gwendolen's and Cecily's dispute over the proposal by 'Ernest'—that Gloria, her sister, and her mother have all received proposals from the same ship's officer. The play continues to have serious fun with Wilde's premises in Act III when Mrs Clandon interrogates Valentine. Reversing the position taken by Lady Bracknell when interrogating Jack, Mrs Clandon says that she cares little about money and that Valentine has a right to amuse himself. But then, out-earnesting *Earnest*, she asks: 'On your honour, Mr Valentine, are you in earnest?' 'On my honour', he replies, 'I am in earnest . . . Only I always have been in earnest; and yet—here I am, you see!' Soon McComas will rebuke Dolly by saying, 'I insist on having earnest matters earnestly and reverently discussed'. Then Gloria will rebuke Valentine by saying that if he were really in love it would give him 'earnestness'. And when she turns her back on him, Valentine will retort: 'Ah, you see you're not in earnest'. The word is regaining the emotional force that Wilde's play had removed from it; and by Act IV that force has revealed itself to be more than personal. Valentine explains that he had been tempted to awaken Gloria's heart, to stir the depths in her. 'Why was I tempted? Because Nature was in deadly earnest with me when I was in jest with her.' The earnestness of Nature, at work below our merely personal jests and grievances, supports the play's many references to the 'heart' or 'depths' of a 'common humanity'. We recognize that Crampton's plea to Gloria—'I want you to feel: that's the only thing that can help us'—must be our own plea to ourselves.

As a game of masks *You Never Can Tell* is less symmetrical than *The Importance of Being Earnest* but no less musical. Dolly and Phil, with their swift completions of each other's thoughts, soon establish the presence of a trans-personal choric music. The other pairings of Valentine and Gloria, Mr Crampton and Mrs Clandon, and William and his son Bohun invite us to discern beneath complementary masks a ground of imperfectly acknowledged feeling. And the avuncular odd-man-out, Mrs Clandon's old admirer McComas, joins Crampton, William, and Bohun to make a variously tempered series of father-figures for the Clandon children. As Martin Meisel has shown, Shaw often equipped his plays with an operatic quartet of soprano, alto, tenor and bass.[21] But the quartet of Gloria, Mrs Clandon, Valentine, and Crampton is here supported not only by the twins (soprano and counter-tenor in *allegretto* duets) but also by the Shakespearean William (a baritone with an *andante* melody that, as Meisel remarks, follows precise musical directions.)[22] Shaw rightly called himself 'a pupil of Mozart in comedy much more than any of the English literary dramatists',[23] and his operatic devices here prepare for a finale that is choreographed (thanks to the hotel's fancy ball) as a bold Harlequinade.

Irritated by the reductive terms on which the play achieved popularity, Shaw wrote to Granville Barker: 'It has always seemed merely a farce written around a waiter. It ought to be a very serious comedy, dancing gaily to a happy ending round the grim-earnest of Mrs Clandon's marriage and her XIX century George-Eliotism.'[24] That mixture of tonalities is crucial. Beneath the rigid masks of our inexperience, wounded vanity, old-fashioned proprieties, and so-called 'modern' ideas, the music of this farce repeatedly invites us to discover a common humanity. But it never asks us to indulge ourselves in a warm bath of feeling. William's buoyant equanimity always involves a witty alertness, and the rhetoric of sentiment is here always suspect. After Phil Clandon finally addresses Crampton as 'dad', for example, he bends his gilt hat into a halo and says *sotto voce*: 'Did you feel the pathos of that?' And the *deus ex machina* is quite appropriately not William's twin but his sardonic son. 'It's understood that self is put aside', says Bohun with dead-pan irony. 'Human nature always begins by saying that.' Dismissing all talk of altruism, he urges Valentine to demand of Gloria a practical marriage settlement. Precisely because *You Never Can Tell* avoids the sentimental, its 'happy ending' has disappointed those who want a more Shakespearean reconciliation of all the parties.[25] Though this musical masking breaks the spell of individuation and lets us glimpse the sharable wisdom of the heart, it keeps our usual needs and confusions before us to the very end. That is why the whirling exit of the Clandon-and-Crampton retinue leaves Valentine disconsolately and farcically behind, without a partner for the dance.

IV The Truths of Dionysus

What the Butler Saw is set in a private clinic equipped with the several doors and windows required by the mix-ups of a marital farce in the tradition of Labiche and Feydeau. At the outset a psychiatrist is interviewing a young woman who has applied to be his secretary. His first question is bizarre: 'Who was your father?' Her reply recalls Jack Worthing and the Clandon twins: 'I have no idea who my father was.' The play's revisionary artifice is already in motion, as Dr Prentice's response makes clear: 'I'd better be frank, Miss Barclay. I can't employ you if you are in any way miraculous. It would be contrary to established practice. You did have a father?' The sly non-sequiturs and cobbled clichés of *The Importance of Being Earnest*, which Orton had called 'much more earthy and colloquial than people notice',[26] become yet stronger when uttered by the unmannerly masks of an age without butlers. 'A combination of elegance and crudity', as Orton said, 'is always ridiculous'.[27] Dr Prentice soon learns that Geraldine Barclay's mother, whom she hasn't seen for many years, had been raped in a linen cupboard at the Station Hotel. After remarking that he had stayed there once himself as a young man, Prentice swiftly leads the compliant Geraldine to his curtained couch for a physical examination that seems an obvious prelude to a kind of employment she hasn't forseen. His plan is frustrated, however, by the sudden return of his wife, who soon reveals that *she* has just been raped by a page-boy in a linen cupboard at the Station Hotel. After the arrival of that boy, Nicholas Beckett, the evasive and aggressive tactics of the Prentices produce a frenzied sequence of hidings, disguisings and mix-ups, which are further complicated by the plodding Sergeant Match, who is looking for a missing part of Winston Churchill's statue, and the manic Dr Rance, who declares himself to be an inspector of lunacy from Her Majesty's Government. Before we're through, Geraldine and Nick will have swapped and reswapped costumes and identities, Match will have been stripped, drugged, disguised in Mrs Prentice's leopard-spotted dress, and wounded by gunfire, and Rance will have performed some brutal psychiatric examinations and offered some juicy elucidations of the action— for he wants very much to write a best-seller that will combine psychoanalytic science with soft porn.

Finally, while Rance and Prentice are each attempting at gun-point to certify the other as insane, Rance presses an alarm, metal grilles fall in place to turn the clinic into a locked cage, and the power goes out. After being thus trapped, our masks or contemporary lunacy discover that Geraldine and Nick possess the two halves of a single brooch that proves them to be the twins conceived in that linen cupboard during an earlier power-cut when Prentice had anonymously assaulted a hotel maid who later became his wife. Geraldine's father is in fact her would-be seducer, and Nick has seduced his mother. After this literalizing of the Oedipal theme of New Comedy (which Synge's *The Playboy of the Western World* had treated in its own startling way) Geraldine appears also to be a strange kind of Miss Prism. On Prentice's desk, unnoticed through all the confusion, is an unopened box that she had brought with her to the interview. To her surprise and ours, Sergeant Match now discovers in it a larger-than-life replica of the penis of Sir Winston Churchill, which had been embedded in her foster mother's body by a fatal gas explosion, and which Match has been seeking in order to re-assemble the statue of Britain's leader.

What the Butler Saw obviously combines elements of *The Importance of Being Earnest* with much that is drawn from *The Menaechmi, The Comedy of Errors, Twelfth Night*, Feydeau's farces, Ionesco's absurdism, and Pinter's comedy of menace.[28] And Dr Rance steps out of the tradition of the mad scientist that runs from *Frankenstein* through much popular fiction and film to the more recent *Dr Strangelove*. But Orton brings to this eclectic game a new realism.

While writing the play he watched the National Theatre's televised production of Feydeau's *A Flea in Her Ear* and 'hated it', he said, because it was 'directed and acted with great speed and no reality'. All the 'externals' in farce, he maintained, must be 'believed'.[29] The violence of *What the Butler Saw*, if properly performed, should cut through the blockage of emotions often ascribed to farce: the bleeding wounds of Nick and Match are as 'real' as any theatre. But when Match descends a rope ladder from the skylight, 'the leopard-spotted dress torn from one shoulder and streaming with blood', then finds the misplaced phallic image and holds it up for our startled and admiring view, and finally leads the entire cast—'weary, bleeding, drugged and drunk'—up the ladder into the blazing light, Orton is leading our community of farce into the classical tradition. Like Pentheus, the persecutor of Dionysus in Euripides' *The Bacchae*, Match has been trapped, in drag, among the celebrants of the god. But the *sparagmos* of Euripides' play has been displaced to Churchill's exploded statue, and Match elevating the phallus becomes a satyr figure presiding over a Golden-Bough-ish re-affirmation of Dionysiac fertility on the other side of destruction.[30]

In effect, *What the Butler Saw* moves through Wilde and the Plautine tradition to become a Nietzschean satyr play. Orton's comments on his vacillation between Dionysian and Apollinian impulses as a writer[31] are but one indication of his familiarity with *The Birth of Tragedy*. 'Farce is higher than comedy', he could also say, 'in that it is very close to tragedy'. It differs, he thought, 'only in the *treatment* of its themes—themes like rape, bastardy, prostitution'.[32] That's why the music of this play articulates the truths of Dionysus. Its pattern of aggressive interrogations discloses beneath these farcical masks our unacknowledged, forgotten, or unrecognized sexual impulses. Its dance of opposites—the probably impotent Prentice and his aggressively bisexual wife, the invitingly compliant Geraldine and the nastily forward Nick, the stoic Match and the manic Rance—proceeds to break down through disguises and transformations not only the lineaments of those oppositions but all our assumptions about personal and sexual identity. At one point when Geraldine is pretending to be Nick but can't prove her gender, Rance says brutally: 'Take your trousers down. I'll tell you which sex you belong to.' Her response is pitiful, hilarious, and thematically central: 'I'd rather not know!' Tearing our social masks to shreds, the play's rising frenzy discloses a polymorphous sexuality for which the madly projecting Rance can give only melodramatic pseudo-explanations. 'The ugly shadow of anti-Christ stalks this house', he declares when he thinks the unfindable Geraldine has been murdered. 'Having discovered her Father/Lover in Dr Prentice the patient replaces him in a psychological shuffle by that archetypal Father-figure—the Devil himself . . . The final chapters of my book are knitting together: incest, buggery, outrageous women and strange love-cults catering for depraved appetites. All the fashionable bric-a-brac . . . As a tranvestite, fetishist, bi-sexual murderer Dr Prentice displays considerable deviation overlap. We may get necrophilia too. As a sort of bonus.'

When the dénouement forces Rance to revise this Gothic Freudianism, he is not dismayed but delighted: 'Double incest is even more likely to produce a best-seller than murder—and this is as it should be for love *must* bring greater joy than violence.' In a sense beyond his understanding, he is quite right about the play's meaning: its perverse violence is in the service of an aspect of love. But the Freudian notions that seem to shape its action provide only parodic explanations. The music of our masking discloses beneath our ridiculous, defensive, and bloody masks a perpetually torn and reborn sexuality that is beyond sentiment, moralism, or rational analysis, and that is in essence prior to all individuation. *What the Butler Saw* does not, as some critics have argued, celebrate 'moral anarchy' or mere 'formlessness'.[33] Within an elaborately rational structure of farce, it celebrates the joyful intuition of unity beyond our violent and transient roles that Nietzsche had attributed to the Greek tragic chorus. Having shared that intuition we can hear in the closing lines—whether spoken by Prentice as in the manuscript or by Rance as in the post-production text[34]—a meaning beyond the speaker's intent. 'I'm glad you don't despise tradition', says one of our masks to another. 'Let us put our clothes on and face the world.' And so they climb into the blazing light.

V The Wisdom of Art

We have moved from *The Importance of Being Earnest*, which invites us into the music of self-conscious mask-wearing, to *You Never Can Tell*, which historicizes our masks and discloses their common heart, and on to *What the Butler Saw*, which psychologizes our masks and discloses their primal sexuality. In complementary ways, these serious farces wake us from the spell of a culturally overburdened individuality and enact a hope or intuition of restored oneness. *Travesties*, with its rather Wildean playfulness and panache, may seem in some respects a brilliant step backward. But for several reasons it brings this sequence to an appropriate climax. It vastly increases the amount of serious material that farce now seeks to encompass and assimilate. It proceeds to disclose behind the masks of persons, politics, art, and history the workings of one imperfect but inventive mind. And it locates that mind in one figure who can stand for our entire community of farce. Its intuition of restored oneness in the midst of the fragmentary, fallible, and confused is therefore a scintillating many-in-one.

The music of *Travesties* retraces the plot of *The Importance of Being Earnest* through a theme-and-variations form that makes possible an astonishing literary, political, and historical expansion. Basing itself stylistically on both Wilde and Joyce, it incorporates procedures from Dadaism, Absurdism, Brechtian theatre, the Irish limerick, and Irish-American vaudeville. It includes moments of Shakespeare and Beethoven, and even a 1974 big-band version of 'The Stripper'. Somewhat in the manner of Shaw's *Man and Superman* or *Saint Joan*, its masking leads us through the dialectical interaction of three highly articulate spokesmen for revolutionary art or politics—Joyce, Tzara, and Lenin—each of whom has farcical or poignant limitations.

Except for a prologue that states the leitmotifs (as does the prologue to the
Sirens episode in Joyce's *Ulysses*) and an epilogue that provides a dialogical
critique, all of the action seems to take place in the mind of Henry Carr, an
acquaintance of Joyce later travestied in *Ulysses*, who is recalling and embel-
lishing his experiences in Zurich. The play therefore does five rather different
things at once: it gives its characters detailed historical and biographical
specificity; it reduces them to a kaleidoscopic whirl of changing masks; it
locates them all in the mind of one sympathetically and ironically portrayed
narrator; it expands that mind beyond its realistic capacities to include the full
stylistic resources and historical knowledge of the playwright; and it renders
that expanded mind through the shared action of our community of farce.[35]

Perhaps the most remarkable effect of our musical masking here is the way it
transforms Carr's memories, which stammeringly shape themselves according
to the plot of *The Importance of Being Earnest*, into a world beyond his talents
and understanding. The prologue implies that Joyce, Tzara, and Lenin are
creating their potent world-visions out of bits and pieces. Carr will obviously
do the same, but his vision soon acquires a strangely independent life. His
initial conversation with Bennett (the Lane to his Algernon) suggests through
'time slips' and replays a potentially endless process of reinterpretation and
expansion. Then the arrival of Tzara, Joyce, and Gwendolen as nonsense
versions of themselves who speak not in Wildese but in shared limericks
signals for us the presence of a poetic mind that is immanent in the action. The
replay of their entrances in the style of *The Importance of Being Earnest* soon
leads to a vigorous debate between the philistine Carr and the Dadaist Tzara,
and soon thereafter to an interrogation of Tzara by Joyce that (in a catechetical
form drawn from *Ulysses*) elicits the history of Dada as it is documented by
contemporary and even later sources. By the end of Act I both Tzara and Joyce
have expressed their aesthetic positions with considerable eloquence. Though
Carr is still the ostensible narrator, he is now clearly but one mask among many
through which a more comprehensive imagination is shaping its world.

That impression is further complicated in Act II, which renders Lenin and
his wife through a documentary realism that seems to make no concession
either to *The Importance of Being Earnest* or to what we may have identified as
the Stoppardian imagination. As Act I moved beyond Carr, Act II seems to
move beyond Stoppard. The play's world is calling up its own antithesis. But if
Lenin's political urgency offers one possible critique of our playfulness, the
play's more inclusive dialectic shows Lenin to be the confused and dangerous
victim of a deadly earnestness. No less a philistine than Carr, he is quite
unaware of the fact—illustrated by *Travesties* itself—that art can include a
more richly sensitive dialectical process than political theory. After *Travesties*
has disclosed with some poignancy Lenin's serious limitations, it can return to
a lighter music that we won't mistake for the whole truth. Our masking now
translates Wilde's symmetries into heightened form. Gwendolen and Cecily
fight out their amorous, aesthetic, and political differences in stanzas
composed in imitation of 'Mr Gallagher and Mr Shean', a patter song from the
Ziegfeld Follies of 1922. As the dénouement approaches, the young ladies echo

that Gilbertian moment in Act III of *The Importance of Being Earnest* by a rather sustained stretch of speaking and moving in unison. The play's complex dissonances are moving toward a final consonance, which seems to be reached when Gwendolen and Cecily regain the folders that they had mixed up in the prologue. There is a rapid but formal climax, with appropriate cries and embraces. The epilogue, however, turns away from that closure to restate the theme of the fragmentary and fallible: Old Cecily criticizes the accuracy of Old Carr's memories, and Carr himself confesses in effect that he doesn't understand or even quite remember the play's main issues.

In this game of masks all masks seem to be one mask, and that mask we all wear in our different ways. At one point Tzara has demanded the 'right to urinate in different colours', and Joyce responds: 'Each person in different colours at different times, or different people in each colour all the time? Or everybody multi-coloured all the time?' Cecily later translates that phrase into 'ruminate in different colours'—and with that amendment the answer to Joyce's question as it applies reflexively to *Travesties* is probably: 'All of the above.' This 'multi-coloured micturition'—to use Carr's yet later translation of the phrase—suggests that the grounding unity of our earnest play is one multiform player—not Carr, though he seems our main representative, nor even Stoppard, though he is our primary agent of imagination, but the player constituted by our community of performance. The play's scrappy unity-in-multiplicity and its prismatic effects—for Miss Prism is here our symbolic producer of the multi-coloured—constitute a living model of the community mind without which the larger worlds of art and history could not exist. (We're not far, of course, from the ground-bass of *Finnegans Wake* and more specifically its 'Anna Livia Plurabelle' section, where each of seven dams has seven crutches, and every crutch has seven hues, and each hue has a differing cry, and where the riddle runs: 'howmulty plurators made eachone in person?')[36] In mirroring that prismatic mind, which seems both the mind of persons-in-community and that of community-in-each-person, *Travesties* exemplifies the 'mystery doctrine of farce' in a way that also fulfils Schiller's prescription for artistic form. 'The most frivolous subject matter', he had said in the letters *On the Aesthetic Education of Man*, 'must be so treated that we remain disposed to pass over immediately from it to the strictest seriousness. The most serious material must be so treated that we retain the capability of exchanging it immediately for the lightest play'.[37] Such playing in earnest is for *Travesties* the wisdom of art.

These four enactments of a 'mystery doctrine of farce', these complementary intimations of a oneness that grounds our communities of serious farce, lead toward a final question. Because they are histrionic through and through, these plays seem to endorse Wilde's dictum that even the 'truths of metaphysics are the truths of masks'. But as we share their disclosures of a unity that must exceed all formulations, we may suspect the adequacy of that dictum. Should we play Wilde's own game of reversals against him? Should we at least entertain the hypothesis that finally the truths of masks must be the truths of metaphysics?

Richard Ellmann: A Chronology

Personal:
Born Highland Park, Michigan, USA, 15 March 1918.
Died Oxford, England, 13 May 1987.
Attended schools in Highland Park, Michigan.
Married Mary Donahue, 12 August 1949.
Children: Stephen Jonathan, Maud Esther, Lucy Elizabeth.

Education:
1939 B.A. Yale. Honours with exceptional distinction in English.
1941 M.A. Yale.
1947 B.Litt. Trinity College Dublin.
1947 Ph.D. Yale. John Addison Porter prize for best dissertation of the
year.

Other degrees:
1970 M.A. Oxford.
1976 D.Litt (hon) National University of Ireland.
1978 Ph.D. (hon) University of Gothenburg.
1979 D.H.L. (hon) Boston College.
1979 D.Litt (hon) Emory University.
1980 D.Litt (hon) Northwestern University.
1981 D.H.L. (hon) University of Rochester.
1986 D.Litt (hon) McGill University.

Teaching:
1942-43 Instructor, Harvard.
1947-48 Instructor, Harvard.
1948-51 Briggs-Copeland Assistant Professor of English Composition,
Harvard.
1951-64 Professor of English, Northwestern.
1964-68 Franklin Bliss Snyder Professor of English, Northwestern.
1968-70 Professor of English, Yale.
1970-84 Goldsmiths' Professor of English Literature, Oxford (Emeritus
1984).
1982-86 Woodruff Professor of English, Emory.

Other teaching:
Frederick Ives Carpenter Visiting Professor, University of Chicago, 1959,
1967, 1975-77.
Fellow, School of Letters, Indiana University, 1956, 1960: senior fellow,
1966-72.

Other work:
  1943-46 US Navy and Office of Strategic Services.
  1961 Chairman, English Institute.
  1961-65 Member, Executive Council, Modern Language Association.
  1968-73 Member, Editorial Committee, Modern Language Association.
  1971-85 Member, US-UK Educational Commission.
  1980 Advisory Board, American Trust for the British Library.
  1980 Adviser in Modern Literature, Guggenheim Foundation.
  Various dates: Advisory Board, *New Literary History, Critical Inquiry, University of Georgia Review.*

Awards:
  Fellow, Royal Society of Literature.
  Fellow, British Academy.
  Member, American Academy and Institute.
  Rockefeller Post-War Fellow in Humanities, 1946-47.
  American Philosophical Society grant, 1953.
  Kenyon Review Fellow in Criticism, 1955.
  National Book Award for Non-Fiction, 1960.
  Guggenheim Fellow, 1950, 1957, 1970.
  Fellow, New College, Oxford University, 1970-84; Honorary Fellow, 1984-87.
  National Endowment for the Humanities grant, 1977.
  James Tait Black Prize, 1983.
  Duff Cooper Memorial Prize, 1983.
  Extraordinary Fellow, Wolfson College, Oxford, 1984-87.

Richard Ellmann: A Bibliography

Lonnie Weatherby and Elaine Yarosky

This bibliography is a selective, partially-annotated list of Ellmann's publications. It includes monographs, pamphlets, edited works, articles, essays, introductions, poetry and his translations of Michaux. It excludes translations of Ellmann's books and articles as well as most interviews, correspondence and critical studies about Ellmann. Additional work remains for future Ellmann bibliographers in these areas as well as in the examination of little magazines at Yale, Northwestern and Oxford for which readily-available indexes do not exist.

The bibliography is arranged in categories according to type of publication then subdivided chronologically with the exception of section VIII *Collections* which is arranged alphabetically. Citations were taken from standard reference works such as periodical and newspaper indexes, bibliographies of English and Irish Literature as well as bibliographies devoted to Joyce, Yeats, Eliot, Wilde and Stevens. The bibliographers were unable to examine all the citations included and regret any inconvenience which the inevitable errors may cause.

Publications are cited according to the McGill-Queens University Press *Style Guide* and the *Chicago Manual of Style* 13th edition.

I Theses

'The Social Philosophy of Thomas Carlyle'. M.A. thesis. Yale University, 1941.
'William Butler Yeats: The Fountain Years'. B. Litt. thesis. Trinity College, Dublin, 1947.
'Triton Among the Streams: A Study of the Life and Writings of William Butler Yeats'. Ph.D. dissertation. Yale University, 1947.

II Poetry

'Admonition'. *Furioso* 1, no. 4 (Summer 1941): p. 18.
'The Simplified Future'. *Furioso* 1, no. 4 (Summer 1941): pp. 16-17.
'Tarzan; Winter Prospect'. *Furioso* 1, no. 4 (Summer 1941): p. 16.
'Your Loveliness, I Say'. *Furioso* 1, no. 4 (Summer 1941): p. 17.
'Behind the Lines'. *Kenyon Review* 7, no. 1 (Winter 1945): p. 74.

'The Last Man on Earth'. *Kenyon Review* 7, no. 1 (Winter 1945): pp. 74-75.

'The Long and the Short of It'. *Furioso* 3, no. 4 (Fall 1948): p. 45.

'The Patterned Land'. *Furioso* 3, no. 4 (Fall 1948): pp. 44-45.

'The Hivinizikis'. (prose poem) *Hudson Review* 1, no. 4 (Winter 1948): pp. 539-45.

'My Properties'. (prose poem) *Hudson Review* 2, no. 1 (Spring 1949): pp. 56-60.

'Status of the Kingdom'; 'What Lady Knows'. *Sewanee Review* 57, no. 2 (April 1949): pp. 261-2.

III Translations

Michaux, Henri. 'And More Changes Still'. (poem) *Partisan Review* 13, no. 2 (Spring 1946): pp. 213-14.

——. 'Revelations'. (poem) *Partisan Review* 13, no. 5 (November-December 1946): p. 567.

——. *Selected Poems*: 'Cries'; 'Enanglom' (excerpt); 'Heroic Age'; 'Night of the Bulgarians'; 'Plume Travels'; 'Simplicity'; 'Man'; 'Bridal Night'; 'In the Land of the Hacs'. *Sewanee Review* 56, no. 1 (January 1948): pp. 24-35.

——. 'Jetty'. (poem) *Poetry* 73 (February 1949): pp. 258-9.

——. 'In the Land of Magic'. (poem) *Kenyon Review* 11, no. 2 (Spring 1949): pp. 173-86.

——. 'The March Into the Tunnel'. (poem excerpt) *Partisan Review* 16, no. 7 (July 1949): pp. 698-701.

——. 'I Am Writing to You From a Distant Country'. (poem) *Sewanee Review* 57, no. 4 (Autumn 1949): pp. 660-64.

——. 'Birth' (poem) *Furioso* 4, no. 3 (1949): p. 36.

——. 'Ecce Homo'. (prose poem) *Wake* 12 (1953): pp. 90-92.

——. 'The Executioner'. (prose poem) *Wake* 12 (1953): pp. 88-89.

——. 'The Lock-Eating Animal'. (prose poem) *Wake* 12 (1953): p. 88.

——. 'Nature Faithful to Man'. (prose poem) *Wake* 12 (1953): p. 89.

——. 'Ulp and Alp'. (poem) *Wake* 12 (1953): p. 87.

——. 'A Very Small Horse'. (poem) *New Directions* 14 (1953): p. 343.

——. 'Vision'. (fiction) *Wake* 12 (1953): pp. 89-90.

——. 'Properties'. (prose poems) *TriQuarterly* 12 (Spring 1968): pp. 109-114.

Michaux, Henri. *L'Espace du Dedans. The Space Within. Selected Writings*. Translated with an introduction by Richard Ellmann (New York: New Directions, 1951; London: Routledge and Kegan Paul, 1952).

IV Monographs and Pamphlets

Yeats: The Man and the Masks (New York: MacMillan, 1948). Based on E.'s B.Litt. and Ph.D.

The Identity of Yeats (London: Macmillan; New York: Oxford University Press, 1954).

Joyce in Love (Ithaca, N.Y.: Cornell University Library, 1959), 14 p.

James Joyce (New York, London: Oxford University Press, 1959).

The Identity of Yeats 2nd. ed. (London: Faber and Faber; New York: Oxford University Press, 1964).

Yeats and Joyce. Yeats Centenary Papers. 1965, no. 11. (Dublin: Dolmen Press, 1965). Reprinted in Miller, pp. 445-79.

Wilde and the Nineties: an Essay and an Exhibition by Richard Ellmann, E.D.H. Johnson and Alfred L. Bush. Edited by Charles Ryskamp (Princeton, N.J.: Princeton University Library, 1966), 64 p. Exhibition held in Princeton, Library 15 Feb-15 Apr. 1966; contains E.'s 'The Critic as Artist as Wilde'.

Eminent Domain: Yeats among Wilde, Joyce, Pound, Eliot and Auden (New York: Oxford University Press, 1967). Contents: 'Oscar and Oisin', pp. 9-27; 'The Hawklike Man', pp. 29-56; 'Ez and Old Billyum', pp. 57-87; 'Possum's Conversion', pp.89-95; 'Gazebos and Gashouses', pp. 97-126.

James Joyce's Tower (Moran Park, Dun Laoghaire, Dublin: Eastern Regional Tourism Organization Ltd., 1969), 24 p.

Literary Biography: an Inaugural Lecture Delivered Before the University of Oxford on 4 May 1971 (Oxford: Clarendon Press, 1971), 19 p. Reprinted in E.'s *Golden Codgers*, pp. 1-16.

Ulysses on the Liffey (New York: Oxford University Press; London: Faber and Faber, 1972).

Golden Codgers. Biographical Speculations (New York, London: Oxford University Press, 1973). Contents: 'Literary Biography', pp. 1-16; 'Dorothea's Husbands', pp. 17-38; 'Overtures to Salome', pp. 39-59; 'The Critic as Artist as Wilde', pp. 60-80; 'Corydon and Ménalque', pp. 81-100; 'Discovering Symbolism', pp. 101-112; 'Two Faces of Edward', pp. 113-131; 'A Postal Inquiry', pp. 132-154; 'He Do the Police in Different Voices', pp. 155-168.

Ulysses on the Liffey, Revised paperback edition (London: Faber, 1974).

The Consciousness of Joyce (London: Faber and Faber; New York: Oxford University Press, 1977).

Oscar Wilde: Two Approaches: Papers Read at a Clark Library Seminar, April 17, 1976 (Los Angeles: William Andrews Clark Memorial Library, University of California, 1977), 50 p. Contents: 'A Late Victorian Love Affair', by E. and 'Resources for Wilde Studies at the Clark Library', by John Espey.

Yeats: The Man and the Masks, Corrected edition with a new preface (Oxford: Oxford University Press, 1979).

James Joyce, New and revised ed. (London; New York: Oxford University Press, 1982).

James Joyce's Hundredth Birthday: Side and Front Views: a Lecture Delivered at the Library Congress May 10, 1982 (Washington: Library of Congress, 1982), 27 p. Reprinted in *New York Review of Books*, 18 November 1982, pp. 58-65 and in E.'s *Four Dubliners*, pp. 53-77.

Oscar Wilde at Oxford: a Lecture Delivered at the Library of Congress on March 1, 1983 (Washington: Library of Congress, 1984), 30 p. Previously published in briefer form under the title 'Oscar at Oxford' in *New York Review of Books*, 29 March 1980, pp. 23-28.

Ulysses on the Liffey. With corrections, reissued with further corrections (London: Faber and Faber, 1984).

Henry James Among the Aesthetes, The Sara Tryphena Phillips Lectures in American Literature and History (Wolfboro, N.H.: Longwood Pub. Group, 1985). Text of Lecture read 19 May 1983, previously published in *Proceedings of the British Academy* 69 (1983): pp. 209-28.

W.B. Yeats's Second Puberty: a Lecture Delivered at the Library of Congress on April 2, 1984 (Washington: Library of Congress, 1985), 29 p. Reprinted in *New York Review of Books*, 9 May 1985, pp. 10, 12, 14-16, 18 and E.'s *Four Dubliners*, pp. 27-51.

Samuel Beckett, Nayman of Noland: a Lecture Delivered at the Library of Congress on April 16, 1985 (Washington: Library of Congress, 1986), 30 p. Reprinted in *New York Review of Books*, 24 April 1986, pp. 27-28, 34-37 and in E.'s *Four Dubliners* pp. 79-104.

Four Dubliners: Wilde, Yeats, Joyce and Beckett (Washington, D.C.: Library of Congress, 1986).

Four Dubliners: Wilde, Yeats, Joyce and Beckett (London: Hamish Hamilton; New York: Braziller, 1987). Contents: 'Oscar Wilde at Oxford', pp. 1-25; 'W.B. Yeats's Second Puberty', pp. 27-51; 'James Joyce In and Out of Art', pp. 53-77; 'Samuel Beckett: Nayman of Noland', pp. 79-104.

Oscar Wilde (London: Hamish Hamilton; New York: Knopf, 1987).

V Edited Works

Stanislaus Joyce. *My Brother's Keeper: James Joyce's Early Years.* (London: Faber; New York: Viking Press, 1958).

James Joyce. *The Critical Writings of James Joyce*, edited by Ellsworth Mason and Richard Ellmann (London: Faber and Faber; New York: Viking, 1959).

Edwardians and Late Victorians, English Institute. Essays, 1959 (New York: Columbia University Press, 1960).

Masters of British Literature. 2 Vol., edited by Robert A. Pratt, D.C. Allen, F.P. Wilson, James R. Sutherland, Carlos Baker, Frances E. Mineka and Richard Ellmann (Boston: Houghton-Mifflin, 1962).

James Joyce. *A Portrait of the Artist as a Young Man*, corrected from the Dublin holograph by Chester G. Anderson (New York: Viking Press, 1964).

The Modern Tradition: Backgrounds of Modern Literature, edited by Richard Ellmann and Charles Feidelson, Jr. (New York: Oxford University Press, 1965).

James Joyce. *Letters of James Joyce*, Vol. 2 and 3 (London: Faber and Faber, 1966).

The Poet as Critic, edited by Richard Ellmann and Frederick R.W. McDowell (Evanston Ill.: Northwestern University Press, 1967).

James Joyce. *Giacomo Joyce*, with an introduction and notes by Richard Ellmann. (London: Faber and Faber; New York: Viking Press, 1968).

Oscar Wilde. *The Artist as Critic; Critical Writings of Oscar Wilde* (New York: Random House, 1969).

Oscar Wilde: A Collection of Critical Essays (Englewood Cliffs, N.J.: Prentice-Hall, 1969).

The Norton Anthology of Modern Poetry, edited by Richard Ellmann and Robert O'Clair (New York: Norton, 1973).

James Joyce. *Selected Letters of James Joyce* (London: Faber, 1975).

Modern Poems: An Introduction to Poetry, edited by Richard Ellmann and Robert O'Clair (New York: Norton, 1976).

New Oxford Book of American Verse (New York: Oxford University Press, 1976).

Oscar Wilde. *The Picture of Dorian Gray and Other Writings* (New York: Bantam, 1982).

VI   Reviews

'Atonic and Archaic Verse from England'. Review of *Selected Poems* by Sacheverell Sitwell and *Selected Poems* by Elizabeth Daryush. *Poetry* (Chicago) 74, no. 5 (August 1949): pp. 304-07.

'Philandering with the Sixth Sense'. Review of *The Permanence of Yeats: Selected Criticism*, edited by James Hall and Martin Steinmann. *Saturday Review of Literature* 33 (14 April 1950): p. 49.

'From Renishaw to Paterson'. Review of *The Canticle of the Rose: Poems 1917-1949*, by Edith Sitwell and *Paterson (Book Three)*, by William Carlos Williams. *Yale Review* 39, no. 3 (March 1950): pp. 543-45.

Review of *The Golden Nightingale: Essays on Some Principles of Poetry in the Lyrics of William Butler Yeats*, by Donald A. Stauffer and *W.B. Yeats: Man and Poet*, by Norman A. Jeffares. *Modern Language Notes* 66, no. 5 (May 1951): pp. 335-36.

Review of *W.B. Yeats: Collected Poems*, 2nd ed. *Kenyon Review* 13, no. 3 (Summer 1951): pp. 512-19.

'Three Ways of Looking at Triton'. Reviews of *The Lonely Tower: Studies in the Poetry of W.B. Yeats*, by T.R. Henn; *W.B. Yeats, Self-Critic: A Study of His Early Verse*, by Thomas Parkinson; and *W.B. Yeats: The Tragic Phase, A Study of the Last Poems*, by Vivienne Koch. *Sewanee Review* 61, no. 1 (January-March 1953): pp. 149-54.

'Cranly's Memoirs'. Review of *The Silent Years; an Autobiography with Memoirs of James Joyce and Our Ireland*, by John Francis Byrne. *Saturday Review* 37 (13 March, 1954): pp. 18-19, 46.

'Yeats Without Panoply'. Reviews of *W.B. Yeats: Letters to Katherine Tynan*, edited by Roger McHugh; *W.B. Yeats: The Letters of W.B. Yeats*, edited by Allan Wade; *W.B. Yeats: Letters on Poetry from W.B. Yeats to Dorothy Wellesley*, edited by Dorothy Wellesley; *W.B. Yeats and T. Sturge Moore: Their Correspondence 1901-1937*, edited by Ursula Bridge; and *Letters: Florence Farr, Bernard Shaw and W.B. Yeats*, edited by Clifford Bax. *Sewanee Review* 64, no. 1 (Winter 1956): pp. 145-51.

'American Aristocracy of James Gould Cozzens'. Review of *By Love Possessed* by James Gould Cozzens. *Reporter* (New York) 17 (3 October 1957): pp. 42-44.

Review of *The Masterpiece and the Man: Yeats as I Knew Him*, by Monk Gibbon. *Chicago Sunday Tribune* (13 March 1960): p. 2.

'Mariner's Land Legs'. Review of *Joseph Conrad: A Critical Biography*, by Jocelyn Baines. *The Reporter* (New York) 22 (26 May 1960): pp. 50-52.

Review of *Essays and Introductions*, by W.B. Yeats. *New Statesman* 61 (23 June 1961): pp. 1011-12.

Review of *The Senate Speeches of W.B. Yeats*, edited by Donald R. Pearce. *New Statesman*, 62 (8 December 1961): pp. 887-88.

Review of *W.B. Yeats: Images of a Poet*. Catalogue of the Exhibition held at the Whitworth Art Gallery, University of Manchester from 3 May to 3 June, 1961; at the Building Centre, Dublin from 17 June to 1 July and at the National Book League, London, 17-22 July. Later republished by Manchester University Press, 1961 ed. by D.J. Gordon. *New Statesman* 62 (8 December 1961): pp. 887-88.

'Under the Ritz'. Review of *A Moveable Feast*, by Ernest Hemingway. *New Statesman* 67 (22 May 1964): pp. 809-10.

'Beckett's Testament'. Review of *Testament of Beckett* by William R. Mueller and Josephine Jacobsen. *Commonweal* 80 (26 June 1964): pp. 416-18.

'The Hemingway Circle'. Review of *Ernest Hemingway, A Life Story*, by Carlos Baker and *Hemingway in Michigan*, by Constance Cappel Montgomery. *New Statesman* 78 (15 August 1969): pp. 213-14.

'The Collected Works of Samuel Beckett'. *New York Times Book Review* (27 December 1970): pp. 1-2, 14. Review of a series of Grove Press separately-published works by Beckett.

'Warped Innocence'. Review of *Behind the Door*, by Giorgio Bassani. *New York Review of Books* (15 November 1973): p.23.

'Garden Party'. Review of *The Faber Book of Irish Verse*, by John Montague. *The New Review* 1, no. 4 (July 1974): pp. 70-71.

'Zealots of Zurich'. Review of *Travesties*, by Tom Stoppard. *Times Literary Supplement* (12 July 1974): p. 744.

'Under Tom Tower'. Review of *Thank You, Fog: Last Poems* by W.H. Auden. *New York Review of Books* (12 December 1974): pp. 26-27.

'Pieces of Ulysses'. Review of *James Joyce's 'Ulysses'*, edited by Clive Hart and David Hayman. *Times Literary Supplement* (30 October 1975): p. 1118.

'Richard Ellmann on Biography'. *New Republic* (29 November 1975): p. 28. E. offers brief reviews of some biographies published in 1975.

'Richard Ellmann on Biography'. *New Republic* (20 November 1976): pp. 31-33. Brief reviews of some of the year's biographies.

'Richard Ellmann on Biography'. *New Republic* (26 November 1977): pp. 26-29.

'The Life of Sim Botchit'. Review of *Samuel Beckett: A Biography*, by Deirdre Bair. *New York Review of Books* (15 June 1978): pp. 3-8.

Review of *The Penquin Book of American Verse*, edited by G. Moore. *Notes and Queries* 26, no. 6 (1979): pp. 586-87.

Review of *Lives of the Modern Poets*, by W.H. Pritchard. *New York Times Book Review* (27 April 1980): p. 11.

'Getting to Know You'. Review of *W.H. Auden—The Life of a Poet* by Charles Osborne. *New York Review of Books* (23 October 1980): p.35.

Review of *The World of Charles Ricketts*, by Joseph Darracott. *Times Literary Supplement* (26 December 1980): p. 1469.

Review of *The Life of Villiers-De-Isle-Adam*, by A.W. Raitt. *Times Literary Supplement* (23 October 1981): pp. 1223-24.

Review of *John Ruskin—The Passionate Moralist*, by J. Abse. *New York Times Book Review* (22 November 1981): p. 9.

Review of *60 Stories*, by Donald Barthelme. *New York Review of Books* (21 January 1982): p. 39.

Review of *Bernard Shaw and Alfred Douglas—A Correspondence*, edited by Mary Hyde. *New York Times Book Review* (14 November 1982): p. 12.

Review of *Robert Lowell A Biography*, by Ian Hamilton. *New York Times Book Review* (28 November 1982): p. 1.

'The Ghost of Westerly Terrace'. Review of *Parts of a World, Wallace Stevens Remembered—An Oral Biography*, edited by P. Brazeau. *New York Review of Books* (24 November 1983): pp. 16-19.

Review of *The Name of the Rose*, by Umberto Eco. *New York Review of Books* (24 November 1983): p. 11.

Review of *The Collected Letters of John Millington Synge*, Vol. 1, 1871-1907, edited by A. Saddlemyer. *New York Times Book Review* (15 January 1984): p. 25.

'The Nation's Conscience'. Review of *An American Procession*, by Alfred Kazin. *Atlantic Monthly* (June 1984): pp. 121-24.

Review of *Ulysses—A Critical and Synoptic Edition*, edited by H.W. Gabler, et al. *New York Review of Books* (25 October 1984): p. 30-31.

'Heaney Agonistes'. Review of *Station Island*, by Seamus Heaney. *New York Review of Books* (14 March 1985): pp. 19-20.

Review of *The Collected Letters of W.B. Yeats*. Vol. 1, 1865-1895, edited by J. Kelly and E. Domville. *New Republic* (12 May 1986): pp. 33-35.

Review of *Ulysses—A Critical and Synoptic Edition*, edited by H.W. Gabler, et al. *Georgia Review* 40, no. 2 (1986): pp. 548-56.

VII Articles, Essays in Collections and Introductions

'W.B. Yeats: The End of Youth'. *Furioso* 3, no. 3 (Spring 1948): pp. 25-31.

'Robartes and Aherne: Two Sides of a Penny'. *Kenyon Review* 10, no. 2 (Spring 1948): pp. 177-86. Reprinted in Ransom, pp. 98-107.

'W.B. Yeats, Magician'. *Western Review* 12, no. 4 (Summer 1948): pp. 232-40.

'Black Magic Against White: Aleister Crowly Versus W.B. Yeats'. *Partisan Review* 15 (September 1948): pp. 1049-51.

'The Ductile Universe of Henri Michaux'. *Kenyon Review* 11, no. 2 (Spring 1949): pp. 187-98.

'Joyce and Yeats'. *Kenyon Review* 12, no. 4 (Autumn 1950): pp. 618-38. Reprinted in E.'s *Eminent Domain* under title 'The Hawklike Man', pp. 29-56.

'William Carlos Williams: The Doctor in Search of Himself'. *Kenyon Review* 14, no. 3 (Summer 1952): pp. 510-12.

'Lawrence and His Demon'. *New Mexico Quarterly* 22 (Winter 1952): pp. 385-93.

'The Art of Yeats: Affirmative Capability'. *Kenyon Review* 15, no. 3 (Summer 1953): pp. 357-85.

'The Backgrounds of "Ulysses"'. *Kenyon Review* 16, no. 3 (Summer 1954): pp. 337-86.

'The Limits of Joyce's Naturalism'. *Sewanee Review* 63, no. 4 (Autumn 1955): pp. 567-75.

'The Grasshopper and the Ant: Notes on James Joyce and His Brother Stanislaus'. *Reporter* (New York) 13 (December 1955): pp. 35-8.

'A Portrait of the Artist as Friend'. *Kenyon Review* 18, no. 1 (Winter 1956): pp. 53-67. Reprinted in Connolly, pp. 88-101; Schorer, pp. 60-77.

'Ulysses, the Divine Nobody'. *Yale Review* 47 (September 1957): pp. 56-71.

'Wallace Stevens' Ice-Cream'. *Kenyon Review* 19, no. 1 (Winter 1957): pp. 89-105. Reprinted in Ludwig, pp. 203-22.

'The Backgrounds of "The Dead"'. *Kenyon Review* 20, no. 4 (Autumn 1958); pp. 507-28. Reprinted in Beja (1973), pp. 172-87; Chace, pp. 18-28 and Scholes and Litz, pp. 388-403.

'Introduction' to *The Symbolist Movement in Literature* by Arthur Symons (New York: Dutton, 1958).

'Joyce's Letters'. *Times Literary Supplement* (27 May 1960): p. 344. Reprinted in *New York Herald Tribune Books* (4 September 1960): p.12.

'Ulysses and the Odyssey'. *English Studies* 43 (October 1962): pp. 423-26.

'A Chronology of the Life of James Joyce'. In Morris and Nault (1962), pp. 4-11.

'James Joyce'. In *Masters of British Literature* (1962) Vol. 2, pp. 873-79.

'James Joyce's "Ulysses"'. *Inventario* 17, no. 1 (1962): pp. 22-33.

'T.S. Eliot'. In *Masters of British Literature* (1962) Vol. 2, pp. 983-88.

'William Butler Yeats'. In *Masters of British Literature* (1962) Vol. 2, pp. 823-31. Reprint of a chapter from E.'s *James Joyce*.

'Romantic Pantomime in Oscar Wilde'. *Partisan Review* 30, no. 3 (Fall 1963): pp. 342-55.

'Palinurus at Sixty'. *Encounter* 22 (February 1964): pp. 67-70.

'Yeats Without Analogue'. *Kenyon Review* 26, no. 1 (Winter 1964): pp. 30-47. Reprinted in Hollander, pp. 395-410.

'Gazebos and Gashouses: Yeats and Auden'. *Irish Times*, Yeats Centenary

Supplement (10 June 1965): p.3. Reprinted and expanded in E.'s *Eminent Domain*, pp.97-126.

'James Joyce's Addresses'. *American Book Collector* 15 (June 1965): pp. 25, 27-29.

'Yeats and Eliot'. *Encounter* 25 (July 1965): pp. 53-55.

'Odyssey of a Unique Book'. *New York Times Magazine* (14 November 1965): pp. 56-57, 92, 94, 96, 102, 104, 106.

'Eliot's Conversion'. *TriQuarterly* 4 (1965): pp. 77-80. Also published in *Encounter* 25 (June 1965): pp. 53-55, under title 'Yeats and Eliot'.

'Ez and Old Billyum'. *Kenyon Review* 28, no. 4 (September 1966): pp. 470-95. Reprinted in E.'s *Eminent Domain*, pp. 57-87 and Hesse, pp. 55-85.

'Joyce: A Postal Inquiry'. *New York Review of Books* (8 September 1966): pp. 24-28. Reprint of the Introduction to James Joyce. *Letters*. Full text reprinted in E's *Golden Codgers*, pp. 132-54.

'The Critic as Artist as Wilde'. *Encounter* 29, no. 1 (July 1967): pp. 28-37. Reprinted in Ellmann (ed.) *The Artist as Critic* (1969), pp. ix-xxviii; Ellmann (ed.) *The Poet as Critic* (1967), pp. 44-59 and in E.'s *Golden Codgers*, pp. 60-80.

'James Joyce: Irish European'. *TriQuarterly* 8 (Winter 1967): pp. 198-204. Reprinted in *Umana* 20 (May-September 1971): pp. 13-15. Special Issue on the Third International James Joyce Symposium. Trieste.

'Joyce Letters'. *TriQuarterly* 8 (Winter 1967): pp. 166-76.

'The Letters of James A. Joyce'. *Northwestern Review* 2, no. 2 (1967): pp. 8-16.

'Italo Svevo and Joyce'. *New York Times Book Review* (21 January 1968): pp. 2,22.

'Contemporary Directions in Literature'. *The Barat Review: A Journal of Literature and the Arts* 3 (June-September 1968): pp. 63-68.

'Overtures to Wilde's "Salomé"' *Yearbook of Comparative and General Literature* 17 (1968): pp. 17-28. Reprinted in *TriQuarterly* 15 (Spring 1969): pp. 45-64; Ellmann (ed.) *Oscar Wilde: A Collection . . .* (1969) pp. 73-91; and E.'s *Golden Codgers* pp. 39-59.

'The Structure of the "Portrait"'. In Schutte (1968): pp. 38-40. Reprinted from E.'s *James Joyce*.

'Yeats'. In *Encyclopedia Americana*. (1968), Vol. 29, pp. 659-60.

'A Curious Case of Amalia Popper'. *New York Review of Books* (20 November 1969): pp. 44-47. Lengthy exchange between E. and H. Barolini on Amalia Popper who Joyce tutored in English while in Trieste. In *Giacomo Joyce* she was apparently the cause of some 'erotic excitation'.

'Forward' to *The Poetry of W.B. Yeats* by Louis MacNeice (New York; London: Oxford University Press, 1969).

'Michael-Frank'. In Sheehy (1969), pp. 23-27.

'Why Does Stephen Dedalus Pick His Nose?' *Times Literary Supplement* (21 May 1971); pp. 591-3. First T.S. Eliot Lecture for 1971, University of Kent, Canterbury on 11 May.

'The First Wasteland'. *New York Review of Books* (18 November 1971): pp. 10-16. Reprinted in Litz, pp. 51-66.

'Yeats and Auden: An Imaginary Conversation'. In Cowell (1971): pp. 98-101.

'Why Molly Bloom Menstruates'. *New York Review of Books* (23 March 1972): pp. 25-30. Reprint of chapter from E.'s *Ulysses on the Liffey* (1972) and later reprinted with slight alterations in Chace, pp. 102-112.

'Uses of Adversity'. *American PEN* 4, no. 1 (Winter 1972): pp. 15-17.

'Dorothea's Husbands: Some Biographical Speculations'. *Times Literary Supplement* (16 February 1973): pp. 165-8. Reprinted in E.'s *Golden Codgers* pp. 17-38.

'Oxford in the Seventies'. *American Scholar* 43 (Autumn 1974): pp. 567-75.

'Two Faces of Edward'. In Wimsatt, (1974), pp. 560-75. Reprinted from Ellmann (ed.) *Edwardians and Late Victorians* (1960): pp. 188-210.

'Love in the Catskills'. *New York Review of Books* (5 February 1976): pp. 27-28. E.'s explanation of a particularly intriguing episode in Washington Irving's *Rip Van Winkle*.

'Publishing Joyce's Letters to His Wife'. *American Scholar* 45 (Autumn 1976): pp. 582-86.

'W.B. Yeats'. In Sinfield (1976): pp. 170-83. An interview with E. on Yeats, conducted by Peter Wilson.

'A Late Victorian Love Affair'. *New York Review of Books* (4 August 1977): pp. 6-10. Reprinted from *Oscar Wilde: Two Approaches*, 1976 (see Monographs section).

'Joyce and Homer'. *Critical Inquiry* 3 (1977): pp. 567-82.

'At the Yeatses'. *New York Review of Books* (17 May 1979): pp. 22-25. Reprint, in slightly different form, of E.'s preface to *Yeats: The Man and the Masks*, (1979).

'Sense of Ireland'. *Times Literary Supplement* (15 February 1980): pp. 172.

'Oscar at Oxford'. *New York Review of Books* (29 March 1980): pp. 23-28. Expanded version later published as separate under title *Oscar Wilde at Oxford*, 1983 (see Monographs section) and reprinted in E.'s *Four Dubliners*: pp. 1-25.

'How Wallace Stevens Saw Himself'. In Doggett (1980): pp. 149-70.

'O'Connor's Crabapple Jelly'. *New York Review of Books*, 8 October 1981, pp. 21-22. Reprint of E.'s introduction to *The Collected Stories of Frank O'Connor*. (New York: Knopf, 1981).

'An Old-fashioned Radical'. *Times Literary Supplement* (5 February 1982): p. 136. Transcript of unbroadcasted parts of an interview conducted by Craig Raine for BBC Radio and entitled 'James Joyce: A Touch of the Artist'.

'Joyce and His Women'. *Sunday Times* (7 February 1982): p. 43.

'On Joyce's Centennial'. *New Republic* (17 February 1982): pp. 28-31.

'Ellmann Rejoycing'. *New York Times Book Review* (19 September 1982): p.7.

'Joyce at 100'. *New York Review of Books* (18 November 1982): pp. 58-65. Originally published as a separate under the title *James Joyce's Hundredth*

Birthday (see Monographs section). Reprinted in E.'s *Four Dubliners*, pp. 53-57.

'Forward' to *James Joyce: an International Perspective: Centenary Essays in Honour of the late Sir Desmond Cochrane*, with a message from Samuel Beckett, edited by Suheil Badi Bushui and Bernard Benstock (Gerrards Cross, England: Colin Smythe, 1982).

'Forward' to *James Joyce's Schooldays*, by Bruce Bradley (Dublin: Gill and Macmillan; New York: St Martin's, 1982).

'Joyce's Aunt Josephine'. *Library Chronicle of the University of Texas* 20-21 (1982): pp. 60-63.

'Joyce's Religion and Politics'. *The Aligarth Journal of English Studies* 7, no. 2 (1982): pp. 101-07.

'Henry James Among the Aesthetes'. *Proceedings of the British Academy* 69 (1983): pp. 209-28. Later published as a separate in 1985 (see Monographs section).

'Yeats and Vico'. *Irish Literary Supplement* 2, no. 2 (1983): pp. 1, 19.

'Freud and Literary Biography'. *American Scholar* 53 (Autumn 1984): pp. 465-78.

'Introduction' to *The United States of America* v. *One Book Entitled 'Ulysses'* by *James Joyce: Documents and Commentary: a 50-Year Retrospective*, edited by Michael Moscato and Leslie Leblanc. (Frederick, Md: University Publications of America, 1984).

'Two Perspectives on Joyce'. Prologue to . . . *Light Rays: James Joyce and Modernism*, edited by Heyward Ehrlich (Far Hills, N.J.: New Horizon Press, 1984).

'Yeats's Second Puberty'. *New York Review of Books*, 9 May 1985, pp. 10, 12, 14-16, 18. Originally published as separate under the title *W.B. Yeats's Second Puberty*, 1985 (see *Monographs* section). Reprinted in E.'s *Four Dubliners*, pp. 27-51.

'Two Perspectives on James Joyce: I. His Religion and Politics; II. His Women'. In Backman and Kjellmer (1985): pp. 128-37.

'Nayman of Noland'. *New York Review of Books* (24 April 1986): pp. 27-28, 34-37. Originally published as separate (see Monographs section). Reprinted in E's *Four Dubliners*, pp. 79-104.

'Finally, the Last Word on "Ulysses", the Ideal Text, and Portable Too'. *New York Times Book Review* (15 June 1986): pp. 3, 37. Reprint of part of E.'s introduction to *Ulysses—the Corrected Text*.

'In Defense of Dr Hoeppli'. *Times Literary Supplement* (26 November 1986): pp. 1484. E. objects to H. Trevor-Roper's portrayal and description of Dr Hoeppli in *A Hidden Life: The Enigma of Sir Edmund Backhouse*.

'A Crux in the New Edition of "Ulysses"'. In Sandulescu and Hart (1986): pp. 28-34.

'Preface' to James Joyce. *Ulysses, The Corrected Text*. Edited by Hans Walter Gabler with Wolfhard Steppe and Claus Melchior (New York: Random House, 1986).

'Yeats and Joyce'. In Beja, et al. (1986): pp. 21-30.

'Wilde in New York: Beauty Packed Them In'. *New York Times Book Review* (1 November 1987): pp. 15-16.

VIII   Collections

Backman, Sven and Goran Kjellmer, (eds.) *Papers on Language and Literature: Presented to Alvar Ellegard and Erik Frykman* (Goteborg: Acta Universitatis Gothoburgensis, 1985).

Beja, Morris, (ed.) *James Joyce, 'Dubliners' and 'A Portrait of the Artist as a Young Man': a Selection of Critical Essays*, (London: Macmillan, 1973).

Beja, Morris, et al. (eds.) *James Joyce Centennial Symposium* (Urbana, Ill.: University of Illinois Press, 1986).

Chace, William M., (comp.) *Joyce: A Collection of Critical Essays* (Englewood Cliffs, N.J.: Prentice-Hall, 1974).

Connolly, Thomas Edmund, (ed.) *Joyce's 'Portrait': Criticisms and Critiques* (New York: Appleton, 1962).

Cowell, Raymond, *Critics on Yeats: Readings in Literary Criticism* (Coral Gables, Fla.: University of Miami Press 1971).

Doggett, Frank and Robert Buttel, (eds.) *Wallace Stevens; a Celebration* (Princeton, N.J.: Princeton University Press, 1980).

Encyclopedia Americana. International Edition (New York: Americana Corporation, 1968).

Hesse, Eva. *New Approaches to Ezra Pound; A Co-ordinated Investigation of Pound's Poetry and Ideas* (Berkeley, Calif.: University of California Press, 1969).

Hollander, John, (ed.) *Modern Poetry: Essays in Criticism* (Oxford: Oxford University Press, 1968).

Horden, Peregrine, (ed.) *Freud and the Humanities* (New York: St Martin's Press, 1985).

Litz, A. Walton, (ed.) *Eliot in His Time: Essays on the Occasion of the Fiftieth Anniversary of the Waste Land* (Princeton, N.J.: Princeton University Press; London: Oxford University Press, 1973).

Ludwig, Richard Milton, (ed.) *Aspects of American Poetry: Essays Presented to Howard Mumford Jones* (Columbus, Ohio: Ohio University Press, 1962).

Masters of British Literature, 2 vols, edited by Robert A. Pratt, D.C. Allen, F.P. Wilson, James R. Sutherland, Carlos Baker, Frances E. Mineka and Richard Ellmann (Boston: Houghton-Mifflin, 1962).

Morris, William E. and Clifford A. Nault. (eds.) *Portrait of an Artist: A Casebook on James Joyce's 'A Portrait'* (New York: Odyssey Press, 1962).

Ransom, John Crowe, ed. *The Kenyon Critics: Studies in Modern Literature* (New York: World Publisher, 1951).

Sandulescu, C. George and Clive Hart, (eds.) *Assessing the 1984 Ulysses* (Gerrards Cross: Colin Smythe Ltd; New York: Barnes and Noble, 1986).

Schorer, Mark, (ed.) *Society and Self in the Novel*, English Institute Essays, 1955. (New York: Columbia University Press, 1956).

Schutte, William M., (ed.) *Twentieth Century Interpretations of 'Portrait of the Artist as a Young Man'* (Englewood Cliffs, N.J.: Prentice-Hall, 1968).

Shapiro, Charles. *Twelve Original Essays on Great English Novels* (Detroit, Mich.: Wayne State University Press, 1958).

Sheehy, Maurice, (ed.) *Michael/Frank: Studies on Frank O'Connor* (New York: Knopf, 1969).

Sinfield, Alan. (ed.) *English Poetry* (London: Sussex, 1976).

Wade, Allan, (ed.) *Some Letters from W.B. Yeats to John O'Leary and his Sister, from Originals in the Berg Collection* (New York: New York Public Library, 1953).

Wimsatt, William K., (ed.) *Literary Criticism: Idea and Art—The English Institute, 1939-1972; Selected Essays* (Berkeley, Calif.: University of California Press, 1974).

Notes

Ellmann's Road to Xanadu

ELLSWORTH MASON

1   The state of Joyce studies at the same time is illustrated in Harry Levin's *James Joyce* (1941), which Levin told me in 1948 was the product of writing up his lecture notes during two weeks of Spring break plus one week's revision at the end of Spring semester. It throws more light on Levin's mind and methods than it does on Joyce; it is riddled with factual errors, it juxtaposes deep observations with profound follies (and both sound convincing), and interprets *Ulysses*, one of the grandest comedies in all literature, as a tragedy.

2   This was especially true of the Americans, since American literature was not highly considered at the time. American authors considered worthy of dissertation research at Yale before the war were Melville, Hawthorne, Poe, and Henry James. The surge of patriotism in the country after the Japanese attack on Pearl Harbour made the importance of American literature soar. For the first time, graduate students taking oral exams in the Spring of 1942 were harried by Stanley Williams and occasionally failed for meagre knowledge of American literature, which had previously been taken for granted. No one could have forseen that after the war we would herald as literature every American wall-scrawl and exhume the scrofulous corpses of writers whose unmarked graves were well deserved.

3   For some years in the mid-30s a full page ad in the *New Yorker* presented a photograph of a fresh and attractive infant lying in the holder of a butcher's scale under the large-print rubric: HOW MUCH IS HE WORTH A POUND? Below the photograph the argument for peace (in the face of Hitler's atrocities) was presented in blowsy detail.

4   Letter from Ellmann to me, 20 April, 1942. All citations to 'Letter' below are from Ellmann to me.

5   Letter, (no day given) May, 1943.

6   Letter, 15 February, 1944.

7   Letter, (no day given) June, 1944.

8   Letter, 19 March, 1945.

9   Letter, 19 March, 1945.

10 Letters, 7 and 23 February, 1945.

11 Sean O'Faolain wrote to John Kelleher complaining about this fact and inquired 'which do you think would be the best defense, breechloaders or breechclouts?'

12 Letter, 27 October, 1946.

13 How many people could write as Ellmann did, 'U. of Chicago asked me to come there but may not be able to meet the salary which Illinois forced Northwestern to give me.'?

Richard Ellmann's Michaux: A Publisher's Recollections

JAMES LAUGHLIN

1   R.E. drew most of his selections from the Gallimard volume *L'Espace du Dedans* (1944) but added two sequences of later work from *Epreuves, Exorcismes* (also 1944).

2 Although some of the poems are poems in prose, R.E. chose 'writings' for his title with intent. In René Bertelé's *Panorama de la Jeune Poésie* (1942) we find Michaux insisting:

I do not know how to make poems, or regard myself as a poet, or find, particularly, poetry in my poems . . . Poetry, whether it is transport, invention, or music is always an imponderable which can be found in no matter what genre—a sudden enlargement of the World . . . Poetry is a gift of nature, a grace, not a labour. The mere ambition to make a poem is enough to kill it . . . I write with transport and for myself.

3 I've not attempted to check these texts. I prefer to have them stand as I remember them.

4 Villon was one of Pound's great heroes. His translations of him will be found in Chapter 8 of *The Spirit of Romance*. When in 1924 he wrote his first opera, *Le Testament*, picking out the monodic line with one finger on his Dolmetsch clavichord, the arias were drawn entirely from Villon's texts.

5 Because in 1968, nine years after he had finished the *Joyce*, Ellmann became seriously interested in doing a biography of Pound, let me give more detail on Pound's concerns in French poetry. In his *Translations* volume we find versions of: Charles D'Orleans, du Bellay, La Marquise de Boufflers, Rimbaud, Tailhade and Laforgue. Around 1916-17 he did extensive reading of modern French poets and produced the long essay-cum-anthology 'French Poets' (*Little Review*, 1918, collected in *Instigations*, 1920). Here he dealt at length with Laforgue, Corbière, Rimbaud, DeGourmont (his favourite among contemporary prose writers), Verhaeren, Stuart Merril, Tailhade, Jammes, Moreas, Spire, Jules Romains, Vildrac, Cros and the poets of the 'La Wallonie' group.

During his Paris years (1921-24) Stock reports that Pound 'lead a busy social and literary life' but there is no evidence of his becoming enthusiastic about his contemporaries, except for 'Marse Jean' Cocteau, who became a close friend. DeGourmont had died in 1915. Pound found the Dadaists amusing and at one time hoped he could 'do something with them', but they were not prepared to be told what to do. The only one he made friends with was Picabia, though he admired him more as a thinker and writer than as a painter. He had no use for the Surrealists; he linked them with the hated Freud. He once told me that he had read a bit of Valéry but didn't take to him. I never heard him mention Apollinaire, Reverdy—or Michaux.

After Pound's move to Rapallo in 1924 he seems to have abandoned the new French poetry; it was as if he had put on blinkers. This was natural enough because he was busy with the *Cantos* and growing increasingly obsessed with economics and monetary reform. Such books were now his reading.

6 In his *Henri Michaux* (Oxford, 1973) Malcolm Bowie points out that the work with drugs preoccupied Michaux for an entire decade and replaced almost all other activity. Michaux surely knew De Quincey's *Opium-Eater*, Baudelaire's 'Le Poème du Haschisch', and Cocteau's *Opium*. The four drug books are *Miserable Miracle* (1956, English translation by Louise Varèse, *City Lights*, 1963); *L'Infini Turbulent* (1957, translated as *Infinite Turbulence* by Michael Fineberg, Calder and Boyars, 1975); *Les Grandes Epreuves de l'Esprit* (1966, translated as *The Major Ordeals of the Mind* by Richard Howard, Harcourt Brace, 1974), and *Connaissance par les Gouffres* (1967). As best I can recall, R.E. never expressed much interest in Michaux's drug books.

'Oranges—Apples—Sugarsticks . . .' Joycean Associations: An Interview with Richard Ellmann

CHRISTIE McDONALD

1 The first draft of this interview was written in English, but it was destined for publication in French in an issue of *Études françaises* (eds. Christie McDonald and Ginette Michaud, 22/1, Spring, 1986), entitled 'Ça me fait penser . . .', on the question of the association of ideas and

free association. Christie McDonald and Ginette Michaud translated the interview. Richard Ellmann made all of his own subsequent changes on the text in French, and discussed the problems of passing from one language to another with Christie McDonald. This version in English poses a different problem: translating his and their changes back into English; there are also two paragraphs on page 4 for which the English draft has been lost, and the English has been reconsituted from the French. In a sense, the French publication may be considered to be 'the original' and this the first 'translation'.

2 Richard Ellmann, *James Joyce* (New York and London: Oxford University Press, 1982).
3 Joyce knew well both works by Dujardin, *Les Lauriers sont coupés* (Paris, 1924) and *Le Monologue Intérieur* (Paris, 1931). The two authors dedicated texts to one another, and Joyce went so far as to call Dujardin 'Master' in his letters, qualifying the *Lauriers* book as 'evergreen'. Joyce understood very early what the consequences of the internal monologue would be if used extensively and systematically: 'in that book', he wrote apropos of Dujardin's novel, 'the reader finds himself established, from the first lines, in the thought of the principal personage, replacing the usual form of narrative, conveys to us what this personage is doing or what is happening to him'. In Richard Ellmann, *Op. cit.*, pp. 519-520. In Dujardin's work Joyce found this new form of narration which he would take over in the last chapter of *Ulysses*.
4 These last two paragraphs have been translated from the French, with the exception of the quotations which always were presented in English.

The Concept of Modernism

CHRISTOPHER BUTLER

1 Cf. Stephen Kern, *The Culture of Time and Space 1880-1918* (London 1983).
2 Cf. Suzi Gablik, *Has Modernism Failed?* (London 1984).
3 Peter Gay, *Art and Act* (London 1976), p.108.
4 Eugene Lunn, *Marxism and Modernism* (London 1985). Peter Bürger's *Theory of the Avant-Garde* (Manchester 1984) makes an even more tendentious selection of the avant garde tradition, for political purposes.
5 This in itself involves accepting Anglo-American usage, as Continental writers for the most part have no such specific view of Modernism as an artistic movement, and prefer to use the terms 'modern', 'avant garde' and 'modernité' to cover a much wider range of post 1880 phenomena. Cf. Monique Chefdor, in Monique Chefdor, Ricardo Quinones and Albert Wachtel, (eds.), *Modernism: Challenges and Perspectives* (Urbana, Illinois 1986), p. 1f.
6 On the division of generations, cf Robert Wohl in Chefdor, *ibid.*, pp. 69ff. Modernism as a continuation of Romanticism is associated with the work of Harold Bloom, Northrop Frye and Geoffrey Hartmann; as a continuation of Symbolism with that of Edmund Wilson, Frank Kermode, and others.
7 Northrop Frye, *Anatomy of Criticism* (Princeton 1957), p. 49.
8 Pierre Boulez, *Relevés d'apprenti* (Paris, Seuil 1966), pp. 33f.
9 Malcolm Bradbury, *The Social Context of Modern English Literature* (Blackwell: Oxford, 1971), p. 16.
10 Wassily Kandinsky, *Concerning the Spiritual in Art*, trans. Michael Sadler (1914, repr, New York, 1977), p. 14.
11 Ezra Pound, 'A Few Don'ts' (1913) in *Literary Essays of Ezra Pound* (London, 1954), p. 4.
12 Matthew Arnold, 'Heinrich Heine' in R.H. Super, (ed.), *Lectures and Essays in Criticism* (Ann Arbor, 1962), p. 109.
13 Thomas Mann, *Tonio Kröger*, trans. H.T. Lowe-Porter (Harmondsworth: Penguin, 1955), pp. 153f.
14 James Joyce, *Stephen Hero* (London, 1969), pp. 184, 190, 96.
15 Irving Babbit, *Rousseau and Romanticism* (Boston, 1919), p. xi.

16 Carl E. Schorske, *Fin de siécle Vienna* (Cambridge, 1981), p. xxvi.
17 Thus Louis Kampf, in his study of Modernism back to Descartes, asserts that 'criticism and the destruction of foundations has become a permanent and logical part of our historical development'. *On Modernism* (London, 1967), pp. 12. Cf 33f.
18 Robert Musil, *The Man without Qualities I*, trans. Eithne Wilkinson and Ernest Kaiser (London, 1979), p. 59.
19 Jean-Francois Lyotard, *The Postmodern Condition* (Minneapolis, 1984).
20 Cf. Mario Praz, *The Romantic Agony* (London, 1960), pp. 322-41.
21 J.K. Huysmanns, *Against Nature*, trans. Robert Baldick (Harmondsworth: Penguin, 1959), pp. 65f.
22 Georges Braque, 'Personal Statement 1908-1909' in Edward F. Fry, *Cubism* (London, 1966), p. 53.
23 Cf Christopher Butler, *After the Wake: an Essay on the Contemporary Avant Garde* (Oxford, 1980).

A Modernist Noesis

BRUCE JOHNSON

1 Virginia Woolf, *To The Lighthouse* (New York: Harcourt, Brace and World, 1955), p.38. Subsequent references will be cited within the text.
2 See Sanford Schwartz, *The Matrix of Modernism* (Princeton, N.J.: Princeton University Press, 1985), chap. IV.
3 Schwartz, p. 159.
4 Schwartz, p. 163.
5 Schwartz, p. 223, fn 9.
6 William Barrett, *The Illusion of Technique* (Garden City, N.Y.: Anchor Press/Doubleday, 1979), both quotations, p. 127.
7 Gayatri Spivak, 'Unmaking and Making in *To the Lighthouse*', in *Women and Language in Literature and Society*, (eds.) Sally McConnell-Ginet, Ruth Borker, and Nelly Furman (Praeger, 1980), pp. 310-327.
8 Jeffrey M. Perl, *The Tradition of Return: The Implicit History of Modern Literature* (Princeton, N.J.: Princeton University Press, 1984). Perl's complex sense of modernism as *nostos* is best seen in chaps I and II.
9 See my discussion of this tendency in Hardy: Bruce Johnson, *True Correspondence: A Phenomenology of Thomas Hardy's Novels* (Tallahassee: University Presses of Florida, 1983), particularly chap. 2 on *The Return of the Native*.
10 See Bruce Johnson, 'Conrad's Impressionism and Watt's "Delayed Decoding"', in *Conrad Revisited: Essays for the Eighties*, (ed.) Ross C. Murfin (University of Alabama Press, 1985), pp. 51-70. Reprinted in the new third edition of the Norton Critical Edition of *Heart of Darkness*, (ed.) Robert Kimbrough, (1988). See also Richard Shiff, 'The End of Impressionism', in *The New Painting: Impressionism 1874-1886* (Geneva, Switzerland: Richard Burton SA, 1986), pp. 61-89, and esp. pp. 72-75. This is the catalogue and discussion of the memorable exhibition at the National Gallery of Art and the Fine Arts Museums of San Francisco which largely reconstructed the catalogues of the original eight Impressionist exhibitions and managed to hang many of the original paintings. The University of Washington Press, Seattle, distributed the book in the United States and Canada.
11 See Bruce Johnson, *True Correspondence*, chap. 2.
12 *Thomas Hardy's Personal Writings*, (ed.) Harold Orel (Lawrence: University of Kansas Press, 1966), p. 226, in a piece for *The Times* on Maumbury Ring (October 8, 1908).
13 Schwartz, p. 18.

Northrop Frye and the Bible

FRANK KERMODE

This paper was read at a conference honouring Northrop Frye, held at the University of Rome in May, 1987.

1 See Marjorie Reeves and Warwick Gould, *Joachim of Fiore and the Myth of the Eternal Evangel in the Nineteenth Century* (Oxford: OUP, 1987).

2 A.C. Hamilton, 'Northrop Frye and the Recovery of Myth', *Queen's Quarterly* 85 (Kingston, Ontario, 1978), pp. 66-77.

Poe's Angels

CHARLES A. HUTTAR

1 Cf. Thomas Hobbes, *Leviathan* (1651), (ed.) W.G. Pagson Smith (Oxford: Clarendon Press, 1909), pp.17 and 302-12; Denis Diderot, *Encyclopédie* (Paris: Briasson, 1751-65), p. 1,458; Voltaire, 'Ange', *Dictionnaire Philosophique* (1764), (eds.) R. Naves and J. Benda, 2 vols. (Paris: Garnier 1936).

2 See, for example, Paul Valéry, *Oeuvres*, (ed.) Jean Hytier, 2 vols., Bibliothèque de la Pléiade (Paris: Gallimard, 1957-60), Vol. 1, pp. 153–6, 205–6, 1580–1, 1592–3; Rafael Alberti, *Sobre Los Ángeles* (Madrid: Compañía Ibero-Americana, 1929); Stefan George, *Der Teppich des Lebens* . . . (Berlin: Holten, 1899); Aleksandr Blok, 'Artist' (1913), trans. C.M. Bowra, *A Book of Russian Verse*, (ed.) C.M. Bowra (London: Macmillan, 1947), pp. 105-6; Rainer Maria Rilke, *Duineser Elegien* (Leipzig: Insel-verlag, 1923); Rilke, *Neue Gedichte* (1907-8), ed. and trans. J.B. Leishman as *New Poems* (New York: New Directions, 1964), pp. 68, 74, 92; Wallace Stevens, *Collected Poems* (New York: Knopf 1975), pp. 136-8, 389, 403-6, 496-7.

3 William Wordsworth, 'The World is Too Much With Us' (1807), *Poetical Works*, (ed.) Thomas Hutchinson (London: Oxford Univ. Press, 1911), p. 259.

4 Percy Bysshe Shelley, 'Hymn to Intellectual Beauty' (1817), *Complete Poetical Works*, (ed.) G.E. Woodberry (Boston: Houghton Mifflin, 1901), pp. 346-7.

5 All citations of Poe refer to Edgar Allan Poe, *Collected Works*, (ed.) Thomas Ollive Mabbott, 3 vols. (Cambridge, Mass.; London: Harvard Univ. Press [Belknap Press] 1969-78).

6 Stephen L. Mooney, 'Poe's Gothic Waste Land', *The Recognition of Edgar Allan Poe: Selected Criticism Since 1829*, (ed.) Eric W. Carlson (Ann Arbor: Univ. of Michigan Press, 1966), p. 282.

7 Allen Tate, 'The Angelic Imagination', *The Recognition of Edgar Allan Poe: Selected Criticism Since 1829*, (ed.) Eric W. Carlson (Ann Arbor: Univ. of Michigan Press, 1966), p. 246.

8 Harry Levin, *The Power of Blackness* (New York: Vintage Books, 1960), pp. 162-3.

9 Levin, *The Power of Blackness*, pp. 128-30.

10 See his *The City of Dreadful Night* (1874), especially sec. 20, in *The City of Dreadful Night and Other Poems*, (ed.) Henry S. Salt (London: Watts, 1932), pp. 41-2.

11 See Stéphane Mallarmé, *Oeuvres Complètes*, (eds.) H. Mondor et G. Jean-Aubry, Bibliothèque de la Pléiade (Paris: Gallimard, 1945), pp. 53-54, 70, 1383-4.

Isabel Archer: The New Woman as American

DECLAN KIBERD

1 Leon Edel, *The Life of Henry James*, Vol. 1 (Harmondsworth: Penguin, 1977), p. 522.
2 Edel uses the phrase 'absentee husband' to illustrate this idea, *ibid.*, p. 523.
3 William Bysshe Stein, '*The Portrait of a Lady:* Vis Inertiae', *Perspectives on James's* Portrait of a Lady, (ed.) William T. Stafford (New York: Columbia, 1967) pp. 168-83.
4 Arnold Kettle, 'An Introduction to the English Novel', quoted in Stafford, *Perspectives*, p. 99.
5 Philip Rahv, 'The Heiress of all the Ages', *Perspectives*, p. 142. The essay appeared in Rahv, *Literature and the Sixth Sense* (London: Faber, 1970), pp. 104-125.
6 Philip Sicker, *Love and the Quest for Identity in the Fiction of Henry James* (Princeton: Princeton University Press, 1980).
7 Joseph Warren Beach, 'The Method of Henry James', in Stafford (ed.), *Perspectives*, p. 49.
8 Carolyn Heilbrun, *Towards Androgyny:Aspects of Male and Female in Literature* (London: Harper, 1973), pp. 90ff. See also Edel, Vol 1, p. 359.
9 Edel, *op. cit.*, pp. 615-6.
10 Patricia Stubbs, *Women and Fiction:Feminism and the Novel 1880-1920* (Sussex: Harvester, 1979), p. 159.
11 *Ibid.*, p. 165.
12 William Bysshe Stein, *op. cit.*, p. 182.
13 Dorothy Van Ghent, 'From *The English Novel—Form and Function*', in Stafford, (ed.), *Perspectives*, p. 124.
14 See how similar is Gabriel Conroy's aestheticisation of his wife as beautiful object in 'The Dead' by James Joyce.
15 William Bysshe Stein, *op. cit.*, p. 180.
16 Edel, *op. cit.*, p. 618.
17 Sicker, *op. cit.*, p. 123.
18 Discussed extensively by Stein who cites almost a dozen correspondences in the named article.
19 Quoted in Edel, *op. cit.*, p. 620.
20 Patricia Stubbs, *Women and Fiction*, p. 160.
21 Kettle, in Stafford (ed.), *Perspectives*, p. 111.
22 Stubbs, *op. cit.*, p. 158.
23 *Ibid.*, p. 158.
24 Edel, p. 674.

Henry James, History, and 'Story'

CHARLES FEIDELSON

1 *William Wetmore Story and His Friends* (1903) (New York: Grove Press, n.d.), II, pp. 205-11.
2 *Italian Hours* (1909) (New York: Grove Press, 1959), p. 359.
3 *The Art of the Novel: Critical Prefaces*, (ed.) R.P. Blackmur (New York: Scribner's, 1953), pp. 160, 164. Hereafter cited as *P*.
4 *The Complete Tales of Henry James*, (ed.) Leon Edel (Philadelphia and New York: Lippincott, 1962), I, pp. 321-67. The story dates from 1868.
5 F.O. Matthiessen, *The James Family* (New York: Alfred A. Knopf, 1947), p. 318.
6 *A Small Boy and Others* (New York: Scribner's, 1913) and *Notes of a Son and Brother* (New York: Scribner's, 1914). Hereafter cited as *SBO* and *NSB*.
7 The following paragraph summarizes the argument of my essay on 'James and the "Man of

Imagination"', *Literary Theory and Structure: Essays in Honor of William K. Wimsatt*, (eds.) Frank Brady, John Palmer, and Martin Price (New Haven: Yale University Press, 1973), pp. 331-352.

8   *Letters*, (ed.) Leon Edel (Cambridge, Mass.; London: Belknap Press of Harvard University Press, 1984), IV, pp. 705f.

9   *The Letters of Henry James*, (ed.) Percy Lubbock (New York: Scribner's, 1920), II, pp. 360f.

10   *The Middle Years* (London: W. Collins, 1917), pp. 75, 114-117.

11   *The Notebooks of Henry James*, (eds.) F.O. Matthiessen and Kenneth B. Murdock (New York: Oxford University Press, 1947), cited as *N*.

Lytton Strachey and the Prose of Empire

S.P. ROSENBAUM

1   Richard Ellmann, 'Two Faces of Edward', *Edwardians and Late Victorians*, (ed.) Ellmann (New York: Columbia U.P., 1960), pp. 188-220.

2   Barbara Strachey, *The Strachey Line* (London: Victor Gollancz, 1985), pp. 156, 164.

3   Leslie Stephen, *The Life of Sir James Fitzjames Stephen*, 2nd ed. (London: Smith, Elder 1895), p. 429. Sir James Fitzjames Stephen's book was *The Story of Nuncomar and the Impeachment of Sir Elijah Impey*, 2 vols. (London: Macmillan, 1895), and Sir John Strachey's was *Hastings and the Rohilla War* (Oxford: Clarendon Press, 1892).

4   Permission to quote from 'Warren Hastings' has been kindly granted by the Strachey Trust in London which owns the unpublished essay.

5   The 370-page typescript of Strachey's dissertation follows closely a holograph manuscript of more than 800 pages, except for the introduction. A partly cancelled draft preface to the holograph became the basis for the typed introduction, which is on different paper than the rest of the typescript. The table of contents for the typescript mentions a preface but not an introduction. Though Holroyd and Levy date the introduction 1905 in *The Shorter Strachey*, (eds.) Michael Holroyd and Paul Levy (London: Oxford U.P., 1980), p. 232, it seems obvious, as Bruce B. Redford has argued, that it was done sometime later when Strachey was planning to make a book of his dissertation: 'The Shaping of the Biographer: Lytton Strachey's "Warren Hastings, Cheyt Sing, and the Begums of Oude"', *The Princeton University Library Chronicle*, 43 (Autumn, 1981), p. 48. I am grateful to the Taylor Collection for allowing me to read the dissertation and to the Strachey Trust for permission to quote from it. Parenthetical references to the dissertation in the text give the part and page numbers of the typescript.

6   Quoted in Redford, p. 47.

7   Lytton Strachey, *Eminent Victorians* (London: Chatto and Windus, 1918), p. ix.

8   Michael Holroyd, *Lytton Strachey: Biography*, rev.ed. (Harmondsworth, Middlesex: Penguin Books, 1971), p. 265.

9   Redford, p. 46.

10   P.J. Marshall, *The Impeachment of Warren Hastings* (London: Oxford U.P., 1965), p. x.

11   Holroyd, p. 228.

12   Quoted in Holroyd, p. 228.

13   Quoted in Redford, p. 51.

14   Thomas Babington Macaulay, 'Warren Hastings', *The Works of Lord Macaulay* (London: Longmans Green, 1907), Vol. 9, p. 488.

15   Holroyd, *Strachey*, p. 265.

16   The first paragraph of the introduction which Strachey took from his holograph preface, has been dropped from the published version in *The Shorter Strachey*, pp. 225-32. (References to Strachey's introduction given in parentheses are to this text). The other omissions, marked by ellipses, are statements of Strachey's purpose in the dissertation.

17   The manuscript of 'The Historian of the Future': is owned by the Strachey Trust.

18 Lytton Strachey, 'The Prose Style of Men of Action', *Spectator* 100 (25 Jan. 1908), p. 142. Strachey may have written this text in collaboration with his uncle-editor St Loe Strachey according to Charles Richard Sanders, *Lytton Strachey: His Mind and Art* (New Haven, Conn.: Yale U.P., 1957), p. 169.
19 Leslie Stephen, *History of English Thought in the Eighteenth Century*, 3rd ed. (New York: Harcourt Brace and World, 1962), Vol. 2, p. 169.
20 Edmund Burke, *The Speeches of the Right Honourable Edmund Burke* (1816), Vol. 4, p. 302.
21 Richard Brinsley Sheridan, *Speeches of the Late Right Honourable Richard Brinsley Sheridan*, (ed.) A Constitutional Friend (London, 1816), Vol. 1, p. 288.
22 Macaulay, Vol. 5, p. 529.
23 Leonard Woolf, *Imperialism and Civilization* (London: Hogarth Press, 1928), p. 57.
24 Lytton Strachey, *Characters and Commentaries* (London: Chatto and Windus, 1933), pp. 10, 46-9.
25 Lytton Strachey, 'The Guides', *Spectatorial Essays*, (ed.) James Strachey (London: Chatto and Windus, 1964), pp. 10, 46-9.
26 Strachey, 'Warren Hastings', *Spectatorial Essays*, p. 45.
27 A.P. Thornton, *Doctrines of Imperialism* (New York: John Wiley and Sons, 1965).
28 Strachey, *Eminent Victorians*, p. 309.
29 Marshall, *Impeachment*, pp. 87, 109, 181-3, 189.
30 John Strachey, *The End of Empire* (London: Victor Gollancz, 1961), p. 46-8.

'The Writing "I" Has Vanished':
Virginia Woolf's Last Short Fictions

SUSAN DICK

I am grateful to the following people and institutions for granting me permission to publish passages from manuscript material: Quentin Bell and Angelica Garnett (Virginia Woolf, Vanessa Bell); Mrs Trekkie Parsons (Leonard Woolf); Mrs Mabel Smith and the Backsettown Trustees (Octavia Wilberforce); Nigel Nicolson (Vanessa Bell, Leonard Woolf); The University of Sussex Library (Leonard Woolf Papers [LWP] and Monks House Papers [MHP]); the Henry W. and Albert A. Berg Collection of the New York Public Library, Astor, Lenox and Tilden Foundations (Virginia Woolf, 'Sketches' and 'The Ladies Lavatory'); and to the Social Sciences and Humanities Research Council of Canada for a Research Grant.

References to the following works by Virginia Woolf are cited within parentheses in the text:

AR   Brenda Silver, (ed.), ' "Anon" and "The Reader": Virginia Woolf's Last Essays', *Twentieth Century Literature* 25, no. 3/4 (Fall/Winter 1979), pp. 356-441.
CSF *The Complete Shorter Fiction of Virginia Woolf*, (ed.) Susan Dick (London: The Hogarth Press, 1985).
DV   *The Diary of Virginia Woolf*, (ed.) Anne Olivier Bell, vol. V (London: The Hogarth Press, 1984).
JR   *Jacob's Room* (London: The Hogarth Press, 1976).
LVI *The Letters of Virginia Woolf*, (eds.) Nigel Nicolson and Joanne Trautmann, vol. VI (London: The Hogarth Press, 1980).
MB   *Moments of Being: Unpublished Autobiographical Writings of Virginia Woolf*, (ed.) Jeanne Schulkind (London: The Hogarth Press, revised and enlarged edition, 1985).
MD   *Mrs. Dalloway* (London: The Hogarth Press, 1976).
TL   *To the Lighthouse* (London: The Hogarth Press, 1974).
W   *The Waves* (London: The Hogarth Press, 1976).

In transcribing passages from unpublished manuscripts and letters I have generally omitted cancelled passages and written out abbreviations.

1 Leonard Woolf, *The Journey Not the Arrival Matters: An Autobiography of the Years 1939-1969* (London: The Hogarth Press, 1969), p. 70.

2 Richard Ellmann, *Golden Codgers: Biographical Speculations* (London: Oxford University Press, 1973), p. 16.

3 See especially Susan M. Kenney, 'Two Endings: Virginia Woolf's Suicide and *Between the Acts*', *University of Toronto Quarterly* XLIV, no. 4 (Summer 1975), pp. 265-289, and Mitchell A. Leaska's 'Introduction' and 'Afterword' to his edition of *Pointz Hall: The Earlier and Later Typescripts of 'Between the Acts'* (New York: University Publications, 1983). Responses to Phyllis Grosskurth's ill-considered attempt in her review of the final volume of Woolf's letters (*TLS* 31 October, 1980), pp. 1225-6 to find evidence in *The Years* and *Between the Acts* to support her notion that Leonard Woolf was implicated in his wife's death have been made by (among others) Joanne Trautmann, 'Introduction' to *Virginia Woolf: Centennial Essays*, (eds.) Elaine K. Ginsberg and Laura Moss Gottlieb (Troy, N.Y.: The Whitston Publishing Co., 1983), pp. 1-9, and Harold Fromm, 'Recycled Lives: Portraits of the Woolfs as Sitting Ducks', *The Virginia Quarterly Review* LXI (Summer 1985), pp. 396-417. The question of the exact nature of Woolf's illness, which has engaged the energies of a number of critics, lies outside the scope of my discussion.

4 Octavia Wilberforce to Elizabeth Robins, 27-29 March 1941 (LWP).

5 Noel Annan, *Leslie Stephen: The Godless Victorian* (New York: Random House, 1984), p. 90. The name of the Alpine guide with whom Stephen always climbed, Melchior Anderegg, is echoed, as Lyndall Gordon has observed, in the name of the inn keeper in 'The Symbol', Herr Melchior. *Virginia Woolf: A Writer's Life* (Oxford: Oxford University Press, 1984), p. 279.

6 *Poems of Thomas Hardy*, (ed.) T.R.M. Creighton (London: Macmillan Press Ltd., 1977), p. 107.

7 Quoted in George Spater and Ian Parsons, *A Marriage of True Minds: An Intimate Portrait of Leonard and Virginia Woolf* (London: Jonathan Cape and The Hogarth Press, 1977), p. 61-2.

8 'Reminiscences' is included in *Moments of Being*. In both works Woolf may also have been remembering her father's life of her mother, Julia Jackson Duckworth Stephen, which he wrote after her death in the form of a letter to his children. See *Sir Leslie Stephen's Mausoleum Book*, (ed.) Alan Bell (Oxford: Clarendon Press, 1977).

9 Quentin Bell, *Virginia Woolf: A Biography* (London: The Hogarth Press, 1972), Vol. I, p. 85.

10 *AR* p. 429. Brenda Silver notes that the sentence describing a 'man sitting alone in his college room' is incomplete in the MS. 'In the TS, he is thinking about suicide' (p. 435). It is also interesting that in one version of this chapter Woolf experimented with writing her criticism in the form of a letter (see pp. 433-5).

11 Leonard Woolf, *Journey*, p. 81. In the latter part of 1940, Leonard Woolf writes, Octavia 'had, to all intents and purposes, become Virginia's doctor'. He consulted her professionally early in 1941 when he became alarmed about his wife's health (p. 86). I cannot agree with Roger Poole's claim that Octavia Wilberforce's visits frightened Virginia because she 'could easily see through Leonard's motive in asking Octavia so often to tea . . . ' *The Unknown Virginia Woolf* (Cambridge: Cambridge University Press, 1978), p. 249. The letters make it clear that Virginia Woolf saw these visits as a welcome diversion. Stephen Trombley makes no reference to Octavia Wilberforce in his book, *'All that Summer She was Mad': Virginia Woolf and Her Doctors* (London: Junction Books, 1981).

12 Octavia Wilberforce to Virginia Woolf, 2 March and 9? March 1941 (LWP).

13 Octavia Wilberforce to Elizabeth Robins, 14 March 1941 (LWP). The 'story' Octavia refers to could be 'The Symbol' or 'The Watering Place' or, perhaps, *Between the Acts*. Woolf's growing depression is reflected in her decision two weeks later that *Between the Acts* was 'too silly and trivial' to be published (*LVI*, p. 486).

14 Octavia Wilberforce to Elizabeth Robins, 22 March 1941 (LWP).

15 Octavia Wilberforce to Elizabeth Robins, 14 March 1941 (LWP).

16 Lyndall Gordon, *Virginia Woolf: A Writer's Life*, pp. 271-80.

17 The holograph drafts are located at the back of the writing book which contains the holograph drafts of 'The Symbol' and 'The Watering Place', which precede them (Berg). The typescript page is located among fragments of other late writings ('The Telescope' ['The Searchlight'], 'Mrs Thrale', 'The Legacy', and 'Anon') and is typed on the back of page 6 of a typescript draft of 'Mrs Thrale' (MHP/B5c).

18 Octavia Wilberforce also recounted this incident, much as Woolf tells it, in her unpublished

autobiography, *The Eighth Child*. I am grateful to Dr Pat Jalland, who is editing the autobiography, for sending me a copy of the relevant passage.

19 References to suicide do appear in Woolf's diary during the spring and summer of 1940. She and Leonard had planned to kill themselves, either by asphyxiation in their garage or by lethal doses of the morphine supplied by her brother, should the Germans invade. She accepted the necessity of this plan, but had no wish to die. 'No, I dont want the garage to see the end of me', she wrote in May. 'I've a wish for 10 years more' (*DV*, p. 285). Once the threat of invasion lessened, references to suicide stopped appearing in her diary.

20 Octavia Wilberforce to Elizabeth Robins, 27–29 March 1941 (LWP). It is difficult to tell from this letter exactly when Woolf made this offer.

21 Vanessa Bell to Vita Sackville-West, 2 April 1941 (Nigel Nicolson).

22 *LVI*, p. 485, where 'in' has been omitted (LWP).

23 Octavia Wilberforce to Leonard Woolf, 29 March 1941 (LWP).

24 Leonard Woolf used this phrase in the letters he wrote to Vita Sackville-West on 28 March 1941 (Nigel Nicolson), to William Robson on 29 March (LWP), and to John Lehmann on 29 March (British Library) to tell them what had happened. She drowned herself in the River Ouse on 28 March; her body was found on 18 April near the place where Leonard had found her walking stick floating in the water. Virginia Woolf left three suicide letters: two to Leonard Woolf, one which he found in the sitting room on 28 March (a Friday) headed 'Tuesday', and one with no heading or date, which he later found on the writing block in her lodge; and one to Vanessa Bell, headed 'Sunday', which Leonard Woolf also found in the sitting room on 28 March. While no reconstruction of the chronology of these letters is entirely satisfying, I tend to agree with the one that Nigel Nicolson and Joanne Trautmann have carefully set out in 'Appendix A' of the final volume of Woolf's letters. They have concluded that these letters were written on three separate days, 18 March (a Tuesday), 23 March (a Sunday), and 28 March. The first letter may coincide with an earlier attempt Leonard Woolf believed she may have made to kill herself (see *LVI*, p. 490).

Strange Meetings: Eliot, Pound and Laforgue

A. WALTON LITZ

1   Arthur Symons, *The Symbolist Movement in Literature* (London, 1911), p. 101.

2   *Ibid.*, pp. 108, 107, 109.

3   *Harvard Advocate*, 88 (26 Jan. 1910), p. 114. Reprinted in *Poems Written in Early Youth* (1950).

4   *Criterion*, 9 (January 1930), p. 357, in a review of Peter Quennell's *Baudelaire and the Symbolists*.

5   First published in the *Southern Review*, 21 (Oct. 1985), pp. 873–884, see p. 879.

6   *Egoist*, 6 (July 1919), p. 39.

7   Jules Laforgue, *Moral Tales*, translated and introduced by William Jay Smith. Introduction, p. xii.

8   Peter Ackroyd, *T.S. Eliot: A Life* (New York, 1984), p. 80.

9   *Pound/Joyce*, (ed.) Forrest Read (New York, 1967), p. 112.

10 *To Criticize the Critic* (New York, 1965), pp. 22–23.

11 *Shama'a*, 1 (April 1920), p. 13.

12 Ronald Bush, *T.S. Eliot: A Study in Character and Style* (New York, 1983), pp. 84, 10, 82. The first two quotations are drawn from Bush's paraphrases of unpublished materials; the third comes from Eliot's introduction to Valéry's *Le Serpent* (1924).

13 Warren Ramsey, *Jules Laforgue and the Ironic Inheritance* (New York, 1953), p. 204.

14 *Ezra Pound and Dorothy Shakespear: Their Letters, 1909–1914*, (eds.) Omar Pound and A. Walton Litz (New York, 1984), p. 302.

15 *Little Review*, 4 (May 1917), pp. 11-12; *Poetry*, 11 (Nov. 1917), pp. 93-98; *Little Review*, 4 (Feb 1918), pp. 3-61.

16 *Little Review*, 5 (July, 1918), pp. 3-12.

17 Included in *Personae: The Collected Poems* after 1949.

18 Pound obviously typed out his 'translation' in great haste. The typescript in the Beinecke Rare Book and Manuscript Library, Yale University, contains many cancellations and typographical errors. I have regularized it to some extent. Eliot himself made a straightforward translation of the poem which bears no resemblance to Pound's (now in the Berg Collection).

19 *New Age*, 25 (7 Aug. 1919), p. 252.

20 Smith, p. xxiv.

21 *The Collected Works of Paul Valéry*, Vol. 9 (Princeton, 1968), pp. 224-25.

22 *Little Review*, 4 (March 1918), p. 57.

23 In 'Irony, Laforgue, and Some Satire' (Nov. 1917). See *Literary Essays*, (ed.) T.S. Eliot (New York, 1954), p. 282.

24 Smith, pp. xiv-xv.

'Sufficient Ground to Stand on': Pound, Williams, and American History

CAROL H. CANTRELL

This is a revised version of a paper presented at the Conference on Politics, Economics, and Literature at Hamilton College, April 1985. Many thanks to my colleague, Ward Swinson, for numerous useful conversations about Pound and history.

1 A comparison of the indexes of the two biographies is instructive: Paul Mariani's *William Carlos Williams: A New World Naked* (New York: McGraw Hill, 1981) a book of 874 pages, lists over a column of references to Pound in the index; Noel Stock's *Life of Ezra Pound* (New York: Pantheon, 1970), a book of 472 pages, lists less than half an inch of references to Williams.

2 This photograph serves as the frontispiece to Mike Weaver's important book, *William Carlos Williams: The American Background* (London: Cambridge University Press, 1971).

3 Geoffrey H. Movius, 'Caviar and Bread: Ezra Pound and William Carlos Williams, 1902-1914', *Journal of Modern Literature* 5 (Sept. 1976), pp. 383-406.

4 *The Autobiography of William Carlos Williams* (New York: New Directions, 1967), pp. 53 and 65; Mariani, *Williams*, pp. 48-9.

5 Donald Gallup, *Ezra Pound: A Bibliography* (Charlottesville: University of Virginia Press, 1983), pp. 14-5.

6 William Carlos Williams, 'Prologue' to *Kora in Hell* (1918), reprinted in *Imaginations* (New York: New Directions, 1970), p. 35.

7 'Yours, O Youth' (1921), reprinted in *Selected Essays of William Carlos Williams* (New York: New Directions, 1969), p. 35.

8 In *The Cantos of Ezra Pound* (New York: New Directions, 1970), he twice (93/685 and 102/728) uses the phrase to refer to writers he thought lacked a proper understanding of economics. Throughout this essay I will refer to specific passages within the *Cantos* by identifying canto and page number within the text.

9 Ezra Pound, *Selected Letters 1907-1914*, (ed.) D.D. Paige (1950; reprint, New York: New Directions, 1971), p. 160.

10 'Indiscretions' (1918); reprinted in Ezra Pound, *Pavannes and Divagations* (New York: New Directions, 1958), pp. 3-51.

11 *The Great American Novel* (1923); reprinted in Williams, *Imaginations*, p. 158-227.

12 William Carlos Williams, *In the American Grain* (1925: reprint, New York: New Directions, 1956).

13 Contained in *Eleven New Cantos XXXI-XLI*, in Pound's *Cantos*, pp. 151-252.

14 See Williams, *Selected Essays*, pp. 38-54.

15 'The Jefferson-Adams Letters as a Shrine and a Monument' (1937); reprinted in Ezra Pound, *Selected Prose, 1909-1965*, (ed.) William Cookson (New York: New Directions, 1973), pp. 147-158.

16 *Many Loves and Other Plays: The Collected Plays of William Carlos Williams* (Norfolk, Conn.: New Directions, 1961), pp. 301-358.

17 Cantos 62-71 of *The Fifth Decad of Cantos* in Pound's *Cantos*, pp. 341-421.

18 William Carlos Williams, *Paterson* (1946-1958; reprint, New York: New Directions, 1963).

19 Pound, *Pavannes*, p. 50.

20 Pound's description of the writings of Henry James in 'Henry James' (1918), reprinted in *Literary Essays of Ezra Pound*, (ed.) T.S. Eliot (New York: New Directions, 1968), p. 391.

21 The August 1918 issue of *The Little Review* was a special Henry James number edited by Pound, to which he contributed three essays. See Stock, *Life*, p. 216.

22 Williams, *The Great American Novel*, p. 175.

23 Pound, *Selected Letters*, p. 124.

24 'Dr Williams' Position' (1928); reprinted in *Literary Essays of Ezra Pound*, p. 391.

25 *Ibid.*

26 *The Malatesta Cantos (Cantos IX to XII of a Long Poem)*, *Criterion* I (July 1923), pp. 363-84, were published on the eve of Williams' year-long sabbatical from medical practice, during which time he wrote *In the American Grain*. See Mariani, *Williams*, pp. 207-08.

27 See Michael Harper, 'Truth and Calliope: Ezra Pound's Malatesta', *PMLA*, XCVI (Jan. 1981), p. 88.

28 Williams, *American Grain*, n.p.

29 *Ibid.*, p. 63.

30 Steven Weiland, 'Where Shall We Unearth the Word? William Carlos Williams and the Aztecs', *Arizona Quarterly* 35 (Spring 1979), pp. 42-48.

31 Stock, *Pound*, p. 338.

32 *Ibid.*, p. 294.

33 Williams, *Autobiography*, pp. 146, 174.

34 Philip Furia, *Pound's Cantos Declassified* (University Park, Pa.: Pennsylvania State University Press, 1984), p. 51.

35 Ezra Pound, *Jefferson and/or Mussolini* (1933; reprint, New York: Liveright, 1970), p. 12.

36 Williams, *Selected Letters*, p. 108.

37 William Carlos Williams, *A Voyage to Pagany* (1928; reprint, New York: New Directions, 1970). The inscription reads, 'To / the first of us all / my old friend / EZRA POUND / this book is affectionately / dedicated'. Williams' essays on Pound include 'Excerpts from a Critical Sketch: *A Draft of XXX Cantos* by Ezra Pound' (1931), 'A 1 Pound Stein' (1935), and 'Pound's Eleven New "Cantos"' (1935), all reprinted in Williams' *Selected Essays*.

38 See Stock, *Pound*, pp. 221-36 and Mariani, *Williams*, pp. 348 and 352-53 for accounts of the two poets' early involvement with Social Credit. Their differences are recorded in the pages of *New Democracy*, a U.S. Social Credit publication, in which Pound attacks Williams for trying to avoid the underlying unities between Fascism, Communism, and Social Credit; Williams replies that Pound is confused by his 'dogged idealism' (Mariani, *Williams*, pp. 352-53). By 1956 one of Williams' milder criticisms of Pound was 'YOU DON'T EVEN BEGIN TO KNOW what the problem is'. (Williams, *Selected Letters*, p. 338).

39 'American Background', p. 137.

40 *Ibid.*, p. 141.

41 *Ibid.*, p. 151.

42 *Ibid.*, p. 157.

43 Mariani, *Williams*, p. 388.

44 *Ibid.*, p. 374.

45 William J. Mahar, 'Williams vs. Washington: the Relationship betweem the Libretto and History', *William Carlos Williams Review* 7 (Spring 1981), p. 18.

46 Williams, 'The First President', pp. 306-07.

47 Mariani, *Williams*, p. 357.

48 See David Frail, '"The Regular Fourth of July Stuff": William Carlos Williams' Colonial Figures as Poets', *William Carlos Williams Review* 6 (Fall 1980), pp. 7-9.

49 Pound urged others to read William E. Woodward's *George Washington: The Image and the*

Man (New York: Boni and Liveright, 1926) for its perceptive presentation of early U.S. history (see Pound's *Jefferson and/or Mussolini*, p. 78). Woodward pictures Washington as a rather dull businessman.

50 Williams was responding to a request for an essay from Louis Zukofsky on behalf of a leftist group, The American Federation of Writers. The group folded; the essay went into Williams' files. See Mariani, *Williams*, p. 390.
51 Williams, 'Writers of the American Revolution', p. 45.
52 Pound, 'Jefferson-Adams Letters', pp. 147-78, 152.
53 The date of acquisition is not known. Internal and external evidence suggest that Pound must have written the Adams cantos in less than three months in early 1939. See Cantrell and H. Ward Swinson, 'Cantos LII-LXI: Pound's Textbook for Princes', unpubl. ms, pp. 27, 116 n. 20.
54 A typical example of Pound's reiterated condemnation of Roosevelt: ' "War is his only way out", phrase pronounced by a Congressman to signify that Roosevelt had made such a mess of things that war was his only way of escape.' ('An Introduction to the Economic Nature of the United States' [1941], reprinted in *Selected Prose*, p. 180.)
55 Adams' family settled in 'Braintree, a plantation near Weston's' (62/341), and both sides of Pound's mother's family, the Westons and the Wadsworths, had settled in Duxbury, Massachusetts, in the early 1600s. According to James Wilhelm, Braintree is 'Adams country, but the paths of the Wadsworths and the Westons run through it . . . Pound is saying . . . that his family's ties go back to the origins of the nation and that they are interwoven with that family he admired so greatly, the Adamses'. See 'The Wadsworths, the Westons, and the Farewell of 1911', *Paideuma* 12 (Fall and Winter 1983), p. 307.
56 See Cantrell and Swinson, pp. 105-10.
57 Cf. 'We read: not the flames / but the ruins left / by the conflagration' (Williams, *Paterson*, p. 148).
58 Pound's 'Usura canto' begins, 'With usura hath no man a house of good stone' (45/229); Williams' passage begins, 'Without invention nothing is well spaced' (*Paterson*, p. 65) and continues to echo Pound's cadences.
59 Benjamin Sankey, *A Companion to William Carlos Williams'* Paterson (Berkeley: University of California Press, 1971), pp. 95-7.
60 Williams, 'American Background', p. 134.
61 Williams, 'Excerpts from a Critical Sketch', p. 106.
62 Williams, *Great American Novel*, p. 226.
63 Williams, *The First President*, p. 303.
64 Joel Conarroe, *William Carlos Williams'* Paterson: *Language and Landscape* (State Park, Pa.: University of Pennsylvania Press, 1970), p. 114.
65 For an illuminating discussion of the differences between Pound's and Williams' use of sources, see Stephen Fender, 'Ezra Pound and the Words Off the Page: Historical Allusions in Some American Long Poems', *Yearbook of English Studies* 8 (1978), pp. 95-108.
66 Pound, *Selected Prose*, n.p.

D.H. Lawrence's Physical Religion:
The Debt to Tylor, Frobenius, and Nuttall

DANIEL J. SCHNEIDER

1 *The Letters of D.H. Lawrence*, (ed.) Aldous Huxley (New York: Viking Press 1930), p. 466.
2 D.H. Lawrence, *Etruscan Places*, in *D.H. Lawrence and Italy* (New York: The Viking Press, 1972), p. 20.
3 *Phoenix: The Posthumous Papers of D.H. Lawrence*, (ed.) Edward D. McDonald (Harmondsworth, Middlesex: Penguin Books Ltd., 1978), pp. 146-47.
4 Edward B. Tylor, *Primitive Cultures: Researches into the Development of Mythology,*

Philosophy, Religion, Language, Art and Custom, 2 vols (New York: Henry Holt and Co., 1889), 1, pp. 427, 426.

5 *Ibid.*, 1, p. 500.
6 *Ibid.*, 1, p. 479.
7 *Ibid.*, 1, p. 457.
8 *Ibid.*, 1, p. 298.
9 *Ibid.*, 2, p. 225.
10 *Ibid.*, 2, p. 341.
11 *Ibid.*, 2, p. 341.
12 *Ibid.*, 2, p. 255.
13 *The Complete Poems of D.H. Lawrence*, (eds.) Vivian de Sola Pinto and Warren Roberts (New York: The Viking Press, 1971), p. 706.
14 *Primitive Cultures*, Vol. 2, p. 360.
15 *Ibid.*, 2, p. 360.
16 *Ibid.*, 2, p. 89.
17 *Ibid.*, 2, p. 90.
18 *Ibid.*, 2, p. 101.
19 *Ibid.*, 2, p. 97.
20 *Mornings in Mexico and Etruscan Places* (London: William Heinemann Ltd., 1956), pp. 52, 53.
21 *Ibid.*, p. 53.
22 *Ibid.*, p. 53.
23 *Etruscan Places*, p. 56.
24 Leo Frobenius, *The Voice of Africa: Being an Account of the Travels of the German Inner African Exploration in The Years 1910-1912* (New York and London: Benjamin Blom, Inc., 1968), pp. 262, 263.
25 *Ibid.*, p. 393.
26 *Ibid.*, p. 397.
27 *Ibid.*, p. 674.
28 *Ibid.*, p. xiv.
29 Zelia Nuttall, *The Fundamental Principles of Old and New World Civilization: A Comparative Research Based on a Study of the Ancient Mexican Religious, Sociological and Calendrical Systems* (Cambridge, Mass.: Peabody Museum of American Archaeology and Ethnology, 1900), p. 47.
30 *Ibid.*, p. 54.
31 *The Plumed Serpent* (New York: Vintage Books, Inc., 1951), p. 129.
32 *Fundamental Principles*, p. 13.
33 *Plumed Serpent*, p. 134.
34 *Ibid.*, p. 136.
35 *Ibid.*, p. 131.
36 *Fundamental Principles*, p. 33.
37 *Voice of Africa*, p. 674.

Notes on a Late Poem by Stevens

DENIS DONOGHUE

1 Jean-Paul Sartre, *The Psychology of Imagination* (London: Methuen, 1972) pp. 11–12.
2 Philip Wheelwright, *The Burning Fountain* (Bloomington: Indiana University Press, second edition, 1968) p. 33.
3 Paul de Man, *The Rhetoric of Romanticism* (New York: Columbia University Press, 1984) p. 6.

The Difficult Debut of Denis Johnston's 'Old Lady'
JOSEPH RONSLEY

1 *Did You Know that the Gate*, an unsigned, undated pamphlet published some time after 1940.
2 *Ireland's Abbey Theatre* (London: Sidgwick and Jackson, 1951), p. 121.
3 *The Dramatic Works*, Vol. I (Gerrards Cross: Colin Smythe, 1977), p. 17.
4 *Ibid.*, p. 79.
5 'Waiting for Emmet', *Denis Johnston: A Retrospective*, (ed.) Joseph Ronsley (Gerrards Cross: Colin Smythe, 1981), p. 30.
6 *The Mantle of Harlequin* (Dublin: Progress House, 1958), p. 31.
7 *The Dramatic Works*, Vol. I, p. 76.
8 Harold Ferrar, *Denis Johnston's Irish Theatre* (Dublin: Dolmen Press, 1973), p. 11. Christine St. Peter, 'Denis Johnston, the Abbey and the Spirit of the Age' *Irish University Review*, Vol. 17, No. 2 (Autumn, 1987), p. 190.
9 'Letter to a Young Dramatist', *The Listener*, Vol. LVI, No. 1431 (30 August 1956), p. 305.
10 In conversation, Montreal, 20 March 1975.
11 *Plays of Changing Ireland* (New York: Macmillan, 1936), p. 28.
12 *Denis Johnston's Irish Theatre*, p. 28.
13 *Ibid.*, pp. 14-15.
14 *The Dramatic Works*, Vol. I, p. 87.
15 In conversation, Montreal, 29 November 1976.
16 'Letter to a Young Dramatist', p. 305.
17 'What Has Happened to the Irish', *Theatre Arts*, XLIII (July 1959), p. 72.
18 'Joxer in Totnes', *Irish Writing*, 13 (December 1950), pp. 52-53.
19 In conversation, Toronto, 17 February 1976.
20 *Lady Gregory's Journals*, (ed.) Lennox Robinson (New York: Macmillan, 1947), p. 117.
21 *Ibid.*, pp. 112-13.
22 'Opus One', *The Dramatic Works*, Vol. I, p. 16.
23 Foreword by Roger McHugh, *Our Irish Theatre*, Lady Gregory (Gerrard's Cross: Colin Smythe, 1972).
24 In conversation.
25 A review of a production of *The Old Lady Says 'No!'*, 'Drama: The Dublin Theatre', *The Bell*, Vol. 3, No. 5 (February, 1942), p. 359.
26 *Ibid.*
27 *Journals* (Gerrards Cross: Colin Smythe, 1988), pp. 306-07.
28 In conversation, Toronto, March 1976.
29 In conversation, Toronto, February 1986. Christine St Peter thinks the words were never written at all. She may very well be right; I myself have never seen the inscription, 'Denis Johnston, The Abbey and the Spirit of the Age', p. 194.
30 Quoted by Robert Hogan, *After the Irish Renaissance* (London: Macmillan, 1968), pp. 11-12.
31 *The Dramatic Works*, Vol. I, p. 16.
32 *All for Hecuba* (London: Methuen, 1947), p. 82.
33 *Journals*, p. 346.
34 *The Mantle of Harlequin*, p. 31.
35 'Sean O'Casey: A Biography and an Appraisal', *Modern Drama* (December 1961), p. 326.
36 See notes 5 and 32.
37 *Joseph Holloway's Irish Theatre*, Vol. 1, (ed.) Robert Hogan and Michael J. O'Neill (Dixon, California: Proscenium Press, 1968), pp. 48-50.
38 4 July 1929.
39 Stephen Williams, 'A Visit to Ireland's Theatre', mid-June 1929.
40 3 July 1929.
41 10 July 1929.
42 *Ibid.*
43 Early July 1929.
44 13 July 1929.
45 20 July 1929.
46 17 May 1930.
47 *Plays of Changing Ireland*, p. 36.
48 'Denis Johnston', *The Bell*, Vol. XIII, No. 1 (October 1946), p. 11.
49 *Theatre in Ireland* (Dublin: Cultural Relations Committee of Ireland 1950, 1964), pp. 38-39.

In Search of Horatio's Identity (via Yeats)

R.W. DESAI

1   *Hamlet* references are to *The New Penguin Shakespeare*, (ed.) T.J.B. Spencer (Harmondsworth: Penguin, 1980).

2   'It is regularly observed that Hamlet values in Horatio what he knows to be lacking in himself', Harold Jenkins, (ed.) *Hamlet*, Arden (London: Methuen, 1982), p. 290.

3   Robert R. Wilson argues that of all the characters in the play 'Horatio meets the narrative demands . . . he will make the story heard, tell it again and again', 'Narratives, Narrators and Narratees in *Hamlet*', *Hamlet Studies*, 6 (1984), p. 39.

4   *The Autobiography of William Butler Yeats* (New York: The Macmillan Co., 1953), p. 87. For the dating of this section, see Joseph Ronsley, *Yeats's Autobiography: Life as Symbolic Pattern* (Cambridge, Mass.: Harvard University Press, 1968), p. 25.

5   *On the Boiler* (Dublin: The Cuala Press, 1938), pp. 33-34.

6   *The Variorum Edition of the Plays of W.B. Yeats*. (ed.) Russell K. Alspach (New York: Macmillan, 1966), pp. 11, 229-31.

7   *Ibid.*, sc. III, 11, 10-22.

8   *Autobiography*, pp. 70-1.

9   *Ibid.*, p. 48.

10   Anne Barton notes that 'the cool and rational Horatio behaves surprisingly at the end' ('Introduction', *The New Penguin Shakespeare*, p. 52).

11   William W. Main observes that 'Horatio cannot command the Ghost to speak. The low-frequency wave length of reason cannot tune in on the high-frequency band of revelation. The mediator between these two wave lengths of knowing . . . will be Prince Hamlet', 'Intertextual Commentary', *Hamlet* (New York: The Odyssey Press, 1983), p. 6.

12   In *The Renaissance in England: Non-dramatic Prose and Verse of the Sixteenth Century*, (ed.) Hyder E. Rollins and Herschel Baker (Boston: D.C. Heath, 1954), p. 477. Yeats, in 'A Prayer for My Daughter', celebrates the soul's solipsism: 'The soul recovers radical innocence / And learns at last that it is self-delighting'.

13   *Boiler*, p. 27.

14   'I wish Hamlet had made some other defence; it is unsuitable to the character of a good or a brave man, to shelter himself in falsehood', *Johnson: Prose and Poetry*, (ed.) Mona Wilson (Cambridge, Mass.: Harvard University Press, 1951), p. 617.

15   For a perceptive analysis of Hamlet's relationship with the gravedigger, see R.S. White, 'The Spirit of Yorick, Or the Tragic Sense of Humour in *Hamlet*', *Hamlet Studies*, 7 (1985), p. 14.

16   M.C. Bradbrook, review of *Hamlet Closely Observed* by Martin Dodsworth, in *Hamlet Studies*, 8 (1986), p. 111.

17   This contradiction has been noted by James P. Hammersmith, '*Hamlet* and the Myth of Memory', *ELH*, 45 (Winter 1978), p. 597. It has been pointed out that before parliamentary reform came from 1840 to 1855, 'in the churchyards coffins were placed tier above tier in the graves until they were within a few feet (or sometimes even a few inches) of the surface, and the level of the ground was often raised to that of the lower windows of the church. To make room for fresh interments the sextons had recourse to the surreptitious removal of bones and partially decayed remains' ('Cemetery', *Ency. Brit.* 11th ed.).

18   *Autobiography*, p. 318.

19   *Essays and Introductions* (London: Macmillan, 1961), pp. 215-16.

20   *A Vision* (2d ed. 1937; London: Macmillan, 1962), p. 181.

21   *Uncollected Prose* by W.B. Yeats, (ed.) John P. Frayne (London: Macmillan, 1970), vol. I, p. 266.

22   *Vision*, p. 294.

23   *A Vision*, (ed.) George Mills Harper and Walter Kelly Hood (1st ed. 1925; London: Macmillan 1978), pp. 171-2.

24   Richard Ellmann, *James Joyce* (New York: Oxford University Press, 1965), p. 87.

25   Horatio states that he saw old King Hamlet 'once' (1.2.186), the occasion being the vanquishing of 'ambitious Norway' and 'the sledded Polacks' (1.1.59-64). According to the Gravedigger this victory coincided with Hamlet's birth (5.1.142-45) as well as with his own

appointment as sexton thirty years ago (5.1.141, 160). If, at that time, Horatio was a young soldier in the Danish army, he must be considerably older than Hamlet. For an incisive exploration of Horatio's role in the drama, see Alethea Hayter, *Horatio's Version* (London: Faber, 1972).

26 Though, for Harold Jenkins, 'Shakespeare seems undecided whether Horatio is in Elsinore as a visitor or a denizen' (*Hamlet*, Arden, p. 123).

27 Most persuasively by Maynard Mack, 'The World of *Hamlet*', *The Yale Review*, XLI (1952), pp. 520-21.

28 *Essays and Introductions*, p. 240.

29 I am grateful to my colleague, Professor A.N. Kaul, for having given me several excellent suggestions for the improvement of this paper.

Labour and Memory in the Love Poetry of W.B. Yeats

ELIZABETH BUTLER CULLINGFORD

The following works by Yeats will be cited within parentheses in the text:

Autobiographies (London: Macmillan, 1955).
Collected Plays, 2nd ed. (London: Macmillan, 1952).
Essays and Introductions (London: Macmillan, 1961).
Variorum Poems, (eds.) Peter Allt and Russel K. Alspach assisted by Catherine Alspach (London: Macmillan, 1966).
A Vision, Rev. ed. (London: Macmillan, 1962).

1 Sigmund Freud, *The Standard Edition*, trans. James Strachey, 24 vols. (London: The Hogarth Press, 1974), II, pp. 188-9.

2 Kurt Heinzelman, *The Economics of the Imagination* (Amherst: University of Massachusetts Press, 1980), p. 153.

3 William Morris, *Collected Works* (ed.) May Morris. 24 vols. (London: Longmans Green and Co., 1910-15), XXIII, p. 203.

4 John Ruskin, *Collected Works* (eds.) E.T. Cook and Alexander Wedderburn, 39 vols. (London: Allen and Unwin, 1903-12), XVII, p. 183.

5 James Olney, *The Rhizome and the Flower* (Berkeley: University of California Press, 1980), pp. 259-60.

6 Harold Bloom, *Yeats* (London: Oxford University Press, 1970), p. 167.

7 George Santayana, *The Life of Reason* (New York: Scribner's, 1955), p. 290.

8 William Earle, 'Memory', *The Review of Metaphysics* 10 (1956), pp. 14, 15.

9 Plato, *Symposium*, trans. Walter Hamilton (Harmondsworth: Penguin, 1951), p. 95.

10 Quoted in A. Norman Jeffares, *A New Commentary on the Poems of W.B. Yeats* (London: Macmillan, 1984), p. 251.

11 Plato, *Symposium*, pp. 60, 64.

12 See Cleanth Brooks, 'Yeats's Great Rooted Blossomer', *The Well Wrought Urn* (New York: Reynal and Hitchcock, 1947), p. 168; John Wain, 'Among School Children', *Interpretations*, (ed.) John Wain, 2nd ed. (London and Boston: Routledge and Kegan Paul, 1972), p. 197.

13 Plato, *Phaedrus and Letters VII and VIII*, trans. Walter Hamilton (Harmondsworth: Penguin, 1973), p. 58.

14 Thomas Parkinson, *W.B. Yeats: The Later Poetry* (Berkeley: University of California Press, 1971), p. 102.

15 Plato, *Phaedrus*, pp. 57, 55.

16 Plato, *Symposium*, p. 87.

17 David Lynch, *Yeats: The Poetics of the Self* (Chicago and London: University of Chicago Press, 1979), p. 47.

18 Plato, *Phaedrus*, p. 60.

19 Morris, *Works*, XXIII, p. 17.

W.B. Yeats and That High Horse

JON STALLWORTHY

1   Seamus Heaney, *Preoccupations: Selected Prose 1968-1978* (London: Faber and Faber, 1980), p. 101.
2   'If I were Four-and-Twenty', 1919, reprinted in *Explorations* (London: Macmillan, 1962), p. 263.
3   See Stallworthy, *Vision and Revision in Yeats's Last Poems* (Oxford: Clarendon Press, 1969), pp. 170-1.
4   My italics, here and in the quotation that follows.
5   Allan Wade, (ed.) *The Letters of W.B. Yeats* (London: Rupert Hart-Davis, 1954), p. 63.
6   Wade, *Letters*, p. 379.
7   *Ibid.*, p. 397.
8   'Dust hath closed Helen's Eye', 1900, reprinted in *Mythologies* (London: Macmillan, 1959), pp. 22-30.
9   *Discoveries*, 1906, reprinted in *Essays and Introductions* (London: Macmillan, 1961), p. 291.
10   He wrote a fourth, 'Reprisals', in late 1920, but did not print it in his *Collected Poems* for fear of offending Lady Gregory. See Peter Allt and Russell K. Alspach, (eds.) *The Variorum Edition of the Poems of W.B. Yeats* (London: Macmillan, 1957), p. 791, and Richard J. Finneran, 'The Manuscripts of W.B. Yeats's "Reprisals"', *Text: Transactions of the Society for Textual Scholarship*, vol. 2, (1985), pp. 269-77.
11   I am indebted for this information and much illumination of Yeats's poems of this period to Daniel A. Harris, *Yeats / Coole Park and Ballylee* (Baltimore: The John Hopkins University Press, 1974).
12   See Curtis Bradford, *Yeats's 'Last Poems' Again*, Dolmen Press Centenary Paper VIII, edited by Liam Miller (Dublin: The Dolmen Press, 1966), pp. 257-88.

'What Can I But Enumerate Old Themes'

PETER KUCH

1   W.B. Yeats, 'Reconciliation', in Peter Allt and Russell K Alspach (eds.), *The Variorum Edition of the Poems of W.B. Yeats* (1956: rpt New York: Macmillan, 1973), p. 257. Hereafter Yeats, *V.P.*
2   Yeats, 'Friends', *V.P.*, pp. 315-316.
3   W.B. Yeats to John Quinn, 15 May 1903, in Allan Wade (ed.) *The Letters of W.B. Yeats* (London: Rupert Hart-Davis, 1954), p. 403. Hereafter Wade, (ed.) *Letters*.
4   W.B. Yeats to G.W. Russell, April 1904?, in Wade, (ed.) *Letters*, pp. 434-435.
5   Yeats, *V.P.*, p. 849.
6   W.B. Yeats, 'Discoveries', *Essays* (London: Macmillan, 1924), p. 366.
7   Denis Donoghue (ed.), *W.B. Yeats: Autobiography—First Draft Journal* (London: Macmillan, 1972), p. 184. Hereafter Yeats, *Memoirs*.
8   Unlocated.
9   Yeats, 'A Coat', *V.P.*, p. 320.
10   W.B. Yeats, *A Vision* (London: Macmillan, 1925), p. xii.
11   Yeats, 'The Circus Animals' Desertion', *V.P.*, p. 629.
12   Quoted in A.N. Jeffares, *A New Commentary on the Poems of W.B. Yeats* (London: Macmillan, 1984), p. 251. My Italics.
13   Yeats, *Memoirs*, pp. 230-231. My Italics.
14   Yeats, 'The Song of the Happy Shepherd', *V.P.*, pp. 66-67.
15   Yeats, 'His Dream', *V.P.*, pp. 253-254. See also Yeats, *Memoirs*, pp. 231-232.

16   George Mills Harper, *Yeats's Golden Dawn* (London: Macmillan, 1974), p. 161. See also Yeats, *Memoirs*, p. 141.
17   Yeats, *Memoirs*, p. 49.
18   *Ibid.*, pp. 47-48. Parnell died in Brighton on 6 October 1891, and was buried in Glasnevin Cemetry, Dublin, on 11 October. See also Yeats, *Memoirs*, p. 133.
19   See Yeats, 'Mourn—And Then Onward!', *V.P.*, pp. 737-738.
20   Yeats, 'The Song of the Happy Shepherd', *V.P.*, p. 66.
21   Yeats, 'The Madness of King Goll', *V.P.*, pp. 81-86.
22   Yeats, 'Fergus and the Druid', *V.P.*, p. 103.
23   Yeats, 'Who Goes with Fergus?', *V.P.*, pp. 125-126.
24   Yeats, 'The Hosting of the Sidhe', *V.P.*, pp. 140-141.
25   Yeats, 'The Song of the Happy Shepherd', *V.P.*, p. 67.
26   Douglas Hyde, *A Literary History of Ireland* (London: T. Fisher Unwin, 1906), pp. 281-282.
27   Yeats, 'The Grey Rock', *V.P.*, p. 275.
28   *Ibid.*, pp. 276.
29   W.B. Yeats, *Autobiographies* (London: Macmillan, 1956), p. 303.
30   *Ibid.*, pp. 222-223.
31   Yeats, 'Ego Dominus Tuus', *V.P.*, p. 369.
32   Yeats, 'The Grey Rock', *V.P.*, pp. 272-273.
33   Yeats, 'The Hosting of the Sidhe', *V.P.*, pp. 140-141.
34   Yeats, 'The Three Beggars', *V.P.*, p. 279.
35   Yeats, 'Fergus and the Druid', *V.P.*, p. 104.
36   Yeats, 'Under the Moon', *V.P.*, p. 210.
37   Yeats, 'The Circus Animals' Desertion', *V.P.*, p. 629.
38   Yeats, 'No Second Troy', *V.P.*, p. 257.
39   Yeats, 'The Rose of the World', *V.P.*, p. 111.
40   *Ibid.*, p. 112.
41   Yeats, 'No Second Troy', *V.P.*, p. 257.
42   *Ibid.*, p. 256.
43   Yeats, 'Old Memory', *V.P.*, p. 201.
44   Yeats, 'Reconciliation', *V.P.*, p. 257.
45   Yeats, 'When You are Old', *V.P.*, pp. 120-121.
46   Yeats, 'The Folly of Being Comforted', *V.P.*, p. 200.
47   Yeats, 'Peace', *V.P.*, pp. 258-259.
48   Quoted in Richard Ellmann, *Yeats, The Man and the Masks* (London: Faber, 1948), p. 161.
49   Yeats, 'Words', *V.P.*, pp. 255-256.
50   Yeats, 'He thinks of those who have Spoken Evil of His Beloved', *V.P.*, p. 166.
51   Yeats, 'Against Unworthy Praise', *V.P.*, pp. 259-260.
52   Yeats, 'A Woman Homer Sung', *V.P.*, pp. 254-255.
53   W.B. Yeats to Olivia Shakespear, 30 June 1932 in Wade, (ed.) *Letters*, pp. 797-798.

Yeats's Stream of Consciousness

TERENCE DIGGORY

1   Balachandra Rajan, 'Its Own Executioner: Yeats and the Fragment', *Yeats: An Annual of Critical and Textual Studies* 3 (Ithaca: Cornell University Press, 1985), p. 78. For Ginsberg, O'Hara and Dorn, see Marjorie Perloff, *The Poetics of Indeterminacy: Rimbaud to Cage* (Princeton: Princeton University Press, 1981), p. 156.
2   Rajan, 'Its Own Executioner', pp. 74, 85, 73. In a fuller presentation of his thesis, focused on poets other than Yeats, Rajan distinguishes his approach from Perloff by noting 'that Perloff is specifically concerned with undecidability embedded in the fabric of discourse', a concern that I share. See Rajan, *The Form of the Unfinished: English Poetics from Spenser to Pound*

(Princeton: Princeton University Press, 1985), p. 301. All dates given in parenthesis in the text are those of first publication.

3 *PMLA* 82 (1967), p. 446.
4 *Ibid.*, p. 454.
5 Perloff, *Poetics*, p. 18.
6 Perloff, 'Spatial Form', p. 446.
7 Perloff, *Poetics*, p. 33.
8 *Ibid.*, p. 177.
9 Quoted in *Ibid.*, p. 197.
10 (Oxford: Clarendon, 1936). The section on Pound appears on pp. xxiii-xxvi.
11 Perloff, *Poetics*, p. 156.
12 *Ibid.*
13 W.B. Yeats, *Autobiographies* (London: Macmillan, 1955), p. 461.
14 *The Poems of W.B. Yeats*, new ed., (ed.) Richard J. Finneran (New York: Macmillan, 1983), p. 181.
15 *A Critical Edition of Yeats's* A Vision (1925), (eds.) George Mills Harper and Walter Kelly Hood (London: Macmillan, 1978), p. 212.
16 Yeats, *Essays and Introductions* (New York: Macmillan, 1961), p. 405.
17 Richard Ellmann, *Eminent Domain: Yeats among Wilde, Joyce, Pound, Eliot and Auden* (1967; rpt. New York: Oxford University Press, 1970), p. 52.
18 *Oxford Book of Modern Verse*, p. xxviii.
19 *Ibid.*, p. xxix.
20 *The Letters of W.B. Yeats*, (ed.) Allan Wade (London: Hart-Davis, 1954), p. 651.
21 Ellmann, pp. 49, 52.
22 Yeats, *Essays and Introductions*, p. 235-6.
23 *Ibid.*, p. 225.
24 Ellmann, p. 59.
25 *Ibid.*, p. 85.
26 *Poems*, pp. 181, 179, 194.
27 Hugh Kenner, 'Some Post-Symbolist Structures', in Frank Brady, John Palmer and Martin Price, (eds.), *Literary Theory and Structure: Essays in Honor of William K. Wimsatt* (New Haven: Yale University Press, 1973), p. 392.
28 *Poems*, pp. 210, 196, 216.
29 William E. Baker, *Syntax in English Poetry 1870-1930* (Berkeley: University of California Press, 1967), pp. 85, 45, 51.
30 Dorrit Cohn, *Transparent Minds: Narrative Modes for Presenting Consciousness in Fiction* (Princeton: Princeton University Press, 1978), pp. 90-1.
31 *Ibid.*, p. 92.
32 *Critical Edition of* A Vision (1925), p. 211.
33 Perloff, 'Spatial Form', p. 452.
34 Cleanth Brooks, *The Well Wrought Urn: Studies in the Structure of Poetry* (1947; rpt. New York: Harvest-Harcourt n.d.), pp. 179-80. For the poem, see Yeats, *Poems*, p. 215-17.
35 Brooks, p. 191; Brooks's emphasis.
36 Hugh Kenner, *A Colder Eye: The Modern Irish Writers* (New York: Knopf, 1983), pp. 185-6.
37 *Poems*, p. 80.
38 Thomas Parkinson, *W.B. Yeats, The Later Poetry*, combined ed. with *W.B. Yeats, Self-Critic* (Berkeley: University of California Press, 1971), p. 97.
39 John Wain, 'Yeats: *Among School Children*', in John Wain, (ed.), *Interpretations* (London: Routledge, 1955), p. 198.
40 See Parkinson, pp. 97-9, for the manuscript evidence; Yeats, *Poems*, p. 597, for Yeats's notes.
41 Robert Langbaum, *The Poetry of Experience: The Dramatic Monologue in Modern Literary Tradition* (1957; rpt. New York: Norton, 1963), p. 146.
42 Roman Jakobson, 'Two Aspects of Language and Two Types of Aphasic Disturbance', in Jakobson, *Selected Writings 2: Word and Language* (The Hague: Mouton, 1971), pp. 258-9.
43 James Joyce, *Ulysses: The Corrected Text*, (ed.) Hans Walter Gabler (New York: Random, 1986), pp. 23-4.

44 *The Variorum Edition of the Plays of W.B. Yeats*, (ed.) Russell K. Alspach (New York: Macmillan, 1969), p. 399.
45 *Critical Edition of* A Vision (1925), pp. 211, 215.
46 *Poems*, p. 205.
47 *Critical Edition of* A Vision (1925), pp. 211-12.
48 Frank Kermode, *Romantic Image* (London: Routledge & Kegan Paul, 1957; rpt. New York: Vintage, 1964), pp. 83, 164.
49 Paul de Man, 'Semiology and Rhetoric', in de Man, *Allegories of Reading* (New Haven: Yale University Press, 1979), pp. 10-12.
50 Yeats, *Essays and Introductions*, p. 332.
51 Michael P. Gallagher, 'Yeats, Syntax, and the Self', *Arizona Quarterly* 26 (1970), pp. 5-16.
52 Quoted in Yeats, *Essays and Introductions*, p. 332.
53 'Lyric and Modernity', in de Man, *Blindness and Insight: Essays in the Rhetoric of Contemporary Criticism*, 2nd ed., rev. (Minneapolis: University of Minnesota Press, 1983), pp. 170-1.
54 *Ibid.*, pp. 186, 171.
55 *Ibid.*, p. 183.
56 Yeats, *A Vision* (London: Macmillan, 1962), p. 302.
57 Yeats, *Essays and Introductions*, p. 419.
58 *Ibid.*, p. 420.

Yeats: The Masker and the Masks

JAMES FLANNERY

This essay was first delivered as a lecture at the Yeats International Summer School, Sligo, on August 19, 1987.

1 J.A. Barish, *The Anti-Theatrical Prejudice* (Berkeley and Los Angeles: University of California Press, 1981), p. 1. I am indebted to a perceptive essay by David E.R. George ('Letter to a Poor Actor', *New Theatre Quarterly*, Vol. II, No. 8, pp. 352-363) for many insights that effectively counter the negative associations with the concept of theatricality.
2 Plato, *The Dialogues*, 4th ed., trans. B. Jowett (Oxford: Clarendon Press, 1953), pp. 241, 479-480.
3 W.B. Yeats, *Autobiographies* (London: Macmillan, 1955), pp. 461, 470.
4 L.A.G. Strong, 'William Butler Yeats', in Stephen Gwynn, (ed.) *Scattering Branches: Tributes to the Memory of W.B. Yeats* (London: Macmillan, 1940), pp. 195-196.
5 See Elinor Fuchs, 'The Theatricalization of American Politics', (*American Theatre*, Vol. 3, No. 12, January 1987, pp. 17-21, 44) for a brilliant anyalysis of how theatrical techniques are widely appropriated to manipulate our lives in contemporary society.
6 Erving Goffman, *The Presentation of Self in Everyday Life* (Garden City, New York: Doubleday, 1959), p. 244. Cf. George *op. cit.*, pp. 353-354, for a refutation of Goffman's theories on solid theatrical ground.
7 George points out that Stanislavsky, in fact, breaks down the process of acting into three stages: finding personal experiences that overlap with the given circumstances of the character; exploring in the rehearsal process the best technical means of demonstrating the character's feelings to the audience; and mobilizing the resources of self, character, and actor in the act of performance. *Ibid.*, pp. 359-361.
8 Norman Holland, *Five Readers Reading* (New Haven: Yale University Press, 1975), pp. 60, 227-228. As A.W. Meisner explains, the self 'implies a larger frame of reference within which . . . interaction between the . . . id, ego, and superego [takes place]. The self comprises the basic drives of libido—the force that seeks union with others—and of aggression—the force that separates one from others, or individuates; various defenses against the immediate expression of these drives; and the ego, the structure or process that organizes the manifes-

tations of drives and defenses, trying to satisfy as many of them as it can in face of numerous obstacles. The parts of the self do not exist in an isolated or pure state; they are interwoven with and actually formed by, internal objects, or 'introjects', the psychic residue or precipitates of a person's experience with significant others. As representations populating our 'inner world', introjects colour our perceptions of the external world and even determine the strategies we use to satisfy conflicting drives; as structural forces introjects decide the specific aims and intersities of the drives themselves.' *Internalization in Psychoanalysis* (New York: International Universities, 1981), p. 67.

9 *Autobiographies*, pp. 354, 274.

10 *Ibid.*, p. 465.

11 Through his doctrine of the mask Yeats believed that a person could oppose the tyranny of a fated self. 'A writer must die every day he lives, be reborn, as it is said in the Burial Service, an incorruptible self, that self opposite of all that he has named "himself".' Yeats described this process as 'an intellectual daily re-creation of all that exterior fate snatches away, and so that fate's antithesis'. Even in defeat there was psychic triumph, if one truly grappled with the imperatives of the mask. Thus 'We begin to live when we have conceived life as tragedy'. *Autobiographies*, pp. 457, 189.

12 *Mythologies* (London: Macmillan, 1972), p. 331.

13 *Yeats and the Theatre*, (eds.) Robert O'Driscoll and Lorna Reynolds (Toronto: Macmillan of Canada, 1975), pp. 18-19.

14 *Essays and Introductions* (New York: Macmillan, 1961), p. 270.

15 *Yeats and the Theatre*, pp. 17-18.

16 *A Critical Edition of Yeats's* A Vision (1925), (eds.) George Mills Harper and Walter Kelly (London: Macmillan, 1978), pp. 17-18.

17 *Essays and Introductions*, pp. 292-293. Yeats's concept of Unity of Being parallels Carl Jung's idea of individuation, that is, an integration of mind, body, sensibility, and imagination through a deliberate effort to energize the total resources of the conscious and unconscious mind. Cf *Memories, Dreams and Reflections*, (ed.) Aniela Jaffe (New York: Vintage Books, 1963), pp. 335-337.

18 *A Critical Edition of* A Vision, *op. cit.*, pp. 18-19.

19 Letter to John Butler Yeats (February 23, 1910), *The Letters of W.B. Yeats*, (ed.) Allan Wade (London: Rupert Hart-Davis, 1954), pp. 548-549.

20 *Autobiographies*, p. 125.

21 *Yeats: The Man and the Masks* (London: Faber and Faber, 1961), pp. 186-187.

22 'Eightieth Birthday Interview', *Mime Journal*, (ed.) Thomas Leabhart (Nos. 7 and 8, 1978), p. 61.

23 My knowledge of the LeCoq system of mask training derives from workshops in 1973 and 1974 with Fred Euringer, Professor of Drama at Queen's University, Kingston, Ontario, and with Richard Pochinko, then in charge of the Youth Theatre Company of the National Arts Center, Ottawa. Euringer and Pochinko each studied with LeCoq in Paris. My further knowledge of neutral and character masks derives from a series of experiments I have carried out as a teacher of acting and as a director of seventeen of Yeats's plays, several of them more than once, over the past twenty years at professional theatres in Canada, the United States and Ireland.

24 *Essays and Introductions*, p. 266.

25 *Memories for Tomorrow: The Memoirs of Jean-Louis Barrault* (New York: E.P. Dutton, 1974), p. 205.

26 See William Arrowsmith, 'Translator's Memo to the Director', *Theater* (Vol. II, no. 3, Summer 1980, pp. 16-17). See also the introduction to his translation of Euripides' *Alcestis* (New York: Oxford University Press, 1974, pp. 4-10) for a discussion of how masks were employed in Greek theatre to express what Arrowsmith terms a 'modal' rather than individualistic form of psychology.

27 Yeats equated the process of writing with methods he learned in the Order of the Golden Dawn for 'skrying', or evoking visions, through a highly disciplined meditation on selected symbols. Through a similar process the poet purified his mind so that 'the little ritual of his verse' more and more resembled 'the great ritual of nature . . .' In this way the poet became,

'as all the great mystics have believed, a vessel of the creative power of God'. *Essays and Introductions*, pp. 201-202.

28 (Berkeley: University of California Press, 1986), p. 18.
29 *Mythologies*, p. 339.
30 *Essays and Introductions*, pp. 287-288.
31 Israel Regardie, *The Tree of Life: A Study in Magic* (New York: Samuel Weiser, 1973), pp. 68-69. Cf. *The Portable Jung*, (ed.) Joseph Campbell (New York: Viking Press, 1971), p. 60.
32 Virginia Moore, *The Unicorn* (New York: Macmillan, 1954), pp. 187-188.
33 *Man and the Masks*, p. 199.
34 This is the idea lying behind Gordon Craig's controversial concept of the *Ubermarrionette* as the ideal actor—an idea with which Yeats concurred and later experienced in the art of the Japanese dancer-actor Michio Ito. See my discussion of Yeats's relationship with, respectively, Craig and Ito in *W.B. Yeats and the Idea of a Theatre: The Early Abbey Theatre in Theory and Practice* (New Haven: Yale University Press, 1976), pp. 266-268, 207-208.
35 See *Masks in Modern Drama*, Susan Harris Smith (Berkeley: University of California Press, 1984) for a comprehensive analysis of these forms of masking as utilized by dramatists as diverse as Büchner, Jarry, Andreyev, Brecht, O'Neill, Cocteau, Goll and Genet. Yeats is unique among modern dramatists in that his plays involve all of the main masking forms discussed by Smith.
36 Robert Avens, *Imagination is Reality: Western Nirvana in Jung, Hillman, Barfield and Cassirer* (Dallas: Spring Press, 1980), p. 8. According to Corbin the 'imaginal' functions as an intermediary between the sensible world and the intelligible, or intellectual and spiritual, world.
37 'A People's Theatre' (1919), *Explorations* (London: Macmillan, 1962), p. 255.
38 Preface to *The Collected Works of W.B. Yeats* (Stratford-on-Avon: A.H. Bullen, 1908).
39 *Samhain* Number Three (September 1903), pp. 30-31. *Samhain* was the literary organ of the Irish dramatic movement.
40 *Yeats, Ireland and Fascism* (London: Macmillan, 1981), pp. 234.
41 This passage is quoted by Seamus Deane in his *Celtic Revivals* (London: Faber and Faber, 1985), p. 112 and attributed to *A Vision*, revised edition (London: Macmillan, 1962), p. 126. Unfortunately, I have not been able to verify this source, though, whether or not the statement is actually by Yeats, it sheds new light on his ironic view of Cuchulain in relation to modern Ireland.
42 *The Irish Mind: Exploring Intellectual Traditions* (Dublin: Wolfhound Press, 1985), pp. 9-10.
43 Fragment, dated October 1913, quoted in A. Norman Jeffares, *W.B. Yeats: Man and Poet* (London: Routledge and Kegan Paul, 1962), p. 318.
44 *Yeats* (London: Oxford University Press, 1970), pp. 471-472.
45 *Explorations*, p. 28.
46 *Samhain* Number Seven (November 1908), p. 8.
47 See note 37.
48 'O'Casey and Yeats: Exemplary Dramatists', *Celtic Revivals*, p. 116.
49 *Ibid.*, p. 122.

Joyce and Mythology

TERRY EAGLETON

1 See Walter Benjamin, *Charles Baudelaire: A Lyric Poet in the Era of High Capitalism* (London, 1973).
2 See Walter Benjamin, *The Origin of German Tragic Drama* (London, 1977).
3 See Claude Lévi-Strauss, *The Savage Mind* (London, 1966).
4 See Roland Barthes, *Mythologies* (London, 1973).

5   See Walter Benjamin, 'The Work of Art in the Age of Mechanical Reproduction', in
    Illuminations (London, 1970).
6   Franco Moretti, 'The Long Goodbye', in *Signs taken for Wonders* (London, 1983).
7   Sean Golden, 'Post-traditional English literature: a polemic', in *The Crane Bag Book of Irish
    Studies* (Dublin: Blackwater Press, 1982).
8   Walter Benjamin, 'Theses on the Philosophy of History', in *Illuminations*.

Mr Leopold Bloom and the Lost Vermeer

MARY T. REYNOLDS

1   Citations to *Ulysses* are given for two editions. *U* 78 refers to the Random House Modern
    Library edition of 1934/1961. VP 5.289 refers to the Viking Press-Penguin paperback edition
    of the 1984 revised edition issued in three volumes. *Ulysses: Student's Edition*. The Corrected
    Text edited by Hans Walter Gabler with Wolfhard Steppe and Claus Melchior. With a new
    preface by Richard Ellmann. (Penguin Books, Viking Press and The Bodley Head. New York
    and London, 1986) Citations in the text will give page numbers for the Random House
    edition; for the Penguin edition, episode number and line number will be given. Thus *U* 78
    will indicate page 78 of the Random House edition; VP 5.289 will indicate Episode 5 (Lotus
    Eaters), line 289. Citations to *A Portrait of the Artist* will be given in the text as P; to *Stephen
    Hero* as SH.
2   I am greatly indebted to Professor J. Michael Montias, of Yale, for suggesting to me that the
    picture of Martha and Mary cited in *U* 78/*U-G* I.159 might be the painting of this subject by
    Vermeer in the Edinburgh Museum. Professor Montias's research in the Dutch archives has
    made him the leading authority on Vermeer's family and his life. See his *Vermeer and His
    Milieu: A Web of Social History* (Princeton: Princeton University Press, 1988).
3   A.B. deVries, *Jan Vermeer de Delft* (Paris: Editions Pierre Tisne, 1948), from Willem van de
    Watering's *Catalogue* in Albert Blankert, *Vermeer of Delft: A Complete Edition of the
    Paintings* (London: Oxford University Press, Phaidon Books, 1978). The most objective
    dating is 1653-1655, and the painting is probably Vermeer's first known painting. The design
    of the rug was discovered by Blankert, who is now the leading authority on the paintings of
    Vermeer.
4   Edward A. Snow, *A Study of Vermeer* (Berkeley: University of California Press, 1979), pp.
    122-124. Nanette Salomon, in 'Vermeer and the Balance of Destiny', discusses a later
    Vermeer which is thematically linked to Martha and Mary, in *Essays in Northern European
    Art*, presented to Egbert Havekamp-Begemann on his Sixtieth Birthday (Doornspijk, 1983),
    pp. 216-221.
5   Blankert, *op. cit.*, p. 13; and C. Hofstede de Groot, *Catalogue of Dutch Painters: The Works of
    the Most Eminent* (London: Macmillan, 1908), Vol. I, p. 582. It is possible that Joyce saw de
    Groot's book.
6   From the unnamed Bristol furniture dealer the painting went to the collection of Arthur
    Leslie Collie in London. It was bought by Forbes and Paterson, who sold it to W.A. Coats.
    Catalogue of Paintings and Sculpture, National Gallery of Scotland, 51st edition, Edinburgh
    1957.
7   Don Gifford and Robert J. Seidman, *Notes for Joyce: An Annotation of James Joyce's Ulysses*
    (New York: Dutton, 1974), p. 69; Weldon Thornton, *Allusions in Ulysses* (New York: Simon
    and Schuster and University of North Carolina Press, 1973), p. 81; Stuart Gilbert, *James
    Joyce's Ulysses* (New York: Knopf, Vintage Books, 1955), p. 154; and Frank Budgen, *James
    Joyce and the Making of Ulysses* (New York: Harrison Smith and Robert Haas, 1934), p. 83.
8   Philip Herring, 'Lotus Eaters' in (eds.) Clive Hart and David Hayman, *James Joyce's Ulysses*
    (Berkeley: University of California Press, 1974), p. 82 note 12.
9   Michael Groden, *Ulysses in Progress* (Princeton: Princeton University Press, 1977), pp. 27-30,
    67, 77, 217-220. When the fourth chapter reached Ezra Pound, he deleted some twenty lines

before sending it on to Jane Heap; the fact that Joyce made no objection to Pound's arbitrary action indicates the strong anxiety Joyce felt about getting his book published.

10 Richard Ellmann, *James Joyce*, new and revised edition (New York, OxfordUniversity Press, 1982), pp. 421-22, 472, 497, 502-504.

11 Sylvia Beach, *Shakespeare and Company* (New York: Harcourt Brace, 1959), pp. 47-49; Ellmann, *op. cit.*, 504-508, 523-526.

12 Groden, *op. cit.*, p. 217. A full account of the evolution of the Lotus Eaters episode is given in Walton Litz, *The Art of James Joyce*, pp. 6, 10, 11, 46-49, 143. There is early evidence of the Vermeer motif in Joyce's British Museum notesheets, not in the Lotus Eaters section but under Nausicaa. Joyce writes 'Mary and Martha, picture', a note that is crossed out in blue crayon, at Nausicaa 6 line 65; 'Martha gives virility to man' at Nausicaa 6 line 105; and 'Molly lustful only when well dressed' at line 80. The latter two are crossed out in red.

Studies of Joyce's practice in using crayons of different colours suggest, without being definitive, that items cancelled in blue 'formed the heart of the Rosenbach manuscript'; in any case, these items have all been found to enter the text later than the *Little Review* serialization. *Joyce's Ulysses Notesheets in the British Museum*, (ed.) Philip Herring (Charlottesville: University of Virginia Press, 1972), pp. 29, 151, 152, 523-531.

13 For the *Ulysses* MS in facsimile, see *James Joyce's Ulysses: The MS and Final Printings Compared*, annotated, with a Preface by Clive Driver (New York: Octagon Books, 1975), Vol. II, at P75-76/L96-97/N78-79. The page is marked '9' in Joyce's hand. Clive Driver adopted a system of paging the facsimile by reference to the (then) three printed editions of *Ulysses*: P for the Paris edition of 1922, L for the 1960 London edition by Bodley Head, and N for the 1961 New York edition by Random House.

The *Little Review* version is in Vol. 5, No. 3 (July 1918), pp. 44-45. The *Little Review* is outside the text's line of transmission, and therefore was omitted from the facsimile edition of Joyce's manuscripts, the *James Joyce Archive*. Joyce did make revisions of the serialized chapters on some numbers of *The Egoist*, which are included in the *Archive* but do not include the Lotus Eaters episode.

14 There is one exception, but it would not have come to Joyce's notice. This is the painting by Jan Steen, a Delft painter of the mid-seventeenth century, who portrayed the three figures around a table in the same pose, a composition manifestly derived from Steen's study of Vermeer. His painting came to light some thirty years after the 1901 discovery of Vermeer's 'Christ in the House of Martha and Mary'. Blankert, *op. cit.*, p. 13.

15 Cheryl Herr, in 'Nature and Culture in the Sirens Episode', *Essays in Literature*, Vol. 11, No. 1 (Spring 1984), argues that stereotyped ideas and behaviour surface in Bloom's thoughts and in the narrative commentary of the Sirens episode. This is quite correct, but her sociological approach ignores the finely drawn distinctions Joyce has made between Bloom's silent monologue and his spoken words, and between Bloom's lines in general in comparison with the lines attributed (in a variety of ways) to the other characters in the episode. She also ignores the technical comments on music that Joyce has given to Bloom, and therefore misses the subtlety of Joyce's point on absolute pitch and the pianist, 'Father' Cowley.

16 Budgen, *op. cit.*, p. 17.

17 My information comes from investigations made for me by Eileen O'Brien and David Wickens. I have not been able to consult the *Weekly Irish Times*; the National Library in Dublin does not have it, and the only complete file between 1901 and 1904 is in the British Library in London.

18 For the Vermeer painting see National Gallery of Scotland, *Catalogue of Paintings and Sculpture*, 51st ed., Edinburgh 1957; for the Rubens, with a photograph of the painting, National Gallery of Ireland, *Concise Catalogue*, 1964, pp. 62, 113.

See also *The Athenaeum* (London), No. 3831 (March 30, 1901), p. 409, 'The Newly Discovered Vermeer'. The article is taken from D.S. MacColl, A Note on Vermeer of Delft and the Picture 'Christ with Martha and Mary' (London, 1901); MacColl was Keeper of the Tate Gallery, and his reminiscences are in Dugold Sutherland MacColl, *Confessions of a Keeper* and Other Papers (London: Macmillan, 1931).

19 'Ibsen's New Drama', in *Critical Writings of James Joyce*, (eds.) Ellsworth Mason and Richard Ellmann (New York: Viking Compass Books, 1965), pp. 47-67. The date of the essay is April 1, 1900. See also Ellmann, *James Joyce*, pp. 74-88.

20 *The Complete Dublin Diary of Stanislaus Joyce*, (ed.) George H. Healey (Ithaca: Cornell University Press, 1971), pp. 24, 78.
21 'Royal Hibernian Academy "Ecce Homo"', *Critical Writings*, pp. 31-37 at p. 35. Professor Montias reminds me that it is amusing to find the great modernist of English literature beginning his career by writing an essay on one of the most conservative painters of his time.
22 My Italics. 'A Neglected Poet', *Ibid.*, pp. 128-129 at p. 129.
23 *The Workshop of Daedalus: James Joyce and the Raw Materials for a Portrait of the Artist as a Young Man*, (eds.) Robert Scholes and Richard M. Kain (Evanston: Northwestern University Press, 1965), pp. 72, 98. The notebook reproduced here contains the early essay (1904), 'A Portrait of the Artist as a Young Man', followed by the notes Joyce made when it was rejected by the Dublin journal *Dana*, at which time he began to enlarge the essay into a novel.
24 *Ibid.*, p. 49; Epiphany No. 39/71. The epiphanies were written between 1900 and 1903.
25 *Letters of James Joyce*, Vol. I, (ed.) Stuart Gilbert (New York: Viking Press, 1957, 1966), p. 256; to Michael Healy, July 1, 1927. Vermeer is not listed in Stuart Gilbert's index to the book, but in a letter of May 31, 1927 Joyce writes to Harriet Shaw Weaver, from the Hague, 'Do you know Johannes Vermeer's *View of Delft?*' *Letters* I, p. 256.
26 Ellmann, *James Joyce*, p. 592 and note 60, a letter to Sylvia Beach on June 6, 1927. The Beach letters have now been published by Indiana University Press, Bloomington.
27 Groden, *op. cit.*, p. 217.
28 *James Joyce's Trieste Library*: A Catalogue of Materials at the Harry Ransom Humanities Research Centre, by Michael Patrick Gillespie with the assistance of Erik Bradford Stocker, Austin, University of Texas 1986. For Joyce's Paris library, see *The Personal Library of James Joyce*: A descriptive Bibliography, by Thomas E. Connolly (Buffalo: The University Bookstore 1957).
29 Ellmann, *James Joyce*, p. 592.
30 *The Encyclopaedia Britannica*, Eleventh Edition (Cambridge: Cambridge University Press, 1911), Vol. XVIII, p. 72. The article on Vermeer is unsigned.
31 Robert Martin Adams, *Surface and Symbol: The Consistency of James Joyce's Ulysses* (New York: Oxford University Press, 1961), p. 250.
The words used in Bloom's description of the Vermeer painting seem to be an echo of a letter written by Joyce to his wife, Nora, at the end of a prolonged separation in 1909: 'Get ready. . . . Get some kind of cheap common comfortable armchair for your lazy lover. Do this above all, darling, as I shall not quit that kitchen for a whole week after I arrive, reading, lolling, smoking, and watching you get ready the meals, talking, talking, talking to you . . . God in heaven I shall be happy there!' *Letters of James Joyce*, Vols. II and III, (ed.) Richard Ellmann (New York: Viking Press, 1966); Vol. II (December 16, 1909), p. 276.
32 Ellmann reports that Joyce said to Louis Gillet, 'Don't make a hero out of me. I'm only a simple middle-class man'. Ellmann adds to this, 'The initial determinant of judgement in his work is the justifiction of the commonplace . . . Bloom is a humble vessel elected to bear and transmit unimpeached the best qualities of the mind'. *James Joyce*, pp. 5, 6.

'There's A Medium in all Things': Joycean Readings

FRITZ SENN

1 All printed texts up to 1987 read 'green'. Joyce meant Stephen to say 'geen', without the liquid that children learn late to pronounce; proof-readers interfered and substituted a wrongly correct form for the correctly wrong one. See Hans Walter Gabler, 'Zur Textgeschichte und Textkritik des "Portrait"', in Wilhelm Füger (ed.) *James Joyce's 'Portrait'* (München: Wilhelm Goldmann Verlag, 1972), p. 20.
2 Parenthetical references are as follows: D=Dubliners (New York: Viking Press, 1969); P=*A Portrait of the Artist as a Young Man* (New York: Viking Press, 1964). FW=*Finnegans Wake* (London: Faber and Faber, 1954); U=*Ulysses*: The Corrected Text edited by Hans Walter

Gabler with Wolfhard Steppe and Claus Melchior (New York: Random House, 1984). The numbers refer to chapter and line within the chapter: 'U9.766' is line 766 in the ninth chapter. The Bodley Head (London) and the Penguin (Harmondsworth) editions follow the same line count and have identical pagination.

3   Richard Ellmann, *Ulysses on the Liffey* (London: Faber and Faber, 1974), p. 8ff.

4   Another passage in *A Portrait* puts 'mass' as quantity right in the context of 'The church is not the stone building nor even the clergy and their dogmas. It is the whole mass of those born into it' (P245). Eveline Hill, about to embark *en route* to, perhaps, Buenos Ayres, catches a glimpse of the 'black mass of the boat' ('Eveline', D40), and some readers cannot help imposing a demonic phantom configuration on what, on the surface, is nothing but a looming bulk. In the same vein, 'Epps's massproduct' (U17.369) has been eucharistically extended, at least in the symbolistic readings that were current in the sixties. Joyce's words have a way of encroaching upon each other, in *Finnegans Wake*, almost inextricably so.

5   Horace, *Satires, Epistles and Ars Poetica*, trans. H. Rushton Fairclough, Loeb Classical Library (Cambridge: Harvard University Press, 1926), pp. 12-3.

6   Its sequel is one that pointedly has no 'fines'—*fin(em) negans*.

7   That aspect has been sketchily dealt with in a talk given at the Tenth International James Joyce Symposium in Copenhagen, 'Joyce the Verb'.

8   Bloom reads the letter he has received from his daughter first summarily, then in its complete wording, and 'Then he read the letter again: twice' (U4.281, 397, 427).

9   Joyce wrote 'called *out*', the form preserved in Hans Walter Gabler's edition. All previous editions perpetuated 'called *up*', which first appeared in the galleys (*placards*) of Darantière, printer in Dijon.

10 *ULYSSES, James Joyce*: An unabridged recording in stereo by Radio Telefis Eireann Players and Guest Artists (Dublin, 1982).

11 *Ulysse*, traduction intégrale par Auguste Morel, assisté par Stuart Gilbert, entièrement revue par Valery Larbaud et l'auteur (Paris: Gallimard, 1948), p. 285.

12 Joyce may have heard Taylor make a similar speech, but he seems to have used printed sources, a newspaper account and a pamphlet, 'The Language of the Outlaw', to confect what essentially pretends to be spoken. See Richard Ellmann, *James Joyce* (New York: Oxford University Press, 1982), p. 90-1, 755-6. In *Ulysses* the question of memory is implicitly posed: how does J.J. O'Molloy remember *verbatim* a speech that was not 'prepared' and not recorded, as there was not 'even one shorthandwriter in the hall' (U7.815)? In medial paradox, a well balanced speech, model of its kind, that has all the appearance of being carefully constructed on paper is said to be unprepared or 'IMPROMPTU'.

13 Bloom does not get through to Alexander Keyes from the newspaper office. The media are joined when, using the telephone, Bloom announces the '*Evening Telegraph* here', and is not understood: ' . . . Yes, *Telegraph* . . . ' (U7.411). Bloom 'phoned from the inner office'. The new invention soon produced a new word, to *phone*, by back-formation, of which the O.E.D. does not list entries before 1900. So 'phoned' (as at U7.62, 411) was still a relatively new word.

14 How can you remember . . . 'Eyes, walk, voice'? (U6.962). These are the characteristic, individual, features that Morpheus, the shaping mimetic god of dreams, knows how to imitate: '*exprimit incessus vultumque sonum loquendi*' (Ovid, *Met.* 11:636), 'gait features sound of speech'.

15 The OED dates 'hallo' 1840, and 'hello' 1854.

16 Compare Gerty MacDowell's mental notation '*tantumer gosa cramen tum*' (U13.499).

17 Stephen Dedalus, in his imaginary telephone call, linked himself with the past, a remote origin: 'Hello! Kinch here. Put me on to Edenville' (U3.39); Bloom imagines a connection with a vague, but possible future.

18 The whole 'Kraarharrk' evocation (from 'After' to 'krpthsth') was inserted at a late stage, on the *Placards* (*James Joyce Archive* 17, 260). The revisions were made, at the earliest, in late August 1921, after Joyce had written 'Circe'.

19 The voice that says these words is that 'of a great multitude, and as the voice of many waters, and as the voice of many thunderings' in *Revelation* (19.6). It would be practically incomprehensible, but scripture has no difficulty in lucidly spelling out what no ear would perceive.

20 If the o's in 'Goooooooooood' (eleven of them) should carry numerical meaning, again this would be lost in pronunciation.

21 'Ce point doit être plus visible', Joyce instructed on a page proof (*James Joyce Archive 27*, 212).

22 This discovery was made by Franz Cavigelli in Zürich.

23 By one of these odd coincidences that no poet has designed, Ovid used the phrase '*filo relecto*' (VIII.173), a thread that has been 'gathered up again, wound up', from *re-legere* (pick up again) which of course also means to read again.

24 There is temptation to enlist a verbal metaphor like '*exercere*', which encapsules a notion of relieving (*ex*) constraint (*arcere*), therefore 'to set in motion': this is certainly what happens in inquisitive reading (to say nothing of *exercise*).

25 Even free and poetic translations could be misapplied to the reading process: 'Appearances/ were all confused; he led the eye astray/ By a mazy multitude of winding ways,/ Just as Maeander plays among the meads/ Of Phrygia and in its puzzling flow/ Glides back and forth and meets itself and sees/ Its waters on their way and winds along,/ Facing sometimes its source, sometimes the sea./ So Daedalus in countless corridors / Built bafflement, and hardly could himself/ Make his way out, so puzzling was the maze'. *Metamorphoses* translated by A.D. Melville (Oxford, New York: Oxford University Press, 1987), p. 176.

26 Letter to Frank Budgen, 16 August 1921 (*Letters* I p. 170).

27 The French version decides Molly is laughing and trying: 'que j'étais à la PI que je riais et j'essayais d'entendre' (*Ulysse*, p. 669); in Italian it looks like Boylan: 'quando ero at DBC con Poldy rideva e cercava di tender l'orecchio' (*Ulisse*, traduzione di Giulio de Angelis, Milan: Arnoldo Mondadori Editore, 1961, p. 971); other versions seem to leave it open.

Transition Years: James Joyce and Modernist Art

ALISON ARMSTRONG

1   Richard Ellmann, *James Joyce* (New York: Oxford University Press, 1982), p. 587.

2   'Transition Days', *Transition Workshop* (New York: Vanguard Press, 1949), p. 21.

3   Eugene Jolas, *I Have Seen Monsters and Angels* (Paris: Servire, 1938), p. 17.

4   Eugene Jolas, *The Language of Night* (The Hague, 1932), p. 17.

5   Eugene Jolas, 'On the Quest', *transition* No. 9, p. 193.

6   See Dougald McMillan, *transition 1927-38: The History of a Literary Era* (London: John Calder, 1975), pp. 180-1.

7   See Jolas, 'Homage to James Joyce', *transition* No. 21, pp. 250-2; see also No. 10, p. 152; No. 14, p. 275.

8   Richard Ellmann, *James Joyce*, p. 601.

9   Carola Giedion-Welcker, *Jean Arp* (New York: Harry N. Abrams, 1957), pp. xxxii, xvi.

10 Arthur Power, *The Joyce We Knew*, (ed.) Ulick O'Connor (Cork, 1950), np. See also Padraic and Mary Colum, *Our Friend James Joyce* (London, 1958), p. 18.

11 *Ibid.*, p. 102.

12 Wassily Kandinsky, *Concerning the Spiritual in Art* (New York: George Wittenborn, 1955 rpt.), p. 35. Written in 1910, this book was first published in German in 1912. Also, as Jolas was to do, he stressed the importance of the instinctive life in the artist: ' . . . that which belongs to the spirit of the future can only be realized in *feeling*, and the talent of the artist is the only road to feeling . . . the most advanced principles of aesthetics can never be of value to the future, but only to the past'. (31)

13 See Paul Ricoeur, *The Rule of Metaphor* (Toronto: University of Toronto Press, 1977), pp. 207-10.

14 Samuel Beckett said of 'Work in Progress' in his 1929 essay, 'Dante . . . Bruno. Vico . . Joyce': 'Here form *is* content, content *is* form. You complain that this stuff is not written in English. It is not written at all. It is not to be read—or rather not only to be read. It is to be

looked at and listened to. His writing is not about something; *it is that something itself.' Our Exagmination . . .* (London: Faber and Faber 1972), p. 14.
15 Paul Ricoeur, *The Rule of Metaphor*, p. 209.
16 Eugene Jolas, *I Have Seen Monsters and Angels*, p. 17.
17 Eugene Jolas, *Secession in Astropolis* (New York, 1929), p. 15.
18 *Ibid.*, p. 84.
19 Dougald McMillan, *transition 1927-38*, p. 184.
20 Thomas McGreevy, 'Note on Work in Progress', *transition* No. 14, p. 216; the essay was retitled 'The Catholic Element in Work in Progress', in *Our Exagmination . . .'* pp. 117-27.
21 Dougald McMillan, *transition 1927-38*, p. 195.
22 In Charles L.P. Silet, *transition: an Author Index* (Troy, N.Y.: Whitston Publishing Company, 1980), p. ix.
23 'James Joyce, Ad-Writer', reprinted in *transition* No. 21 (March 1932), p. 18; originally 'Written apropos of the publication of *Haveth Childers Everywhere* and *Anna Livia Plurabelle* in the *Criterion Miscellany*, Faber and Faber: London'.

'All That Fall': Samuel Beckett and the Bible

VIVIAN MERCIER

1 The following works by Beckett are cited in the following editions: *All That Fall*, in *Krapp's Last Tape and Other Dramatic Pieces* (New York: Grove Press, 1960); *How It Is* (Grove, 1964); *Endgame* (Grove, 1958); *Murphy* (London: Routledge 1938); *More Pricks Than Kicks*, Collected Works (Grove, 1970); *Waiting for Godot* (Grove, 1954); *Happy Days* (Grove, 1961); *Molloy* and *The Unnamable*, in *Three Novels* (Grove, 1959); *Lessness*, Signature Series (London: Calder and Boyars 1970); *That Time* (London: Faber and Faber 1976).
2 Augustine Martin, 'Anglo-Irish Literature', in *Irish Anglicanism 1869-1969*, (ed.) Michael Hurley (Dublin: Allen Figgis, 1970), pp. 120-21.
3 Tom Driver, 'Tom Driver in "Columbia University Forum"', in *Samuel Beckett: The Critical Heritage*, (eds.) Lawrence Graver and Raymond Federman (London: Routledge and Kegan Paul 1979), p. 220.
4 This reference has eluded me, but I presume I found it in *TLS c.* Nov.-Dec. 1986.
5 Samuel Beckett, *En attendant Godot*, (ed.) Colin Duckworth (London: Harrap, 1966), p. lvii.
6 *Church Hymnal*, new ed., rev. and enlarged, by permission of the General Synod of the Church of Ireland (Dublin: Association for Promoting Christian Knowledge 1922). The hymns but not the pages are numbered: No. 710, 'Safe in the arms of Jesus'; No. 587, 'Jesu, lover of my soul'; No. 611, 'Gentle Jesus, meek and mild'; No. 557, 'Jesu, my Lord, my God, my All'. The full name of the publisher, used only on the title-page, is the Association for Discountenancing Vice and Promoting the Knowledge and Practice of the Christian Religion.
7 *The Jerusalem Bible* (Garden City, N.Y.: Doubleday 1966); *The New American Bible* (New York: Nelson 1971); *The New English Bible with the Apocrypha* (Oxford University Press; Cambridge University Press, 1970).
8 James Knowlson, 'Foreword', in Eoin O'Brien, *The Beckett Country: Samuel Beckett's Ireland* (Dublin: Black Cat Press; London: Faber and Faber 1986), p. xvii (both quotations).

Beckett's Recent Activities: The Liveliness of Dead Imagination

DANIEL ALBRIGHT

1 In the original German text, it is clear that Beckett has populated the forest of symbols from Baudelaire's 'Correspondances' with the little birds from Goethe's 'Wanderers Nachtlied'.

The Consolation of Art: Oscar Wilde and Dante

DOMINIC MANGANIELLO

1 John Ruskin, *The Stones of Venice* (London, 1898), vol. III, p. 156.
2 Perhaps following his mother's linguistic idiosyncrasies, Wilde mixed Dante with modern slang in his own Italian conversation. See *The Letters of Oscar Wilde*, (ed.) Rupert Hart-Davis (London, 1963), p. 664. See also Robert Keith Miller, *Oscar Wilde* (New York, 1982), p. 2.
3 *Letters*, p. 480.
4 *Complete Works of Oscar Wilde* (London and Glasgow: Collins, 1971), p. 827.
5 *Ibid.*, p. 784.
6 Dante Alighieri, *The Paradiso* (London: J.M. Dent, 1900), XVII, pp. 58-60. In a letter to his mother dated 24 and 25 June 1875, Wilde underlined the pun on *stairs* and *Scaliger* ('scale' meaning 'stairs' in Italian) in Dante's passage. See *Letters*, p. 9.
7 In 1315 the Angevin vicar in Florence issued a decree of amnesty for exiles like Dante. He changed their death penalty to that of temporary confinement, provided the exiles put up a cash guarantee and agreed to be 'offered' as penitents to St John by the bishop. Dante responded in forceful terms to 'a Florentine friend' that he would not return disgraced in the eyes of his fellow-citizens. See *Dantis Alagherii Epistolae*, (ed.) Paget Toynbee (Oxford, 1966), pp. 158-159.
8 Compare the plight of Wilde's 'Happy Prince' who, despite his earthly misery, will be eventually welcomed, God says, in his 'city of gold'. See *Works*, p. 291.
9 *Letters*, p. 471.
10 *Ibid.*, p. 474.
11 *Ibid.*, p. 115.
12 *Ibid.*, p. 413. While in prison Wilde also asked for Franz Hettinger's book on Dante. See *Letters*, p. 523.
13 Frank Harris, *Oscar Wilde* (Lansing: Michigan State University Press, 1959), p. 194.
14 *Works*, p. 853. The entire episode of his trial and imprisonment seemed to Wilde, in fact, as a Victorian version of the *Inferno*. In his second trial, for instance, Wilde sat listening to the Solicitor-General's denunciation as if it were an outburst from Dante's poem (*Letters*, p. 502). Similarly, the apparent aloofness of Lord Alfred Douglas towards Wilde during his imprisonment prompted the latter to compare the former to those who are morally neutral and 'shallow of intention' in *Inferno* III (*Letters*, p. 458). Wilde in turn placed himself in the lowest mire of the Malebolge, the eighth circle of the *Inferno*, between Gilles de Retz and the Marquis de Sade (*Letters*, p. 414). In his letter to the editor of the *Daily Chronicle* (*Letters*, pp. 568-9), Wilde protested the cruelty practiced on children at Reading Gaol and he distinguished ordinary cruelty from the deliberate infliction of pain which gave men like Dante's Ezzelino (or Azzolino) da Romano perverse pleasure (see *The Inferno*, London: J.M. Dent, 1900, XII.p.110). Later, when he was released from prison and revisited Paris, Wilde likened his journey through the 'Circle of the Boulevards' to Dante's journey through the *Inferno* (*Letters*, p. 737).
15 *Works*, p. 785.
16 In *The Picture of Dorian Gray*, (ed.) Isobel Murray (London: Oxford University Press, 1981), p. 110, Dorian tells Basil he wants to understand Sybil Vane's death from a 'proper artistic point of view', from what Gautier used to call *la consolation des arts*.
17 *Works*, p. 811.
18 Compare Wilde's line in 'Flower of Love': 'the Cytheraean like an argent lily from the sea' (*Works*, p. 803). Cytheraean is Aphrodite's frequent title because she was said to have landed on the island of Cythera in the Ionian Sea after her birth.
19 In 'The Garden of Eros' Wilde surveys English literature as culminating with Rossetti, of whom he writes: 'He bears his name / From Dante and the seraph Gabriel' (*Works*, p. 722).
20 *Works*, p. 732.
21 *Paradiso*, XXI. p. 13ff.
22 *Works*, p. 774. In this poem Wilde also makes 'Sordello's passion' his own. Sordello, a Provençal writer of the thirteenth century, admonished the rulers of his time in his verse.

Dante follows suit in *Purgatorio* (London: J.M. Dent, 1900), VI, by railing against the Pope and Emperor. Wilde was probably thinking of the passion he had displayed in his early political verse, such as the 'Sonnet to Liberty', 'Ave Imperatrix', and 'To Milton'.

23 *Works*, p. 802.
24 *Ibid.*, p. 802.
25 *Paradiso* XXV, pp. 8-9; *Works*, p. 803.
26 *Works*, p. 987.
27 Richard Ellmann, *Eminent Domain* (London: Oxford University Press, 1967), p. 21.
28 *Works*, p. 1035.
29 Cf. *Paradiso* I. p. 22; XXX. p. 78.
30 *Purgatorio* XXI. pp. 133-136. In a letter dated March 1899 Wilde told More Adey that he would find Statius, traditionally the first Christian poet, in heaven but wished he was a better poet than was suggested in the *Divine Comedy* (*Letters*, p. 785).
31 Marcia Colish, *The Mirror of Language* (Lincoln and London, 1982), p. 8.
32 *The Picture of Dorian Gray* (London: Oxford University Press, 1981), pp. 19, 107, 57, 35, 45, 36.
33 For an elaboration of this point and others that I make subsequently see my 'Ethics and Aesthetics in *The Picture of Dorian Gray*', *Canadian Journal of Irish Studies* IX (December, 1983), pp. 25-33.
34 *The Picture of Dorian Gray*, pp. 86, 87.
35 *Ibid.*, p. 167.
36 This is from *Jerusalem*, plate 43. See Northrop Frye, *The Secular Scripture* (Cambridge: Cambridge University Press, 1976), p. 108).
37 John Freccero, 'Dante's Medusa: Allegory and Autobiography' in *By Things Seen*, (ed.) David L. Jeffrey (Ottawa, 1979), pp. 33-46.
38 *Purgatorio* XXXIII. pp. 73-75.
39 *The Picture of Dorian Gray*, pp. 216, 217, 215.
40 This is Wilde's phrase taken from *De Profundis*. The full sentence reads: 'Blindness may be carried so far that it becomes grotesque, and an unimaginative nature, if something be not done to rouse it, will become petrified into absolute sensibility, so that while the body may eat, and drink, and have its pleasures, the soul, whose house it is, may, like the soul of Branca d'Oria in Dante, be dead absolutely' (*Letters*, p. 461). The reference is to *Inferno* XXXIII pp. 135-147.
41 In this context Wilde quotes *Purgatorio* XVI. pp. 86-87 in *De Profundis*: 'Dante describes the soul of man as coming from the hand of God "weeping and laughing like a little child", and Christ also saw that the soul of each one should be "*a guisa di fanciulla, che piangendo e ridendo pargoleggia*"' (*Letters*, p. 485).
42 Jacques Maritain, *Art and Scholasticism*, trans. J.F. Scanlan (London, 1943), p. 96.
43 'Introduction' to *The Picture of Dorian Gray and Other Writings* (New York: Bantam, 1982), p. ix.
44 R.A. Shoaf, *Dante, Chaucer and the Currency of the Word: Money, Images and Reference in Late Medieval Poetry* (Norman: University of Oklahoma Press, 1983), p. 21.
45 We can compare the story of Francesca's adulterous affair with Paolo which eventually landed them in Dante's hell. In *Inferno* V.134 Francesca remarks that a book of chivalrous romance acted as their go-between and lead to their ruin.
46 See *Inferno* XV. pp. 88-90; *Paradiso* XXXIII. pp. 85-90.
47 Cf. *Paradiso* I. p. 70; *Works*, p. 1018.
48 Dorian seemed to the very young men who were his guests at dinner parties 'to be of the company of those whom Dante describes as having sought to "make themselves perfect by the worship of beauty"' (p. 129). The quotation seems to be from Pater's *Marius the Epicurean* rather than from Dante (see p. 230fn). In his chapter on St Augustine's influence on Dante, however, E.K. Rand argues that the reader who follows the medieval philosopher 'will attain a region where beauty is truth, truth beauty'. Unlike Keats, Augustine would not hold that is all we know on earth and all we need to know. Rand also points out that in one of his early works (*Contra Academicos*, II.3.7) Augustine called the love of beauty (*philocalia*) and the love of truth (*philosophia*) two sisters. See *Founders of the Middle Ages* (New York, 1928; rept. 1957), pp. 264 and 345 fn. 29. Dorian's tragedy, from this perspective, lies in his inability to link the two loves.
49 *Letters*, p. 784. In the same letter to More Adey, dated March 1899, Wilde explains that Dante

had succeeded the Greek tragedians who had dealt with 'the elemental difficulties of life—the terrible things external to us'. This perhaps explains why in his poem entitled 'A Vision' (*Works*, p. 772), Wilde has Dante's Beatrice identify Aeschylus, Sophocles, and Euripides as the sad figures in the poet's dream.

Wilde's Criticism: Theory and Practice

JONATHAN CULLER

1 Richard Ellmann, 'The Critic as Artist as Wilde', in Oscar Wilde, *The Artist as Critic*, (ed.) Richard Ellmann (Chicago: University of Chicago Press, 1982), p. x.
2 René Wellek, *A History of Modern Criticism, 1750-1950*, vol. 4 (New Haven: Yale University Press, 1965), p. 408.
3 'Mr Swinburne's Last Volume', in Wilde, *The Artist as Critic*, (ed.) Richard Ellmann, p. 146.
4 *Ibid.*, pp. 147-8.
5 'Dostoevsky's The Insulted and the Injured', *Ibid.*, p. 77.
6 'The Decay of Lying', *ibid.*, p. 299.
7 'Mr Pater's Last Volume', *ibid.*, p. 234.
8 'The Decay of Lying', *ibid.*, p. 319.
9 'The Critic as Artist', *ibid.*, p. 359.
10 'The Decay of Lying', *ibid.*, p. 294.
11 'The Decay of Lying', *ibid.*, p. 305.
12 *Idem.*
13 'The Critic as Artist as Wilde', p. x. In particular he was 'one of the first to see that the exaltation of the artist required a concomitant exaltation of the critic', p. ix.

Playing in Earnest

THOMAS R. WHITAKER

1 Jessica Milner Davis, *Farce* (London: Methuen, 1978), p. 86; Albert Bermel, *Farce* (New York: Simon and Schuster, 1982), p. 14; Maurice Charney, (ed.), *Classic Comedies* (New York: New American Library, 1985), p. viii; Eric Bentley, 'Farce', in Robert W. Corrigan (ed.), *Comedy: Meaning and Form* (2nd ed.) (New York: Harper and Row, 1981), p. 210; Barbara Freedman, 'Errors in Comedy: A Psychoanalytic Theory of Farce', in Charney, (ed.), *Classic Comedies*, p. 590.
2 Stark Young, *Immortal Shadows* (New York: Hill and Wang, 1958), p. 177; W.B. Yeats, *Explorations* (New York: Macmillan, 1962), pp. 153f, 448f.
3 Friedrich Nietzsche, *The Birth of Tragedy and the Case of Wagner*, trans. Walter Kaufmann (New York: Random House, 1967), pp. 104, 74.
4 *Ibid.*, pp. 119, 157; Nietzsche, *Thus Spake Zarathustra*, in *The Portable Nietzsche*, trans. Walter Kaufmann (New York: Viking, 1951), p. 153.
5 Morton Gurewitch, *Comedy: The Irrational Vision* (Ithaca: Cornell University Press, 1975), pp. 127f. Gurewitch offers a suggestive anatomy of 'The Imagination of Farce'.
6 Stuart E. Baker, *Georges Feydeau and the Aesthetics of Farce* (Ann Arbor: UMI Research Press, 1981), p. 22f. Though my interpretation of the game of farce goes in a rather different direction, I have learned much from Baker's study.

7   Michael Booth has speculated on the French connections between Morton's play and Ionesco's in 'Early Victorian Farce', in Kenneth Richards and Peter Thomson, (eds.) *Essays on Nineteenth Century British Theatre* (London: Methuen, 1971), p. 109n.

8   John Maddison Morton, *Box and Cox*, in Michael R. Booth, (ed.) *'The Magistrate' and Other Nineteenth-Century Plays* (London: Oxford University Press, 1974), p. 198.

9   Davis, *op. cit.*, p. 56.

10 W.S. Gilbert, *The Complete Operas*, preface by Deems Taylor (New York: Random House, 1932), p. 135. I can't resist noting here that David Lodge's *Small World* recapitulates much in the farcical tradition that I am commenting upon. Its identical-but-antithetical twins (Angel and Lily) have been found in the lavatory of a KLM airplane by its Prism-figure (Sybil Maiden), who in this version *is* their natural mother. Though not literally mixed up with a manuscript, these twins are fathered by a literary critic (Arthur Kingfisher) who is among other things the impotent king of the Waste Land, and they are themselves quite self-consciously 'textual' as topoi of romance.

11 See Joseph W. Donohue, Jr., 'The First Production of *The Importance of Being Earnest*: A Proposal for a Reconstructive Study', in *Essays on Nineteenth Century British Theatre*, pp. 125-143.

12 From Gilbert's note to the play, in Michael R. Booth, (ed.), *English Plays of the Nineteenth Century* (London: Oxford University Press, 1973), III, pp. 330. On Wilde's debt to *Engaged*, see Lynton Hudson, *The English Stage, 1850-1950* (London: Harrap, 1951), pp. 101-105.

13 For Shaw's recognition of Gilbertian elements, see *Our Theatres in the Nineties*, in *The Works of Bernard Shaw* (London: Constable, 1931), I, pp. 44f.

14 Oscar Wilde, *The Importance of Being Earnest*, with commentary by Patricia Hern (London: Methuen, 1981), p. xxxiii.

15 John Russell Taylor, *The Rise and Fall of the Well-Made Play* (New York: Hill and Wang, 1967), p. 90; Eric Bentley, *The Playwright as Thinker* (New York: Meridian 1955), p. 144; Morton Gurewitch, *op. cit.*, p. 118.

16 *Complete Works of Oscar Wilde*, (ed.) Robert Ross (Boston: 192-), IV, p. 270.

17 Shaw, *Plays: Pleasant and Unpleasant* (New York: Brentano's, 1922), II, p. x.

18 For excellent discussions of the play's eclectic style, see Martin Meisel, *Shaw and the Nineteenth Century Theatre* (Princeton: Princeton University Press, 1963), pp. 249-259; Margery M. Morgan, *The Shavian Playground* (London: Methuen, 1972), pp. 83-99; and Daniel J. Leary's introduction to *You Never Can Tell: A Facsimile of the Holograph Manuscript* (New York: Garland, 1981).

19 See 'The Dentist' in *Scenarios of the Commedia dell'Arte: Flaminio Scala's 'Il Teatro delle favole rappresentative'*, trans. Henry F. Salerno, with foreword by Kenneth McKee (New York: New York University Press, 1967), p. 85ff. For a discussion of *The Toothache*, see Matthew N. Coughlin, 'Farce Transcended: George Fitzmaurice's *The Toothache*', in *Eire-Ireland*, X:4 (1975), pp. 85-100.

20 Shaw, *Works*, XXIII, 10, p. 44f.

21 Meisel, *op. cit.*, pp. 47-50.

22 *Ibid.*, pp. 58-59.

23 A letter of 1902 quoted by Meisel, *op. cit.*, p. 54.

24 Bernard Shaw, *Letters to Granville Barker*, (ed.) C.B. Purdon (New York: Theatre Arts, 1957), p. 45.

25 See, for example, Arthur Ganz, *George Bernard Shaw* (London: Macmillan, 1983), pp. 118-119.

26 John Lahr, *Prick Up Your Ears* (New York: Limelight Editions, 1986), p. 106.

27 *Ibid.*, p. 155.

28 See Maurice Charney, *Joe Orton* (London: Macmillan, 1984), pp. 107-110, for a summary of the play's eclecticism. See Lahr, *op. cit.*; p. 233, for Orton's close study of Feydeau.

29 Lahr, *op. cit.*, p. 143.

30 The use of a prop phallus that could be elevated by the mime fool goes back to classical times. See, for example, the Roman statuette reproduced in Anthony Caputi, *Buffo: The Genius of Vulgar Comedy* (Detroit: Wayne State University Press, 1978), p. 178. Caputi also has suggestive comments (p. 159ff) on elements of madness and rebirth in Plautine farce. Albert

Bermel (*Farce*, p. 39f) brings *The Bacchae* into analogous relations with farce. For Orton's own recognition of 'a "Golden Bough" subtext' in this play, with castration of the father-figure and descent of the god, see the diary notes quoted in Lahr, *op. cit.*, p. 21.

31 Lahr, *op. cit.*, p. 15.

32 *Ibid.*, p. 187.

33 See C.W.E. Bigsby, *Joe Orton* (London: Methuen, 1982), pp. 56-58, and Lahr, *op. cit.*, p. 273. Katherine Worth, in *Revolutions in Modern English Drama* (London: G. Bell, 1972) had already offered more finely balanced judgements. She notes 'a faint sense of poignancy as the chase works up to its desperate climax' and 'a real longing for the alluring, hermaphroditic wraith that has been created out of the hopeless confusion between Gerald and Geraldine' (p. 154). And she calls the play 'a great id-releasing experience and a reassuring demonstration of the power of wit to control it' (p. 156).

34 Lahr, *op. cit.*, p. 273.

35 For an extended reading of the play, see Thomas R. Whitaker, *Tom Stoppard* (London: Macmillan, 1983), pp. 108-129. See also John William Cooke, 'Perception and Form in "Travesties"', in *Tom Stoppard*, (ed.), Harold Bloom (New York: Chelsea House, 1986), pp. 87-100.

36 See James Joyce, *Finnegans Wake* (New York: Viking, 1939), p. 215.

37 Friedrich Schiller, *On the Aesthetic Education of Man*, trans. Reginald Snell (New York: Ungar, 1965), p. 106.

Contributors

DANIEL ALBRIGHT. Ellmann's student at Yale. Teaches at the University of Rochester. Author, *The Myth Against Myth: A Study of Yeats's Imagination in Old Age; Personality and Impersonality: Lawrence, Woolf, Mann; Representation and the Imagination: Beckett, Kafka, Nabokov, and Schoenberg; Lyricality in English Literature; Tennyson: The Muses' Tug-of-War.* Editor, *Poetries of America: Essays in the Relation of Character to Style*, by Irvin Ehrenpreis. Editor and translator (with Irvin Ehrenpreis and Heinz Vienken), *Amerikanische Lyrik: Texte und Deutungen.*

ALISON ARMSTRONG. Ellmann's student at Oxford. Teaches at The Cooper Union (New York City). Co-editor of the *Irish Literary Supplement.* Author, *The Joyce of Cooking: Food and Drink from James Joyce's Dublin.*

CHRISTOPHER BUTLER. Ellmann's student at Oxford. Teaches at Christ Church, Oxford. Author, *After the Wake; Interpretation. Deconstruction and Ideology: An Introduction to Some Current Issues in Literary Theory; Number Symbolism; Topics in Criticism: An Ordered Set of Positions in Literary Theory.*

CAROL HELMSTETTER CANTRELL. Ellmann's student at Northwestern. Teaches at Colorado State University. Has recently completed a monograph on the China-Adams Cantos in collaboration with Ward Simpson.

JONATHAN CULLER. Teaches at Cornell University. Author, *Flaubert: The Uses of Uncertainty; Structuralist Poetics: Structuralism, Linguistics, and the Study of Literature; Ferdinand de Saussure; The Pursuit of Signs: Semiotics, Literature, Deconstruction; On Deconstruction: Theory and Criticism after Structuralism; Roland Barthes.*

ELIZABETH BUTLER CULLINGFORD. Ellmann's student at Oxford. Teaches at the University of Texas. Director of the Yeats International Summer School, Sligo, Ireland. Author, *Yeats, Ireland and Fascism.* Editor, *Yeats's Poems, 1919-1935: A Casebook.*

ANDONIS DECAVALLES. Ellmann's student at Northwestern. Teaches comparative literature at Fairleigh Dickinson University. Books: *Nimule-Gondonkoro* (Greek poems); *Akis* (Greek poems); *T.S. Eliot: Ta Tessera Kouarteta* (Greek translation of Eliot's *Four Quartets*); *Amerikaniki Piisi* (*American Poetry*, a series of broadcasts over the Voice of America); *The Voice of Cyprus: An Anthology of Cypriot Literature* (as co-editor and co-translator); *Okeanidhes* (*Oeanids*, Greek poems); *Armoi, Karavia, Lytra* (*Joints, Ships, Ransoms*, Greek poems, awarded Poetry Prize of the Academy of Athens in 1977); *Pandelis Prevelakis and the Value of a Heritage; Ransoms to Time: Selected Poems* (translated from the modern

Greek by Kimon Friar); *Isaghoyi sto loghotehniko ergho tou Pandeli Preve-laki* (*Introduction to the Literary Work of Pandelis Prevelakis*).

RUPIN W. DESAI. Ellmann's student at Northwestern. Teaches at the University of Delhi. Editor of *Hamlet Studies*.

SUSAN DICK. Ellmann's student at Northwestern. Teaches at Queen's University, Kingston, Ontario. Editor, critical editions of George Moore's *Confessions of a Young Man*; Virginia Woolf's *To the Lighthouse: The Original Holograph Draft*; and *The Complete Shorter Fiction* of Virginia Woolf.

TERENCE DIGGORY. Ellmann's student at Oxford. Teaches at Skidmore College. Author, *Yeats and American Poetry: The Tradition of the Self*.

DENIS DONOGHUE. Teaches at New York University. Author, *The Third Voice: Modern British and American Verse Drama; Connoisseurs of Chaos: Ideas of Order in Modern American Literature; The Ordinary Universe: Soundings in Modern Literature; Jonathan Swift: A Critical Introduction; Emily Dickinson; William Butler Yeats; Thieves of Fire; The Sovereign Ghost: Studies in Imagination; Ferocious Alphabets; The Arts Without Mystery*. Editor, *An Honoured Guest: New Essays on W.B. Yeats* (with J.R. Mulryne); *Swift Revisited; Jonathan Swift: A Critical Anthology; Memoirs*, by W.B. Yeats.

TERENCE EAGLETON. Teaches at Wadham College, Oxford. Author, *Shakespeare and Society; The New Left Church; Exiles and Emigrés; The Body as Language; Myths of Power: A Marxist Study of the Brontës; Marxism and Literary Criticism; Criticism and Ideology; Brecht and Company* (play); *Walter Benjamen: or, Towards a Revolutionary Criticism; The Rape of Clarissa; Literary Theory; The Function of Criticism; Against the Grain; Saints and Scholars* (novel).

ROSITA FANTO. Collaborated with Ellmann to produce the Oscar Wilde Playing Cards. Artist, publisher, and originator of a unique visual and tactile publication, *Presages*. Film producer, including a programme for French television on Henry Moore.

CHARLES FEIDELSON. Classmate of Ellmann's at Yale. Collaborated with him on *The Modern Tradition*. Teaches at Yale University. Author, *Symbolism and American Literature*.

JAMES FLANNERY. Teaches at Emory University. Theatre director, especially of Yeats's plays. Author, *W.B. Yeats and the Idea of a Theatre: The Early Abbey Theatre in Theory and Practice*.

CHARLES A. HUTTAR. Ellmann's student at Northwestern. Teaches at Hope College, Holland, Michigan. Author, *The Myth of David in Western Literature*.

BRUCE JOHNSON. Ellmann's student at Northwestern. Teaches at the University of Rochester. Author, *Conrad's Models of Mind*.

JOHN V. KELLEHER. Ellmann's friend and travelling companion in the 1940s. Professor Emeritus of Irish Studies, Harvard University. Has written extensively on the use of Irish history and mythology in modern Irish literature.

BRENDAN KENNELLY. Teaches at Trinity College, Dublin. Poet. Author, poems: *Cast a Cold Eye; The Rain, The Moon* (with Rudi Holzapfel); *The Dark about Our Loves* (with Rudi Holzapfel); *Green Townlands* (with Rudi Holzapfel); *Let Fall No Burning Leaf; My Dark Fathers; Up and At It; Collection One: Getting up Early; Good Souls to Survive; Dream of a Black Fox; Selected Poems; A Drinking Cup: Poems from the Irish; Bread; Love-Cry; Salvation, The Stranger; The Voices: A Sequence of Poems; Shelley in Dublin; A Kind of Trust; New and Selected Poems; Islandman; The Visitor; A Small Light; In Spite of the Wise; The Boats Are Home; The House That Jack Didn't Build; Cromwell.* Novels: *The Crooked Cross; The Florentines.* Editor, *The Penguin Book of Irish Verse.*

FRANK KERMODE. Fellow, Kings College, Cambridge, teaches at Columbia University. Author, *Romantic Image; Wallace Stevens; Puzzles and Epiphanies; The Sense of an Ending; Continuities; Shakespeare, Spenser, Donne; Modern Essays; D.H. Lawrence; The Classic; The Genesis of Secrecy; The Art of Telling; Forms of Attention.* Editor, *English Pastoral Poetry;* Shakespeare, *The Tempest; The Living Milton; Discussions of John Donne; Edmund Spenser; Four Centuries of Shakespearean Criticism; Selected Poetry* of Andrew Marvell; *The Metaphysical Poets; King Lear: A Casebook; Poems* of John Donne; *The Oxford Reader* (with R. Poirer); *Oxford Anthology of English Literature* (general editor with J. Hollander); *Selected Prose* of T.S. Eliot; *The Literary Guide to the Bible* (with Robert Alter).

DECLAN KIBERD. Ellmann's student at Oxford. Teaches at University College, Dublin. Formerly Director of the Yeats International Summer School at Sligo, Ireland. Collaborated with Ellmann on the award-winning RTE film *Samuel Beckett: Silence to Silence.* Author, *Man and Feminism in Modern Literature; Synge and the Irish Language.* Writes a weekly column on politics and culture in *The Irish Times.*

PETER KUCH. Ellmann's student at Oxford. Teaches at Avondale College, New South Wales, Australia. Author, *Yeats and AE: 'the antagonism that unites dear friends'.*

JAMES LAUGHLIN. Founding Editor and President, New Directions Publishing. Author, *Some Natural Things; Skiing: East and West* (with H. Fischer); *Report on a Visit to Germany* (poetry); *A Small Book of Poems; The Wild Anemone and Other Poems; Confidential Report and Other Poems; Pulsatilla; Die Haare auf Grossvaters Kopf; Quel che la Matita Scrive; The Pig: Poems; The Woodpecker; In Another Country: Poems 1935-1975; Selected Poems 1935-1985.* Editor, *Poems from the Greenberg Manuscripts; A Wreath of Christmas Poems* (with A. Hayes); *Spearhead: Ten Years' Experimental Writing in America; A New Directions Reader* (with H. Carruth); *The Asian Journal of Thomas Merton* (with N. Burton and P. Hart).

A. WALTON LITZ. Teaches at Princeton University. Author, *The Art of James Joyce; Modern American Fiction; Essays in Criticism; Jane Austen; The Poetic Development of Wallace Stevens; Eliot in his Time; Major American Short Stories; Scribner Quarto of Modern English and American Literature.* Editor, James Joyce, *Dubliners* (with Robert Scholes); *Modern*

Literary Criticism 1900-1970; The Collected Poems of William Carlos Williams (with Christopher MacGowan); *Ezra Pound and Dorothy Shakespear, Their Letters 1909-1914* (with Omar Pound); *The Jane Austen Companion* (consulting editor with Brian Southam).

DOMINIC MANGANIELLO. Ellmann's student at Oxford. Teaches at the University of Ottawa. Author, *Joyce's Politics; T.S. Eliot and Dante.*

ELLSWORTH MASON. Classmate of Ellmann's at Yale. Collaborated with him in editing *The Critical Writings* of James Joyce. Teaches at the University of Colorado. Author, *James Joyce's Ulysses and Vico's Cycle.* Editor, *Recollections of James Joyce; The Early Joyce.*

CHRISTIE MCDONALD. Colleague and collaborator of Ellmann's at Emory. Teaches at the Université de Montréal. Author, *The Extravagant Shepherd: A Study of the Pastoral Vision in Rousseau's Nouvelle Héloîse; The Dialogue of Writing: Essays in 18th Century French Literature; Dispositions: Quatre essais sur les écrits de Rousseau, Mallarmé, Proust, et Derrida.*

DOUGALD MCMILLAN. Ellmann's student at Northwestern. Taught at the University of North Carolina, Chapel Hill. Publisher, Signal Books. Author, *Transition: The History of a Literary Era; Beckett at Work in the Theatre.* Presently editing Samuel Beckett's production notebooks and text of *Waiting for Godot.*

VIVIAN MERCIER. Taught at the University of California, Santa Barbara. Author, *Irish Comic Tradition; The New Novel: From Queneau to Pinget; Beckett/Beckett.* Editor, *1,000 Years of Irish Prose,* part 1; *Great Irish Short Stories.*

SEÁN O'MÓRDHA. Former Head, Arts and Documentaries at RTE, Ireland's National Broadcasting Service, now a freelance film director. Produced and directed, in collaboration with Ellmann, documentary films: *James Joyce: Is there One Who Understands Me?; Oscar Wilde—Spendthrift of Genius; Samuel Beckett: Silence to Silence.* Recipient of an Emmy Award for his television work.

MARY T. REYNOLDS. Compiler of indexes for Ellmann's books. Teaches at Yale University. Author, *Interdepartmental Committees in the National Administration; Joyce and Dante: The Shaping Imagination.*

WILLIAM K. ROBERTSON. Columnist for *The Miami Herald.*

JOSEPH RONSLEY. Ellmann's student at Northwestern. Teaches at McGill University. Past President, Canadian Association for Irish Studies. Author, *Yeats's Autobiography: Life as Symbolic Pattern.* Editor, *Myth and Reality in Irish Literature; Denis Johnston: A Retrospective; The Selected Plays* of Denis Johnston; *Irish Drama Selections* (co-general editor with Ann Saddlemyer).

S.P. ROSENBAUM. Teaches at the University of Toronto. Author, *Victorian Bloomsbury: The Early Literary History of the Bloomsbury Group; Concordance to the Poems of Emily Dickinson.* Editor, *The Bloomsbury Group: A Collection of Memoirs, Commentary, Criticism;* Henry James, *The Ambassadors; English Literature and British Philosophers.*

ANN SADDLEMYER. Teaches at the University of Toronto. Past

Chairman, International Association for Study of Anglo-Irish Literature, Past President, Association for Canadian Theatre History. Author, *Synge and Modern Comedy; In Defence of Lady Gregory, Playwright.* Editor, *The World of W.B. Yeats* (with Robin Skelton); *The Plays* of J.M. Synge; *The Plays* of Lady Gregory; *A Selection of Letters from John M. Synge to W.B. Yeats and Lady Gregory; Letters to Molly: J.M. Synge to Maire O'Neill; Theatre Business, Management of Men: The Letters of the First Abbey Theatre Directors; Irish Drama Selections* (co-general editor with Joseph Ronsley). Presently writing a biography of George Yeats.

SYLVAN SCHENDLER. Ellmann's student at Northwestern. Director, American Studies Research Centre, Hyderabad, India. Formerly Editor of the *Indian Journal of American Studies.* Author, *Living Language; American Pantheon; Eakins.*

DANIEL J. SCHNEIDER. Ellmann's student at Northwestern. Teaches at the University of Tennessee. Author, *Symbolism: The Manichean Vision; The Crystal Cage: Adventures of the Imagination in the Fiction of Henry James; D.H. Lawrence, The Artist as Psychologist; The Consciousness of D.H. Lawrence: An Intellectual Biography.*

FRITZ SENN. Has taught at universities throughout Europe and North America. President, Zurich James Joyce Foundation. Co-editor and co-founder of *A Wake Newslitter* and European editor of the *James Joyce Quarterly.* Editor, *A Wake Digest* (with Clive Hart); *Materialian zu James Joyce 'Dubliners'* (with Klaus Reichert and Dieter E. Zimmer); *Briefe an Nora; New Light on Joyce from the Dublin Symposium; A Conceptual Guide to 'Finnegans Wake'* (with Michael H. Begnal); *Materialien zu James Joyce's 'Ein Portraet des Kuenstlers als junger Mann'* (with Klaus Reichert); Arthur Schopenhauer, *Zurcher Ausgabe* (complete works in 10 volumes, with others).

JON STALLWORTHY. Teaches at Wolfson College, Oxford. Author, *Between the Lines: W.B. Yeats's Poetry in the Making; Vision and Revision in Yeats's Last Poems.* Poetry: *Root and Branch; Hand in Hand; The Apple Barrel: Selected Poems 1956-63; A Familiar Tree; Complete Poems and Fragments; Book of Love Poetry; Anzac Sonata: New and Selected Poems.* Editor, *Penguin Book of Love Poetry; Yeats's Last Poems: A Casebook; Oxford Book of War Poetry*; Wilfred Owen, *The Complete Poems and Fragments*; Boris Pasternak, *Selected Poems* (translated, with Peter France).

LONNIE WEATHERBY. Reference Librarian and English Literature Bibliographer. McLennan Library, McGill University.

THOMAS WHITAKER. Teaches at Yale University. Author, *Swan and Shadow: Yeats's Dialogue with History; William Carlos Williams; Fields of Play in Modern Drama; Tom Stoppard.* Editor, *Twentieth Century Interpretations of the Playboy of the Western World.*

ELAINE YAROSKY. Reference Librarian and English Literature Bibliographer, McLennon Library, McGill University.

Index

O'Neill, Eugene, 190; *The Fountain*, 176
O'Neill, Joseph, 286, 287
O'Reilly, James, 187, 188
Orton, Joe, 408, 409; *What the Butler Saw*, 408, 411, 413, 418-421
Orton, Leonie, 408
O'Sullivan, Seumas, *see* Starkey, James
Oude, Begum of, 122-132
Oude, Vizier, Asuph-ud-dowla, 122, 123, 126, 127, 128
Our Exagmination Round his Factification for Incamination of 'Work in Progress', 357
Ovid, Metamorphoses, 346, 347
Oxford, University of, xvii, 7, 12, 28, 29, 30, 31, 43, 47, 48, 188

Pahlavi, Muhammed Reza, Shah of Iran, 23
Palace Bar, Dublin, 15
Palmer, Eileen, 298
Palmer, Gladys, 290, 298
Palmer, Phyllis, 290, 298
Panker, John, 4
Parnell, Charles Stuart, 240
Pascal, Blaise, 25
Pater, Walter, 124, 173, 257, 304, 402, 403; *Appreciations*, 403; *Marius the Epicurean*, 294, 295
Patrick, Sara, 285, 286
Pauker, John, 4
Paul, Elliot, 353
Payne, Ben Iden, 285
Peacock Theatre, Dublin, 177, 184, 186, 188, 189, 301
Pearse, Padraig, 232
Pearson, Norman Holmes, 4, 10; (ed. with W.R.Benét) *The Oxford Anthology of American Literature*, 4
Peirce, Charles Saunders, 67
Peoples' Rights Association (Dublin), The, 290
Perl, Jeffrey M., 64, 67
Perloff, Majorie, 253, 254, 255, 259, 265; *The Poetics of Indeterminacy*, 253-254, 255; 'Spatial Form in the Poetry of Yeats: The Two Lissadell Poems', 253
Perrin, John H., 281, 282, 286, 288, 289, 301

Philpotts, Dulcie (née Childers), 290
Photo-Bits, 332
Picasso, Pablo, 50, 53, 351, 359, 380; 'Les Demoiselles d'Avignon', 51, 53, 58, 65; 'Saltimbanques', 52; 'La Vie', 52
Pinter, Harold, 419; *The Birthday Party*, 408
Pirandello, Luigi, 256, 274; *The Game as He Played It*, 176; *Six Characters in Search of an Author*, 295, 408
Plato, 77, 204-205, 209, 213, 214, 217, 218, 219, 259, 398, 399, 401; *Phaedrus*, 216, 218; *The Republic*, 216, 267; *Symposium*, 215-216; *Timaeus*, 78
Plautus, *The Menaechmi*, 411, 419
Poe, Edgar Allan, 82-84, 146, 402; *Al Aaraaf*, 82; 'Al Aaraaf', 82; 'Annabel Lee', 83', 'Dreamland', 83; 'The Colloquy of Monos and Una', 82; 'The Conversation of Eros And Charmion', 82;'Lenore', 82; 'The Power of Words', 82, 83; 'The Raven', 82; 'Sonnet: To Science', 82
Pollexfen, George, 227
Pontius Pilate, 366
Portora Royal School, Enniskillen, 364, 365
Pottle, Frederick, 7
Pound, Ezra, 5, 24, 25, 28, 52, 53, 55, 56, 57, 61, 64, 67, 146, 148-160, 234, 253, 254, 255-256, 257, 258, 259, 265, 317, 353; 'The Age Demanded', 151; *Cantos*, 59, 152, 154, 155, 156, 158-160, 254, 255-256, 265, 317; Cantos LII-LXXI, 5; trs. 'Dans le Restaurant', 149-151; 'Dr Williams' Position', 154, 156; *Eleven New Cantos*, 156; 'Ezuversity', 24; 'La Fraisne', 258; *Homage to Sextus Propertius*, 151; *How To Read*, 24; *Hugh Selwyn Mauberley*, 151, 152; *Indiscretions*, 154; 'Irony, Laforgue and Some Satire', 149; 'The Jefferson-Adams Letters as a Shrine and a Monument', 154, 158; 'Our Tetrarchal Précieuse', 149; 'Pastiche: The Regional', 151; 'Pierrots', 149, 151; *Ripostes*, 153; *Selected Prose*,

Sainte-Beuve, Charles-Augustin, 56
Sand, George, 76
Santayana, William, 160
Santayana, George, 210
Sartre, Jean-Paul, 313; *The Psychology of Imagination*, 169
Satie, Erik, *Parade*, 51
Saturday Review of Literature, The, 189
Saussure, Ferdinand de, 311, 312
Savile Club, London, 290
Scala, Emilio, 283, 284
Scaligeri, Can Grande, 395
Schendler, Gigi, xi, xiii, 28
Schendler, Sylvan, xi, xii, 28
Schiller, Friedrich, *On the Aesthetic Education of Man*, 423
Schiller Theatre, The, 391
Schlegel, Friedrich, 355
Schlovsky, Viktor, 66
Schmitz, Ettore, 40
Schoenberg, Arnold, 53, 58, 359, 376-377; *Die Gluckliche Hand*, 55; *Erwartung*, 51, 52, 53, 54; *Gurrelieder*, 52; *Harmonienlehre*, 54; *Pelléas and Mélisande*, 52; *Pierrot Lunaire*, 51, 52; *Verklärte Nacht*, 52
Schorske, Carl E., 56
Schwartz, Sanford, 60, 61, 69
Scott, Michael, 301
Scott, W.L, 298, 299
Scriabin, Alexander, 56
Scrutiny, 314
Seale, Rev. E.G., 364
Serly, Tibor, 157
Shakespear, Dorothy, 28, 149
Shakespear, Olivia, 210, 287
Shakespeare & Co. (Paris), 24, 325, 357
Shakespeare, William, 191, 196, 198, 199, 200, 202, 220, 307, 308, 324, 326, 333, 339, 407, 421; *Anthony and Cleopatra*, 410; *Comedy of Errors*, 411, 412-413, 419; *Hamlet*, 191-203, 231, 269, 334, 374. 410; *Julius Caesar*, 202; *King Lear*, 176, 182, 287, 374, 381, 410; *Macbeth*, 200, 390; *Othello*, 139; *The Tempest*, 381-382; *Twelfth Night*, 419
Shama'a, 148
Shaw, George Bernard, 6, 54, 177, 183, 187, 303, 409, 413; *Fanny's First Play*, 176; *In Good King Charles's*

Golden Days, 5; *Major Barbara*, 176; *Man and Superman*, 421; *Saint Joan*, 421; *You Never Can Tell*, 408, 413, 416-418, 421
Shawe-Taylor, Captain John, 229
Shelley, Mary, *Frankenstein*, 419
Shelley, Percy Bysshe, 82, 84, 209, 231, 266; *Prometheus Unbound*, 266
Sheridan, Richard Brinsley, 129, 130, 132
Shields, Arthur 'Boss', 182
Shri Purohit Swami, *An Indian Monk*, 303
Sicker, Philip, 91
Sing, Cheyt, Rajah of Benares, 122, 123, 124, 125, 126, 127, 128, 129, 132
Sing, Ranee of Benares, 126
Sitwell, Edith, 5; *Poems New and Old*, 5; *Street Songs*, 5
Slattery, Dr R.V., 301, 302
Smith, William Jay, 147, 149, 151
Smyth, Dame Ethel, 138, 142
Society for the Prevention of Vice, USA, 325
Society of Useful Manufacturers, 189
Socrates, 216, 267
Solomons, Bethel, 281
Solomons, Estella, 288
Sophocles, 383
Spanish Civil War, 6
Speaker, 131
Spectator, The, 122, 129, 131, 132, 295, 302
Spengler, Oswald, 54
Spinoza, Benedict, 308
Spivak, Gayatri, 63
Stange, Stanislaus, *The Chocolate Soldier*, 229, 300
Starkey, James (pseud. Seumas O'Sullivan), 288, 290, 291
Starkie, Walter, 176, 182, 285, 286, 288, 289, 295, 296, 298, 299, 300, 301, 302
Starkie, Mrs, (née Itaia Augusta Porchietti) 288, 289
Stein, Gertrude, 351, 353, 354, 356, 359
Stein, William Bysshe, 86-87, 101
Steinberg, Leo, 254
Steiner, George, 363